WHITE SEA
FINLAND
RUSSIA
WEDEN
ESTONIA
STOCKHOLM
LATVIA
MOSCOW
LITHUANIA
BELARUS
KAZAKHSTAN
POLAND
WARSAW
UKRAINE
CZECH
EPUBLIC
CASPIANSEA
SLOVAKIA
MOLDAVIA
USTRIA
HUNGARY
ROMANIA
GEORGIA
AZERBAIJAN
ARMENIA
CROATIA
BLACK SEA
BOSNIA
& HER.
SERBIA
IRAN
BULGARIA
MACE-
DONIA
TURKEY
DRIATIC SEA
ALBANIA
GREECE
AEGEAN
SYRIA
IRAQ
IONIAN
SEA

GLIMPSES OF EUROPE

GLIMPSES OF EUROPE

A crucible of winning ideas, great civilizations and bloodiest wars

Bindeshwar Pathak
S.P. Singh

KALPAZ

Glimpses of Europe

Rs. 750

ISBN: 978-81-7835-831-4

Published in 2010 in India by
Sulabh International
Social Service Organisation
Sulabh Gram, Mahavir Enclave
New Delhi-110045
Co-Publishers
Kalpaz Publications
C-30 Satyawati Nagar
New Delhi-110052
E-mail: kalpaz@hotmail.com
Website : www.kalpazbooks.com

Laser Type Setting by: Quick Media, Delhi
Printed at : Salasar Imaging Systems, Delhi-35

Dedicated to
HRH the Prince of Orange of the Netherlands, Willem-Alexander

OF THE HOUSE OF ORANGE — a very ancient dynasty which has led the country in stormy times and helped establish peace when the Netherlands needed it most. Through his personal initiatives, the Prince has been able to transfer technologies and knowhow from Europe to the developing countries, acting as a bridge between the East and the West.

I hope historians will forgive me; for, I am going to write history.

-Sir Winston Churchill

Europe had been the source of the best and the worst in human history. It invented practically everything that matters: from Greek philosophy to Roman law, from the Renaissance to the fax machine, or to anything that has changed the way we live and think. But this was also where the world's deadliest wars were fought, killing tens of millions. It was in Europe that the most murderous ideologies were invented: communism, fascism and Nazism, complete with the Gulag, the Gestapo, and Auschwitz.

Contents

Everything worth telling has been told already, but no one listened. So, let us start telling it again. For, study of history is the beginning of political wisdom and social change.

-Andre Gide (1869-1951)

Preface

This book has been written to introduce Europe specially to non-Europeans. This is a popular and rapid reading, a summary and a reference history book on Europe, particularly for those who seem to be indifferent to the affairs of the continent, seduced as they are by the glitzy New World and its ways of living and thinking. It is a loose encyclopedia of everything about the countries under discussion. There cannot be a Gibbon to write "*The Decline and Fall* ....", nor is one needed now because today we have a lot more things to know about than the British historian had to. His was an age of leisure while we are in a perpetual hurry if only to go nowhere. This is the popular history of Europe.

It is meant to be read straight forwardly, almost as a novel is read. It gives in the most general way an account of European history, shorn of elaborations and complications, providing the reader a framework for the study of a particular country. It may be found useful as preparatory to reading more about Europe. But its special objective is to meet the needs of the busy general reader, too work - driven to study detail, and who wishes to refresh and repair his faded or fragmentary conceptions of the great adventures of mankind. This is a generalized history, planned and written afresh with non-European perspective. It will interest history students, general reader for ready reference, policy makers, travellers, diplomats, speech writers and even the uninitiated, keen on knowing about Europe. This book is the staccato rendition of European history which seeks to intellectually link common Indians with Europe which is hugely ignored while working out our areas of concern. It is a quick look at over 2,000 years of history, marked by periods of conquest, defeats, civil wars, crusades, concentration camps, two global wars and great achievements unmatched by any before.

Thus, we seek to take yet another look at the European history, telling the same story differently, giving a perspective to it and relating it to the wider issues of our times, going beyond the fixed narratives because history has to be continually constructed and reconstructed, making room for different interpretations against different backgrounds. This is a Euro-centric period-piece but free from the certainties of earlier times. History thrives on revisionism. However, to compress more than 2,000-year-old stories of Europe and extract what matters in post-modern times has been a daunting job which we have tried to do if only to hurriedly tell how history has happened to Europeans and how the good life that they enjoy today is also the consequence of long and bloody struggles, in the making of which millions of innocent men, women and children had perished.

In sum, we play storytellers for Europe, helping readers understand the outstanding people of the continent which has been the home of great artists, intellectuals, reformers, revolutionaries, painters, scientists, caudillos and killers and seek to re-tell their stories in easy, readable and understandable ways. We have kept the book free from commitment to any single interpretation of history. Unafraid to write it interestingly, we take the risk of being criticised for many imperfections (a perfect book is still to be written), repeats and borrowing of ideas and facts which nobody can recreate. We have taken facts and opinions from different sources, authentic and the latest, and the sources are gratefully acknowledged. If history is an assembly of dates, names of kings, queens and killers, of course, they cannot be changed. What can, however, change is the interpretation and perspective of events in the changing social and political context. And, we have sought to do that in order to make the old Europe relevant to the post-modern world. The book provides a reading on everything that goes into making modern Europe – its geography, history, political, social and intellectual developments. In all, the book covers 25 countries in separate chapters. The book has two sections - *Profile of European Continent* and the *Profiles of Core European Countries*. The first section is about the defining features and major events of the continent while the second one is the country - specific narratives.

The focus is largely on 25 core countries within Pyrenees in the west and the Elbe in the east which make for "European home". And the other countries on both fringes, Spain, Portugal and Gibraltar, in the west and those beyond the Elbe, though included in the original version of the book, have been kept out of the revised copy on the advice of the publisher to make the book easy to handle. Spain and Portugal are not quite the European countries as others are, so also Poland and the Balkan countries although they have close relations with mainland Europe. (It may be noted both world wars started in Eastern Europe - first in Sarajevo, Bosnia, on June 28, 1914 and second in Poland on Septemebr 1, 1939). Together, these constituted an explosive mix which the Balkans have been since Alexander the Great. We have also not included, in this abridged version, Hungary, Romania and Bulgaria which were epistemological sources of the collapse of the USSR after which 15 countries, held in the tight-embrace, were freed. We wanted to leave out the Mediterranean countries also but we could not do that entirely because the narrative of Europe started with *Europa* and her stories around the Mediterranean. Or, how can one ignore Greece, the inventor of democracy, and still claim to talk about Europe!! Impossible. Greece was the source of greatness of Rome on whose fall in 476 AD, Gibbon said: *"The world collapsed in one city"*. A chapter on the Ottoman Empire is given along with the Balkans where the Turks were a major power and the single most important source of conflict in the region.

This book is neither a classical nor a popular narrative; it is something like John Gunther's *"Inside"* series. Gunther was a reporter with *The New York Times*, and he converted his reports into the *Inside* series (Inside Europe, Inside Africa, Inside Latin America etc.) which had become among the most popular accounts of people and places of his time (1950s and 1960s). Our attempt is also to tell the story of Europe in the same appreciative manner. Choosing the facts and events to be included in this book has not been easy either. The events are too near to see them in right perspectives. Some of them will soon be left behind by the march of time. Hence, we make no claim to have written a definitive history.

To begin with, we could not determine as to what constitutes the European boundaries. Far too long, Europe has been an abstraction which still remains to be defined in precise terms. Commenting on Turkey joining the EU, a French politician said: "If Anatolia (Turkey in Asia), can join EU why not the entire Middle East? Europe is after all an abstraction." But we have drawn a line – very traditional one at that – from the Atlantic, in the west, to the Baltic, in the north, and the Black Sea, in the south. Best known Italian historian Carlos Ginzburg says history is "located knowledge" and one should avoid preaching. We have done that by strictly limiting the narrative to facts, leaving "preaching" for professionals to do.

The Core Countries

But what is very special about the core countries in the European mainland? There is a lot. Between 1880s and 1980s, these relatively small number of countries governed nearly all of the world. On the eve of the First World War, Britain, France, Belgium, Holland and Germany, which among them accounted for less than 1 percent of the world's land surface and less than 8 percent of its population, ruled in the region of a third of the rest of the world's area and more than a quarter of its people. All of Australasia, 90 percent of Africa and 56 percent of Asia were under some form of rule of these mainland European countries, as were nearly all the islands of the Caribbean, the Indian Ocean and the Pacific. And although only around a quarter of the American continent mainly Canada found itself in the same condition of dependence, nearly all the rest had been ruled from Europe at one time or another in the seventeenth and eighteenth centuries. In both the north and the south, the polity of the American republics were fundamentally shaped by the colonial past.

Nor do these calculations about the extent of the West European maritime empires tell the whole story of nineteenth-century empire. Most of Central and Eastern Europe was under Russian, German or Austrian imperial rule. Indeed, the Russian empire stretched from the Baltic to the Black Sea and from Warsaw to Vladivostok. Independent nation-states, in short, were the exception to a worldwide imperial rule.

Even Japan, the best-known example of an Asian state that had resisted colonization (though its economy had been forcibly opened to trade by the United States), had itself already embarked on empire building, having conquered Korea. The United States, though forged in the crucible of anti-imperial war, had taken its first steps on the road to an empire, having annexed Texas in 1845, California in 1848, Alaska in 1867 and the Philippines, Puerto Rico, Hawaii and Guam in 1898. Indeed, its nineteenth-century history can be told as a transition from continental to hemispherical imperialism. The First World War had already dismantled three empires, the Habsburg, Hohenzollern and Ottoman, but many of their possessions had ended up in the hands of other empires, having enjoyed only the most fleeting taste of independence. After 1945 it was different. Not only the British but also the French, Dutch, Belgian and Portuguese empires were wound up, rapidly in some regions of the world, slowly and painfully elsewhere, until the 1970s when little more than their vestiges remained.

In short, these core countries virtually ruled the world. They set up institutions, changed customs, spread their languages, lifestyle value systems and everything else that go into the making of modern world. Americans were late-comers, and despite their awesome power, technology and attractive culture, they could nowhere influence the way we live and think today as the core West European countries did in the past. The countries left out of the scope of the book, the Iberian countries and those in the eastern Europe, also influenced history in considerable ways but again not as much as the core countries of central Europe. Hence, the discussion is limited to these countries. For that matter, it is not about whole of Europe but that part which matters most.

Acknowledgements

In the course of research and preparation of this book, *Glimpses of Europe,* we depended on a variety of sources which we have liberally used but only after due acknowledgements and attribution. These sources are a mix of the old and new because of the scope of the book which is a vignette of Europe in all its complexities – institutional, geographical, historical, political and cultural. Since the European history changed enormously after the collapse of Communism (1989-91), a large number of contemporary publications have provided the background materials for this book which include narratives on basic European values, international relations, European history, geography, people and places and much else besides.

For this reason, different kinds of source materials were necessary. And, combining them together in a structured book form was harder still to do. Since we have lived through the momentous period since 1989 and much before, we have rich collections of reports, paper cuttings, comments and contemporary opinion articles of leaders and commentators to guide us through this project which was taken up after extensive tour of the Continent. It took us about a decade to complete the project because we did not figure our how to go about selecting from plethora of materials from various soures and compress them into a popular history book. And, still we are not sure if the full story of Europe is adqualety told -a job which we leave to professional historians.

We acknowledge our debts to many writers whose works we have virtually pillaged and whose ideas and opinions we have borrowed. These include a large number of books, including The State of Europe (Howard K. Smith), Evolution of Nationalism, and Patriotism (R. Paul and Yuwa Wong), Contemporary Europe (Editor Joseph S. Roucek), The Age of Empire (Erick Hobsbawm), and the book edited by Graham Bateman and Victoria Egan. The other classics on Europe include books by Anthony Pagden, Robin Briggs, William I. Hitchcock (The Struggle for Europe), Alison Rowlands, R.A.

Houston and James C Riley. All the books written by distinguished historian Niall Ferguson have been extensively studied and consulted on facts and comments. We are hugely indebted to them.

We would also like to make special mention of the following sources. Jan Morris, Over Europe; James B. Collins and Karen L. Taylor, Early Modern Europe, Issues and Interpretations; John Hale, The Civilization of Europe in the Renaissance (London 1993); Norman Davies, Europe, A History; R.R. Palmer; Joel Colton & Lloyd Kramer, A History of the Modern World; Robert Ergang, Europe in Our Time; Ernest Barker (and others), The European Inheritance; Fritz Morstein Mark, Foreign Governments; John Canning, 100 Great Lives; Strategicus, A short History of the Second World War; C. Grove Haines, European Integration; Paul Kennedy, Rise and Fall of Great Powers; Herbert Feis, Between War and Peace; J.S. Roucek, Contemporary Europe; Liddell Hart, The War in Outline; Glbert Murry, The Deeper Causes of the War and its Issues; The Economist; Newsweek; Foreign Affairs; Time; Encyclopaedia Britannica; Hutchinson Encyclopaedia; (all national indicators are from Hutchinston Encyclopaedia) and UN documents. The list is not complete.

We are profoundly grateful to Mr. S.P.N. Sinha, IAS (retd.) and an academic, who has thoroughly revised the script, making significant changes and corrections on fact, grammar and language which are critical to credible narratives. We are also thankful to Prof. Sidheswardhari Sinha, a Commonwealth Education Fellow, who has revised the script and made many valuable corrections. We also owe immense thanks to Mr. Shashi Dhar and Ms. Babita who revised and typed out the copy many times over, so also to Mr. Debabrata Chatterjee for his guidelines on make-up and use of photos. They have been part of the team constantly at work with us. We commend their patience and good work.

A Continent of Destiny

For Greeks, Europe was a distant, cold and misty land beyond their northern horizon where feuding princes, dukes and dictators ruled over kingdoms with messy borders which Romans united in a huge empire with Britannia in the north, from Egypt to Morocco in the South, Asia Minor in the South-East, Dacia (Romania) in the North-East, and Hispania (Iberian peninsula) in the west, and ruled over it for about three centuries (753BC 476 AD). And, when the last of the Roman Emperor was caught and deposed by marauding tribals Vandals and Huns, Gibbon writes; *"The entire world collapsed in one city"*. This is their heritage much of which was reflected when Europeans played Romans and again conquered almost the entire world and held the humankind hostage to theor glory. But the better part of their history is that Europe is a land where great and glorious ideas of liberty, art, science, architecture and other find things of human glorious ideas of liberty, art, science, architecture and other fine things of human civilization were born and nourished. No wonder even in its much diminished avatar today, Europe remains the Continent of Destiny. Let's see how?

The Shaping of Europe

Nothing moves today; no political system, no system of technology, of law, or science that is not European in origin.

-D.W. Brogan

Introduction

In more ways than is often recognized, the one hundred years after the death of Elizabeth I in 1603, broadly marks the beginning of the first century of the modern world. A number of developments, peculiar to modern European thought, took place within these years. They are beginnings of modern science in the work of Galileo and Newton, Harvey and Boyle; the first expression of modern democratic ideas by the Levellers and the English Civil Wars; the end of the wars of religion and the achievement of representative government in England after the Glorious Revolution of 1688. But, Europe existed before these events took place. Although, these cannot be re-invented or compressed in this book but a brief perspective for rapid reading of the European history should be in order.

When the Greeks first talked of Europe, they were thinking of a distant mainland inhabited by barbarians who did not deserve a "mention" in Greek literature. For them, *Europa* was an invention and not a great landmass that extends from the Atlantic Ocean to the China sea, arbitrarily defined and called a continent. There is, however, something special about Europe. In the west, it lies romantically away beyond the Atlantic. In the south, it is bounded by the Mediterranean which has legendary islands like Crete, Malta and Corsica. In the north, it vanishes into the wastelands of the Arctic. Only in the east are its limits less marked. Europe, about the size of Brazil, is the smallest of all the continents except Australia. But, in riches, trade, education and civilization, it is the world leader. It lies, for the most part, in the temperate zone.

Earlier, the continent ended dramatically where the former Soviet Union began. Not now. Thus, Europe has 37 countries which includes the Balkans, Poland, Czech Republic, Slovakia and Hungary of East Europe with the total population of about 540 million (1991 estimate). However, only core countries are covered in the book. The line from the Baltic to the Black sea separates Western Europe from the Eastern Eurasian landmass. Six European countries (Britain, France, Italy, Germany, Spain, and Poland) account for 75% of the total European population, with others making up the rest. To be true, Europe consists largely of these countries and Scandinavia and the rest is geography. From the Atlantic and Arctic Oceans to the Mediterranean and Baltic Seas lay Europe in all its diversities, and with all the signs of its common bonds and shared values.

Much of Europe is gently rolling country, watered by perennial rivers, and temperate weather. There are, however, the marshes of the Danube, the forests of Finland and the formidable Hungarian plains. "There are snow, peaks and tundras and patches of moorland wilderness, bears, bison, water buffalo, wild cats, wolves, jackals, Arctic foxes, reindeer, wild pigs and even a few wild camels – are all to be found in Europe somewhere, and along its coastlines which range from the subtropical Mediterranean to the fierce fiords of the frozen north." says travel writer Jan Morris. European civilization has been nurtured in towns and cities and along the river valleys, on estuaries and bays or wherever the soil was rich, the terrain safe, welcoming those who settled in urban centres. No wonder, half the big cities of the world are in Europe. Europeans constitute about one-tenth of the earth's total population. The primitive people, who lived here before history began, were overwhelmed by successive streams of immigrants from Asia, gradually dissolving themselves into linguistic and racial groups, including the Teutons, Latins, Slavs, Celts and the Greeks. These again evolved into Germans or Italians or Serbs or Norwegians and also many other ethnic and linguistic splinters, like the Lapps or the Basques.

Europe is a brilliant mosaic of cultures and characteristics of the counties, kingdoms, principalities, empires, republics and city-states. It brought democracy, Christianity and the Renaissance, industrial, agricultural, social and intellectual revolutions. Europeans could be Danish, Irish, Sicilian, Belgian, Austrian and Welsh. Now in the expanded Europe, they may be Poles, Romanians or even Turks. They are, however, not Europeans as others are Chinese or Americans who share common purpose or conscience. Europe does not evoke loyalty or patriotism; *it is only a geographical definition,* an abstraction and the notion of European unity has been a pipedream. However, Europeans felt themselves integrated by a common civilization which, they thought, was superior to others. This concept of a common civilisation and European exceptionalism is impugned in the expanded Europe.

In the last century, Europe seemed less united than ever before. The Iron Curtain between communism and capitalism made one half of the continent feel permanently estranged from the other half. To travel from Brussels to Bucharest at the height of the Cold War was a medieval experience. It was less of a culture shock for Europeans to go to Cairo or Delhi than to any city in eastern Europe. Now that the Curtain has dissolved, and the concept of being European has acquired a new validity, a new continent seems to be in the making when it may not be entirely a Christian Europe. And, the members of the European Union, entirely different from the "Christian club", may change the basic character of the continent. The New Europe from the Western Isles of Ireland to the eastern reaches of Transylvania, with 540 million people and an economy of $ 9 trillion, rivalling the US (2006) may not be at one with Europe's shared values and common bonds. But that is, still, a guess.

35 MAJOR LANGUAGES

Ms Morris says the Europeans have never been homogenized into a distinctive type. "There are Europeans pale-faced, olive-skinned, congenitally tall, genetically squat – Europeans who look like Arabs or like Eskimos – Europeans habitually reserved, like Englishmen, or famously volatile like Italians or emotional like Poles or stubborn like Turks". At least, thirty-five major languages are spoken in the continent, and almost all have their own literature. Architecture, cuisines, tastes and attitudes – all vary widely. Switzerland is constitutionally neutral. There are eight European hereditary monarchies, besides princedoms and dukedoms. Francs, marks, pounds, dinars, drachmas, lire, leva, schillings, pesetas, crowns, florins, zlotys and escudos were European currencies before the *euro* hit the market.

ROMANS UNITED EUROPE WITH MESSY BORDERS

The Romans united the continent. From Istanbul, in the east, to Rome in the west, they imposed a common system, common laws and customs, enabling them for the first time to travel safely. At that time, the concept of Europe was born. But when the Roman legions withdrew, Europe fell apart again. It was also the time when the nation-States were born, and for hundreds of years the kingdoms, principalities and republics of Europe fought each other for supremacy or survival, inflamed by dynastic jealousies, border disputes, the grievance of minorities, or water rights. Sometimes simply for the sake of enhanced grandeur. The second smallest continent has complicated borders, some of which are, however, geographically obvious: the Rhine is one, the

English Channel is another; the Danube separates Bulgaria from Romania, the Pyrenees divides Spain from France, the summit of the Matterhorn (a peak on the Alps) draws a line between Italy and Switzerland. The Channel Islands, close to the coast of France, are British. Rhodes, near the coast of Turkey, is Greek and Gibraltar, near Spain, is British. Some states have population speaking several languages; in France alone eight languages are spoken.

Patriotism has been at once the glory and disgrace of Europe. Patriotism is not an innocuous pride in the beauty of a countryside, the success of an economic system, the glory of its history or the splendour of its literature. More often, it is the irrational devotion to a state, a particular patch of territory, enclosed within man-made limits and taught to think of itself as different from others. Part of the problem of Europe is its display of nationalism. It is hard not to feel the spirit of Frenchness, for instance, while walking down the Champs-Elysees in Paris on a public holiday when the traffic is cleared, flags are flying, and you can march towards the Arc de Triomphe feeling great like de Gaulle himself.

Every kind of state flourishes in Europe, and demands its own allegiance. In and among the great kingdoms and republics are many semi-states, hardly less proud of their dignity. Liechtenstein and Monaco, Andorra and San Marino and the Vatican, for instance, are town-size states with their own stamps, their own laws and their own ceremonial figureheads – a prince, a grand duke, state president or the pope. And far fiercer is patriotism among these small nations of Europe which had never been forcibly integrated into greater political entities, like those in Eastern Europe or the Balkans.

NO ORIGINAL EUROPEANS, ONLY IMMIGRANTS

Europe's original inhabitants came from somewhere else, and repeatedly threatened to master it. In the thirteenth century, the Mongols, storming out of the Asian heartlands, advanced far into Poland and Hungary and swarmed across the entire continent. In the fifteenth century, the Muslim Turks seized the Byzantine capital of Constantinople and established an Islamic toehold in Europe which still survives in the European part of Turkey. And in the eighth century, the Arabs and Berbers came from Africa to create an enclave in Europe. The Muslim Moors ruled much of Spain for seven centuries, and would perhaps have ruled France too, if they had not been defeated in 732 AD, near Poitiers, in one of the most crucial battles of history. By the end of the fifteenth century, they were out of Spain and out of Europe altogether, but they left behind relics of the synthesis they had achieved during their long presence. "It is an ironic truth that of all the cultures of Europe, the forcibly imposed culture of the alien Moors, blended so well with the Spanish genius and got absorbed so well into Christian Spain," says Ms. Morris.

AXIS OF CIVILIZATIONS

Europe has been central to the growth of human civilization even before Herodotus (c.485 – c.425 BC) started writing history as a critical pursuit of knowledge. For instance, when Columbus discovered America in 1492 (or, was it Amerigo Vespucci, a Florentine navigator), Europe was passing through the Renaissance period (14th to 17th century) which laid the foundation of the modern world. This is not to talk about Greek and Roman civilizations, without which living in today's world would have been a medieval experience. Europe was talking about science and art when immigrants were killing the native Indians to create a new country to which Tom Paine, a British cobbler, (later a maverick thinker, a celebrated writer and defender of *The Rights of Man*, writer of *The Age of Reason* and a believer in deism) gave a name, the *United States of America*.

There are many curious facts about Europe. For instance, there was no country like Germany until 1870; it was East Prussia. And, Belgium was born in 1839, conquered and re-conquered by many invading countries. Italy emerged in its present form only after Garibaldi united five major feuding city-states and proclaimed himself King at Turin in 1861, the date when the modern United Italy was born. There are six principalities, Andorra, Monaco, Liechtenstein, San Marino (founded by a stone-cutter) and the Vatican City with a population of about 1,000 people, all Catholic priests and unmarried. Nine of the 16 West European countries had most of the world's empires, including Belgium, (population 10 million in 1994) smaller than Delhi and the Netherlands (population 15 million in 1996), about the size of Mumbai. Europe had captured world's people and territories twice its population and twenty times its size. Still they are all Europeans – Latins, Slav, Tutons and Anglo-Saxons – flaunting Magna Carta (1215), Petition of Rights (1628); Habeas Corpus (1679), Glorious Revolution (1689) and Bill of Rights (1689) to claim that Europeans are the upholders of human rights and dignity.

However, whatever one may say about Europe, and very rightly so, the opposite is equally true. All great and glorious achievements, for instance, can be rightly attributed to Europe, including science, technology, human rights, art, painting, music, political and economic thought systems since Greeks and the Roman law. Then, what is the unchanging truth about the European history? None!! There are several fundamentally contrary ideas and images of Europe and they have quite distinct roles in understanding the continent. A country (or a people), has many identities; it depends what one likes to write about. Samuel Huntington of the *Clash of Civilisations* fame has put the world into a single identity mode – religion. They are Christian, Islamic and Hindu civilisations, etc. And, that they cannot co-exist peacefully, says the Pentagon think-tank member. (Huntington says that multiculturalism at home will harm the US and the West). This approach is flawed, imperfect and even dangerous. For instance, a man can be a priest, but he is also a father, social activist, painter and may be a bird watcher, besides being many other things. Huntington's segregation has done considerable harm to the understanding of global history of man and ideas.

EVENTS THAT SHAPED EUROPE

Among the major events which have created the present-day Europe was Treaty of Westphalia (1648) that marked the end of the Thirty Years' War after which emerged the nation-states of Europe; the treaty also defined the principle of non-interference in the internal affairs of other states. The Congress of Vienna (1814-15), attended by Austrian Foreign Minister Metternich, Alexander I of Russia, the British Foreign Secretary Castlereagh, military commander Wellington, and the French diplomat Talleyrand, created the Kingdoms of the Netherland and Poland and the German confederation of 39 states. Monarchs were re-instated in Spain, Naples, Piedmont, Tuscany and Modena; Louis XVIII was confirmed as

TIMELINE OF COLLAPSE

June 4: ((1989) Solidarity won Polish elections.

September 10: East Germans crossed Hungary's borders into Austria in droves.

November 9: the Berlin Wall fell;

November 24: Velvet Revolution succeeded in Czechoslovakia;

December 25: Ceausescu executed. The "Autumn of Nations" lasted only a few months; in its aftermath, two Germanys reunited, the Soviet Union collapsed and the Cold War ended.

king of France. The events of World War I accelerated the 1917 October Revolution (which took place on November 6), and the rise of Bolshevism, directly leading to the collapse of the Austro-Hungarian Empire and the creation of new nation-states in central Europe. After World War I, the Ottoman Empire collapsed and on its ruins were created Syria (1918-19), Iraq (1921), Iran (1935) and Lebanon (1922). These were the UN mandated territories, out of which Israel was also carved out (1948) under the Balfour Declaration (1917) to re-settle the Jews from Europe. The main consequence of the World War II was the collapse of the British empire. Its break-up freed the colonies but divided Europe by what Winston Churchil called an Iron Curtain, stretching from the Baltic to the Adriatic. This imaginary line, drawn between the countries occupied by the Soviet Union after 1945 and those nations liberated by the Western allies, dominated postwar politics.

Then came December 1991, when the USSR collapsed out of sheer exhaustion and the Commonwealth of Independent States (CIS) was joined by 12 former republics (the Baltic states remained outside). The Warsaw Pact and Comecon had already vanished with the breakaway of the Central European satellites in 1989. The meltdown of Communism also ended the Cold War which brought the world closer to nuclear conflicts many times, specially during the Cuban crisis. Thus, the European boundaries were drawn – again, again and again, ushering in the postmodern Europe The emergence of the US as the sole superpower reduced Europe to the status of a satellite continent, living on American dole (Marshall Plan) and protected by US defence networks (NATO). One doesn't know how long the "*American Century*" will last. The Third Reich was set up to last for "a thousand year" and the British and the Soviet Empires were supposed to last forever, but they melted away in history. That the bloodbath during these conflicts could have been avoided if European leaders had behaved differently will continue to be debated.

A CHRISTIAN CONTINENT

Pope Benedict XVI did not say a word too many when he declared in September 2006 that Europe was a Christian continent. He linked Islam with violence, quoting Byzantine Emperor Manuet II Paleologas of the Medieval Age. (The Pontiff later regretted the remark.) The fact is that Christianity, Judaism and Islam have a common prophet, Abraham (c2300 BC), whom the Jews consider the founder of the Jewish nation, followed by Moses who led the Israelites out of Egypt to the Promised Land of Canaan (Palestinian area between the Mediterranean and the Dead Sea) in the Exodus – a story which has the Biblical ring. Jesus Christ was also born a Jew but when Judas (Iscariot), an Apostle, cheated Jesus for 30 pieces of silver, Judaism split and Christianity was born. There is, however, no consensus on this explanation of the dispute between the Jews and Christians; for, Judaism is based on Old Testament, the first part of the Bible, corresponding to the Hebrew Bible, while Christianity is based on the second part of it, the New Testament, recording the life and teachings of Christ and his earlier followers.

FALLIBLE POPE

While criticising Islam, the Pope ignored history. Christianity, beginning with Constantine and continuing through the Crusades up to the Enlightenment, was "spread by the sword of the faith" it preached while Islam promoted religious amity among Jews, Christians, and Muslims. Christian theology's claim to rational method came about by St. Thomas Aquinas' appropriation

AVERROES WHO?

Ibn Rushd, known as Averroes, (1126-1198), was an Arab philosopher and physician, a master of philosophy and of Islamic law, mathematics, and medicine. He was born in Cordoba, Spain, and died in Marrakech, Morocco.

Averroes is most famous for his translations and commentaries of Aristotle's works, which had been mostly forgotten in the West. Before 1150 only a few translated works of Aristotle existed in Latin Europe, and they were not studied much or given much credence by monastic scholars. It was through the Latin translations of Averroes' works, beginning in the 12th century, that the legacy of Aristotle was recovered in the West.

Averroes' work on Aristotle spans almost three decades. He wrote commentaries on almost all of Aristotle's work except for Politics, to which he did not have access. Hebrew translations of his work also had a lasting impact on Jewish philosophy. Famous scholastics such as Thomas Aquinas believed him to be so important they did not refer to him by name, simply calling him '*The Commentator*' and calling Aristotle *The Philosopher*.

Without Averroes, the Greek knowledge would never have reached Europe. And, without Greek knowledge, Europeans would have been not far too different from those living in caves. Hence, while denigrating Arabs for many things, Europeans should remember that Averroes, an Arab, was among the founders of European civilization.

of Aristotle, as was made known to the West through Islamic scholars, including Arabian philosopher Averroes (1126-98), whose translations of Aristotle rescued the Latin West from the Stone Age. The other Muslim thinkers who made considerable contributions in the evolution of the European civilization include al-Farabi (10th century), Avicenna (11th century), al-Ghazali (12th century), Ash-Shatibi (13th century) and Ibn Khaldun (14th century).

The Pope also made no mention of the Islamic provenance of European and Christian culture. The European rejection of coercion in religion came about not through religion but through the secular impulses of the Enlightenment. The separation of church and state, in defence of the primacy of individual conscience, was an idea that the Catholic Church continued to oppose into the 20th century. Even now, the Pope campaigns against Enlightenment politics, condemning pluralism, and what he calls the "dictatorship of relativism". In all of this, the Pope seems to say that faith is superior to reason, Christian faith is superior to other faiths and Roman Catholicism is superior to other Christian faiths. Finally, the Pope is the supreme among Catholics and, by implication, all faiths, specially Islam. Such narcissism of power comes attached to a fuse.

Whatever the Biblical conundrum, the Pontiff, however, only sought to re-assert the fact that despite the claim of godless secularism, like that of France and many other European countries, the historical fact remained uncontested that the continent is built upon the immense foundation of Christianity which is the "cornerstone" of Europe where the Christian faith was formalized, institutionalized, intellectualized and popularized. It is true that even within the faith, the Europeans continued to quarrel – the Reformation, which split the continent in the sixteenth century, reverberates still on Europe's western fringe where the Catholics and Protestants of Ireland are locked in a "frozen" conflict. The Protestant Church, the Eastern Orthodox Church, and the Evangelical communions have, since the Reformation, repudiated the authority of the Pope. The schism between Eastern and Western churches was finally effected in 1054. The Reformation of the 16th century also gave rise to two large groups of reformed churches – those which followed Martin Luther and those which regarded John Calvin as their teacher. The Protestant movement has since given birth to a very large number of smaller sects. But, Europe is still the headquarters of the Christian world and, hence, it can be called a Christian continent although a handful of Jews, Muslims and immigrants can declare themselves anything else. Most pictures of Europe include the towers and steeples of churches and often the pattern of a city is built around their presence.

EUROPE IS PLURAL AND MULTI-RACIAL

Europe might be Christianity's flagship but the Continent is also the most mutinous, multi-racial and plural. Europe has three images; the first is Graeco-Roman Europe which is the core of Western civilization. Yet another image is that of the Christian Europe of the Middle Ages when Church held Europe in its iron grip, so much so that anyone found "guilty of heresy" was burnt at the stake. In that era, jurisdiction of the church and monarchs often overlapped. The level of literacy was low. The Middle Age Europe also witnessed the Christianisation of barbaric tribes like the Franks, Goths, Angles, Saxons, Vandals, Avars, Magyars, and Lombards who were physically and militarily mightier than the sinking Romans. But, through evangelisation, Graeco-Roman values of free-thinking, democracy and education were inculcated in those wild tribes and their descendants which produced a civilization far more advanced than the Greeks' and Romans'. Another feature of the Middle Age Europe was the continent's defence against aggressive Islam.

The third image of Europe has been Renaissance (1325-1525), Protestant Reformation (16th century) The Enlightenment (17th & 18th cent), Industrial Revolution (18th & 19th cent) and the French Revolution (1789-1802). The only church-friendly feature of it was the colonization that took Christianity to far-off lands, including South America which is now home to world's largest Catholic community. However, despite the post-War rhetoric of universalism, secularism and multi-culturalism, there is an abiding relationship between the church and state in all Christian nations, notwithstanding a formal separation of powers between Church and the State. Christianity powerfully supports Western civilization, as was evident in the pronouncement of Pope Benedict XVII, unlike in India where it is fashionable to undermine the native religiosity. And, condemn Indian religions as anti-modern, medieval and narrow-minded although heterodoxy, atheism (a la Buddhism) and pluralism have been the Indian traditions since Ashoka, 200 years before Christ, and Akbar the Great, some 400 years ago.

EMPIRE–BUILDERS, THESE

To be true, the last millennium belonged to Europe, which has exported worldwide its soldiers, missionaries and empire-builders, its religion and ideas, arts and sciences, goods and technology, its political and business systems and even its currencies. The Spaniards swept away the Inca and the Aztec civilizations. The French spread their culture from Indo-China to the Caribbean. Thousands of French citizens marched in Paris in early 2006 to commemorate the Setif and Guelma massacres in 1945 in which up to 45,000 Algerians were slaughtered by French troops. The Portuguese declared themselves rightful landlords of Brazil. Their cruelty is blood-curdling. The Dutch commanded an enormous empire in the eastern sea. And, the British sailed out from their islands to rule nearly a quarter of the earth's landmass and govern a quarter of all its inhabitants. English, French and Spanish became world languages. European systems of law, education, religion and technique were distributed among the indigenous population. "It became commonplace to find soldiers marching in turbans, hats and flowing robes under the Union Jack. In fact, Europe is a continent of empire-builders, unlike the US where the debate on social morality, human rights and freedom has been noisier than in Europe," says Ms Morris.

The European history is also marked by "postmodernism" which is a movement in art, culture and politics against the imperfections of modernism. Prof. Malcom Bradbury says, the term "postmodernism" broadly defines the decline of modernism since 1945. Particularly associated with post-industrial society, it suggests relativism, cultural crossover and multicultural borrowing. In generalised term, it is all about knowing the contemporary society and how different it is from the one that we have described as ancient, medieval and modern. For historical analysis, this epistemological obfuscation does not clearly determine the line between modernism and postmodernism. The French Revolution (and the American Revolution 13 years earlier) ushered in equality, liberty and human rights as an intellectual and empirical basis of modernism. But, it accepted feudalism and imperialism as facts of life. World War I demolished the Ottoman Empire but European imperialism remained intact. The World War II demolished imperialism also but communist empires were created. It was only after the collapse of Communism in 1991 that a free world was born in the true image of French Revolution ideas. And, that is the beginning of the postmodern world, according to historians. These landmark years are important also because during these periods, European boundaries were drawn and redrawn.

WORLD CAST IN EUROPE'S IMAGE

Europe almost always dominated the world. More important still, it created new worlds of its own. The empires fell one after another as the twentieth century ended, but Europeans stayed throughout North America and in the distant territories of Australasia where sovereign settlements of Europeans grew to finally become the governing class. Great new nations grew up in Europe's image in distant lands. When in the 1960s the Common Market came into existence in western Europe, people in New Zealand, on the other side of the globe, felt quite unhappy to be excluded from it. To be true, Europe is kaleidoscopic, moulded by different national origins, rooted in thousands of regional customs, embodied in disparate cultures and sealed by the effects of countless wars. One does not know any tiny piece of land on this planet where European explorers, conquerors, or buccaneers have not reached. Yet, there is more than the mere geography which binds this continent into a whole. Even Europe's most ardent nationalists would not say there is anything like the European patriotism. However, despite conflicts, they have a common inheritance. Europeans have mostly fought the same wars, on one side or another, and endured similar political or ideological processes. Common depressions and catastrophes have oppressed them and common tyrants have killed them. The wind that sweeps Ireland also makes people on the Polish plains shiver. When the Chernobyl reactor blew up in 1986, it polluted both the vineyards of Bulgaria and the sheep-farms of Wales. This is a case of common geography also.

MOST CONFLICT PRONE

Europe has also been a continent of conflict. There are few cities in the continent that have not, at one time or another, been razed, looted, fought over or bombed. The rivalry and ambition of Europeans have embroiled the whole world. An obscure assassin killed an Austrian aristocrat in a small town, Sarajevo, in the Balkans, and men were slaughtering each other in East Africa, Iraq and in the Indian Ocean. A demagogue came to power in Germany, and twelve years later the nuclear bomb fell on Japan. The plagues of Europe became the curse of humanity, and in our own time mass murder of Jews has become a paradigm of suffering itself. This continent has more reasons to cry than to celebrate. The lovely landscapes of the continent were soaked in blood and tears, more often than was the case anywhere else in the world.

As a matter of fact, the two world wars were essentially European wars, fought all over the world although they started in Europe and ended there. Yet the Europeans always thought of themselves as the arbiters of right and wrong. In the Middle Ages, (the period between the fall of the Roman empire and the Renaissance of the 5th and 15th centuries) the Pope had no qualms about dividing the unexplored world between Spain and Portugal. Europe seized the countries of other continents, declaring their inhabitants subjects to itself and exploiting their resources for its own use. At one time, European powers ruled the entire African continent, the whole of India, the two Americas and Australia. A vast aggressive energy flowed from Europe for a thousand years and more to conquer other peoples and impose its rule, culture, lifestyle, languages and everything else.

AMERICAS ARE EUROPEAN "DISCOVERY"

Whatever the pretentions, the Americas remain Europeans' achievement of the past four centuries. British explorer Martin Frobisher (1535-94) led the first expedition to North-West Passage (sea route from the Atlantic to the Pacific) in 1576 and helped defeat Spanish Armada; Walter Raleigh (1552-1618) organized exploration and colonization of America before he was executed by his own King James I for conspiracy; Italian-Spanish born Christopher Columbus (1451-1506) landed in many Caribbean islands in 1492 and in 1498, he was the first European to reach South American mainland and Jacques Cartier (1491-1557) was the first man who established the French claim to North America and also made many voyages to Canada. Just after Easter in 2007, the British Queen visited Virginia to mark the 400th year of the founding of Jamestown, the first English town in the New World. The English, French and the Spanish explorers have left behind their languages, cultures and cuisines which have now become the rich heritage of Americans. What started in Jamestown in 1607 is even more intimately bound up with African slavery. The first African slaves arrived at Jamestown in 1619, just 12 years after the three ships, *Discovery*, *Godspeed* and *Constant* carrying the 105 original pioneers, dropped anchor in the James River. Even the horror, shame and cruelty of slavery cannot undo the fact that the building of the 21st century Americas – specially the modern United States itself which is a pioneer of law, democracy, and freedom – has proved to be the single greatest achievement of the past four centuries. Columbus, Cartier, Frobisher, de Soto, and many more represented something that, in the fullness of time, changed the world. But the truth is that the Europeans have influenced the world for good or ill.

"ALTERNATIVE HISTORY"

Although the European primacy is established but not without opposition from many historians who reject the triumphalist Eurocentric view of history according to which the technological changes, that emanated in Europe, not only brought about Industrial Revolution that changed the world, but it also created a new "civilization". These economic historians, including Mr. A.K. Bagchi, say that in terms of human achievements, the two most populous countries of the world, India and China, did not do any worse than the best performing countries of Europe in the middle of the 19th century. In terms of commercialization, craft production, and agricultural growth also, China, India and Japan were performing no worse than major European countries during the Industrial Revolution period. In many areas, India had a leading position. Indian textile and craft production had to be suppressed to enable Britain to industrialise. For, India was the biggest exporter of textile manufactures in the world in the middle of the 18th century. Thus, the de-industrialisation of India and the economic deprivation and human suffering, accompanying it were the costs of the Europeans achievements. Therefore, the Europeans did not have the burden of lifting humanity from poverty. The contrarians say that the sudden increase of wealth in Europe, following the Industrial Revolution, did not have much positive effect on the welfare of most people. On the contrary, men and women suffered a decline in their biological well-being and standard of living during the meridian years of the English Industrial Revolution, and male illiteracy remained stagnant for 50 years between 1750 and 1800, although female illiteracy declined steadily from 1750 onwards. To those who say that freedom had been associated with capitalism, these historians point out that most slave exports from Africa took place between 1700 and 1900, when Europeans virtually ruled the world.

How then did Europe (or the lands settled by Europeans, such as the U.S., Canada and Australia) achieve unprecedented progress during the past two centuries, while the rest of the world had the opposite experience? That is because, it is argued, Europeans made striking economic advancement at the expense of the rest of the world. These economic historians add that in Europe, economy grew under intense national rivalries and wars, and because of the technical advance trade wars could be readily taken to other parts of the world in the quest for profits. It was in warfare that the rest of the world was inferior to Europeans and it was through wars and not by trade or economic or intellectual superiority that Europeans established dominion over the world. "Capitalism was from the beginning a system of fomenting wars and conflicts for new markets and colonies. No wonder, even today the U.S.

military expenditure accounts for close to 50 per cent of global military expenditure which is a major source of the Western supremacy", says Mr. Bagchi, in his book "Perilous Passage." Amartya Sen calls it an "alternative history.".

"History is written by victors; accept it or reject it", says Churchill. We have done neither, by giving the viewpoints of both – the winner and the loser, leaving the reader alone to make his own judgment. But whatever the contrarians may say, this is the absolute truth that Europeans have changed the world, for good or bad, in ways few had imagined before. Europeans have always been feared and admired both. Americans and Australians have often thought Europe as a decadent civilization. Activists of the Third World have thought it unwholesome because during the past centuries, Europe has given the rest of humankind as much tragedy as blessing. Nor could anybody boast of the continent's general behaviour in our own time.

However, time heals. It is the state, not the people, who commits atrocities. And, as the eventful twentieth century ended, Europe seemed at last half-reconciled to its past. The nations of the West, so long enemies, are slowly coalescing. The nations of east Europe, so long estranged, are beginning to see themselves as part of the continent. It may deteriorate again, the Balkans may relapse into discord, the old enemies across the Rhine may come to blows again, the British may turn their backs on the continent again and look to the sea once more. But, at least, we see in Europe today the hope of a peaceful continental community. Nobody but the gods and the angels can say that Europe is a sinless continent, but it is a continent where great things happened – good and bad. And, both make it an interesting continent to know about.

> ***The most persistent sound which reverberates through humanity's history has been the beating of war drums.***
> – *Arthur Koestler 1978*

Collapse of Old European Order

During more than 5,000 years of recorded human history, there had been 14,531 wars. And, most of them were fought in Europe which became a veritable burial ground of a generation of young Europeans during World War II. Now that there is no war to fight, no enemy to kill, nor any fortress to conquer, Europe is looking a strange place.

After the World War I, peace treaty was signed on June 29, 1919, Allied Chief of General Staff Marshal Ferdinand Foch said : "Let the German soldiers have their weapons and uniforms and go home with dignity. After all, they are brave soldiers who fought well." Displaying high spirits and unbroken discipline, the famished and defeated German soldiers cried, *"Hail Fatherland,"* and walked past the dais. Marshal Foch turned sad and told his British counterpart: "This is not peace but a truce for twenty years. Germans are unconquerable." And, exactly after 20 years, (September 1, 1939), Germans attacked Poland which started World War II in which more than 50 million people died or were injured, maimed or crippled for life. The global war was fought on five continents, involving more than two-thirds of the total world's population fighting on land, sea and in the air, setting new records in ferocity and cruelty, the like of which was never seen before and since. Soldiers in uniform rampaged European areas between the Pyrenees, in the east, and the Volga, in the West.

Elvin Toffler says: "Since World War II, there was the Korean War (1950-53), the Vietnam War (1957-75), the Arab-Israeli wars (1967, 1973, 1982), the Persian Gulf War (1990-91), and many in Africa. Thus, between 150 and 160 wars and civil conflicts had raged around the world since peace was achieved in 1945. And, an estimated 7.2 million soldiers were slaughtered in the process. That is the figure for deaths alone – not for the wounded, tortured, or mutilated. Neither does it include the far larger number of civilians sacrificed. Or, those who perished in the aftermath of combat. Ironically, in the World War I, the number of soldiers killed was only moderately larger : approximately 8 million. This means, amazingly enough, that in terms of combat deaths, even allowing for a wide margin for error, the world has fought almost the equivalent of World War I all over again since 1945. When civilian deaths are added, the total reaches an astronomical 33 to 40 million – again, not counting the wounded, raped, dislocated, diseased, or impoverished.

"People have shot, stabbed, bombed, gassed, and otherwise murdered one another in Burundi, Rwanda, Nigeria, Bolivia, Cyprus, Sri Lanka, Madagascar and Morocco. There are today nearly 200 members of the United Nations (191 in 2006) and war has been waged in well over sixty of them. SIPRI, (the Stockholm International Peace Research Institute) counted thirty-one armed conflicts took place in 1990 alone. In other words, in the 2,340 weeks that passed between 1945 and 1990, the earth enjoyed a grand total of only three weeks that were truly war-free. To call these peaceful years (from 1945 to the present post-War era) is, therefore, to compound tragedy with irony," says the futurist writer.

MAN IS WAR-PRONE

Arnold Toynbee says that war is a normal condition of man. Before the reign of Emperor Augustus, the Romans were seldom at peace with their neighbours; for 267 years (32 BC to 235 AD) peace was generally preserved; that prior to the invasion of the Nazis in 1940, Norway had peace for 126 years. In 1960, a Norwegian statistician, with use of computers, announced that in the 5,560 years of recorded human history, there had been 14,531 wars and that of the 185 generations of man's recorded experience, only ten have known peace. And, most of these wars were fought in Europe, the bloodiest of them being the one which ended on May 9, 1945. All changes involved ruthless killing without which nothing was settled in Europe. No wonder twice in twenty years, European boundaries were re-drawn; first at Versailles (South of Paris) on June 29, 1919 and again at Potsdam (outside Berlin) on August 2, 1945. At the Congress of Vienna 1815, three manifestly crafty statesmen and diplomats, Metternich (Klemens First van), an Austrian; Talleyrand (Perigord Chavles Maurice de), a French, and Castlereagh (Viscount Robert Stewart), a British, re-drew the boundaries of Europe ravaged by Napoleon during the 12 years he held the continent hostage to his glory.

WANDERERS MAKE HISTORY BY UNITING TWO GERMANYS

Earlier still, Europeans fought a 100-year war, a 30-year war and a series of battles which produced nation-states in Europe. The overseas conflicts between the European powers also sparked off conflicts at home. However, what happened in the early 1990s was never known in European history before. On November 5, 1989, a couple of wanderers crossed over the Berlin Wall and the drunken guards let them go west. Then came the other groups of determined men and women when the guards referred the matter to the Communist Government in East Berlin. The order came that the Berlin question was being discussed in Moscow. Again came hundreds of thousands of men and women from East Germany, chanting *"freedom"*. No order had come from Berlin yet and the surging crowds tore down the Wall for the entire people to escape to freedom in the west. And that was the end of the German question. Thus, the truncated country was informally united again (formal unification took place on Sept. 3, 1990). Weeks of huge demonstrations in October 1989 following mass exodus via Hungary and Czechoslovakia led to the collapse of the hard-line regime in the Communist ruled German Democratic Republic. The opening of the Berlin Wall, built in 1961, came next and then the promise of free elections. November 5, 1989, when the Berlin Wall fell, is a great day in European history. (*Detail in later chapters*)

The GDR was led by men such as Erick Honecker, who had spent ten years in a Nazi concentration camp. Which was why the brightest and best of Germany's exiled left-wing and liberal intelligentsia, such as Bertolt Brecht and Arnold Zweif, chose to live in the GDR at the end of the War. Germany's best spirits have always warned of the dangers of a unified Reich. Goethe had predicted at the beginning of the 19th century that once united, the Germans would be guilty of the most appalling barbarities *("Germans are so worthy as individuals, so worthless as a united nation")*. Nietzsche, at the end of the 19th century warned his fellow-Europeans of the *"deceiving folk"* in Germany. "There are", he said, "dark corridors in the German soul, a labyrinth in which one never quite knows what is going to be in the next corner". The king of Bavaria told the Archbishop of Cologne in 1871, when the crown was handed over to the King of Prussia, "future generations might well curse me for handing over the crown to the King of United Germany, no peace-loving country this." The unification of Germany has caused many justifiable fears among millions of people – Jewish, Russian and Polish. The creation of a *Fourth Reich* has demonstrated that a united Germany was a danger to the world. Whatever its faults, the German Democratic Republic (East Germany) was an essential component of the peace and stability of Europe since 1945 and the only German state in which the full horrors of the Nazi regime (1933-45) were fully revealed. Two world wars and millions of dead have proved how prophetic were Nietzsche's words.

EAST EUROPEAN DOMINOES FELL LIKE NINE PINS

In Czechoslovakia, the regime collapsed after a week of huge demonstrations, triggered by police violence against protesters on November 17, 1989. Mr. Vaclav Havel, in jail at that time, became the first president of a non-communist Czechoslovakia. At the beginning of the year 1989, Solidarity (a dock workers' union) was a banned organisation in Poland. By the end of August, Poland had a Solidarity Prime Minister (Lech Walesa), East Europe's first non-Communist leader in 40 years. In Romania, protest in the western city of Timisoara was crushed on December 17, 1989, an incident of violence in which thousands died in army action. Protest spread to Bucharest and within five days, President Nicolae Ceausescu and his wife were executed. In Bulgaria, demonstrations in November 1989 were soon followed by sacking of Todor Zhivkov, in power since 1954. This led to free elections in 1990 when the communist system was abolished in the country forever. Hungary was the only country where impetus for reform came mostly from above – specially from the leading communist radical, Mr. Imre Pozsgay. Budapest's Parliament was torn down.

To say this, however, is not to suggest that communism has failed and capitalism will last forever to mark the "*End of Civilization*", *a la* Francis Fukuyama. In the beginning of the new century, the Left has won significant majority in Brazil (with President Inacio Lula da Silva in 2002), Argentina (with President Néstor Kirchner in 2003), Uruguày – (with President Tabaré Vásquez in 2004), the Dominican Republic (with President Leonel Fernández in 2004), Bolivia (with President Evo Morales in 2005) and Chile (with President Michelle Bachelet in 2006) and President Hugo Chávez of Venezuela who has been in power for quite some time now, and keeps winning elections. To have a metal worker, who lost one of his fingers on the factory floor, as President of Brazil; an aboriginal leader as President of Bolivia, and an agnostic, single mother as

President of Chile, all of them elected with more than 50 per cent of the popular vote, indicates a major shift in the patterns of social and political behaviour when it was believed that Marxism was dead forever. With social inequality and poverty most glaring in the 14 mainland countries of Latin America, Karl Marx will begin to turn in his grave. As he does today in many poor countries. (Reporting year 2006).

And, thus, the Old Order set up at Potsdom and Yalta in 1945, collapsed. This also marked an end to Marxist orthodoxy which ruled half of Europe for 70 years and more. Between 1945 and 1989, European relations were largely determined by the Cold War which, ironically enough, was a powerful matrix for solving problems. To be true, East-West (European) tension had been the centrepiece of the foreign policy of superpowers who stood across the defeated and humiliated continent, like Colossus. A Europe, without an enemy was looking truly a strange place. For, Europeans have always learnt to live with enemies and resources and scientific skills had been invested in raising armies and making bombs. The best brains of the continent, the youth and enormous sums of money had been set apart by each country for conflicts, many of which never took place at all. Now, there is no war to fight, no enemy to kill nor any fortress to conquer; what do Europeans do now? Trade.

This is the "New Order" in Europe which has been the le ıder of the peoples of the world. "Where can we look for assurance that it is not the same old world which we loved to hate," said a European commentator after the collapse of the Berlin Wall. "If there were no Gorbachev, history would have created one because Communism had lived far too long in organised boredom and avoidable indigence," said another political commentator on changes in Europe. If it is the Europe that mattered in the shaping of world events, let us know more about its people, history, geography, resources, and everything else that go into making it a continent of destiny.

PART – I
PROFILE OF EUROPEAN CONTINENT

1

What is Europe?

"What is Europe?", Winston Churchill asked in 1946, "A rubble heap, a charnel house, a breeding ground for pestilence and hate".

There had been so many wars in the World, but nothing happened. But, the mere assassination of Archduke Ferdinand of Austria on July 28, 1914, sparked off a global war. Again attack on Poland, a country about the size of Bangladesh, caused a second global war in which some 50 million people were killed. Very clearly, Europe is a continent of destiny which always set the trend for global events.

Europe is neither a landmass, nor a single people, nor was it ever a single political unit. Europe has been a cultural space. European culture, which combined constituents inherited from various peoples in the ancient Mediterranean world, gave its people a sense of belonging more closely to each other than to the rest of humanity. The Greeks bequeathed to Europe a philosophical outlook, and a belief in the value of city life for developing the human personality to the full. The Roman Empire gave a common language and a legal system. Christianity gave a shared faith. Ancient learning instilled the belief that free Europeans possessed the skill, the craft, and knowledge to master the world through ingenuity and technology. This belief gave early Europeans the confidence that they were destined to dominate the rest of the world.

One may detect a sorry contrast between the shared destiny for Europeans and other peoples with whom they fought for colonies and trading-posts. However, it is an inescapable fact of history that European culture and government expanded over much of the world, in a way that Asian cultures did not. Towards the end of the 18th century, European writers were beginning to think of themselves as belonging to a wider humanity, bearing responsibility for the world as a whole (white men's burden). Aspirations for a supranational unity of the whole continent had been expressed as early as in the sixteenth century. And, this sets the background for the European story which is still far from complete, despite the expansion of the European Union in the east to make it a 27-member Christian and white men's club. (It is still expanding east)

EARLY EUROPEANS

Europa: In Greek mythology, the daughter of the king of Tyre, carried off by Zeus (in the form of a bull); she personifies the continent of Europe.

The survival of early Europeans depended on land. Crop yields were poor and left little leeway for bad harvests or the exactions of state and Church. Family structures were shaped by the customs and conventions inherited by different regions of Europe: nuclear households in the north and extended families in the south. The overwhelming majority of people who lived close to the soil used ingenious systems of borrowing to tide over bad times. The old world, or pre-industrial society, was marked by misery. The sixteenth century had increased numbers of mouths to feed and that put pressure on land. Rents increased and wages declined. A minority of wealthy tenant farmers exploited the rise in food prices to become peasant aristocracies, while their neighbours sank into poverty. The economy, as a whole, expanded in the sense that more was bought and sold at higher prices but this expansion only made the poor poorer. In the seventeenth century, this pattern changed. The slowing down of the population growth, combined with the continued effort to grow more food, stabilized basic food prices. Crop yields increased although in certain areas, particularly the Netherlands and England, to the point where the agricultural economy produced more than was needed for subsistence. Economic factors did not determine people's lives absolutely, but interacted with the social and political structures of the region. The better-fed bourgeoisie of the Low Countries were fed with grain grown by enslaved peasants. By the end of the eighteenth century, liberalism and laissez-faire were beginning to take over from *mercantilism*, the economic doctrine which justified restricting trade in national interest. It also supported colonial exploitation. However, laissez-faire sought to cut regulations and allowed free flow of goods, in the belief that the wealth of a nation was not fixed, but that diligence and cooperation could make the total cake larger for all to share. The fear of the mortal sin of greed and its consequences, which had governed price-fixing and market-rigging for several centuries, was replaced by the belief that everything would work out well if left to itself. This was the background against which modern Europe grew, not far too different from the one found in Asia.

TRADE LED TO WARS AND COLONISATION

During that period, Europeans also discovered that they were operating an industrial economy on the basis of old principles, fashioned during the French Revolution. The chief mechanism of the commercial principle, the market, was too limited to absorb technology. It was found inadequate for distributing the produce of the machines. Hence, the population was pressing for new openings. Production, too great for internal markets to absorb, caused depression in the industrialised countries which led to colonisation of what is now called the *Third World*. Through their conquests, the nations sought either new markets or cheap labour which would allow them to undersell their competitors in the domestic market. And, they also sought strategic positions from which both could be defended by force, if necessary. During the years just before 1914, the pressure became very intense and World War I broke out.

Esme Winsfield Stratford, a historian, said: "If the war peril from Germany delayed longer to materialise, it seemed that it would be forestalled by revolution." Similar sentiments were expressed by the US Ambassador to Britain, Mr. Walter Hines Page, when he said in 1917: "Perhaps our going to war is the only way in which our present prominent trade position can be maintained". This was true of the World War II also which was fought not only to eliminate Jews from Germany or to seize *"living space"* (*a la* Hitler) for Germans but also to contain Germany which was fast becoming a threat to British trade in Europe and outside it. Eventually, the forces making for war won the race. Germany, with vigorous and swiftly expanding industry but a late-comer in the trade competition, found all the outlets occupied. And, hence, it proceeded with the Prussian tradition of war for trade expansion.

Europe was first named *"Europa"* by the Greeks which means *"mainland,"* though its earlier interpretation was "sunset." (Detail given in the chapter: How it all began?) It appears to have been suggested by the Greeks as an appropriate name of the extensive northerly lands that lay beyond, – the lands with characteristics clearly different from those inherent in the concept of Asia and Libya (Africa), both of which were prosperous civilisations then. Traders and travellers reported that Europe possessed distinctive physical features, with mountain systems and lowland river basins much larger than those known to the inhabitants in the Mediterranean region. It was also clear that climates were different from those in other parts of the then known world.

A PROFILE

Europe is a small outgrowth on the rump of Asia. The frontier separating Europe from Asia, (the Urals), is a far less formidable obstacle than the Himalayas and Hindu Kush, or even the Pyrenees and the Alps which cut off Europe's south-western and southern parts from the main body. The slits of the Bosphorus and the Dardanelles are small streams compared to the English Channel. The only imposing frontier is the Caucasus which is not a clear-cut geographical line of demarcation between Europe and Asia. The Aegean Sea separates Europe from Asia in the eastern Mediterranean. Europe is less than a quarter size of Asia and less than half the size of North America. If European Russia be excluded, it is not much larger than Australia or India. Looking closely at the world map, Europe seems appendixed to *Eurasia*. It is quite hard to believe that this small peninsula, not quite one-fifth of the total land surface of the globe, could for so long dominate the rest of the world.

SECOND SMALLEST – ABOUT SIZE OF BRAZIL: Though second smallest of the seven continents, except Australia, Europe has twice as many people as North and South America put together. (The seven continents are: North America, South America, Asia, Africa, Australia, Antarctica and Europe). Europe, spread over 10.5 million sq.km., is about the size of Brazil (8.4 million sq.km) which is the largest country in South America. The population density is twice as great as Asia's and nine times that of the US. For centuries, Europe's principal export has been its population. The Asian immigration into Europe is a recent development, sharply noticed after the end of World War II when European powers had to abandon their colonies in Asia and Africa from where earlier a sizable number of people, most of them by force, were brought to the continent and England to do the work which whitemen could not.

ETHNIC GROUPS: Europe has three large ethnic groups, Latins, Teutons and Slavs, who intermarried to produce a common European stock. For instance, Adolf Hitler was a crossbred between Slav and Teuton. "*The greatest German who ever lived* would have been far less conspicuous among the Slovene mercenary on the Carinthian border than among the blond blue-eyed Bavarian mountaineers of Germany", says historian Robert Ergang.

GEOGRAPHY: Europe's pre-eminence in history also flows from geography; its thin and long structure has attracted men and animals to come and multiply. No point west of the Russian border is farther than 500 miles from sea. And, almost the entire area of Europe lies in the narrow strip of moderate temperature and mean rainfall, a situation enjoyed by no other continent. The soil is rich and even after centuries of exploitation, most European countries produce more grain to an acre than Americans do in the midwest. Almost the entire area between the Elbe, in the east, and the Pyrenees, in the west, has precipitation enough to produce a variety of grains without irrigation, except in the highlands.

Travelling deep into French villages, along the Alps or up in Sweden from Copenhagen or still to the east of Berlin, one can see endless stretches of land producing grain without irrigation. Lush green forests, hills and orchards produce fruits and timber for all, whatever the climatic vagaries. People sow crops and go to the fields only to harvest them. This is a tremendous advantage specially when viewed against tropical areas in India where almost nothing grows without irrigation.

EUROPEAN RIVERS, SEAS AND HARBOURS

In the dawn of history, civilisation advanced by piracy and trade, both moved by water. And no continent had so much water and harbours as Europe which is surrounded on three sides by easily navigable seas and another – the Baltic – goes deeper into the northern landmass. Along most of its coastlines, the seas are nearly tideless. Although Europe is less than a third of the size of Africa, her coastlines are three times its length. It is irregular almost everywhere. These were immense advantages for the movement of men, goods and also ideas in the days of primitive navigation. And, there is no continent so thoroughly laced with rivers. In the heart of the continent, the headwaters of four great rivers, leading to all the surrounding seas, run within a few miles of one another. When the Mediterranean civilisation exhausted its resources, Europe had a rich continental hinterland to inherit its seeds and nurture them to growth.

RIVERS: The main rivers flow into northern or inland seas. The Volga, the Don, the Dnieper, the Northern Dvina, and the Western Dvina rise on the Valdaian plateau, to the north-west of Moscow, and the Danube, the Rhine, the Rhone, the Po, and the Adige flow from the Alps. The East has many lakes, notably Geneva, Constance, Lucerne, Neuchatel, Maggiore, Garda, and Como in the Alps; Vanern, Vattern, Malar, Mjosa, and Randsfjord in the peninsula formed by Norway and Sweden; Ladoga, Onega, Peipus, and Ilmen in North Russia; Salma and innumerable others in Finland. The largest islands are Spitsbergen, Iceland, Britain, Ireland, Sardinia, Corsica, Sicily, Novaya Zemlya, and Crete.

VEGETATION: South of the Alps, the trees are mainly ever-green. Rice, maize, millet, and wheat are among the cereals cultivated in this region, and olives, grapes, oranges, lemons, figs, and chestnuts thrive. Central East is particularly rich in cereals and also produces large quantities of fruit. Most of its forests are deciduous, oak, beech, etc. In the North the chief trees are pines, larches, birches, and willows.

MINERALS: Coal is found in Great Britain, Germany, France, Belgium, former Czechoslovakia, Poland, and Russia. Great Britain, Germany, France, Belgium, Sweden, Austria, former Czechoslovakia, Russia, and Spain have deposits of iron ore. Copper, lead, zinc, gold, platinum, silver, salt, sulphur, and graphite are all obtained in the east. There are large oilfields in the Caucasus and west Ukraine and both oil and natural gas offshore beneath the North Sea. Industrialization began in the west because of the aptitude of the people, presence of minerals and accessibility to overseas territories, offering both raw materials and markets. Industrial development spread east wards, and was accelerated after World War II especially in the Ukraine and other countries of the former USSR or under Russian influence.

MAJOR LANDMARKS OF EUROPE

In order to understand the geography of Europe, which has also political implications, let us know about these major geographical landmarks.

ODER RIVER: It is in central Europe, rising in east Sudeten mountains of former Czechoslovakia and flows north through Poland, along the former

East German frontier to meet the Baltic Sea, near Szczecin. The length is 854 km. The *Oder-Neisse Line* is the border between Poland and Germany drawn by the Allied in 1944-45, involving the transfer to Poland of large areas of pre-War Germany, a source of major contention between former east and west Germany. This was recognised as the formal boundary in 1970.

ELBE: It is east of the Oder river and one of the principal rivers of Germany (1,166 km), rising on the southern slopes of the Riesengebirge of Czech Republic, and flowing across the German plain, west of Berlin, into the North Sea.

RHINE RIVER: It is in the centre and west of Europe, rising in south-east Switzerland, forming part of the Germany-France border; it divides into two major branches in the Netherlands before entering the North Sea; length 1,320 km. It is main waterway in west Europe, flowing through major industrial areas and widely connected by canals to other rivers. It promotes tourism in the Rhine Valley.

COUNTRIES OF EUROPE

Countries	Capitals
Norway	Oslo
Sweden	Stockholm
Finland	Helsinki
Denmark	Copenhagen
Iceland	Reykjavik
The United Kindgom	London
Ireland	Dublin
France	Paris
Andora	Andorra la Vella
Monaco	Monaco
The Netherlands	Amsterdam
Belgium	Brussels
Luxembourg	Luxembourg
Spain	Madrid
Portugal	Lisbon
Italy	Rome

Vatican City	Vatican City
San Marino	San Marino
Greece	Athens
Malta	Valletta
Cyprus	Nicosia
Germany	Berlin
Switzerland	Bern
Liechtenstein	Vaduz
Austria	Vienna

(These 25 countries are treated as European countries for purpose of discussion in this book).

PYRENESS: The mountain range in south-west European boundary between France and Spain; length about 435 km; highest peak Aneto (French Nethon) 11,172 feet. Andorra is entirely within the ranges. Hydroelectric power has encouraged industrial development in the foothills. The *Pyreness Treaty* of 1659, was signed between France and Spain ending the hostilities of the *Thirty Years' War* and followed a series of Spanish Habsburg defeats since 1643. Austrian Habsburgs, however, made a separate peace in the *Treaty of Westphalia* (1648) which marked the end of Spanish military and political dominance in West Europe.

SEINE: It is essentially the French river, rising on the Langres plateau north-west of Dijon, flowing 774 km to join the English Channel, near Le Havre. It passes through Paris and Rouen.

DANUBE: It is the second longest European river, rising on the eastern slopes of the Black Forest and flowing 2,858 km across Europe to enter the Black Sea in Romania. A canal connects the Danube with the Main river and, thus, with the Rhine river system. In 1992, the river was diverted in Slovakia to feed the controversial Gabcikovo Dam. It is considered as the Balkan river.

URAL MOUNTAINS: This is the mountain system running from the Arctic Ocean to the Caspian Sea, traditionally separating Europe from Asia in the east. The highest peak is Naradnaya at 6,214 feet. It has vast mineral wealth. The middle Urals is one of the most industrialised regions of Russia. Perm, Chelyabinsk, Ekaterinburg (Sverdlovsk), Magnitogorsk and Zlatoust are major industrial centres.

AEGEAN SEA: This separates Europe from Asia in the eastern Mediterranean. It is the eastern end of the Mediterranean Sea, bounded in west and north by Greece, north-east and east by Turkey, south by islands of Crete and Rhodes. It is dotted with islands on which the Aegean Civilization (of 3000 1000 BC) flourished. Its length (north-south) is 645 km; width 320 km and the greatest depth is 2013 m/6604 ft. The Aegean civilization was the Bronze Age culture which flourished in the third and second millennia BC on the islands of the Aegean Sea and around its coasts. Aegean Islands have the population (1981) of 428 533; area 9122 sq. The Island group and region of Greece is the name applied to the islands of the Aegean Sea, including Lesbos, Chios, Samos, Limnos, and Thasos.

HOW EUROPEANS GREW

The population of Europe advanced from a mere 10 million in 1000 BC to 36 million in the Roman period and 80 million by the end of the 15th century. The development of a healthier society from the 16th century onwards led to a much lower death rate, pushing the population of Europe up to 400 million by 1900. The contemporary trend of a low birth rate is stabilising the total at around 700 million, including Eurasia.

FRONTIERS AND BOUNDARIES

Europe had been highly unstable in the sixteenth and seventeenth centuries and the boundaries between nations were indistinct. Only the Atlantic and the Mediterranean provided obvious frontiers. For the Greeks, Europe had been only the area in which the Greeks lived – a vaguely defined region which paled into what was once Yugoslavia, in the north, and Turkey, in the east. Beyond Europe lay Asia and Africa. And, Africa, south of the Atlas mountains, was dark. Only the north coast, which had once been part of the Roman Empire and the home of marauding Portuguese and Spaniards, was a recognisable territory. And if Europe's southern frontiers were indeterminate, her eastern ones were forever undecided. Between eastern Europe and the *recognisable* Orient was the unsettling presence of Russia.

PROFILE AT A GLANCE

Some defining features of the European continent

Europe is the second smallest continent, occupying 8% of the Earth's Surface, spreading over an area of 10,400,000 sq km. (4,000,000 sq. mile).

COUNTRIES – The core 25 countries have been covered in this book.

POPULATION – (1991) 540 million (excluding Turkey-in-Europe and the former USSR); annual growth rate 0.3 per cent (average). In some countries, including France, population is declining.

LARGEST CITIES – (population over 1.5 million) Athens, Barcelona, Berlin, Birmingham, Bucharest, Budapest, Hamburg, Istanbul, Kharkov, Kiev, Lisbon, London, Madrid, Manchester, Milan, Moscow, Paris, Rome, St. Petersburg, Vienna and Warsaw.

FEATURES – Mount Elbruz 5,642 m (18,517 ft) in the Caucasus Mountains is the highest peak in Europe; Mont Blanc 4,807 m (15,772 ft) is the highest peak in the Alps; lakes (over 5,100 sq km/2,000 sq mi) include Ladoga, Onega, Vanern; rivers (over 800 km/500 mi) include the Volga, Danube, Dnieper, Ural, Don, Pechora, Dniester, Rhine, Loire, Tagus, Ebro, Oder, Prut, Rhone. The largest river is the Volga (3,687 km).

PHYSICAL – Conventionally occupying the part of Eurasia to the West of the Ural Mountains, North of the Caucasus Mountains, and North of the Sea of Marmara, Europe lies entirely in the northern hemisphere between 360^0 North and the Arctic Ocean. About two-thirds of the continent is a great plain which covers the whole of European Russia and spreads through Poland to the Low Countries and the Bay of Biscay. A line from the Baltic to the Black Sea divides Europe between an eastern continental region and a western region, characterized by a series of peninsulas that include Scandinavia (Norway and Sweden), Jutland (mainland Denmark and a small part of Germany), Iberia (Spain and Portugal), and Italy and the Balkans (Greece, Albania, Croatia, Slovenia, Bosnia-Herzegovina, Serbia and Montenegro (former Yugoslavia), Bulgaria and Turkey-in-Europe.

CLIMATE – Most parts of Europe fall within the northern temperate zone which is modified by the Gulf Stream in the north-west. There are four main climate zones: the north-west region (stretching from north Spain through France to Norway), the Mediterranean zone, central Europe, and eastern Europe. The north-west region has mild winters, cool summers, and cloud and rain all the year round.

LANGUAGES – Mostly Indo-European, with a few exceptions, including Finno-Ugric (Finnish and Hungarian), Basque, and Altaic (Turkish); apart from a fringe of Celtic, the North-West is Germanic; Letto-Lithuanian languages separate the Germanic from the Slavonic tongues of Eastern Europe; Romance languages spread east-west from Romania through Italy and France to Spain and Portugal. In all, there are 50 key languages, and many dialects.

RELIGION – Christian (Protestant, Roman Catholic, Eastern Orthodox), Muslim (Turkey, Albania, Bosnia-Herzegovina, Serbia and Montenegro, Bulgaria) and Judaism.

Roman empire, Roman law, Christianity and the Latin language have emotionally united Europe, instead of a common history which Europeans had never had one.

– Anthony Pagdon

2

Europe's exceptionalism and sources of its primacy

The old and tired Europe has been seeking new ways to reshape history, in the making of which it had a hand in a manner unmatched by any before. To be true, European science, technology, law and languages have been imposed on most parts of the world by force. And, it is too late to waste time regretting it. After all, the ideas and techniques of the Graeco-Roman world were also imposed on Europe by force. – Arnold J. Toynbee

The culture of Europe centred on city, although most people lived and worked in the countryside until well into the nineteenth century. Community, village and the "small homeland" were cultural congregations of the people with a shared and historically determined culture. "Politics" and "polity" have their root in the Greek term *polis*. Similarly "civil", "civility", "civilization" have their origins in the Latin word – *civitas* – for the same spatial, political, and cultural groups. Both *polis* and *civitas* became "the state". City defined European culture which originated in Asia. Man is "made for good life in the *polis,*" said Greeks. Civility was the best attainable existence. It was what the Greeks called "good life", the only life in which it was possible for man to achieve his elusive goal which Aristotle termed *eudaimonai*, or "happiness" or "human flourishing".

For Aristotle, there could be no life beyond the limits of the city, but that of "beasts and gods". Since humans were distinct from both beasts and gods and were guided by rules, laws and customs, the city was also the source of law. Those who lived within it had to abide by its rules. Beyond it, there was wilderness described as "the state of nature". In the Greek world-view, to live in the state of nature was to live like a "barbarian" or a "savage". The *polis* was a bounded space with a community which had the power to transform all those who entered it. So long as you were outside, you were a barbarian (Ironically Aristotle, who said it, was himself an outsider). Once inside, however, you would in time become "civilized". Once inside, you would also become a "citizen" – that is a member of the *civitas* or city. Rome was a city in the Greek concept. Hence, Rome was the source of law, the place of customs and mores, and it was encircled and protected by its massive walls. And, even more than the Greek city-states, Rome welcomed outsiders within its walls.

Through conquest and colonisation, Europe had carried her culture to the other continents. In America, Australia, the northern part of Asia and the southern tip of Africa, she had invaded huge, sparsely inhabited areas and had taken to them her sons and daughters, who carried their home culture along with them and established genuine *daughter societies.* At their fringes, where a strong native population survived, a composite pluralist society arose and race admixture took place. The *daughter societies* became more or less faithful replicas of the mother country, even though they were separated by huge oceanic distances. The social development of such societies was more rapid than that of their parent stock because the hand of tradition lay less heavily upon them. Yet they retained their cultural affinities with the old countries. Kansas, or Toronto, Ontario, or even Cape Town breathe a far more European atmosphere than Budapest or Belgrade ever did.

The thickly populated, highly cultured areas of Asia and the northern fringes of Africa which had come under European domination could not be settled by Europeans. They remained "native", but the contact with European traders, officials and missionaries attracted their higher strata of society to the ways of the West. Christian missions had not been very successful as far as the numbers of converts were concerned, but the ideas, if not the ideals, of western democracy and capitalism had been accepted nearly everywhere. Today, all over Asia and North Africa the leaders of anti-European movements talk in terms of West European political philosophies and clamour for American-European institutions.

POLITICS AND HISTORY

History of Europe usually began with politics, according to which power had tended to coalesce in the central governments of a relatively small and easily identifiable number of nation-states. Some countries, including England, had become centralised before others like Germany or Italy which acquired central government in the latter half of the nineteenth century. However, the prevailing trend of the years around 1500 was one of aggregation rather than disintegration. France had seized the lands held by the English and re-absorbed most of the Duke of Burgundy's French possessions in the fifteenth century. The whole of the Iberian peninsula accepted one sovereign between 1580 and 1640. German Emperors tried to unite Europe under the Holy Roman Empire.

There was also an illusion of superhuman dignity around the kings and princes of Europe. Royal courts were known for their ceremonial symbolism. Courts worked through favour and petitions and allowed courtiers to carve out careers for themselves by cultivating patrons and showing their worth in service which was part personal, part political. It has been said that one of the last courts was the ruling clique around Adolf Hitler. The aggregation of power had grown up through binding together of separate political units with often diverse traditions. The Habsburg dynasty was one such case.

The rise of centralised states was the prime mover behind the growth of the nation-state in early modern Europe which resulted in expanding armies which exceeded the capacity of the empires to support them. The State which wished to maintain large forces on a permanent basis had to find money without which these huge armies became impoverished and destroyed the countries which they were supposed to defend. Most countries raised taxes and borrowed money to keep permanent army. Historian Paul Kennedy calls it "*strategic overstretch*," a single most important reason for "The Rise and Fall of Great Powers."

WILSON'S DREAM AND BRITISH IMPERIALISM

Woodrow Wilson expressed in many addresses during 1918–1919, his conviction that in the closely-knit world of the 20th century the peace in all countries, including the United States, depended upon the establishment of a League of Nations that would be able to protect all countries, weak and strong, against aggression by a system of collective security. He made it clear that two great aims animated the soldiers who fought the war. Although European imperialism in the second half of the nineteenth century made possible not only an economic exploitation by the European nations but it also fulfilled the educational mission of bringing to the non-European population the message of liberty and equality underlying Western civilisation. Sometimes, British imperialism unintentionally carried with it the liberal attitude and the *Magna Carta.* From the example set by individual Englishmen and from the reading of English texts, a feeling of individual dignity, a new appreciation of civic and personal liberty, and social responsibility began to change the thinking of the educated classes of the native population. The message of modern civilisation, as developed in the Anglo-Saxon and French revolutions, has been universal in its scope, destined for all classes and all races and, therefore, carried a powerful appeal for all those who were excluded from its full benefits. Thus, European domination, as long as it rested on liberal foundations, carried with it the seeds of its own gradual destruction, replacing, at least in theory, domination and exploitation by trusteeship and partnership. And, finally, the collapse of European imperialism.

The wave of democratization, a new feeling of social responsibility, and the rising demand for liberty, brought about by World War I, did not remain confined to Europe. It produced even greater changes among the non-European peoples. The people in Egypt and Turkey, in India and in China, awakened for the first time from their age-old lethargy, from the narrow bounds of their traditionalism, and under the leadership of men like Saad Zaghlul in Egypt, Mustafa Kemal in Turkey, Mahatma Gandhi in India and Sun Yat-Sen in China organised themselves for political action for reforms. As a result of this revolt in the East, the political and economic domination of Europe was shaken off in the Near and Far-East. The undisputed hold of Europe over Asia and Africa began to weaken. Even more important than the struggle for political independence was the effort of the non-European countries for a gradual modernization of their economic and social life, so as to put them on a footing of equality with the European countries.

The four years of World War I had broken the flow of economic goods between Europe and the non-European continents; many of the non-European countries had started a process of industrialization to make themselves economically independent of Europe and to retain the gains derived from manufacturing raw materials for their own national economy. This process of a transformation of backward agrarian countries into modern industrialized nations went ahead, with great differences in speed and energy, in the vast and semi-Oriental regions of the former Soviet Union as well as in Turkey, China and in Latin America. This beginning of the economic re-organization of the world destroyed the equilibrium between highly industrialized and mainly agricultural countries, as it had developed in the late 19th century, a system which had benefited the European countries which possessed large industrial plants, trained skilled workers, and sufficient capital for investment abroad.

Thus, the World War I broadened the area of world political decisions. The economic relations of the different countries and continents became more and more complex, with the rise in the standard of living all over the world and, with the greater intensification of production, the economic interdependence of all peoples grew. At the same time, new means of communication, unknown in the 19th century, changed the traditional concepts of time and space even more strikingly than railroads and telegraph did one hundred years ago. Railroads had integrated nations into closely-knit administrative and economic units; the telegraph had made the fast transmission of news possible. After World War I, airplanes began to perform for the globe the task of close connection and fast communication which in the nineteenth century railroads had done for individual countries; the radio broadcast news and views with an immediacy and a width of territory covered infinitely surpassing all performances of the printing press and the telegraph. And, now with TV, computer and a large number of other contraptions for rapid communication and transportation, the world has changed beyond recognition, globally united in a tight squeeze – sometimes too tight to be comfortable.

The 16th, 17th and 18th centuries were the age of colonial imperialism; during which period the Spanish, Portuguese, Dutch, British, French and Russian colonial empires were founded. About the middle of the 19th century, overseas colonisation came to a standstill. Free trade was to unite the nations of the world in a businessman's commonwealth. Trade expansion was to make territorial expansion superfluous; commercialism was to replace colonialism. The political frontiers separating countries need not be abolished; they would, so to speak, be sterilised and would no longer foster and protect national jealousy. And, peace, free trade, and goodwill among nations were to prevail. The rise of Germany and Italy through the wars in the third quarter of the nineteenth century put an end to these hopes. A new scramble for colonial possessions began. This interval has often been called *"The Age of Imperialism"*. Expansion, however, concentrated on Black Africa, Polynesia (Pacific Ocean Islands) and the crumbling Turkish and Chinese empires. The struggles over their partition led to armed conflicts between the European powers. These empire-breaking activities contributed to a national awakening of the hitherto subjugated non-European nations, who demanded liberation from their masters.

GROWING INFLUENCE OF EUROPEAN POWERS

Until World War I, Europe had been, politically, economically, and culturally, the dominant and decisive factor in world politics. Its influence had grown during the 19th century. On an unprecedented scale, tens of millions from all parts of Europe migrated across the oceans and populated vast territories in the New World and in the South Seas. Africa was opened up by European explorers, mapped and divided among European powers. The Far East, secluded until then in its own mysterious and ancient civilisations, was brought into the comity of nations. The dynamic economic system of Europe, increasing its productive capacity with each new discovery and invention, demanded ever larger colonies to meet its ever-growing needs for industrial raw materials and foodstuff, and to serve as captive markets for the ever-growing flow of its manufactured goods.

That was the period when European history was world history and European affairs were world affairs. All recognised great powers were European powers. European civilisation was on the way to becoming the universal civilisation of mankind. The European countries in north-western Europe, specially in England, France and the Netherlands, believed in man's perfectibility and in human progress; man was regarded as a rational being who had the ability to subject existing institutions and traditions to the scrutiny of his mind, to inquire into causes and consequences of social relations, and to change existing conditions for the good of the common man. A new emphasis on the equality before the law and of equal opportunities for all, on the dignity of individual and on his liberty to think and to speak according to his own conscience, and on a common destiny for mankind had increased the self-reliance and the spirit of activism of the individual. This new attitude toward life expressed itself in the writings of Milton and Locke, Voltaire and Condorcet. It was the foundation of the *Bill of Rights* and the *Declaration of the Rights of the Man and of the Citizen.* In its name, the people claimed and received the right to participate in legislation; government by laws replaced government by men; arbitrariness and inequalities before the law were abolished.

During the 19th century, this new evaluation of man and of his place in society spread, in spite of much resistance, from western Europe to central and eastern Europe. At the beginning of the 20th century, it was accepted even beyond the boundaries of Europe. Revolutions in China, Persia, and Turkey destroyed the ancient theocratic monarchies with their Oriental despotism and tried to introduce modern constitutional reforms. Japan accepted, although haltingly, the Western outlook of government and of individual rights. Throughout Asia, even in Africa, the non-European peoples demanded liberty and self-determination, after the example and under the influence of 19th century Europe. This whole era of the growth of liberal institutions all over the world was under the influence of Anglo-Saxon traditions of representative government and individual rights. Progressive statesmen and thinkers in the 18th and 19th centuries looked to British institutions for guidance and norms; the industrial and maritime leadership of the British went hand in hand with the spread of Anglo-Saxon ideals.

EUROPEAN REVOLUTIONS (1848)

In 1848 every important country in Europe, except Britain, was shaken by revolt. The frustration of popular liberal and national ambitions formed the background; an economic slump, with failed harvests and rising unemployment, provided more immediate causes. The revolts were not planned, though they took place as a chain reaction following outbreaks in France and the Austrian empire. Revolutionaries like Marx were taken by surprise; The Communist Manifesto had little effect.

The first outbreaks occurred in northern Italy and Sicily. The French revolt followed in February, and it was promptly echoed in Belgium, Holland, and various German states, including Prussia. Within the Austrian empire, the Hungarians and the Czechs rebelled, and Metternich fell from power after almost forty years. Venice seized brief independence, and the Papal States gained constitutional government.

None of these revolutionary movements was wholly successful, and in two years the old systems of government were restored nearly everywhere. However, the despots of Europe were never again able to feel quite so secure.

EUROPE GREW ON ROMAN RUINS

The growth of European civilisation is no less interesting. The collapse of Roman administration left Rome's European colonies in chaos, forcing them to create their own social organisations. In a purely functional response to the times, they created feudal structures where local groups of men gathered around their strongest leaders and agreed to give them money in return for protection. Feudalism performed an invaluable service, and stability emerged out of chaos. In primitive ways, Europe prospered and its people multiplied in conditions of security. But then, the decline set in. The nobles outstayed their usefulness. With the decrease in barbarian pressure, their social usefulness declined. In general, they needed a broader way of life than was permitted in the feudal system. In the resulting clash of new needs with outdated institutions, Europe became a troubled world of unemployed warlords and jobless wanderers.

The Crusade attracted dissatisfied and jobless warlords. Commercial contacts awakened curiosity and destroyed old values and patterns of behaviour. In the end, the long tumult of cultural Renaissance, religious Reformation and the rise of traders to power destroyed the feudal values and replaced them with much broader and richer ways of life dominated by commercial principles. Through this long transition, Europe remained a secondary influence in the world; it was still the Mediterranean basin from where most culture and wealth flowed. The Balkans, a backward region now, enjoyed, due to their Mediterranean proximity, greater wealth and culture than Britain which was then a dim Island of "vulgar inhabitants", said the Greeks.

Europe came into the limelight through its commercial activities. The Muslim Turks held an extensive monopoly on trade with the Indies. The Mediterranean peoples, pressed to the limits of their resources, sought a free access to the trade with the Indies by way of the western seas. When the Italian sailor, Columbus, returned from a westward voyage to claim that he had discovered a new free route to the Indies, stock markets collapsed in Italian city-states. There was never a more justified market crash. For the next two centuries, the world's centre of gravity moved steadily from the Mediterranean to the Atlantic seaboard.

GREEK SCIENCE, ROMAN LAW, LATIN LANGUAGE AND CHRISTIANITY

Rome believed in a single law for all humanity. If the Greeks had given to Europe philosophy and mathematics, it was the Romans who gave it law. And although, the concept of Europeans as law-governed peoples originated in Greece, it was the Romans who elevated the law to become the sole guarantor of civilisation. Roman law remained, and remains, the single most unifying feature of Europe. Edmund Burke, a good European, thought of a world with independent states "united in a common culture, based upon the Roman law". For this reason, the creation of a united Europe remained an ambition of the most Europe's rulers – from Emperor Justinian, in the sixth century, through Philip-II of Spain and Louis XIV and Napoleon. The Roman Empire, Roman Law, Christianity and Latin language united Europe.

After the triumph of Christianity, ancient Greek and Roman notions of exclusivity were further enforced by the Christian insistence upon the uniqueness of the Gospels and Church as a source of moral and scientific authority. Christianity was thought of as coextensive with the Roman Empire. Christendom had become the buzz-word of Europe. In 1761, Rousseau, a non-believer, conceded that "Europe is indebted more to Christianity than to any other influence which survives among Europeans." He hated European unity but could not quite escape the reality. The scattered, diverse, and plural cultures had grown up in the ancient world to become what we now call Europe. The Europeans shared a single identity bound together by a common system of law and Christianity which became a common religion and a common culture of the continent. They also shared a common language – Latin – which remained both as the language of the Church (it still does) and of the elite of the continent. In sum, Europe possessed three unifying features: the Roman Law, Christianity, and the Latin language.

FRENCH REVOLUTION MARKED THE END OF OLD EUROPE

The *ancien régime* of kings, nobles, and priests died after the industrial society gradually emerged to replace agriculture. The upheavals which created the first industrialised society in Europe depended on the intellectual changes which finally destroyed the political and social structures, so absolutely that the collapse was sudden and shocking. That collapse was triggered off by the French Revolution which gave a thrust to a more rational ordering of society. The respect for authority vanished and ideas replaced power. The wholesale military mobilisation during the Revolution led to resources problems which, in turn, led to the insistent demands for equality, an unheard of concept. Society became more rational and less restrained. The way was, thus, cleared for both liberalisation, and the horrendous acts of totalitarian brutality which have marked the coming of modern Europe that began with the end of the

French Revolution. *(Separate chapters on France)*

EUROPE, ALWAYS A CULTURE

Despite the religious, cultural, and linguistic unity, neither the Roman Empire nor Christendom was identical with Europe. Much of the Roman Empire lay in Asia and in North Africa. Not only had Christianity begun as an Asian religion, but some of the first Christian churches had been established in North Africa. After the fall of Rome, and the attempt by Charlemagne to rebuild the empire in the west, it shrank to what is today's continental Europe. Charlemagne, although frequently claiming some kind of world sovereignty, also called himself *pater europae* – "the father of the Europeans" – and Emperor Charles V who, in the early sixteenth century, came closer than any other ruler to uniting Europe under one sovereign, was addressed as *totius europae dominus* – "lord of all Europe", an obvious allusion to Rome's Antoninus Pius' claim to be *dominus totius orbis* (Lord of the World).

Europe was considered as the place of civility and of free men living in secure urban communities under the rule of law. The rest lived under tyrannies governed according to the caprice of individual rulers, or in nomadic or semi-nomadic groups never far from the primordial "state of nature". By the late seventeenth century, this sense of *exceptionality* had found expression in a theory of stages in human development according to which all human societies began as *hunter-gatherers*. They, then, become *pastoralists*, less mobile than their predecessors. Finally, they invented agriculture and, in time, transformed themselves into city-dwellers, traders and into modern civilized social beings. All the peoples on the globe were bound to pass through each of these stages. Only the Europeans had reached the final stage of "commercial society," without becoming nomadic region. Or, so it was believed. This has been the European fallacy.

Russia, sometimes friend, more frequently foe, threw into occasionally stark relief the fact that Europe was a culture, a shared way of life, rather than a place. Russia had many of the features of a European society, and it was undeniably Christian. Yet in its vast size, it also lay beyond the formal limits of Romanized "civilization". While it remained oriental despotism, Russia existed firmly within Asia, the "backward barbaric empire of the steppes". Russia's relationship with the rest of Europe was determined not only by dress code and religion but also by a powerful European sense of *exceptionality*. Russians share some features of European culture. For, to be exceptional, a culture has also to be whole. No people can be permitted to acquire part of its trappings without also acquiring the iaws and customs, political structure, and the social organisation. As a matter of fact, Russia has been neither fully European nor fully Asian. When Charles de Gaulle crossed the Elbe, he used to grumble: "I am in Asia."

WORLD MIND: The Roman Empire had trade relations beyond its frontiers which also brought remote regions into its sphere of influence. However, it was only in 19th and 20th century that science produced what is the modern Europe today. The European Enlightenment created *world mind,* believing in continuity and unity of human thought. Europe is not culturally homogeneous; for example, the British Isles, the Scandinavian, Iberian and the Balkan people have different cultural ethos. The cultural polarisation is also one reason for conflicts among nation-states. However, the religions have great unifying effect. Christianity has taken over almost the whole of Europe with exception of the Islamic pockets in the Balkans and the Turco-Tatar South-east. The great branches of Christendom – Catholicism, Protestantism and Orthodoxy – are linked with German and Slavic cultures.

SOURCES OF EUROPEAN PRIMACY

All human beings are shaped by cultural and moral norms. Distinguished journalist Walter Lippmann said 65 years ago: "People don't become happy by satisfying their desires but by living within a belief system that gives coherence to their desires. Above satisfaction of any other need, above hunger, love, pleasure, fame, even life itself - what a man needs most is the conviction that he lives within the discipline of an ordered society where he is accepted and loved."

People need the togetherness which culture provides. Culture shapes behaviour; cultural differences mostly explain why some nations develop quickly while others don't. Some cultures encourage development while others retard it; some cultures check corruption, while others permit it; some cultures focus on the future, while others focus on the past. Some cultures encourage the belief that individuals can control their own destinies, while others encourage fatalism. It is culture, not politics, that determines the success of a society.

This is truer largely of Hindu and the Islamic cultures where change is resisted in the conviction that what we believe is eternal and the best. Not true. Change does not pollute culture; it enriches life. The world's richest culture is Greek and that is most mixed. The European culture, which has been shaped by social revolutions, the Enlightenment, Renaissance, mass education, social conflicts, technology and its imperial heritage, is forever changing, even today when immigration threatens to change indigenous culture. For instance Muslim veil threatens the Britishness in Britain. It is true also of France, Scandinavian countries and the Balkans. The ever-changing culture is one important source of European primacy.

There are many other profound reasons for Europe's world primacy. To be true, Europe is the centre of the first *universal civilisation.* All the basic modes of thought and expression, the key institutions, the unconsciously accepted values, by which the world is judged today, were formed in Europe. And, almost nothing new has been added to it since Plato. The European whitemen carried these standards around the globe, planting their banners at the Poles and in the forests. And, thus, the whitemen became the world's ruling class. (Most Americans are of European origin.) Europeans ruled almost the entire Africa and Oceana. Republicanism was born in Switzerland, Communism was born in London Museum and Capitalism was born in Manchester. The Third World, specially Africa, suffers almost permanent food shortage and there is hardly any mention in the world; let there be a temporary shortage of food in Europe and the world Press will carry screaming headings. The other four continents were as much destroyed in the last global war, but all the aid under Marshall Plan, *"lease-lend"*, and UNRRA went to Europe.

The second reason for the European primacy in world affairs is economic. Until recently, Europe was the most productive industrial area in the world. She has now lost that position to America and probably to Japan. But, still it remains the most important factor in world trade, specially after the setting up of the European Union. Even today, it is impossible for any large area in the world to enjoy economic health if the economy of Europe fails.

The third reason is the accident of global strategy in a world which spends so much of its resources on war. Eighty per cent of the land surface of the globe is situated in the northern hemisphere and Europe lies smack in the middle of the area of the easiest communication. The distance from London westward to San Francisco is nearly the same as the distance from London eastward to Vladivostock. A single power in control of Europe will be in a good position to dominate four other larger continents. No wonder, for much of her history, Europe has dominated Asia, Africa, North America and South America.

For this significant reason also, the rest of the world is far more sensitive to small changes in Europe than big changes elsewhere. For the past so many years, both South-East Asia, West Asia, Africa and Latin America have been torn by wars, conflicts and revolutions without causing any global effect. There have been so many wars but nothing happened. The mere assassination of Archduke Francis Ferdinand of Austria on June 28, 1914 sparked off a global war; again, an attack on Poland, a country as small as Bangladesh, caused another world war in which some 60 million people were killed or injured. Since the last war, the Chinese have seized Tibet and other areas, but nothing happened, but the Berlin Blockade (1948-49) brought the world close to yet another world war. Europe is a continent of destiny.

INVENTIONS FUELLED SOCIAL REVOLUTIONS

Europe found a broad outlet for human energies as population increased. Commerce, however, alone was not an adequate outlet. The pressure of population and the accumulation of surplus capital from trade was combined with enterprise and the flourishing of science to bring in a new age of invention and machinery which created jobs and wealth. Until that time, mankind had known only one period of technical improvement. That was the wheel, invented 4,000 years before Christ. Later, animals were domesticated for locomotion and metal spades, axes and knives devised. The subsequent civilisation of Mesopotamia, Egypt, Rome and Medieval Europe added virtually no new principle to these techniques. It was only in the eighteenth century Europe that mechanical evolution took place rapidly. It is beyond the scope of the book to discuss industrialisation which will need a separate book altogether, but it may be briefly stated that the coming in of steam power, internal combustion engine and electricity outdated all medieval technologies just as the later-day atomic power made the earlier sources of energy look primitive.

However, modern Europe matched its blessings with its curses. It has enriched material life beyond its dreams and has expanded leisure time. Within the last two centuries or so, the literacy of western man has risen from a mere five per cent to 90 per cent and more. Despite all the scorn poured on modern man and his follies, he is much more curious and wiser today than before; asks more questions and is harder to fool than his ancestors. Democracy, the political system which requires leaders to win assent for their actions from the people, was the natural consequence. If the modern man is in a worse mess than his forefathers, it is not because he has not made great intellectual progress but because the machine has created an infinitely more complicated world whose changes are too rapid for institutions to respond adequately.

For the first time in history, the basic cause of social discontent does not seem to be poverty which is an absolute lack of means of livelihood. Although poverty exists in pockets, most West Europeans enjoy a much higher standard of life than their forefathers did before. The main source of discontent in Europe seemed to be the fear of poverty and insecurity. And to combat this frustration, arms were piled up and two superpowers stood eyeball-to-eyeball until the Berlin Wall fell in 1989 and a new era descended on Europe. The source of today's conflict, including the one in Iraq (2003), is to avert the danger – real and imagined.

DISCOVERIES AND INVENTIONS MADE WORLD MYSTERIOUS

Whereas the discoveries of the 15th and 16th centuries had widened the earth to such an extent that it gave to contemporary mankind the feeling of an infinite and unending adventure, even in the 19th century frontiers remained open for expansion. The period after the World War I witnessed a fast shrinking of the earth as the result of the new inventions. The globe became finite and mapped out, formerly unknown deserts were easily crossed by car and plane; man conquered the mysteries of air; thus, realizing one of the oldest and most daring dreams of flying. This unprecedented and fantastic situation needed the establishment of some new form of world order to maintain peace among the nations and continents, and to assure to all peoples freedom and equality.

World War II laid the foundations on which a global society, based upon democracy and peace, could be built. The victory of the three great Western democracies over the monarchies of central Europe, the introduction of democratic constitutions in almost all countries in the long oppressed and stagnant nations like Mexico and Ireland, Spain, Egypt, Poland and Bohemia, Turkey and China – all that pointed in the direction of the fulfilment of the hopes which had animated many people in the Western democracies in 1918 for a lasting peace and for a secure growth and spread of democratic institutions. The League of Nations, the most important contribution made by the United States, under the leadership of Woodrow Wilson, became the instrument of a *"universal dominion of right by such a concert of free peoples as shall bring peace and safety to all nations and make the world free"*. It was upon the insistence of Woodrow Wilson that the Covenant of the League of Nations became not only an integral part of all the peace treaties concluded after the World War I, but occupied the place of honour at their beginning, thus turning them into a great promise for the future. If the League of Nations failed, it was not for want of idealism, but because the ideals were too lofty for the imperial nations to practise.

TECHNOLOGY IS PRIME SOURCE OF EUROPEAN DOMINANCE

The European notion that Europe was distinctly superior to all other cultures of the world is derived from the Graeco-Roman cultures and technological superiority. In the physics of Aristotle, which remained dominant in Europe until the early seventeenth century, nature has enormous potentiality which can be realised only through human intervention. Aristotle says a tree is also chairs. It required man's art, his *techne,* to release from the tree its essential "chairness". *Techne,* or technology, was called *scientia* (or science) which is the human capacity to transform the world according to human needs. This, for the Greeks, was a form of knowledge (*logos*). *Techne* is from the word *tikto*, which means to "generate;" humans are the *teknotes*, or generators; and the *tekne* (technology) is their offspring. *Techne* has the potential to acquire power and skill which humankind and gods alone possess. This power could also be exercised by one human group over another. The development of humankind within the *polis* was the human manipulation of the natural world. Men were, thus, encouraged to see in the natural world a design of which they were the final beneficiaries.

The European sense of superiority is also derived from the conviction that only those who lived in law-governed and free urban communities (read Europe) would possess the capacity to harness nature to its advantage. The others, the "barbarians", bogged down by the demands of their rulers, remained forever in unenlightened herds. In Europe, arts were "liberal". Although it began in Asia, in Babylon and Egypt, it was only in Europe that nature's potential had been fully realised. "The liberal arts", writes English travel writer Samuel Purchas (1577-1626), "are more liberal to us, after they have left their places in Asia and Africa".

And, this led to the assumption that science would always be superior to simple force. It had been human skills – their *techne* – which had enabled the vastly outnumbered Spartans to defeat the Persians, an enslaved people. The Turks – archetypal Asians – were not merely denied freedom of action by their rulers, but they were also denied access to knowledge. Their military success had been due, in part, to their ferocity and, in part, to the lack of skill of their opponents. Throughout the sixteenth century, it was said that European science and technology would never fail against Asian ignorance. It is true that Asia has never been able to resist even the most mediocre European force because of the technology-gap. And when in the thirteenth century, Europeans set out to convert the world to their religion, their technological superiority made them the masters of the world and Christianity became the dominant religion of Europe, driving out Islam which had enormous following in the continent.

COLUMBUS HIGHLIGHTED THE USE OF TECHNOLOGY

After Columbus' discovery of America and the rounding of the Cape of Good Hope – famously declared by Adam Smith to be "the two greatest and most important events recorded in the history of mankind" – the European belief in the capacity of European science to dominate the world became more assertive. For, both these oceanic journeys had been made possible through the use of the compass and the skill of European navigators and cartographers. Only the West had been able to achieve such a triumph. Asians and Africans had been capable of limited navigational feats. The Europeans claimed that they have civilized peoples of the "inferior worlds".

The early sixteenth and the late eighteenth century marked Europe's triumpth over the known world which only science could achieve. Europeans believed that they had discovered and subdued the world through science. The stories of the conquest of Mexico and Peru where vast numbers of men had been vanquished by a handful of adversaries armed with canon, horses, and swords, or of the victory of the Portuguese over the peoples of the West African coast and southern India, only enhanced the European sense of superiority achieved through technology. "Natives", the British say, fell down in awe before European firearms, and mistook them for gods. Even the great critics of the European colonial venture in the eighteenth century could not quite avoid taking pride in the success of their science. However, Denis Diderot (1713-84) has lamented; "Technology had fallen into criminal hands."

(Diderot was a French philosopher who brought out first *encyclopedia* in the world). The ability to control the resources of the world had given Europe its assumed superiority. This is the origin of the belief that Europe, (read the West,) is *exceptional*. There can be little doubt that the West has exercised technological and political mastery over much of the world because of the power of European technology. The historical truth is, however, that there is nothing like European exceptionalism; it is the technology that has given them an edge over others. ***(Based on inputs from the writings of historian Anthony Pagden.)***

Nationalism is neither wholly logical nor wholly rational; it is a response to grave threats, real or perceived, to nation-states.

– *Palmer Perkins*

3

The origin and growth of nation-states in Europe

Nationalism is a state of mind, an emotion stirred up to fight for a cause defined in terms of territory, language, culture, religion or a common history. It is a feel-good ideology which is both dangerous and absurd.

The nation is a geographical group possessed of a common sentiment of solidarity. Psychologically, it is like a flock of crows, or a herd of cattle. The sentiment of solidarity may be due to common language, common culture, common interests or common danger. As a rule, all these play a part in producing national sentiment. The devotees of nationalism tend to think of a nation as a race in the biological sense. Shakespeare speaks of the English as *"this happy breed of men,"* and subsequent nationalists have followed suit. Since nations were conceived as races, the differences between them were thought to be, at least in part, congenital.

In simpler terms, a nation is a body of men and women, inhabiting a definite area who possess a common stock of thoughts and feelings acquired during the course of a common history; who have a common religious belief, who use common thoughts and feelings, cherish a common will, and tend to form a separate State for the expression and realization of that will. What constitutes a nation is, however, not always speaking the same language or belonging to the same ethnic group, but also having accomplished great things together in the past and the wish to accomplish them in future.

The nation is not necessarily a state which is a political unit. In fact, even in a modern sense we may conceive of a state being composed of several nations. We often speak of the *multinational state,* but the terms "nation" and "state" are used interchangeably, and the major political units which exist today may appropriately be called nation-states. *The nation needs a state.* One nation and one state is ideal. Britain, Germany and France like many others have one language, one religion etc. and they are ideal nation-states. However, no less ideal is the US and India which are multi-ethnic and multi-religious states. But, they are cohesive and united emotionally.

HOW DANGEROUS IS PATRIOTISM

Patriotism is commonly defined as love of country. From the historical point of view, it is not necessarily associated with the nation-state. The addresses of Pericles to the Athenians, of Hannibals to the Cartheginians and of Cicero to the Romans are among the greatest examples of patriotic oratory. Today, however, patriotism, like nationalism, is associated almost exclusively with loyalty to the nation-state. It is capable of inspiring some of the finest human sentiments, but it can become as intense and as narrow as that which prevailed among the city-states of ancient Greece and infinitely more dangerous. In its exaggerated form, it is known as *chauvinism.* Nationalism is a dangerous concept.

However, no satisfactory single definition is possible. Perhaps the most revealing is Hayes's statement that nationalism consists of "a modern emotional fusion and exaggeration of two very old phenomena – nationality and patriotism." Or, as Hans Kohn puts it, "nationalism is first and foremost a state of mind, an act of consciousness." In the twentieth century, nationalism became the common form of political life all over the world, but everywhere nationalism differs in character according to the specific historic conditions and the peculiar social structure of each country. In eastern Europe and later in Asia, nationalism tended toward the closed society, in which the individual counted for less than the strength and authority of the nation as a whole. Professor Louis L. Snyder advances the following definition. "Nationalism is a condition of mind, feeling, or sentiment of a group of people living in a well-defined geographical area, speaking a common language, possessing a literature in which the aspirations of the nation have been expressed, attached to common traditions and common customs, venerating its own heroes and, in some cases, having a common religion."

Throughout history, men have been attached to their native soil, to the traditions of their parents, and to the established territorial authorities. But, it was not until the end of the 18th century that nationalism began influencing public and private life to become one of the important most single determining factors of history. Because of its all-pervading character, nationalism is mistakenly regarded as the powerful manifestation of the sentiment of togetherness. After Latin America, it spread in the early 19th century to central Europe and from there, toward the middle of the century, to eastern and south-eastern Europe. At the beginning of the 20th century, nationalism flowered in Asia and Africa. Thus, the 19th century has been called the *Age of Nationalism* in Europe, while the 20th century witnessed the struggle for power by the national movements in Asia and Africa.

LOVE FOR IDENTITY: Nationalism, translated into politics, implies the identification of the state or nation with the people according to ethnographic principles. In the age of nationalism, the principle generally recognised was that each nationality should form a state and that the state should include all members of that nationality. Formerly, states or territories under one administration were not delineated by nationality. Men did not give their loyalty to the nation-state, but to other forms of political organizations: the city-state, the feudal fief and its lord, the dynastic state, the religious group, or the sect. The nation-state was non-existent during the greater part of history, and for a very long time it was not even regarded as an ideal. In the first 15 centuries of the Christian Era, the ideal was the universal world-state, not loyalty to any separate political entity. The Roman Empire had set the great example which survived not only in the Holy Roman Empire of the Middle Ages, but also in the concept of the *republica christiana* ("Christian republic" or community) and in its later secularized form of a united world civilization.

CIVILIZATIONS WERE NEVER NATIONALLY DETERMINED

The political allegiance, before the Age of Nationalism, was not determined by nationality, nor was civilization thought of as nationally-determined. During the Middle Ages, civilization was determined religiously because with all the different nationalities of Christendom and of those of Islam, there was but one civilization – Christian or Muslim – and one language of culture – Latin (or Greek) or Arabic (or Persian). Later, in the periods of the Renaissance and Classicism, it was the ancient Greek and Roman civilizations that became a universal norm, valid for all peoples and all times. Still later, French civilization was accepted throughout Europe as the valid civilization for educated people of all nationalities. It was only at the end of the 18th century that, for the first time, civilization was considered to be determined by nationality. It was then that the principle was put forward that a man could be educated only in his own mother tongue, not in the languages of other civilizations.

Since the end of the 18th century, the nationalization of education and public life went hand-in-hand with the nationalization of states and political loyalties. Poets and scholars began to emphasize cultural nationalism first. They reformed the mother tongue, elevated it to the rank of a literary language, and delved deep into the national past. Thus, they prepared the foundation for the political claims for national statehood, soon to be raised by the people in whom they had kindled the spirit of nationalism. Before the 18th century, there had been evidence of national feeling among certain groups at certain periods, specially in times of stress and conflict. The rise of national feeling to major political importance was encouraged by a number of complex developments: the creation of large, centralized states ruled by absolute monarchs who destroyed the old feudal allegiances, the secularization of life and education which enriched the vernacular languages and weakened the ties of church and sect and the growth of commerce, and demanded larger territorial units for the rising middle classes and their capitalistic enterprise. And, this weakened the sentiment of nationalism.

EUROPEAN NATIONALISM–
BRITAIN IS THE LEADER

The first full manifestation of modern nationalism occurred in the 17th century England when she had become the leading nation in scientific spirit, commercial enterprise, political thought and activity. Swelling with pride and by an immense confidence in the new age, the English people felt upon their shoulders the mission of history, a sense that they were at a turning point from which a new true reformation and a new liberty would begin. In the English revolution, an optimistic humanism merged with Calvinist ethics; the influence of the Old Testament gave form to the new nationalism by identifying the English people with ancient Israel. The new message, carried by the new generation not only for England but for all mankind, was expressed in the writings of John Milton in whose famous vision the idea of liberty was seen spreading from Britain, "as a soil most genial to the growth of liberty", to all the corners of the earth. English nationalism was, thus, much nearer to its religious matrix than to the nationalism that rose after secularisation of the state. The nationalism of the 18th century was about liberty, humanitarian character, emphasis on the individual rights and on community above national divisions. The rise of English nationalism coincided with the rise of the English trading middle classes. It found its final expression in John Locke's political philosophy which influenced American and French nationalism in the following century.

AMERICAN AND FRENCH NATIONALISM

American nationalism was a product of the 18th century. British settlers in north America were influenced partly by the traditions of the Puritan revolution, the ideas of Locke and by the new rational interpretation given to English liberty by contemporary French philosophers. American settlers became a nation engaged in a fight for liberty and individual rights. They based their fight on current political thought as expressed by Thomas Jefferson and Thomas Paine. It was a liberal and humanitarian nationalism that regarded America as in the vanguard of mankind on its march to greater liberty, equality, and happiness for all. The ideas of the 18th century found their first political realization in the *Declaration of Independence* and in the birth of the American nation. Their deep influence was felt in the French Revolution.

ROUSSEAU'S GENERAL WILL: Jean-Jacques Rousseau had prepared the soil for the growth of French nationalism by his stress on popular sovereignty and the general cooperation of all in forming the *national will,* and also by his regard for the common people as the true depository of civilization. The nationalism of the French Revolution was more than that: it was the triumphant expression of a rational faith in common humanity and liberal progress. The famous slogan *"liberty, equality, fraternity"* and the *Declaration of the Rights of Man* and of the Citizen were thought valid not only for the French people but for all peoples. Individual liberty, human equality, fraternity of all peoples were the cornerstones of all liberal and democratic nationalism. Under their inspiration, new rituals were developed that took the place of the old religious rites and ceremonies, festivals and flags, music and poetry, national holidays and patriotic sermons. In the most varied forms, nationalism permeated all aspects of the French life.

Like the rise of American nationalism, the rise of the French nationalism produced a new phenomenon in the art of warfare. In America and France, *citizen armies,* untrained but filled with a new fervour, proved superior to highly trained professional armies that fought without the incentive of nationalism. The revolutionary French nationalism stressed free individual decision in the formation of nations. Nations were constituted by an act of self-determination of their members. The plebiscite became the instrument to determine will of the nation. In America and revolutionary France, nationalism meant the adherence to a universal progressive idea, looking toward a common future of freedom and equality, not toward the past characterized by authoritarianism and inequality. Napoleon's armies spread the spirit of nationalism throughout Europe and even in the Near East and across the Atlantic, it aroused the sentiments of Latin Americans. But Napoleon's conquest turned the nationalism of Europeans against France. In Germany, the struggle was led by writers and intellectuals who rejected all the principles upon which the American and the French revolutions had been based, as well as the liberal and humanitarian aspects of nationalism.

NATIONALISM BROUGHT THE UNIFICATION OF GERMANY, ITALY

German nationalism began to stress instinct against reason; the power of historical tradition against rational attempts at progress and a more just order; the historical differences between nations rather than their common aspirations. The French Revolution, liberalism, and equality were regarded as a brief aberration against which the eternal foundations of societal order would prevail. Or, so it was thought.

However, that German interpretation was proved to be false by the developments of the 19th century. Liberal nationalism reasserted itself; it permeated the rising middle class and the new proletariat. The revolutionary wave of 1848, the year of *"the spring of the peoples,"* seemed to realize the hopes of nationalists such as Giuseppe Mazzini, who had devoted his life to the unification of Italy by democratic means. Nationalism brought the unification of Germany by Bismarck. And the 1860s saw progress in liberalism in Russia and Spain. The victorious trend of liberal nationalism, however, was reversed in Germany by Bismarck who unified Germany on a conservative and authoritarian basis and defeated German liberalism. The German annexation of Alsace-Lorraine against the will of the inhabitants was contrary to the idea of nationalism which was based upon the free will of man. The people of Alsace-Lorraine were held to be German by race, independent of their will or of their allegiance to any nationality of their choice.

In the second half of the 19th century, nationalism disintegrated the supernational states of the Habsburgs and the Ottoman Sultans, both of which were based upon loyalties. In Russia, nationalism produced two opposing schools of thoughts. Some nationalists proposed a westernized Russia, associated with the progressive, liberal forces of Europe. Others stressed the distinctive character of Russia, its independent and different destiny based upon its autocratic and orthodox past. These Slavophiles, influenced by German romantic thinkers, saw Russia as a saviour of the West undermined by liberalism and the heritage of the American and French revolutions.

BALKAN NATIONALISM

One of the consequences of World War I was the triumph of nationalism in central and eastern Europe. From the ruins of the Habsburg and Romanov empires, emerged the new nation-states of Austria, Hungary, Czechoslovakia, Poland, Yugoslavia and Romania. These states, however, were to be ravaged by their own internal nationality conflicts and by nationalistic disputes over territory with their neighbours. Russian nationalism was in part suppressed after Lenin's victory in 1917, when the Bolsheviks took over the old empire of the Tsars. But the Bolsheviks also claimed the leadership of the world communist movement which was to become an instrument of the national policies of the Russians. During World War II, Stalin appealed to nationalism and patriotism in rallying the Russians against foreign invaders. After the war, he found nationalism one of the strongest obstacles to the expansion of Soviet power in eastern Europe. National communism, as it was called, became a divisive force in the Soviet bloc. In 1948 Tito, the Communist leader of Yugoslavia, was denounced by Moscow as a nationalist and a renegade; nationalism was a strong factor in the rebellious movements in Poland and Hungary in 1956; and subsequently its influence was also felt in Romania and Czechoslovakia.

NATIONALIST LEADERS IN ASIA AND AFRICA

As stated earlier, nationalism began to appear in Asia and Africa after World War I. It produced such leaders as Kemal Ataturk in Turkey, Sad Pasha Zaghul in Egypt, Mahatma Gandhi in India, and Sun Yat-sen in China. Ataturk succeeded in replacing the medieval structure of the Islamic monarchy with a revitalized and modernized secular republic in 1922. Demands for Arab unity were frustrated in Africa and Asia by British imperialism and in Africa by French masters. Britain demonstrated a gift for accommodation with the new forces by helping to create an independent Egypt (1922-1936) and Iraq (1932), and displayed a similar spirit in India, where the Indian National Congress, founded in 1885 to promote liberal nationalism, became radical after 1918.

And, finally India became independent in 1947. Japan, influenced by Germany, used modern industrial techniques to promote authoritarian nationalism.

NATIONALISM, A SOURCE OF TWO WORLD WARS

In Europe, the spirit of nationalism appeared to wane after World War II with the establishment of international economic, military and political organizations such as NATO, and the European Union. But the policies pursued by France under Charles de Gaulle, and the problem of a divided Germany showed that the appeal of the nation-state was still very much alive. Nationalism prepared the minds of the people for the world war. Its immediate cause was the murderous activity of a secret nationalistic society of Yugoslavs. Its fighting was done by *"nations in arms,"* whose morale was sustained by nationalist propaganda. Its immediate result was the acceptance of principle of the nationalism and self-determination in central and eastern Europe. The last of the world empires on the European continent, the Austrian, Russian and Ottoman, were destroyed in the World War I which was caused by nationalism and which led to more intense nationalism and finally, the distintegration of three global empires and many nation-states. In Europe, the newest national states almost instantly passed from liberal to illiberal conduct and vied with older nation-states in establishing nationalised tariffs, armies, schools and other agencies of propaganda and in discriminating socially, if not legally, against dissident minorities.

TOTALITARIAN NATIONALISM

In the years following World War I, the internationalism, built across the world by the League of Nations and by such agreements as the Locarno and Kellogg pacts, proved to be too weak to keep the world together. Fascism gained power in Italy only three years after Versailles and later in Germany, Japan and Spain. With fascism, the world witnessed the first flowering of modern totalitarianism, bringing a form of nationalism more powerful, more brutal, and more dangerous than of any previous variety. Eventually, World War II was brought on by totalitarian nationalism and it is by no means certain that the fascist threat has been eliminated forever. Moreover, another form of totalitarianism, the communist totalitarianism of the Soviet Union and her satellites, and of communist China, had become more firmly entrenched, more restless, and more aggressive. Now that communism is unravelling, the world can breathe easy.

To speak of communism as a form of totalitarian nationalism may seem to be a contradiction in terms because communism, unlike fascism, is an international and not a national gospel. In practice, however, communism has become increasingly nationalistic. The Soviet rulers had posed as champions of nationalism in Asia and as enemies of colonialism and imperialism, and they had considerable success in identifying communism with nationalism. Native communist leaders captured nationalist movements, and they scored notable successes in Indo-China, Indonesia, Korea, and, above all, in China. The Chinese communists succeeded in taking over the nationalist revolution which had been under way since the fall of the Manchu dynasty in 1911-1912. In spite of the collapse of the Soviet Union, the Chinese communists still pretend to be national leaders, without being elected.

MOTHER RUSSIA

During World War II, when German armies were occupying the western part of Russia, the Russian people were exhorted to rise up in defence of *"Mother Russia"* – not of communism or world revolution. Soviet rulers had harped on the danger of "foreign encirclement." In the post-War years, the Soviet government had encouraged nationalism of Russia's many nationalities, permitting their cultural, political, and economic institutions to be "national" as long as they were "proletarian" in substance. In the satellite states of Eastern Europe, it had encouraged dissident nationalist groups while denying liberties and independence to those countries. Operating behind the war fronts, communist leaders used pressures and promises, and brutality to protect Mother Russia. Of all the hypocrisies of communist leaders, this was the most cruel.

YUGOSLAV NATIONALISM

When Tito was denounced by the *Cominform* for his "heresy", the situation changed because Tito was more nationalist than the Communist USSR. Since his open break with the Communist world, Tito had relied totally on Yugoslav nationalism. Titoism also occurred elsewhere, and nationalistic tendencies grew stronger within the communist camp. Modern nationalism was associated with democracy and liberty, and, for some time, it was believed that the relationship was more than historical. Now we know that nationalism, far from always promoting democracy and liberty, as in case of colonies, often supported autocracy and totalitarianism and it tended to restrict the area of human freedom. In sum, nationalism hurts liberty. ***(Read more about it in separate chapters on Yugoslavia and Balkans).***

NATIONALISM, A THREAT TO HUMAN CIVILISATION

Since nationalism tends to become a major cause of war, it is condemned as an evil force. Hayes Ruthford, 19th President of the US, distinguished between nationalism as a historical fact and nationalism as a belief. As a belief, he says, nationalism has been "a curse and nothing but a curse." Rabindranath Tagore held that nationalism was a great menace because it called for a "strenuous effort, strength and efficiency and thereby drains man's energy from his higher nature, where he is self-sacrificing and creative." Victor Gollancz writes: "Of all the evils I hate, I think I hate nationalism most." Arnold Toynbee's ten-volume work, *A Study of History,* contains many references to crimes committed in the name of the nation-state. Professor Shafer closes his careful study of nationalism with a fervent attack on the whole concept of nationalism and pleads for *brotherhood of man.* Many students of nationalism have commented on its apparent tendency to exclusiveness and its incompatibility with international cooperation. Thus, Vladimir Solovyev, a Russian philosopher, of the nineteenth century, writes about nationalism: "In its extreme form, nationalism destroys a nation; for, it makes mankind its enemy."

Contrary to the hopes of many optimists, the twentieth century has become an age of virulent nationalism. Internationalists think that the tide of nationalism is ebbing, but the evidence to the contrary is overwhelming. However, there are encouraging signs of a slow but steady growth of internationalism. The conclusion seems unavoidable, that nationalism is still very much with us and may even be increasing in intensity. And, this is the challenge and a threat to our Age of Reason.

THIRTY NEW NATIONS SINCE 1984 AND MORE ON CHOPPING BLOCK

Europe has been splitting since the Treaty of Westphalia (1648) and before but none came so rlapidly as the birth of 30 new nations since 1984. The primary culprit was the dissolution of the Soviet Union — which bestrode the earth like a colossus occupying one-sixth of the world's and mass — in 1991. In what must have been a cartographer's nightmare, as many as 15 new countries appeared on the map after the break-up of the USSR. This include Russia as well as several smaller nations from Armenia to Uzbekistan.

The disintegration of the Soviet Union along with the fall of the Barlin Wall had a domino effect in countries behind the Iron Curtain. True to their name, the Balkans were the first to get affected. The former Yugoslavia was riven by bitter ethnic strife to break up into five different countries — Sloenia, Bosnia and Herzegovina, Serbia and Montenegro, Croatia, and Macedonia. Czechoslovakia too split into the Czech Republic and Slovakia. It wasn't just all bitter partings though. East and West Germany merged to form a unified Germany in 1990.

The Balkanization countinues. Montenegro split from Serbia in 2006 after a referendum and Kosovo became independent last year. The last 25 years have witnessed the birth of 30 new countries. There are, as of now, 192 member states in the United Nations.

You can be sure that this number won't remain constant for very long.

I love my dreams of the future more than the history of the past.

– *Thomas Jefferson*

4

European unity-a dream that refuses to die

Europe had many kings, conquerors and killers and all of them had dreamt of unity but nothing happened until March 1957 when the Treaty of Rome was signed, setting off the process of the European unification. And, it seems to be happening well.

History has it that much of the world's problems have been caused by romanticising history and mixing cold facts with emotion. Patriotism (and nationalism) is one such dangerous emotion. Patriotism, according to Bernard Shaw, is an emotional feeling that the country in which one is born is the best in the world. No less dangerous are the irrational emotions which have moved more people and shaped more events in the world than cold economic, scientific and social motivations. One such irrational emotion is called the *"European dream"* which never came true. Yet it never dies. It was the dream conceived by Kant, Novalis, Voltaire, Rousseau, Victor Hugo, Mazzini and Garibaldi. The European cause was embraced equally by conservatives like (Klemens) Metternich, and revolutionaries like Napoleon. Aristide Briand, the French Foreign Minister, who first proposed the creation of the *United States of Europe* in 1929 in the belief that in spite of infinite diversities, separate histories, religions, cuisines and languages, Europeans were basically the same kind of people. It has been a heart-warming idea that has made European eyes shine. The concept for *"European unity,"* has deep historical origins. Indeed, they do stretch back to the dissolution of the Roman empire.

Ever since the fall of Rome, Europeans have longed for the recreation of an over-arching political structure for Europe, and used the Roman empire as a model. In 800 AD – more than three centuries after the fall of Rome –

Charlemagne, the king of the Franks, had been crowned in Rome by the Pope. His empire stretched from the Pyrenees to the Danube and from Hamburg to Sicily, and his imperial seal bore the words *Renovatio Imperii Romani*, "the renewal of the Roman Empire". Charlemagne's empire fell apart soon after his death. But, the memory of Charlemagne continued to inspire those who sought to unite Europe by fair means or foul. Napoleon created the Legion of Honour, an order of distinction, in 1802 on the model of the *Roman Legio Honoratorum* and invoked Charlemagne at his imperial coronation in 1804. Hitler's loyalists gave the Roman salute and their cry *"Heil Hitler!"* was modelled on *"Heil Caesar!"* When the Nazis formed a new SS division for French volunteers they called it the Charlemagne division.

Of course, the Romans have inspired not only despots but also democrats, among them the architects of the US Capitol in Washington DC. The Romans and Charlemagne also inspired the founders of the EU, whose objectives were the exact opposite of war. The founding treaty of their creation was signed in Rome in 1957 and their successors were hoping to return to the eternal city to put their names to a new constitution. The expansion of the European club was finalised at the Charlemagne Building in Brussels. It is easy to see common elements in the Roman empire that might appeal to modern-day builders of Europe. Most obvious is sheer territorial expanse. To that may be added the creation of a common legal code, a common currency (euro) as a symbol of imperial rule, the building of roads linking the empire. And all this is based upon supposedly lasting peace within the empire – for the Romans, the *Pax Romana*.

UNITY, FRATERNITY, CREATIVITY

The notion that unity and peace in Europe are two sides of the same coin is an article of faith for modern pro-Europeans. A large exhibition about the history of the idea of European unity was staged in late 2003, at the German History Museum in Berlin. It was argued that the "idea of unification and peace are linked." The Berlin exhibition emphasised the intellectual origins of the idea of European unity. Behind the shifting alliances between nations, there were always people who thought and wrote about the utopia of a united Europe, even though they were never really taken seriously until after the World War II.

There was Pierre Dubois, a counsellor for the Duke of Burgundy, who called for a European federation in 1306; Immanuel Kant, the German philosopher who made a celebrated call for "perpetual peace;" William Penn, the founder of Pennsylvania, and an early advocate of a European parliament; and Victor Hugo, the French 19th-century novelist who proclaimed in 1849 that "a day will come when you, France, you, Russia, you, Italy, you, Germany, you, all nations of the continent, without losing your distinctive qualities and glorious individuality, will be merged within a superior unit." Lest any utterly dim-witted visitor miss the political, and moral message, the Berlin exhibition closed with a quotation from former French President Valery Giscard d'Estaing. "Let us imagine a continent at peace, freed of its barriers and obstacles where history and geography are finally reconciled."

The European unity was also the concern of serious historians in France and Germany. Hagen Schulze, a professor of history at the Free University of Berlin, ends his scholarly study of the evolution of the European nation-state, *"States, Nations and Nationalism"*, with the thought that the "ancient states and nations" of Europe "may gradually fade away and recede into the background to make way for one united Europe." This, he says, is likely to be a considerable improvement on previous efforts to restore the unity of this continent by elevating one of its major powers to a position of hegemony – first Spain, then France, then Germany.

Jacques Boussard in *"The Civilisation of Charlemagne"* (1968) says that "Charlemagne's achievement was the realisation of a united Europe. There were no wars except at the frontiers." (This is an important qualification, given the fact that the great man fought some 53 military campaigns, expanding the boundaries of his empire). In Boussard's view, it was only the "stable society created by Charlemagne" that allowed for an "extraordinary growth of cultural, artistic and intellectual activity." It is sometimes observed that the countries that once formed part of Charlemagne's empire – France, Germany, Italy, the Netherlands – have been much more at ease with the modern-day drive for European unity than the areas that fell outside it, notably Britain and Scandinavia. As a consequence, British historians are less likely than their French or German counterparts to assume that European unity is necessarily synonymous with peace and cultural progress.

WHO THOUGHT IT FIRST?

Hitler, for example, told the Reichstag in 1936; "It is not very intelligent to imagine that in such a cramped house like that of Europe, a community of peoples can maintain different legal systems and different concepts of law for long." Mussolini said in 1933 that, "Europe may once again seize of the world, if it can develop a modicum of political unity." Oswald Mosley, the leading British fascist of the 1930s, was also a champion of the idea of a European union. Many British Eurosceptics are inclined to see the modern promoters of European unity not as idealistic peaceniks, but as the heirs of Hitler who have simply devised a new and subtler plan for taking over Britain. Perhaps, they forgot the speech of Winston Churchill in Zurich in 1946, in which he called for a *United States of Europe*. When Mr. Giscard d'Estaing published his draft constitution in 2003, the Sun, Britain's bestselling newspaper, greeted it with a cartoon showing Hitler and Napoleon squabbling over a copy of the document, each claiming, *"I thought of it first."* Hitler, however, does not feature prominently in the making of a United Europe. Hitler sought to subjugate the European continent to the Third Reich in the name of *New Europe*. But, it is unfair to link Hitler to the modern movement for European unity because Hitler based his ideas on notions of the superiority of the Germanic race and conquest, whereas modern Europe is being built on the idea of equality between peoples. The French are much keener on the idea that Napoleon was a "builder of Europe." Some French historians, however, are much less bashful about claiming Napoleon as the cause of European Unity. Since the French still regard Napoleon as a "good thing" to happen – he was a hero to Churchill, too – they are less likely to fear that the cause of European unity will suffer by association with the emperor.

Historia, a monthly French magazine, published an article (in 2002) under the title "Napoleon – the real father of Europe," with a cover illustration of the great man crossing the Alps wearing a hat decorated with the insignia of today's EU. According to the article, many of the EU's features – federal law, the common market, the dismantling of frontiers, the promotion of the idea of the rights of man – can be traced to the Napoleonic heritage. Even the Grand Army brought together 20 nations. And such musings are not confined to popular history magazines, Dominique de Villepin, the French Foreign Minister, published a book in 2003 on Napoleon in which he argued, "History has vindicated Napoleon's vision of a "great European family" of the future. Napoleon himself had little doubt that he deserved to be counted as a great European. In his memoirs, he lamented that had he only won his war in Russia, Europe would soon have been one people, and anyone who travelled anywhere would have found himself always in the common fatherland." Moreover, "Paris would have been the capital of the world, and the French the envy of the nations." The architects of modern Europe hope that, one day the EU will be a great power – a peaceable, liberal, law-based and generous great power in the best traditions of their forefathers. And, not without reason.

UNIFICATION PROCESS BEGAN AFTER WORLD WAR II

The process of unifying a continent, divided by political and economic conflict for centuries, began at the end of the World War II as leaders of West European capitalist countries began to converge in an alliance against the Communist East. It was the perceived threat from the Soviet Union, rather than any intrinsic feeling of unity, that brought these countries together though the process came close to the goal set by Sir Winston Churchill who envisaged a *"United States of Europe."* What the Soviets never succeeded in doing, the Japanese did with the commercial threat, proving themselves to be more formidable than the military or political challenge from the Eastern bloc. Admittedly, the creation of a single European market was still a far cry from the Churchillian vision of post-war united Europe.

Undeniably, the unification of the European market was a policy initiative inspired by the requirements of European businessmen. In their struggle to catch up with the US, the Japanese and new East Asian rivals were looking at ways of improving their competitive position. The credit for this, must firmly rest with a group of economists and civil servants in Brussels who were involved in the production of the White Paper and the subsequent EC Report: *"The Economics of 1992 – an Assessment of the EC"* (Brussels, 1988). A popular version of the latter, written by its principal author, Paola Cecchini, (The European Challenge, 1992) had become a best seller worldwide having run into four editions in one year!

Those who were still sceptial about the benefits of a single market saw the report as a mere bravado. "1992 is not simply a date. It is a programme, and a strategy," the report said. "A strategy not simply for the revival of the sagging West European economies but for the creation of the largest territory for capitalist industrialisation." The report said this strategy "will propel Europe onto the blustery world stage of the 1990s, in a position of competitive strength and on an upward trajectory of economic growth lasting into the next century." Europe has been divided into small economies which hurt each other through *"beggar thy neighbour"* policies. These have prevented the exploitation of economies of scale and have increased the cost of European manufactured goods, resulting in the shrinking of the domestic market for many goods, and preventing Europe from competing effectively with the US and Japan. A single market, it was expected, would remove barriers to growth in Europe, speed up industrial rationalisation, reduce costs of production and increase employment.

SINGLE EUROPEAN ACT 1992

In the process, it was hoped, political and cultural unification may occur, helping to restore Europe's economic pre-eminence in the 21st century. The supporters of the 1992 deadline saw other fringe benefits as more and more European nations outside the EC discovered the advantages of unification. Western capitalist Europe finally succeeded in re-absorbing Eastern Europe. However, the spurs for unification were not the grandiose dreams but the business benefits. What precisely were then the barriers that 1992 sought to eliminate? The *EC Report on The Economics of 1992* saw these as (i) differences in technical regulations between the countries which impose extra costs on intra-EC trade; (ii) delay at frontiers for customs purposes, related administrative burdens for companies and public administration which imposed further costs on trade; (iii) restrictions on competition for public purchases through excluding bids from other community suppliers which often resulted in high cost of purchase; and (iv) restrictions on freedom to engage in certain service transactions or to become established in certain service activities in other European countries.

The *Single European Act,* signed in February 1986 and later ratified by the then 12 EC governments, set the deadline for the creation of the single market on the last day of 1992. The Act had a wider scope than the simple integration of the market; for, it sought to create a more cohesive political and economic entity in Europe. In the process, it was hoped that the European industry would witness a significant reduction in costs, due to a better rationalisation of industrial structures and the establishment of more competitive markets. As many as 300 different non-tariff barriers to intra-EC trade were eliminated by 1992 – the barriers which added to the inefficiency of production in Europe. The removal of trade barriers, the EC report said, would "liberate resources for alternative productive uses and when they are so used the total sustainable level of consumption and investment in the economy will be increased." This was the criterion of economic gain.

Sceptics of 1992 came mostly from the backward economies of Europe that were afraid of being sidelined in a united Europe by the Germans and the French. Businessmen in some countries feared that unification would strengthen labour and push wage cost while workers feared that rationalisation would mean loss of jobs. Procedural delays in the unification process aimed at giving more time for the sceptics to be convinced had irritated the French, Germans and the Belgians who were exerting pressure for a faster pace of unification. It was not surprising that these countries first initiated procedures for the elimination of border controls.

ECONOMY BEHIND UNIFICATION

The original plan was to integrate 12 West European countries which had influence well beyond the world economy. Turning the European Community – from Lapland (Arctic Circle) to Sardinia, from the Algarve (Southernmost province of Portugal on the Atlantic coast) coast to the Dodacanese (south-east Aegean) islands – into a single political entity, as the USA or the Soviet Union, will have an impact far beyond its borders. Culturally, it could affect the 21st century world as much as the European colonisation of North America affected the first half of 20th century, or the rise of Japan affected the second half. The principal interest was on the immense economic effect of the 12-nation integration: the removal of legal barriers not only to trade, investment and travel but also to banking, insurance and employment. In the 1990s, a common currency was expected to evolve and the *euro* later became a reality. Much of Europe's economic integration had already been achieved in 1992. Intra-European tariffs were created, modified only by some controversial, protectionist price supports, especially in agriculture. By and large, a Japanese or Indian or Brazilian company in Ireland could export without excise to Denmark or Greece. It was made easier for foreign companies to make money in Europe by establishing factories there than by exporting non-European products to Europe. However, even those who could export from outside benefited from the standardisation of requirements. What was acceptable in Milan was also acceptable in Manchester and Madrid.

Just as the Industrial Revolution destroyed forest in England to build "*dark, satanic mills*", so the homely little groceries of small-town and "village Europe" would be thrown out by faceless supermarts. But, the driving factor behind European integration – to be larger and to raise material standards – was not entirely without unattractive values. W. Somerset Maugham says that money is a sixth sense, without which it is difficult to appreciate the other five senses completely. There is more than cynicism in this; those of us who get more pleasure from sitting on a rock and thinking than driving a Mercedes are a minority, and must respect the majority will. The love of beauty does not relieve hunger pangs of the starving people, or improve the homes of the indequately housed.

FEAR OF GYPSY INFLUX

West Europeans also feared the influx of gypsies into the European heartland. The Gypsies, were a ragged settlement of 20,000 people, about 20 km southeast of German border town of the Czech city of Most. The towns people were convinced that these newly-minted Europeans will assert their right to move freely within the Union. They foresee Gypsy caravans, with clanking pots and shoeless children, next to their backyards. Even Europeans, whose "yards" are half a continent away, share an atavistic fear of the invading horde from the East. While the EU welcomed its 75 million new residents on May 1, 2004, tabloids in Britain published reports about the coming deluge. "Britain won't let us starve," "They can't wait to arrive in a land of dole and benefits," reported newspapers. The fear, ingrained through generations, persisted. "I couldn't drive them out if they set up a camp in our town," said Mr. Heinz-Peter Haustein, the mayor of Deutschneudorf (2002). "Germany has a special responsibility toward the Roma because of our history." History is on the side of gypsies. The hilly terrain across the Czech border was once known as Sudetenland. It stands as a tragic example of how Europe failed in earlier efforts to integrate wandering peoples. More than three million Germans once lived in Sudetenland, which emboldened the Nazis to annex it in 1938. After Germany was defeated in World War II, the territory was ceded to Czechoslovakia and many Sudeten Germans were expelled – in some cases brutally – to border towns.

GYPSIES WHO?

It is a widely held belief that gypsies were Egyptian in origin who arrived in Basel, Switzerland, with a great horde of followers in 1422. A.L. Basham and S.A.A. Rizri, in their book, "*The Wonder that was India*," quote historical legends to suggest that the 5th century Sassanian king (Persia) Bahram Gur invited ten thousand Indian musicians to his realm and gave them cattle, corn and asses, with the hope they would settle down and teach his subjects music and dance. They, however, ate up all his gifts and wandered about as nomads. The language that the gypsies speak have similarities with Indian languages.

It is also believed that the gypsies originated in the Gangetic plains from a low caste called *Doms* and are, thus, called Roma. This is what the gypsies call themselves, hence, the term Roma or Romani gypsies – no connection to Rome or Romania.

The gypsies are an independent people. They jealously guard their language, customs and social practices. They marry among themselves and, thus, belong to an endogamous gene pool. Basham describes how several of their customs and rituals of birth, death and animal slaughter are remarkably similar to Indian ones. The gypsies, largely inbred have certain traits. The Australian researchers were able to show a particular mutation in the gene which occurs in a Roma gypsy family, leading to early childhood blindness (cataract) in the family. There are about 8 million of them today, mostly in south-eastern and Central Europe, and a smaller number in Russia and North Africa.

Gypsies were, however, not the only ghosts that haunted Europe. Germans also warned that low-cost Czech and East European labourers will cross the border to take away their jobs. It was also feared that an integrated Europe could lead to the disappearance of secondary European languages such as Dutch or Portuguese, much as Gaelic and Provencal are nearly dead, and ensure the supremacy of Standard English over American English while restoring French as an international tongue.

The convergence of Greek philosophy and the Biblical faith, with the subsequent addition of Roman heritage, created Europe and remains the foundation of what can be called Europeanism.

– H.G. Wells

5

Sources of European unity- a mystique or reality?

Why is Europe being united at all when it has been so different, so divided and so quarrelsome? Nothing is common among its countries except the experience of fighting bloody wars and killing one another. Together now, the old and exhausted Europe cries out; "Enough is enough." And, the European Union was born although its growth does'nt seem to be trouble-free as was made clear by the rejection of EU Constitutional draft by France and the Netherlands in 2005.

Unlike the United States, with its *"In God We Trust,"* engravings on coins and in courtrooms, most countries of Europe keep religious rituals outside of European governments. Europeans are less religious than Americans and uneasy about the US foreign policy driven by faith. There are two sides of the argument. In one camp are the mostly Catholic countries, Ireland, Spain, Italy and Poland which have been demanding a more emphatic recognition of Europe's religious roots. They are joined by other countries, including Slovakia, the Czech Republic, Malta and Lithuania. They support a Christian (or a Judeo-Christian) reference in the preamble of the European Constitution. *"Either Europe is Christian or it is not Europe at all"*, was the bold formulation of this group. On the other side is a conviction, held most tenaciously by France and Belgium, which have perhaps the fiercest attachments to the idea of a total church-state separation or secularism. They say that religion is not the founding principle of the European Union.

There was plenty of support in Europe for a specific mention of Christianity, or the Judaeo-Christian tradition, or even the Judaeo-Christian-

Islamic heritages of Europe. Certainly, at least some on the pro-religion side of the issue, have voiced support for including all the three major religions as a gesture of inclusiveness. But, this did not happen. And, the question of a common European heritage remains unsettled.

The Renaissance, Enlightenment, Industrialisation, state-system, Judaism, Islam (until it was thrown out of Europe), Christianity, and the Latin language (which was widely spoken in Europe) are the common European experiences. However, to speak of a European heritage is not to suggest that the continent has been at peace with itself. No, it never was. On the other hand, it has been the most quarrelsome, and divided continent, that had become the killingfield many times in the past. The concept of European cultural unity means common European experiences, history and geography which finally resulted in the setting up of the European Union.

When France and Germany decided to co-operate and end all wars, they were actually trying to make the past and its inherited prejudices irrelevant for the future of Europe. It must be admitted that nation-states thrived on hostility, which was why it was so difficult to separate jingoism from patriotism. Over the centuries, Europeans fought against each other, goaded on by economic interests, territorial ambitions or sectarian passion. In the 19th and 20th centuries alone, nearly half a dozen major wars were fought between Germany and France. As late as the 1950s, children in the Alsace region of France were admonished never to speak German, even though the Alsatian dialect is closer to German than to French. Today all this seems so remote. Yet, the memory lingers.

The *euro,* however, does not mean that the boundaries between countries have collapsed. It is possible that Europe may, in the long run, become one nation-state, like the US. What is of interest, however, is that countries like France, Germany and Italy are increasingly defining themselves in terms other than those taken from cultures, traditions, and memories. If this logic is allowed to proceed, it will in due course change the contours and definition of the nation-state.

In France and Germany, for example, cultural distinctions still exist. But a closer look will reveal that these differences are not quite as dominant as they used to be. The French and the Germans are beginning to define themselves in terms of how they harness and enhance their knowledge base which is reflected, among other things, in the social policies that these countries have adopted with regard to health, education, nuclear energy and the corporate sector. The French have been very proud of their public health system, of their nuclear energy programme, and of their many *Grand Ecoles* that produce the elite of their country. Likewise, Germany, too, has its own ways of handling knowledge related to such areas. In France, there is a strong commitment towards maintaining a super efficient transport system even if it runs at a loss. They are proud of the knowledge they have created and put to use in this regard. The high speed TGV train is not a profit-making enterprise but the French want it anyway.

Thus, while France and Germany are leading nations of the European Union, it is not as if they are about to merge all their differences. True, language will continue to separate the two countries, but that too will lose its salience over time. More and more people in the manager and technical sectors are already moving between countries and picking up languages as they go along. Language, in such cases, is not a cultural cache worth acquiring for its own sake, but a means of securing a job and earning money. For instance, young French people are much more eager to learn English than their fathers a generation before.

SOURCES OF CONFLICT

The Catholic church gained power in Western Europe on the decline of the Roman Empire, after which it never again had a single "emperor" of Europe. Instead, the Catholic church was able to play one European prince against another, becoming the *"swing vote"* in the power struggle of the day. Had one monarch emerged across the continent, he could have crushed the church's independence, turning it into a handmaiden of the state power. That is what happened to the Greek Orthodox church and later the Russian Orthodox Church. But no ruler ever conquered all of Europe, or even the greater part of it. Over the millennia, only a few tried - Charlemagne, Charles-V, Napoleon, Kaiser Wilhelm, and Hitler. All of them failed. What explains this? Probably, geography. Europe has rivers with barriers that divide its highlands into river valleys, bordered by mountain ranges. Its rivers flow into sheltered, navigable bays along the long, indented Mediterranean coastline-all of which means that small regions could exist, indeed thrive, on their own. Hence, Europe has a long history of many independent countries. They are hard to conquer, easy to cultivate, and their rivers and seas provide ready trade routes. Asia, by contrast, is full of vast flatlands - the steppes in Russia, the plains in China and India - through which armies could march unhindered. Not surprisingly, these areas were ruled for millennia by centralized empires.

ONCE, EUROPE HAD 500 STATES; GEOGRAPHY IS ITS HISTORY

Europe's topography made possible the rise of communities of varying sizes- city-states, duchies, republics, nations, and empires. In 1500, Europe had within it more than 500 states, many no larger than a city. This variety had two effects. First, it allowed for diversity. People, ideas, art, and even technologies that were unwelcome or unnoticed in one area would often thrive in another. Second, diversity fuelled competition between states, producing innovation and efficiency in political organization, military technology, and economic policy. Successful practices were copied; losing ways were cast aside. Europe's spectacular economic and political success – what the economic historian Eric Jones has termed "the European miracle" – might well be the result of its odd geography.

Africa is particularly unlucky in its geography. Despite being the second-largest continent in the world, it has the shortest coastline, much of which is too shallow to develop into ports. So it has historically little trade. Its rivers are not navigable, because they are either too shallow or too deep, scarred by rapids and waterfalls. Add to this, tropical heat and accompanying diseases and one gets a sad structural explanation for Africa's under-development. This is also the case with India that has no natural harbour or port comparable to any in Europe.

Geography and history also combined to help shape Europe's political structure. The fall of the Roman Empire and the backwardness of the German tribes that destroyed it resulted in decentralized authority across the continent; no ruler had the administrative capacity to rule a far-flung kingdom, comprising many independent tribes. By contrast, Ming and Manchu of China, Mughals of India, and the Ottoman Empire controlled vast lands and diverse peoples. But in Europe, local landlords and chieftains governed their territories and developed close ties with their tenants. This became the distinctive feature of European feudalism; no wonder its landowning classes were independent. From the Middle Ages until the seventeenth century, European sovereigns were distant creatures who ruled their kingdoms, mostly in name. The king of France, for example, was considered only a duke in Brittany and had limited authority for hundreds of years. In practice, if monarchs wanted to do anything (start a war, build a fort) they had to borrow money and troops from local chieftains who became earls, viscounts, and dukes for giving them money, troops or other favours.

Thus, Europe's landed elite became an aristocracy with power, money and legitimacy–a far cry from the grovelling and dependent courtier nobles in other parts of the world. This near-equal relationship between lords and kings deeply influenced the course of European history. As a historian has said, "Without the effective resistance of privileged classes, the monarchy would have created nothing but slaves." In fact, monarchs did just that in much of the rest of the world. In Europe, on the other hand, as the Middle Ages progressed, the aristocracy demanded that kings guarantee them certain rights that even the crown could not violate. They also established representative bodies likes parliaments, estates-general and *diets* to give permanent voice to their claims. In these medieval bargains lay the foundations of what we today call *"the rule of law."* Building on Roman traditions, these rights were secured and strengthened by the power of the nobility. Like the clash between the church and the state, the conflict between the aristocracy and the monarchy is the second great power struggle of European history that helped provide, again unintentionally, the raw materials for freedom.

The English aristocracy was the most independent of them all. Lords lived on their estates, governing and protecting their tenants. In return, they extracted taxes which kept them both powerful and rich. It maintained its position not through elaborate courtly rituals but by taking part in politics and government at all levels. England's kings, recognized that their rule depended on co-opting the aristocracy. When monarchs pushed their luck too far, they resisted. Henry-II, crowned king in 1154, extended his rule across the country, sending judges to distant places to enforce royal decrees. He sought to unify the country and create a common imperial law. To do this, he had to strip the medieval aristocracy of its powers and special privileges. His plan worked but, only up to a point. Soon the nobility rose up in arms and after forty years of conflict, Henry's son, King John, was forced to sign a truce in 1215, in a field near Windsor Castle. That document, the *Magna Carta*, was regarded at the time as a charter of baronial privilege detailing the rights of feudal lords. It also had provisions guaranteeing the freedom of the church and local autonomy for towns. It came out against the oppression of any of the king's subjects.

Over time, the document was interpreted more broadly by English judges, turning it into a quasi-constitution that enshrined certain individual rights. But even in its day, the Magna Carta was significant, being the first written limitation of royal authority in Europe. As such, the historian Paul Johnson notes, it is "justly classified as the first of the English statutes of the empire. "This was the first collection of English laws that make up British unwritten constitution from which English and American liberties flow," says Fareed Zakaria in his widely acclaimed book, "The Future of Freedom". Now, the Magna Carta has become a *mantra* for the freedom of man. It is ironical that democracy flows from the behaviour of privileged nobility, rightly accused of anti-democratic practices, of which slavery, oppression and inhumanity had been the defining features.

There is nothing like Europe; we have to create one.
– Jean Monnet, (1888-1979), First President of the European Coal and Steel High Authority, precursor of the EU.

6

European Union fit at 50 and expanding east

The European Union at 50 is still an unfinished story. Starting with six members in 1957, it has become a community of 27 sovereign nations today (March 2007). And still, other countries are waiting to join.

The European Union is an extraordinary experiment in shared sovereignty, creating a zone of peace that now stretches from Britain to the Balkans. The union of 27 countries is the world's most formidable economic bloc, incorporating about 500 million people in an integrated market that produces nearly a third more than the United States.

On March 25, the European Union (EU) completed 50 years of the signing of the *Treaty of Rome*, which established the European Community. The EU is an extraordinary system in governance, without parallel in history. Five hundred million people stretching across 27 different countries, from the Irish Sea to the doorsteps of Russia, have come together in less than three generations to create the world's first transnational political space. More blood has been spilled in Europe than in any other region of the world. But after 2,000 years of conflict and strife, Europe emerged form the World War II, determined to turn a new chapter in the way human beings behave to one another. And, they have succeeded.

Unlike past forms of governments, whose *raison d'etre* has always been the extension of power and the expropriation of people, resources, and territory, the EU was conceived with a different end in mind: the pooling of collective interests, the extension of reciprocity, and the desire to create a lasting peace based on trust between peoples. The European dream is so utterly different from the American dream which set the gold standard for the world in the 19th and 20th centuries. The American dream is all about individual opportunity which Americans define in terms of freedom, autonomy and mobility, which is, Americans have a love affair with the automobile and freedom on top of their agenda. Americans are taught that pursuing one's self-interest in the marketplace is the preferred path to personal happiness and societal progress. However, Europeans have a different dream. When pressed about their vision of the future, they will inevitably say that they dream of a happy and prosperous Europe. The EU's institutions were initially designed for six, not today's 27, and no wonder there is no agreement about what to do about the constitution. Some countries want a bigger treaty with social provisions; others a smaller one with no new powers for Brussels and others want to reopen all the institutional compromises. And, because of these differences, EU has no constitution. Not yet.

However, the EU works well even without a constitution. It takes longer to make decisions with 27 than with six or 15, but that is not necessarily a bad thing. It is true that a new deal is likely by 2009 on the size of the European Commission and on votes and parliamentary seats for new entrant. But, the plea that no new members can join EU without a constitution is political, not legal. It is made by those who don't want Turkey to join Europe and are using the constitution's absence as an excuse.

However, the European Union did not happen in a day; rather, it is the result of a series of steps taken over a long period to build networks of institutions and bind together the nation-states, almost all of whom have been fighting among themselves to acquire supremacy in the affairs of the Continent.

The process of European integration was launched on May 9, 1950 when France officially proposed to lay "the first concrete foundation of a European federation." Six countries (Belgium, Germany, France, Italy, Luxembourg and the Netherlands) joined in the beginning. And, after four waves of accessions (1973: Denmark, Ireland and the United Kingdom; 1981: Greece; 1986: Spain and Portugal; 1995: Austria, Finland and Sweden) the EU had 15 member states until May 1, 2004, when 10 new countries joined the EU with a population rising from the 370 million earlier, to 450 million after the new accessions. Bulgaria and Romania became full members in 2007.

The EU decided on December 14, 2003 that Latvia, Lithuania, Estonia,

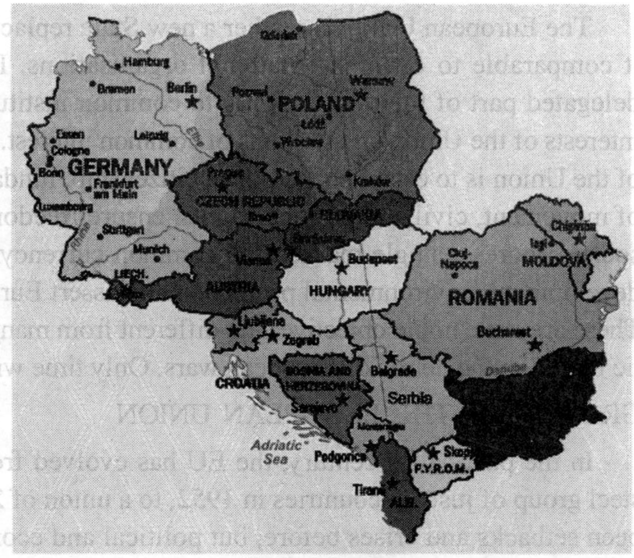

Central Europe

Poland, Hungary, Czech Republic, Slovakia, Slovenia, Malta and Cyprus will become members by 2004, which they did amid fanfare. The expanded Europe stretches from Portugal, on the Atlantic coast, to the borders of Russia in the heartland of the Eurasian continent. The 27-member EU is structured on a common economic and political heritage, based on the key principles of multi-party democracy, rule of law, free market economy and tariff-free and borderless trade. Poland, the largest of the new entrants, was to come last on board after finally accepting new financial arrangements. A visibly emotional Prime Minister of Poland, described the occasion (May 1, 2004) as a historic one and said, "Today, Poland comes from a '*Poland of Solidarity*' to a Europe of Solidarity".

The expanded EU came into being 15 years after the fall of the Berlin Wall in November 1989 after which the Soviet Union melted away, marking the end of the Cold War. As an ecstatic President of the European Commission Romano Prodi put it (May 1, 2004): "The accession of 10 new member-states brings to an end the divisions of Europe."

Turkey, with a population of close to 70 million, however, remains a big question mark on the map of the expanded EU, but EU leaders accept that Turkey could become a full member of the Union provided it meets European standards of good governance and secularism. The bombing in London on June 7, 2005 by Muslim terrorists has strengthened the resistance against Muslim Turkey joining the Union. The rise of Islamic fundamentalism has created fear in Europe, specially in France which has the largest Muslim population in Europe. The entry of Turkey has also been resisted by some other member-countries because of its Islamic identity. *(read more about it later).*

The European Union is neither a new State replacing existing ones nor is it comparable to other international organisations. Its member-states have delegated part of their sovereignty to common institutions, representing the interests of the Union on questions of common interest. The principal objective of the Union is to establish European citizenship, fundamental rights, freedom of movement, civil and political rights, ensure freedom, security and justice, social progress, single market, the common currency, job creation, regional development, environmental protection and assert Europe's role in the world. These are quite noble objectives, no different from many such covenants which lie buried in the debris of European wars. Only time will tell how it works.

GROWTH OF THE EUROPEAN UNION

In the past half a century, the EU has evolved from a modest coal-and-steel group of just six countries in 1952, to a union of 27 members. There had been setbacks and crises before, but political and economic logic has driven the project forward, forcing many reluctant countries to join the Union. Denmark and Sweden have rejected the *euro* in referenda while the UK has taken no decision yet.

European Union Member-States

1. Belgium	2. Denmark
3. Germany	4. Greece
5. Spain	6. France
7. Ireland	8. Italy
9. Luxembourg	10. The Netherlands
11. Austria	12. Portugal
13. Finland	14. Sweden
15. United Kingdom	16. Czech Republic
17. Estonia	18. Cyprus
19. Latvia	20. Lithuania
21. Hungary	22. Malta
23. Poland	24. Slovenia
25. Slovakia	26. Bulgaria
27. Romania	

Note: Bulgaria and Romania became full members in 2007. Hence, officially it is a 27-member European Union. And the Turkey case is pending.

(Reporting Year 2007)

The original six members – Belgium, France, West Germany, Italy, Luxembourg, and the Netherlands – were joined by the UK, Denmark, and Ireland (1973), Greece (1981), and Spain and Portugal (1986). East Germany was incorporated after German re-unification in 1990. Austria, Finland, and Sweden joined in 1995. Cyprus applied in 1990 as one member. Hungary and Poland in 1994; Bulgaria, Estonia, Latvia, Lithuania, Slovakia and Romania in 1995; and the Czech Republic in 1996. A customs pact with Turkey approved in 1995 was seen as the first step towards full membership but the move was criticized by human-right activists. In 1995, there were more than 360 million people in the EU countries. Now with expanded EU, the population is 450 million.

A European Charter of Social Rights was approved at the Maastricht Summit. The same meeting secured an agreement on a treaty framework for the European Union, including political and monetary union, and for a new system of police and military cooperation. After the initial rejection by Denmark in a national referendum in 1992, the Maastricht Treaty on European Union came into effect on November 1, 1993 and the new name, *European Union*, was adopted. In 1995 the EU's members affirmed their commitment to the attainment of monetary union, and in December of the same year, they agreed to call the new currency, the *euro*. The European Union is run by mainly five institutions: The European Parliament (elected by the peoples of the member-states); Council of the Union (composed of the governments of the member-states); European Commission (executive body); Court of Justice (compliance with the law); Court of Auditors (sound and lawful management of the EU budget). There are other outfits also.

The European Economic and Social Committee expresses the opinions of organised civil society on economic and social issues; the Committee of the Regions expresses the opinions of regional and local authorities on regional policy, environment, and education. The European Ombudsman deals with complaints from citizens concerning maladministration by an EU institution or body; the European Investment Bank contributes to EU objectives by financing public and private long-term investments and the European Central Bank is responsible for monetary policy and foreign exchange operations. A number of other agencies and bodies complete the system.

KEY EU INSTITUTIONS

At the heart of the EU, as envisaged by its French founding father Jean Monnet, is the *European Commission*, to which each national government appoints one commissioner for a five-year term. The "college" of 27 commissioners sits atop a 20,000- strong bureaucracy that constitutes the EU's executive. The Commission also has the sole right of initiating legislation, administers the budget and has other independent powers including deciding competition cases and representing the union in trade negotiations.

The European Union			
Older members	**Date joined**	**Older members**	**Date joined**
Belgium	1958	United Kingdom	1973
France	1958	Greece	1981
Germany	1958	Spain	1986
Italy	1958	Portugal	1986
Luxembourg	1958	Austria	1995
Netherlands	1958	Finland	1955
Denmark	1973	Sweden	1995
Ireland	1973		
Newer members	**Date joined**	**Newer members**	**Date joined**
Cyprus	2004	Lithuania	2004
Czech Republic	2004	Malta	2004
Estonia	2004	Poland	2004
Hungary	2004	Slovakia	2004
Latvia	2004	Slovenia	2004
Bulgaria	2007	Romania	2007

The Commission takes its political cue from the *European Council*, made up of the 27 heads of government, which meets four times a year and also nominates the commission president. The European Council is, in practice, the highest incarnation of the *Council of Ministers*, the main law-and budget-making body, which brings together national ministers (e.g., for finance, foreign affairs, agriculture). The presidency of the council rotates every six months. The Council often makes decisions by qualified majority, a weighted system of national votes, but on some issues (e.g., taxation) it has to be unanimous. As part of the council, the *high representative* for foreign policy reports to national governments and may (or may not) work closely with the commissioner for external affairs. The common foreign and security policy he runs is not part of the classic Monnet machinery (sometimes known as the "community method"), but is formulated by the member governments. The same is true for policies on justice and home affairs.

> **YALTA AND SINCE**
>
> While the celebrations were held on May 1, 2004 in Dublin to mark the joining of ten East European countries expanding the European Union to 25, historians were wondering how times had changed. For, those who ended up on the wrong side of the armistice line after the World War II, the D-Day (June 6, 1944) had nothing to celebrate. However, the ten new east European countries remembered the Yalta Conference (February 4-11, 1945) in the Crimea where Stalin, Churchill and Roosevelt consigned half of Europe to poverty and dictatorship of the Soviet Union which they suffered until the Communism collapsed in 1991. After so many years of sufferings, the east Europeans had finally had the taste of the forbidden fruit – *freedom*. And, now Poland, Slovakia and Hungary are the new frontline states of Russia, Belarus and Ukraine – a new geostrategic orientation of old Europe, now being *re-invented*.

The other law-and budget-making body is the *European Parliament*. It has 785 members, directly elected in rough proportion to each country's population. Like the commission, the parliament serves for five years; unlike the commission, which is in Brussels, it holds its plenary meetings mostly in Strasbourg,though committees meet in Brussels. Most EU laws are subject to "co-decision" by the council and parliament, but in some areas, including justice and home affairs, the parliament has no say. The parliament has to approve the choice of commission president and can dismiss the entire commission, but not individual commissioners.

The *European Court of Justice*, based in Luxembourg, acts as the EU's supreme court in areas for which the union is responsible (which does not include criminal law, for example). There is one judge per country. A court of first instance helps with the caseload. Cases are decided by simple majority. Luxembourg also hosts the Court of Auditors, which checks EU spending- and qualifies the accounts every year. The EU has plethora of other agencies, as well as the Luxembourg-based European Investment Bank, the word's biggest multilateral borrower. Among the more puzzling are two Brussels-based advisory bodies: the Economic and Social Committee, which brings together the "social partners", and the Committee of the Regions.

EURO IS BORN

The single currency for Europe was dreamt of by many, including Charlemagne and Napoleon. The plan for a single currency was abandoned in the 1970s. The decision was, however, taken at a European Union summit in the Dutch town of Maastricht in 1991. And, finally the European currency, *euro,* was born on January 1, 2002. It is said that *euro* is primarily about politics and not economics. Defenders of the common currency, point out that countries can share a currency without political unity. The gold standard, a *de facto* common currency, operated for decades without any movement towards a political union and indeed through several wars. On a smaller scale, Britain and Ireland long shared a currency, as did Belgium and Luxembourg, as also a clutch of West African countries, with no suggestion that monetary marriage should inevitably lead to political fusion. Currency unions that do not follow on to political union existed among France, Belgium, Italy, Switzerland, Greece and Bulgaria between 1865 and 1914, but they came to grief with the World War I. However, the currency union was described as a "profoundly political act."

EUROPEAN UNION – A PROFILE

(Total members 27)

✹ Population	:	Above 500 million
BIG SIX EU COUNTRIES:		
✹ Germany	:	82.17 million
✹ Britain	:	59.63 million
✹ France	:	59.30 million
✹ Italy	:	57.68 million
✹ Spain	:	39.44 million
✹ Poland	:	38.20 million
AREA:		
✹ EU 15	:	3.23 million sq kms
✹ EU 27	:	3.94 million sq kms

The four largest economies of the EU (Germany, UK, Italy and France) account for 67 per cent of the gross domestic product of the EU-27 in 2007. (Reporting Year 2009)

When the new continental currency, *euro,* was introduced on Jan 1, 2002 some 320 million people in the 12 nations exclaimed *"Happy New Euro."* And, thus, rang out old currencies like the French franc, German mark, Dutch guilder and Italian lire. The idea of a single currency and single market for the EEC member-states had evolved steadily over almost half a century. The original proposal by economist Jean Monnet in the 1940s was made long before globalisation had become the buzzword. Europe had suffered two World Wars

THE EURO COUNTRIES	
Austria	Belgium
Cyprus	Finland
France	Germany
Greece	Ireland
Italy	Luxembourg
Malta	The Netherlands
Portugal	Slovakia
Slovenia	Spain
	(Reporting Year 2009)

and, hence, it was important that it never went to war again. The idea in the 1950s was to employ economic integration as the catalyst for European political unity, breaking the tariff barriers between closed national economies. It began innocuously with the customs union in the 1950s, first reducing and later eliminating tariffs and took 30 years to create the single market.

The currency of any nation acquires an emotional, patriotic value and many people resisted change. There was also the risk of fake currencies being circulated over a larger area. Some 14 billion brand new *euro* notes had been printed and over 50 billion coins minted. Campaigns were launched to familiarise the man in the street with the *euro* equivalent of older currencies. Elaborate plans were also afoot to "round up" the older currency. Across Europe, 350,000 tonnes of coins were collected, stored and melted down for recycling. Coin-mangling operations were in full swing for older currencies while raw metal discs were being sent to national central banks for minting new *euro* coins.

323 million people of 16 Countries have one currency: It was the largest-ever logistical peacetime operation – the transition to the *euro* now in 15 countries. Inevitably, there were some glitches, but by and large things went off well. Sweden and Denmark have rejected *euro* regimes in referenda, while the UK has still to take a decision. So out of the then 15 member-countries, 12 had adopted the *euro* until 2004. Ms. Anna Lindh, the Swedish Foreign Minister, and a campaigner of the *euro* regime in the September (2003) referendum, was stabbed to death on September 11, 2004 in Stockholm which sent a shockwave through Europe where many had started questioning the wisdom of European integration. The arrival of the *euro* in physical form was a landmark in the movement towards a larger pan-European identity. And the ease with which 12 nations gave up their currencies, indicated the willingness to discard old, narrow identities that could provide a model for the rest of the world.

This was broadly the European scenario until 2005, with all its complexities and hopes. It is hard to judge what a united Europe will look like, now that 10 more countries of Eastern Europe have joined the Union, but if history is any guide, unified Europe will be a safer and better place than the divided one in which one nation sought to conquer the other and, in the process, starting wars, many of which crossed the European boundaries, causing devastation and miseries to peoples around the world.

Besides the fifteen Member-States of the *euro* area, Europe's single currency also circulates, officially or informally, in a number of other countries and territories in the world. Special monetary agreements have been concluded with Monaco, the Vatican City and San Marino which enable each of these countries to issue euro coins. This follows the tradition of earlier agreements between France and Monaco, between Italy and San Marino and Italy and the Vatican which had previously allowed these countries to issue their own coins in French francs and Italian lira respectively. In Andorra, the *euro* has replaced the Spanish peseta and French franc, both of which previously circulated in the Principality. The *euro* is also used as means of payment in Kosovo and Montenegro, replacing the German mark which was formerly used as the de facto currency.

EXPANDED EUROZONE

The eurozone expanded to 16 countries after Malta and Cyprus adopted the European Union's common currency in January 2008 and Slovakia in 2009. The entry of the Mediterranean islands and Slovenia in 2007 was in line with the expectation that in eurozone smaller economies would also meet the so-called convergence criteria. This coincided with the steady rise of the euro as the second global currency after the US dollar, with over 25 per cent share in the world's foreign exchange reserves. The growing tendency among third country governments to spread risk and hold an increasing proportion of their forex reserves in euro is due to the eurozone's global attractiveness as the world's largest trading destination and its stable currency. The single currency, first introduced as a unit of account in 1999 and as banknotes and coins in 2002, enables consumers (about 450 million) in the 16 states to compare prices of goods and services and do away with the cost of changing currency for travel within the euro area.

EURO, A DECADE OLD NOW

The euro, the European Union single currency that has turned 10-year-old in Jan 2009, is arguably the single most visible symbol of post-war European integration that enables the free movement of persons and services across national borders. Euro has eliminated the cost of currency exchange during internal travel and facilitated the comparison of prices in cross-border trade. The euro, as of now (2009), is the world's second largest global currency after the United States dollar, with about a quarter of the share of foreign exchange reserves. The eurozone's attractiveness as the world's largest single trading destination has led emerging economies to rethink the greenback as the sole currency peg for exchange rates. Notwithstanding the limited room for manoeuvre for countries with profligate spending records and high public debt, the benefits of staying inside far outweigh the pain of exiting from the eurozone. To that extent, the predictions of doom that greeted the euro a decade ago have been belied. For EU countries that are yet to adopt the euro, which include the United Kingdom, Hungary and Poland, the message from it all is to create the political climate to expedite an early entry.

Euro will, however, not evoke national pride or nostalgia like the US dollar and the British pound did at one time. EU has no geographical unit like a nation-state. Hence, there is no issue of loyalty to a common currency with no common flag existing. How can there be a battle without flag, a national anthem or a shared language? A body like the European Union could, however, develop into a powerful and effective structure because it has no electorate other than a small number (albeit growing) of member governments. The EU would be nowhere without its *'democratic deficit'* and there can be no future for its parliament for there is no 'European people' but only a collection of 'member peoples' less than half of whom bothered to vote in the 2004 EU parliamentary elections.

Europe is now a functioning entity, but unlike the member-states, it enjoys no popular legitimacy or electoral authority. Unsurprisingly, problems arose as soon as the EU moved beyond negotiations between governments and became the subject of democratic campaigning in the member-states. Democracy, however desirable, is not an effective device for solving global or transnational problems, even in Europe, the Balkan is a case in point.

EUROPEAN UNION at a glance

TWENTY SEVEN COUNTRIES have joined together to form the European Union (EU). But Europe was not always united. Between 1870 and 1945, France and Germany were at war three times. Determined to ensure that their two countries never fought again, the French and German decided to link coal and steel industries so that their nations would be forced to work together. The creation of the European Coal and Steel Community (ECSC) in 1951 led to today's European Union.

Uniting Europe

In 1957, the ECSC evolved into the wider European Economic Community (EEC). Ten years later this became the European Community (EC). In 1991, EC leaders signed the Maastricht Treaty, which started Europe towards full economic and monetary union. When the treaty came into force in 1993, the EC became the European Union (EU).

The Growing Union

The European Union has 27 members now. A number of states have applied for membership, with more considering joining. Trade and cooperation agreements are already in place between the EU and many applicants. Switzerland has close trade links with the EU, but a national referendum in 2001 rejected joining.

Jean Monnet

Jean Monnet (1888-1979) was a French economist who convinced the French foreign minister, Robert Schuman (1886-1963), that the only way to avoid another war between France and Germany was to integrate their coal and steel industries. The ECSC was set up with Monnet as its first president. His vision led directly to the development of today's EU.

What the EU does

The European Union has many different roles covering economic, financial, commercial, political, industrial, agricultural, social and cultural matters. Its two main achievements have been to establish free trade between the member states by abolishing customs duties, and set up a common agricultural and fisheries policy.

The Euro

On 1 January 2002, a single currency, the euro, was fully launched in 12 countries of the European Union (EU). The notes and coins of this new currency replaced the national currencies of those nations. The only EU countries to stay out of the monetary union were Britain, Denmark and Sweden.

Structure of the EU

The EU has three main institutions; the Commission, based in Brussels, Belgium, is the civil service which runs the EU; the Parliament, in Strasbourg,

France and Brussels, provides control over the EU; the European Court of Justice, in Luxembourg, makes sure EU laws are applied properly.

European Parliament

Every five years, adults throughout the EU go to the polls to elect 732 Members of European Parliament (MEPs) to represent their interests. Although it does not have the same powers as a national parliament, the European Parliament advises the Commission and supervises its work and annual budget.

EU aid

The EU provides subsidies to the less well-off regions of Europe, for projects such as developing new industries. Much EU aid is targeted towards improving transport links in Europe, such as building roads and railways, so all regions can share in the benefits of the single market.

Agricultural Policy

In order to guarantee food supplies and increase agricultural productivity, the EU runs a very complex Common Agricultural Policy (CAP). This has established free movement of farm produce throughout the EU.

Social Policy

The EU tries to improve workers and young people by investing in education and training in deprived regions. It has also established a common Social Chapter of Workers' Rights.

Timeline

1951 European Coal and Steel Community (ECSC) is set up.

1957 The ECSC nations sign the Treaty of Rome, setting up the European Economic Community (EEC).

1967 ECSC, EEC, and Euratom merge to form the European Community (EC).

1979 European Monetary System set up to link currencies.

1991 Maastricht Treaty sets out timetable for full economic union.

1993 EC becomes the European Union (EU).

2002 The euro replaces existing currencies in 12 EU countries.

2004 Ten additional countries become members of the EU.

> ***The European state system evolved through armed competition, trade, market and colonial exploitation.***
>
> *– A.K. Bagchi*

7 The state system since Treaty of Westphalia

The Treaty of Westphalia marked the formal end to the Thirty Years' War and the beginning of the rivalries between and among the nation-states that came into being after the Treaty.

Scholars commonly designate 1648, the date of the Treaty of Westphalia, as the time when the state system began to take its modern form. States had existed before Westphalia, and they had conducted a relationship with each other, but they had done so on quite a different basis. The ancient world had known a succession of sprawling dynastic empires and tiny city-states. It had known the vast Roman Empire which had encompassed the Western world. But it had never known a national state or a system of independent states resting upon something akin to the theory of sovereignty. Notable changes had come on the eve of the Treaty of Westphalia; England, France, and Spain had grown as nation-states and others were well on the way to becoming ones. The Roman church had failed to assert and make good its universality and Machiavelli, Bodin, Grotius,

> **THE TREATY**
>
> Westphalia was an independent medieval duchy, incorporated in Prussia at the Congress of Vienna in 1815, and made a province in 1816 with Munster as its capital. Since 1946, it has been part of the German Land (region) of North Rhine-Westphalia. The kingdom of Westphalia, created by Napoleon (1807-13), did not include the duchy, but was made up of Prussian lands west of the Elbe – Hessen, Brunswick, and Hanover. The Treaty of Westphalia (1648) ended the Thirty Years' War. The peace also marked the end of the supremacy of the Holy Roman Empire and the emergence of France as a dominant power. It recognised the sovereignty of the German states, Switzerland, and the Netherlands. And, Lutherans, Calvinists, and Roman Catholics were given equal rights.

Luther, Calvin, and a host of other theorists had together provided justification for the independent secular state.

With the Thirty Years' War and the Peace of Westphalia, a notable landmark was reached in the history of the nation-state system. The war resulted from the Protestant-Catholic schism caused by the Protestant Reformation and promoted by the Catholic Counter-Reformation. In addition to its religious aspects, the war involved dynastic rivalries of the Habsburgs and the Bourbons as also some German princes. The struggle established no dominant religious group, but it did result in a mutual tolerance which lasted until the present time. In spite of enormous destruction, the wrecking of the universal Church, and the fragmentation of Europe into well-defined nation-states, the resulting Peace of Westphalia paved the way for European stability.

The settlement at Westphalia formalised the nation-state system through its recognition that the Empire no longer commanded the allegiance of its parts and that the Pope could not everywhere maintain the final authority, even in spiritual matters. Henceforth German princes were to rule as they saw fit, and they were to be free to choose Calvinism, Lutheranism, or Roman Catholicism. Holland and Switzerland were recognized as independent republics. The enlargement of Brandenburg started an expansion that produced the Kingdom of Prussia and, eventually, the German Empire. France and Sweden also were given additional territory. One historian has summarized the results of the Peace of Westphalia as follows: "By 1648 the state system was fully established in Europe. The Empire was an empty shell. The claim of the Pope to temporal sovereignty in Europe was a thing of the past."

TREATY CREATED NATION-STATES

In 1648, England, France, Spain, and Sweden were great powers. England had not been a party to the Thirty Years' War and was largely unaffected by it; France was about to enter a period of continental dominance; Spain was in decline; Sweden, in control of the Baltic area, was only momentarily a first-rate military power. Russia had not yet emerged as a strong state. Poland, large and populous, was too poorly governed to count for much in international politics. Italy, a conglomeration of small states, was only a geographical expression. The Ottoman Empire, important for strategic rather than military reasons, had exhausted its expansive force and was soon to decay. Germany, nominally unified as part of the Holy Roman Empire, was actually disunited, although some of the larger states (Brandenburg, Bavaria, and Saxony) wielded considerable influence. The emperor was also ruler of the Habsburg dominions, but he never succeeded in making a nation of them. The most important of these were Austria, Spain, and the Spanish Netherlands. The independent small powers were Denmark (which then included Norway), Holland, Portugal, and Switzerland,

(It may be noted that the Seven Years' War of 1756-63 took place between Britain and Prussia on the one hand, and France, Austria, and Russia, on the other. Its military interest centered on the successful struggle of Frederick II of Prussia against great odds. Britain's role in the war, under the direction of Chatham, was mainly confined to operations at sea, notably the victory of Quiberon Bay (1759), and in the colonies. The victories of Wolfe and Clive resulted in the conquest of Canada and the foundation of the Indian empire. Robert Clive (1725-74) was the founder of the British Empire in India by defeating Siraj-ud-Daulah at Plassey in 1757. Clive suspected that the Nawab of Bengal was assisting the French in the Seven Years' War. After this victory, Bengal fell to the East India Company and, finally, to British control.

While it is true that the state system that came into being after Westphalia still remained unchanged in its basic pattern of "sovereign" states, but it is also true that the passing of time had brought many developments which had affected the system. These included the rise of representative government, the Industrial Revolution, population changes, the growth of international law, the evolution of diplomatic methods, the increase in the economic interdependence of states, the setting up of procedures for the peaceful settlement of disputes, and many others.

TREATY OF UTRECHT

The international relations of the years between the Treaty of Westphalia in 1648 and the Treaty of Utrecht (a city in Central Netherlands) in 1713 were dominated by the ambition of Louis XIV (1643-1715) to establish French hegemony on the continent of Europe and by the rivalries of Great Britain, France, Holland, and Spain for colonial supremacy in the Western Hemisphere. Britain provided the chief link between the two areas of conflict, for she joined with continental states to preserve the balance of power in Europe and reduce the capacity of France for fighting on the seas and overseas. Louis XIV possessed a magnificent army and a consuming urge to use it. He was remarkably successful in extending his domains, but finally a coalition of powers, headed by Britain and Austria, stopped him in the War of the Spanish Succession (1701-1713). France suffered heavy losses following the Treaty of Utrecht (1713). While France managed to keep a Bourbon on the throne of Spain, she was forced to pledge that France and Spain would never be united. She lost Nova Scotia to Britain. Austria was given Naples, Sardinia, Milan and the Spanish Netherlands; and Britain won Gibraltar from Spain. The Treaty of Utrecht also gave further impetus to the unification of Prussia which later became the pivot of the European balance, and the agreement made it clear that Sweden, Russia, and Poland could no longer resolve issues in the East without involving the West. In fact, it is not too much to say that after Utrecht, no European state could act alone.

BALANCE OF POWER CONCEPT HAS ITALIAN ORIGIN

A key concept in international relations had been defined as a power equilibrium among States achieved by maintaining military strength that be sufficient to deter aggression by the others. A balance of power may be established between individual states of similar strength or through alliances, when several smaller states unite to offset the power of one or more larger ones. It may be bipolar, between two states or alliances, or multipolar, among several competing centres of power or within an alliance. The term is used in other, sometimes conflicting, terms; when a nation seen as the linchpin of an alliance, or one possessing a preponderance of military force, is said to "hold the balance of power." It can also refer to a balanced structure or situation in domestic politics. Although the balance of power arrangements are at least as old as the classical Greek city-states, the doctrine was first articulated in the 16th century by *Francesco Guicciardini,* who described in his *"History of Italy,"* the Florentine city-state's policy of preventing any one state from dominating the Italian peninsula. The term first appeared in the 1713 Treaty of Utrecht, which attempted to restore stability among European nations after the War of the Spanish Succession. Between the 16th and the 19th centuries, Europe was the scene of shifting alliances because the emerging nation-states combined to thwart single powers dominating others. In the wake of World War I, the formation of the League of Nations was in part an effort to replace the old balance of power status in Europe with a system of collective security.

While a balance of power was intended to promote stability, it had also provoked an arms race and inevitable war. In the mid-18th century, the French philosopher Montesquieu criticized European alliances as a "disease" that could only lead to "mutual ruination." During the Cold War, the nuclear threat of mutual annihilation created a "balance of terror" between the United States and the Soviet Union. While it made all-out war "unthinkable", it did not prevent conflict between the two superpowers but merely channelled it into economic and technological competition and "proxy wars" in poorer countries.

The balance of power, set up at Utrecht, was often imperilled during the next hundred years, but it was not destroyed. No state was able to establish permanent hegemony over Europe. By 1733, France had recovered enough to fight the War of the Polish Succession, by which she forced the Habsburgs to cede to her the Duchy of Lorraine. After five years of peace, she undertook to partition Austria, only to be thwarted by the courage of Maria Theresa in the War of the Austrian Succession (1740-1748). The primacy of France and Austria, which forced them to clash whenever a continental issue arose, was disturbed by the development within Prussia of a powerful military machine. Fearing Frederick the Great (1740-1786) and his fine army, France quickly reversed her strategy and concluded an alliance with Austria. Russia, alarmed by Frederick, also joined the coalition against Prussia. Seeing an increase in French strength, England quickly jumped on the scales to counterbalance the combination against Prussia. In 1756, the Seven Years' War began when Frederick invaded Saxony. Only the defection of Russia gave him victory, as he was outnumbered by the forces set against him. His ally, Britain, won a clearer victory in North America, virtually eliminating France from the New World.

The defeat of Austria, France, and Spain in the Seven Years' War, together with the exhaustion of Prussia, left no state powerful enough to dominate Europe: the balance of power, essentially a European concept, had been restored. The next threat was precipitated by the French Revolution, an internal convulsion brought on by the fact that the demands of the rising bourgeoisie had been left unanswered by a reactionary monarchy. When the rebels sought to carry the new gospel of liberalism to the rest of Europe, they touched off a conflagration that was to last for twenty-three years. The war was several years old when the "Little Corporal" strode upon the scene, asserted his mastery of France, and set out upon the conquest of Europe. Napoleon held the continent under control, and Russia was his ally. For a time, Britain fought alone. Then, as *"Liberty, Equality, Fraternity"* deteriorated into aggressive French nationalism, vigorous rival nationalism sprang up under the heel of Napoleon's conquering armies. British naval supremacy, "General Winter" in Russia, and the combined might of Britain, Russia, Prussia, Austria, and Sweden finally brought about the defeat of the Corsican adventurer and the end of the most formidable of all French attempts to conquer Europe. *(More about Napoleon later)*

THE US JOINS THE EUROPEAN POWER GAME

Overseas, a group of new states joined the United States of America in the Western Hemisphere. The removal of Ferdinand VII from the throne of Spain by Napoleon provided an occasion for the assumption of sovereign power by some of Spain's American colonies. Brazil declared her independence of Portugal in 1822, with the son of the Portuguese king as emperor; the monarchy flourished until 1889, when a republican form of government was established. During these years, the United States of America was growing steadily. By the sixties, she had a population and resources sufficient to wage one of the most colossal wars of the century. Certainly an important power by the end of the Civil War, the US was recognized as one of the major world powers after the Spanish-American War in 1898. In the Far East, Japan emerged from feudalism in 1867-1868 with the overthrow of the *shogun* (military strongmen). Copying the techniques of the Western world, she was able to parry the imperialistic thrusts of the European powers and build a strong nation-state. As a result of her victory over China in 1894-1895, her alliance with Great Britain in 1902, and particularly her defeat of Russia in 1904-1905, Japan was admitted to equality with the major powers. Once small states of Europe got sovereignty without resources to protect it, bigger states, including the US, joined others in winning them over. And, that kept European politics boiling.

The Renaissance was marked by balance, clarity and proportion in architecture and scientific and enquiring mind which created a "world man".

8

An age of adventure and classical learning

It was not the creation of knowledge but revival and expansion of it so also its application in science and technology which has given Europe importance far beyond its resources and size.

The Renaissance (rebirth) is the period in European civilization immediately following the Middle Ages, which is characterized by a surge of interest in classical learning and values. The Renaissance was also an age of adventure and discovery which witnessed the exploration of new continents, the substitution of the Copernican for the Ptolemaic system (which said the earth was fixed and not moving) of astronomy, and the invention and application of powerful innovations such as paper, printing, the mariner's compass, and gunpowder. To the scholars and thinkers of the day, however, it was primarily a time of the revival of classical learning and wisdom after a long period of cultural decline and stagnation during the Middle Ages.

Renaissance began in Italy around 1400 AD and lasted until the end of the 16th century; elsewhere in Europe it flourished later, and lasted until the 17th century. A characteristic of the Renaissance was the exploration of the world and the rediscovery of pagan classical antiquity (led by Giovanni Boccaccio and Francesco Petrarch). Central to the Renaissance was humanism, the belief in the active rather than the contemplative life and a faith in the republican ideal. The greatest expression of the Renaissance was in arts and learning.

Leon Alberti, in his writings and painting, created a method of painting – using perspective to create an illusion of a third dimension – and a classically inspired, non-religious subject matter. In architecture, he created a system of simple proportion that was to be followed for hundreds of years. Alberti's contemporaries Masaccio and Filippo Brunelleschi exemplified these ideas in painting and architecture respectively. In arts, critics regard the years between 1490 and 1520 as a peak period in the Renaissance, with the work of Leonardo da Vinci, Raphael Sanzio, and Michelangelo Buonarotti in painting, and Michelangelo and Donato Bramante in architecture. The highpoint of Venetian painting was to come some years later. Leonardo has been described as a *"universal man"* for his enormously wide-ranging studies, including painting, architecture, science, and engineering. The enormous achievements of creative artists were made possible by the patronage of wealthy ruling families such as the Sforza in Milan, and the Medici in Florence, by the ruling class of Venice, and by popes, notably Julius-II and Leo-X.

In literature, both Boccaccio and Petrarch wrote major works in Italian rather than Latin, a trend that continued by the creation of epic poems in the vernacular by Ludovico Ariosto and Torquato Tasso. Progress from the religious to the secular was seen in the creation of the first public libraries, and by the many translations from the classics published in Venice in the 16th century. In philosophy, the rediscovery of Greek thought took the form of neo-Platonism in such figures as Marsilio Ficino. Niccolo Machiavelli in *The Prince* founded the modern study of politics.

NEW ART AND ARCHITECTURE

Renaissance art and ideas became widespread throughout Europe. Desiderius Erasmus, from the Netherlands, embodied humanist scholarship for northern Europe; Netherlandish painters include Albrecht Durer and Hans Holbein. In France, Renaissance writers include Francois Rabelais, Joaquim Du Bellay, and Michel Eyquem de Montaigne; in Spain, Miguel de Cervantes, in Portugal, Luis Vaz de Camoens, and in England, William Shakespeare. The term Renaissance, to describe the period of cultural history, was invented by 19th-century historians. In the visual arts, the end of the High Renaissance is marked by a late-15th century movement known as Mannerism, a tendency to deliberately elongate the body, and a wilful distortion of perspective; but the true end of the Renaissance ideal only came with the late-17th century rise of the enlightenment.

Renaissance architecture which began in 15th-century Italy, based on the revival of classical, especially Roman, architecture was developed by Brunelleschi. It is characterized by a concern with balance, clarity, and proportion, and by the external use of columns and fluted pilasters. Many Roman buildings were still extant in Renaissance Italy and artists and scholars studied their proportions and copied their decorative motifs. The architectural books of the Roman Vitruvius (1st century AD) were popularized by Leon Battista Alberti in his influential treatise *De re aedificatoria* (On Architecture) (1486) but the first major work of the age was the successful construction by Brunelleschi of a dome (1420-34) on Florence Cathedral. Alberti himself designed a new facade for Santa Maria Novella, completed in 1470, in Florence, and redesigned a church in Rimini subsequently called the Tempio Malatestiano, (C.1450). Bramante came closest to the recreation of classical ideas with works such as the Tempietto of San Pietro in Montorio, Rome, and the new basilica of St Peter's in Rome in 1506. Other Renaissance architects in Italy include Michelangelo, Giulio Romano, Palladio, Vignola, Sangallo, and Raphael.

In northern Europe, the Renaissance spirit is apparent in the painting of the Van Eyck brothers in the early 15th century. Later, Durer demonstrated a scientific and inquiring mind and, after his travels to Italy, brought many Renaissance ideas back to Germany. The Italian artists Cellini, Rosso Fiorentino, and Primaticcio took the Renaissance to France through their work at Fontainebleau. Hans Holbein, the Younger, carried some of the concerns of Renaissance art to England in the 16th century, but it was not until the 17th century that English taste was significantly affected. Much of good and beautiful things that we see today can be attributed to when human creativity flowered best during the Renaissance, considered the most beautiful chapter in human history.

The Pope cannot peddle the blessings of God (papal indulgences) for money.
– Martin Luther (1483–1546)

9

New faith challenges the Church

Europe was torn asunder in the 16th century by the ideas of a German monk who sought a direct relationship with God without brokers. The political and religious conflicts that followed shattered the certainties of the medieval world. The Reformation saved Christianity and its followers and also created space for science and reason which mark the modern times.

At the start of the 16th century, all European Christians were Roman Catholics and accepted the spiritual rule of the pope. Within 50 years, the continent was bitterly divided between Catholics and those who protested against the authority of Rome, called Protestants. Historians use the term Reformation to describe this split and the religious and civil conflicts it provoked. At its heart, the Reformation was an ecclesiastical and spiritual revolution, but there were also economic and political elements. Its roots can be traced to the late 14th century when the Englishman John Wycliffe and the Bohemian John Huss attacked the corruption of the papacy. Simmering discontent came to the boil in 1517 when a German Augustinian friar, Martin Luther, challenged the Church to respond to his 95 'theses', or propositions, about its condition. Luther was outraged by the sale of *"papal indulgences"*, (or pardons for sin), which had increased to help to pay off the debts of Pope Leo X. Luther nailed his theses at the door of the chapel of Wittenberg Castle, so lighting the fuse that led to the Reformation.

Martin Luther (1483–1546)

Germany was then in the grip of an agricultural recession. The peasantry and lesser nobility were ready to vent their anger on the great landlords, especially ecclesiastical landlords who controlled the wealth of the Church. The temporal authorities of many European states, such as England with its increasingly powerful central monarchy under the Tudors, also saw in Luther's challenge an opportunity to press their claims for independence, and for an end to the payment of various taxes to the Vatican. Their political ambitions found justification in Luther's assault on the worldliness of the Church.

Luther's message was purely spiritual. He proclaimed a doctrine of *'justification by faith alone'* and 'the priesthood of all believers'. Formal religious observance would not bring eternal salvation; a man was justified by his belief in the redemptive power of Jesus Christ alone. And every man was his own priest, with direct access to God and the truth of the Gospels. It followed that the rigid hierarchy of the Church was an irrelevance to spiritual health.

Luther was excommunicated by the *Diet of Worms* in 1521 after refusing to recant his opinions, declaring *"Ich kann nicht anders"* – 'I can do no other.' By siding against the German peasants in their revolt of 1525, he helped to stifle the democratic implications of his teachings, but nothing could stop the spread of Protestant ideas. The invention of movable press by Johann Gutenberg in the mid-15th century had made the Bible accessible to readers who spoke no Latin. Only the extremities of Europe – Russia and Ireland, for instance – remained almost untouched by the new ideas. The counter Reformation, a renewal of the Catholic Church through reform, kept Spain, Portugal, Italy and France loyal to the papacy. But in northern Europe, Protestantism gained sway – often in the extreme form preached by John Calvin who establied a Puritan theocracy in Switzerland in 1541. National churches, such as the Church of England, established by Henry VIII in the 1530s, asserted their independence, and for the next century Europe was thrown into turmoil by a series of bitter religious wars. *(More about it in the chapter on Germany)*

REFORMATION at a glance

IN THE 16TH CENTURY, Europe's Christians relied on the Roman Catholic Church to guide them through their lives on Earth, and show them the way to reach Heaven. However ordinary priests were often poor and ignorant. Scholars began to demand reforms that would restore the Church's old purity. The authorities, however, were slow to respond, so the protesting scholars – backed by certain kings and princes – made their own Reformation by creating an alternative Protestant Church.

Early Protests

Forerunners of the Reformation included the English scholar, John Wyclif (c. 1329-84) and the Bohemian (Czech) priest Jan Hus (c. 1369-1415). Wyclif accused the Catholic Church of incompetence and corruption. After his death, many of his followers, known as the Lollards, were put to death for continuing to support his beliefs.

Hussites

Hus supported Wyclif's views, called for reform, and was burnt at the stake as a heretic. His followers, the Hussites, proclaimed him a martyr and started an armed struggle against the Church. The Hussites were defeated, and Bohemia was forced back to Catholicism.

Protestantism

Protestants wanted to reform the Catholic Church which, they believed, had deviated from the Christian ideals set down in the Bible. Their reforms included a return to simple ceremonies, with less emphasis on priestly intervention and more on each worshipper's quest to find God. They also wanted services in the local language, rather than Latin, and an educated, uncorrupted clergy.

Christendom, c. 1560

When a country's ruler became Protestant, the population usually followed suit. However, in France and the Netherlands, many ordinary people turned Protestant of their own accord, and were then persecuted by Catholic rules.

Martin Luther

German university teacher and priest, Martin Luther (1483-1546) started the Reformation. From 1517, he challenged aspects of the Catholic Church's teaching and behavior. He wanted people to find their own personal faith in

God by individual Bible study. Luther was protected by sympathetic German princes, and his message was spread by the advent of printing.

Dissolution of Monasteries

In the 1530s, the Reformation reached England. Monastic life had no place in Protestantism, so between 1536 and 1539, King Henry VIII dissolved (shut down) all England's monasteries and took their lands for himself.

Protestant Division

The Protestant Church had divisions within itself as people in different countries followed the teachings of reformers, such as Ulrich Zwingli (1484-1531) and John Calvin (1509-64). Calvin greatly influenced the Swiss, Dutch, French, Scottish, and Polish Reformations.

Puritans

English followers of Calvin were called Puritans, after their desire for a "pure" form of worship. Some Puritans wielded great political power and were persecuted; others crossed the Atlantic to establish "godly" colonies in America.

Huguenots

France's Catholic authorities tried to quash the Huguenots (French followers of Calvin). In August 1572, Catholic mobs in Paris killed 3,000 Huguenots, an event that became known as the St. Bartholomew's Day Massacre. In 1789, the Huguenots won the right to worship freely.

Counter-Reformation

During the 1500s, the Counter-Reformation set out to reclaim Protestant Europe for the Church. The Society of Jesus, a major part of this movement, was formed by Ignatius Loyola (1491-1556) in 1534. The Jesuits, as they were called, became famous for foreign missionary work and education.

Reason, not faith, should be the foundation of a society which is formed on the belief in the natural rights of man.

– *Voltaire*

10

Thinkers of the new era

In the 17th and 18th centuries, the radical ideas of the philosophers of the Age of Enlightenment overturned established beliefs, reflecting the intellectual mood of the time and changed the ways people think.

The Enlightenment was an intellectual movement inspired by the resurgence of the sciences in 17th century Europe. It tried to apply the methods of the natural sciences to social and political affairs. The English poet Alexander Pope spoke for the Enlightenment when he said : *"Presume not then the ways of God to scan/The proper study of mankind is man."* No European nation and no sphere of culture escaped its influence. Its main doctrines say that man is, by nature, rational and attains perfection by education and use of his reason; that men and women are equal, and should be given equality before the law and individual liberty; and that beliefs are to be accepted not on the basis of authority or tradition, but only if they pass the test of reason. This emphasis on reason favoured atheism or deism, the belief that God's existence can be established by reason. The *'Age of Enlightenment'* or *'Age of Reason'* began in Britain in the 17th century with the lawyer, politician and thinker Francis Bacon, and the political philosophers Thomas Hobbes, John Locke, David Hume and Adam Smith. In 18th-century France, it became an organised movement, which influenced the French Revolution in 1789. The publication between 1751 and 1780 of the *Encyclopaedia* edited by Jeal le Rond d'Alembert and Denis Diderot, with contributions by Voltaire, Jean-Jacques Rousseau and others, provided a focal point for Enlightenment. It was advertised as a "systematic dictionary of the sciences, arts and trades," and was marked by anti-clericalism and political radicalism.

KANT, VOLTAIRE AND FICHTI

In Germany, the Enlightenment achieved its most significant philosophical expression in the writings of Moses Mendelssohn, Gotthold Lessing, Immanuel Kant and Johann Fichte. Kant described Enlightenment as the "emergence of man from his self-imposed infancy": its watchword was: "Have the courage to use one's own reason!" The most typical, if not the most distinguished, representative of Enlightenment was Francois Mariee Arouet (1694-1778), better known by his pen name, *Voltaire*. He was a playwright, historian and novelist, and a gifted populariser of scientific and philosophical ideas. His sometimes spiteful but invariably witty assaults on authority were rewarded with lawsuits, imprisonment and exile. Voltaire was a deist rather than an atheist, but he believed that the world contains much pointless evil, and in his novel *Candide* attacked, in the person of 'Dr. Pangloss,' the doctrine of Gottfried von Leibniz that God has created the best of all possible worlds. *Voltaire was a relentless critic of established religion, and waged a lifelong war in defence of justice, humanity, tolerance and liberty. He was a true spokesman of the Enlightenment.*

ENLIGHTENMENT IN THE EAST; BUDDHISM IS CORE

The state or process of coming to the truth out of ignorance – illumination after darkness. In Eastern religion, especially Buddhism and Hinduism, enlightenment is the fulfilment of the human quest for perfect understanding. In European and American history, the Enlightenment refers to the predominant intellectual mood of the 18th century, exemplified by confidence in the power of reason. While the two concepts share the image of light overcoming darkness, they are in many ways opposites: in Eastern traditions, enlightenment involves shedding earthly knowledge and attachments in order to achieve perfect understanding of cosmic reality, whereas the Western Enlightenment was focused on rational thought and human progress. "Enlightenment" translates the Sanskrit word *"bodhi"*, denoting awakening, wisdom, and awareness; *bodhi* is the root of Buddha, "enlightened one." The Buddhist concept of enlightenment derives from the Buddha's seven-week meditation seated under a tree, during which he attained progressive levels of awareness, arriving finally at perfect enlightenment, or Buddhahood. Enlightenment is seeing the world and the self as they really are, free from the veils of illusion. It is the precondition and passageway to *Nirvana*. The Age of Enlightenment challenged many of the assumptions that had prevailed throughout the Middle Ages.

"DARE TO KNOW," SAYS KANT IN THE AGE OF ENLIGHTENMENT

The enlightenment was characterized by cosmopolitanism, secularism, distrust of traditional authority, and superstition, respect for human dignity, and the conviction that reason would illuminate mankind and lead to perpetual social, political, and scientific progress. Although the term "Enlightenment" (*Aufklarung)* was first used in this context in Germany – where Immanuel Kant proposed the motto *"Dare to Know"* – the movement had its echo in England and Scotland in the work of David Hume and Adam Smith. Its greatest flowering was in France where it was closely associated with philosophers, the foremost among whom was Voltaire. The philosophers were for the most part not "philosophers" as such, but popularisers of the 17th century doctrines that inspired them, particularly the Rationalism of Descartes and Spinoza and the Empiricism of Bacon and Locke's *theory of natural rights*.

Much of the philosophers' agenda consisted of the repudiation of the dogmatism and authoritarianism of the Roman Catholic Church. The *Encyclopaedia* was intended to be a compendium of all human knowledge, particularly the "new knowledge" promoted by the philosophers. Thomas Jefferson who wrote the American constitution included in it the thoughts which inspired the *Enlightenment* movement in the West. No wonder, the American constitution has become a reference book for rational thinkers and republicans. The thought contained in the Enlightenment was tremendously influential in colonial and post-revolutionary America. As envoys to Paris, Thomas Jefferson and Benjamin Franklin befriended many of these philosophers, and were influenced by them also. What we see in the American constitution, a model for republicanism, is the loud echo of the basic sentiments of the Enlightenment Revolution, the epicentre of which was Paris, always the intellectual leader of Europe.

People in the pre-modern time lived and died as their forefathers did - without much change in their lifestyle – until Newton (1642-1727) saw the falling apple and Scottish engineer James Watt (1736-1819) turned steam engine into economic use, after which life was never the same again.

11

Industrial Revolution that made the modern world

The changes that turn a country from reliance on basic agriculture and commerce into a modern industrial society using powered machinery are known as an industrial revolution. There have been three kinds of industrial revolutions and together they paved the way for the emergence of the modern world.

French visitors, investigating Britain's innovations at the end of the 18th century, coined the phrase "industrial revolution" as a counterpoint to the French Revolution in their own country. The term describes a decisive advance in the way technology is used. With each such revolution economic growth rates have greatly increased and human life changed for the better. Pre-industrial economies were not unchanging, when spurts of growth were followed by periods of decline. The main constraint was shortage of energy. In 17th-century England, for example, two-thirds of the land area was needed to provide basic subsistence. The remaining had to produce the principal source of energy, wood, animal feed and raw materials. The land could produce little more than 20 kg of wood per person per week, which was equivalent in energy to just half that amount in coal. The only abundant energy sources were wind and water; everything else had to be accomplished by muscle power. It was the introduction of fossil fuels, initially coal, that enabled economies to escape these limitations.

FIRST INDUSTRIAL REVOLUTION

The first industrial revolution, in the late 18th and early 19th centuries,

James Watt (1736-1819)

occurred in the most prosperous continent. Western Europe was then the richest part of the world and Britain, which had the most productive agriculture, was its wealthiest country. As an island, Britain had been protected from the worst ravages of continental wars and it had cheap coastal trade, a major reason why London was the biggest city in Europe. The process of industrialisation started in the richest country because it was there that demand was putting the greatest pressure on resources. Britain also had ample supplies of coal. By 1850, pre-industrial energy levels had been augmented by 560 kg of coal per person per week, making the extra energy available to get industry started.

In general, technical change is not caused by the "inventions" of inspired individuals. The steam engine was introduced not because James Watt, observed the boiling of a kettle but because it was profitable. The wealth of the 18th-century Britain had created a demand for new technology which would be profitable. Similarly, textile production was mechanised because cotton entrepreneurs such as Sir Richard Arkwright and James Hargreaves could not satisfy the market with existing technology. Most inventors were really entrepreneurs. Once one industrial country came into being the world was transformed; for, it was not necessary to invent the steam engine twice. Businessmen could copy or adapt British technology. Governments also became important agents of industrial change as pressure grew to emulate Britain.

But industrialisation spread quickly through trade and investment. It became possible for a country to export raw materials and food in return for industrial products. The 19th century development of the United States was a classic example of industrialisation spreading to a "follower" country. The US exported cotton, timber, wheat and beef to Britain in exchange for manufacture. This allowed the US to develop faster. Once industrialisation was under way, the United States erected tariffs to "capture its own market" and to force its people to buy American goods. Russia, Germany and Japan all followed suit. Industry created a new kind of urbanisation. Large cities had existed for thousands of years but, in the main, industrial cities were where the govt. was and where rich people lived. By the late 19th century, industry in most countries had become highly concentrated, creating dirty, overcrowded cities, housing a large population of impoverished workers. It was a long time before the poor benefited from industrialisation. In the beginning, they were the victims.

SECOND INDUSTRIAL REVOLUTION

Most of the classic products of the first industrial revolution – steam engines, locomotives, machinery, ships and reapers – were capital goods, the items which are used to make other goods rather than the goods to be consumed by their purchasers. Technical change in consumer goods was often difficult to achieve and in most countries consumers remained poor. As long as a small number of wealthy people formed the main market for sophisticated consumer goods, such as early cars, it was not profitable to mass-produce them. The 'second industrial revolution' came about because of the rise of a mass consumer market even the middle income group buying things.This happened first in the USA where, in the late 19th century, the consumers were the world's richest. The essential advance was the development of new production processes. On the production line, each operator carried out only one task. The system required great coordination to perfect the work – it took, for instance, three years to make the *Model T Ford* car. The growth in the size of firms and the revolution in management techniques, associated with the rise of the business corporation and eventually the multinational company, came later. And, that was the real revolution.

Computer technology also helped communications to become faster and cheaper. The result was that markets became global, making it easier for other countries to acquire technology and allowing investment to flow to the most dynamic economies. In combination with state planning, these two factors explained the late 20th century success of the countries of the Pacific Rim. Japan developed into one of the world's major economic powers within 30 years after its defeat in the World War II. South Korea was able to develop a huge export trade in heavy engineering products, notably ships. Taiwan concentrated on exporting consumer goods. The success of countries such as Singapore, Malaysia, Hong Kong, South Korea and Taiwan was based on the combination of quality technology with low-cost labour, undercutting and destroying some industries in the older industrial countries. In the developed world at the end of the 20th century, people took economic growth for granted. They expected their incomes to rise each year and would vote only for governments offering the prospect of greater prosperity. Yet continuous growth began in Europe 200 years ago. It was the crude technical breakthroughs of the first industrial revolution that made the silicon chip possible. And, the modern world in which we live today.

IMPACT OF INDUSTRIAL REVOLUTION

The power of the Old World was human power; everything depended ultimately upon the driving power of human muscle, the muscle of ignorant and subjugated men. A little animal muscle, supplied by draft oxen, horse traction, and the like, contributed. Where a weight had to be lifted, men lifted it; where a rock had to be quarried men chipped it out; where a field had to be ploughed, men and oxen ploughed it; the Roman equivalent of the steamship was the galley with its banks of sweating rowers. A vast proportion of mankind in the early civilizations were employed in purely mechanical drudgery. Men were employed in excavating canals, in making railway cuttings and embankments, and the like. The number of miners increased enormously. And as the nineteenth century went on, the plain logic of the new situation asserted itself more clearly. Human beings were no longer wanted as a source of muscle power. What could be done mechanically by a human being could be done faster and better by a machine. The human being was needed now only where choice and intelligence had to be exercised. Human beings were wanted only as human beings. The drudge, on whom all the previous civilizations had rested, the creature of mere obedience, the man, whose brains were superfluous, had become unnecessary to the welfare of mankind.

This was as true of such ancient industries as agriculture and mining as it was of the newest metallurgical processes. For ploughing, sowing, and harvesting, swift machines came forward to do the work of scores of men. The Roman civilization was built upon cheap and degraded human beings; modern civilization is being rebuilt upon cheap mechanical power. For a hundred years, power has been getting cheaper and labour dearer.

As the nineteenth century went on, it became more and more plain to the intelligent people that the common man had now to be something better than a drudge. He had to be educated, if only to secure 'industry efficiency'. He had to understand what he was about. From the days of the first Christian propaganda, popular education had been growing in Europe, just as it had smouldered in Asia wherever Islam had its foot, because of the necessity of making the believer understand the belief by which he was saved. With the industrialisation, also grew education, marking a beginning of the modern world.

The economic revolution of the Roman republic had never been clearly apprehended by the common people of Rome. The ordinary Roman citizen never saw the changes through which he lived, clearly and comprehensively as we see them today. But the industrial revolution of the nineteenth century was more distinctly seen as one whole process affecting the common people, and the rich alike, because they could read, discuss and could go about to see things as nobody did before. The Industrial Revolution also encouraged people to think differently and independently. To that extent, humankind was freed from superstition and biind faith although these changes were largely in centres where machinery worked instead of men, most specially slaves.

The combination of new industrial technologies, coal power, and market forces created the Industrial Revolution. The Industrial Revolution in turn, led to the most revolutionary economic events in human history since the start of agriculture ten thousand years earlier. Suddenly, economies could grow beyond long-accustomed bounds without hitting the biological constraints of food and timber production. Industrial production grew rapidly, and the power of economic growth spilled out from Great Britain to all parts of the world. Societies the world over were fundamentally changed, often tumultuously. It may be noted that the Industrial Revolution first started in Britain after James Watt invented steam engine. *(Read also chapters on Britain)*

The Industrial Revolution, and the modern economic growth that followed, has changed the way people live in every fundamental sense: where and how they live, what kind of work or economic activity they perform, how they form families. In Britain first, and then elsewhere, industrialization meant a shift of people from overwhelmingly agrarian activities to industrial activities, giving rise to urbanization and social mobility. The single most important reason why prosperity spread, and why it continues to spread, is the transmission of technologies and the ideas underlying them. Even more important than having specific resources in the ground, such as coal, was the ability to use modern, science-based ideas to organize production. The beauty of ideas is that they can be used over and over again, without ever being depleted. Economists call ideas nonrival in the sense that one person's use of an idea does not diminish the ability of others to use it as well. This is why we can envision a world in which everybody achieves prosperity. The essence of the first Industrial Revolution was not only coal; it was how to use the coal. Even more generally, it was about how to use a new form of energy. The lessons of coal eventually became the basis for many other energy systems as well, from hydropower, oil and gas, and nuclear power to new forms of renewable energy such as wind and solar power converted to electricity.

The *FIRST* wave of the Industrial Revolution was the development of the steam engine and related technologies, including the organization of large-scale factory production, new machinery in the textile and apparel sector, and new techniques to produce steel. A second wave of technological breakthroughs came in the middle of the nineteenth century with the rail, and even more notably the telegraph, which offered the first instantaneous telecommunications around the world, a phenomenal breakthrough in the ability to diffuse information on a large scale.

The *SECOND* technological wave also included ocean steamers, globalscale trade, and two huge infrastructure projects: the Suez Canal, completed in 1869, which significantly shortened the trade time between Europe and Asia, and the Panama Canal, completed in 1914, which dramatically reduced the trade time between the U.S. eastern seaboard and destinations in the western United States, much of Latin America, and East Asia. Epidemics of yellow fever and malaria that killed thousands of workers delayed the first attempt to build the canal in the 1880s. Once scientists understood that mosquitoes were transmitting those killer diseases, the canal builders made a full-fledged effort to control the mosquito breeding alongside the construction of the canal and thereby completed the project in 1914.

The *THIRD* wave of technological advance involved electrification of industry and urban society at the end of the nineteenth century, including Edison's invention of the incandescent bulb and other electronic appliances. Edison, Westinghouse, and others championed large power plants that could bring electricity into homes, office buildings, and factories by wire, which was the defining new infrastructure of the early twentieth century. The development of the internal combustion engine was also critical, as was the pivotal advance in the chemical industry, mainly in Germany, with the new process for taking atmospheric nitrogen and converting it into ammonia for fertilizer (the Haber-Bosch process). This use of fossil fuel energy to create nitrogen-based fertilizers was the breakthrough advance in raising food production in the twentieth century, enabling a great proportion of humanity, though still not all of it, to overcome chronic hunger and the risks of famine that had forever plagued humankind.

INDUSTRIAL REVOLUTION at a glance

MORE THAN 200 YEARS AGO, changes took place in industry that transformed society, and altered the way goods were made. The changes, which began in Britain in about 1760, are known as the Industrial Revolution. They included the use of water and steam power, the invention of new machinery, increased coal and iron production, the introduction of factories, the growth of towns, and a revolution in transport. Industrialization also created new types of work and new social groups. By 1850, the Industrial Revolution was spreading to the rest of the world.

New Technology

The textile industry was the first to be mechanized. In the 1700s, new water or steam-driven machines replaced the old spinning wheels. This change meant that cloth, particularly cotton, could be produced faster than ever before.

Ironbridge

In 1779, the world's first iron bridge was built across the River Seven, England.

The Spinning Jenny

James Hargreaves, an English weaver, invented the spinning jenny in 1764-1767. Worked by one person, it consisted of a frame and a number of spindles that spun several threads at once.

Factories

People used to make good in their homes, but the invention of new machinery took manufacturing into factories. The first factories were cotton mills powered by water wheels, and the factory owners employed huge numbers of people to operate the machines. Most employees worked 16 hours a day, six days a week, and were subjected to harsh discipline. The work was hard and sometimes dangerous, but, for the first time, workers received regular wages.

The Water Frame

As the name suggests, the water frame was a spinning frame powered by water. It replaced the spinning jenny, and was used in the first factories.

New Industrial Towns

As industrialism increased, new towns sprang up around coal mines and factories. Many people arrived from the countryside in search of work.

Living conditions in the new towns were dreadful, with poverty, overcrowding, poor sanitation, and illness. After the 1850s, urban conditions began to improve.

Transport

A revolution in transport was stimulated by the need to move raw materials and finished goods cheaply and quickly. From 1760, a network of canals was built to carry coal, iron and steel to and from the new industrial centers. However, by the 1840s, one of the greatest achievements of the industrial age had appeared – the railways.

Railways

After the ironmaster Abraham Darby discovered how to smelt iron cheaply, using coke rather than charcoal, the way was clear for the mass production of iron. The world's first public railway opened in 1825, linking the coal mines of Darlington with the port of Stockton, England. By the 1870s, there were 25,000 km (15,000 miles) of railway track in Britain alone.

Iron Goods

Developments in the iron industry meant that cast iron could be moulded into any shape, from pots and pans to iron bedspreads and machine parts.

Soap

The growing textile industry stimulated a demand for soap and bleach. When a process was invented that turned table salt into baking soda, soap could be mass produced.

Matches

The first friction matches were produced in the 1830s. To make the matches, women dipped splinters of wood into white phosphorus, an inflammable chemical. As the phosphorus ate away the skin of their faces, many suffered "phossy jaw".

Gas lighting

Coal provided steam for new machinery, and heated coal produced a combustible (burnable) gas. By 1850, gas lamps were common in the streets of most towns and cities.

Child labour

Factory owners employed children in mills and mines because they could enter cramped spaces, and their small hands could operate delicate machinery. Dangerous conditions meant that many children died.

New products

As mass production increased in factories, new goods became available. Cheap cotton clothing was the first product to be made completely by machinery. Soaps, dyes, and iron goods became widespread. However, many of the industrial processes were harmful to the workers' health.

Social Change

The Industrial Revolution transformed society. It created a new social group, the industrial, waged, working class. A new army of industrial workers sprang up, including railway workers, dockers, textile workers, engineers, and factory girls. Industrialization also produced a new, wealthier middle class. The separation of work from home had profound effects. For the first time, and for the middle class only, the home became a place of peace and leisure.

Middle Classes

The middle classes included merchants and industrialists. Middle-class men worked as managers and owners in industry, middle-class women remained at home, living lives of enforced idleness. Some of these women, irritated by boredom, worked with the poor and needy, or began to fight for women's rights.

A middle-class girl's dress was usually made of delicate material, such as silk, or had a lot of handiwork on it, such as a lace collar.

Working Classes

Most working people lived lives of relentless drudgery in the early years of the Industrial Revolution. Men worked long hours in the new industries, and women had a double burden of work both inside the home, and outside in the mills and factories. A factory girl's clothing had to be warm and hard wearing. It was often made of cheap material, such as wool or cotton.

Popular Protest

The early years of the Industrial Revolution were hard for the workers. Social unrest increased as different groups fought for improvements in working conditions. Some, such as the Luddites, attacked the new machines that were taking away their jobs and skills. Trade unions, which emerged after 1824, sought better working conditions and workers' rights.

Co-operative Movement

The followers of this political and social movement challenged the competitiveness of the new industrial society. They argued instead for co-operation, and a form of socialism, or common ownership. In 1844, the movement established the first co-operative shop in Rochdale, Lancashire.

Robert Owen

Born in Wales, Robert Owen (1771-1858) was an early socialist. His book *A New View of Society* (1813) argued for co-operation instead of competition in all levels of society. His ideas led to the first co-operative shop in England, which sold fresh, cheap food, on a non-profit basis. He also set up one of the first trade unions, and created model working communities in Lanark, Scotland, and New Harmony, USA.

Timeline

1709	Abraham Darby uses coke to smelt iron ore.
1733	John Kay develops the flying shuttle, which speeds up weaving.
1764-1767	Spinning jenny invented.
1761	Bridgewater canal links coal mines to Manchester.
1768	Richard Arkwright develops a water-driven spinning frame.
1769	James Watt improves the steam engine.
1789	Steam-powered loom introduced in Britain.
1830s	Industrial Revolution in Belgium and USA under way.
1833	Factory Act bans children under nine from working in cotton mills, to allow time for school.
1842	Coal Mines Act bans women and children for mines in England.

Society is produced by our want and government by our wickedness.

– Thomas Paine

12

Libertarianism is the foundation of European democracy

"Who should rule the State?", asks Plato in his book, Republic, and this question has not been finally settled since it was first asked some 2,400 years ago. In medieval times, it was the divine right of the king (my king, right or wrong); Marx talked of the rule of the proletatriat, Adam Smith talked of capitalism (invisible hands) and the European philosophers have combined the two in libertarianism, a concept which flows from the theory of social contract as advocated by John Locke, the English philosopher, who also talked of checks and balances.

Libertarianism is the 20th century social and political theory, stressing individualism, limited government and free market. Libertarians advocate the Lockean notion of the individual's inalienable right to life, liberty and property, holding that each person has the sovereign right to live the way he or she pleases as long as the equal right of others is not violated. Drawing on Adam Smith's theory that economic competition creates an optimal allocation of resources libertarians insist that the state, if it exists at all, should be no more than a *"night watchman."* In their view, the government's only legitimate role is to ensure protection of the individual's rights and safety, to enforce valid contracts, and to provide for the national defence. By the same token, taxation is considered coercion and public services should be privatised and paid for by those who use them, say libertarians.

The ideological foundations of libertarianism are found primarily in 19th-century anarchist thought and in classical and neo-classical economics, including the Laissez-faire philosophy of Austrian economists *Ludwig von Mises* and *Nobel Laureate Friedrich von Hayek,* who contended, in *"The*

Road to Serfdom" (1944) that economic planning would lead to totalitarianism. Among American academics, the most prominent libertarian thinker is *Robert Nozick* whose *"Anarchy, State and Utopia"* affirms the principle that government should be limited to the protection of persons and their property and argues that any attempt to regulate economic activity is unjust. The libertarian emphasis on *rational self-interest* is echoed in the works of the novelist Ayn Rand whose philosophy of objectivism asserts the moral right and duty of the sovereign individual to live for himself or herself.

"A true democracy cannot be reached by voting, nor by sabotage, nor general strike or through revolution and class struggle. It will come by individual initiative first on a small scale, and then on an ever-increasing and expanding basis. Voting may bring a political change; sabotage may drive capital owners from industry; general strike may cause industrial upheaval; taxing may equalise wealth; but not one of these can bring a permanent economic change which will come by evolution alone," says Ayn Rand. In libertarianism, a structure is built which holds the promise of efficiency. Cooperation is part of libertarianism.

ABOLISH THE STATE BASED ON BRUTE FORCE

While hunger for freedom is widely prevalent, desire for power prompts people to deny liberty to others which they want for themselves. And, they use coercion for compliance. People have suffered restrictive laws for so many generations that it is now accepted as natural. In the development of a society ruled by industrialism, the individual has lost control of the job at which he earns his livelihood. So, gradually and insidiously has this control been lost that its loss is not yet realised. But, that loss marks the difference between freedom and dependence. Punishments and forcible restraints by governments are largely called for because of the existence of an inequitable distribution of resources of nature. To maintain an established state of inequity, use of force is necessary. The philosophy of libertarianism is based on the theory that all forms of government *rest upon violence* and are, therefore, wrong and harmful as well as unnecessary. It demands the absence of government in the political and coercive sense. It is opposed to the authority based on force.

The social functions of the state produce a narrow and irresponsible individualism. As the obligations to the state increase, the citizens are relieved of their obligations to each other. The state taught the individual that his responsibility was to the state, and the state would protect the individual. The citizen, for instance, pays taxes which absolves him from his life-long responsibility to do things for himself and society. As a result, there arises the theory that man can and must seek his own happiness, ignoring the needs of others that may be left to the state. This leaves the citizen free from the old and natural human obligations to society which have become the business of the state. The generally accepted theory is that the security of society depends upon *"law and order."* There is a prevalent idea that if the restraints of the law were removed – policemens' clubs, soldiers' bayonets, battleships, armoured cars, poison gases, bombing airplanes, and the executioner's noose – people would fly at one another's throats, and chaos would reign. It is not true.

The just dispensation of a society is the one in which democracy prevails; in which the worker is rewarded with the full value of the service he renders; in which production and distribution are for service and not for profit and in which the people are equal citizens in a democratic state, and in which private income from interest, rent, and dividends has been abolished. The way to achieve these is to capture power through election or by revolutionary overthrow or by the disintegration of the capitalist system, or by the gradual socialization of industries. Voting does not bring about a change in the economic system. The economic systems are changed only by evolution. A permanent change is brought about by the edict of neither rulers nor voters. Nor does the earnest belief in a theory qualify or prepare workers to direct the industrial affairs of a nation. In which case, something more than belief, revolution or voting is necessary.

REVOLUTIONS FAIL, WHY?

Revolutions fail because the owners of property hold surplus wealth surplus food, guns, and the power of coercion. It is not a question of what i right or what is wrong; it is a question of the forces which cannot be controlle nor changed overnight. Apparently, the way to change the economic syster is to go to work day by day and change the economic system by so doing Experience shows that there is no easy way of removing the state. Electio is a dubious way to bring about a change. If the people want a change, the must train themselves to do things themselves in the way they would wa them done in a changed society. As to voting, the most important voting being done every day in the economic "elections". Shall one buy this or th shirt, patronize this shop or that, rent an apartment or build a house, buy a ticket and ride? The political voting which comes once a year or after five years is upon the results of these small economic decisions taking place daily in homes and market places.

STATE, A COMPULSORY ORGANISATION

The state is a compulsory organisation set up to secure justice. The state was created as an organisation in which the dominant forces in society protected themselves against the suppressed forces. The state developed as an institution for the protection of the privileged. Its perpetuation depends upon force. A state without repressive laws, police, soldiers, and jails is not conceivable; a people who can get along without these instruments need no state. When we go back far enough, we find that states and governments started not so much as movements of the people, but rather as the efforts of a privileged class – chiefs, kings, lords – to have their privileges, which were got by force of arms, legalised and made secure.

JOHN LOCKE (1632-1704)

The English philosopher and a political theorist helped lay the foundation of liberal democracy; his ideas were reflected in the American Declaration of Independence and the US Constitution. Trained in science and medicine as well as philosophy, Locke was influenced by the scientific revolution; his epistemological theories were aimed at "removing some of the rubbish which lies in the way to knowledge." Locke's political theory was outlined in his *Two Treatises on Government (1690),* written in defence of the Glorious Revolution of 1688 that established the sovereignty of the British parliament over the monarch. In the Treatises, he attacked the notion of the divine right of kings and proposed a constitutional monarchy based on *social contract.* The State, he says, is created by the will of the people who retain sovereignty by virtue of their God-given rights: *life, liberty and property.* If the state abuses power, it may be overthrown. Locke also advocated a system of checks and balances, central to the American Constitution.

The state, since the beginning, has been a physically powerful social organisation. It could do much for its citizens. It did everything for those citizens in whose interest it existed. It protected their property and their privileges against the demands of the unpropertied and unprivileged. It made laws or interpreted them on their behalf. The concern of the state has been for property rather than for people. The state has looked upon property as the most important basis of social organisation. And, it still does. But, if we depart from the interest of the few, who own most of the property, and consider the many, we find that the state today does much for them also. But the things the state does for the masses, are chiefly in the interest of the law. Discontent, strikes, unemployment, poverty, crime, disease, prostitution, and slums are all disagreeable. The world is small, the poor may be neighbours of the rich, disease is contagious, unruly mobs are annoying to the rich. Therefore, it is wiser to do something for the poor also. And so the state does good things, not because of natural virtue or intention, but because it wants the rich and privileged protected.

In some cases, the state is responsive to the will of the people to a large degree. But the dominant voice in the control of the state is not the people but those few who control finance, property, and industries. With the property-owning minority as the dominant influence in the banks, the press, the courts, the police power, the voting of the majority is also not free. Generation after generation of thought-control and induced patriotism compel approval of things by the people as they are. This was illustrated by the action of the masses in World War I. People were made to approve that War through the thought control system, rhetoric or sheer lies. And, Europe became a killing field for the innocent people who did not know those whom they killed. And why? The people are, therefore, not free to act through the state because they are not capable of acting together. They do not know how to move together and operate the complicated political machine and make it serve them. It is beyond their genius.

TOM PAINE (1737-1809)

Tom Paine, an Englishman, was a cobbler, a tobacconist, a maker of stays, and whalebone corsets worn both by men and women of the upper class in the 18th century. It is ironic that the man who did these strange things also wrote in 1776 *"Common Sense"*, a republican pamphlet. He advocated republicanism, deism, abolition of slavery and emancipation of women. His *"Rights of Man"* made a great impact in America and Britain. He went to France to fight for the Revolution and barely escaped the guillotine. Again, he wrote *"Age of Reason"* when he was tried for treason in France and escaped to America where he died in poverty. He was the man who coined the name *"The United States of America"*. A formidable writer, he laid the foundation of a free society in Europe. He called kings "crowned ruffians."

GOD IS HIGH IN THE HEAVENS

AND KING IS FAR AWAY

Politics usually is remote from the lives of the people. God is high in the heavens and the king is far away. The people, therefore, think of them as foreign to them. The government is surely remote from their daily problems of bread and butter and the crying baby in the slum. The politicians make the people think that political affairs are vital matters. But, the people are absorbed with the real problems of the family paying the rent and buying food and clothes. The economic life is closer. Politics is, therefore, an agent of corruption, not reform. For a citizen to prosecute a state for its crimes is impossible. The state may commit murder – either in retail or wholesale. Were it possible to hold it to account, as the individual is held to account, the governments would become the arch criminals at the bar of justice, the world over. The growing power of the state has been described by Herbert Spencer as *"the coming of slavery."* This is based on the fact that the state has demonstrated itself to be the greatest of tyrants in the suppression of liberties and justice.

UNEQUAL CONFLICT BETWEEN INDIVIDUAL AND STATE

The conflict between the citizen and the state is an unequal one. It is also demoralizing. The free spirit of the individual is constantly subjected to insult by the arrogance of office-holders who have behind them the authority and force of the state. Political hypotheses, however, are built upon the idea that the purpose of the state is to do good for its citizens. Good must be the state's first responsibility. It provides entertainment, cinema shows, cricket, builds monuments in the public places, parks and playgrounds, free education, free lunches, old-age pensions, free hospitals and the dole. Social legislation is the gesture to the people by the Govt. in distress. The more of these things the state does, the better it projects itself. If the state is not more prodigal with its benefactions, it is because the money comes out of the pockets of those who control the government. And, they want to spend just enough to save themselves from the collapse of their economic system and their state. And, not to benefit the poor.

"Fidelity to the Republic" is a typical constitutional requirement. This political demand takes precedence over fidelity to justice or to ideals. It assumes that the state is superior to fundamental virtues.

For want of other organisations, the state provides many necessary things. The government builds bridges, provides electricity, builds roads, issues weather reports, prevents animal diseases, regulates traffic, grants divorce and makes war and peace. And also does thousand other good things. The people need the state and its government because they have not organised themselves to do things themselves. The state exists with the approval of the people and serves them in such manner as they desire – or deserve. If it fails, it is more due to the indifference of the many than to the wickedness of the few. Its deficiency is that it is capable of being controlled by one section and used in the interest of another. But this can be said of any institution in which the majority is indifferent. The state now exists, and clings to the body of society as a parasite. It takes its sustenance from the weakness of society, from the inability of the masses to do things for themselves. But as society makes itself more healthy, as the people become more efficient in their own affairs, the grip of the parasitic state will relax. Or, so say libertarians.

The libertarians say the voluntary and cooperative action alone will be a substitute for the State. Libertarianism as a concept, however, is only a theoretical analysis of the individual initiative to reduce the role of the state. And, promote cooperation among the peoples of the world. This concept is the antithesis of a political state, on which turns the existence of organised political and social life. In the European context, libertarianism is critical to political philosophies.

Libertarianism, however, is no positive philosophy to fully meet the need of the people and society. The cooperative movement offers an alternative philosophy based on liberty and unrestricted by man-made laws. It is the philosophy of a society regulated by voluntary agreements, instead of by political government. It is the one movement which directs the world away from the expansion of the political state and development of social cooperation which is the basis of civil society on which the democratic structure can be built.

Unequal distribution of property and income is inherently an unequal distribution of freedom and social justice.

– *Communist Manifesto*

13

Western economic systems and Eurocommunism

Europe has developed many economic systems, including mercantilism, to give an ideological support to colonial exploitation. But, all of them failed by default or design, in part because not one of them, acting alone, could ensure the continued prosperity of Europeans although capitalism has emerged as the closest approximation of what Europeans need. But this capitalism is far too different from what was conceived by Scottish social philosopher Adam Smith, some 250 years ago. And, Eurocommunism is not a spent force still.

Economics has often been referred to as a dismal science because it deals with scarcity and alternative ways of allocating resources. It is also filled with numbers and calculations. Economists turn flesh-and-blood human beings and their busy social and commercial lives into money and abstractions such as supply and demand, says historian Lewis Lipsitz. Economists rise from the real world of people – sweating and working, haggling in the market-place – to dismal realm of inflation and recession, money markets, gold standards and so forth. In the course of European history, the governments have pursued three major types of economic policy: mercantilism, which involved direct government intervention to facilitate economic exploitation and political colonialism; laissez-faire capitalism, in which government gives relatively a free hand to business; controlled capitalism, in which government intervenes to regulate functioning of the economy.

MERCANTILISM

The economic theory of mercantilism was evolved in the seventeenth-century Europe. Operating under its tenets, the rulers of nation-states such as England and the Netherlands established government chartered corporations and encouraged their growth through subsidies, or financial support. The corporations had their growth through subsidies, or financial support. The corporations had protected from competition through grants of monopoly status, and their production and distribution were extensively controlled to keep out honest competitors. They were formed overseas to provide raw materials and markets for exports. The East India Company was one such chartered corporation. In exchange for protection and subsidization, the semi-public corporations gave the government a share of their income. Mercantilism benefited both the government and the businessman, but profits were often made at the expense of the general public. This concept provided an ideological support to colonialism and facilitated exploitation of the poor. Here, the thrust was on profit, at any cost. The Americans rebelled against the British taxation policies (No taxation without representation) and regulations. In developing their own political system, however, Americans and Europeans eventually resorted to many of the same mercantilist devices, which aided business growth at the expense of farmers, artisans and workers. Operating under the Constitution, governments imposed high taxes on imported goods (protective tariffs), gave subsidies to business, and granted monopoly powers to national banks.

LAISSEZ-FAIRE CAPITALISM

The principal tenet of laissez-faire capitalism which, by the mid-nineteenth century had replaced mercantilism, was the belief that national wealth would be increased if only government restrictions on economic activities were kept to a minimum. In theory, this policy called for the abolition of such mercantilist strategies as government-backed corporate monopolies, detailed regulatory laws, and high protective tariffs. In practice, the laissez-faire movement "democratized" capitalism by throwing open all those sectors of the economy previously restricted to the government-chartered corporations. The new, privately-held corporations that emerged under the laissez-faire doctrine, wanted to be free of competition from government enterprises and from the regulations imposed on the previously chartered companies.

The irony of the laissez-faire period, however, was that as it progressed, business competition declined and monopolies returned. As the more successful corporations expanded, they either bought out their competitors or drove them out of business. As the public monopolies of the 1820s were replaced by the private monopolies of the 1880s, public protest, particularly from farmers and small businessmen, led to the passage of regulatory legislation. In the 1880s, many states, bowing to the demands of Western farmers and Eastern merchants, imposed restrictions on the rates charged by corporations. In 1890, US Congress passed the Sherman Anti-Trust Act, which was designed to prevent monopolies and trusts, and the pooling of resources by several companies for the purpose of controlling a market. Such laws were also passed by most European countries earlier although without much effect.

One hundred years ago, as industrial capitalism was rapidly developing everywhere in the Western world, defenders and opponents of this economic system predicted an intense struggle over its future. Capitalism and socialism were seen as the great alternatives. Socialists believed their system held out the prospect of genuine economic equality combined with democratic politics. Capitalists contended that only their system would protect individual freedom and promote economic growth and high productivity. There often seemed little way of conflating the two alternatives.

A JUST SOCIETY - FACT OR FANTASY

By comparing the theories of socialism and capitalism, we can clarify the debate about the "just society" that has preoccupied Western political thinkers since the eighteenth century. It must be borne in mind, however, that the socialist alternative has not been a very preferred one in the United States, at least in comparison to Western Europe. In the US, the debate over the political economy has been carried on not so much between socialists and capitalists as between the more liberal reformers of capitalism and the more conservative defenders of it. Generally, U.S. liberals have sought to amend, humanize, or improve the capitalist system, rather than to substitute socialism for it. Neoconservatives (neocons), however, stick to the radical concept of capitalism, supporting lower taxer, lower subsidy or welfare support for high production. And, leaving the poor alone and struggle to get out of poverty. Republicans support this approach while Democrats oppose it. However, both the principal parties support free enterprise with differences in details.

The essential elements of a capitalist system are private ownership of the means of production and a competitive market system, driven by the profit motive, through which wealth and resources are distributed. The major capital goods in such a society like factories, machines, land, and money are owned by individuals or groups who have the right to use this property for private gain. What goods are produced, what they cost, and who will receive them are determined by the competitive operations of the marketplace regulated by supply and the demands. According to eighteenth-century exponents of capitalism, the ideal capitalist society would be made up of many small enterprises, competing for a portion of the market. Government would play a minor role in this society: basically, it would provide various public services, such as the building and maintenance of roads; conduct foreign policy and provide for the national defense: and enforce the law. The liberal-capitalist concept of minimum government was espoused by many early leaders of the West. They, along with many other eighteenth-century liberals, saw government as the chief potential enemy of freedom. Freedom to do business as one pleased was linked in their minds, and in their actions, with other freedoms, such as freedom of conscience and freedom of speech. For them, the ideal government was one that functioned as a "night watchman" – a guardian of the existing distribution of property.

THE POOR LEFT OUT IN CAPITALISM

In the early nineteenth century, it was widely believed that laissez-faire (unregulated) capitalism would liberate society from the tyrannies of political oppression, bureaucratic control, and stifling traditions. Capitalism, many held, would create a new world of immense wealth, a far more efficient and productive economy, without any conscious direction from government. Each person could attempt to profit as much as possible; for, in doing so he or she would create wealth, and this would benefit the whole society. Selfishness, in other words, would serve social ends. In this ideal capitalistic world, individuals would be judged on their merits, meaning the value of their skills in the marketplace – not on such non-economic criteria as social status, colour, sex or religion.

Capitalism's achievements were almost immediately evident. The new economic system was enormously productive. It revolutionised the production and distribution of goods, stimulated worldwide trade, and broke down ancient and often oppressive traditions and social barriers. For many, the economic freedom of capitalism and the political freedom of democracy seemed necessarily to go hand-to-hand. Yet from the first, the capitalist system had many critics. Conservative critics viewed capitalism as inimical to social bonds. Conservatives were also unhappy with capitalism's anti-government stance.

Government was needed, nineteenth-century conservatives argued, to protect the weak (such as children who worked fourteen-hour days in mines and factories) and to limit the ferocity of competition. There were some values, conservatives argued, more important than profit.

More radical opponents of capitalism attacked it as a system that proclaimed the value of equality but, in fact, created inequality. Under nineteenth-century capitalism, wealth was very unequally distributed, and it seemed likely to remain that way. Capitalism exploited the workers and it was highly inefficient, radicals argued. Cycles of inflation and depression caused great suffering and wasted vast resources. Another major criticism of capitalism was that it made real democracy difficult to achieve. As long as wealth was so unequally distributed, the few who were rich would have excessive political power and the many who were poor would have too little power. Then, the fact that in a capitalist economy decisions affecting the lives of millions were made by a handful of powerful capitalists who controlled the means of production, was inherently undemocratic. For these reasons, most radicals called for some form of collective ownership of the main means of production, in order to democratize economic decision making. And, thus, came the concept of socialism.

SOCIALISM, AN ALTERNATIVE?

There is less agreement on the meaning of socialism than on that of capitalism. Most socialists, however, would agree that private ownership of the means of production should be replaced by some form of social ownership; that the market system should be replaced by some sort of planned economy; and that the distribution of wealth should be considerably more equal than it is under capitalism. Some early socialists – including Karl Marx and Friedrich Engels – expected that capitalism would inevitably collapse under the weight of its internal problems and that socialism would automatically take its place. Others were gradual reformers who favoured a slow transition from capitalism to socialism through parliamentary processes. Almost all traditional socialists, however, expected to use the vast productive apparatus created by capitalism to achieve a more just social order. Socialism would work in a more rational, planned fashion than capitalism, avoiding the problems of economic boom and bust. Socialism would allow for a more just social order, since wealth would be more equally distributed and large concentrations of wealth abolished. The system would also create a more compassionate and community-minded

ADAM SMITH, A MISUNDERSTOOD MESSIAH

Smith Adam (June 5, 1723 and July 17, 1790), a Scottish social philosopher and political economist, is best known for his major work, *An Inquiry into the Nature and Causes of the Wealth of Nations* (1776), the first major work of laissez-faire economics.

After receiving his elementary education in Kirkcaldy, Smith went to the University of Glasgow in 1737 to study moral philosophy and, subsequently, studied at Balliol College, Oxford. In 1748, he began delivering public lectures in Edinburgh under the patronage of Lord Kames. In 1750, he met David Hume who became one of the closest of his many friends. Smith was appointed professor of logic and later of moral philosophy at Glasgow. In 1759, he published, *The Theory of Moral Sentiments,* which was on human nature.

From 1764 to 1766, Smith travelled as tutor with the young Duke of Buccleuch. Returning to Kirkcaldy in 1767, he spent much of the next nine years there and in London working on The Wealth of Nations. This work contained, among other things, Smith's famous exposition of the "Invisible hand" of competition as guiding an economic - system based on individual self-interest. After being appointed commissioner of customs and of salt duties for Scotland in 1777, he went to live in Edinburgh with his mother. He died there in 1790 after a painfull illness. He had apparently devoted a considerable part of his income to numerous secret acts of charity.

Shortly before his death, Smith had nearly all his manuscripts destroyed. In the last years, he seemed to have been planning two major treatises, one on the theory and history of law and one on the sciences and arts. The posthumously published Essays on Philosophical Subjects (1795) probably contains parts of what would have been the latter treatise. Ironically, 'the fallen sons of Adam Smith' today have forgotten the moral and philosophical message and concentrate on immoral ways of making money in the name of the free market enterprise which has become credo of capitalism.

society characterised by a strong concern for those who were not economically productive. Socialism would enable individuals to pursue values more worthy than profit and would neutralize the crass commercialism of capitalism.

The critics of socialism predicted disaster. How could any planner manage the complexities of a modern economy, they asked. Attempts at government planning, they argued, would only result in inefficiency and in the concentration of power in the hands of government. Socialism would, thus, threaten democracy and freedom itself. Some critics pictured socialism as a new kind of tyranny, with government planners as the tyrants. Others feared that socialism, in attempting to bring life's uncertainties under control and provide security for all, would succeed only in producing stultification of human creativity. The utopian forecasts of the early supporters of capitalism and socialism turned out to be very wide of the mark. Rather than evolve into strictly socialist or strictly capitalist societies, the Western industrial democracies came to adopt a mix of capitalist and socialist methods. The exact mix of elements differs from one society to another: the United States, for example, is more capitalist in orientation; Great Britain and Sweden, more socialist.

MIXED SYSTEM

These mixed systems developed in fits and starts, often spurred by desperate efforts to deal with the crises of capitalism. In many countries, socialist-type reforms, backed by growing trade union movements and socialist political groups, began gathering momentum in the late nineteenth and early twentieth centuries. The first steps toward what we now call the welfare state were taken then, including systematic government aid to the poor and the unemployed, public housing, and government provision for old age pensions. As government became more and more involved in regulation of the economic marketplace,

EMPLOYMENT IN THE PUBLIC SECTOR (1982) (% OF LABOUR FORCE)

	Public enterprises	Total public sector
Austria	13.7	33.0
Belgium	5.2	19.6
Britain	8.1	28.5
Denmark	3.4	18.7
France	7.3	21.0
W. Germany	7.2	20.6
Holland	3.6	16.6
Ireland	7.3	12.8
Italy	6.6	18.5
Japan	2.8	12.9
Spain	2.9	na
Sweden	8.2	29.6
United States	1.5	18.8

Sources : European Centre for Public Enterprises (CEEP), OECO, National Statistics (2006)

new governmental agencies were created to protect consumers and workers. There also were some attempts to break up large concentrations of industrial power, and a few tentative efforts to protect the environment.

MANY FACES OF SOCIALISM

The *Great Depression* of the 1930s represented a watershed in the evolution of mixed economics. As governments sought to deal with widespread unemployment and social dislocations, they became far more active in intervening in the market and in creating new social programs. This trend was reinforced by the experience of World War II, during which governments were forced to do extensive economic and social planning. The Western democracies emerged from the war with new capabilities for dealing with modern economic life. In the post-World War II period, the proponents of socialism enjoyed some measure of success in Western Europe. In Great Britain and Scandinavia, socialist parties held the reins of government in the immediate postwar era, and in West Germany, France, the Netherlands, and other countries they became political forces to be reckoned with. The Labour Party of Great Britain nationalised the failing coal mining industry, as well as the steel industry, road transport, and other major industries. The British also created a socialised medical system and generally increased the reach of the welfare state.

Generally speaking, socialist parties in power proved more moderate than many had expected. In Scandinavia, for example, there was very little nationalisation. Instead, Scandinavian socialists concentrated on keeping employment and economic growth high and in extending the scope of government benefits. The goal was still equality, socialists argued; the exact means used didn't matter that much. In addition, most workers found their lives little changed by the shift from private to government ownership. During the prime ministership of Mrs. Margaret Thatcher (1979-90), the UK switched back to capitalism. Privatisation was the high point of her regime. And, her party lost election after she ceased to be the Prime Minister.

CONTROLLED CAPITALISM

The third era of European economic policy marked by 'controlled capitalism,' began around the turn of the last century and still evolving today. During this era, the government, rather than dismantling large corporations or allowing them to operate unfettered, has created regulatory agencies to oversee and control their activities. One of the chief characteristics of this period has been the transfer to the federal government many of the regulatory and productive activities formerly handled by the states. Federal regulatory agencies multiplied first during the Progressive Era (1900-17) and again during the New Deal of the 1930s, as the nations of Europe tried to cope with the Great Depression which represented a turning point in economic management. As such, it is worth looking at in detail.

THE GREAT DEPRESSION

There was no single cause for the depression, which swept over all industrialised nations and lasted for close to a decade. Its onset usually is linked to the collapse of the U.S. stock market in October, 1929. But that event was only the crystallisation of many other factors that had been building for some time. During the 1920s, there had been a vast expansion of credit buying and a "get-rich-quick" attitude had led to extensive land and stock speculation. As the decade progressed, the production of goods increased more rapidly than the incomes required to buy those goods. The distribution of income in the United States also grew increasingly unequal during the 1920s. In 1929, the richest one percent of the population received as much income as the bottom 42 percent. All these factors fuelled the situation that developed into the depression. Much of European economic life operated on the faith that large profits would continue into the indefinite future. But demand could not keep up with supply. As incomes grew more unequal, even with installment buying, demand for goods began to dry up. The Great Depression was also a cause for the World War II. At one time, a sack full of mark could not buy a kg. of vegetable. Hitler was waiting for this to happen. And, when this did, the stage for the global upheavel was set.

EUROCOMMUNISM

Eurocommunism indicates a trend among European Communist parties toward independence from Soviet Communist Party doctrine. The term Eurocommunism was coined in the mid-1970s and received wide publicity after the publication of Eurocommunism and the State (1977) by the Spanish Communist leader Santiago Carrillo. A spirit of independence among non-ruling European Communist parties had already appeared shortly before World War II with the growth of Popular Fronts in Socialist politics. The excesses of the Stalin regime and such Soviet repressions as the crackdown in Hungary in 1956 and the invasion of Czechoslovakia in 1968 alienated many Communists in the Western countries and tended to accelerate the movement toward independent policies and autonomy.

The Eurocommunist movement avowedly rejects the subordination of Communist parties to the Soviet doctrine of one monolithic world Communist movement. Instead, every party is expected to base its policies on the traditions and needs within its own country. Eurocommunism supports the establishment of socialism only through legitimated political means and free elections. The need for revolution is abjured, and parliamentary democracy in the Western sense is embraced as essential for true Communist government. The Eurocommunist parties advocate pluralistic alliances with other parties that support similar social and economic programs. In addition, Eurocommunists reject atheism as an essential ingredient of Communism and, with it, the Soviet form of Marxism-Leninism.

The promotion of Eurocommunism seemed to coincide with the stagnation or decline of many European Communist parties. The "revival" of Communist strength, such as had existed in most Western European countries in the immediate postwar era, was a hoped-for event. First, public opinion in Western Europe had become overwhelmingly anti-Soviet, or anti-Communist. Dissociation from the Soviet Communism for this reason may have seemed desirable to Eurocommunists. Second, blue-collar industries, whose workers had formed the bases of most Western Communist parties, were declining in favour of service and high technology industries, whose employees were generally unreceptive to the Marxist idea of class struggle. Eurocommunists may have wished to play down the old Marxist-Leninist premise that the Soviet Union, still was the best.

In some countries - such as Portugal, Greece, and Cyprus - new industries had not significantly displaced the old workers and Communist parties still fared moderately well, pulling 15 to 25 percent of the vote. In most other countries, the trend was different. In Belgium, for example, the Belgian Communist Party, once the third largest in the country after World War II, had shrunk to insignificance, with scarcely any more importance than the American or British Communist parties.

In Spain, after Francisco Franco's death in 1975, the Communist Party of Spain (founded in 1920) re-emerged but, within a few years, splintered into several factional parties. By the early 1980s, the Spanish Communists in elections were reduced to less than 5 percent of the popular vote, and the spirit of Eurocommunism had collapsed. Moscow spurned the "nonaligned"

Communist Party of Spain and began favouring politically and, financially, one of the pro-soviet splinter parties, called, the Communist Party (Partido Comunista), founded by Ignacio Gallego, a former leading member of the old nonaligned party. In France, the once-powerfull French Communist Party, which in the early postwar era would command about a third of the French popular vote, experienced a severe decline in later years. Its leader Georges Marchais and his comrades briefly flirted with Eurocommunism in the late 1970s without any success and retreated to fidelity to Moscow. The French Communist share of the popular vote had declined to less than an eighth of the national total.

The chief exception to the ill-fate of Eurocommunist was found in the Italian Communist Party, which remained Italy's second largest party, stressed its independence of Moscow, and seemed to be evolving into a kind of social democratic party. Its foreign contacts and sympathies seemed more with the West German Social Democrats, the British Labour party, and the social democratic parties in The Netherlands and Scandinavia and less with such pro-Soviet groups as the French Communists. Thus, it is clear that Eurocommunism has no future, in part because it had no past. Leader Romano Prody's Victory in April, 2006 general election over Capitalist flamboyant Prime Minister Silvio Berlusconi has proved that Eurocommunism is not dead. At least not fully dead, yet, for Capitalists to celebrate.

Europe is literally the creation of the Third World; its gold, spices, ivory and slaves were shipped across to enrich the European continent.
-Frantz Fanon,
(The Wretched of the Earth 1965)

14

European empires, motives and the missions

What Columbus discovered as new lands, later became empires where people were captured, enslaved and exploited to add to the glory of the conquerors.

The motives that encouraged enterprising men and women to examine their environment are many, strong among them, were curiosity, trade, spreading religion, desire for security or political power. At different times and in different places, different motives were dominant. Sometimes one motive inspired the promoters of discovery and another motive inspired the individuals to do research. Still other motives drew settlers to the new territory. The period of European colonization had its origin with the Renaissance, marked by the development of science, and the great voyages of discovery. This period began in about 1500 and reached its peak in the early 1900s, when the last independent territories of Asia and Africa were colonised. Following World War II, the freedom movements opposed colonialism. Modernization of economic systems also brought about the decline of the colonial empires. Colonialism is a political and economic phenomenon, whereby various European nations discovered, conquered, settled, and exploited large areas of the world.

Colonialism commenced with the emerging European nation-states including England, France, Portugal, Spain, and the Low Countries. After the opening of a sea route around southern Africa in 1488 and the discovery of America in 1492, voyages of colonization and conquest were sent out by most nations of Atlantic Europe. Portugal led the way in discovery. When Prince Henry, the Navigator, died, in 1460, his quest for gold, ivory, spices, and slaves had yielded the discovery of the Cape Verde Islands and the colonization of the Madeira Islands. Bartolomew Dias sailed around the Cape of Good Hope to the Indian Ocean, and in 1498 Vasco da Gama brought back spice from the Indies. The Portuguese expanded westward to Brazil and eastward to the Indian Ocean, where they traded without competition until Philip-II of Spain seized the throne of Portugal in 1580 and other nations began to move in on its monopoly.

After Columbus discovered Cuba, the Bahamas and Hispaniola (West Indian islands) for Spain in 1492, other Spanish voyagers staked claims to Brazil and the Isthmus of Panama; Magellan, a Portuguese ship sailed under the Spanish flag in 1519 around South America and across the Pacific. Spanish conquest of the Americas began with the occupation of the larger West Indian islands. Later, encouraged by the occupation of Aztec Mexico, by Hernan Cortes, which yielded much gold and silver, the Spanish established an American empire stretching from Chile, in the South, to Mexico in the north, including the present-day Florida.

DUTCH EAST INDIA CO AND ROBERT CLIVE

Early in the 16th century, the Dutch became the leading European naval and commercial power, with an Oriental empire that developed rapidly after the chartering of the *Dutch East India Company* in 1602 and the Company's founding of Batavia (now Jakarta), Java as the centre of trade with China, Japan, India, Ceylon (Sri Lanka), and Persia. France, beset by problems on the continent, was a weak administrator of its overseas empire. The French New World settlement began after Verrazano's trip in 1524 and the exploration of the St. Lawrence River, Samuel de Champlain went to New France (Canada) in 1603 and founded Quebec in 1608, but despite the status of royal province granted in 1663, the colony grew slowly, with only 55,000 people by 1754.

England's East India Company (established in 1600) led to the conquest of India by Robert Clive. The British gain in North America resulted from the colonial wars of the 18th century. With Queen Anne's War with Spain ending in 1713, England won Newfoundland, Nova Scotia, and part of northern Canada. The French and Indian War in 1763 gained for Britain all of North

America, east of the Mississippi. The first colonial era ended with Britain becoming the most wealthy of all European colonial nations. British sea power propelled the empire to the South Pacific, Far-East and South Atlantic, and the African coast. The loss of American colonies in 1783 was a blow, although offset by the consolidation of India after the defeat of the Marathas in 1803 and by the settlement of Australia and the Caribbean.

In contrast, the colonial growth of Spain and Portugal suffered setbacks during the Napoleonic wars and the French occupation of the Iberian peninsula in 1807 resulting in an estrangement between South American colonies and their mother countries, both of which were too pre-occupied to intervene effectively in nationalized movements, civil wars, and revolutions. By 1825, Brazil had freed itself from Portugal and Spain. The late 19th and early 20th century saw new colonial powers emerge. The United States, Belgium, Italy, and Russia, another new colonial power, expanded overland displacing indigenous cultures. Russia penetrated Siberia, the Far–East, the Caucasus, and Asia as far as the Korean coastline but was stopped by the Russo-Japanese war in 1905. Western Europe began the partitioning of China with the Opium Wars, waged by Britain to protect British merchants who were exporting opium from India to China. After the Treaty of Nanking (1842), the United States, France and Russia secured similar treaties of entry.

IN 20 YEARS, ALMOST ENTIRE AFRICA WAS CAPTURED

Before 1880, there were very few colonial possessions in Africa, but by 1900 the continent was almost wholly controlled by European powers, beginning from French Algeria and the subsequent British takeover of Egypt, Belgian Congo, French Equatorial Africa, Tanganyika (German East Africa), and South Africa where Britain gained control over the Transvaal and the Orange Free State after the Boer War (1899-1902). Between World War I and World War II, most colonial systems were, however, on the verge of collapse. The Russian Revolution (1917) and various nationalist movements created revolt against imperialism. The process of economic modernization also helped erode the old military dominance of European powers.

From 1945, decolonization acquired momentum. Great Britain, in particular set about dismantling its empire. India and Pakistan were granted independence in 1947, followed by Britain's black African colonies after 1956. Cyprus and Malta were freed in 1960s. Britain pulled out of Persia (Iran) in 1971, and the Royal Navy left Singapore in the same year, ending British Far East presence. France's decolonization process was less peaceful, marked as it was by wars in Indochina, Morocco, Tunisia, and Algeria. Belgium, Portugal, and the Netherlands divested themselves of their overseas possessions during the 1950s, 1960s, and 1970s although not without violence. Thus, the age of imperialism was reaching its end, paving the way for self-governance.

Nelson Mandela waited for 30 years in bushes and 27 years in jail for his moment to arrive. And, when it did on April 10, 1994, instead of crying foul, he pleaded with the British, his tormentors, to stay on and forget the past to build together a new South Africa. History has many strange stories to tell, but this was the strangest of them all.

15

European imperialism; warts and all

European states possessed colonies with twice their own total population and 20 times their areas. And, the area of the colonial empires of the world in the 1920s was roughly the size of the United States, and their population was more than five times as much.

In Tolstoy's *War and Peace,* Natasha sits on the gutted ruins of the once imperial palace and says to Andre, also half-destroyed in the war: "You are like this house; you suffer; you show your wounds and still you stand unbent." So did Nelson Mandela. And, on April 10, 1994 the once convicted guerilla leader became the first black president of South Africa after 300 years of slavery, exploitation and plunder, also marking the end of imperialism.

Modern imperialism may be divided into the old imperialism, usually called colonialism, for which we might set the arbitrary dates of between 1492 and 1763, and the new imperialism between 1870 and 1918. Between these two periods, there was a full century of comparative quiet in the rivalry between states over building colonial empires. Imperialism died also because it did not bring money which it did in earlier times. It was estimated that the loss to the Netherlands because of loss of her Indonesian possessions was more than compensated by two years of her economic growth.

To be true, the old imperialism was the consequence of mercantilism and its tools were innovations and force that ensured Europeans victory over the peoples in America, Africa and Asia. (Mercantilism is the opposite of free trade. This was the imperial philosophy of European powers to exploit colonies and store gold which was the index of power and wealth). Gunpowder, printing and banking gave immense advantages to Europeans, so did advances in building ships, roads, and fortifications and development in the science of navigation. The principal gainer was Britain, but Spain, Portugal and the Netherlands also built colonial empires.

While European states were engaged in dividing the backward areas of the earth, some of them were also advancing their interests in less backward regions through more subtle methods. Seeking special rights, several of them acquired "leaseholds" in China; Great Britain and France divided Siam (now Thailand) into "spheres of influence"; and Britain and Russia did the same with Persia (Iran). Britain, France, Germany, Russia and Japan established spheres of influence in China, so did Britain, France, Germany, and Italy in Turkey. In some cases, spheres of influence preceded annexation; this was often the case in Africa. The advantages sought were economic or military, and the forms of control were various tariff regulation, financial supervision, or military occupation. The United States has carefully avoided this subtle kind of imperialism in non-American areas and, in fact, in 1899-1900 she sponsored the *Open Door Policy* in China to protect American interests against colonial powers.

EMPIRES BY MANY NAMES

The areas controlled by imperialists were known by many names, like possessions, colonies, protectorates, semi-protectorates, and dependent states. Colonialism has also been a status symbol and a source of rivalries and inter-state conflict. However, the main motive was the economic gains that included conquest for the sake of loot, quest for competition-free markets, sources of raw materials, the search for virgin lands for investment by the capitalists of the capital-glutted countries, and also captive manpower (read slaves). Colonies also provided goods that could not be obtained otherwise and at much lower price and with less likelihood of interruption by war. While the nineteenth-century imperialists' declaration that *"trade follows the flag"* may not be entirely true, this has been the main motive for conquering foreign lands and exploiting their people. Defenders of imperialism have believed that a state must achieve its *"manifest destiny"* or its "place in the sun." Generations of Englishmen gloried in the boast that *"the sun never sets on the British Empire."* Benito Mussolini loved to move his hand over the map of vast expanses of African desert and hill that he sought to bring under the Italian flag. And, finally, he failed, so also all conquerors after the coming of democracy at the end of World War II.

The Europeans changed the course of world history, also by planting white populations overseas. In 1800, large European populations of Spanish and Portuguese stocks lived in Central and South America. There were British and French settlers in Canada, Dutch in the Cape of Good Hope, and a few British – mainly convicts – in New South Wales. By 1914, these people became new and mature nations. Great Britain was their progenitor. For much of the 18th century in which the British flag flew over an empire on which the sun never set, Englishmen viewed the large pink spaces on the map with imperial pride and arrogance.

As profits from colonies usually depended upon the use of native labour, and as colonial peoples were strangers to capitalistic propaganda on the dignity of labour, imperialist powers forced the natives to till soil, dig for gold, gather rubber, hunt for ivory, or collect coconuts. The colonial powers did that through slavery, forced labour, heavy taxation, and confiscation of land. Sometimes, the natives were forced to give a share of their crops to the government; sometimes troops managed forced labour; sometimes a *hut tax* (or poll tax) was imposed, payable only in labour, sometimes native chieftains were rewarded according to their success in mobilising their tribesmen for labour and sometimes labourers were imported from distant lands. Small countries like Mauritius, Guyana, Haiti, Surinam and many floating atolls and islands in South Pacific are inhabited by imported labour.

At one time, about half the revenue from French West Africa came from taxes on hard liquor. The British profited from the gambling and opium trade in the Far East. Everywhere, there were sharp

EUROPE HAD CAPTURED ONE-THIRD OF HUMAN RACE

As late as the mid-1920s, half the world's land area and one-third of the human race had been captured and made subjects to colonial powers. European states possessed colonies with twice their own total population and 20 times their own area. To put it another way, the area of the colonial empires of the world in the 1920s was roughly the size of the United States, and their population was more than five times as much.

discriminations against the natives and in favour of white men, black leaders were ordered to enlist natives to be sold into slavery, and the yellow men of Japan and China had proved amazingly resourceful in the techniques of human torture and abuse. Morality is certainly not a matter of race, and the brutalities of imperialism suggest the disheartening conclusion that it may have little to do with "culture" or with what passes for Christian virtues.

IMPERIALISM IS A DIFFERENT GAME; IT IS A POWER RELATIONSHIP

Imperialism is use of the engines of government and diplomacy to acquire territories, protectorates, or spheres of influence occupied by other peoples only to promote industrial, trade, and investment opportunities and make money by exploitation. Imperialism is a power relationship between the weak and the strong, the poor and the rich. J.A. Hobson defines imperialism, as a natural overflow of nationality; its test is the power of colonists to transplant their culture to a new social environment in which they find themselves ruling over others. It is also a master-subject relationship; it is the occupation of a territory by force by the Europeans. Imperialism has also fuelled nationalism. The colonial system broke down following the rise of national self-consciousness which produced a desire to be free. The rise of nationalism saw the end of both imperialism and colonialism.

The Industrial Revolution attracted the European states to the prospect of huge profits from the sale of their newly invented machinery. Spain and England tried to resist the efforts of their colonial subjects to achieve independence. Spain, however, was a decadent empire, having used her fabulous treasure chest of colonial gold and silver in foreign wars and in maintaining an extravagant court rather than in building an economy. England had already had her fingers burnt in the American War of Independence. Bankrupt France experienced the savage consequences of the French Revolution and the Napoleonic wars. Napoleon's ambitions for overseas dominions ended after his defeat at Trafalgar on October 21, 1805. By 1829, however, France had recovered enough to dream again for an expanding empire. Germany and Italy had not yet entered the ranks of colonial powers.

Empires have existed almost from the beginnings of civilization, but different empires at different times have meant different things in practice. Chinese imperial officials, for instance, seemed to have been satisfied that subject peoples acknowledged the empire's superiority by providing tribute and showing respectful behaviour and that was all. But, the European empires of the nineteenth century had some special features. The most obvious was their geographical reach, with some of them spread over frozen wastes of Antarctica while others over the deserts of the Sahara. There seemed to be no part of the world in which empire-builders were not interested, including a huge rock, Gibraltar. This was partly because of technology and science, and the new military capability of empire-builders. The only non-European nations which stopped them before 1914 and kept their independence intact were the poor Ethiopians, who defeated an Italian army that invaded their country in 1896, and the Japanese who, however, adopted the European ways in order to survive.

These facts indicate that the nineteenth-century imperialism was overwhelmingly European. Only one Asian country – Japan – took part in the empire-building of the age; the older Chinese, Ottoman and Persian empires had made great conquests in the past but were losers in the nineteenth-century, and they contracted in area considerably. Some of them – Russia, Great Britain, France – had long been in the business of empire. One of the old European imperial powers, Spain, lost more than she gained during the nineteenth century. The Portuguese and Dutch, were in much the same position. But two European states which did not exist in 1850, Germany and Italy, were acquiring new territory overseas, so was Belgium, which had only appeared in 1830 and built an overseas empire many times its size. Therefore, nineteenth century was an age of European imperialism. American acquisition and addition to the mainland (like those of Russia) did take place but they were not the case of empire building which is a different exercise altogether. Imperialism was largely the work of the peoples of European stocks and cultures. *(Italian unification finally took place in 1870 when Italian forces captured Rome under Garibaldi. Earlier, Italy was divided in states including Milan, Florence, Venice & Kingdom of Naples. German unification also took place under Bismark in 1870-71 after Franco–Prussian war. Earlier, it was Prussia, east and west.)*

16 EUROPEAN COUNTRIES HAD MOST EMPIRES

Sixteen countries of Western Europe, had empires which they exploited to build their economies or satisfy their ego. While the loss to the colonies in terms of money cannot be calculated, the series of conflicts before and after

1945 had been the consequence of the colonial world order which began soon after the discoveries of many countries in the 15th century. Since then, it has become the trend of advanced and adventurous nations to discover new lands and conquer them and retain them as long as they did. The Hundred Years' War between France and England (1337 to 1453), the Thirty Years' War in Germany (1618-48), and a series of wars and conflicts in between were fought to build colonies and set up empires. The two world wars were also the cause and consequence of colonial ambitions. The conquest of Latin America is a classic example of imperialism practised on behalf of a religious mission for the Catholic sovereigns of Spain and Portugal and thousands of humble priests who went willingly to do God's work in the wilderness. Most of them perished. And, many unwittingly served the cause of militarism and economic exploitation, while sincerely believing in the idealism of the *White Man's Burden,* particularly during the Age of Imperialism (1870 to 1914).

It is absurd to say that imperialism was inspired by the desire to improve the lives of the subject people, although there had been a number of instances where governments had established political systems for humanitarian work. It is said that the occupation of New Zealand in 1833 was to stop the debauching and robbing of the natives by white men; that direct British rule in India after Battle of Plassey in 1757, was partly to end the abuses of indirect administration by the British East India Company; that British jurisdiction over some Pacific islands in 1872 was to stamp out the slave traffic; and that thousands of Americans supported the war against Spain in 1898 because Spain was pursuing a policy of oppression and exploitation in Cuba and Puerto Rico.

MANHATTAN WAS BOUGHT FOR $ 24: BOMBAY GIVEN IN DOWRY

The new imperialism began in 1870, when England began to feel the competition of other industrial rivals, and the manufacturing nations began to raise protective tariff walls around their own markets. Steamships and railways created facilities for world commerce and conquest, and hungry factory towns called out for raw materials. Imperialist control was asserted through military conquest. They also used gold and gunpowder, bribe to threaten native leaders to make room for them. Manhattan, for instance was "purchased" from the Red Indians for 24 dollars' worth of trinkets. In other such dealings, Europeans also acquired most of Africa without fighting and resistance. In addition to fraud, the imperialists also threatened to use force against the established regimes. This was how Hawaii was acquired in 1894. Colonies had also been transferred as spoils of war as was the case with Guam which was acquired by the United States after victory in war with Spain. *(More about the US later).*

Bombay (Mumbai) was given to Britain in 1662 as part of Catherine of Braganza's wedding dowry. We know of the famous *Louisiana Purchase*. Plebiscites have also been used in a few instances to allow a small population to choose its master as a colony or possession, as with the Ionian Island, St. Bartholomew, and the Danish West Indies. It was said that "independent" states agreed by plebiscite to subordinate themselves to another state. The Soviet Union was the creation of such "independent plebiscites," a cruel farce. And, the media reported that very faithfully. The story of conquest by deceit and fraud is, however, not complete.

PROFILES OF IMPERIALISTS

GREAT BRITAIN: The Industrial Revolution had filled warehouses with surplus manufactured goods in Britain. Sale abroad was possible, but it was not easy to compete with industrial states, particularly those with high tariff walls, like the United States and Germany. It was easier in English colonies where England could manipulate the tariff control. She might also acquire a protected source of supplies of cotton, rubber, coca, coffee, tea, sugar, iron, hemp, oil, phosphate and nitrate which were crucial to British industry. British transportation, communication, and banking facilities had also produced surplus capital, ready for investment. Greed, patriotism, jingoism, militarism, Christianity or sheer adventure – all these whipped Englishmen into a state of mind in which they were willing to accept the imperialist plan announced by Disraeli in 1872. Even Gladstone's Liberal Party supported imperial expansion which had become a holy mission, and very profitable at that. The British territorial expansion in Africa alone covered more than two and a half million square miles, with a population of nearly 50 million. In 1914, the British empire was still the world's largest and the richest, so made specially by the size and resources of India.

BRITAIN RULED OVER A FIFTH OF THE WORLD'S POPULATION

Although the presence overseas of people of European stocks and culture was crucial for much of the future development of the world, European ascendancy was most obvious in the form of colonial empires and the direct rule over non-European nations. The British empire contained some 400 million people - about a fifth of humanity at that time – of whom about 35 million lived in the United Kingdom. The French, with over 50 million overseas colonial subjects, also ruled more people of other nations than their own, and millions more and vast areas of land were ruled by other European powers. Outright control of so much of the earth and its inhabitants marked the beginning of the twentieth century Europe. In the year 1900, the only places outside the Americas still not under direct white rule were China, the much-shrunken Ottoman and the Persian empires, Japan and a handful of smaller countries. In 1900, people were talking more about empires and 'imperialism,' than fifty years earlier. There had never been so imperialist a century or seemingly such successful empires.

FRANCE: France joined the imperialistic programmes of the early eighties and, within 40 years, planted its flag on nearly three million square miles of soil and sand. Her prizes were largely in Africa, with lesser ones in Southeast Asia, specially Indo-China. These impressive conquests gave France the world's second largest empire on the eve of World War I. But, the French colonies were small, scattered and resources poor, unlike Britain which had large colonies, including India, America, Australia and many in Africa. The French Equatorial Africa was a federation of French territories in West Africa. Founded in 1910, it consisted of Gabon, Middle Congo, Chad, and Ubangi-Shari (now the Central African Republic). It was ruled from Brazzaville.

The federation supported the Free French in World War II and was given representation in the French Fourth Republic (1944-58). In 1958, the states voted for autonomy and the federation was dissolved. The *French West Africa* was a group of French colonies administered from Dakar (1895-1958). They are now Senegal, Mauritania, Sudan, Burkina Faso, Guinea, Niger, Cote d'Ivoire, (Ivory Coast) and Benin. French Overseas Territory in the South Pacific consisted of five archipelagos: Windward Islands, Leeward Islands (the two island groups comprising the Society Islands), Tuamotu archipelago (including Gambier Islands), Tubuai Islands, and Marquesas Islands. Total area 1,521 sq mi; capital *Papeete* on Tahiti. The French Guiana (*French Guyane Francaise*) was French overseas department from 1946, and the administrative region from 1974 on the north coast of South America, bounded in the West by Surinam and East and South by Brazil; area 32,230 sq mi; capital is *Cayenne*.

GERMANY: Bismarck, father of the German empire, reluctantly turned away from continental politics to imperialism. Within six years (1884-1890), he acquired Togoland (Togo now), Kamerun (Cameroon), German South-West Africa (Namibia) and German East Africa, (with a total of a million square miles), and a portion of New Guinea; She had also extensive economic rights in the Shantung Peninsula in China, and scattered groups of islands in the Pacific. Germany woke up rather late in the day when there was very little of Africa left for occupation. Only Tanganyika, part of West Africa, and the sun-drenched *savannah* and semi-deserts of South-West Africa remained unclaimed. (Tanganyika and Zanzibar were united in 1964 to form Tanzania).

GERMAN COLONIES MADE UN "MANDATED" TERRITORIES

The progress of nationalism in Asia and Africa is reflected in the history of the League of Nations after World War I and of the United Nations after World War II. The Treaty of Versailles, which provided for the constitution of the League of Nations, also reduced the empires of the defeated Central Powers, mainly Germany and Turkey. The League distributed Germany's African colonies as *"mandates"* to Great Britain, France, Belgium and South Africa, and its Pacific possessions to Japan, Australia, and New Zealand under various classifications. Among the League's original members, there were only five Asian countries (China, India, Japan, Thailand and Iran) and two African countries (Liberia and South Africa), and it added only three Asian countries (Afghanistan, Iraq, and Turkey) and two African countries (Egypt and Ethiopia) before it was dissolved in 1946. Of the "mandated" territories under the League's control, only Iraq, Lebanon, and Syria achieved independence during the League's lifetime.

Of the original 51 members of the United Nations in 1945, eight were Asian (China, India, Iraq, Iran, Lebanon, Saudi Arabia, Syria, and Turkey) and four were African (the same as in the League). By 1980, 35 years after its founding, the United Nations had added more than 100 member-nations, most of them Asian and African. Whereas Asian and African nations had never totalled even one-third of the membership in the League, they came to represent more than one-half of the membership of the United Nations. Of these new Asian and African nations, several had been created, entirely or in part, from *"mandated"* territories.

ITALY HAD ERITREA, SOMALILAND AND LIBYA: Italy, like Germany, was a late-comer. Although she lacked the strength, she was able to carve out three colonies in Africa: Eritrea, on the Red Sea, Italian Somaliland, on the eastern tip of Africa, and Libya in North Africa. Libya was the unification of Tripoli and Cyrenaica, taken from Turkey in the Italian-Turkish War of 1911-1912. It is a large, barren tract of about 600,000 square miles. Italy tried to absorb Ethiopia and, unify East African colonies, but she suffered a crushing military defeat at the hands of the Ethiopians at Aduwa in 1896. Just before World War II, she tried again and succeeded in organising Italian East Africa, only to lose everything later.

ZAIRE WAS PERSONAL PROPERTY OF BELGIAN KING: The little Belgium was put on the road to imperialism through the venture of Leopold-II, who staked out for himself the Congo Free State, now Zaire. Acquired as a personal possession by the King in the 1880s, it became a Belgian colony in 1908 when the Belgian Government, responding to outside criticism of Leopold's abuse of the Congo natives, forced the King to relinquish his proprietorship. It had an area of nearly one million square miles and a population of more than 26 million.

SMALL EUROPEAN STATES HAD LARGE COLONIES: Austria-Hungary also found an outlet through expansion into contiguous territory rather than in overseas conquest. The lesser powers of Europe – Spain, Portugal, the Netherlands, and Denmark – lacking capital and power to compete with major powers, kept control of the colonies they had acquired earlier, but only Spain and Portugal made efforts to expand their holdings, with some modest successes in Africa. Thus, five lesser powers – these four and Belgium – possessed colonies at the outbreak of World War I, but of these, only one was of great economic value – the rich Netherlands' East Indies which antedated the new imperialism. Norway later established the title to the Spitzbergen Archipelago.

RUSSIA: The Russian imperialism differed from the imperialistic expansion that had sliced up North and South America, Africa and much of Asia. Russia spread out over contiguous territories rather than pursue imperialism of commerce, sea power, and investments over the ocean highways. The Russian expansion was aimed at acquiring new areas and not colonies. She manifested some interest in Africa, particularly in Ethiopia, but gained nothing there, nor did she ever possess any non-contiguous territory, after the sale of Alaska to the US by the Czar in 1867 for $ 7.2 million. Her continental gains between

1850 and 1914 amounted to more than a million square miles of contiguous areas. She also had spheres of influence in Persia, Manchuria and Mongolia. During the inter-war years, the Soviet Union concentrated on building her industrial and military strength. She, however, made no serious effort for territorial expansion. She did put some pressure on Turkey in 1939, and also dabbled in Iranian politics and, she had a brief period of success in getting her foot on the Chinese door. She fought a "semi-war" with Japan over Manchuria, but brought no additional land or people under her control.

Since World War II, however, the threat of Soviet imperialism expanded. At a time when Britain, France, and the Netherlands had been expelled from vast areas in Asia and Africa, the imperialism of the Soviet Union had expanded until it included virtually all of Eastern Europe and parts of Asia. Under the Communist regime, the Soviet Union had annexed 264,000 square miles as satellite parts or all of eleven countries of more than five million square miles and a population in excess of seventy million people. Russians comprised only 58 per cent of the population of the former Soviet Union. And, that created its own problems, finally resulting in the collapse of Communism.

JAPAN: While Japan was rapidly becoming industrialised, she was also learning to play Western games. And, she rejected democracy and accepted industrial capitalism, militarism, and imperialism. Supported by an astonishing industrial development, she began her variety of imperialism in 1894 after a war on China. After victory, she annexed Formosa, now Taiwan, and the Ryukyu Islands and absorbed Korea completely in 1910. Following the victory in the Russo-Japanese War (1904-1905), she annexed southern Sakhalin; acquired a leasehold on Port Arthur on the Liaotung Peninsula, and eliminated Russian influence from Korea and southern Manchuria. This was her position when she entered World War I as an ally of Britain. She took no part in the division of Africa and, indeed, confined herself to regional imperialism. During World War II, she took advantage of the preoccupation of the Western powers with the conflict in Europe to move into the Shantung Peninsula and demand far-reaching concessions from China in 1915.

CANADA WAS SET UP IN 1867: British Canada lived next door to America whose citizens believed Canada should simply be absorbed by the United States. A war between the US and Great Britain, 1812 to 1814, was the only attempt to bring this about, but it did not happen. Inside Canada, there was the difficulty in governing two groups of settlers; the French, who had settled in Quebec, and the British in the West. The setting-up of the Dominion of Canada as a federal state in 1867 set the seal on the process by providing a national government. From that moment, Canada can be reckoned as an independent nation in its own right even though tied by many practical and sentimental links to Great Britain. In 1867, Canada was poor and underpopulated. The 500,000 new Canadians who arrived from Europe between 1815 and 1860 combined with natural increase in population pushed the population up to 3 million and this figure doubled by 1900, when a new burst of settlement and faster growth began. In 2005, Canada's population was more than 32.2 million – almost all of them of European stock. Canada may be the world's second-biggest country by area, one of its dozen largest economies and a founding member of the G7 club of rich countries. But much of its vast land is frozen waste. Nearly all of its 32.2m people cling to a narrow belt along its border with the United States.

The making of Australia had been spectacular. The 736 convicts, who arrived in the first shipment in 1788 multiplied into 100,000 in the 1830s and a million by about 1860. Australia presented fewer problems of governance than Canada and had no powerful neighbours, but the precarious economy and the continuing transport of convicts (the last were landed only in 1867) gave the British governors difficulties. The Merino sheep was one answer. In 1850, Australia was divided into colonies and each given internal self-government. British troops were withdrawn in 1870, and the commonwealth of Australia (like Canada, a federal state) came into being on January 1, 1901.

SAILORS SET UP NEW ZEALAND: In New Zealand too, there appeared a new nation predominantly British in culture. The first settlers, sailors or escaped convicts from Australia or traders seeking to make money by supplying the native Maori people with guns, had been so notorious that the British government had resisted taking responsibility for the islands at all. Then missionaries came, vigorous and hard-working, and they were received with no encouragement until the French threatened to seize the islands. Under a treaty in 1840, Maori chiefs accepted British sovereignty. Thus, New Zealand's short colonial history began. The colony grew fast; there were 300,000 settlers in 1875 and over 10,000,000 sheep in the south island alone. New Zealand found in wool a staple commodity for export. With the introduction of refrigerated cargo ships in 1882 the sheep farmer could think of raising stock for meat as well as for wool for export. Export of dairy produce also became profitable. Both islands were under one local government from 1875, London retaining responsibility only for native affairs. The New Zealanders, like the

Australians, took steps to keep out Asiatic immigrants, prescribed an eight-hour working day and an old age pension scheme in the 1890s. And also gave vote to women. Finally, in 1907, New Zealand was recognized as an independent "dominion" within the British Empire.

SOUTH AFRICA

Australia and New Zealand enjoyed slightly different degrees of legal sovereignty in 1899, but they had freedom from British control. In that year, Canada, Australia and New Zealand sent troops to fight war in South Africa for Britain. This was the consequence of the Anglo-Dutch conflict. The Dutch had arrived in South Africa in the seventeenth century. They numbered about 25,000 by 1800 and settled in a country in which there was already a large native population which would not go away or die out. Even in 1900, when many more white people (mainly British) had gone to South Africa, its white population was only about one-quarter of the black. The British and Dutch farmers did not come to terms. The Dutch were closely-knit by custom, language and religion.

BOER WAR (1880-81 AND 1899-1902): Trouble began soon after 1815 when the British (who had occupied the Cape because of its strategic importance during the war with Napoleon) annexed the area. Later, British settlers began to arrive. They were accompanied, to the annoyance of the Dutch, by missionaries who almost at once took up the question of the defence of the rights of the native population, whom they sought to convert. English became the official language instead of Dutch, and the old judicial arrangements were replaced by British. When slavery was abolished throughout the British Empire in 1834, there was much grumbling among the Dutch over the terms of compensation. In 1835, there began the *Great Trek*, a migration to the north of some 10,000 Boers (as the Dutch were often called) with their families, cattle and possessions, across the Vaal river. This was the origin of the Boer republic of the Transvaal. A few years later, another British authority was established in Natal to protect natives against the Boers.

Meanwhile, diamond was found on the Orange river and later on the Rand in the Boer Transvaal. Native wars (in particular, with the Zulu) sent up the cost of government. By the 1890s, the Boer leaders were convinced that the British were intent on destroying their republics, while the British thought that the Boers might obtain a seaport on the Indian Ocean and then threaten imperial communications with India. This led to two wars with Boers one in

1880-81 and the second Boer war of 1899-1902. Finally, the British took over the Dutch republics, and set up representative institutions. On 31 May 1910, the British parliament passed the South Africa Act and a new state came into existence within the British empire.

In other major areas of European settlements this did not happen, though Frenchmen and Italians settled in large numbers in north Africa during the nineteenth century. With the exception of Algeria (which ended up being treated legally as a part of France) these settlement areas either remained formally under the native authorities (as in Tunisia) or were made colonies as was the case with Libya and Tripolitania (a former province of Libya) which was later seized by the Italians from the Ottomans before 1914.

LATIN AMERICAN COUNTRIES

Latin America includes countries of South America and North America (including Central America and the islands of the Caribbean Sea) south of the U.S. However, the term is often restricted to countries where either Spanish or Portuguese is spoken. The colonial era in Latin America began in the 15th-16th centuries when explorers such as Christopher Columbus and Amerigo Vespucci made voyages of discovery to the New World. The *conquistadores* who followed, including Hernan Cortes and Francisco Pizarro, brought Spanish rule to much of the region. In 1532, the first Portuguese settlement was made in Brazil. The Roman Catholic church soon established many missions in Latin America. Roman Catholicism is still the chief religion in most Latin American countries, though the number of Protestants and Evangelicals has grown.

Spanish and Portuguese colonists arrived in increasing numbers and they enslaved the native Indian population, which was soon decimated by ill-treatment and disease, and came imported African slaves to replace them. A series of movements for independence, led by Jose de San Martin, Simon Bolivar, and others, swept Latin America in the early 19th century. Federal republics were promulgated across the region, but many of the new countries collapsed into political chaos and were taken over by dictators or military juntas, a situation that persisted into the 20th century. In the 1990s a trend toward democratic rule re-emerged; in socialist-run countries many state-owned industries were privatized, and efforts toward regional economic integration were accelerated. Now, most countries in mainland Latin America are democratic.

The only other place where nation-states appeared as consequence of European settlement was South America. French occupation had brought about a virtual severing of ties between Spain, Portugal and the Americas during the Napoleonic wars. Some of the *creoles* (as the American-born of European blood were called) had already noted that the North Americans had shaken off British rule. In 1810, a series of risings in widely separated places began what were to later become the Latin wars of independence. Two outsiders then entered the story. One was the United States, which declared in 1823 that no European power must contemplate the Americas as a place for further conquests or colonies. This *'Monroe Doctrine'*, as it was called after the name of the president who declared it, depended on another outsider, Great Britain, whose government was quite happy, for commercial reasons, to see South and Central America independent of Spain and Portugal. As the Royal Navy was the only naval force which could thwart any attempt to reconquer them, the survival of the new republics was assured.

LATIN AMERICA: MAINLAND COUNTRIES

Countries	Capitals
Venezuela	Caracas
Guyana	George Town
Sourinam	Paramaribo
French Guiana	Cayenne
Brazil	Brasilia
Argentina	Buenos Aires
Chile	Santiago
Bolivia	La Paz
Paraguay	Asuncion
Uruguay	Montevideo
Peru	Lima
Equador	Quito
Colombia	Bogota
Offshore Countries	
Falkland Is.	Pt. Stanley
Trinidad & Tobago	Port of Spain
Barbados	Bridgetown
Grenada	St. George's
Dominica	Roseau
St. Lucia	Castries
St. Vincent & the Grenadines	Kingstown
Antigu & Bermuda	St. John's.

NAPOLEON III GAVE THIS NAME

After the wars of independence, emerged a collection of new states often ruled by soldier-dictators though Brazil, for some time, had an emperor of the Portuguese royal family. Geography and history made a federation like that of the northern continent impossible. Quarrels and wars finally resulted in the appearance by 1900 of four mainland central America republics (of which Mexico was the biggest), two island states in the Caribbean (soon to be joined by a third, Cuba) and ten republics in South America whose politicians seemed remarkably like their European equivalents. French Emperor Napoleon-III, therefore, coined the term '*Latin America*' for the continent where Spanish, Portuguese and French are spoken.

South America attracted European emigrants much more than Central America, though it was less of a draw than North America; only 6 of the 41 million Europeans who crossed the Atlantic between 1845 and 1914 went south of the Rio Grande. Still, this helped to confirm the expansion of European societies many of whose inhabitants were American or (in the case of Brazil and some Caribbean islands) African in descent. Population in Central and South America did not, however, grow so rapidly as that in the United States. Overall, there were about 80 million people in Latin America in 1914.

COLONIES FREED AFTER WORLD WAR II

After World War II, India, Pakistan, Ceylon (Sri Lanka), Burma, and Malaya (Malaysia) in Asia, and Ghana in Africa achieved independence peacefully from Britain. The Malay states formed a federation in February 1948, but a Communist guerrilla campaign delayed its independence until 1957. Other territories had to fight hard for their independence in bitter colonial wars, as in French Indo-China (Vietnam, Laos, Cambodia) and French North Africa (Tunisia, Algeria). Communism recruited supporters from within the ranks of the new nationalist movements in Asia and Africa, first by helping them in their struggle against Western capitalist powers and later, after independence was achieved, by competing with Western capitalism in extending financial and technical aid. Chinese nationalism under Chiang Kai-shek (Jiang Ji Shi 1887-1975) during World War II was diminished with the takeover of the Chinese communists. But Chinese communism soon began to drift away from global communism, as the European communist countries did before. By the late 1960s, mutual recriminations between the Russians and Chinese revealed a Chinese nationalism in which Mao Zedong had risen to share the place of honour with Lenin.

British influence also waned in Australia and New Zealand which looked increasingly to the United States for security in the Pacific. The Philippines, an American-ruled semi-independent state, was granted full independence in July 1946. Indonesia, formerly the Dutch East Indies, became independent in November 1949 after four years of guerrilla warfare. The French lost Indochina: Laos became independent in October 1953, Cambodia in November. In 1945, the Communist leader Ho Chi Minh had claimed independence for Vietnam and after an exhausting struggle the French withdrew in July 1954. But the country remained divided and, like Berlin and Korea, became the arena for a bitter confrontation between the postwar enemies - the Communist world and the West.

Ambitions among new Asian and African nations clashed. The complex politics of the United Nations illustrated the problems of the new nationalism. The struggle with Dutch colonialism that brought the establishment of Indonesia continued with the UN mediation of the dispute over West Irian (Irian Jaya). In the Suez crisis of 1956, UN forces intervened between those of Egypt and Israel. Continuing troubles in the Middle East, beginning with the establishment of Israel and including inter-Arab state disputes brought on by the establishment of the United Arab Republic, also concerned the UN. Other crises involving the United Nations included, the India-Pakistan dispute over Jammu and Kashmir, the Korean partition and subsequent war; the four-year intervention in the Congo, the struggle of Greece and Turkey over newly independent Cyprus and Indonesian and The Philippine objection to the inclusion of Sarawak and Sabah (North Borneo) in the newly formed Malaysia.

Many new nations, all sharing the same pride in their independence, faced difficulties. As a result of an inadequate preparation for self-rule, the first five years of independence in the Congo passed with no semblance of a stable government. The problem of varying peoples and languages was exemplified in Nigeria where an uncounted population included an uncounted number of tribes (at least 150, with three major divisions) that used an uncounted number of languages (more than 100 language and dialect clusters). The question of whether the state of Jammu and Kashmir should go with Pakistan or India lasted for more than 50 years and still continuing after the Indian Independence Act became effective in 1947. Desperate economic competition caused trouble, as in Israel where the much-needed waters of the Jordan River kept it in constant dispute over its water-hungry Arab neighbours.

The year 1945 marked the death of colonialism in the world. Exceptions are not many. Earlier there had been wars, revolts and revolutions, an era of profound identity crisis for the bourgeois classes whose traditional moral foundations crumbled under the pressure of their own accumulations of wealth and comfort in the midst of new and sudden mass labour movements that rejected capitalism and the new middle classes which rejected western liberalism. The world empires built by the small countries of Europe lasted barely a lifetime, and, ironically, the European domination of world history was

DECOLONIZATION IN ASIA

Indian sub-continent	
1946	March 14; British offer of full independence to India.
1947	February 20: British set terminal date for withdrawal. August 15 set for inauguration of dominions of India and Pakistan.
1948	Ceylon (Sri Lanka) becomes free.
South-East Asia	
1948	Burma becomes independent.
1949	Independence of Vietnam within French Union.
1954	France concedes complete independence to South Vietnam, Laos, Cambodia, Vietnam.
1957	Federation of Malayan states made independent.
1959	Self-government for Singapore.
Indonesia	
1949	Dutch transfer of sovereignty to Indonesia.
East Asia	
1943	The UK and the US relinquish extra-territorial rights in China.
1945	Division of Korea between the USSR and the USA.
1946	The Philippines became free.
1948	Republic of Korea (South) and Korean Peoples' Democratic Republic (North) set up.

never more evident than at the moment when it was about to disappear forever. It was the era of Queen Victoria, Madame Curie and the Kodak Girl, Nietzsche, Carnegie, William Morris and Dreyfus, and the terrorist who killed the heir to the Austrian throne, Archduke Franz Ferdinand, on June 28, 1914 which started World War I. To be true, the history of mankind is the history of exploitation of man by man. There are no moral lessons to learn from the colonial masters, who had been working overtime to set up a different kind of colonial order with much less pain. But, it did not happen.

HOW BRITAIN LEFT BLOOD TRAILS

Most of today's festering conflicts can be traced to colonial-era meddling – through partition, or worse, indiscriminately corralling unrelated ethnic groups into a single, quarrelsome country.

SRI LANKA: During their 150-year rule, the British favoured Tamils and other minority ethnic groups over the majority Sinhalese. After 1947's national elections, the Sinhalese tried to reverse the discrimination, culminating in a quarter-century-long civil war.

INDIA/PAKISTAN: When the Brits arrived, the subcontinent was a patchwork of princely states. When they left, they divided it up by religion, prompting mass migration and perhaps a million deaths. Kashmir, which had a Hindu leader and a Muslim majority, has been contested ever since.

IRAQ: Border disputes and ethnic tensions have been rife since 1920, when the British forged modern-day Iraq out of three Ottoman states of Baghdad, Basra, and Mosul. The Brits decamped after a 1958 revolution, but their handiwork lives on.

SUDAN:A British-Egyptian alliance ruled North and South Sudan separately until 1946, when the Brits abruptly changed their minds and decided the two should merge. The north was economically and politically favoured over the south, and civil war has been on and off ever since.

ISRAEL/PALESTINE: As anti-Semitism gained ground in Europe, an influx of Jews complicated land claims, but the Brits flip-flopped on the declaration of Isreal as the Jewish homeland and proposed partition, which was rejected by both sides. In 1948 they left it up to the UN.

NIGERIA: The West African nation was once two distinct states – officially joined in 1914, but administered by the British separately until independence in 1960. Here, the British favoured the south, setting the stage for decades of strife.

The Holy Roman Empire was neither holy, nor Roman, nor an empire, in any way. It was a succession of German rulers, all of whom fell into the dustbin of history, one by one.

– Voltaire

16

The Holy Roman Empire

It is the name applied to the empire of Charlemagne and his successors. And, also to the German Empire (962-1806), both being regarded as the Roman Empire. Which is not true.

It was the Roman imperial title which had lapsed in western Europe in the 5th century, and revived in 800 by Pope Leo III and conferred on Charlemagne, king of the Franks. Since then, the title was held by successive dynasties of German kings almost continuously from the mid-10th century until its abolition. The Latin phrase *Sacrum Romanum imperium* (Holy Roman Empire) actually dates only from 1254, though the term was used in 1157, and the words Roman Empire in 1034 denoted the lands under the emperor Conrad-II. Otto-II (died in 983) was called Roman emperor, but his predecessors were simply called *imperator augustus* (august emperor). The form Holy Roman emperor is a convention adopted by modern historians; it was never officially used. The heir to the throne was called king of the Romans. It is the name applied to the Empire of

This gold bust of Charlemagne was made in 1349 for Charles IV, as Holy Roman Emperor.

Charlemagne and his successors and to the German Empire (962-1806), both being regarded as a revival of the Roman Empire.

The territory of the Empire originally included what is now Germany, Austria, former Czechoslovakia, Switzerland, eastern France, Low Countries, and parts of northern and central Italy. But its sovereign was usually the German king, and the German lands were always its chief component; after the mid-15th century, it was known as the Holy Roman Empire of the German Nation.

Originally allied with the papacy, the Empire became involved in a long struggle with the popes for the leadership of Christian Europe between the mid--11th and the mid-13th century. Weakened by the effects of this struggle, the Empire was further shaken by the 16th century Reformation, during which a split developed between the Catholic emperor and the German princes who adopted Protestantism. A series of conflicts followed, climaxed by the Thirty Years' War, which devastated Germany in the period 1618-48. After 1648, the Empire was simply a loose collection of semi-independent states under the nominal authority of the emperor. In this period, the French writer Voltaire described it as "neither holy, nor Roman, nor an Empire."

In spite of their bitter quarrels, the Empire and the papacy remained closely associated throughout the Middle Ages, and until the beginning of the 16th century the German king, having been elected emperor by the leading German princes, was then crowned by the pope. Maximilian-I (reigned 1493-1519) was the first emperor not to be so crowned; his successor, Charles-V, did have a papal coronation in 1530, but the custom was abandoned in the war-torn period that followed, and it was never revived.

GERMAN REICHS

Beginning in the early 15th century, the imperial title and the German kingship became virtually hereditary in the Austrian House of Habsburg although formal elections were still held. In 1804, when Napoleon Bonaparte declared himself emperor of the French in a bid to usurp the Holy Roman Emperor's traditional primacy among European monarchs, Francis-II, last of the imperial line, adopted the title "Emperor of Austria." Two years later, he resigned the old title altogether. For this reason, the German Empire of 1871-1918 was often called the *Second Reich* (Empire) to indicate its descent from the medieval Empire and by the same reasoning, Adolf Hitler referred to Nazi Germany as the *Third Reich.*

CHARLEMAGNE CROWNED HOLY ROMAN EMPEROR (AD 800)

Christmas Day, AD 800, can be regarded as one of the most important dates in history; for, it was on that day that Charles, King of the Franks, was crowned by Pope Leo III to become known as Charles the Great, or Charlemagne (*c.* AD 742-814). This date is often looked on as the beginning of the Middle Ages.

Charlemagne was the grandson of Charles Martel, who defeated the invading Saracens in the battle of Tours (AD 752), and his father was *Pepin the Short* who seized the Frankish kingdom from Childeric, the last of the Merovingian kings. On Pepin's death in AD 768, his kingdom was divided between his two sons, Charles and Carloman, but the latter died three years later and Charles became king of all France.

He faced a grim world. Europe was torn apart by dissension, ignorance, greed and superstition which surrounded him on all sides. With a Cross in one hand and a sword in the other, he began his great work. He conquered the Saxons and the Lombards, subdued the barbarian Avars on the Danube, fought in Spain against the Muslims and in Germany against the Magyars. By the time of his death, he ruled an empire that stretched from the Baltic to the Spanish Marches, from Brittany to the Lower Danube.

He was not only a soldier, however. He encouraged scholarship and music and also built many churches and palaces. At his death, only one of his sons, Louis the 'Pious' (AD 778-840) was living. By the Treaty of Verdun (AD 843) the empire was divided amongst Louis' sons, and split into quarrelling fragments.

The Holy Roman was conceived as a replacement for the Carolingian Empire in the Christian imperial tradition of the Roman emperor Constantine. It has been called the greatest mistake of the medieval popes; for, instead of establishing a powerful secular deputy to rule Christendom, they created a rival. From Otto-I's coronation in 962, the Empire became associated with the German crown, even after it passed to the Austrian Habsburgs in the 15th century. The Empire consisted of duchies, counties and bishoprics owing formal allegiance to the emperor. But clashes occurred between the emperor and the nobility, specially over the emperor's claims to sovereignty in Italy. Emperor Henry-IV struggled with the Church over the right to appoint bishops and senior clergy in the 11th century. Frederick-I made a sustained attempt to bring Italy and the papacy under his military control but was finally defeated at the Battle of Legnano in 1176. Open warfare broke out between the Guelphs (allies of the pope) and the Ghibellines, the imperial party. After the death of Emperor Frederick-II in 1250, German imperial power waned. The first Habsburg emperor was Rudolph-I from 1274, and the Empire remained in the family's hands until its dissolution in 1806.

This title was revived in 1530 when King Charles-I of Spain was crowned as Holy Roman Emperor. His Empire included Spain, Germany, the Netherlands, Sardinia and Sicily, together with newly conquered territory in the Americas. But the Reformation and the Thirty Years' War caused upheavals which challenged the power of the Catholic Habsburgs, and the emperors lost power during a series of wars against Louis XIV. In the 18th century, Prussia under Frederick- II emerged as the leading German power, and the imperial crown was surrendered to Napoleon in 1806. The Empire was not revived after his downfall. This was the infamous end of the Holy Roman Empire which is seen as the first attempt to unite Europe.

END OF THE HOLY ROMAN EMPIRE (1806)

The Holy Roman Empire is sometimes regarded as originating with Charlemagne although some claim it began with the coronation in AD 962 of Otto the Great, King of Germany, as Roman Emperor. The last emperor, Francis-II of Austria, abolished the title following the defeat at Austerlitz, so that it would not pass to Napoleon.

The lamps are going out all over Europe; we shall not see them lit again in our lifetime.
– Lord Grey of Falloden, August 3, 1914 (on the eve of Britain's declaration of war)

17

World War I
When Europe became killing field

The World War I was fought as a local conflict to suppress Serbian nationalism and contain Balkan revolt against the Austria-Hungary empire. But, it caught up like a bushfire to involve about 90% of the world's population and the colonial powers over the issues which were never clearly known.

Austria-Hungary's declaration of war against Serbia on July 28, 1914, precipitated the most widespread war in human history up to that time. Before the end came in 1918, about 90 per cent of the world's population was to become involved in the conflict. The causes of the struggle go far back into the past and deep down into the subsoil of European political, economic, ethnic, and geographical conditions. As President Wilson put it in 1917: You can explain most wars very simply, but the explanation of this war is not simple. Its roots run deep into obscure soils of history.

Three main conflicts went to produce the war. The first arose from the French desire to recover Alsace and Lorraine, and the struggle of French and German industrialists to control the iron of Lorraine and the coal of the Ruhr. The second was caused by the desire of Russia to dominate the Balkans as an outlet to the Mediterranean, and of Germany to do the same as a step to economic control of the area. The third lay in the colonial ambitions of the powers, who had partitioned Africa and divided China into spheres of influence, especially in the ambitions of Germany which had been left behind in the scramble for colonies. The powers were divided into two rival alliances: the Triple Alliance of Germany, Austria, and Italy, formed in 1882, and the Triple

Entente of Britain, France, and Russia, formed in 1895-1907. To be true, the period preceding the world conflagration was international anarchy. Among the other important causes of World War I, the following may be listed.

SECRET ALLIANCES: During the decades before 1914, a strong feeling of insecurity gripped the European nations. Separated by language, national traditions, and by different ways of thought as well as by political lines, they found it difficult to understand one another. These differences, coupled with conflicting ambitions, gave rise to suspicion, fears and mistrust. These fears caused the citizens of every country, great or small, to seek protection against the "evil designs" of other nations. Since national alliances appeared to offer security, the nations gradually entered into treaties with other states which considered themselves threatened by the same enemies. The war was fought between the Allied Powers (the British Empire, France, Russia, Italy, the USA, Japan, Belgium, Serbia, Montenegro, Greece, Romania and Portugal) and the Central European Powers (Germany, Austria-Hungary, Turkey, and Bulgaria).

The two rival groups were called Triple Alliance and Triple Entente. Of the two, the *Triple Alliance* was the older. It was the handiwork of Bismarck. Having achieved his purpose of unifying Germany, Bismarck wanted to become a man of peace and also to consolidate the new empire. Keeping the peace was, however, not an easy task, for, he had made a number of enemies in creating German unity. One nation alone he did not fear; what he feared most was a coalition against Germany. Consequently, it became the primary purpose of his diplomacy to prevent the formation of such a coalition. The nucleus of any combination of powers against Germany, he knew, would be France, for the French could not forget that Prussia had taken Alsace and Lorraine from them in 1871. Bismarck himself had said during the Franco-Prussian war, "France will consider any peace simply as an armistice." At first, he tried to make the French forget the lost provinces by encouraging them to embark on imperialist ventures and when this failed, he decided to isolate France. "So long as France has no alliances," he said, "she is no danger to Germany."

DUAL ALLIANCE

Believing that colonial interests would sooner or later lead to a clash between France and Great Britain, Bismarck concluded a defence alliance with Austria-Hungary in 1879, known as the Dual Alliance. The main provisions of the treaty were that in case of an attack on either ally by Russia, the other was bound to come to its defence; in case of attack on either by any other power, the other was bound to maintain a benevolent neutrality. In 1882, Bismarck expanded the Dual Alliance into a Triple Alliance which included Italy. The treaty signed by the three nations provided that if Italy were attacked by France, the other signatories were bound to give full assistance; Italy, in turn, was to come to Germany's aid if the latter were attacked by France; if one or two signatories were attacked by two or more great powers, all were to join against the attackers.

ARMS RACE: Alliances sparked off arms race. Careful, and persistent preparations were regarded as essential to success. In many countries periodicals cited with relish such statements as that of Theodore Roosevelt: Victory in any contest will go to the nation that has earned it through preparation. Consequently all the great powers of Europe, with the exception of Great Britain, modelled their armies on the Prussian system of compulsory service. Ever-increasing sums were lavished on things military and ever more formidable weapons were heaped up until all Europe was armed to the teeth. In time, the burden of military expenditures became so heavy that it deprived the governments of the means for dealing with domestic ills. Nevertheless, the armament race continued. No nation, not even the most peaceful one, dared withdraw for fear of annihilation. Paradoxically, none of them wanted war. Most of them were building arms because they believed that the maintenance of large armies and navies was the sure way of preserving peace. Finally, all the nations were so much armed that they started searching for enemy.

ECONOMIC IMPERIALISM: The bad relations between the European states during the decades preceding 1914 were further aggravated by economic competition. This was particularly true of the relations between Germany and Britain. Probably the most striking feature in the history of the German Empire between 1870 and 1914 was its development from an agricultural to a manufacturing and commercial nation. An agricultural nation in 1870, Germany had by 1914 come to be second only to the United States in manufacturing and Britain in shipping. During this period, Germany's export trade had increased three-fold. Germany produced twice as much steel as Great Britain. But, German industries not only produced goods in quantity; they also manufactured them so cheaply that German merchants were able to undersell their competitors in the world markets. While practically all the European nations raised tariff barriers against German goods, the British still adhered to a policy of free trade. With the result, the markets in the United Kingdom were flooded with goods, bearing the legend, "*Made in Germany.*" In other words Britain, which for decades had been "the workshop of the world," now saw its industrial and commercial supremacy threatened. Thus, German economic rivalry, by arousing British apprehension and antagonism, became one root cause of the war between the two countries. The development of industry and commerce in Germany was accompanied by a growing desire to seek colonial adventures. While her industrialists loudly demanded colonies as a source of raw materials and an outlet for surplus products, insisting that the prosperity of the empire would not be secure without colonies, jingoists asserted that Germany by reason of her greatness must play a major role in colonial affairs.

While Bismarck was content to make Germany the dominant power on the continent, the young Kaiser Wilhelm II (1859-1941) decided to transform Germany into a world power. So, the Germans began to look about for undeveloped territories which might be exploited with profit. But, they found that all the colonies had been captured by others. When the German government sought to share the exploitation of some of these territories, trouble ensued. In Asia, German interests clashed with those of Japan and Russia; in northern Africa German activities caused difficulties with France, Great Britain and Spain, and when Germany turned to the Far-East, both Russia and Great Britain saw their plans for the domination of that part of the globe menaced. All in all, Germany's efforts generated much friction but gained few profitable colonies. Kaiser William-II forced Bismarck to resign in 1890. On the outbreak of revolution in 1918, the King fled to Holland and died there.

NATIONALISM: Another factor which intensified the hostility between the Triple Alliance and the Triple Entente was the spirit of nationalism which is an idea that people of the same nationality should be united in one state which had contributed to the unification of Italy and Germany but it also excited political desire in the smaller national groups. Italians in the Austrian Empire and French in Alsace-Lorraine, to mention only two, wished to be united with their "mother states." In the Balkans, this spirit was working like a leaven. By the end of the century, nationalism had disrupted the Ottoman Empire and was threatening the Austro-Hungarian Empire with disintegration. A conglomeration of nationalities and creeds, which the Habsburgs had been unable to fuse into one nation, (the Austro-Hungarian Empire) contained many ardent nationalists who were desirous of joining their brethren, living in independent states.

Action on the lines of trenches through Ypres, Arras, Albert Rheims to Verdun was most intense during World War I.

There were, for example, more than five million Serbs who wanted to be united with Serbia. When pan-Serb propaganda was circulated in its southern provinces, the Austro-Hungarian Empire wanted to suppress it. But, the agitators were being encouraged by Russia, who posed as the big brother and protector of the Slavic peoples. Having, in large part, achieved its purpose of weakening the Ottoman Empire, the Russian government planned to undermine the strength of Austria-Hungary in the hope of being able to get control of Constantinople and the Straits, so that it would have a warm-water port in the south and an outlet in the Mediterranean. This was, of course, incompatible with ambitions of Germany which had become the most influential of the great powers. Thus, the Balkan question was a fertile source of antagonism between the two great alliances. Austria - Hungary (also Austro - Hungarian empire) was the dual monarchy established in 1867 by the Austrian emperor Franz Josef, according to which Austria and Hungary became autonomous states under a common sovereign.

THE STORM BREAKS

The European situation was distinctly critical by 1914: "The feeling that the nations are moving toward a conflict, urged by an irresistible force grows by the day," a Frenchman wrote at the close of 1913. Several months earlier, an Englishman had written: "Very likely, we stand close to a great war." In May 1914, Colonel House, who had been sent to Europe to promote better relations between the European states and the United States, reported: "The situation is extraordinary. The whole of Germany is charged with emotion. Everybody's nerves are tense. It only needs a spark to set the whole thing off." And, the spark came with the murder on June 28, 1914, of the Archduke Francis Ferdinand, heir-apparent to the Habsburg throne, and his wife in Sarajevo, capital of Bosnia. The actual assassin was a twenty-year-old Serbian youth, Gavrilo Princip, but the crime was instigated by the Narodna Qdbrana, a powerful pan-Serbian society whose main object was to break up the Habsburg Empire so that the Serbs under Austrian rule could be included in a Greater Serbia. The Serbs hated the archduke because he was planning to convert the Dual Monarchy into a Triple Monarchy in which the Serbs within the empire were to have self-government. It was feared that the success of this plan would make the Serbs under Habsburg rule less desirous of becoming a part of Serbia and, thus, frustrate the dream of a Greater Serbia. Hence, when it was announced that the archduke and his wife would attend military parade at Sarajevo on June 28 of 1914, plans were laid to assassinate him. A group of young men, inflamed by the pan-Serbian propaganda, armed themselves with bombs and pistols. Although a number of members of the Serb cabinet, including the prime minister, knew of the plot, they made no attempt to warn the Austrian government. The archduke and his wife reached Sarajevo on schedule and after the attempt to blow them up with a bomb failed, they were shot with a pistol.

The news of the assassination shocked Europe, but the Austrian ministers shed no tears. To them the death of Francis Ferdinand not only meant the removal of a figure whose accession they had feared but also offered to put an end to the anti-Austrian movement which was threatening the existence of the empire. The day after the crime Count Berchtold, the foreign minister is reported to have told the chief of the general staff that the time had come to settle the Serbian question once for all by making war on Serbia. The chief of staff eagerly supported the idea, stating that the Dual Monarchy must "choose between allowing itself to be strangled and making a last effort to prevent its destruction."

ONLY PEACE BETWEEN EQUALS LASTS: WOODROW WILSON

What Berchtold wanted was only a local war. Nevertheless, he could not embark upon such a war unless Germany was willing to promise full support in the event of Russia's entry into the conflict on Serbia's side. So, he sent a special envoy to Germany to obtain the promise of German support. The mission was successful. On July 5, 1914 the kaiser gave assurance that Austria "could depend on the complete support of Germany." At least two motives impelled Kaiser Wilhelm II to promise "wholehearted support." First, he was convinced that Russia was not ready for war and would back down as it did in 1908 and 1913. Second, he saw that the Habsburg Empire was Germany's one dependable ally and as such must be kept strong.

Thus, the shots fired by Princip, the Serbian nationalist that killed Archduke Franz Ferdinand, started the First World War. Britain declared war on Germany on August 4, 1914, after Kaiser Wilhelm II's forces had invaded Belgium, whose independence Britain had guaranteed. While the Royal Navy was the world's largest, Britain alone in Europe possessed no conscript army. Britain's secretary of state for war, Lord Kitchener, set about creating a volunteer army which by the end of 1915 numbered 2.5 million men. But, in January 1916, as recruiting figures slumped and casualties rose, Britain was forced for the first time to introduce compulsory military service.

THE TRENCH WARFARE

The German attempt to inflict a knockout blow against France before the Russian mobilisation was completed was checked at the Battle of the Marne (a river near Paris) in September 1914. By then, it had become clear that the range, accuracy and firepower of modern weapons, especially the machine gun, were such that soldiers could survive on the battlefield only by taking shelter in trenches. All attempts by both sides to outflank the other failed. By the end of the First Battle of Ypres in November 1914 the British Expeditionary Force, under Sir John French, was almost wiped out, and by December 1914 opposing lines of trenches extended from the English Channel to Switzerland. For the next four years, the Allies and the Germans tried to find a means of ending the stalemate of trench warfare. This resulted in successive attempts to breach the enemy lines by the use of artillery bombardments, poison gas and the development of the tank. Casualty rates were enormous. In 1916 Allied losses in the Battles of Verdun and the Somme were more than 1.1

million, with the Germans also losing almost as many. In that year, the British Army under Sir Douglas Haig was suffering an average monthly casualty of 44,000 men, a figure which by 1918 had increased to 75,000. The most important theatre of war after France was the Eastern Front, where Austria-Hungary and Germany confronted Russia. The Russians had achieved initial successes, invading East Prussia and even, it was thought, threatening Berlin itself. But with the reinforcements from the Western Front, Generals Paul von Hindenburg and Erich Ludendorff were able to secure a stunning victory over the Russians at the Battle of Tannenberg, where more than 100,000 prisoners were taken.

FEBRUARY REVOLUTION AND ALEXANDER KERENSKY

By 1917, the Russian army had suffered enormous losses and, despite winning a great victory over the Austrians during General Alexei Brusilov's offensive in the summer of 1916, it was exhausted. After the success of the February 1917 Revolution, the Provisional Government under Alexander Kerensky mounted another offensive in the summer of 1917. This failed, due in part to mass disaffection among the troops. The Bolshevik (October 1917) Revolution ended Russia's war effort and in March 1918 concluded a humiliating peace with the signing of the Treaty of Brest-Litovsk. In addition to the Eastern Front, there were a number of "sideshows". More than a million British troops took part in campaigns against Germany's ally Turkey on the Gallipoli peninsula, where Australian and New Zealand forces distinguished themselves, and in Egypt, Palestine and Mesopotamia (now Iraq). In the Balkans, the Serbs threw back the Austrians, but were defeated by a combined force of Austrians, Romanias and Bulgarians in the winter of 1915-16. To assist the Serbs, an Allied force which eventually totalled 600,000 men was landed at Salonika. In May 1915, Italy joined the Allies after having been given lavish promises of enemy territory. The Italian front was stabilised along the River Isonzo for two and a half years before the Italians were forced back from Caporetto to the River Piave in October 1917 by an Austro-German force. An Anglo-French force was sent to aid the Italians, who avenged Caporetto a year later at the Battle of Vittorio Veneto. Farther afield, there were campaigns in Africa to mop up German colonies. Most fell quickly, but in German East Africa, defending forces were still fighting at the time of the Armistice.

The World War I had a profound effect on civilian life in all the warring nations. In Britain, the government introduced the Defence of the Realm Act, which gave it sweeping powers. News was censored, the coal mines were nationalised, property was requisitioned, the sale of alcohol was restricted and Summer Time was introduced. Food rationing was imposed in 1918. Germany suffered greatly from the Allied blockade. In all countries the influx of men into the armed forces caused labour shortages which resulted in women doing jobs in industry, transport, agriculture and commerce that had until then been done by men. In Britain, more than 100,000 women joined the auxiliary services of the forces.

US JOINS WAR

Aircraft were used for the first time in large numbers during the war: the Germans raided British and French cities both with aircraft and Zeppelin airships, while Paris was also bombarded by long-range guns. These raids put the civilian in the front line for the first time, and some 1,500 British civilians died as a result of this new form of warfare. Above the trenches airmen engaged in combat, and "aces" such as Manfred von Richthofen (the "Red Baron"), Albert Ball, Georges Guynemer and Eddie Rickenbacker became national heroes. The Allied blockade made the Germans retaliate with a campaign of unrestricted submarine warfare against merchant shipping. In the spring of 1917, this campaign brought Britain close to defeat, but it also precipitated the USA's entry into the war on April 6, 1917. The adoption of the convoy system and a huge increase in British and American shipbuilding enabled the Allies to overcome the U-boat threat.

After the collapse of Russia, the Germans attempted a knockout blow to defeat the British and French before American aid could become effective. Their offensive, which began on March 21, 1918, was initially successful and the Allies' situation appeared desperate. But the tide turned during the summer of 1918 and the Allies, joined by the US went on to offensive. The British won a spectacular series of battles and the Germans were forced to ask for an armistice. *This came into effect at 11 am on Monday, November 11, 1918*. A final settlement, reached at the Paris Peace Conference dominated by the US president Woodrow Wilson and the British and French premiers David Lloyd George and Georges Clemenceau, was put in the Treaty of Versailles signed in June 1919. Germany lost territory and her army was restricted to 100,000 men. She had to pay huge compensation – $5 billion in gold marks to be paid between 1919 and 1921, with reparations to be fixed later – for war damage and to admit her guilt for starting the conflict. These terms created great bitterness in Germany, where a strong desire to upset the Treaty was soon apparent. As Marshal Ferdinand Foch, the Allied commander, observed: "This isn't peace, but an armistice for 20 years."

CONSEQUENCES: World War I was a watershed for both Europe and the USA and had far-reaching consequences on both sides of the Atlantic. The Treaty of Versailles, mostly at the insistence of France, sought to disarm and punish Germany, and to weaken it with reparations. Industrial assets were taken away from the Ruhr by the French, the Rhineland was demilitarized, and limits were set on the strength of the German Army. These factors, combined with weak government the Weimar Republic, made Germany even more vulnerable to the ravages of the Depression than other European nations. And these combined to form a breeding ground for German resentment and resurgent nationalism. Hitler and National Socialism were the inevitable consequence.

The events of World War I accelerated the collapse of the Russian monarchy, the 1917 revolution, and the rise of Bolshevism. They also led directly to the collapse of the Austro-Hungarian Empire and the creation of new nation states in Central Europe. The war also engaged the USA in Europe's affairs; after the sinking of US ships by German submarines in 1917, the US navy underwent major expansion in 1917-18, confirming the USA as a global naval power. US intervention in 1917 created a precedent for its involvement in 1942 in World War II. The 1914-18 war weakened Europe economically. While Europe struggled to recover, the US prospered. But the disparity between the European and US economies meant that there were no export markets for American goods resulting in depression. The Wall Street crashed of 1929 and the Great Depression. Though the World War I was fought to end all wars, it led directly to the policies of appeasement of Hitler in the 1930s and, hence, World War II.

Why was World War I so dramatic and so traumatic? Because it marked the beginning of the end of European-led imperialism which finally ended 20 years later. Its death toll was staggering, and it led to several cataclysmic events that cast their shadow over the rest of the century. The first side effect was that it destabilized the Russian czarist regime, unleashing the Bolshevik revolution. A relatively backward Russia, which was the last in Europe to come out of serfdom, fell into turmoil under the burdens of war. Vladimir Lenin and a small group of conspirators were able to seize power with very little popular support and institute a revolutionary doctrine that sent Russia on a seventy-five-year detour of enormous brutality and economic waste. At their maximum extent, the communist doctrines that Lenin and Joseph Stalin instituted in Russia ensnared roughly a third of the world's population, including China, the Eastern European states, Cuba, North Korea, and other self-styled revolutionary states aligned with the former Soviet Union.

FINANCIAL INSTABILITY

Another great consequence of World War I was the prolonged financial instability in Europe. The war created a morass of interlocking financial and economic problems, including the mountain of debt incurred by combatant countries; the destruction and break-up of the Ottoman and Hapsburg empires and their replacement by small, unstable, and feuding successor states; and the Allied claims for reparation payment from Germany, which embittered the next generation of Germans and was one of the rallying points for Hitler's rise to power.

WORLD WAR I, at a glance

FOR MORE THAN FOUR years, the world was engaged in a war with a ferocity and on a scale never seen before. World War I arose out of the economic, colonial, and military rivalry of the European empires. The assassination in 1914 of the heir to one of those empires – Austria-Hungary – was the spark that set the rivalries alight. Within months, fighting had broken out in Europe, Africa and Asia. By the time the war ended in 1918, the old empires were in ruins, their place taken by a new world power – the USA. World War I was the first truly international war in history. People from every continent took part in the fighting. In Africa and Asia, the Turkish Empire and former German colonies were overrun by British Empire troops. There was also fighting in the Middle East and in the Pacific. The entry of the USA into the war in 1917 marked the end of European dominance of world affairs.

Outbreak of War

On 28 June 1914, the heir to the Austrian throne was killed in Serbia. Austria invaded Serbia, Russia came to Serbia's aid, and Germany supported Austria. Fearing war on two fronts, Germany invaded Belgium and France. Britain then declared war on Germany.

Western Front

The German plan was to sweep through Belgium and northern France to capture Paris and knock the French out of the war within weeks. This plan was thwarted by the French army at the River Marne. Both sides then dug lines of defensive trenches, which stretched from the English Channel to the Swiss border, to protect their positions.

Eastern Front

The war in Eastern Europe, between Germany and Austria-Hungary on one side, and Russia on the other, was more fluid than in the west. Most battles were held in open country, across what is now Poland and in the eastern Mediterranean. The war expanded into Asia when Turkey attacked Russia at the end of 1914 and the Allies launched the ill-fated Gallipoli campaign. Turkey also posed a threat in Syria and Palestine and so Allied troops were sent from Egypt to defend the region.

The Somme

On 1 July 1916, Allied troops (those on the British and French side) tried to break through German lines near the River Somme, France. By the end of the four-month battle, the Allies had advanced 8 km. One million men were killed.

Passchendaele

In July 1917, the Allies tried again to get through German lines, this time near the village of Passchendaele, Belgium. Bad weather turned the area into a sea of mud, over 300,000 Allied troops lost their lives, and hardly any advance was made.

Manfred von Richthofen

The most famous pilot of the war was the German airman Manfred von Richthofen (1892-1918). He is said to have destroyed 80 Allied aircraft before he was killed when his aircraft was shot over France. He was known as the Red Baron because of his bright red Fokker triplane.

The Civilian War

The huge armies of World War I needed a massive force of back-up workers to provide them with weapons, food and other supplies. The entire civilian workforce was directed towards war work, producing arms and ammunition, growing food, and keeping industry and commerce going at home while millions of soldiers fought at the front.

Women in War

Before 1914, women traditionally worked in jobs men did not want. During the war, women were required to do jobs normally done by the men fighting at the front. Across Europe, women worked in factories and offices, drove buses and trams, dug fields and even joined the police forces.

New Weapons

The main weapons used in the war were the rifle (with its bayonet), the machine gun, and the artillery shell. In April 1941 the German army introduced a new weapon – gas – which both sides larger used to deadly effect. The British first used tanks at the Somme in September 1916, and both sides made more and more use of aircraft – at first for reconnaissance, later for bombing.

Propaganda

To stiffen morale and weaken the enemy's resistance, both sides used propaganda. People were made to believe the worst of the other side, with leaflets, posters, and radio broadcasts, all used for propaganda. Those who refused to fight were given white feathers, a sign of "cowardice".

End of the War

In mid-1918, fresh US troops arrived to fight on the Allied side, and there was increasing hunger and discontent among the German soldiers. The Allies broke through the German lines in August 1918. Austria-Hungary and Turkey collapsed in October, and the Allies finally forced Germany to make peace on 11 November 1918.

The Treaty of Versailles

The peace treaty was signed on 28 June 1919 in the palace of Versailles, France, Germany lost territory, and had to limit the size of its army, as well as pay compensation to the Allies. Subsequent treaties redrew the map of Eastern Europe.

The Cost of War

No one knows how many people died in the war. About 9 million soldiers and possibly 13 million civilians were killed. A further 20 million died in the influenza epidemic that swept Europe during 1918-19. Poppies, which grew on the fields of France, became the symbol of those killed in the war.

War Art

The horrors of the war inspired painters and poets on both sides. The old romantic idea of war as a great cause was replaced by the realization of its cruelty and destructive force. Many young artists and writers fought at the front; some, such as the British poet Wilfred Owen (1893-1918) were killed in the fighting.

Timeline

June 1914 Archduke Franz Ferdinand, heir to the throne of Austria-Hungary, is assassinated; Serbia is blamed.

July 1914 Austria-Hungary invades Serbia in retaliation; France, Germany and Russia mobilize their armies in preparation for war.

August 1914 Germany declares war on Russia and France and invades Belgium; this involves Britain into the war; Germany pushes back Britain at Mons, Belgium; Germany defeats Russia at Tannenberg.

February 1911 German forces try to capture French fortress of Verdun in a 10-month battle.

May 1916 British and German fleets fight inconclusive Battle of Jutland, off Denmark.

July-November 1916 Battle of the Somme; tanks used for first time.

April 1917 USA enters war on Allied side.

July-November 1917 Battle of Passchendaele.

March 1918 Germany and Russia make peace at Brest-Litovsk.

March 1918 German forces make massive advances on the Western Front.

July 1918 German advance halted.

August 1918 With the help of American forces, Allied troops make the decisive break through German lines.

October 1918 Italy defeats Austria-Hungary; both Austria-Hungary and Turkey ask for peace.

November 1918 Armistrice signed between Germany and the Allies.

June 1919 Peace treaty signed at Versailles, France. The conditions imposed on Germany were later to become a major cause of World War II.

Now our follies have ended; all the soldiers, Allied and German, who have died in the war will never know why this war was fought in the first place. Let us forget that and return to work – grow food, raise family and re-build homes.

-Gen Eishenhower, Supreme Allied Commander in Europe, after the end of World War II in May 1945.

18

World War II
The world at arms

The World War II was fought for six years, six months and four days when the entire Europe turned into a slaughterhouse. The area between the Pyrenees, in the east, and the Volga, in the West, became a vast burial ground. And, when the Last Post was sounded at the end of the war, Supreme Allied Commander Eisenhower, looking at the decaying corpses in the battlefield, said; "This is what we have fought to win."

Hopes for lasting peace after the end of the World War I in 1918 were short-lived. The next 20 years witnessed a series of diplomatic crises that foreshadowed a new world war. Fascist dictatorships, bent on territorial expansion and cultural domination, were established in Italy under Benito Mussolini and in Germany where Adolf Hitler became Chancellor in January 1933. Japanese militarism threatened peace in Asia. The basic causes of World War II are no less complex than those which brought about the World War I. Among the factors which made Europe move toward war were;

ECONOMIC CONFLICTS: The struggle for markets, raw materials, and colonies, which had been one of the major causes of World War I, did not abate since; it became more acute. The two countries which, on the eve of World War I, were struggling to acquire colonies as sources of raw materials, and markets were Italy and Germany. Whereas the Italians felt that they should have received a larger share of the spoils, the Germans were disappointed because they had been deprived after World War I of the few colonies they had managed to acquire. The third aspiring country was Japan which was also nursing imperialist ambitions. These three countries were poorest in natural resources. The bulk of the earth's surface, wealth, and population was controlled by Britain, France, the United States, Belgium, Portugal, and the Netherlands. Britain alone controlled nearly a quarter of the world's territory and population and more than a quarter of its wealth. Italy had virtually no coal, little oil, and only small iron resources. The situation was equally bad in Japan, which had limited quantities of coal and iron, no oil, and so small an area of arable land that it was difficult to meet the needs of her growing population.

THE FAILURE OF THE LEAGUE OF NATIONS: After the World War I, the minds of men were fascinated by the hope held out by the League that nations might live in peace together and settle their differences at the common conference table. In other words, the League was to organise a federation of mankind in which national policies were to be voluntarily subordinated to international order. When in January 1920, a group of seven members representing Great Britain, France, Italy, Japan, Belgium, Brazil, and Spain, met in Paris to set up the Council of the League, its chairman Leon Bourgeois, described the meeting as "the birth of a new world." While the United States which had never became a member of the League although it was founded at her initiative (because the US Senate did not approve it), Germany and the other defeated nations were excluded from the Council. Hence, in German eyes the League appeared as a committee of conquerors whose prime purpose was to uphold the Versailles settlements.

The first year of the League's existence was largely occupied in building up the machinery of international administration. Problems referred to it in early years dealt largely with the delimitation of frontiers. Some of these problems were solved with considerable success. But, in 1924 the spirit of the League changed. For the first time, the offer of a seat to Germany was discussed, and in the next year Germany was admitted and the Locarno treaties were adopted. (Locarno treaties were a series of diplomatic documents signed in Locarno, Switzerland, on October 16, 1925 which guaranteed Germany's existing frontiers with France and Belgium. And Germany was made a member of the League of Nations.) The League's greatest failure was its inability to achieve real progress toward disarmament. In disarming Germany, the victorious nations pledged to disarm themselves but it did not happen. There were many conferences but nothing could be done and arms continued to be piled up.

PROBLEMS OF NATIONAL MINORITIES: Another cause of antagonism was the question of minorities. The peacemakers at Paris had tried to settle such problems once and for all by adopting the Wilsonian principle of "self-determination." But its application was conditioned by such factors as economic necessity, military defence, religious and political traditions, and punishment of the defeated nations. Moreover, in many areas of central Europe, they were unable to apply the principles because the national minorities were intermixed in such a way that the drawing of clear-cut frontiers was difficult. In the Soviet Union, the plan of giving cultural freedom and equality to the many minorities ruled out the conflicts between the various language groups, but conditions were different in central Europe. There the national groups became hotbeds of ferment. Encouraged by propaganda from their "homeland," they demanded reunion with the "mother state" or full autonomy.

At the Versaille Peace Conference in 1919, Lloyd George had warned against the inclusion of large numbers of Germans in foreign states. "I am," he said, "strongly adverse to transferring Germans from German rule to the rule of some other nation. I cannot conceive any greater cause of future wars than that the German people . . . should be surrounded by a number of small states . . . each of them containing large masses of Germans agitating for reunion with their native land." His warnings were not heeded. The Nazis seized upon this violation of the principle of self-determination almost at once. They said World War I was fought for the self-determination of nationalities; why was Austria forbidden to unite with Germany and why were a large number of Germans put under foreign rule? In other words, the principle of self-determination furnished them with a convenient pretext for annexing Austria and the Sudeten. In 1939, they employed it as a pretext for the invasion of Poland which started World War II.

RESENTMENT AGAINST VERSAILLES TREATY: Even the severest critics will confess that the settlement made at Paris in 1919 removed many old injustices, but also created new ones. President Wilson's healing message of international justice and cooperation found its way into peace terms. The treaty, however, violated the whole spirit and intention of the Fourteen Points. In depriving Germany of every scrap of colonial empire, in creating the Polish Corridor which severed East Prussia from the rest of the Reich, and in cutting

Danzig away from Germany the settlement created a burning sense of injustice among Germans. More than this, in including the 'war-guilt" clause (Article 231) whereby Germany accepted full responsibility for the war, the peacemakers inflicted a bitter humiliation upon the German people. The German people did not regard the settlement of its frontiers with Poland as anything more than provisional. Like President Wilson, they insisted that the basis of durable peace must be justice, and for them justice was lacking so long as the treaties remained unrevised. Although Article Nineteen of the League Convenant provided for the reconsideration of treaties, it never happened. The Versailles Treaty never allowed the Weimar Republic to succeed. The German Republican Constitution was doomed right at its birth. The economic crisis which had engulfed the Germans was already taking the turn for worse. The heavy reparation clause in the Versaille Treaty had destroyed the viability of German economy, already shattered in the war. The League members never made use of this Article. The French, in fact, never ceased to declare that not a jot or clause of the treaty could be either expunged or altered. Germans regarded it as the chief cause of Germany's post-War difficulties.

TOTAL COLLAPSE OF GERMAN ECONOMY

It was the economic recession that induced Germans to listen to the Nazi blandishments. Economic suffering, combined with a revived consciousness of humiliation, raised their emotions. Convinced that anything would be better than nothing, they called on their leaders to do something toward lifting them out of the depression and despondency. This gave Hitler his long-awaited opportunity. During the years between 1930 and 1933, the Allies could have saved the situation by revising the treaty, but nothing was done. No sooner did Hitler come to power than he began his preparations to demolish the settlement. He did not share the hope that the treaties might be revised through international negotiation. He was convinced that "only force counts." This is the basic idea of *Mein Kampf*. "The reconquest of lost territories cannot be achieved by solemn appeals to Almighty God or pious hopes in a League of Nations, but only by armed force," Hitler said in his book.

The German mark, which had begun to slide in 1921, dropped to 75 to the dollar. The next year it fell to 400 mark to the dollar and by the beginning of 1923 to 7,000. Already in 1922, the German government asked the Allied to grant moratorium on reparation payment. The French Government of

Raymond Poincare (1860-1934) bluntly refused it. And, when the Germans defaulted on the deliveries of timber, the French troops attacked Germany and occupied Ruhr, the industrial heart of Germany which fetched the Reich four-fifths of its coal and steel. It was cut off from the rest of the country after the French attack. The paralyzing blow to German economy united the people. The workers of the Ruhr declared strike and launched passive resistance. The French countered with arrests, deportations and even death sentences. But, not a wheel in the Ruhr turned. The strangulation of the economy hastened the final plunge of the German currency which fell again in 1923 to 18,000 marks to the dollar; by July it dropped to 20,000; by August 1, to a million to the dollar. By November 1923, it took four million marks to buy one dollar!! *And, after that the German currency ceased to buy anything when the Weimar administration came to a standstill.*

RESURGENCE OF NATIONALISM: During the decades preceding 1914 schools, press, churches, literature, art, and other agencies had combined to promote nationalism. But during the war, it lost much of its glamor. The soldiers in the mud of Flanders (Belgium) as well as the civilians, under the desire to prevent another war, became lukewarm converts to international psychology. All realized that if war was to be outlawed, conflicting national ambitions would have to give way to a system of international control. This attitude was reinforced by the speeches of President Wilson and others who advocated a pacific internationalism based on cooperation and the promotion of common interests. But, when the war ended, the spirit of nationalism dictated the peace settlement in large part; with the result the framework of the "New Europe" was reconstructed on strictly national lines.

There were many other causes for the outbreak of war, like the attempt of the Communists to seize power; political instability, interference of the Allied powers in the administration of the German territory etc., but nothing was so hurting for the common man than the total collapse of the national economy. All the savings of the country were made worthless. One had to go to market with many bags of currency only to buy sausages. In the midst of these crisis, democracy ceased to be an issue for Germans. They wanted food and shelter; the former was made scarce and the latter was destroyed in the war for which there was neither money nor material to rebuild or repair. The people were starving and freezing in the open. The war spirit had, however, not died out. Unemployed ex-soldiers, restless and violent youngsters for the most part, liked to wear splendid uniforms and swagger about the streets, armed with clubs and revolvers. The soldiers who fought the war could scarcely respect the moral, ethical and religious teachings which they had learned as youths. And, why should they? The war was over, but the psychological, economic and social damage could not be repaired. Even the fundamental necessities of life were not available. Specially, in Germany which lay prostrate and punished but not punished enough to rule out its role in future.

COMMUNIST PLOT & WANDERING YOUTHS

Led by bold men, they carried on in civil life the warfare so well learnt on the Eastern and Western Fronts. They did not really know what they wanted, but in Germany and Italy, two corporals were eventually to give direction to these wanderers. It was the time when one summer evening in 1919, infantry corporal Hitler, a lonely, unhappy and frustrated man of thirty, who hated the republic, the socialist and the Jews, became the seventh member of an obscure organisation in a Munich beer hall which was later to become the Nationalist Socialist Party (or Nazi). About the time Hitler joined the Nazi Party, Benito Mussolini in Italy was forming the first detachment of Fascist Blackshirts. Europe, unfortunately, provided a fertile soil for these two wicked men who sought a solution to mankind's difficulties by violence, sadism and terror which increased as the post-War difficulties grew.

This, in brief, was the scenario when the World War II broke out, bringing to an end all that the Europeans had stood for. Europe before 1914, had common spiritual foundation; they believed in the Christian Church; took capitalism for granted, set a high value on free speech, free press; scientific inquiry and practised international trade and democratic processes. Most enlightened people believed in liberalism, democracy, parliamentarism and humanitarianism. The optimists believed that this would never end. But, it did. And, what a bloody end at that!! The rise of Hitler to full glory in 1933 (that was the year when Roosevelt took office as the President of the US over which he presided for 12 years) is a long and winding story of blood and tears. It is well to recount rapidly the event, specially for those who had not lived those fateful days.

WAR BREAKS OUT

After the treaty was signed at Versailles on June 29, 1919, Allied Commander General Foch said at a parade: "Let the German soldiers have their uniforms and weapons and go home with dignity. After all, they are brave soldiers who fought well." And, when German soldiers got their arms and uniforms, they turned stiff in salute to their commanders, also prisoners of war, and displaying high spirit and unbroken discipline, they cried *heil* to their Fatherland and walked past the dais on which stood the Allied Commander. General Foch suddenly became sad and said to the colleagues next to him. "This is not peace, but a truce for twenty years. We have only injured the German vanity without breaking it. Germans are unconquerable," said General Foch. And, it was exactly after twenty years, on September 1, 1939 Germans attacked Poland which started World War II in which more than 60 million people died and twice as many injured, maimed or crippled for life.

The global war was fought on five continents, involving more than two-thirds of World's population; fightings took place on land, air and sea, setting a record in ferocity and cruelty, the like of which was never seen before and since. It lasted for six years, six months and four days. One cannot blame Hitler alone for World War II, the situation after the Versailles Treaty was such that if there were no Hitler, Germans would have produced one. Hitler was a product of the post-World War I injustices to Germans as a consequence of which the world had to fight yet another global war, bloodier than the one fought before.

ALLIED & AXIS POWERS; BATTLELINES CLEARLY DRAWN

The war of 1939-45 was between the US, Britain, France, the USSR and China, called Allied, on the one hand, and the Nazi Germany under Hitler and Fascist Italy under Mussolini and Japan under Hirohito, called the Axis Powers, on the other hand. The war was preceded by a series of acts of aggression by the Axis power, the Japanese conquest of Manchuria (1931), the Italian conquest of Ethiopia (1935-36) and the Italian intervention in the Spanish Civil War (1936-39), Japanese invasion of China (1937), the German annexation of Austria (March 1939), Sudetanland (September 1938) and Czechoslovakia (March 1939) and the Italian conquest of Albania (April 1939). Britain and France attempted to meet this menace with an appeasement policy, culminating in the Munich agreement in September 1938. The reaction of public opinion to the annexation of Czochoslovakia forced Britain and France to open negotiations with the USSR.

MOLOTOV-RIBBONTROP PACT

When the talks broke down, the USSR concluded peace with Hitler on

September 1, 1939 – the *Molotov-Ribbontrop* Non-Aggression Pact. And two days later, Germany attacked Poland which brought Britain in the war. And this was the formal beginning of the World War II. Between August and October 1939, the Battle of Britain raged in full fury as the Luftwaffe launched mass day`light raids. When it ended, they had lost nearly 2,000 aircraft. Night raids followed directly against London and many British provinces. The Italian invaded Greece in October 1949 only to be driven back into Albania. Germany in order to complete her control of the Balkans attacked both Greece and Yugoslavia on April 1, 1941 and by May 1, had overrun both and compelled the British forces to withdraw from Greece. A month later, Crete had been invaded and occupied by German parachutists in spite of the stubborn resistance by British and Commonwealth troops.

A new front opened on June 22, 1941 when Germany, in alliance with Finland, Rumania, Hungry, attacked Russia. By December, the invaders, standing on a line from Lake Ladoga to the mouth of the Don were within 40 km of Moscow and Leningrad was besieged. A Russian counter-offensive (December 1941 - March 1942) forced the Germans to retreat. But, in June they launched a new offensive designed to secure the control of the Caucasian oilfields. Savastopol was stormed and by August they had reached the Caucasus and were attacking Stalingrad. Since the Battle of Britain, American opinion had inclined strongly towards the policy of Roosevelt of making the US an "arsenal of democracy" which was put into the operation with the passage of Lease-Lend Act in March 1941. On December 7, 1941, Japan attacked the US naval base in Pearl Harbour and declared war on Britain and the US and four days later Germany and Italy declared war on the US. Thus, the war in Europe and the Sino-Japanese war which had been in progress since 1937, now became two aspects of single world-wide conflict.

AFRICA AND THE NEAR-EAST (1940-43)

The long campaign in North Africa opened in September 1939 with an Italian drive from Libya into Egypt. General Wavel counter-attacked in December 1940 and 1941 and advanced into Cyrenaica. The withdrawl of troops for the Balkan campaign then weakened his army while German forces under Rommel were poured into Africa. During March-April, Germans pushed the British back into Egypt. A new offensive by the 8th Army in November 1942 drove them into Libya but was halted at Gazala when during May-July Rommel launched a counter offensive which ended at a place 115 km from

Alexandria. In October-November, General Montgomery, commanding the 8th Army, won a resounding victory at EL Alamein and began a rapid advance westward, while on November 8, large British and US forces under General Eisenhower landed in Morocco and Algeria. Caught between converging armies, the Axis forces in Africa surrendered in May 1943. The control of the Middle-East was important to the British position in the Mediterranean and vigorous measures proved necessary to counteract German intrigues in that area. Following the seizure of power by a pro-Axis premier in April 1941, British forces occupied Iraq and in June, Syria, where a pro-Vichy administration held power, was also occupied. In August, British and Russian troops entered Persia (Iran) where the Shah was under the German influence and converted it into an important supply-line to Russia.

VICTORY IN THE EAST 1943-45,

LANDING IN NORMANDY

The failure of the Germans to capture Stalingrad together with the victory of El Alamein and the landing in North Africa, marked the turning-point of the war. A Russian offensive in November 1942 and March 1943 cleared the Caucasus and drove Germans back to the Donetz while in Stalingrad 330,000 invaders were killed or captured. A new German drive in July was halted within a week. The Russians then opened the offensive which captured Kiev and Zhitomir during January-April 1944; they liberated the Ukraine and entered Rumania. A general offensive in June-October expelled the invaders from Russian soil, forced Finland, Rumania and Bulgaria out of the war and entered East Prussia, Poland and Yugoslavia. British forces entered Greece in October and by the end of 1994, the Germans had been expelled from the greater part of the Balkans.

The way had been prepared for the opening of the second front in the West by Allied forces, bombing raids on Germany which since 1940 had steadily increased in number and size. On June 6, 1944 the invasion was launched under the Allied Supreme Commander General Eisenhower. A bridgehead was established in North-West France between Cherbourg and Le Havre (Normandy) and after much hard fighting the American broke through the German line at St Lo and the British at Caen. On August 15, the US and French troops landed on the Mediterranean Coast and advanced rapidly northward. The people of Paris compelled the Germans to surrender on August 25, 1944.

THE GERMAN SURRENDER

By the September end, the Allied had liberated most of France, entered Belgium and the Netherlands but the airborne operation was a failure on the German frontiers, they were halted by the Siegfried Line. After a temporary setback caused by Rundstedt counter-offensive in the Ardennes in December, they launched a new offensive in February 1945 which broke the Siegfried Line. In March, the Rhine was crossed, the Canadians advanced through the Netherlands and the British into North Germany, On April 24, the Russians entered Berlin which surrendered on May 2, 1945. And, on May 7, 1945 Germans surrendered unconditionally. The war on the Japanese front was finally ended when Atomic bombs were dropped on Hiroshima and Nagasaki on August 6 and August 9, 1945. Hirohito announced the surrender on August 14, 1945. And, thus ended the greatest conflict in human history. It is 60 years now when the greatest global conflict ended but still the causes of the World War II are being discussed. And, the last word has yet to be said, so intriguing were the human relations and so disastrous were its consequences.

RUSSIA LOST 14 PER CENT OF ITS POPULATION

While the forces of Fascism tormented people in many parts of the world, their most devastating impact was on the inhabitants of Eastern Europe, especially the Soviet Union. With 27 million Soviet citizens killed in the course of the four-year conflict, the multinational socialist country lost about 14 per cent of its population. The destruction stands out in all its staggering scale when contrasted with the losses suffered by the western allies. The United Kingdom lost about 0.6 per cent of its population and the United States about 0.3 per cent. After the fall of France and the Balkans and until the Anglo-Americans landed in Sicily, the Nazi war machine operated almost wholly in the East. Rommel's Afrika Korps was about the only major unit active in the western theatre. While the western allies faced 58 German divisions after landing in Normandy, the Soviet Union never faced fewer than 226 divisions. By the end of the war, there could be no doubt about the fighting ability of the Red Army soldier or the tactical skills of commanders such as Georgi Zhukov, Ivan Koniev, and Konstantin Rokkosovsky. This was the force that destroyed 80 per cent of Nazi Germany's military power. But, at what cost? Even now, Russia has not fully recovered from the war which each Soviet family had to fight and die to win.

CONSEQUENCES

World War II destroyed many institutions and created many new ones. The Third Reich and the British Empire vanished in the thin air, so also the concept of colonialism. In their places, the UN. Atlantic Alliance and Warsaw Pact were set up which started cold war. New inventions like radar, jet aircraft and many devices were made which are widely in use now, for good or bad. The main consequence of World War II was the division of Europe by what Winston Churchill called an Iron Curtain, stretching from the Baltic to the Mediterranean. This frontier between those countries occupied by the Soviet Union in 1945 and those nations liberated by the Western allies dominated post-War politics until the collapse of the Soviet Union in 1991. It resulted in the absence of democratic government in central Europe for 40 years, but also in the creation of a democratic West Germany – which in turn became the driving force for a unified Germany. The war also spawned a host of institutions, notably the United Nations (UN), the North Atlantic Treaty Organisation (NATO), and the European Economic Community (EEC), now the European Union (EU), all of which continue to play a vital role in world politics and economy. In the UK, the welfare state was very much a consequence of the war. And, while nuclear fission would have been discovered eventually, World War II brought about an Angle-American accelerated programme of development which led directly to Hiroshima in 1945. This heralded the age of Mutual Assured Destruction (MAD) for the next 45 years, underpinned by the ideological conflicts of the Cold War. World War I produced World War II which, in turn, produced Cold War. Which the world has survived. One doesn't know when the luck will run out. And, if this does, this will be the last war and deluge.

WHAT COST TWO WORLD WARS

World War I was not like any other war Europe had known before. French and British troops went into it bare-headed. It took them over a year to follow the Germans and wear steel helmets against artillery fire. The first war, fought with mass armies, disrupted society more than any other war since the Thirty Years War in Germany. Perhaps the outstanding consequence of the War was the October Revolution in 1917 (November 6, in Western calendar), in Russia when a small band of radicals, known as *"Maximalist"* and later as *"Bolsheviks"*, seized power in the largest country of the world. Europe, divided against itself, could never get over this event. And, when Hitler was building up a massive war machine, Europeans thought the days of communism were over. This also helped the German corporal, who was shot and injured in the World War I, to seize power, strangely enough by election. Hitler was *"an elected"* dictator who promised all of Europe to the Germans. And, hereby hangs a tale.

World War II was a more complete worldwide war than World War I. More people died in World War II than in all conflicts fought in Europe since the Middle Ages. An estimate in money-term made by the Bank of International Settlements in 1948 (at that level of currency value) set the cost at £ 338,000, or four times the World War I figure of £ 84,000. The US alone spent as much on World War II as all the nations put together spent on World War I. In terms of casualties, 10 million people were killed in World War I against 60 million in the second war. It is reckoned that throughout the war, over a quarter of the people of Europe, were uprooted, either made slave labour in victor countries or forced to flee their homes. This does not include Jews, 60 million of whom perished in German gas chambers. That apart, between seven and 13 million civilian non-combatants were killed. There was not a house in Europe which did not nourish its injured or mourn its dead. In the World War I, tank was first invented and it got the victory for the Allied. In World War II, Germans could not make radar and they lost the war again. These two equipment finally clinched the issue, besides everything else.

European wars in the past, almost always, were followed by plague and famine, but no internal upheavals took place after World War II. There was no starvation; no mass deaths. Rather, most nations of the continent, except Germany, acquired the pre-war level of production within one year. This was largely because of the exploitation of colonies. In India, the Bengal famine of 1942-43 is still fresh in our minds. So also of Ethiopia (formerly Abyssinia) and other countries of Asia and Africa. As a matter of fact, 750 million people (or more than the population of Western Europe) suffered from hunger, which was the legacy of World War II. This, in brief, is the story of madness of man.

2.5 MILLION INDIAN SOIDIERS DIED FIGHTING FOR BRITISH EMPIRE

The untold stories of gutsy Indian soldiers, killed in World War II, were told in Britain in Feb 2008 to commemorate the day when, in 1944, Naik Yashwant Ghatge was killed and later awarded the Victoria Cross, UK's highest military decoration, for his superhuman valour in one of the fiercest battles of the Italian campaign. The generations across Australia, Canada, New Zealand, South Africa, UK and India were finally told how it all happened to the 23-year-old brave Indian soldier.

The Commonwealth War Graves Commission, which maintains graves of the members of the Commonwealth forces killed in the two wars, has produced educational resources for schools in these countries to tell Ghatge's story. Its Director-General Richard Kellaway said on the occasion: "It is a salute to Ghatge's duty and sacrifice; we hope his saga inspires the younger generations." Literature, CD-ROMs and DVDs on Ghatge were circulated in schools by the Commission. Ghatge, from the 5th Maratha Light Infantry, was one of the two and a half million Indian men who fought alongside the British soldiers during World War II. The VC was awarded to 20 soldiers in the Italian campaign. Eight of them, including Ghatge, lie buried near battlefields in which they fought and fell.

This is, however, only the story of one gallant Indian soldier and those of others remain untold. Indian soldiers also fought in North Africa, Central Europe and in France and Flanders. In World War-I, Indian soldiers fought on the Western Front along the *Maginot Line* and in what was then Mesopotamia, between the rivers Tigris and Euphrates, and also in the Middle East. All died unknown and unsung.

WORLD WAR II at a glance

WORLD WAR II was the most devastating war in history. For the first time ever in warfare, more civilians than soldiers lost their lives. In total, more than 50 million people were killed, including 20 million Russians, 6 million Poles and 6 million Jews. The war, which lasted from 1939-45, involved every continent, and few countries or people remained untouched by the carnage. In Europe, the strength of the Russian and American armies war was used for the first time to defeat Japan.

How war began

Adolf Hitler took power in Germany in 1933 and set out to restore German power in Europe. He built a strong army and air force, and began to expand German territory in central and Eastern Europe. On 1 September, 1939, German troops invaded Poland. In response, Britain and France declared war on Germany.

Blitzkrieg

The German army moved tanks quickly into enemy territory, supporting them by aerial bombardment. This strategy, called Blitzkrieg, (lightning war), was successful in 1939-40.

Battle of Britain

For four months in 1940, British aircraft fought against the German air force. After heavy causalities, Germany cancelled in plans to invade Britain.

Invasion on Russia

In June 1941, German troops invaded Russia. Six months later, Japanese aircraft bombed the US naval base at Pearl Harbor, bringing the USA into the war. By the end of 1941, an international alliance of the USA, Russia, and Britain confronted the Axis powers of Germany, Italy and Japan. On June, 1941, 79 German divisions invaded Russia in the biggest military operation in history. At first they made good progress, but Russian resistance ensured that they failed to capture Moscow and Leningrad.

Pearl Harbor

On 7 December, 1941, Japanese planes launched a surprise attack on the American Pacific Fleet stationed at Pearl Harbor in Hawaii, and also invaded the Philippines, Hong Kong, and Malaya. The USA then declared war on both Japan and German.

Turning Point

By mid-1942, the Germans occupied most of Europe and northern Africa, and the Japanese controlled most of the Pacific. Three battles turned the tide: Midway, where the USA stopped the Japanese; El Alamein in North Africa; and Stalingrad, where the Russians began to push back the occupying forces.

El Alamein

In 1942, German and Italian troops led by Field Marshal Rommel advanced across North Africa towards Egypt and the Suez Canal. In a lengthy battle, the British 8th Army led by General Bernard Montgomery, or "Money" defeated Rommel at El Alamein, Egypt.

Occupied Europe

Life in German-occupied Europe was hard. Food was rationed, newspapers and radio were censored, and everyone was put to work producing supplies for the German war effort, Jews lived in fear of their lives as more and more of them were rounded up and sent to their deaths in concentration camps, such as Auschwitz and Treblinka.

Civilians at war

For the first time, war was brought into the homes of people far away from the battlefield. Bombing of towns and cities meant that civilians became the targets of enemy action and often had to take refuge in shelters. At sea, submarine warfare stopped ships bringing in food and other supplies, causing severe shortages.

Rationing

Shortages all over Europe led to many types of food being rationed. Everyone was given a ration card stating what food he could buy each week. People with gardens grew their own food.

Hiroshima

The war against Japan seemed likely to continue as the Japanese fought hard to protect their country. On 6 August 1945, the US air force dropped an atomic bomb on the Japanese city of Hiroshima, and a second on Nagasaki on 9 August. The Japanese surrendered five days later.

Labour camps

In Germany, millions of Jews, gypsies, and prisoners of war were incarnated in camps. Some camps held slave labourers, who produced munitions and other supplies; others were concentration camps to exterminate Jews and other "undesirables". Conditions were inhumane, and many died of ill-treatment and starvation. Prisoners of war were also often kept in appalling conditions.

D-Day

On 6 June 1944, more than 100,000 Allied troops, supported by thousands of ships and aircraft, crossed the English Channel and landed on the beaches of France. At first they met fierce German resistance, but by 25 August the Allies had liberated Paris. By the end of the year, they had retaken the whole of France.

End of the War

By 1944, the war had turned in the Allies' favour. Italy had surrendered, and the Russians were making slow progress towards Berlin. In June 1944, the Allies invaded France, opening up a new western front. The Russians entered Berlin in April 1945, and Germany surrendered in May 1945.

Winston Churchill

Churchill (187-1965) became prime minister of Britain in May 1940. A fine orator whose speeches boosted British morale during the Battle of Britain and the rest of the war, Churchill led Britain to victory in 1945, but lost power in July 1945. He was elected prime minister in 1951-55.

Timeline

March 1936 Germany begins to expand her territory by sending troops into the Rhineland.

October 1936 Germany had Italy make an alliance – the Rome-Berlin Axis.

November 1936 Germany becomes allied with Japan.

March 1939 German troops invade Czechoslovakia.

September 1939 Germany and Russia invade Poland; Britain and France declare war on Germany.

April 1940 Germany occupies the Netherlands, Belgium and France, forcing the British to retreat.

July-October 1940 British air force defeats Germany in the Battle of Britain; preventing Germany's invasion.

December 1941 Japan bombs US Pacific Fleet, leading to US entry into the war.

1942 US fleet stops Japanese advance across the Pacific at the Battle of Coral Sea and the Battle of Midway.

November 1942 British defeat German forces at El Alamein in North Africa.

January 1943 German siege of Stalingrad (Volgograd) broken.

June 1944 Italian fascist dictator Mussolini resigns.

June 1944 D-Day landings; the Allies invade France.

June-August 1944 Russian armies reach Warsaw, Poland, and eastern Prussia.

April 1945 Adolf Hitler commits suicide, as the Russian army reaches Berlin.

May 1945 Germany surrenders.

August 1945 Atomic bombs on cities of Hiroshima and Nagasaki, Japan surrenders.

When you go home tell them of us and say: "For your tomorrow we gave our today."

– Inscription on the British 2nd Division Memorial at Kohima

19

Shaping Europe after the war

World War II continued for six years and the war of attrition, no less exhausting, lasted for 45 years, largely because of the political immaturity of Americans who won the war but lost peace. The US President Roosevelt was in hurry to bring his soldiers back home and Britain was too battered and bruised to fight the communist expansion in the east alone. Thus, the East European case for a just political order was lost by default.

Europe's future increasingly figured in Allied discussions as the war drew to a close. Poland's postwar frontiers had been mapped out in rough and ready fashion when the Big Three Allied leaders met in Tehran in November and December 1943. There, as always, Stalin knew what he wanted. This time, it was a slice of eastern Poland up to 300 km wide, an area traditionally claimed by the Russians. Poland was to be compensated by getting a slice in the west, a cut from Germany's eastern boundary, extending Poland to the Oder and Neisse rivers.

Less than a year later, Churchill met Stalin in Moscow in October 1944 and with an approach based on the old imperial concept of *'spheres of influence'*, casually suggested to Stalin a trade-off that the Soviet Union should have 90 per cent influence in Romania, 10 per cent influence in Greece, 75 per cent in Bulgaria and 50 per cent in Yugoslavia, with the remaining percentages controlled by Britain. Churchill scrawled these figures on a piece of paper and passed it to Stalin, who simply ticked it and passed it back. Churchill said that the paper should be burned as it might be thought that these issues were disposed of in an offhand manner. To this Stalin replied: "No, you can keep it".

Stalin kept his side of the bargain when it came to Greece, and did not intervene in the six-week Greek civil war in the winter of 1944-5 but the same was not true when fighting resumed in 1946. And, between the summer of 1944 and spring of 1945, the Red Army occupied all eastern Europe and the Balkans excepting Greece, Albania and Yugoslavia. By the end of the war, the Soviet Union reoccupied the Baltic states of Lithuania, Estonia and Latvia, which it had first seized in 1940; annexed much of East Prusia; took the ice-free part of Pestsamo and part of the Karelian isthmus from Finland; acquired the Ruthenian region from Czechoslovakia, and Bessarabia and parts of Bukovina from Romania; and occupied eastern Poland. All these lands were to become integral parts of the USSR. Thus, beyond the Soviet borders would stretch a protective buffer of eastern European nations that the Soviet Union had either liberated (Poland and Czechoslovakia) or invaded (Romania, Hungary and Bulgaria). Stalin gave his view in a speech in July, 1944, "Everyone imposes his own systems as far as his army can reach. It cannot be otherwise".

POLAND WAS LOST AT YALTA

In February 1945, with the German Army on the retreat and the Red Army inside the Reich, it became an urgent matter for the Allies to settle the future of Europe. They met at Yalta in the Crimea and disagreements quickly surfaced. The Americans – under great pressure to bring the soldiers home quickly once the war was over – were less forceful than the British. Roosevelt, as chairman, was perhaps more conciliatory to the calm, unshakable Stalin than he would otherwise have been. He reserved most of his suspicion not for Stalin but for the old-fashioned imperialist notions of Churchill. One of the first arguments was over the Tehran proposals for the German-Polish border. Should Poland be allotted territory up to the eastern branch of the Neisse – as Churchill and Roosevelt believed – or to the western branch 100 km nearer Germany, which was the Russian suggestion? A decision was put off until an eventual European peace conference which never took place. In any case, Stalin was determined that Poland, a traditional invaders' route into Russia, must be controlled by the USSR or its friends.

At Yalta, the Americans submitted a *Declaration on Liberated Europe;* among its provisions was the right of all peoples to choose the form of government under which they wanted to live. In reality, Poland's prospects of democracy had long since been shattered. When the Polish government-in-exile in London called for a Red Cross inquiry into the massacre of more than 4,000 Polish officers at Katyn, revealed in 1943, the Soviet Union immediately broke off relations with the London Poles and set up their own Polish provisional government in Moscow. From then on, they backed the Polish National Liberation Committee, a Communist-controlled underground military organization in Poland, rather than the London-based Polish Home Army. The provisional government moved to Lublin in 1944 and to Warsaw in 1945. Many exiled Poles chose to remain in exile rather than return to a distrusted regime.

In Yugoslavia, the situation was different. Marshal Tito's Communist-led partisans had liberated Yugoslavia with little outside help, and by the end of the war had established a self-confident Communist regime of their own. They saw no reason to exchange German occupation for Russian domination. Much the same happened in Albania; at first the new Communist regime there was friendly to Moscow, but after Stalin's death in 1953 it switched its allegiance to China. However, over the few years following the war the Russians made sure that subservient regimes were installed in Bulgaria, Romania, Hungary and Czechoslovakia.

GERMANY DIVIDED AT POTSDAM

As well as settling boundaries – and recognizing realities – in eastern Europe, the Allies had to decide what to do about Germany itself. As early as 1943, the British had been working on a plan for a three-way division of Germany and joined occupation of Berlin, code-named *'Rankin C'*. The Allies did not plan to make the division long-term, but better a divided Germany than a powerful but undependable nation of 79 million at the heart of Europe with the potential to become a Fourth Reich. The plan gave Moscow control of almost 40 per cent of Germany's postwar area, 36 per cent of its population and 33 per cent of its resources.

At Yalta, the Big Three formally agreed to the zones outlined in "Rankin C", with the addition of a smaller French zone in the Saarland, carved from the British and American areas. Berlin was divided into four sectors and was to house the Allied Control Council for supervising the occupying powers. Moscow gave informal guarantees of access by air, road, canal and rail by the Western powers. Austria was split up in similar fashion, with Vienna providing the headquarters for a four-power commission. The Allies met at Potsdam in the southern suburbs of Berlin in the summer of 1945 for their final great conference. Germany, now surrendered, was the main subject for discussion. On August 2, 1945 the leaders signed an agreement which put into effect the zoning arrangements agreed at the Yalta conference.

Roosevelt died on April 12, 1945, and his successor Harry Truman was untried in the international arena. However, Truman held a trump card. During the conference, on July 23, 1945, he announced that the United States' new secret weapon, the atomic bomb, had been successfully tested at Alamogordo, New Mexico. Churchill's reaction was: "It gives the Americans the power to shape the world; if the Russians would have got it, it would mean the end of civilization". Stalin was impassive at the news conference though he knew that the Soviet Union would also, in time, have its own nuclear arsenal. With Churchill replaced by Attlee on July 27, 1945 after Britain's general election, Stalin was the only one of the original Big Three still in office. He was the one constant factor during all the planning of postwar Europe – at the height of his power at home and unfettered by the democratic process. The outcome, settled by war and words, was that his Red Army, immensely powerful and with no other major strategic commitments, garrisoned in central Europe and held Germany's industrial areas. And, thus, ended the freedom of the countries of Eastern Europe who suffered most in the war. That things would have been different if the US had not trusted Stalin will continue to be debated, but that President Roosevelt did not give to Europe what he had promised is a fact of history.

ON TRIAL AT NUREMBERG

It was fitting that leading German war criminals should be brought to book at Nuremberg, the city where Hitler declared war. In the vast Nuremberg arena, built by Albert Speer, Hitler had roused his audiences to new fervour, their eyes shining back at him in the firelight from thousands of torches. There were practical reasons for the venue, too. Although pulverized by Allied bombing, Nuremberg still had a jail and a courthouse, the Palace of Justice, big enough to accommodate a major trial.

The 21 defendants, representing the German General Staff, government and Nazi party, were charged with crimes against peace, war crimes, crimes against humanity and conspiracy. Three more had been indicted but Martin Bormann, Hitler's secretary, had eluded capture; Robert Ley, leader of the Labour Front (the Nazi workers' and employers' organization), had committed suicide; and armaments magnate Gustav Krupp was unfit to stand trial. The prosecutors and judges were drawn from the 'Big Four' – Britain, France, the USA and USSR. In the dock, Rudolf Hess stared fixedly into space, Julius Streicher was sweating and decrepit, Field Marshal Keitel sat stiff-backed. Goring, weaned off morphine and now too thin for his uniform (stripped of all insignia), dominated the trial with a brave defence of Nazism. The trial continued, with short recesses, from November 1945 until the end of August 1946. The evidence seared the names of places such as Belsen, Buchenwald and Dachau into the conscience of the world. The defence, more often than not, was: *'I was only obeying orders'*. The judges' findings were delivered on September 30, 1946 and the sentences on the following day. Ten want to the gallows in the Nuremberg prison gymnasium in the early hours of October 16, 1946. Goring forestalled the hangman the previous evening by taking cyanide. His body and those of the other executed Nazis were incinerated in the freshly lit ovens of Dachau concentration camp and their ashes scattered in the Isar river.

SENTENCED TO DEATH: Martin Bormann (Hitler's secretary; in absentia), Hans Frank (governor of Poland), Wilhelm Frick (Interior Minister; later governor of Bohemia-Moravia), *Hermann Goring* (Luftwaffe chief), Alfred Jodl (chief of staff to Keitel), Ernst Kaltenbrunner (security chief), Wilhelm Keitel (Chief of Staff), Joachim von Ribbentrop (Foreign Minister), Alfred Rosenberg (Minister for Occupied Eastern Territories), Fritz Saukel (in charge of slave labour); Arthur Seyss-Inquart (governor of the Netherlands); Julius Streicher (owner of anti-Semitic newspaper Der Sturmer).

SENTENCED TO IMPRISONMENT: Karl Donitz (U-boat and navy chief; Hitler's successor; 10 years) Walther Funk (president of Reichsbank; life); Rudolf Hess (Hitler's secretary to 1941; life); Konstantin von Neurath (governor of Bohemia-Moravia to 1941; 15 years); Erich Raeder (navy chief to 1943; life, commuted to 10 years); Baldur von Schirach (Youth Leader and Gauleiter of Vienna; 20 years); Albert Speer (Armaments Minister; 20 years).

ACQUITTED: Hans Fritzsche (radio propaganda chief); Franz von Papen (Chancellor in 1932; Vice-Chancellor in Hitler's first government); Hjalmar Schacht (Economics Minister in 1930s). That those who were convicted and put to death were the only offenders and the winners were sinless in shining armours is a debateable point.

In eighteenth century, Europeans spread their empires and, along with it, their ideas, law, philosophy and way of life which have become symbols of modern world.

20

World wars created new states and destroyed old order

After the last two global wars, Europe divided the Ottoman empire which stretched from Turkey to north Africa. The Allied powers destroyed old countries and created new ones in their image in messy manners. No wonder the Middle East is the most troubled spot in the world; oil has fuelled rivalries more than it has created wealth.

The defeat of the Axis and the victory of the Allied powers in 1945 did not bring immediate peace to the world. The advance of the Soviet Union in Eastern and Central Europe and the retreat of the Western colonial empires in Asia and Africa posed grave problems in these regions. The Middle East, Asia and Africa had their share of post-war upheavals. Peace in these regions was fitful, uneasy, and frequently interrupted by struggles against internal and external enemies. However, the troubles were less intense and less traumatic than those which followed the clamping down of Soviet rule in Central and Eastern Europe, or the winding down of British rule in South and Southeast Asia. In the post-colonial world, the first issue of public concern was independence.

In the aftermath of the World War I, Turkey, Iran and Afghanistan had full independence and had experience in managing it. The inter-war period created four new Arab states, Saudi Arabia, Yemen, Iraq and Egypt. The first two already enjoyed a large measure of independence, but the last two were bound to their former rulers by unequal treaties and by the presence of foreign forces. The departure of France from the Levant (name applied to eastern

Mediterranean region, including Turkey-in-Asia, Syria, Lebanon and Israel) added Syria and Lebanon to the list of Arab free states. The League of Arab States was formed in March 1945 by Egypt, Iraq, Syria, Lebanon, Saudi Arabia, Yemen and Transjordan, though the last was still part of the British-mandated territory of Palestine. A year later, in March 1946, Transjordan, was renamed as Jordan, and was granted independence.

SAUDI ARABIA BORN IN 1927: Saudi Arabia was assembled by Ibn Saud in 1927 after conquest of different tribal and regional groups. It was all Arab, all Muslim and overwhelmingly Sunni. Most of the other newly created states lacked this advantage, and were riven by inner rivalries and hatred. Sometimes these broke out into armed conflicts, variously described as rebellion, revolution, or civil war – the differences between these are of perspective as well as of dimension. The contact with the West after the World War II so much transformed the divided countries of the Middle-East, Asia and Africa that the ruling elite of these countries became Western-minded. And, a new Western culture emerged over the ashes of old civilizations of the East which have been reduced to mere historical curiosities now. Oil was discovered in the Persian Gulf in the 1940s and that made the Middle East an important player in the world politics. Oil is their fortune and nemesis, both.

MORE STATES FREED: The process of regime change was extended to the rest of the Arab world. Libya became independent in 1951; Morocco in 1956; Mauritania in 1960; Kuwait in 1961, Algeria in 1962; South Yemen (the former Aden colony and Protectorate) in 1967, (North and South Yemens were united in 1990) and the Gulf States in 1971. All of them joined the Arab League. Some, notably South Yemen and Algeria, acquired their independence only after a long and bitter struggle. In most other cases, independence was achieved more or less peacefully. They all were once part of the Ottoman empire. The wave of freedom spread farther east. With the break-up of the Soviet Union in 1991, the Transcaucasian and Central Asian territories, seized by the *tsars* in the nineteenth century and retained by the Soviets in the twentieth, became free. Historically, these countries had been part of the Middle East. Two of them, Armenia and Georgia, were Christian but had, for many centuries, been part of Muslim empires, either Turkish or Persian. The rest, Azerbaijan and the five republics of Central Asia, were predominantly Muslim. Tajikistan was Persian by speech and culture. The other four – Kazakstan, Uzbekistan, Kyrgyzstan, and Turkmenistan – spoke languages related to Turkish.

Though officially neutral, Iran was overrun by foreign soldiers. The Crimean War (1853-6) brought Iran's intense involvement with Europe and an acceleration of the process of change. The World War II also ended in defeat of Turkey, and the Turks were compelled to relinquish their Arab territories and give them to Britain and France. Only in the Anatolian Turkish homeland, did they manage to defy the victors and, after a struggle, establish an independent Turkish republic. The French set up two republics after World War II, of which one was called Lebanon while the other retained the name, Syria. And, the British split their area in two: they formed an Arab emirate renamed *Transjordan*, (which later became Jordan) and set up direct administration in Israel in 1948 after the termination of the Palestine mandate. And, the British and the French had created new states in their own images. The French set up parliamentary republics and the British set up constitutional monarchies. After their departure, however, almost all of them collapsed or were abandoned to the people of the region who adopted their own models of dictatorship.

END OF CALIPHATE

The World War II ended the Islamic Caliphate. Caliphate (Arab *khalifah* or successor) was the title adopted by Mohammed's successors as civic and religious heads of the world of Islam. The first Caliph was Abu Bekr (d.634) father-in-law of the Prophet. The Caliphate was earlier elective, but became hereditary in practice, being held by the Unmayyad dynasty (661-770), and then by the Abbasids. During the 10th century the political and military power passed to the leader of the Caliph's Turkish bodyguard; about the same time an independent Fatimite caliphate sprang up in Egypt. After the death of the last Abbasid (1258) the title was claimed by a number of Muslim chieftains in Egypt, Turkey, and India. The most powerful of these were the Turkish sultans of the Ottoman Empire. In 1924 the last Turkish Caliph was deposed by Kemal Ataturk and that ended the Caliphate regime.

The Turks originated in Mongolia, whence in the 6th century, they spread into Turkestan. During the 7th century, they adopted Islam. The Seljuk Turks in 1055 secured political control of the caliphate, and established an empire in Asia Minor. The Ottoman Turks, driven from Central Asia by the Mongols, entered the service of the Seljuks, and Osman-I in 1299 founded a kingdom of his own. Having overrun Asia Minor, the Ottomans began their European conquests by seizing Gallipoli in 1354, captured Constantinople in 1453, and by 1480 Turks were masters of the Balkans. And, by 1550, they had conquered

Egypt, Syria, Arabia, Mesopotamia, Tripoli, and most of Hungary; thereafter the empire ceased to expand, although Cyprus was taken in 1571 and Crete in 1669.

RISE & FALL OF TURKISH EMPIRE: The Christian counter-offensive opened in 1683 with the defeat of the Turks by the rulers in Vienna; in 1699 the Turks lost Hungary and, in 1774, Russia ousted Turks from Moladavia, Wallachia, and the Crimea. In the Balkans, there was an unsuccessful revolt in Serbia in 1804, but in 1821-9 Greece threw off Turkish rule. Russia's attempts to exploit this situation were resisted by Britain and France, which in the Crimean War (1854-6) fought on the Turkish side. The Bulgarian rising of 1876 led to a new war between Turks and Russia, and the Treaty of Berlin (1878). Turks lost control of Bulgaria, Bosnia, and Herzegovina. Meanwhile, Italy took advantage of the crisis and seized Tripoli in 1911-12, while the Balkan states in 1912-13 expelled the Turks from Albania and Macedonia. To be on the winning side, the Turks joined Germans in 1914, only to again lose Syria, Arabia, Mesopotamia, and its nominal suzerainty in Egypt. A succession of defeats and tactical blunders finally sealed the fate of the Turkish empire.

ATATURK, A SAVIOUR

The Greek occupation of Smyrna (Izmir) in 1919 produced patriotic reaction among Turks. Mustapha Kemal (Atatürk) came on the scene; and established a provisional government at Angora (Ankara) in 1920, defeated the Greeks in battles and, in 1923, Turkey was declared a republic, with Kemal as its first President. The new republic carried out a sweeping policy of westernization: Islam ceased to be the state religion, polygamy was abolished, and a new legal code was introduced. Kemal's People's Party ruled until 1950, but then government subsequently became less stable, frequently under coalitions, and the military intervened in 1960, 1971, and 1980. Terrorism by extremists of right and left had led to violence in 1979-80. A junta under General Kenan Evren took unlimited powers under an interim constitution. Turkey is now a member of NATO, seeking to become a member of the European Union.

TURKS AND YOUNG TURKS: The first self-styled revolutions in the Middle East were those of the constitutionalists in Iran in 1905 and the militant *Young Turks* in the Ottoman empire in 1908. Since then, there had been many other militant organisations, and by the last decade of the last century, most states in the region were governed by regimes installed by means of the violent removal of their predecessors. In early days, this was accomplished by nationalist struggles against foreign overlords; later, it was largely achieved by military officers deposing the rulers. All of these laid claim to the title "revolutionary," which in time became the most widely accepted claim to legitimacy in the Middle East. So also in other countries, including Africa. Even today, many dictators in the developing countries call themselves revolutionaries to acquire legitimacy. 'Young Turks' has since symbolised fight for lawful govts. *(India had also seen Young Turks during emergency 1975-77).*

IRAN IS MIDDLE EAST'S YOUNGEST NATION: Persia, among the oldest empires, was renamed Iran in 1935 to become the youngest country in the Middle East. Persia was overrun by Aryans in 1600 BC and from that comes the name, *Iran.* Cyrus-II seized the throne from Medes and set up the large Persian empire which included Babylonia, Syria, Asia Minor (Turky), Egypt, Thrace (modern Bulgaria), Georgia, Armenia and Macedonia. In 334-338, Persia was conquered by Alexander the Great. During World War I, Persia was occupied by Britain and Russia. Riza Kha seized power in 1921 and established the Pahlavi dynasty which was overthrown by Ayatollaha Khomeini in the Iranian Revolution. The rest is known history.

NATIONALISM ALSO GRIPS NON-EUROPEAN COUNTRIES

Patriotism and nationalism were never known to non-European countries because there was no idea of nation and country, sovereignty or national identity. The introduction of these Western ideas after the treaty of Westphalia in 1648 has changed the world, destroying feudalism and kingship. That had impact on the Asian and Middle Eastern countries also. Patriotism united the different peoples in Britain, France and the US, speaking different languages, and practising different religions, into powerful nations. This idea also served to bind together the different ethnic and religious communities of the Ottoman Empire in a common loyalty to their homeland and Government, although in Islam, there is no concept of nationhood; it is Islamic brotherhood. It is for this reason that Muslims outside Islamic countries say (as was evident in the July 2005 London bombing) that they have loyality to Islam first and to others afterwards. Patriotism was more attractive in Syria, Iraq and Egypt because they had well-defined national boundaries. The two Yemens (north and south) in southern Arabia, Libya and Algeria in North Africa, were also attracted to these ideas.

> **WHERE IS MIDDLE EAST?**
>
> So powerful had Europe become after World War I that instead of calling the countries by their names, the western geographers divided the orient into regions.
>
> Middle East was the lands around the southern and eastern shores of the Mediterranean Sea, extending from Morocco to the Arabian Peninsula and Iran and sometimes beyond. The central part of this general area was formerly called the Near East, a name given to it by modern Western geographers and historians, Near East applied to the region nearest to Europe, extending from the Mediterranean Sea to the Persian Gulf; Middle East, from the Gulf to Southeast Asia; and Far East, those regions facing the Pacific Ocean.
>
> The change in usage began to evolve prior to World War II and tended to be confirmed during that war, when the term Middle East was given to the British military command in Egypt. Thus defined, the Middle East consisted of the states or territories of Turkey, Cyprus, Syria, Lebanon, Iraq, Iran Palestine (now Israel), Jordan, Egypt, Sudan, Libya, and the various states of Arabia proper (Saudi Arabia, Kuwait, Yemen [now Yemen Arab Republic], Oman, Bahrain, Qatar, the United Arab Emirates and Aden Protectorate (now the People's Democratic Republic of Yeman Republic)
>
> Occasionally Greece is included in the compass of the Middle East because the Middle Eastern (then Near Eastern) question in its modern form first became apparent when the Greeks rose in rebellion to assert their independence from the Ottoman Empire in 1821. Turkey and Greece; together with the largely Arabic-speaking lands around the eastern end of the Mediterranean, were called the Levant.

The idea of the nation, defined not by the geographical boundary but by language, culture, and presumed common descent, was European and it came to the Middle East and India later where the well-defined State of the European kind was more visible than the patriotism which was an abstraction. Both patriotic and nationalist ideas produced resistance movements. Patriotism produced nationalism which sought to subvert the existing political order. For a patriot, independence of his country comes first, and freedom of individuals later. People in India think they had freedom under autocratic Hindu rulers and loss of independence came after Babur's attack in 1525. Not true; people were "unfree" in both. Freedom means self-governance, an unknown concept in the ancient world. But, people believe differently.

The notion of revolution is another powerful western idea, developed in the sixteenth-century Holland, seventeenth-century England and eighteenth-century America. However, for France, it was alien until the French Revolution which was the first movement of ideas in Europe. It had a significant impact on the world that brought about change in the processes of thought and action. This was the first major upheaval in Europe that expressed its ideas in secular and not Christian terms. Liberty, equality, and fraternity were not entirely new ideas for the peoples of the world. Fraternity – the brotherhood, although of the believers has been basic principle of Islam. In the course of human affairs, such privileges have been uniting people in all countries. Marx says it is unity of class, not caste or colour. The French Revolution opposed the dominant Western ideologies and practices, including feudalism, slavery, aristocracy, property-based privileges and the consequent exploitation. After the French Revolution, the World was never the same again.

In Asia, the French Revolution produced dissidence and rebellions. It caused most dramatic changes in Egypt where in 1954, King Fârûq was deposed and exiled. The monarchy was abolished and a republic was proclaimed. The first ruler, General Muhammad Neguib, the nominal leader of the revolution, was replaced by Colonel Nasser, the head of the group of so-called "*Free Officers*," who had planned, organized and executed the regime change. In time, other Arab states were affected by the revolutionary wave. In 1958, the monarchy in Iraq was overthrown and replaced by a series of military dictators. In Syria, the army rule gave way to a party dictatorship run by the *Ba'ath* party. First, the Greeks and Serbs, later the other Balkan states responded to French revolutionary ideas which continue to dominate human mind even today. *(Read more about it in following chapters).*

REVOLUTIONARY IDEAS SPREAD

However, in a very few cases, the regime change had resulted from profounder ideology, with deeper causes and greater consequences, than the simple replacement of the men at the top. And, for the pursuit of self-interest. One such was the Islamic Revolution of 1979 in Iran, which may be compared with the French and Russian Revolutions in its origins. What happened in Iran can be seen as a revolution in the classical sense: a mass movement with wide popular participation that resulted in a major shift in economic as well as political power and that started a process of social transformation. The revolution in Iran was, however, called Islamic. Its leaders cared nothing for the models of Paris or Petrograd, and saw European ideologies (of the left no less than of the right) as part of the infidel enemy design against whom they were waging struggle. The symbols and slogans of the revolution were Islamic because these alone could mobilize and emotionally unite the masses for struggle. But, this revolution was not for equality, fraternity or liberty; it was to bring in Islamic regime which is denial of all these. Hence, it was a revolution only because there was mass participation. Islam defined the enemies and objectives; it was aimed against the infidel abroad, and the apostate at home. The apostate meant all those Muslims who did not share Khomeini's interpretation of Islam and who, in his perception, were importing western ways. In principle, the aim of the Islamic revolution in Iran was to sweep away all the Western and infidel rules that had been imposed on Muslim lands and restore the true Islamic order. Unlike the French Revolution, Iran's revolution sought to re-establish slavery although of different kind. However, the Islamic revolutionaries seek analogy with the French Revolution which is false.

HARMONY ELUDES MIDDLE EAST

Historian Bernard Lewis says, the division and conflict have been built into the way the Middle Eastern Muslim States were created after the end of Turkish caliphate. The difference is conceptual also. In the Western world, the basic unit of human organization is the nation. For Muslims, it is religion subdivided into nations. The nation-states that make up the modern Middle East are new creations, left over from the era of Anglo-French imperial domination that followed the defeat of the Ottoman Empire, and they preserve the frontier demarcations of their former imperial masters. Even their names reflect this artificiality: Iraq was a medieval province, with borders very different from those of the modern republic, excluding Mesopotamia in the north and including a slice of western Iran; Syria, Palestine, and Libya are names from classical antiquity revived after a thousand years with different boundaries by European imperialists in the twentieth century. Algeria and Tunisia do not even exist as words in Arabic. Most remarkable of all, there is no word in the Arabic language for Arabia, and present-day Saudi Arabia is spoken of as "the Saudi Arab kingdom" or "the peninsula of the Arabs," depending on the context. This is not because Arabic is a poor language – the reverse is true – but because the Arabs simply did not think in terms of combined ethnic and territorial identity.

Both Arabs and Turks struggled against Christian Europe, from the first Arab incursions in the eighth century to the final Turkish retreat in the twentieth. But until the modern period, when Europe became dominant, Islamic soldiers, officials, and historians referred to their opponents not in territorial or national terms but simply as infidels (kafir). Similarly, they never referred to their own side as Arab, Persian or Turkish; they identified themselves as Muslims. In Islam, there is no concept of nation-state or country; they have only *Muslim brotherhood* which is also a Sunni Islamic movement founded in Egypt in 1928. But much of the Islamic solidarity is however, undermined by the internal divisions, including that of Shia and Sunni, the name Pakistan, a twentieth-century invention, designates a country defined entirely by its Islamic allegiance although the country and people of Pakistan have always been part of India. But an Afghanistan, defined by its Islamic identity would be a natural ally of Pakistan. An Afghanistan defined by ethnic nationality, by contrast, may be a dangerous neighbour, advancing irredentist claims on the Pashto-speaking areas of northwestern Pakistan and perhaps even allying itself with India to achieve this objective, says Bernard Lewis.

SOME LANDMARK YEARS OF THE COUNTRIES

SAUDI ARABIA: *18th Century* Al Saud family united tribesmen of Nejd in Central Arabia in support of Wahhabi (radical) religious movement; *1830C* Riyadh is made capital; *1927 Saudi Arabia was assembled by Ibn-Saud; 1932* Hesaz and Nejd joined to constitute the United Kingdom of Saudi Arabia; *1933* Saudi Arabia allowed American-owned Standard Oil Company to prospect for oil which was discovered in Hisa in 1938; *1940s* Commercial exploitation of oil begins; *1991* Saudi Arabia fought on the Allied side against Iraq in Gulf War; *1996* Fahd becomes King.

IRAQ: *1921* Britain created this Kingdom out of the former Mesopotomia (land between two rivers – Tigris and Euphrates) though the border was messy, so also ethnic groups. Sunni, Shia and Khurds are major groups and that is the problem. *1932* became free from the UK; *1941-45* occupied again by the UK during World War II; *1968* Saddam Hussein takes power; *1980-88* Iran-Iraq war; *2003* Saddam toppled by US forces after invasion.

IRAN: *In 1935,* its name was changed from Persia; *1946* Allied forces left Iran; *1951* oilfields nationalised by Muhammad Mossadeq and anti British-US sentiment increased; *1980* Iraq invades Iran; *1978* Iranian revolution puts Ayotollah Khomeini in power; *1971* the Shah leaves the country; *1993* Rafsanjani becomes president; *1996* re-elected and introduced free market;

1997 Seyyed Mohamad Khatami elected President. In 2006, Mahmoud Ahmadinejad elected president, re-elected in 2009.

SYRIA: *1916* Agreement between France and Britain to partition the Turkish empire and Syria was allotted to France; *1918* British expelled Turks; *1941* British forces ousted pro-Nazi Vichy French regime in Damascus; Syria was occupied by British, fighting with Free French forces; *1944* Syrian freedom proclaimed; *1946* Full freedom after French forces withdrew; *1961* Syria seceded from United Arab Republic (UAR); *1973* Syria attacked Israel (Yom Kippur War); *1991* Syria supported US in Gulf-war.

YEMEN: *In 628* Islam was introduced; *1538* North Yemen came under control of the Turkish Ottoman empire; *1839* Aden became a British Protectorate *1870s* the Ottomans re-establish control over North Yemen; *1918* North Yemen becomes independent; *1937* Aden (South Yemen) became a British crown colony; *1990* North and South Yemens re-united.

JORDAN: *13thC* The oldest state of Jordan was set up; *C1000* Southeast Jordan was part of Israel under David and Solomon; *64BC* conquered by Romans; *16th century* on, it came under the Turkish Ottoman empire, ruled from Damascus; *1946* achieved independence from Britain; *1948* British mandate expired; *1950* Jordan annexed West Bank; *1951* King Abdullah assassinated *1967* Israel defeated Egypt, Syria, and Jordan in the six-day war and re-occupied West Bank; *1999* King Hussein dies, son becomes King.

ISRAEL: It was the ancient kingdom north of Palestine, formed after the death of Solomon, by Jewish peoples seceding from the rule of his son Rehoboam and electing Jeroboam as their leader. It is named after the descendants of the Old Testament patriarch *Jacob*, whose name was changed to Israel. Jews believe that the land of Israel was given to them forever by God when He brought them out of Egypt under Moses' guidance. The name is, therefore, sometimes used to refer to the Jews themselves, as in the 'people of Israel' or, in the context of historical times, 'Israelites". It was created in 1948 after the termination of Palestine mandate which is the source of running battle between the peoples of Palestine and Israel.

KUWAIT : The nomadic 'Anizah' tribe of central Arabia founded Kuwait city in 1710, and 'Abdal-Rahim of the Sabah dynasty became sheikh in 1756; the family continues to rule Kuwait. In 1899, to thwart German and Ottoman influences, Kuwait agreed to give Britain control to rule Kuwait. In 1899, outbreak of war with the Ottoman Empire in World War I (1914-18), Britain established a protectorate there. In 1961, after Kuwait gained full independence from Britain, Iraq laid claim to Kuwait. British troops were sent to defend Kuwait; the Arab League recognised its independence, and Iraq dropped its claim. Iraq reasserted these claims in the aftermath of the Iraq-Iraq War and invaded and occupied Kuwait in 1990. A U.S.-led military coalition drove the Iraqi army out of Kuwait the next year.

The earth moves round the sun 30 km per second and rotates at its axis at 1,666 km per hour – or faster than the speed of sound. But, map-makers don't show it for imperial reasons, says Arno Peters, a German cartographer.

21

Eastern Europe is a geographical error?

Europe exists, according to Encyclopaedia Britannica, between the Atlantic in the West and the Urals in the east. In which case, what is now called eastern Europe is in the centre of the Continent. This error, however, was contrived by the Capitalist west to condemn the Communist east calling it as part of Asia – backward, poor and disenfranchised.

Until the end of the Cold War in 1990, the countries we know as Eastern Europe had hardly seemed to be part of the European continent. They stood beyond the Iron Curtain and looked for their economic, cultural and military support not from their old partners in the West, but to the "mostly Asiatic Soviet Union", with which they all share frontiers to the east. Yet, they have been partners in Europe's Christian heritage and are linked to it by common history. The countries of eastern Europe for purpose of this book are : Poland, Hungary, Romania and Bulgaria. (The Balkans are treated separately). The west has been treating only the area between the Elbe river and the Pyrenees mountains, as Europe, keeping out even Spain and Portugal and the US official Defence Secretary Donald Rumsfeld called it (2005) as Old Europe.

In 1938, British Prime Minister Neville Chamberlain, refusing to defend former Czechoslovakia, described it as *"a far–away country that we know little of."* Nevertheless, these countries have never been beyond the concerns of Europe. Almost landlocked (only Poland has a sea-coast on the Baltic), with Russia on one flank, Germany on the other, they have been battlegrounds throughout their history and have been plagued by all the old European problems of minorities and disputed boundaries.

Ethnically mixed, they are nevertheless among the most strongly nationalistic countries of the continent. The Poles look back to centuries of defiance, as their country has been divided, enlarged or diminished at the will of stronger powers. French writer Hilaire Belloc once called Poland "*the hope of the half-defeated.*" Hungary remembers the days when it was an equal partner in the Austro-Hungarian Empire, and still further back to its own pre-eminence under the Magyar kings of the Middle Ages. Former Czechoslovakia has been a State only since 1918, when it was created out of the fragmented Habsburg empire, and divided between the predominantly urbanized Czechs and the chiefly rural Slovaks, but its loyalties are centred on the magnificent and historic city of Prague, one of the most beautiful in all Europe and in itself an exhibition of European civilization.

A range of mountains dominates former Czechoslovakia, but Poland and Hungary are mostly flat, allowing the easy entry of armies. Here successive waves of invaders from the east have reached the limits of their expansion-Mongols, Muslims, Soviet Communists-and here before the World War II lived the world's largest population of Jews, most of them murdered in the concentration camps of Nazi-occupied Poland.

The people of these countries have always lived austerely. Traditionally, these have been agricultural lands with a labour force of peasantry. Only in the west of former Czechoslovakia, old Bohemia and Moravia, is there an old-established industrial base, and even now,

NEW COUNTRIES EVOLVED AFTER THE COLLAPSE OF THE FORMER U.S.S.R

Country	Capital	Area (Sq.km.)
BALTIC STATES		
1. Estonia	Tallinn	45,100
2. Latvia	Riga	63,700
3. Lithuania	Vilnius	65,200
RUSSIA AND OTHER 11 INDEPENDENT STATES (CIS)		
* Russia	Moscow (Europe)	1,70,75,000
1. Armenia	Yerevan (Europe)	29,800
2. Azerbaizan	Baku (Europe)	86,600
3. Belarus	Minsk (Europe)	2,07,700
4. Georgia	Tbilisi (Europe)	69,700
5. Moldova	Kishinev (Europe)	33,700
6. Ukraine	Kiev (Europe)	6,03,700
7. Kazakhistan	Alme-Ata (Asia)	27,17,300
8. Kirgizstan	Frunze (Asia)	1,98,500
9. Tazhikistan	Dahanbe (Asia)	1,43,100
10. Turkmenistan	Ashkhabad (Asia)	4,88,100
11. Uzbekistan	Tashkent (Asia)	4,47,400

* The Russian Federation lies in Europe as well as Asia.

when the whole area had been homogenized by nearly half a century of communism, the gilded cities of the old regimes contrast piquantly with the poor villages of the countrysides. Yet these are States with strong loyalties, and forming a kind of buffer, extending north and south across much of Europe, between the venerable and elaborate cultures of the west and Asia's ever-threatening influence.

IMPERIAL CARTOGRAPHY

The fact is that the East European countries are geographically not in the east but in the centre of Europe situated between the Urals and the Atlantic. They are, however, so called to indicate their backwardness or that they were under Soviet control. West Europeans called them East Europeans, also because the West never counted Russia as part of Europe. After crossing the Elbe, de Gaulle would murmur: *"We are headed for Asia."*

However, not every country in the east is poor and small. Slovenia is seven times the size of Luxembourg and 70 times that of Malta. The three Baltic countries are bigger in area than Belgium, the Netherlands and Denmark although less populous. Poland is the sixth-largest country in the European Union, in both area and population. The three Baltic countries were occupied by the Soviet Union for half a century. Poland, Hungary, the Czech Republic and Slovakia (the latter two were one country until 1993) had titular independence, but they were governed from Moscow. Slovenia was part of Yugoslavia which sparred ideologically with the Soviet Union.

Now let us know about cartographical inaccuracies. Even after repeated partitions – the separation of Burma in 1935 and the creation of Pakistan in 1947 – modern India is still the seventh largest in the world. But maps do not show it. Greenland and Scandinavia, for instance, appear to be ten and three times larger than India respectively. In reality, Greenland is only 80% India's size, and Scandinavia three times smaller than India. Russia appears bigger than the entire continent of Africa; Alaska larger than Mexico, and Europe seems larger than the entire South America. Northern hemisphere occupies two-thirds of the space, and the southern hemisphere one-third.

This discrepancy in books and atlases is because it is the Mercator map, made during an age when Europe dominated and exploited the world. (Geradus Mercator, was a Flemish map-maker who first published a map in 1568). The white-dominated countries are, thus, portrayed to be extraordinarily large while non-white countries become extraordinarily small. It seems that the Mercator map was made to artificially portray the territorial "superiority" of the colonial powers, and psychologically influence the gullible minds of the colonised people into greater submission. Surprisingly, even today maps in India reflect this inaccuracy.

Our planet is moving around the sun in an elliptical orbit at 30 kilometres per second, and rotating around its axis at 1,666 kilometres per hour, which is faster than the speed of sound. Such high-speed rotation has resulted in the polar areas being compressed towards the centre and the equatorial areas bulging out. This explains the Earth not being a perfect sphere. Acknowledging this discrepancy, the UN in 1974 accepted a new map made by a German, Arno Peters. It is called the Peters' map which shows countries in their relative sizes.

The imperial powers had many ways to expand their economic and political powers and rule peoples. Wars, alliances, divide-and-rule policy, imperial architecture, pomp and pageantry, conspiracy and seductive slogans were among them. Not always by superior force. British, for instance, ruled India more by pomp, pageantires and parades (with kings and queens in glittering clothes at Delhi's India Gate being carried in buggies by famished Indians or overfed British horses) than by superior army whose strength seldom exceeded 20,000 (except during emergencies and wars). But, cartographical imperialism is a novel idea used by the Western Europe to rule the world.

SOME LANDMARK DATES

Unification of Germany	Oct. 3, 1990
Croatia declared independence from Yugoslavia	June 25, 1991
Kirgizstan and Uzbekistan declared their independence	Aug. 31, 1991
Baltic states recognised by the Soviet Union	Sept. 6, 1991
Estonia, Latvia, Lithuania became members of UN	Sept. 17, 1991
That it has changed its name to Belarus	Sept. 19, 1991
Soviet Union collapsed, Russia and 11 other independent states formed	Dec. 26, 1991
Armenia, Azerbeizan, Kazakhistan, Kirgizstan, Maldova, Tazhikistan, Turkmenistan and Uzbekistan became members of United Nations. Bosnia-Herzegovina, Croatia, Slovania became members of UN	May 22, 1992
Bifurcation of Czechoslovakia	Jan. 1, 1993

Whoever may win now, Spaniards have lost. They have seen faces of bad dreams. Look at them down a levelled gun; how sad, how defeated are they !!

– *Margot Heinemann,*
"On the Spanish War"

22

The Spanish Civil War

During the civil war, hostilities were conducted with extreme ruthlessness; neither side allowed any compassion to govern its decision on death. And, after the civil war ended in 1939, World War II began which left Spain among the poorest countries of the continent.

The Spanish civil war began on July 17, 1936 and ended after three years in 1939. This was the war, which was waiting to happen. Following the establishment of the Spanish Republic after election in 1931, Spain was virtually split between the republicans (moderates, socialists, communists, Catalan and Basque separatists), on one side; monarchists, Catholics and the fascist Falange Party, on the other. Spain's brief experience with democracy between 1931 and 1936, polarized the people. In 1936, when a coalition of Left-wing parties formed a popular front government, the army launched a coup. Started by the overseas military forces in Morocco, the uprising spread to northern and central Spain. The working classes, which had welcomed the coming of the Republic, fought fiercely to defend it, and the military faced the prospect of a civil war. The coup leaders turned to the army's chief of staff, Gen. Francisco Franco, who at first was reluctant to join the rebels but in September 1936, accepted the role of commander-in-chief and leader of the nationalist forces. For the next forty years, he ruled Spain as the Caudillo *(leader),* at the head of an authoritarian regime.

On the side of the Republic were grouped a heterogeneous assortment of communists, socialists, and workers, as well as untrained but zealous Leftists and intellectuals who came to Spain from Europe and the US to fight against the forces of Fascism. The Republicans, without an army or material,

GENERAL FRANCO
(1892-1975)

Francisco Bahamonde Franco, a ruthless dictator, had been an exemplary soldier. Born into a devout middle class family in Galicia in 1892, Franco decided to pursue a military career at an early age and entered the Infantry Academy in Toledo at 14. He served in Spain's colonial campaigns in Morocco where he was recognized for his integrity and moved up the ranks swiftly, becoming the youngest captain in the army in 1915. After leading the Spanish Foreign Legion to victory over rebels in Spanish Morocco in 1926, he won national acclaim and was promoted to brigadier.

He was deeply dismayed by the dissolution of the monarchy in 1931. Yet, he remained on active duty, and in May 1935 became chief of the general staff. Though not a politician, his instincts were conservative, monarchical, and religious. He became the perfect symbol for the reaction of the Right-wing elites against the Leftist Republic.

He was appointed Chief of staff in 1935 and the governor of Canary Islands in 1936. Dismissed by the popular front Government, he plotted an uprising with German and Italian assistance and organised invasion of Spain by Moorish troops and foreign mercenaries. He took command of insurqents (nationalists) proclaiming himself Caudillo (leader) of Spain. He died in 1975.

welcomed military aid from the Soviet Union, which allowed them to face Franco's forces with surprising effectiveness. Yet Franco had many more assets. The army was under his command and the Right-wing political parties supported him. Nazi Germany and Fascist Italy provided Franco with a steady supply of weapons. And the Church gave Franco's campaign against the secular Marxist "barbarians" its full support. The Nationalist cause was depicted as a just war to save Spain from an unholy alliance of Communists, foreigners, atheists, and anarchists.

200,000 DIED IN

CIVIL WAR

Unlike the divided Republicans, Franco in 1937, forged his supporters into a unified party called the *Falange Espanola Tradicionalista* (FET, or traditionalist Spanish Phalanx). In March 1939, despite the determined resistance of Republican forces, Franco's army marched into Madrid. Through the dreary months of 1938, Franco's German and Italian allies poured supplies and men into Fascist Spain while American, British, and French statesmen discussed neutrality and non-intervention. Eventually, Russia ceased to give effective aid to the Loyalist. Madrid suffered hunger, disease, and terrorism. Barcelona, under Communist and separatist leadership, was isolated from Madrid. The end came during the winter of 1938-1939, with Loyalist officials fleeing for safety and refugees streaming into France. Franco's triumphant entry into Barcelona (January 26, 1939) ended the Civil War, marked by atrocities, mass arrests, concentration camps, and famine. It cost at least 200,000 lives.

FOR WHOM THE BELL TOLLS

Robert Merriem was once a White House aide to US President Dwight Eisenhower (1890-1969). He went to Europe in 1936 to fight the Spanish Civil War. He commanded the Lincoln Battalion and fought the Civil War on the Aragon Front in 1938. He was killed. Ernest Hemingway (1899-1961) made him immortal in his novel *"For Whom the Bell Tolls"* (it was made into a movie later). Merriem died for *"Republicanism"* which became a rallying cry of the continent. And, a dominant faith of the time.

Franco and his political allies immediately established the foundations of the dictatorship. First came the settling of scores: anyone who had supported the Republican cause was subject to arrest, imprisonment, and death. Communists, leftists, labour activists, and peasants were punished for their Republican sympathies. Perhaps 400,000 people spent time in jail over the next four years, and, at least, 28,000 people were executed. Franco worked swiftly to reward those who had supported his cause, returning lost property and wealth seized during the Republican period, giving the military a central place in the new state, and restoring the rights and privileges of the Catholic Church in Spain, including the right to maintain its own educational system, the control of marriage, and a role as the arbiter of morality. In economic matters, Franco faced great difficulties, since the war had destroyed the economy and Spain's trading partners in Europe and North America were by 1939, embroiled in World War II. The country suffered 200,000 deaths from malnutrition and disease between 1940 and 1944. During the War, Franco kept Spain neutral, though his sympathies clearly lay with the Fascist states.

The Spanish Republic fell, overwhelmed by an alliance of Spanish clericals, military men, landowners and wealthy industrialists; supported lavishly with men and munitions by Mussolini and Hitler. The disorganised Popular Front, together with the hesitancy of the democracies in Europe and America in coming to the aid of the Loyalists, helped to nullify the courageous defence of the republic. Fighting against overwhelming odds, the Loyalists showed the world a magnificent example of valour and tenacity. As for Franco, the fortunes of victory had catapulted him from the command of a comparatively unpopular military faction into the leadership of a nation of 25 million people. This conflict shook the world not so much for the scale of battles but for the fact that for the first time in history the intellectuals of the world united to fight Fascism. And lost.

FASCIST CONSTITUTION

Early in 1937, the *Falange (Espanola Tradicionalista)* emerged as a strong party of the new Fascist state which was embodied in a twenty-six point constitution, which summoned all individuals to bow to the nation's collective will. "The nation must develop a strong army and navy, and a *"spiritual axis"* with Spanish America; banks and public utilities must be nationalised, and church and state co-ordinated but without impairing the dignity of the state". In carrying out these ideals, Franco's leadership was supreme. He appointed a council to supervise industry, labour, and agriculture. In January 1938, the military Directorate gave way to a ministry, of which Franco was President and also Minister of War. So far, the dictatorship could be viewed as a revival, in a more brutal fashion, of the Fascist regime. In August, 1939, however, Franco proclaimed himself absolute dictator.

By 1945, Franco's Spain faced enormous difficulties. The country was isolated in international affairs; it was kept out of the United Nations, the Marshall Plan, and NATO, despite Franco's anti-communism. The UN launched an economic boycott of Spain between 1946 and 1953. Economically, the country was a "*basket case*", and Franco's total ignorance of economic matters made matters worse. His ideological

SPAIN'S RESTLESS NATIONALITIES

Spain's two main ethnic minorities – the Basque and Catalan – have long sought autonomy. Both were repressed during Franco's dictatorship, but in 1980 they gained regional autonomy, each with their own parliament. The Basque country straddles the western Pyrenees into France, its three Spanish provinces having 620,000 people. The Basques speak a language unrelated to any other. A terrorist group, ETA *(Euzkadi ta Azkatasuna* – 'Basque Homeland and Liberty'), has killed more than 800 people since 1968, with brief truces in 1989 and 1998-9.

The four north eastern provinces of Catalonia are home to 6 million people, many speaking Catalan, a distinct Romance language. Catalonia was independent from 1932 to 1939. Today it is Spain's main industrial area, and Barcelona, its capital, is one of Spain's most vibrant cities.

principles dictated that Spain be renewed without recourse to outside aid. Rather, Spain should pursue a policy of autarky, and self-sufficiency, when the state would take command of the economy.

It was like India's *commanding height* for the public sector. Franco's Right-wing supporters rallied to these ideas because they thought that industrialization could move forward under the careful eye of the state, and the class conflict, associated with economic growth and the free market, would be avoided. Strikes, political parties, and unions were banned. Predictably, these policies were disastrous for the economy. Import restrictions resulted in a dearth of raw materials, new machinery, fertilizers, and equipment; agriculture slumped; price controls inhibited output. Corruption, bribery, and the black market prevailed. Basic foodstuffs were in short supply. Franco died in 1975 and things began to change.

AFTER FRANCO

In October 1982, the Socialist Party of Felipe Gonzalez won the general election, and the transfer of power to this party of the Left was done without unrest. Gonzalez, a young lawyer who had joined the Socialist Party when it was still illegal, led Spain as prime minister [1982-96]. He guided Spain's entry into the European Community in 1996 and pursued market-oriented policies that helped the Spanish economy grow at rapid rates. In 1996, he and his party was narrowly defeated in the general election. Spain's entry into NATO in 1982 has provided stability to Spanish politics.

Fourscore and seven years ago our fathers brought forth upon this continent a new nation, conceived in liberty, and dedicated to the proposition that all men are created equal.

– *Abraham Lincoln*
Gettysburg Address
November 19, 1863

23

American imperium was not empire

At the peak of Britain's empire, its popular culture was filled with songs and verse, extolling the glories of its imperial destiny. Across the world, thousands of young Britons delighted in governing India, Malaya, Kenya and other exotic lands. Americans, by contrast, particularly most American soldiers, cannot wait to leave the deserts of the Middle East (Iraq) and the mountains of Central Asia and get back to their suburban homes. Empire? No, thank you.

Empires are built by war and aggression. The British, Spanish, French, Dutch or German – all empires were built by regular wars. But it was not the case with America which got control, say, of the Philippines after defeating Spain in 1898. South Vietnam, small countries or islands in South Pacific and the Caribbean also fell to American control after the rivals were defeated in war to Americans who never lost in any armed conflict during its history. The countries under American control had been part of a system of "*satellite or compliant*" states. Not colonies like the British ones. And America never tried to build an empire like the British against which it fought to get independence.

Hence, it was the American *imperium* (absolute authority) and not empire of the British variety. No wonder the US stayed as a governing power with uneasy conscience and left the occupied countries as soon as they did – free and richer (or less poor) than before. America is the child of revolution which, *de Tocqueville* says, is anti-elitist. This was not the case with other imperial powers. The British left the empire when it was reduced to a near insolvency after World War II; Spain, Portugal, France and other colonial powers were thrown out by force or stiff resistance.

Yes, in all cases, the imperial powers left their cultural imprints on the occupied countries, specially their languages which are the major identities of nations. Most former British colonies, including India, can speak English, have parliamentary system, British land revenue system, the Common Law, liberalism in politics, representative assemblies and idea of liberty. The entire Latin America speaks Spanish except Brazil, a former Portuguese colony where Portuguese is spoken. The French language is freely spoken in Algeria, Mauritania, Mali, Senegal and Morocco. So much so Ivory Coast has a French name, Cote d'Ivoire. Soccer, tennis, golf, racing, skiing, baseball and cricket are colonial legacies which have stayed while the empires have vanished.

FOUNDATION MYTH

The empire is the name of a dream - a dream of doing great things. *Pax Americana* was coined by pro-empire Americans on the pattern of *Pax Britannica* which, in turn, was named after *Pax Romana* of the ancient Roman Empire. Paradoxically, "pax", a Latin word, means peace and all these empires were set up after wars. It is a pure megalomania which America could not afford, also because it has no "*foundation myth*" (a la Eric Hobsbawm) which is provided by history. It was with Britain, France and other colonial powers of Europe that evoked nostalgia and produced nationalism to unite them to conquer other people and other lands.

America has no national identity that could be constructed out of a common English past. Hence, Americans constructed their identity out of its revolutionary ideology and its republican institutions. The European Union countries have always been fighting among themselves and, ironically, their conflict has become their identity to form the Union. The US whose existence has never been threatened by any war, other than the Civil War, has only ideologically-defined enemies – those who reject the American ways of life or its ideology. And those who don't.

Like a flag and an anthem, the nation-state also need a foundation myth, which is conveniently provided by ancestral history. But the US could not use ancestral history as a foundation myth, because it had none white England and even revolutionary France could; even Stalin could use Alexander Nevsky to mobilise Russian patriotism against the Germans (*Mother Russia* or

Iconic visages of America's Founding Fathers

Germany's *Fatherland*). The US had no usable ancestors on its territory earlier than the first English settlers. Native Americans, like slaves, were by definition, outside the Founding Fathers' definition of *"We the People.."*:- So the national identity of the US could not be constructed out of a common English past, even before the mass immigration of non-Anglo-Saxons. It had to be primarily constructed out of its revolutionary ideology and its republican institutions.

The empire was also an essential element for Britain's economic development and its international powers. It was not so for the US. What was crucial for the US was the initial decision to be not a state among other states, but a continental giant. The land, and not the sea, was central to American development. The US was expansionist from the start, but not in the ways of overseas empires like the sixteenth-century Portuguese, the seventeenth-century Dutch, and the British. It was more like Russia, expanding outwards across the plains from a central nucleus in Muscovy until it could also claim to reach *'from sea to shining sea'*, namely from the Baltic to the Black Sea and the Pacific.

The US without an empire would still be the state with by far the largest population in the western hemisphere, and the third most populated country on the globe. Even Russia, reduced as it now is to what it was before Peter the Great, remains a relative giant, not least in terms of the natural resources available on its vast territory. Britain without its empire was and is just one middle-sized economy among many, and knew itself to be so even when it governed a quarter of the world's land and population. The British economy was also essentially linked to the British Empire. There are no significant British colonial territories in Latin America outside the Caribbean area, and Britain deliberately refrained from using its naval or military force to intervene there. Yet until the First World War, Latin America was far more a part of a British-oriented world economy than it was linked to the US. British investments were more than twice as large as those of the US in 1914.

During the 1950s, at least three quarters of Britain's enormous investments were in developing countries. Even between the wars, well over half of British exports went to the British empires. With European and US industrialization, Britain soon ceased to be the world's workshop, but it remained the world's trader, the world's banker, the world's capital exporter. Modest as it was in size and population until as late as the 1880s, it bought most of the internationally traded raw cotton and 35 per cent of internationally traded wool. It also consumed something like half of all internationally traded wheat and internationally traded meat and most of its tea.

The US economy, on the contrary, had and has no such organic connection with the world economy. Being by far the largest industrial economy on the globe, it made, and still makes, its impact on it through sheer continental size and the American originality in technology and business organisation that made it a model for the rest of the world from the 1870s on, and especially in the twentieth century, when it emerged as the first society of mass consumption. Hence, the US never needed colonies to grow and become prosperous as was the case with European countries where small countries like The Netherlands and Denmark had empires many times their size. To be true, the two world wars, which were essentially European wars, were fought over empires. And, America participated in both wars more by inadvertence than by compulsion. Americans had no empire to protect or build; it was the case of lost innocence. Or outright declit by wily European politicians.

US OVERSEAS EXPANSION: The story of American expansion may be divided into three parts : continental expansion, overseas expansion, and intervention. Most of the American territory was acquired by purchase or by other "voluntary procedures," but some of it was gained by conquest, notably the Mexican Cession in 1848. Happily, the precedent had been established that possession and settlement should be followed by full political equality.

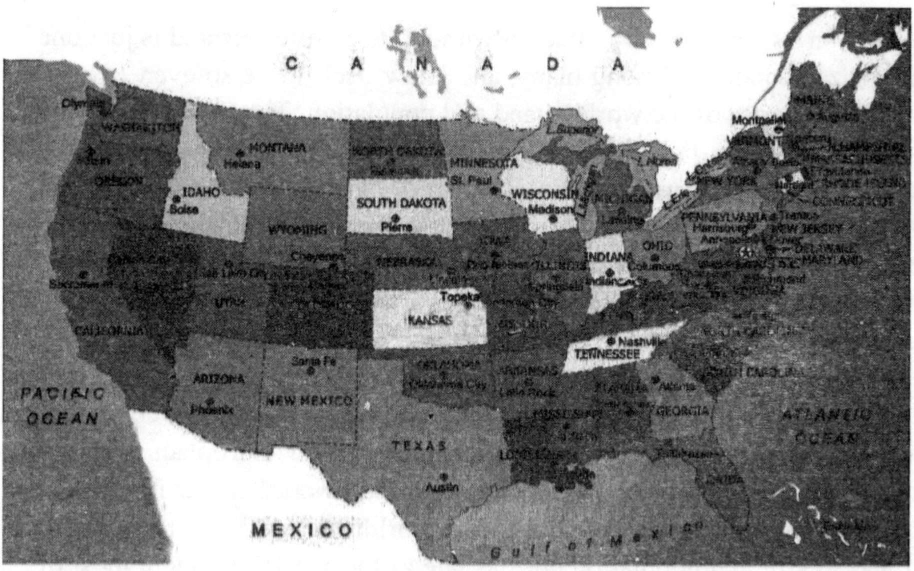

Consequently, American continental imperialism was short-lived; and it now seldom occurs to anybody to think of America as an imperialist power.

Many non-contiguous areas, which had come under the American flag, had been acquired through a variety of processes. Alaska and the Virgin Islands were purchased; the Hawaiian Islands and the Canal Zone were acquired by the "voluntary acts" of de facto governments, although there was chicanery in both cases; Puerto Rico, Guam and the Philippines went to the US as a reward for the victory in the Spanish-American war of 1898. The Canal Zone (Mexico) was leased for the building of a canal, regarded as necessary for American defence and commerce. Many other lands, mostly uninhabited islands in the Pacific, had been picked up from time to time. Except for the Philippine Republic, all these areas are politically subordinate to the United States, although some of them now have a large measure of self-government. The Philippines has been independent since 1946, and Puerto Rico now enjoys a very special status as a commonwealth country associated with the United States.

NAPOLEON SOLD LOUISIANA TO US: Louisiana, which takes its name from the old French province of Louisiana, was explored by La Salle and claimed for Louis XIV, in whose honour this was so named in 1682. The province extended from the British colonies, in the East, to the Spanish colonies, in the West, and from what is now Manitoba to the Gulf of Mexico.

France lost to Britain the part of Louisiana east of the Mississippi in 1763, and it became part of the USA in 1783; the part west of the Mississippi (2,144,500 sq.km in area), passed to Spain in 1762, but by a secret treaty in 1800, it was restored to France. In 1803, Napoleon sold this area to the USA for $ 3 million; it was divided into the Territory of New Orleans, which became the state of Louisiana in 1812. The present-day states of Louisiana, Missouri, Arkansas, Iowa, Nebraska, North Dakota, South Dakota and Oklahoma were also part of the French Louisiana.

This purchase doubled the size of the USA and marked the end of Napoleon's plan for a colonial empire. Guam, ceded to the US by Spain in 1898, has now full US citizenship. It was given self-Government in1950 and now it is the headquarters of US Pacific Strategic Air Command. Japan had captured it in World War II. Hawai, now the 50th state of the US, was a kingdom until 1893; it became a republic in 1894 and admitted to the Union in 1959 after a plebiscite in 1898. This island of North Pacific came into the headlines after an attack on Pearl Harbour by the Japanese on Dec. 7, 1941 which brought the US into the War. Pearl Harbour is one in the chains of islands in the North Pacific of which the other chief islands are; Maui, Oahu, Kanai, Molokai, Lanai and Niihau.

CALIFORNIA CEDED TO US: California was colonised by Spain in 1769 and ceded to the US after the Mexican War in 1848 and became a state in 1850. The discovery of gold in the Sierra Nevada in 1848 was followed by the *gold rush* (1848-56). The completion of the first transcontinental railroad in 1869, speeded up economic development. The Los Angeles areas flourished with the growth of the film industry after 1910, oil discoveries in the early 1920, and the development of aircraft plants and shipyards during World War II. It is today the leading agricultural state with fruit (peaches, citrus, grapes in the valley of the San Joaquin and Sacramento rivers), nuts, wheat, vegetables, cotton and rice, all mostly grown by irrigation; beef cattle; timber; fish; oil; natural gas; aerospace technology; electronics *(Silicon Valley);* food processing; films and television programmes; great reserves of geothermal energy have made the State richest in the Union. With the population (1990) at 30 million, California is the most populous state in the USA (69.9% white; 25.8%% Hispanic; 9.6% Asian and Pacific islander, 7.4% black; 0.8% Native American. Now the whites are close to becoming a minority). Famous people include Luther Burbank, Walt Disney, William Randolph Hearst, Jack London, Marilyn Monroe, Richard Nixon, Ronald Reagan and John Steinbeck.

PUERTO RICO: The Island is a commonwealth in association with the USA. It is situated in the easternmost part of the Greater Antilles, West Indies: there are a number of small islands nearby. Discovered by Columbus in 1493, it was annexed by Spain in 1509, and ceded to the USA by a treaty in 1898. In 1952, it achieved a commonwealth status, and confirmed this, by a referendum in 1967. It should be noted that many of these areas are so small that they could never achieve independence and keep it.

MONROE DOCTRINE: The Monroe Doctrine was first announced in President James Monroe's address to Congress in December 1823 which declared, among other things, that the United States would oppose the transfer of any land on the American continent from one European state to another, the acquisition or further expansion of holdings by a European state, or the interference by European states in the political affairs of the independent states of the New World. President Monroe (Fifth President 1816-1824) was prompted to take this position by the threatening actions of the Holy Alliance and by the evident interest of Britain and other European states. The declaration was merely an announcement of executive policy while Monroe was President. Nevertheless, the Doctrine took an increasing hold of the American mind until late in the last century when it became the basic principle of the nation's foreign policy. The newly-born states of Latin America welcomed President Monroe's pronouncement. Only much later, when the danger of the Spanish re-conquest had passed and they themselves had grown in strength and national consciousness, did they begin to resent the imperialistic implications of the Doctrine. While disliking the unilateral character of the Doctrine, Latin American states had never quarrelled with its objective of preventing foreign intervention in the Western Hemisphere. But, while shielding the Latin Americans from the European states, the Doctrine did not shield them from the United States herself. Indeed, the Doctrine became the moral basis for American interventions.

THE PHILIPPINES

Earlier, the US was a colonial power in the Philippines (and other former Dutch colonies) which she left

ALEXIS DE TOCQUEVILLE

In the United States, the majority undertakes to supply a multitude of ready-made opinions for the use of individuals who are, thus, relieved from the necessity of forming opinion of their own. America is God's crucible, the great melting pot where all the races of Europe are melting – God is making America, said Alexis de Tocqueville (1805-59), the French historian, in 1831.

on her own, a better organized and prosperous country. It fought in the Korean peninsula in 1950 and left the southern part, down the 38th Parallel, a rich country while its northern counterpart is biting its nuclear bullet and starving. Truer still is case of Guam, Puerto Rico, and of the 2,360 islands, islets, atolls and bays (small lowlands) acquired or purchased by the US between 1856 and 1945. But, not one of them was treated as colony, nor kept under control by force. Today, they govern themselves through various democratic ways while many of them stay federated to the US system.

US has always been uncomfortable as a colonial power because it is against the founding principles of America, *"conceived in liberty"*. It is also because of the fact that the US does not need a colony to prosper and support its superpower status; its prosperity is home-grown unlike that of Europeans. Colonial powers, including Holland (Dutch West Indies) and Belgium (Belgium Congo) and for that matter Russia since Peter the Great, had always depended on colonies to draw their resources. Now that it has lost colonies, Russia is not able to grow food on its vast land area (17 million/sq. km. which is four times larger than India's about 4 million sq. km.) enough to feed its population which is equal to India's one province, say U.P. All colonial powers fell because of what Paul Kennedy calls, "*strategic overstretch*"; that is they have expanded their areas of control more than their resources could support. Not so with America.

Wilson fought World War II in which 60 million people died and Kennedy fought in Vietnam in which 58,000 Americans and one million Vietnamese died in 10 years but they remained most loved Americans in the world. Bill Clinton also used force in Bosnia, Haiti and Kosovo, but, he remained the darling of Americans and the world. Bush has only toppled a dictator. Why is so much uproar, then? Simple; it is because President Bush has ignored the founding principles on which the Republic has been built.

British Historian Nicolas B. Dirks says in his powerful critique, *The Scandal of Empire,* "It is impossible not to be deeply disturbed by the continuities of historical mistakes, manifest in scandals most evident in U.S. relationship with Iraq. Imperialism has not yet been consigned to the past tense once and for all. Rather, empire is transforming itself into new forms of global power that uses markets, corporate influence, international banking system, (IMF, World Bank, etc.) and law rather than military conquest, colonial occupation, or direct economic domination to control the affairs of other countries."

The Boston tea party (1773) was a revolt of the Boston merchants against the English who had waived off the import duty exclusively for their own companies to protect their tea monopoly. This was the beginning of the American War of Independence.

THE CARIBBEAN POLICY: American influence of the early 20th century in the Caribbean area soon came to be spoken of as resting on what some writers call the Caribbean Policy and others the Panama Policy. This was simply the resolution of the United States to defend the Isthmus and its approaches, even if need be, by violating the sovereignty of the Caribbean republics. The first step was the establishment of a protectorate over Cuba in 1901, while the United States was still in military occupation of the island as a result of the Spanish-American War.

America has devised a system of Government with a strong stress on freedom, free speech and democracy. The political debate in the US is noisier on morality than in Europe. It includes free speech, democracy and pluralism, more than on benefit and income. The country is full of voices supporting political legitimacy and human rights, more than can be found in Europe which is also a continent of empire-builders, sailors, plunderers and adventurers. It is true that the US has been *"unmoral and unprincipled"* during the Cold War when its sole aim was to defeat communism and supported dictators from Saddam in Iraq to Papa Duvalier in Haiti, but democratic values and political morality have never ceased to be central to American foreign policy. Wilsonianism has long been the creed and those who wavered from it were not accepted by Americans who "decide on their political affiliation less on income and more on, say, church- going, attitude to abortion, race relations, freedom, democracy and dualism. In America, even technical matters become moral questions, like human cloning." It is not possible to have laws on gun regulation without debating about the right to self-defence. In Europe, even moral questions are treated as technologies as happened on stem-cell research.

In America, patriotism and religiosity are the core values, linking them with the defence budget and global security. Americans see foreign policy often in moral terms. Europeans have a different worldview which is largely amoral, hard-core pragmatic, colonial and more dominating than democratic. Americans fought two world wars on moral grounds while Europeans went to war to acquire colonies. When Henry Truman asked Churchill, after World War II was over, to give India independence, the British Prime Minister said he would not preside over the liquidation of the British empire. He said it quite ignoring the promise given to Roosevelt and Mahatma Gandhi. But, the US held referendums before the annexation of small islands and freed them if they so wanted.

Most European colonial powers did not leave colonies until they were thrown out unlike America which enriched its colonies and made them free on its own like the Philippines. Almost all problems in Africa, south and southeast Asia (including Kashmir), the Balkans and also in Latin America are the legacies of the European policy. The secularisation and immorality of Europe are the forces setting it apart from the United States where religion plays a potent role in politics and society, shaping the American worldview. Young Europeans say religion is irrelevant. Americans are more comfortable with notions of good and evil, right and wrong than Europeans who often see such views as expediency.

CATHOLIC FRANCE

In France, which is predominantly Catholic but emphatically secular, about one in 20 people attend the religious service every week, compared with one in three in the United States. Drift from Christian values and disparity with the United States hold true in much of Europe where faithful attendance at Christian services is small. One reason may be that Christian churches now face competition. The Rev. Enzo Bianchi, a Catholic theologian of Italy, says that in today's heterogeneous European capitals, there are more morals and ethics in the market than in the Church. "There's Buddhism, Hinduism, new age spiritualism and consumerism. With all these competitors around, it is hard for the church to sell Christianity," he says (2005).

However, to say that America is sinless in the power game of winning lands and capturing peoples is historically incorrect. Nothing like American slavery had ever happened in the world. President George W. Bush's Abu Ghraib in Iraq in 2003 or Guantanamo Bay in Cuba (2005) or Mai Lai massacre in 1968 match any that we know of Soviet *gulags*. But the American concern for democratic and religious values gives a cutting edge to its claim for global leadership, leaving way behind the united Europe though their income may be almost the same. The world still trusts America, despite its many moral aberrations, more than it trusts Europeans whose history of colonial exploitation will continue to hurt the developing countries.

AMERICA, A MELTING POT

Spaniards came in Florida in 1565, the first white settlement in what later became the USA. The first permanent English settlement was at Jamestown, Virginia, in 1607. In 1620, the *Pilgrim Fathers* landed at Plymouth, and eventually founded Massachusetts. English Roman Catholics founded Maryland in 1634; English Quakers (members of Religious Society of Friends) founded Pennsylvania in 1682. A Dutch settlement (1611) on Manhattan island, named New Amsterdam in 1626, was renamed as New York after it was taken by the English in 1664. Throughout most of the 18th century, the English colonies were threatened by French expansion from the Great Lakes, in Canada, to Louisiana, but the threat from the French ended with the Seven Years War (1756-63). In 1775, the 13 colonies, were New Hampshire, Massachusettes, Rhode Island, Connecticut, New York, New Jersey, Pennsylvania, Delaware, Virginia, North Carolina, South Carolina, Maryland, and Georgia. And, they were against the home govt, and declared themselves in 1776 to be "free and independent states." Led by George Washington, they defeated Britain's George-III's armies in the War of American Independence. By the Treaty of Paris, 1783, Britain recognized the independence of the 13 colonies. A constitution, drawn up in 1787, came into force two years later in 1789. In 1803, Louisiana was bought from Napolean and in 1819 Florida from Spain. Later expansion westward carried the territories of the USA to the Pacific. The war with Mexico, 1846-8, secured from that country the vast lands which were reorganized as California, Utah, New Mexico, and Texas.

Alaska was purchased from Russia in 1867. This is how the 13 colonies expanded to become among the largest nations in the world. And, the strongest too.

AMERICAN CIVIL WAR: The American Civil War was fought in 1861-5. It was the war between 11 of the Southern States, the *Confederate States*, which wished to maintain their rights to be independent, in particular the peculiar institution of Negro slavery, and claimed the right to secede from the Union; and the Northern or *Federal States* which fought to maintain the Union. The Confederate States chose Jefferson Davis as President; the leader of the North was President Lincoln. For four years, the conflict went on. At first the Confederates were successful under Gen Lee at the battles of Bull Run (1861–1862), but Gen Lee was defeated at Gettysburg in 1863; Gen Grant overran the Mississippi states and Gen Shreman marched through Georgia to the sea. On 9 April 1865, Gen Lee surrendered to Gen Grant at Appomattox Court House, and a month later the war was over. Casualties on both sides includes 600,000 dead. Slavery was ended, but the war left behind bitterness that lingered until much later. The war had stimulated the industrial development of the North which led to the construction of roads and railways. The country's vast natural resources were exploited. Thousands more miles of railway were laid. The prairies were inhabited. Americans referred with pride to '*God's own country*', and extolled the virtues of private enterprise. Occasional depressions broke the tide of prosperity, but progress was vast and rapid until 1929 when the greatest of slumps engulfed America. And, F.D. Roosevelt who became President in 1933, embarked on a '*New Deal*' with enormous expenditure plan to revive economy.

US EMERGES A WORLD POWER

Between its independence in 1776 and 1850, Americans took control of half of a continent and 6 million of Americans in 1800 became 23.5 million fifty years later. They were by then already the products of what a nineteenth-century writer called a *melting pot*; they were being moulded into a new nation by the common experience in setting up of a new continent and by the institutions of the republic. During the nineteenth century, the United States took as many European emigrants as the rest of the world combined. Many of them were unable to speak English. Yet English remained the language of the country, and, for a long time, Americans continued to look to England for their cultural inheritance and their ideas. Only in 1837, was an American president (Andrew Jackson) elected who did not have an English, Scotch or

Irish name (there was not to be another until 1901, Theodore Roosevelt). Many basic institutions, too, were English; English legal ideas, an English emphasis on Protestant Christianity and English belief in the sanctity of property were the foundation of the American Republic which, since then, continued to be the leading nation of the world.

PRESIDENTS OF UNITED STATES

1.	George Washington (Independent)	1789
2.	John Adams (Federalist)	1797
3.	Thomas Jefferson (Democrat Rep.)	1801
4.	James Madison (Democrat Rep.)	1809
5.	James Monroe (Democrat Rep.)	1817
6.	John Quincy Adams (Democrat Rep.)	1825
7.	Andrew Jackson (Democrat)	1829
8.	Martin Van Buren (Democrat)	1837
9.	William Henry Harrison (Whig.)	1841
10.	John Tyler (Whig)	1841
11.	James Knox Polk (Democrat)	1845
12.	Zachary Taylor (Whig)	1849
13.	Millard Fillmore (Whig)	1850
14.	Franklin Pierce (Democrat)	1853
15.	James Buchanan (Democrat)	1857
16.	Abraham Lincoln (Republican)	1861
17.	Andrew Johnson (Democrat)	1865
18.	Ulysses Simpson Grant (Republican)	1869
19.	Rutherford Birchard Hayes (Republican)	1877
20.	James Abram Garfield (Republican)	1881
21.	Chester Alan Arthur (Republican)	1881
22.	Grover Cleveland (Democrat)	1885
23.	Benjamin Harrison (Republican)	1889
24.	Grover Cleveland (Democrat)	1893

25.	William McKinley (Republican)	1897
26.	Theodore Roosevelt (Republican)	1901
27.	William Howard Taft (Republican)	1909
28.	Woodrow Wilson (Democrat)	1913
29.	Warren Gamaliel Harding (Republican)	1921
30.	Calvin Coolidge (Republican)	1923
31.	Herbert C. Hoover (Republican)	1929
32.	Franklin Delano Roosevelt (Democrat)	1933
33.	Harry S. Truman (Democrat)	1945
34.	Dwight D. Eisenhower (Republican)	1953
35.	John F. Kennedy (Democrat)	1961
36.	Lyndon B. Johnson (Democrat)	1963
37.	Richard M. Nixon (Republican)	1969
38.	Gerald R. Ford (Republican)	1974
39.	'Jimmy' Carter (Democrat)	1977
40.	Ronald Reagan (Republican)	1981
41.	George H.W Bush (Sr.) (Republican)	1989
42.	W.J. Clinton (Democrat)	1993
43.	George W. Bush (Republican)	2001
44.	Barack Obama (Democrat)	2009

UNITED STATES OF AMERICA – WHEN THE STATES JOIN THE UNION!

States with dates of Capitals admission to Union Union		***Capitals***	***States with date of admission to***
Alabama (1819)	Montgomery	Pennsylvannia	
Alaska (1959)	Juneau	(1787)	Harrisburg
Arizona (1912)	Phoenix	Rhode Island	
Arkansas (1836)	Little Rock	(1790)	Providence

California (1850)	Sacramento	South Carolina	
Colorado (1876)	Denver	(1788)	Columbia
Connecticut (1788)	Hartford	South Dakota (1889)	Pierre
Delaware (1787)	Dover	Tennessee (1796)	Nashville
Florida (1845)	Tallahassee	Texas (1845)	Austin
Georgia (1788)	Atlanta	Utah (1896)	Salt Lake City
Hawaii (1959)	Honolulu	Vermont (1791)	Montpelier
Idaho (1890)	Boise	Virginia (1788)	Richmond
Illinois (1818)	Springfield	Washington	
Indiana (1816)	Indianapolis	(1889)	Olympia
Iowa (1846)	Des Moines	West Virginia	
Kansas (1861)	Topeka	(1863)	Charleston
Kentucky (1792)	Frankfort	Wisconsin (1848)	Madison
Louisiana (1812)	Baton Rouge	Wyoming (1890)	Cheyenne
Maine (1820)	Augusta	District of	
Maryland (1788)	Annapolis	Columbia	
Massachusetts (1788)		Boston	
Michigan (1837)	Lansing		
Minnesota (1858)	St. Paul	Outlying Territories:	
Mississippi (1817)	Jackson	Puerto Rico,	
Missouri (1821)	Jefferson City	CW. of	San Juan
Montana (1889)	Helena	Guam	Agana
Nebraska (1867)	Lincoln	Virgin Islands	Charlotte
Nevada (1864)	Carson City	American Samoa	Fagatogo
New Hampshire (1788)		Concord	Wake Island --
New Jersey (1787)	Trenton	Midway Islands	--
New Mexico (1912) Saipan		Santa Fe	Marians, CW. of the Northern
New York (1788)	Albany	Micronesia,	
		Fed. States of	Moen Is.
North Carolina (1789)		Raleigh	Marshall Islands

North Dakota (1889)		Bismarck	Belau
Ohio (1803)	Columbus	Johnston and Sand Island	–
Oklahoma (1907)	Oklahoma City		
Oregon (1859)	Salem		

NATIONAL INDICATORS - U.S.

Area 9,372,610 sq. km.; capital Washington DC; major towns: New York, Los Angeles, Chicago, Philadelphia, Detroit, San Francisco, Washington, Dallas, San Diego, San Antonio, Houston, Boston, Baltimore, Phoenix, Indianapolis, Memphis, Honolulu, San Jose; territories: the commonwealths of Puerto Rico and Northern Marianas; Guam, the US Virgin Islands, American Samoa, Wake Island, Midway Islands, and Johnston and Sand Islands; political system: liberal democracy; administrative divisions, 50 states; political parties, Democratic Party, liberal centre; Republican Party, centre-right; population 270,312,000 (1998); population growth rate 0.8% (2000-05); ethnic distribution approximately three-quarters of the population are of European origin, including 29% who trace their descent from Britain and Ireland, 8% from Germany, 5% from Italy, and 3% each from Scandinavia and Poland; 12% are African-Americans, 8% Hispanic, and 3% Asian and Pacific islander; African-Americans form 30% of the population of the states of the 'Deep South', namely Alabama, Georgia, Louisiana, Mississippi and South Carolina; Asians are most concentrated in California; life expectancy men 73, women 80; education: (compulsory years) 10; literacy rate 99%; languages English and Spanish; religions, Christian 86.5% (Roman Catholic 26%, Baptist 19%, Methodist 8%, Lutheran 5%); Jewish 1.8%; Muslim 0.5%; Buddhist and Hindu less than 0.5%; currency US dollar; GDP (US $) 7,819.3 billion (1997); GDP per capita (PPP) (US $) 26,525 (1995) growth rate 2.0% (1994-95); average annual inflation 2.6% (1994); major trading partners Canada, Japan, Mexico, EU (principally UK and Germany); resources coal, copper (world's second-largest producer), iron, bauxite, mercury, silver, gold, nickel, zinc (world's fifth-largest producer), tungsten, uranium, phosphate, petroleum, natural gas, timber; industries: machinery, petroleum refinery and products, food processing, motor vehicles, pig iron and steel, chemical products, electrical goods, metal products, printing and publishing, fertilizers, cement; exports: machinery, motor vehicles, agricultural products and foodstuffs, aircraft, weapons, chemicals, electronics. Principal market: Canada 20% (1993); imports: machinery and transport equipments, crude and partly refined petroleum, office machinery, textiles and clothing, Principal source: Canada 18.5% (1993); arable land 18.9% (1993).

HISTORY

c. 15,000 BC First evidence of human occupation in North America.

1513 Ponce de Leon of Spain explored Florida in search of the Fountain of Youth; Francisco Coronado explored south-west region of North America 1540-42.

1565 Spanish founded St. Augustine (Florida), the first permanent European settlement in North America.

1585 Sir Walter Raleigh tried to establish an English colony on Roanoke Island in what he called Virginia.

1607 English colonists founded Jamestown, Virginia, and began tobacco growing.

1620 The Pilgrim Fathers founded Plymouth Colony (near Cape Cod); other English Puritans followed them to New England.

17th-18th Cs Millions of Africans were sold into slavery on American cotton and tobacco plantations.

1763s declared independence; France and Spain supported them in war with Britain.

1781 Americans defeated British at Battle of Yorktown; rebel states formed loose confederation, codified in the Articles of Confederation.

1783 Treaty of Paris: Britain accepted loss of colonies.

1787 'Founding Fathers' devised new constitution for the United States of America.

1789 Washington elected first president of the USA.

1791 Bill of Rights guaranteed individual freedom.

1803 Louisiana Purchase: France sold former Spanish lands between Mississippi River and Rocky Mountains to USA.

1812-14 War with Britain arose from dispute over blockade rights during Napoleonic Wars.

1819	USA bought Florida from Spain.
19th Cs	Mass immigration from Europe; settlers moved westwards, crushing Indian resistance and claiming 'manifest destiny' of USA to control North America. By end of century, number of states in the Union had increased from 17 to 45.
1846-48	Mexican War: Mexico ceded vast territory to USA.
1854	Kansas-Nebraska Act heightened controversy over slavery in southern states; abolitionists formed Republican Party.
1860	Abraham Lincoln (Republican) elected president.
1861	Civil war broke out after 11 southern states, wishing to retain slavery, seceded from USA and formed Confederate States of America under Jefferson Davis.
1865	USA defeated the Confederacy; slavery abolished; President Lincoln assassinated.
1867	Alaska bought from Russia.
1869	Railway linked east and west coasts; rapid growth of industry and agriculture 1870-1920.
1898	Spanish-American War: USA gained Puerto Rio and Guam; also Philippines (until 1946) and Cuba (until 1901); USA annexed Hawaii.
1913	16th amendment to constitution gave federal government power to levy income tax.
1917-18	USA intervened in World War I; President Woodrow Wilson took leading part in peace negotiations 1919, but USA rejected membership of League of Nations.
1920	Women received the right to vote; sale of alcohol prohibited, until 1933.
1924	Native Americans made citizens of USA by Congress.
1929	'Wall Street Crash': stock market collapse led to Great Depression; 13 million unemployed by 1933.
1933	President Franklin Roosevelt launched 'New Deal' with public works to alleviate Depression.
1941	Japanese attacked US fleet at Pearl Harbour, Hawaii, USA

	declared war on Japan; Germany declared war on USA, which henceforth played a leading part in World War II.
1945	USA ended war in Pacific by dropping two atomic bombs on Hiroshima and Nagasaki, Japan.
1947	'Truman Doctrine' pledged US aid for nations threatened by communism; start of Cold War between USA and USSR.
1950-53	US forces engaged in Korean War.
1962	Cuban missile crisis: USA forced USSR to withdraw nuclear weapons from Cuba.
1963	President John F. Kennedy assassinated.
1964-68	President Lyndon Johnson introduced 'Great Society' programme of civil-rights and welfare measures.
1961-75	USA involved in Vietnam War.
1969	US astronaut Neil Armstrong was first person on the Moon.
1974	'Watergate' scandal: evidence of domestic political espionage compelled President Richard Nixon to resign.
1979-80	Iran held US diplomats hostage, humiliating President Jimmy Carter.
1981-89	Tax-cutting policies of President Ronald Reagan led to large federal budget deficit.
1986	'Irangate' scandal: secret US arms sales to Iran illegally funded Contra guerrillas in Nicaragua.
1990	President George Bush declared end to Cold War.
1991	Gulf War: USA played leading part in expelling Iraqi forces from Kuwait.
1992	Democrat Bill Clinton won presidential elections and his running mate Al Gore became vice president.
1996	Clinton re-elected. US missile attacks on Iraq in response to Saddam Hussein's incursions into Kurdish safe havens.
1998	In August, President Clinton testified before a grand jury that he had misled the public for seven months about his 'inappropriate' relationship with the White House intern, Monica Lewinsky. In response to bombings of US embassies in Tanzania and Kenya

	by an Islamic group, the USA bombed sites in Afghanistan and Sudan.
1999	Clinton cleared of perjury and obstruction of justice in an impeachment trial.
2001	George W. Bush elected President.
2005	George W. Bush again re-elected President.
2009	Barack H. Obama elected President.

"Give me liberty or give me death".
– Patrick Henry, March 23, 1775

24

Republic versus democracy; where US, Europe differ

Democracy and republic are often taken as one of the same thing, but there is a fundamental difference. While in both cases, the government is elected by the people, in democracy the majority rules according to their whims, while in the republic the Government rules according to the law framed in the constitution to limit the power of Government and ensure some rights and protection to minorities and individuals.

These succinct definitions of democracy and republic was produced by the US Army in 1928 which was later withdrawn. However the validity of the definition stays. Democracy is a government of the masses where the authority is derived through mass meeting or any other form of "direct" expression which may results in mobocracy. Attitude toward property is negating property rights. Attitude toward law is that the will of the majority shall prevail whether it is based upon cool deliberation or by passion, prejudice, and impulse, without restraint or regard to consequences, according to the US Army definition.

Professor Alexander Fraser Tytler, nearly two centuries ago, had this to say about Democracy: "*A Democracy cannot exist as a permanent form of Government. It can only exist until the voters discover they can vote themselves out of public treasury. From that moment on, the majority always votes for the candidate promising the most benefits from the public treasury; with the result, democracy always collapses over a loose fiscal policy, always to be followed by a dictatorship.*" A democracy is majority rule and harms liberty because there is no law to prevent the majority from trampling on individual rights. Whatever the majority says goes! A lynch mob is an example of pure democracy in action. There is only one dissenting vote, and that is cast by the person at the end of the rope. Socrates was put to death by a majority vote.

Authority in a republic is derived through the election by the people of public officials best fitted to represent them. Attitude toward property is respect for laws and individual rights, and a sensible economic procedure. Attitude toward law is the administration of justice in accord once with *fixed principles and established evidence,* with a strict regard to consequences a greater number of citizens. Avoids the dangerous extreme of either tyranny or mobocracy which results in statesmanship, liberty, reason, justice, contentment, and progress.

REPUBLIC IS GOVERNED

BY FIXED PRINCIPLES

A republic is a form of government under a constitution which provides for the election of an executive and a legislative body, have all the power of appointment, all power of legislation all power to raise revenue and appropriate expenditures, and are required to create; a judiciary to pass upon the justice and legality of their governmental acts and to which recognize and ensures certain inherent individual rights.

Take away any one or more of those four elements and you are drifting into autocracy. Add one or more to those four elements and you are drifting into democracy American Constitutional fathers, familiar with the strength and weakness of both autocracy and democracy, with fixed principles definitely in mind, defined a representative republican form of government. They "made a very marked distinction between a republic and a democracy and said repeatedly and emphatically that they had founded a republic." A republic is a government of law under a Constitution. The Constitution holds the government in check and prevents the majority (acting through their government) from violating the rights of the individual. Under this system of government a lynch mob is illegal. The suspected criminal cannot be denied his right to a fair trial even if a majority of the citizenry demands otherwise, according to Tytler.

Democracy and Republic are often taken as one of the same thing, but there is a fundamental difference. Whilst in both cases the government is elected by the people, in democracy the majority rules according to their

Democracy	Republic
a: government by the people; *especially*: rule of the majority. b: a government in which the supreme power is vested in the people and exercised by them directly or indirectly through a system of representation usually involving periodically held free elections. Attitude toward law is that the will of the majority shall regulate, whether it be based upon deliberation or governed by passion, prejudice, and impulse, without restraint or regard to consequences.	a: a government having a chief of state who is not a monarch and who in modern times is usually a president: a political unit (as a nation) having such a form of government. b: a government in which supreme power resides in a body of citizens entitled to vote and is exercised by elected officers and representatives responsible to them and governing according to law, and not majority.

whims, whilst in the republic the Government rule according to law. This law is framed in the Constitution to limit the power of Government and ensuring some rights and protection to minorities and individuals. The difference between republic and righteous republic is that in the republic the government rules according to the law set up by men, in the righteous republic the law is the Law of God. Only in the righteous republic it can truly be said *"One nation under God"* for it is governed under commandments of the only One True God and there is no pluralism of religions. Autocracy declares the divine right of kings; its authority can not be questioned; its powers are arbitrarily or unjustly administered. Mobocracy: 1. Political control by a mob. 2. The mass of common people as the source of political control.

In sum democracy involves the government ruling and making laws for the "greater good" of all people, they may abolish personal rights in doing so; democracy is government by and for the people. They may or may not be republics-that is, government limited by constitution or charter. The tricky part of "democracy" is defining "the people" and then deciding what counts could be considered the content of democratic practice.

Republic invloves the government using and abiding by the constitution heavily. Personal rights are respected and cannot be taken away. This helps to avoid *tyranny* and *mobocracy* (the majority makes laws and governs by passion, prejudice, or impulse, without restraint or regard to consequences). Republics are the common and "standard" type of governments found today, not democracies, despite what many people think. Just as democracies may or may not be republics, may or may not be democracies.

MAJORITY RULE

Democracy and Republic are two forms of government which are distinguished by their treatment of the minority, and the individual, by the majority. In a democracy, the majority has unlimited power over the minority. This system of government does not provide a legal safeguard of the rights of the individual and the minority. It has been referred to as *"majority over man"*. In a Republic, the majority is limited and constrained by a written constitution which protects the rights of the individual and the minority. The purpose of a republic form of government is to control the majority and to protect. The God-given, inalienable rights and liberty of the Individual. The United States of America is a Republic.

The Founding Fathers who wrote the American Constitution gave a republic. They believed democracies were dangerous and unworkable." On that, they are partly right, but they fail to mention that democracies and republics overlap. They are not opposites. And they fail to account for the history of American government since 1788, much less the debates that took place in America prior to 1788, when the U.S. Constitution was substituted for the Articles of Confederation.

Democracy means rule of the people. The two most common forms of democracy are direct democracy and representative democracy. In direct democracy everyone takes part in making a decision, as in a town meeting or a referendum. The specific rules may vary: perhaps everyone must agree, perhaps there must be consensus, perhaps a mere majority is required to make a decision. The other, better known form of democracy is a representative democracy. People elect representative to make decisions or laws. Again, specifics vary greatly.

ROME WAS REPUBLIC NOT DEMOCRACY

A representative democracy is a kind of republic. What distinguishes a republic is that it has an elected government. Representative democracies are, therefor, a kind of republic. Self-appointed governments such as monarchies, dictatorships, oligarchies, theocracies and juntas are not republics. However, this still allows for a wide spectrum. The classic is the Roman Republic, in which only a tiny percentage of citizens, members of the nobility, were allowed to vote for the Senators, who made the laws and also acted as Rome's supreme court. Most people would say that Rome was a Republic, but not a democracy, since it was very close to being an oligarchy, rule by the few. Although the Roman Republic was not a dictatorship (until Augustus Caesar grabbed power), it did not allow for rule of the people. In both theory and practice the Soviet Union, that late evil empire, was a republic (Union of Soviet Socialist Republics) because the lawmakers were elected, if only by the Communist Party members.

Beginning with the Constitution's adoption, America has been a Republic. But the dominant trend over the last two centuries has been to make it into a democracy as well, a representative democracy, also know as a democratic republic. True, the creation of the Constitution itself was partly a reaction against democracy. In states like Pennsylvania, Rhode Island, and Massachusetts, the situation was getting way too democratic for the monied aristocracy that had, since the American Revolution, refused to share power with ordinary men.

AMERICAN REVOLUTION

The causes of the American Revolution were many, but for the moneyed class there were three principal aims. They sought self-government: that is, they sought to rule the colonies themselves, to further their own interests. They sought to protect the institution of slavery, which had been endangered by Lord Mansfield's ruling against it in the Sommersett case of 1772. And land speculators like George Washington sought to seize more Native American Indian land, which the British had outlawed. But to win the American Revolution this predatory elite needed help. Their own rhetoric about freedom and equality led to widespread demands for the right to vote: universal suffrage. In other words, the people began demanding democracy. Even the slaves (white and black alike) demanded to be freed and allowed to vote.

After the British were defeated a centralized, national government was setup by George Washington and company not as a method of extending freedom and the right to vote, but as a way of keeping control in the hands of rich. They wrote several anti-democratic provisions into the U.S.

Constitution. Slavery was institutionalized. The Senate was not to be elected directly by the people; rather Senators were to be appointed by state legislatures. The President was not to be directly elected by the voters, but elected through an electoral college. The Supreme Court was to be appointed. Only the House of Representatives was elected directly.

The U.S. Constitution left the question of who could vote in elections to each individual state. In most states only white men who owned a certain amount of property could vote. So, on the whole, the first federal government that met in 1789 was a republic with only a fig-leaf of democratic representation. This is what today commentators mean is when they say America is a republic, not a democracy. The early federal government was not very powerful. In state after state it became easier for white males to qualify to vote. And slowly, decade after decade, our republic became a democratic republic.

BILL OF RIGHTS

At the national level the major steps toward democracy can be marked by amendments to the U.S. Constitution. The Bill of Rights guaranteed limits to the power of the federal government. The Thirteenth Amendment abolished slavery. The Fourteenth Amendment effectively extended the vote to all adult male citizens, including ex-slaves, by penalizing states that did not allow for universal male suffrage. The Fifteenth Amendment explicitly gave the right to vote to former slaves. After the Supreme Court ruled that the Fourteenth and Fifteenth Amendments did not extend suffrage to women, a vigorous campaign for the vote was launched by women, who received the vote through the Nineteenth Amendment in 1920. But the main Amendment that tipped the scales from the national government of the United States being a mere republic to being a true representative democracy was the often-overlooked Seventeenth Amendment, which took effect in 1913. Since 1913 the U.S. Senate has been elected directly by the voters, rather than being appointed by the state legislatures. That makes the national government democratic in form, as well as being a republic.

SLAVES COULD NOT VOTE UNTIL 1960s IN AMERICAN REPUBLIC

There will always be anti-democratic forces in any society. The most blatantly undemocratic feature of U.S. Government in the 20th century was the unconstitutional but systematic disenfranchisement of African-American and other non-white citizens. This came to an end in the 1950s and 1960s with a series of Supreme Court decisions against segregation laws, the passage of Civil Rights Acts, and the passage of the Twenty-Fourth Amendment outlawing poll taxes. We even lowered the voting age to 18 with the Twenty-Sixth Amendment in 1971.

There are no longer any voter-qualification impediments to democracy in the United States. But many have noted that the will of the people has tended not to prevail, and that a majority of people eligible to vote are so discouraged that they do not vote. The main reason for this is the buying and selling of elections and politicians by the wealthier class of citizens and their special interest groups. A year or more before elections take place, the winner is decided by those who vote with dollars. But this is a defect in democracy, not a reason to abandon it. The answer is to cure the defect, not to attempt to destroy our representative democracy.

HOW IT ALL BEGAN

'Republic' is derived from the Latin phrase *respublica* — "a public thing". Ancient Romans used this to describe the wellspring of their governance system for their city-state by about 500 BC. Inspired by notions of Athenian democracy, Rome's republic was a noble experiment. The inscription 'SPQR', emblazoned on all Roman standards and public buildings, expanded to *'The Senate and People of Rome'*. It touted to the world that Roman political power was vested in a great many, not concentrated in one ruler or family. Rome's republican tryst, sustained by public elections and classical debate, lasted until Julius Caesar seized control in 44 BC. Being succeeded by his wily nephew, Augustus — who founded a famous empire that lasted a while longer — soon consigned the republican ideal to the dustbin of the world.

Rome took much of its republican template from Greece. In particular, from Athens, most luminous of ancient Greece's many city-states. The notion of moving political power away from an individual to the masses sprang from the need to safeguard the then 'new' notion of personal and individual freedom. It meant citizens would willingly join any battle to safeguard this freedom from any aggressor. But it was a troubled ideal. Athens ran on slave labour; democracy became limited to narrower sections as time went by. Tyranny and mob rule reared their ugly heads; Athenian imperialism overstretched the city-state so much so that even Plato and Aristotle, in effect, argued for enlightened oligarchies in their political philosophy.

Aristotle's star pupil, Alexander of Macedon, soon put paid to all notions of republicanism by conquering large parts of Eurasia to establish an empire so large that it would only truly be eclipsed by Rome's later rise.

Besides the many obvious fruits of Renaissance and Reformation — Europe's two most epochal events in the second millennium — the republican ideal owes much to Niccolo Machiavelli and John Locke. Machiavelli, a 15th century Italian statesman-writer, located sovereignty in a collective exercise of power. The governed would guide actions of their ideal governor, he argued forcefully. Little wonder that Rousseau later referred to Machiavelli's 'The Prince' as "a handbook for Republicans". Locke, 17th century England's most notable philosopher, cut through mythological mumbo-jumbo to argue that true power must formally lie with the people. A 'contract' existed between rulers and people, that bound both to establish laws "directed to no other end but the peace, safety, and public good of the people". The rise of England's parliament soon after injected a strong republican element into its body politic. Modern liberalism — which sprang from Locke's work — did the same in most of the western world.

IT CAME TO EUROPE WITH MACHIAVELLI & LOCKE

Two revolutions, one decade and two continents apart, brought forth two republican models the world still looks to. The American, in 1776, and French in 1789. The first saw England lose its earliest colony. Monarchy was sternly repudiated and the ideas behind the Declaration of Independence exploded onto the western world as a serious alternative whose time had come. That declaration laid the basis for much republican-democratic ideation. The US's new constitution firmly located power with the people by stating that governments derived "their just powers from the consent of the governed".

The French Revolution brought French monarchy, and all its attendant power structures, to a violent end, sending shockwaves through European kingdoms. The new republic's bloody convulsions and military campaigns — for liberty, equality, and national self-aggrandizement — spread the spirit of revolution. Even under Napoleon Bonaparte. France would flirt with monarchy again but remained firmly democratic and republican in spirit ever after.

Nationalism soon proved a potent new force, redrawing Europe's map several times over. Old power structures were found severely wanting. All big European monarchies made room for democratic representation.

Communism brought much churn to notions of republicanism. The republic was integral to all socialist theorizing in late 19th, early 20th centuries, but was markedly different in form and intent from what had by then become the liberal-capitalist model of republican democracy.

All power flowed from the masses in socialism too but political power was clearly vested in one entity: the Communist Party, which represented these masses. Coercive institutions were justified for liberty and greater good, supposedly driven by collective approaches to national growth. But political theorists wonder whether these were true republics, devoid as most were of democratic representation attributed to republicanism. Republicanism too suffered abuse. Many republics today are just so in name and little else, as many before. 'Banana Republics' was coined to describe one such bunch in the Americas, a collection of nations ruled by iron-fisted despots propped up by outside power. Pakistan under military ruler Pervez Musharraf could scarcely be termed a republic, even though Musharraf even got himself duly 'elected'.

More intriguing still are 'republics' of Syria and North Korea, among others. Power passes from father to son here, much like a monarchy, but rulers are presidents and rule in the name of the people. Dynastic rule is not a habit easily rid. Even in the most republican of systems, space is often made for dynastic succession of sorts. The perfect republic, say political theorists, is still work in progress.

IN INDIA, IT IS BHARAT

DISTINCTLY UNDEFINED

Given India's long history of fractious monarchies and mighty empires, the freedom movement set itself in democratic tradition. That wish came to final culmination on January 26th, 1950, when the nation was declared a republic and given the world's most comprehensive Constitution to abide by. But India may not be a stranger to this 'western-inspired' system. Historical research has shown, but not proven, that some city-states in north India between 500 BC and 400 AD might have actually been ancient republics of a sort. The Licchavi state, a Buddhist kingdom with *ganas* and *sanghas* — normally translated as republics, but best referred to as 'self-governing multitudes' — was the most prominent. A good thought to hold as India basks in 60 years of republican glory. After all, that's no mean achievement.

The question of right and wrong of slavery is eternal and throughout the world. And, this question will continue to haunt this country much after Judge Douglas and I are dead and forgotten.

– Abraham Lincoln in his speech during the Senatorial poll campaign against Judge Stephen A. Douglas in 1858.

25

The scramble for Africa for gold and slaves

The Europeans were slow to capture black Africa but very cruel when they had done it. Slavery is the gift of imperialism and also all its consequences from which Africans still suffer. Once cradle of humankind, Africa is today known for poverty, tribalism and conflict.

Of all the targets of European empire-builders, Africa was the nearest; and "Black Africa" (South of Equator) among the most backward and poor. Yet, save for its far south, it was the last to be grabbed although its coast had been known to Europeans for centuries. Until 1860, the interior was protected. Fevers prevented white men from intruding deep into the land; roads were few and large water areas blocked access to places.

However, the unstoppable Europeans started from their posts along the shores; walked the old Arab trade routes and, by 1862, they reached the source of the Nile. A little later, they traced the route of the Niger and confirmed the reality of Africa's fabled riches–ivory, gold, diamonds, emeralds, copper. Europeans found that, instead of buying crops like cotton or palm oil from its villagers, they could set up plantations and use cheap local labour to work them. By that time, Africa had become too valuable to be left to Africans. Besides, Christian missionaries had also the "mission" of civilizing black people because they were "savage, heathen and ungodly". In sum, Africa was ripe for takeover.

Britain at first opposed division but seized the richest parts, including today's South Africa, Ghana and Nigeria. Belgium's King Leopold-II was one of Europe's least powerful rulers. But, once he had carved out the Congo basin as his personal fief, other countries were quick to stake claims. Otto von Bismarck, chancellor of the newly-formed Germany, put in a bid for huge chunks of East and West Africa. Although Europeans were quick to fight each other at home, but they became friends to seize the continent that they barely knew.

Abraham Lincoln (1809-65)
The Emancipator

In 1884, European powers met in Berlin to divide Africa. In some areas, ignorant of people and geography alike, they made frontiers simply by drawing straight lines on the map. The Africa they captured was backward, poor and politically divided into several thousand units, based on language, culture, or conquest, paying tribute to their conquerors. Slaving gangs sent out by some of its own rulers spread war. Thus, arbitrary division of Africa is the principle source of its present-day problems there. Those Africans who resisted the takeover were attacked and brutally crushed. Europeans had guns and Africans had swords. Much of Africa surrendered without a fight; kings signed away their sovereignty with thumb prints. Many allied with the intruders, maybe believing that they would not stay long and would give help against local rivals. Some tried to play one set of Europeans off against another. Others were overawed by technology; the kingdoms of northern Nigeria surrendered to forces, led by a handful of white men, far smaller than their own because of poor weapons.

EUROPEANS CAPTURED AFRICA

By 1914, Europeans had captured all of Africa, except Liberia, the state founded by America for its ex-slaves, and Abyssinia (Ethiopia), an ancient kingdom which was left free because it fought off the Italians in 1896. Europeans counted Africans, taxed them and divided their communities into tribes and constructed new groups to keep them divided. The best land was taken for plantations, and the minerals dug out and shipped off to be processed in Europe. Africans saw little of their wealth and lost all of them. The European occupation of Black Africa was, however, short-lived, barely a generation in some areas. After the World War II in which many thousands of Africans

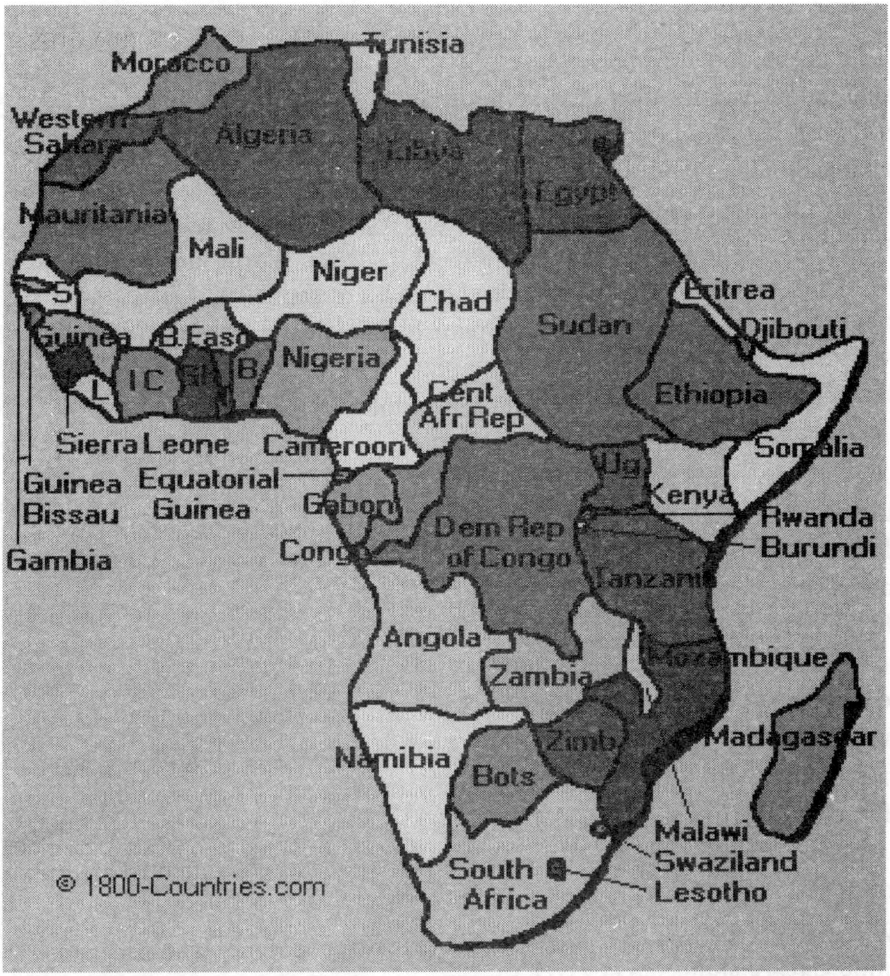

died fighting for the Allies, the US wanted an end to European imperialism, and she was supported by the Soviet Union. In Algeria, Kenya and Rhodesia, white settlers tried to keep power by force, but in fullness of time lost them.

It is hard to draw up a balance-sheet of colonialism but perhaps the Africans' worst loss was not of land or power but self-respect, because Europeans taught them that their ways, cultures and gods were inferior and should be abandoned. Africa was left both psychologically and politically impoverished. Today, it is a continent of states stranded between old and new ways. African rulers set up the European style institutions bequeathed to them by Europeans, ignoring the African traditions and values. No wonder, no African country except South Africa is able to operate democracy although all of them have elections, real or fake.

SLAVE TRADE

The slave trade in Africa began in the 16th century after European settlers started colonizing the New World. And, by the time the Atlantic slave trade was abolished in the 19th century, 12 million African men, women, and children had already been transported as slaves to American colonies, some 70% of them for the sugar fields of Brazil and the West Indies. Black slaves set up new frontiers, converted the wilderness of the New World into fertile land. Sugar, rum, tobacco, rice, and other staples were sent to European market. The beneficiaries were the English, Spanish, Danish and European investors. Slave-grown sugar transformed the Western diet, creating a taste for sweet drinks and food; slave-grown cotton clothed the Western world.

Slavery's economic and social benefits appeared to be so obvious (like India's caste system) that initial ethical doubts were rapidly overcome. Who could deny that slavery brought prosperity to all involved – except, of course, to slaves? Few spoke against it, and their voices were usually drowned by the clamour for yet more slave-grown profit. In 1789, the white found a new world, the US, which needed blacks to work for it. They seized blacks in Africa, force-marched them to the coast, carrying ivory or copper; then inspected them like animals, sold and crammed into ships and made the 40-day voyage to the US, chained and forced to lie in their own vomit and urine. Then taken out of the ship, inspected again and re-sold. They were branded and forced to dig in mines, clear land, plant and harvest sugar. This was the time when Europe was passing through the period of Enlightenment. This was the irony.

William Wilberforce (see box) was the British campaigner who succeeded in getting slavery abolished in 1807. Slavery underpinned the economy of 18th century Britain as oil does business today.

To historians such as Richard Beck, the story of the slave trade is a *morality play* with the British cast as "evil knaves." Profits from the bloody trade secured the imperial hegemony of Georgian England. It was only brought to an end in 1807. "There was nothing noble about abolition," says Beck.

By contrast, champions of Britain's imperial past point to 1807 as symbolic of "our good empire." It was a heroic moment when idealism trumped materialism as the Royal Navy scoured the seas for illegal slave ships. This is the story of the Rule Britannia, William Wilberforce and the Society of

WILLIAM WILBERFORCE
THE PROFILE OF AN ABOLISHIONIST

Campaigned against Slave trade by Wilbeforce

William Wilberforce (1759-1833) - A British reformer born at Hull, he began his attacks on slavery while at school, and from 1788 devoted himself to its abolition. He entered parliament in 1780, his bill for the abolition of the slave-trade was passed in 1807.

He was a leading member of the Evangelical Movement, which sought to promote Christian values in late 18th-early 19th-century English society, William Wilberforce fought from 1788 to abolish British involvement in the slave trade. Having achieved this in 1807, he began campaigning for the abolition of the slave trade abroad and the total abolition of slavery. Slavery in the British Empire ended in 1833, the year of his death.

News of the passing of the act abolishing slavery in British colonies was brought to him as he lay dying. Wilberforce had spent his entire political career fighting against the slave trade. Slavery had been illegal in England since 1772, but the slave trade continued in full flood. About 20,000 Africans were transported to America every year by ships from Liverpool, Bristol and London. The opponents of the trade, called "Abolitionists," fought long and hard against it. Finally, a motion to declare it illegal was carried by Charles James Fox (1749-1806) through British parliament in 1807. The next step was to persuade other countries to abolish the trade, and to stop illegal trading (profits were so large that slave-traders could afford to lose two ships out of three). France, Spain and Portugal soon agreed to stop trading, but as long as slavery itself was legal, illegal slave-trading went on. Britain's abolition of slavery cost the government £20,000,000 in compensation to slave-owners. But it was an important step towards ending an ancient evil.

Friends. Certainly, the slave economy underpinned the riches of 18th century society and it had a dominating influence across the British politico-financial establishment. Among the investors in slave trade were the Hanoverian royal family, numerous colleges of Oxford and Cambridge, universities, and even the Church of England. They made money while black slaves were bought and sold in open markets.

British Professor James Walvin says that the British had shipped extraordinary numbers of Africans across the Atlantic. And in what conditions: "The barbarity of the Middle Passage often led to 30 per cent morality rates among the ten million slaves shipped across the Atlantic. They were shackled together and laid back to back for weeks on end; Christian British captains were to throw sick slaves into water and claim insurance on the lost cargo," James says.

Despite its barbarity, ending this lucrative trade was an uphill struggle. Few today would go so far as to hail it, "the most altruistic act since Christ's crucifixion," but halting trafficking had serious economic costs. Yet the moral certitude of Wilberforce and his evangelical allies convinced MPs in the West minister parliament, many of whom had slaving interests, of the ethical case for abolishing "the foul iniquity." And, slavery was abolished.

Slavery infected the Georgian economy as readily as oil underpins business today. 2007 offers a unique opportunity to say something new to a broad audience about British imperial and post-colonial past. For much of its modern history, Britain has stood at the hub of a series of global networks: religious, commercial, political. Much of it has been exploitative and racist. But it hasn't all been one way. Ideas, people, and cultures have influenced the British metropolis as much as the colonies. "So, while the unrivalled horror of the slave trade should never be diminished, Britishers could use next year's anniversary as much to enlighten 2007 as to commemorate 1807," says Tristram Hunt, author of *Building Jerusalem, the Rise and Fall of our Victorian City*.

SLAVE REBELLIONS

Europe took 300 years to reject it. Christianity and Islam both forbade the enslavement of their own adherents, but saw nothing against enslaving unbelievers; rather, they thought it might bring them salvation. Christians saw black people as descendants of devils, and, therefore, eternally cursed. Later, the slavers, sea captains and ship-owners alike, believed Africans would be better off as slaves in America than free persons in Africa. In the 18th century, an anti-slavery lobby built up in Europe, notably in Britain, the superpower of the seas. In 1772, Lord Mansfield, a judge, ruled that a runaway slave could not be forced back by his master in the West Indies. The ruling was interpreted as confirming that there could be no slavery in Britain. In America, it created fears that Britain might try to abolish slavery in its colonies. The desire to maintain slavery was not the motive for the American War of Independence. But it became one. Slavery did not end in the British Caribbean until 1838, in the United States 1865, in Spanish-owned Cuba, 1886, in Brazil, 1888 and in Mauritania (Africa) until as late as 1980.

Nanny was a legendary figure in the style of Robin Hood or King Arthur who led a band of fugitive slaves in the 18th century and defeated the might of the British empire, at least according to Jamaican folklore. It is said that, under her formidable leadership, her army called *Maroons,* (meaning the wild and untamed), wore bushes as camouflage and used sticks, stones, and machetes to wage guerrilla warfare, killing soldiers, raiding plantations, and giving hope to slaves throughout the Caribbean. The British suffered thousands and thousands of causalities. Nanny is seen as a personification of black resistance to slavery like *Spartacus.* Her armed insurgency challenged the popular image of passive victims who awaited their liberation by white abolitionists such as William Wilberforce, the British MP who led the case against slavery in London and abolished slave trade in 1807.

Ms. Dynamite (Niomi Melean - Daley), who has done a documentary on Nanny, says: "My most emotional moment came at a museum when I was shown sets of small chains and gibbets (gallows) used to kill, incarcerate, and torture slaves. I asked the man who was with me, why the one was so small. He said, those were for children: they would put it round the kids' ankles and then hammer the giant nail into the floor so that they couldn't get under their parents feet while they were at work. That was the hardest thing to see. All I could picture was my son. I was fighting back my tears", Ms. Dynamite, who has Jamaican father and Scottish mother, said in an interview published in Time magazine in March 2007.

COUNTRIES THAT HAVE CHANGED NAMES

Old names	***New names***
Western Samoa	Samoa
Persia	Iran
Rhodesia	Zimbabwae
Zaire	Congo Free State
Upper Volta	Burkina Faso
Belgian Congo	Zaire
Abyssia	Ethiopia
Ottoman Empire	Turkey
Transjorden	Jorden
New Herbidiee	Vanuatu
Gilbert Islands	Tuvalu
Gold Coast	Ghana
Belorussia	Belorus
British Hondourus	Belize
British South Asia	India, Pakistan
Eastern Pakistan	Bangladesh
Burma	Myanmar

200 YEARS AFTER UK ENDED SLAVE TRADE

Britain marked on March 25, 2007 200 years since its first law, abolishing trade in African slaves was passed which was a major step towards ending the practice that shipped more than 10 million Africans into slavery. Many slaves, such as, Samuel Sharpe of Jamaica fought for their freedom. Toussaint L'Ouveture and his army freed an entire country. It was rebellions

ORIGIN OF SLAVERY

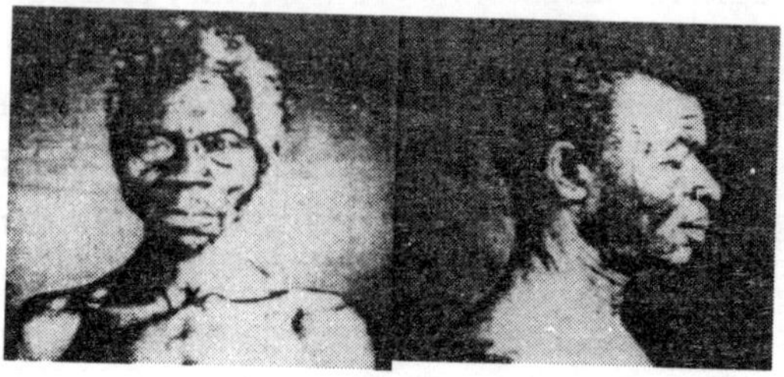

SLAVERY: The earliest known photographs of American slaves, discovered at Harvard University in 1977. On the left, a Congo slave called Renty, and on the right Jack, from the Guinea Coast, who bears ritual scars decorating his cheek.
Photos: Popperfoto

As a legal and economic status of being another's property, slavery probably originated in early agricultural societies when slaves were recruited from among prisoners of war. In Greece and Rome, slavery formed the economic basis of society. From the 2nd century BC, global conquests flooded Rome with slaves who, in the 1st century AD, outnumbered free men in Italy. Several slave revolts occurred. The economic crisis of the 2nd century AD, onwards led to alleviation of the slaves' conditions, and serfdom replaced slavery. It, nevertheless died, out slowly, surviving in England until the 11th century. The colonization of America led to a revival of slavery in the 16th century, and to the establishment of a traffic in Negro slaves. Humanitarian agitation led to the ban on slave trade in the British colonies in 1807 and of slave-holding itself in 1833. Leaders of the movement were Granville Sharp, Thomas Clarkson and Wilberforce. In the USA the Civil War turned largely on slavery, which was declared illegal by Lincoln in 1865. Slavery was, however, not officially abolished in Saudi Arabia until 1963, and in Mauritania until 1930, and it still lingers in some obscure parts of the world.

like these that ultimately forced the Europeans to abolish slavery. During the 19th century slavery continued as "indentured labour", used as a factor of production by colonial trading companies in concert with local agents. Ultimately, it wasn't Protestant conscience that eradicated slavery, but the ascendance of mass-production lines and innovations such as the steam engine. Here are some shocking facts about the slave trade.

TYPES OF SLAVERY

- Most common was domestic slavery.
- Slave labours were employed on plantation, in classical Greece and Rome; in the 19th century Iraq, and in a few areas of sub-Saharan Africa, and across the Americas. It was most practiced in the southern United States.

SLAVERY IN AFRICA

- Up to 18 million Africans were delivered into the Islamic trans-Saharan and Indian Ocean slave trades between 650 and 1905.
- In the 15th century, the Europeans began to trade in slaves. By 1867, at least 10 million- (estimates range as high as 60 million) Africans had been shipped as slaves to the New World.

TRANSATLANTIC SLAVE TRADE

Britain's abolition of the slave trade In 1807 marked the beginning of the end for the transatlantic trade in human beings which, for over 400 years, had witnessed at least 11 million people transported from Africa into slavery in appallingly inhumane conditions. Slave ships from Europe sailed to Africa with textiles, rum, guns and other goods to exchange for slaves, and slaves were transported across the Atlantic to sell to plantation owners.

UNCLE TOM'S CABIN, THE BOOK THAT PRODUCED A CIVIL WAR

Ms Harriet, Beecher Stowe, an American housewife, had written a book in 1852, *Uncle Tom's Cabin*, which was so moving and so enormous that it shook the American conscience on slavery. At one time, all the printing units in England and American were printing this book, still they could not meet the demand. After the Civil War was over, President Lincoln invited Ms Stowe to the White House to know the person who could write like that. Ms Stowe, a simple, not very educated lady either, was nervous and prepared her best to answer all the possible questions the President might ask. But, Lincoln didn't ask any. While leaving her in the porch of the White House after the visit, President Lincoln looked back to the author and said: "Ms Stowe, please don't write any other book like this; I am too old to fight another civil war." In January 2006, the Montgomery Planning Board of Rockville, Maryland, bought the one-acre log cabin for $1 million to preserve it as a reminder of a great event. This log cabin was the home of Josiah Henson, a slave Ms Stowe used as a model for the Uncle Tom character in her book. The cabin and house sit behind a fringe of trees on a busy thoroughfare, a few miles from the Washington Beltway.

Ships returned to Europe with sugar and coffee. The following are some estimated numbers.

West Indies & Caribbean:	:	4,128,000
British	:	2,000,000
French	:	1,600,000

SLAVERY STILL IN MAURITANIA

They do not wear chains, nor are they branded with the mark of their masters, but slaves still exist in Mauritania. In the Saharan Islamic state, the centuries-old system of bondage is resisting the rise of democracy in the largely desert former French colony. Herding camels or goats out in the sun-blasted dunes of the Saharan, or serving hot mint tea to guests in the richly carpeted villas of Nouakchott, Mauritanian slaves serve their masters and are passed on as family chattels from generation to generation. They may number thousands, anti-slavery activists say.

A shocking anomaly in the 21st century, this is widely accepted in a racially diverse, hierarchical society dominated by a Moorish elite. "It's like having sheep or goats. If a woman is a slave, her descendants are slaves," said Boubacar Messaoud, who was born a slave and is now his country's leading antislavery campaigner.

He says a 1981 decree outlawing slavery is a dead letter and slavery is alive in Mauritania, with all its manifestations of non-paid work, punishment, forced sex and other abuses. Mauritania's military rulers shy away from discussing the issue and prefer to talk of "vestiges of slavery *(Source: Reuters – March 2007)*

Dutch	:	500,000
Danish	:	28,000

SLAVE SHIPS

The ships took six to eight weeks to make the crossing from Africa to the New World. Over 600 men, women and children were packed tightly into every available space. During this journey, many slaves died, some committed suicide while others went completely insane.

THE END

- Britain's *"Abolition of Slavery"* Act was passed in March 1807, which forbade trading in slaves with Africa, and in 1833 abolished slavery entirely across its empire.
- The US Congress banned import of slaves from 1808. But it was only after President Abraham Lincon's Emancipation Proclamation and the 13th Amendment to the Constitution that slavery was abolished in 1865.
- Slavery was abolished in Ethiopia in 1931 and Saudi Arabia in 1962.

AMERICAN CIVIL WAR

In 1861-5 was fought the Civil War, or the War between 11 of the Southern States, the *Confederate* which wished to maintain their 'states' rights, in particular the institution of Negro slavery, and claimed the right to secede from the Union; and the Northern, or *Federal States* which fought to maintain the Union. The Confederate States chose Jefferson Davis as President; the leader of the North was President Lincoln. For 4 years the conflict went on. At first, the Confederates were successful under Lee at the battles of Bull Run (1861 and 1862), but Lee suffered a repulse at Gettysburg in 1863; Grant overran the Mississippi states and Sherman marched through Georgia to the sea. On April 9, 1865, Lee surrendered to Grant at Appomattox Court House, and a month later the war was over. Casualties on both sides included 600,000 dead. Slavery was ended.

American anti-slavery movement had become a crusade. But the supporters of slavery dug in, convinced of their own moral, religious, and economic justification. Pro-slavery arguments had taken on a racist colour, but their basis remained economic because slave-based cotton was profitable. The fight against slavery was also seen as an attack on the Southern way of life itself. This siege mentality led to the American Civil War. Although the war was about secession, the conflict focused on slavery. In January 1863, Abraham Lincoln issued the Emancipation Proclamation, granting freedom to all slaves in the rebellious states and two years later, the Thirteenth Amendment to the American Constitution confirmed freedom throughout the USA. Lincoln's assassination sanctified his crusade against slavery and made him the greatest champion of the poor for all time to come.

To write and read the stories of helpless slaves, hungry and chained, may be a professional work, but close your eyes and think of those sad faces, men, women and children, in chain and you will reach for your gun.

White men came to Africa we had the land and they had the Bible. They asked us to close eyes and pray. When we opened eyes, we had the Bible and they had the land.

– Desmond Tutu

26

Africa-where armies followed the Bible

"If you become a Christian now, you will go to heaven," told Father Richards to Lady Nehanda, a condemned African woman warrior, standing at the scaffold. "Is that the place, Father, where white men go," asked the condemned rebel. "Yes, yes, daughter; this is where white men go." Nehanda turned to the executioner and asked him to hurry. The stories of the conquest of the poor man's world by rich Europeans are as painful as they are cruel.

White men believe that they have a moral obligation to carry the blessings of their own religion and civilisation to "backward" peoples. In their view, the white man has a duty to uplift his less fortunate brothers and sisters in the yellow (brown) man's Asia or in the black man's Africa. No wonder, countless missionaries braved the perils of the jungles, unknown seas and hostile people to do this job. US President William McKinley said, God told him "to take them all (the Philippine islands), and educate the Filipinos, and uplift and civilise and Christianize them, and by God's grace do the best we could to them, as we do to our fellowmen for whom Christ died."

Joseph Chamberlain, Britain's leading exponent of imperialism, said in 1893, *"it is our duty to do our share of work in civilising Africa,"* and John Bright, the chief spokesman of the opposition, did not see how Britain could withdraw from India until that country had been made secure against discord and anarchy. Albert J. Beveridge, often regarded as the ablest defender of imperialism in the American Senate during the debate on the peace treaty with Spain, thus interpreted America's responsibility: *"God has made us adept in government and we may administer government among the savage and servile people."*

The defenders of modern imperialism and colonialism have seen white man's burden as the obligation of advanced nations to help the people of backward nations – to *"Civilise and Christianize"* them, to teach them the dignity of labour and to impress upon them the beauties of their own concepts of law and order. They have argued that colonialism was a prelude to democracy in the 20th century. They have talked a great deal about roads, medicine, trade, self-government, science and technology. There may be truth in what they say, but the story of their exploitation remains a fact of history.

LIBERIA WAS CREATED TO RESETTLE FREED US SLAVES

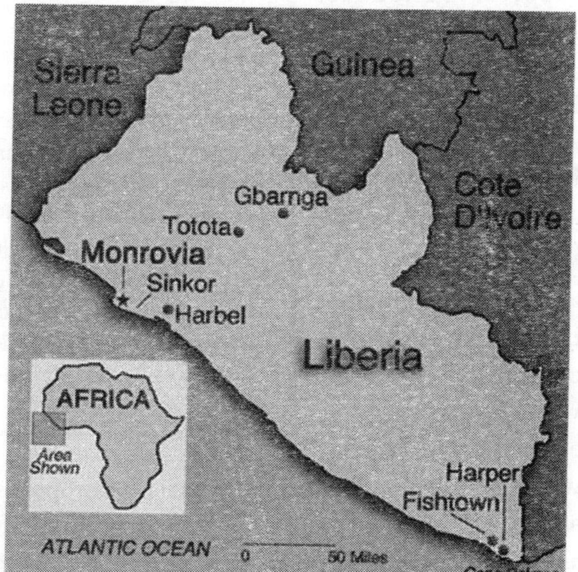

James Mill wrote *"The History of British India"*, in 1817 without ever visiting India and that book became the guide for the British governance. Mill advised Britain to make war and capture the "lesser peoples". Among his ardent supporters was Macaulay who described it as the "best book on history since Gibbon". Besides India-born British poet Rudyard Kipling, there was another British writer Katherine Mayo who wrote "Mother India", which was an extremely derogatory book. These two writers and their books fully reflected the British contempt for India. First published in 1927, "Mother India" was written in the context of official and unofficial British efforts to generate support in America for British rule in India and dissuade the US from demanding freedom for which Gandhiji was fighting. The book gave lurid detail to the image of Hindu India as irredeemably and hopelessly poor, degraded, depraved, and corrupt. Mayo's Mother India echoed not only the views of men like Alexander Duff,

Charles Grant, and John Stuart Mill but also those of Theodore Roosevelt, who glorified in the concept of White Man's burden in Asia and celebrated the accomplishments of imperialism. Mahatma Gandhi, described Mahatma Mayo's book as a "drain inspector's report". (Theodore Roosevelt – 1858-1919 – also known as Teddy President was America's 26th President who was awarded Nobel Peace Prize in 1906).

CECIL RHODES, A PLUNDERER

Cecil Rhodes

Cecil John Rhodes (1853-1902) was a South African politician, born in the U.K., to later become prime minister of Cape Colony (1890-96). Aiming at the formation of a South African federation and the creation of a block of British territory from the Cape to Cairo, he was responsible for the annexation of Bechuanaland (now Botswana) in 1885. He formed the British South Africa Company (1889) which occupied Mashonaland and Matabeleland, thus forming Rhodesia (now Zambia and Zimbabwe).

Rhodes went to Natal in 1870. As head of De Beers Consolidated Mines and Goldfields of South Africa Ltd., he amassed a large fortune. He entered the Cape legislature in 1881 and became prime minister in 1890, but after the exposure of his complicity in the Jameson Raid conspiracy, he was forced to resign in 1896. Advocating Anglo-Afrikaaner cooperation, he violated rights of black Africans, despite his call that : "Equal rights for every civilized man south of the Zambezi." The Rhodes scholarship, was founded at Oxford University, UK, under his will for students from the Commonwealth, the US, and Germany. He symbolises African exploitation and plundering that he indulged in all his life.

Of all the cruelties in history, those committed in Africa were the worst. The entire "dark continent" was pillaged, plundered and ravaged by Europeans who trapped African slaves and sold them as far away as in America. From an Island off Dakar (Senegal), as many as two million slaves were exported to the US. And, when President George Bush visited the Island in July 2003, he apologised to the Africans for slave trade. They divided the continent not on grounds of geography, ethnicity, language and tradition, but on the basis of minerals, forest wealth and other resources. Consequently, Africa continues to be on the boil, even while Europe has the longest spell of peace since the last war. The story of Zimbabwe (former South Rhodesia and Zambia is former North Rhodesia) is the story of practically the entire continent. The central players were David Livingstone (1813-73) and Cecil Rhode (1853-1902) who came to Africa as explorers and missionaries and conquered the entire Black Continent.

Liberia was founded by the American Colonisation Society in 1822 to resettle freed American Negro slaves. It may be noted that most Negroes captured and sold in America's south, where most cotton, tobacco plantation was done, were from the place which later became Liberia. But, this land could not absorb the American culture of freed American slaves, rehabilitated there. And, hence, the conflict between Americo-Liberians and the indigenous population. Now a free country, its political institutions are patterned after America's.

There is a continuing civil conflict. In the 1990s, some books had been written by African authors, expressing bitterness, rage and frustration and they have been suppressed. This write-up on the historical background of the region now called Zimbabwe is largely based on one such book written by *Lawrence Vambe,* great-grandson of the Chief of Mashonaland – *An ill-fated People – Zimbabwe Before and After Rhodes.*

The story begins with the adventures of David Livingstone of the London Missionary Society during 1841-75. He was the "Christian agent of a government bent on conquest". His best friend in his excursions was a slave trader, *Tipu Tibb,* who supplied him with information and assistance. The man's adventurous spirit was unquestionable, but Dark Africa was not anywhere near as dangerous as has been made out to be. There was at that time no hostility towards the white man; and a Scotsman in Zimbabwe was safer than he might be in the streets of contemporary London at night.

Livingstone exchanged his saint's halo for the colonialist's hat in 1858 when he emerged as the British Consul. But, whatever his headgear, his sole aim was advancing Britain's colonial interests. Livingstone was the man who made a plan to shift the whole Makololo people (his hosts at Linyante) from their ancestral lands, *'for the good of their health,'* as he put it, and make room for English settlers. He also explored Zimbabwe in preparation for the colonial aggression that was to follow. He approached the king with a document in English. The king did not know a word of English. When the document was placed before him, he turned for advice to a man he trusted, *Rey Helm,* a local missionary. Livingstone had already bribed Helm with the promise of a life pension. The man of God duly advised the king to sign. King Lobengula signed. Much later Lobengula understood the implications of what he had signed. It was his note of abdication. An appeal to the English queen for annulment of the agreement was made. The queen did not bother to reply.

THE PIONEER COLUMN

The first white settlement (Pioneer Column), unauthorised even by the fraudulent agreement, arrived in Mashonaland (east of Zimbabwe) in 1890. The "ragged freebooters with animal-like hair and beards" set up camps at Harare later called Salisbury, and began to seize the best land. The entire territory of the Washawasha (a tribe) people was handed over for administration to one Father Hartman of the Jesuit Order, and the people thereafter "entirely lived at the pleasure of their white missionary landlords." Their religion was suppressed; their social customs banned, and every aspect of their lives interfered with. The traditional marriage ceremony was declared unlawful, and anyone who performed it was forced to leave home for permanent exile. "The church owned the Washawasha people", says Vambe in his book.

SOME IMPORTANT DATES - LIBERIA

1821	Purchased by the philanthropic American Colonisation Society and turned into a settlement for liberated black slaves from the southern USA.
1847	Recognised as an independent republic.
1869	The True Whig Party founded, which was to dominate politics for more than a century, providing all presidents.
1926	Large concession sold to Firestone Rubber Company as foreign indebtedness increased.
1944	William Tubman, a descendant of US slaves, elected president.
1971	Tubman died; succeeded by William Tolbert.
1980	Tolbert assassinated in military coup led by Sgt. Samuel Doe, who banned political parties and launched a drive against corruption.
1993	Peace agreement signed under OAU-UN auspices, but soon collapsed.
1996	Renewed fighting in capital.
2005	Ellen Johnson-Sirleaf, first African woman from former US slave parents, became president of Liberia after 12 year of Civil War.

In the 1850s, Zimbabwe was divided into four regions. The Matabele, driven from their homeland by the Boers (Dutch settlers), occupied the south-west under their king, Lobengula. The more peace-loving Mashona lived in the north-east to the south-east in the Manyika and Karanga regions. The whole region is rich in minerals, specially gold. The great Zimbabwe ruins, remains of an ancient civilisation, have been dated to the early centuries of the Christian era. It is after this that a new nation has been named. Rhodesia was named after Cecil Rhode. Cecil Rhodes, a native of England, who landed in South Africa in 1870, was the one who followed up the Livingstone policy of loot and plunder. After making a fortune in the diamond trade by unscrupulous methods, he turned his special talents towards the partition of Africa. His declared objective was to turn all Africa, from *"Cape to Cairo,"* into British property and with that end in view he approached the king.

ZIMBABWE WAS SOLD FOR GUNS AND A BOAT

Another missionary was despatched from London, bearing a draft agreement that would give Britain exclusive rights to all minerals in the country, along with unrestricted access in their exploitation. It was an updated version of the *Barber of Baghdad's* agreement with the woodcutter – all the wood on the animal's back – which included the pack saddle! In return, the king would get one hundred pounds sterling a month, a thousand rifles and a boat for which he had no conceivable use. This was all for handing over Zimbabwe to Britain. After six years of silent suffering, the people rose in revolt against their oppressors in 1896. Wielding clubs and spears, they flung themselves against British army units armed with repeating rifles, machine guns and other weapons. They were mown down in the sands. Lobengula was driven out of his country to die in wilderness. The victorious British troops burned down houses, destroyed food stocks, dynamited places where families had taken refuge. Thousands were killed, maimed and hanged. Among those killed was Lady Nehanda, a woman warrior who fought to resist British oppression. Sentenced to death after the usual 'trial' was held in Salisbury jail, she was confronted by one Father Richards, who offered to convert her to the Christian faith. Lady Nehanda was amused.

"Why should I accept your creed which I have opposed all my life," she asked.

"If you die a heathen," she was told, "you will suffer the endless agonies of hell. But if you are a Christian, you will go to heaven."

"This heaven of yours – is that the place where white people go when they die?"

"Yes, if they are true Christians."

"Heaven must be full of white people, then?"

Lady Nehanda turned to the executioner and asked him to hurry.

The war had ended in defeat and destruction. For six decades the people lay sunk in apathy, subject to a government run exclusively for the white settlers. Then, in 1965 came the *Unilateral Declaration of Independence,* a pre-emptive move to perpetuate the racist regime. But world conditions had changed and there was another war of independence and this one was not fought with clubs and spears. Having won it, the people of Zimbabwe gained freedom. This is the story of one country, that has been repeated with greater cruelty in other countries, until Nelson Mandela's exit from jail in 1990 marked the formal end to the white man's rule in Africa. *(This is, however, only a glimpse into the African exploitation. The detailed discussion on it is outside the scope of this book).*

Slavery is neither economics nor politics; it is sheer brutality. Slavers should be fought and punished by all free men and women of the world.

– Abraham Lincolm

27

History and geography are sources of Africa's sufferings

Of the 53 African nations (47 on the mainland and rest are offshore islands), all those south of Equator were colonies – exploited and enslaved. This is where black Africans were hunted and exported to run the economies of rich nations. Geography and history have conspired to reduce this great continent to this pass. Let us see how.

Geography and history go a long way toward providing the explanations for the African riddle. Geographically, the continent spans both the north and south temperate zones. North of Equator is largely the Arab (or Muslim) and South of Equator is black Africa. This simple geographic reality explains a great deal about Africa today.

And this is the place where some seven million years ago the evolutionary lines of apes and protohumans diverged. It remained the only continent our ancestors inhabited until around two million years ago, when *Homo erectus* expanded out of Africa into Europe and Asia. Over the next 1.5 million years, the population of those three continents followed such different evolutionary courses that they became distinct species: Europe's became the *Neandertals*, Asia's remained *Homo erectus*, but Africa's evolved into our own species, *Homo sapiens*. Sometime between 100,000 and 50,000 years ago, our African ancestors underwent some further profound change. Whether it was the development of complex speech or something else, such as a change in brain wiring, we don't know. Whatever it was, it transformed those early *Homo sapiens* into "behaviorally modern" *Homo sapiens*. Those people, probably with brains similar to our own, expanded again into Europe and Asia. Once there, they exterminated or replaced or interbred with Neandertals and Asia's homunculi and became the dominant human species throughout the world.

In effect, Africans enjoyed not just one but three huge head-starts over humans on other continents. That makes Africa's economic struggles today puzzling. It is the opposite of what one would expect from the runner first off the block. Here again geography and history give us answers. It turns out that the rules of the competitive race among the world's humans changed radically about 10,000 years ago, with the origins of agriculture. The domestication of wild plants and animals meant our ancestors could grow their own food, instead of having to kill it in the wild. That allowed people to settle in permanent villages and increase population. With domestication came other advances, including the first metal tools, writing, and state societies.

The world's earliest and most productive farming arose in the Fertile Crescent of southwestern Asia (Muslim areas) where wheat, barley, sheep, cattle, and goats were domesticated. While those plants and animals spread east and west in Eurasia, in Africa they were stopped by the continent's north-south orientation. Crops and livestock tend to spread much more slowly from north to south than from east to west, because of different climates, seasons, days lengths, and diseases. Africa's own native plant species were not domesticated until thousands of years after Asia and Europe had agriculture. And Africa's geography kept oil palm, yams, and other crops of equatorial Africa from spreading into southern Africa's temperate zone. While South Africa today boasts of the continent's richest agricultural lands, the crops grown there are mostly northern temperate crops, such as wheat and grapes, and brought directly on ships by European colonists. Those same crops never succeeded in spreading south through the thick tropical core of Africa. They had to be brought by ship.

ANIMALS AND HUMANS CO-EVOLVED

The long human presence in Africa is probably the reason the big animals survive today. African animals co-evolved with humans for millions of years, as human hunting prowess gradually progressed from the rudimentary skills of our early ancestors. That gave the animals time to learn a healthy fear of man, and with it a healthy avoidance of human hunters. In contrast, North and South America and Australia were settled by humans only within the last tens of thousands of years. To the misfortune of the big animals of those continents, the first humans they encountered were already fully modern people, with modern brains, hunting skills and new weapons. Most of those animals – woolly mammoths, saber-toothed cats, and in Australia marsupials as big as rhinoceroses – disappeared soon after humans arrived. Entire species may have been exterminated before they had time to learn to beware of hunters.

The long human presence in Africa also encouraged something else to thrive – diseases. The continent has produced some of our nastiest diseases like malaria, yellow fever, East African sleeping sickness, and AIDS. These and many other human illnesses arose when the microbes causing diseases in animals crossed species lines to evolve into a human disease. For a microbe already adapted to one species to adapt to another can be difficult and requires a lot of evolutionary time. Much more time has been available in Africa, cradle of humankind, than in any other part of the planet. That's half the answer to Africa's disease burden; the other half is that the animal species most closely related to humans – those whose microbes required the least adaptation to jump species – are the African great apes and monkeys.

AFRICA'S 15 OUT OF 47 COUNTRIES LANDLOCKED

Africa continues to be shaped in other ways by its long history and its geography. Of mainland Africa's ten richest countries – the only ones with annual per capita gross domestic products over $3,500 – nine lie partly or entirely within its temperate zones: Egypt, Libya, Tunisia, Algeria, and Morocco in the north; and Swaziland, South Africa, Botswana, and Namibia in the south. Gabon is Africa's only tropical country to make to the list. In addition, nearly a third of the countries of mainland Africa (15 out of 47) are landlocked, and the only African river navigable from the ocean for long distances inland is the Nile. Since waterways provide the cheapest way to transport cumbersome goods, geography again thwarts Africa's progress.

Is the continent then doomed eternally to wars, poverty, and devastating diseases? Absolutely not. Any visitor can see how harmoniously ethnic groups live together in many countries. Tensions arise in Africa, as they do elsewhere, when people see no other way out of poverty except to fight their neighbors for dwindling resources. Foreign interests are also creating problems there. But many areas of Africa have an abundance of resources: The rivers of central Africa are great generators of hydroelectric power; the big animals are a major source of eco-tourism revenue in eastern and southern Africa; and the forests in the wetter regions are sources of income. Africa's health problems can be greatly alleviated with the right planning and funding.

Within the past half a century several formerly poor countries in Asia recognized that tropical diseases were a major drain on their economies. By investing in public health measures, they have successfully curbed those diseases, and the increased health of their people has led to far healthier economies. Within Africa itself, some international mining and oil companies have been funding successful public health programmes throughout their concession areas because they realized that protecting the health of their workers was an excellent business investment for them.

If the continent can overcome its health problems and the corruption that plague many of its governments and institutions, then it could take advantage of today's globalized, technological world in much the same way China and India are now doing. Technology could give Africa the connections that its geography, particularly its rivers, long denied it. Nearly half of all African countries are English speaking, an advantage in trade relations, and an educated English-speaking workforce could well attract service jobs to many African countries. *(Source: National Geographic)*

The October Revolution did not happen in a day; discontent was brewing for long when Lenin reached Moscow in a sealed wagon and lighted the fire which raged for over 70 years, destroying almost two generations of Russian youth, a tragedy unmatched by any in its dire historical consequences.

28

Bolsheviks seize power in Russia; how it happened

The Russian Tzardom was rotten at the core. The sex maniac monk Rasputin, who ruled the state on behalf of Tsar Nicholas II, was the symbol of decay of the system which just needed a push. And, Bolshevik leader Lenin gave it hard.

Russia collapsed after the War. The Tzardom had been showing signs of profound rottenness for some years before the war; the court was under the sway of a fantastic religious impostor, Rasputin, and the public administration, civil and military, was in a state of extreme inefficiency and corruption. At the outset of the war, there was a great flare of patriotic enthusiasm in Russia. A vast conscript army was raised, for which there was neither adequate military equipment nor a proper supply of competent officers, and this great army, ill supplied and badly handled, was hurled against the German and Austrian frontiers.

There can be no doubt that the early appearance of Russian armies in East Prussia in September, 1914, diverted the energies and attention of the Germans from their first victorious drive upon Paris. The sufferings and deaths of scores of thousands of ill-fed Russian peasants saved France from complete overthrow in that momentous opening campaign, and made all western Europe the debtors of that great and tragic people. But the strain of the war upon this sprawling ill-organized empire was too heavy for its strength. The Russian common soldiers were sent into battle without guns to support them, without even rifle ammunition; they were wasted by their officers and generals in a delirium of militarist enthusiasm. For a time they seemed to be suffering mutely as the beasts suffer; but there is a limit to the endurance even of the most ignorant. A profound disgust for Tzardom was creeping through these armies of betrayed and wasted men. From the close of 1915 onward Russia was a source of deepening anxiety to her Western Allies. Throughout 1916 she remained largely on the defensive, and there were rumours of a separate peace with Germany.

On December 29, 1916, the monk Rasputin was murdered at a dinner-party in Petrograd, and a belated attempt was made to put the Tzardom in order. By March things were moving rapidly; food riots in Petrograd developed into a revolutionary insurrection; there was an attempted suppression of the Duma, the representative body, there were attempted arrests of liberal leaders, the formation of a provisional government under Prince Lvoff, and an abdication (March 15) by the Tzar. For a time it seemed that a moderate and controlled revolution might be possible - perhaps under a new Tzar. Then it became evident that the destruction of popular confidence in Russia had gone too far for any such adjustments. The Russian people were sick to death of the old order of things in Europe, of Tzars and wars and of Great Powers; it wanted relief, and that speedily, from unendurable miseries. The Allies had no under-standing of Russian realities; their diplomatists were ignorant of Russia, genteel persons with their attention directed to the Russian Court rather than to Russia, they blundered steadily with the new situation. There was little goodwill for republicanism among these diplomats, and a manifest disposition to embarrass the new government as much as possible. At the head of the Russian republican government was an eloquent and picturesque leader, Kerensky, who found himself assailed by the forces of a profounder revolutionary movement, the 'social revolution', at home and cold-shouldered by the Allied governments abroad. His allies neither let him give the Russian peasants the land for which they craved nor peace beyond their frontiers. The French and the British press pestered their exhausted ally for a fresh offensive, but when presently the Germans made a strong attack by sea and land upon Riga, the British Admiralty quailed before the prospect of a Baltic expedition in relief. The new Russian republic had to fight unsupported. In spite of their naval predominance and the bitter protests of the great English admiral, Lord Fisher (1841-1920), it is to be noted that the British and their allies, except for some submarine attacks, left the Germans the complete mastery of the Baltic throughout the war.

KERENSKY'S BRIEF RULE

The Russian masses, however, were resolute to end the war. At any cost. There had come into existence in Petrograd a body representing the workers and common soldiers, the Soviet, and this body clamoured for an international conference of socialists at Stockholm. Food riots were occurring in Berlin at this time, war weariness in Austria and Germany was profound, and there can be little doubt, in the light of subsequent events, that such a conference would have precipitated a reasonable peace on democratic lines in 1917 and a German revolution. Kerensky implored his Western allies to allow this conference to take place, but, fearful of a world-wide outbreak of socialism and republicanism, they refused, in spite of the favourable response of a small majority of the British Labour Party. Without either moral or physical help from the Allies, the unhappy 'moderate' Russian republic still fought on and made a last desperate offensive effort in July. It failed after some preliminary successes, and there came another great slaughtering of Russians.

The limit of Russian endurance was reached. Mutinies broke out in Russian armies-and .particularly upon the northern front, and on November 7, 1917, Kerensky's government was over-thrown and power was seized, by the Soviets, dominated by the Bolshevik socialists under Lenin, and it was pledged to make peace regardless of the western powers. On March 2, 1918, a separate peace between Russia and Germany was signed at Brest- Litovsk.

It speedily became evident that these Bolshevik socialists were men of a very different quality from the rhetorical constitutionalists and revolutionaries of the Kerensky phase. They were fanatical Marxist communists. They believed that their accession to power in Russia was only the opening of a world-wide social revolution and they set about changing the social and economic order with the thoroughness of perfect faith and absolute inexperience. The western European and the American governments were themselves much too ill-informed and incapable to guide or help this extraordinary experiment and the press set itself to discredit the ruling classes to wreck these usurpers upon any terms and at any cost to themselves or to Russia.

A propaganda of abominable and disgusting inventions went on unchecked in the press of the world; the Bolshevik leaders were represented as incredible monsters glutted with blood and plunder and living lives of sensuality before which the realities of the Tzarist court during the Rasputin regime paled to a white purity. Expeditions were launched at the exhausted country, insurgents and raiders were encouraged, armed and subsidized, and no method of attack was too mean or too monstrous for the frightened enemies of the Bolshevik regime. In 1919, the Russian Bolsheviks, ruling a country already exhausted and disorganized by five years of intensive warfare, were fighting a British Expedition at Archangel, Japanese invaders in Eastern Siberia, Romanians with French and Greek contingents in the south, the Russian Admiral Koltchak in Siberia and General Denikin, supported by the French fleet in the Crimea. In July of that year an Estonian army, under General Yudenitch, almost got to Petersburg. In 1920 the Poles, incited by the French, made a new attack on Russia; and a new reactionary raider, General Wrangel, took over the task of General Denikin in invading and devastating his own country. In March, 1921, the sailors at Cronstadt revolted. The Russian Government under its president, Lenin, survived all these various attacks. It showed an amazing tenacity, and the common people of Russia sustained it unswervingly under conditions of extreme hardship. By the end of 1921 both Britain and Italy had made a sort of recognition of the communist rule.

AGGRESSION & REVOLT

But if the Bolshevik government was successful in its struggle against foreign intervention and internal revolt, it was far less happy in its attempts to set up a new social order based upon communist ideas in Russia. The Russian peasant is a small land-hungry proprietor, as far from communism in his thoughts and methods as a whale is from flying; the revolution gave him the land of the great landowners but could not make him grow food for anything but negotiable money, and the revolution, among other things, had practically destroyed the value of money. Agricultural production, already greatly dis-ordered by the collapse of the railways through war-strain, shrank to a mere cultivation of food by the peasants for their own consumption. The towns starved. Hasty and ill-planned attempts to make over industrial production in accordance with communist ideas were equally unsuccessful. By 1920 Russia presented the unprecedented spectacle of a modern civilization in complete collapse. Railways were rusting and passing out of use, towns were falling into ruin, everywhere there was an immense mortality. Yet the country still fought with its enemies at its gates. In 1921 came a drought and a great famine among the peasant cultivators in the war-devastated south-east provinces. Millions of people starved.

Under these distressful circumstances it was resolved to slow down the process of reconstruction. A New Economic Policy (the N.E.P.) was adopted, and considerable freedom of private ownership and private enterprise was restored. There ensued a partial restoration of productive activity. It seemed as though Russia was drifting away from constructive socialism and re-producing conditions rather parallel to those of the United States a hundred years earlier. A class of prosperous peasants, the Kulaks, emerged, the equivalent of the small American farmer. Small independent traders multiplied. But the Communist Party was not disposed to abandon its objectives in this fashion, and to allow Russia to follow in the wake of America a hundred years behind. In 1928 it began a powerful effort to bring back the country to the Communist line of development. A Five-Year Plan was evolved, designated to force forward a rapid expansion of State industrialism, more especially in the heavy staple products, while at the same time replacing peasant production by large-scale collective farming. The Plan was put into action in the teeth of immense difficulties; chief of which were the illiteracy and general backwardness of the common people, the lack of a sufficiency of competent foremen and technical workers, and the unhelpfulness and positive antagonism of the western world. None the less, a considerable measure of success was claimed upon the industrial side. There was waste and there was want of proportion, but there was undeniable achievement. The effect of these bold and rapid changes upon agricultural production was not so satisfactory, and the winter of 1933-34 found Russia once again facing a great food shortage.

The rest of the world, which was still working out the results of the system of private-profit capitalism, surveyed the Russian experiment with a mixture of curiosity, distrust, and respect. That older system also was working badly. It was restricting purchasing power to a shrinking moiety of the population, and losing its progressive momentum very rapidly. It was no longer self-complacent. The word 'planning' spread throughout the world. As the economic stresses we shall tell in the next chapter increased, 'plans' multiplied. By 1933 no self-respecting statesman was without a plan. So much homage at least the world paid to Russia. *(Source: H.G. Wells)*

If there were no Gorbachev, history would have invented one because communists had run out of new ideas.

– George Kennan (American diplomat)

29

The Soviet Union fell out of exhaustion

The Soviet empire was a vast ideological iceberg, which melted like ice floes after contact with the democracy of Western Europe. One man has seldom done so much for so many people in such difficult conditions. People will always know Gorbachev as a redeemer.

At the height of its success, between 1945 and 1985, The Soviet Union enjoyed enormous influence in the world. Moscow, the ancient land of Rus Kiev, was the capital of the largest country in the world. That country comprised 15 republics (of which the biggest was Russia itself, with about half the total Soviet population), and it commanded immense natural and industrial resources. The Soviet Union also had three seats in the UN, (one for the Ukraine and one for Belarus, earlier Byelorussia, and a third for Russia and the remaining republics) and a vast military capacity. Russia, in its 20th-century Soviet incarnation, was stronger than at any time in its history, feared or respected by the whole world. But Communist totalitarianism had frozen Russia's empire into one great ideological iceberg, and a long cold war had almost bankrupted it to finally break down without shooting.

Mikhail Gorbachev, who was appointed general secretary of the ruling Communist Party in 1985, introduced *perestroika* (restructuring) and *glasnost* (openness) in the system. These concessions encouraged the Soviet satellites to demand independence, and drift away like ice floes; first the countries of eastern Europe, then the Baltic states, then the other 14 Soviet republics. Small-scale ethnic wars flared up in several corners of the old Soviet state. The bloodiest was in Chechnya in the Caucasus. But the introduction of limited democracy, press freedom, free enterprise, and the release of dissidents, led to an unstoppable drive to overturn Communist rule. As the USSR liberalised, the satellite states of East and Central Europe, one by one, voted in free elections for non-Communist governments (1989-90). Thus, Soviet republics began to break away from the Union. By 1991, the USSR ceased to exist; instead a nominal *'Commonwealth of Independent States'* (CIS) came into being.

With the loss of republics, Russia's stake in Europe was reduced to something less than it had been at the time of Catherine the Great in the 18th century. The Russian economy, exposed to the free market, went into steep decline and Russia became dependent on Western aid. Millions of ordinary citizens were left bitter, destitute and nostalgic about the certainties of the Soviet system which collapsed in the early 1991. Russia has been beset by violent crime and corruption, as well as by economic problems.

STRATEGIC OVERSTRETCH

The Soviet empire fell out of sheer exchaustion in a regime of *"strategic overstretch"* (*a la* Paul Kennedy). Dissatisfied with the system, the Communist rule flared up in the early 1980s in Poland, centred on the Gdansk shipyard where the Solidarity trade union was active. Solidarity was banned in 1982, but the ban was lifted in April 1989, leading to a Solidarity victory in free elections in June, and the first non-Communist government in the Soviet bloc. In September, Hungary opened its border with Austria and a mass exodus began with East Germans heading for the West. The Hungarian government declared a new republic, promising multiparty elections (held in 1990) and disbanding the Communist Party. Soon the spark of reform had become a blaze. By the end of 1989, Erich Honecker had resigned in East Germany and the Berlin Wall was pulled down. In 1990, Czechoslovakia, Romania and some Yugoslav republics acquired non-Communist governments. States of the Soviet Union, starting with Lithuania and Latvia, pushed for independence and in 1991, after an unsuccessful Communist coup, the USSR was dissolved. The new governments of Eastern Europe faced many problems. Centralised economies had to be restructured and regional tensions revived in many places, resulting in wars in the Balkans and Chechnya.

The disintegration of the Soviet Union started in the 1960s. After the Soviet leader Nikita Khrushchev visited the USA in 1959, he promised that communism would match the material success of capitalism by 1981. His endeavour to initiate economic reforms however, failed and during the next three decades the Soviet production fell further behind that of the West. And, the Soviet Union was forced to import grain from the USA. As Western economies accelerated, communist countries became mired in inefficiency. Faults were papered over, and criticism was stifled, often by force. By the late 1980s, the countries of the eastern bloc were burdened with outdated and inefficient factories, failure of the supply systems, huge military budgets, subsidised industries and declining production of consumer goods – all made worse by non-convertible currency.

THE BREAK-AWAY DATES

POLAND

June 5, 1991 Solidarity wins 35 per cent of Polish assembly seats.

August 24 Tadeusz Masowiecki becomes first non-Communist Prime Minister in Eastern Bloc.

HUNGARY

September 11 Government opens borders, allowing 60,000 Germans to migrate to West.

October 10 The Communist Party dissolves itself, renouncing Marxism-Leninism for social democracy.

EAST GERMANY

November 7 Leader Egon Krenz and Politburo resign.

November 9 Berlin Wall opened.

BULGARIA

November 10 Leader Todor Zhivkov resigns.

CZECHOSLOVAKIA

November 17 Police quell demonstrations in Prague.

November 24 Leader Milos Jakes and entire Politburo resign : non-Communist government formed under Vaclav Havel.

ROMANIA

December 22, 1991 President Nicolae Ceausescu overthrown.

December 25 Ceausescu executed.

On May 17, 1985, Mikhail Gorbachev, the just appointed Secretary-General of the Soviet Communist Party, stood in the Smolny Institute, Leningrad, the place from which Lenin had first proclaimed the victory of Bolshevism in 1917, and announced a new revolution : "We must change our attitudes – from the worker to the minister!" His strategy for change comprised two prongs, *glasnost,* (political openness), and *perestroika,* (economic restructuring). The two processes blew apart the Soviet Union's dinosaur-like economy and the established constraints on criticism. Critics, who had previously been suppressed, could now be heard, and were able to gather people behind them. In 1991, the three Baltic republics – Estonia, Latvia and

Lithuania – declared themselves independent. The old economy of the Soviet Union was in tatters, but there was no sign of a new system. Gorbachev, caught in a paradox of his own making, tried to halt the split by sending soldiers into Latvia and Lithuania. Troops were also mobilised into the Ukraine. Protesters crammed Red Square and a civil war seemed imminent. It was, however, too late and too little.

SOME KEY DATES

9thC	State of Kiev Rus founded.
13thC	Mongol invasion.
1480	Mongol rule ends.
1905	Defeat by Japan; parliament established.
1914-17	Fight in World War I against Germany and Austria.
1917	Tsar overthrown in *'February Revolution';* Bolsheviks seize power in October Revolution.
1918-20	Communists win civil war.
1922	USSR established; Stalin rises to power.
1930	Collective farms set up; Stalinist purges.
1939	Stalin and Hitler agree to divide Poland.
1941	German invasion.
1945	Beats Germany on Eastern Front; occupies eastern Europe.
1953	Stalin dies; Khrushchev becomes first secretary of the party.
1956	Invades Hungary to suppress anti-Soviet demonstrations.
1958	Khruschev becomes premier.
1962	Crisis with USA over Soviet missiles based in Cuba.
1964	Brezhnev, Kosygin replace Khruschev.
1968	Soviet forces invade Czechoslovakia to crush reforms.
1979-89	Invades and occupies Afghanistan.
1985	Gorbachev made general secretary; *'glasnost'* (openness) and *'perestroika'* (restructuring) begin.
1989	Open elections.
1991	USSR breaks up; Russia (led by Yeltsin) joins Commonwealth of Independent States (CIS).
1994-2002	Civil unrest and military occupation of Chechnya.
2000	Putin becomes president.

GORBACHEV-YELTSIN SHOWDOWN

The crisis sparked off a confrontation between two once-friendly supporters of change, Gorbachev and Boris Yeltsin, the newly elected first president of the Russian Federation, the union's largest republic. Gorbachev, once a radical, was seen as reactionary, trying merely to fine-tune the old system. The brash, erratic Yeltsin wanted nothing less than the end of the system itself. In August, 1991, to the astonishment of the world, Gorbachev fell victim to a coup by disaffected hardline communists. Briefly, the future seemed to threaten a renewal of oppression and a return to the cold war. After three days, the coup died in the face of popular protests, led by none other than Yeltsin. One after another, the republics broke free from Moscow until all 15 of them became independent. Anarchy threatened. But the republics needed to cooperate as trading partners. It was Yeltsin who brokered a way forward. In December, the republics formed a *Commonwealth of Independent States (CIS),* with its centre in Minsk, capital of Byelorussia (now Belarus). On Christmas Day 1991, Gorbachev resigned. An idealist of a corrupt system, what he intended was a radical change, but, in the process, he destroyed the Soviet system. And, also himself.

GORBACHEV – A MIRACLE MAN

The man who created a strange enemy-free Europe was paradoxically a Russian, Mikhail Gorbachev, whom the world, most specially the West calls one of the greatest men of all time. George Kennan of America who helped re-fashion Europe after the last War, says: "Gorbachev is a miracle man; his mind-boggling decisions led East Europe to break free, to let the people choose their governments, and fold up the Russian empire, in the building of which one generation of Russians were killed in battlefields. It is hard to explain these in conceptual and historical terms. He (Gorbachev) is the man born once in a century," Kennan told US Congress. The elderly American diplomat, who died in 2005 at 92, was not really reciting poetry when he made this statement before the US Congress.

"I will not like to be remembered for demo-lishing communist dictator-ship but for creating conditions when future generations may not have to choose between communism and capita-lism. I have synthesised both".
Mikhail Gorbachev

He was re-telling history to the younger generation of Americans whose fathers and forefathers died in Europe and Africa to build a world order that had vanished into thin air, like a bad dream. The world which the superpowers took 45 years and 60 million people dead and injured to produce, Gorbachev demolished in a sweep. It was just hard to believe. Gorbachev responded to complex situations when the new generation wanted peace, democracy and goods to buy and not arms to kill, and here was a man who could stand up and get counted when he said; "*Freedom of choice is a universal principle and let the people of the world exercise it.*" The Communist dominoes came crumbling down. The revolution was fuelled by information blitz, TV and Radio Free Europe, which united the world as nothing did before.

Boris Yeltsin* *(1931-2007)

In the 19th century, Napoleon had dreamed of the *"continental system"* to integrate the territory he conquered from Spain to Russia. Karl Marx also predicted that a proletarian revolution would sweep Europe. Now Gorbachev, one of Marx's ideological heirs, preached the creation of a *"common European home"* where after years of Kremlin domination, the nations of Eastern Europe would be free to pursue the policies they set for themselves. This was all because of one man, Gorbachev, who will always be remembered in history with respect. Seldom before so much was owed by so many to one man.

Nothing goes right in the Balkans.
– Eleaner Louis Kayser

30

The Balkans—a profile

The Balkan region has been the boiling pot of eastern Europe. Divided between Roman Catholic and Eastern Orthodox Christians, as well as between Christians and Muslims, the Balkan states have for centuries been known for their deep and ancient animosities, resulting in wars and regional conflicts.

Balkan Peninsula is situated in south-eastern Europe. Located between the Adriatic Sea, the Mediterranean Sea, and the Aegean and Black seas, it contains many countries, including Slovenia, Croatia, Bosnia-Herzegovina, Macedonia, Serbia-Montenegro, Romania, Bulgaria, Albania, Greece and European Turkey. From 168 BC to AD 107, part of the area was incorporated into Roman provinces, including Epirus, Moesia, Pannonia, Thrace and Dacia. It was subsequently settled by Slavic invaders including Serbs, Croats, Slovenes and Bulgars, the last of whom were pushed into the Balkan region in the 6th century. It was gradually organised into kingdoms, many of which were overrun by the Ottoman Turks in the 14th-15th century. The factional strife from the early 20th century, provoking the continual breakups and regroupings of different states, introduced the word "balkanize" into English. It means slitting up.

The Soviet leader Mikhail Gorbachev initiated *perestroika* and *glasnost,* which weakened Soviet influence in Eastern Europe. Soviet-supported governments collapsed, and West Germany and East Germany joined to become one nation in 1990. In 1991 the Soviet Union itself collapsed, splitting into fifteen states, with the Russian Federation taking the Soviet Union's seat on the United Nations Security Council.

The most violent breakup happened in Yugoslavia. Four out of six (Slovenia, Croatia, Bosnia-Herzegovina and Macedonia) Yugoslav republics declared independence and a violent war ensued in some parts lasting until 1995. The remaining two republics formed a new Federal Republic of Yugoslavia, under the leadership of Slobodan Milosevic. Milosevic presided over the Kosovo war, and was overthrown after his government was destroyed by NATO airstrikes against Yugoslavia. Following the ouster of Milosevic, the country changed its name to Serbia-Montenegro in order to case the tension between the two federal units.

Most Balkans are mountains. The principal ranges are the Carpathian Mountains in Romania, the Balkan and Rhodope Mountains in Bulgaria, and the Pindus Mountains in Greece. The Dinaric Alps stretch through the region along the Adriatic coast from the Julian Alps in Slovenia to the Yugoslav border with Albania, rising to 8,000 feet above sea level. The Danube river connects the eastern Balkan countries with the Black Sea. The Sava river in the north and the Morava in the east are tributaries of the Danube; the Neretva in the west flows southward into the Adriatic Sea. Other important rivers in the Balkans are the Maritsa in Bulgaria, the Drin in Albania, and the Vardar in Greece, and the large lakes, Ohrid and Prespa, are located near the borders of Albania, Greece, and Yugoslavia.

The Balkan States
The main political divisions of the former Yugoslavia.

In the northern and central parts of the Peninsula forests are deciduous up to about 5,000 feet and coniferous above that. At elevations higher than about 6,000 ft. the forest gives way to scrubs and herbs. In the southern and western coastal areas evergreen and various Mediterranean woods and bushes are common, with oak and conifer forests at higher elevations. Throughout the Peninsula much of the woody vegetation has been destroyed by human occupation, opening the region for continuing conflict.

In the Minoan age, Greece and the Aegean islands had produced a rich civilisation, contemporaneous with that of imperial Egypt and Mesopotamia. The Balkan Peninsula had known the glories of the Periclean Age and of the Hellenistic period. Balkania was part of the provincial structure of the Roman Empire. Through the Balkans, in days of Roman decline, had passed Goths, Vandals, and Huns, traces of these peoples are found today in the history rather than the ethnography of the area. Although the modern Greeks take pride in the cultural tie with the ancient Hellenes and the Rumanians, it is the late-comers who have fixed the present racial character of the Peninsula. To this, there is one outstanding exception; the Albanians, not without some reason, claim descent from the ancient Thracians and Illyrians, although later conquered by other peoples.

Ethnic diversities have made the Balkans a by-word for political conflicts which have led, for example, to the confrontation between Greece and Turkey over Cyprus, and the differing types of communism that prevailed in the region until the early 1990s. More recently, ethnic inter-fighting has dominated the Peninsula, first Slovenia and Croatia, and then Bosnia-Herzegovina, which have battled to win independence from the Serb-dominated Yugoslav Federation. Despite international recognition being awarded to all three republics early in 1992, fierce fighting between Serb, Croat and Muslim factions continued in Bosnia-Herzegovina into the late 1990's. It was one of the bloodiest conflicts in Europe.

FIVE ETHNIC GROUPS

Five major ethnic groups and several scattered minorities are found in the Balkan Peninsula. Southern Slavs, Croats, and Serbs are the most numerous. They live mainly in the western-central and eastern-central parts of the Peninsula. In the north-east are Romanians; in the southeast Turks; in the southwest, Albanians; and in the south Greeks, Gypsies and Balkan Jews are minorities. Largely because of the rural character of the population, the absence of large towns, and industrial areas, the population density averages only about 235 persons per sq. mile throughout the Balkans, except for the Thrace region of Turkeys, where it is about 490 per sq. mill. The largest cities are Istanbul, 2,800,000; Bucharest, 1,950,000; Belgrade, 1,200,000; Sofia, 1,070,000; Athens, 886,000; and Zagrab, 770,000.

In addition to Greek and Turkish, the languages of the Peninsula include Slavic languages spoken by the Bulgarians and southern Slavs of Yugoslavia; Albanian, a mixture of Illyrian, Thracian, Latin, Slavic, and Turkish elements and Romanian, a romance language. Before World War II, a majority of the Balkan peoples belonged to the Greek Orthodox church; Roman Catholics were found mostly in eastern and northern Yugoslavia and northern Romania, and Muslims inhabited Albania and Turkey. After the last war, the suppression of religious practices in the Communist Balkan countries made religious distinctions less important, but about half of Yugoslavia's people are Orthodox and a third Roman Catholics. Greek Orthodoxy and Islam still predominate in Greece and Turkey, respectively.

KNOW THESE REGIONS

Eurasia: A geographical term that consists of Ukraine, Moldova, the Balkans, the Caucasus Balkan. Black sea region has Bulgaria, Romania, Moldova, Albania, Bosnia - Herzegovina, Serbia - Montenegro.

The Balkans: comprise Albania, Bosnia – Herzegovina, Bulgaria, Greece, Croatia Romania, Turkey-in-Europe and former Yugoslavia (Serbia - Montenegro).

Anatolia: It is a alternative name for Turkey-in-Asia.

Levant: Eastern Mediterranean region, including Turkey-in-Asia, Syria, Lebanon and Israel.

Maghreb: It is the name for north-west Africa. It is the Arabic word for sunset. The Maghreb powers are Algeria, Libya, Morocco and Tunisia.

ROMAN EMPIRE – EAST AND WEST

Before the coming of the Slavs into the Balkans, Rome had already been divided into the eastern and western empires, and after the death of the Emperor Theodosius in 395, the two parts were never united. The Eastern and Western Churches were finally severed at the end of the eleventh century. Croats and Slovenes gave allegiance to the Roman pontiff while Rumanians, Greeks, Serbs, and Bulgars looked for guidance to the Metropolitan in Constantinople. As heirs to the Eastern Empire, the Sultans became the overlords of the eastern Balkan peoples, while Croats and Slovenes found their masters in the Habsburgs. Thus, to the divisive influence of Balkan geography were added diverse religious and political traditions.

Of the post-World War Balkan states, only one, Yugoslavia, (land of Slavs) bore a name really descriptive of its racial character. The others, though predominantly Slav, bore non-Slav names. Bulgaria was originally settled by the *Bulgars,* a Mongolian tribe, who conquered the area in the seventh century only to be absorbed later by the numerically superior Slavs. Rumania perpetuated the Rumanian claim to descent from the legions which conquered Dacia in the reign of Trajan. Rome withdrew her legions, but traces of the language remained. The name Greece is justified, in part, by the language of her people, but here again there are mixed racial elements among whom the Slav predominates.

POST-WAR MINORITIES: In the Balkans political lines never coincided with ethnic and geographical ones. And, that is the source of conflict. For example, Macedonia has been aptly described as "a political problem rather than a geographical entity." Bulgarians, Yugoslavs, and Greeks have claimed Macedonia and sought to impress their cultural pattern on its people. Some 600,000 Bulgaro-Macedonians lived in Yugoslavia and more than 80,000 in Greece. Rumania and Yugoslavia had German minorities in the areas formerly incorporated within the Austro-Hungarian Empire. Rumania also had over 1.4 million and Yugoslavia nearly half a million Hungarians before 1918. In Bessarabia and Northern Bukovina, incorporated into Rumania, there were more than half a million Ukrainians. In Greece, Bulgaria, and Yugoslavia, Jews formed a very small part of the population, but Rumania had a Jewish minority of 4 per cent. In Bessarabia and the Dobrudja, Rumania inherited about 300,000 Bulgarians (1918). These, however, represented only the major minorities in an area where, due to the frequent shifting of boundaries, particularly in the last century, minorities seemed to be the rule rather than the exception. Hence, continuing conflict.

TREATIES ON BOUNDARIES: The territorial status of the Balkans was fixed by the Treaty of London (May 30, 1913) between the Balkan nations and Turkey; the Treaty of Bucharest (August 10, 1913) between the Balkan states and Bulgaria, and many World War treaties. The status of Albania was fixed in 1913. Bulgaria, on the losing side in the First World War, failed to get back South Dobrudja and Macedonia which she had lost in 1913, and also had to yield to Greece, the land between the Kavalla and Maritsa rivers, her corridor to the Aegean. Rumania was tremendously increased in size by the addition of the former Hungarian territories, Transylvania, and part of the Banat, Bukovina (previously held by Austria), and Bessarabia (belonging to Russia). *Yugoslavia consisted of Serbia, Montenegro, Bosnia-Herzegovina, Croatia, Slavonia and Macedonia. It may be noted that there was no country like Yugoslavia before. This country was created in 1918. It has vanished again.*

The Balkans once formed the greatest part of Turkey's empire in Europe. And, "to Balkanise" has come to mean "to divide an area into small, mutually hostile states." The rugged terrain of the Balkans and the bitter divisions between its peoples are reflected in history. The region has been frequently invaded by Celts, Romans, Thracians, Slavs, Huns, Goths, Hungarians, Bulgars, Turks, Italians and Germans. The ethnic and religious hatred have frequently boiled over into violence, often generations later. The area is a mosaic of disputed borders, once of kingdoms, principalities and provinces, now of republics. It has suffered as a buffer zone between rival religious empires, marking the divide between the Roman Catholic and Eastern Orthodox Churches, and between Christianity and Islam. There have been periods of stability under the Roman, Byzantine and Ottoman empires, and under post-War Marxist dictatorships, but involvement of great powers have always been destabilising the Balkans.

A TURBULENT HISTORY

The Balkans emerged from prehistory in classical times, with records of civilisation in Greece and contacts between and among various states and peoples of the central and northern regions of the Peninsula. They were later incorporated into the Roman Empire, while the eastern half of the Peninsula became the Byzantine Empire. The Slavs began to penetrate the Peninsula at the end of the 5th century, the Avars in the 6th century, and the Bulgars arrived from the Volga region in the 7th century. The area was part of the Roman Empire until 395. Thereafter, the territories of modern Slovenia, Croatia and Herzegovina remained in the Latin Western Empire, while the rest became part of the Byzantine Eastern Empire. In 1054, the Eastern Orthodox Church broke with the Roman Church. The Byzantine region of the Balkans has remained Orthodox while the Croats and Slovenes are Catholics.

Ottoman Turks began their conquests in Europe in the 14th century. In the region of the former Yugoslavia, only Montenegro could resist the onslaught.

The Serbs were defeated at the *Battle of Kosovo* in 1389, and the last Bulgarian stronghold was overrun in 1396. In 1453, the Turks captured Constantinople and, within seven years, they had taken all of Greece. Until 1477, Romanian-speaking Wallachia and Moldavia put up a fierce resistance under its leaders Vlad Tepes,' the *Impaler',* prince of Wallachia, who inspired the legend of Count Dracula.

Albania was overrun in 1479. The Turks defeated Hungary in 1526, expanding their empire north and west of the Danube. In 1527, Croatia sought the protection of Austria, and remained under Austrian control until 1918. The Turks strengthened their hold on Bosnia-Herzegovina and by the mid-16th century they were masters of most of the Balkans. The exceptions were Croatia and the Adriatic coast, where the Turkish fleet was decisively beaten in 1571 at Lepanto by the Christian League of Spanish, Venetian and Genoese ships.

At the beginning of the 13th century, Greek Byzantine rule was replaced by Roman, except in Epirus. The Ottoman Turks began their onslaught on the Balkans in the 14th century, and by the end of the 15th century, they occupied almost the entire Peninsula. Turkish power began to decline in the 18th century, and the partition of the Balkans into local states or colonies of the great powers of Europe drew international attention. Greece was recognised as independent in 1829, and the state of Serbia was created in 1830. After 1830, three new Balkan states appeared: Romania, Montenegro and Bulgaria.

SERIES OF BATTLES

The Bulgarian occupation of eastern Rumelia in 1885 was followed by the Serbo-Bulgarian war and, by the turn of the century, the Balkans became a scene of international conflicts. In 1908, Austria-Hungary annexed Bosnia-Herzegovina, and in 1912-13 the *Balkan League* of Greece, Serbia, Bulgaria, and Montenegro attacked and defeated Turkey – the first of two conflicts known as the *Balkan Wars.* As a consequence, the Ottoman rule in the Balkans was ended. After World War I, a Serb-Croat-Slovene kingdom of the South Slavs was set up. Italy received the extreme northwest coast of the Balkan Peninsula, including Rijeka, as well as some of the Adriatic islands. Large population exchanges were carried out in an attempt to stabilize the new frontiers. Romania and Yugoslavia allied with Czechoslovakia in 1921 to counter foreign threats, and in 1934 a new Balkan Pact was signed by Greece,

Yugoslavia, Turkey and Romania.

WORLD WAR II AND AFTER

After World War II, the Allied peace treaty with Italy, Romania, and Bulgaria (concluded in Paris in 1947) introduced the present frontiers. Longtime Soviet support for local communist leaders and groups in the region was instrumental in the establishment of the post-War communist governments of Albania, Bulgaria, Romania, and Yugoslavia. Yugoslavia broke with the Soviet bloc in 1948, and in 1961 the Albanians expelled their Soviet advisers and allied themselves with China, an association that lasted until 1978. Bulgaria and Romania were founding-members of *Comecon* in 1949. Greece and Turkey became members of the NATO in 1952. The Turks added a fresh component – Islam – to the existing split between Catholic and Orthodox. Some Christians converted to their conquerors' faith, notably in the regions of modern Albania, Kosovo, Macedonia and Bosnia-Herzegovina. The region was economically and educationally backward, its people reduced to serfdom. After their defeat at the gates of Vienna in 1683, the Ottomans were in retreat. They were driven from Hungary, and many Serbs trekked north into Vojvodian to gain the protection of the Habsburgs and the Austro-Hungarian Empire. Europeans were unhappy with the Muslim domination of Balkan Christians.

> "Rumania, Serbia and Montenegro (Yugoslavia) should be evacuated; occupied territories restored; Serbia accorded free and secure access to the sea and the relations of the several Balkan states to one another determined by friendly counsel along historically established lines of allegiance and nationality and international guarantees of the political and economic independence and territorial integrity of the several Balkan states should be entered into."
>
> ***- Wilson's Fourteen Point For Peace***

SERBIAN REVOLT CAUSED WORLD WAR II: Serbia revolted against the Turks in 1815, and gained autonomy in 1829, though the Turkish troops did not leave until 1867. The Greeks began a war of independence against the Turks in 1821. (The English poet Lord Byron was among those who sought to help them, but he died of fever in Greece in 1823.) The combined British, French and Russian fleets defeated the Turks at Navarino in 1827, and Greece gained freedom two years later. A Bulgarian revolt against Turkish rule in 1876 was brutally crushed, but in the same year Romania, helped by France and Russia, declared its independence from the Ottoman Empire. Serbia, Romania and Russia then declared war on Turkey, which allowed Bulgaria to become autonomous in 1878. Macedonia remained under Ottoman rule, but in the First Balkan War in 1912, Serbia, Greece and Bulgaria formed an alliance to liberate Macedonia and Albania. Turkey in Europe was reduced to a rump. A year later, the Balkan allies turned on each other. Serbia and Greece united against Bulgaria, which had claimed Macedonia for itself. At the same time, Serbia gained control of Kosovo from Albania.

These tensions triggered the World War II. *Archduke Franz Ferdinand,* heir to the Austro-Hungarian Empire, was assassinated by a Serb nationalist in Sarajevo in June 1914. Austria used the murder as a pretext to overrun Serbia. The Russians felt their position in the Balkans was threatened and mobilised their armies, involving their British and French allies in a war against the Central Powers – the Austro-Hungarian Empire and Germany. This was the beginning of the World War I about which we will talk later. After the First World War, Vojvodina, Slovenia and Croatia joined with Serbia, Montenegro and Macedonia to form a new country, ruled by the King of Serbia. In 1929, its name was changed to Yugoslavia, meaning *"land of southern Slavs".* Serbian domination of the government was bitterly resented by the people belonging to minorities, notably the Croats.

YOGOSLAVIA WAS CREATED IN 1918 AND VANISHED IN 2003

Yugoslavia came into existence in 1918 as the kingdom of the Serbs, Croats and Slovenes with the Serbian Peter-I Karageorevich, as King. Peter-I died in 1921 and was succeeded by his son Alexander who, faced with difficulties at home and abroad, established a military dictatorship in 1929. Peter-II (1923-70) succeeded him and a regency under his uncle Paul was set up until Peter assumed power early in 1941. The German invasion followed and the whole country was overrun; the king took refuge in England, and Yugoslavia became an area of grim guerilla warfare until the Germans were expelled with the help of Russian forces. The guerilla leader Josip Broz (Marshal) Tito established a Communist govt. in Yugoslavia independent of the former Soviet Union. It vanished in 2003 and became Serbia and Montenegro *(see later chapters).*

The birth of the Balkan states is also an interesting story. Greece was created in 1829 and Serbia in 1830. The Balkan Federation was created by Tito in 1948 after World War II which brought together the Central Balkan areas under the Communist control. The Balkan League was constituted on the prompting of the then Soviet Union which wanted to contain the expansion of the Austria-Hungary empire. But, this did not happen and Austria annexed Bosnia and Herzegovina in 1948 and after the assassination of the heir to the Austrian throne, Archduke Franz Ferdinand, on June 28, 1914, the first World War started.

By 1990, as communism crumbled in much of Europe, Serbia held on. Slobodan Milosevic, Serbia's leader since 1987, played skilfully on nationalism to stay in power. In Croatia and Slovenia, the desire for independence spread, both among anti-communists and anti-Serbs. The Croats government urged caution. Religious and national rivalries, lack of democracy, ancient feuds, World War genocide – Yugoslavia saw them all. But in the mid-1990s, its economy was creaking. Local communists bossed over people. But, as eastern Europe was liberated, Yugoslavia was left open to international influences. Intellectually and culturally, it seemed a natural part of Europe and that was the beginning of war, first in the minds of feuding groups, and later on the ground in which more than 1.5 million people have lost their lives since 1992.

HITLER'S INVASION AND AFTER

Adolf Hitler invaded Yugoslavia in 1941 and established a fascist puppet regime in Croatia. Armies of the pro-monarchist *Chetnik* and communist partisans under Marshal Tito fought the Germans and each other in a savage war of atrocity and counter atrocity, in which a tenth of the population was killed. Greece was overrun by the Germans in 1941. Bulgaria and Romania entered the war with the Germans, but both countries changed sides in 1944. In September 1944, in a truly Balkan twist of diplomacy, Bulgaria was simultaneously at war with Germany, the Soviet Union, Britain and the USA. With the exception of Greece, the Balkans were liberated by the Soviet Red Army, with the help of communist partisans in Yugoslavia and Albania.

Although the Greek monarchy survived a three-year civil war against communist guerrillas after 1946, communist dictatorships were established throughout the rest of the Balkans. The Albanian, Bulgarian, Romanian and Yugoslav monarchies were replaced by republics. With political dissidence crushed in single-party states, an impoverished stability was attained. But ethnic tensions were only partially submerged under the Tito-led regime which controlled Yugoslavia from 1945. Although the federal government was responsible for major policy areas such as defence, foreign policy, economy and human rights, other powers were devolved from 1970, to the six republics and two autonomous regions of Yugoslavia.

The communist monopoly of power was broken in the aftermath of Mikhail Gorbachev's reforms in the Soviet Union. In November 1989, the day after the Berlin Wall was breached, the 35-year rule of the Bulgarian party leader Tidor Zhivkov ended. After a bloody uprising, the Romanian dictator Nicolae Ceausescu and his wife Elena were executed in December the same year. In December 1990, the ramshackle communist regime in Albania agreed to allow opposition political parties to be form government.

ETHNIC CLEANSING AND DAYTON ACCORD

After Tito's death in 1980, the unwieldy federal structure he had created to unite Yugoslavia proved unable to contain nationalist passions and economic crises. In 1990, the Serbian nationalist leader Slobodan Milosevic campaigned to bring Kosovo and Vojvodina within Serbia, a move resisted by Kosovo's predominantly Muslim Albanians. In 1991, Croatia and Slovenia declared themselves independent, while fighting broke out between Croatians and Serbs of the Krajina region, who wished to join a *'Greater Serbia'*. In Bosnia-Herzegovina, Serbs fought Muslims and Croatians. In December 1991 the federal president, Stipe Mesic, resigned and declared that 'Yugoslavia no longer exists'. Bosnia-Herzegovina and Macedonia declared independence in 1992. Several hundred thousand refugees fled as violence escalated beyond the United Nations' control.

Serbs under Radovan Karadzic 'ethnically cleansed' Bosnia of Croats and Muslims by forced evacuations and mass killings. UN sanctions were imposed on Serbia, and NATO air strikes were used on Bosnian Serb positions around the besieged city of Sarajevo. After much bloodshed, a peace accord was brokered at Dayton, Ohio, (US) in December 1995, with a NATO-led Peace Implementation Force stationed in Bosnia. However, the patchwork of minorities throughout the region – Hungarians in Romanian Transylvania and Serbian Vojvodina; Turks in Bulgaria; Bulgars in Macedonia; Albanians in Kosovo; Serbs in Bosnia – suggested that the Balkans would remain as volatile as ever.

In the Balkans, political lines have never coincided with ethnic lines. However, ethnic differences don't make war but if they are exploited by politicians, yes, they do.

-Galbraith

31

Sources of conflicts in the Balkans

In the complicated history of the Balkans, ethnic groups, geography, history and religion are mixed so inextricably that no nation-states, like those in Western Europe, could be set up. Hence, the perpetual turmoil. In the historical context, it may be noted that the entire region is governed by the Roman law of centralised authority, as a result, minority groups have always faced oppression, resulting in conflict.

The Balkan Peninsula is one of three Peninsulas that juts southward into the Mediterranean, the other two being the Iberian in the west and the Italian in the centre. Political and linguistic unity have long been established in Italy, and the Iberian Peninsula is shared by Spain and Portugal. There has been little unity, however, in the Balkan Peninsula. For centuries it has been inhabited by discordant peoples, whose interests and ambitions clashed fiercely. On this account, someone has aptly called it the *Peninsula of Unrest.* It is "a rough mountainous region, with fertile valleys tucked between boulder-strewn ridges and steep, wooded hills." Its mountainous nature has kept the inhabitants from any commercial development, the main occupation being agriculture.

As constituted after World War I, Romania has an area of 113,889 square miles; in other words, it is only about the size of Tamil Nadu. Former Yugoslavia, with an area of some 96,000 square miles, was nearly the size of Madhya Pradesh. Greece, with about 50,000 square miles, was about the size of Assam. Bulgaria, with some 30,000 square miles, was about the size of Maine, US; Albania, the smallest of these states, has an area of about 10,629 square miles, which is about the size of Tripura before the War. According to the census of 1925, the total population of the five states was 42 million. Since 1920, demographic structure and boundaries have changed, specially after the split of Yugoslavia in 1991 and of Czechoslovakia in 1992.

For many decades prior to the World War I, the Balkan Peninsula had been the danger zone of Europe. It was the scene of plots and counterplots. Time and again, upheavals in this region threatened to involve most of Europe in bloody conflict. For example, war almost broke out when Austria seized Bosnia and Herzegovina in 1908.

CROSSROAD OF GREAT POWERS

The reason for the perpetual turbulence was two-fold. First, because the Peninsula formed the main highway from Europe to Asia and from Russia to the Mediterranean, a number of great powers coveted control of it. This desire caused Russia and Austria to stare at one another eyeball–to–eyeball throughout much of the nineteenth century, toward the end of which Germany also entered the competition. These three powers were ever ready to stir up unrest to gain supremacy. In brief, *"live and let live"* was not the rule. Dealings between the nations were normally regulated in accordance with "the simple plan, that he shall take who has the power and he shall keep who can." The second reason for the perpetual unrest was nationalism and the desire for national union. Some of the nationalists in the Peninsula were still not free. Since freedom had been denied them so long, they continued in their efforts to attain it. On the other hand those, who already had independent governments wished to include all the members of their respective nationality in one state.

WORLD WAR I: It destroyed the Romanov and Habsburg empires and removed the outside influences from the lives of the Balkan peoples. But their main problem was only partially solved by the Versaille Peace Conference, despite the fact that the peacemakers sought to base the settlement on such lofty principles as the right to political freedom. But, the nationalities of the Balkans were so intermingled that it was impossible for the conference to make a clean-cut division on ethnographical lines. Even when allowance is made for this fact, the settlement did not approximate the best possible achievement under the circumstances, other motives also influenced the settlement. One of these was the *doctrine of punishment;* many of the peacemakers were influenced by the idea that the lesser as well as the greater enemy states should pay penalty. Then there was also the desire to block

Germany's drive to the southeast by strengthening the states that had been on the Allied side.

The result was a series of compromises. Romania, as one of the victors, received all of Transylvania and Bucovina, thereby more than doubling her population and becoming the largest of the Balkan states. The territory of Greece was nearly doubled. Serbia nearly quadrupled her population, Serbia and Montenegro being merged into the great commonwealth of Yugoslavia. On the other hand, Bulgaria, being on the losing side, was pared down considerably. Once strong among her neighbours, Bulgaria now became one of the smallest states in the Balkans.

BOUNDARY CHANGES: The political position of these states was far from satisfactory. The victors were determined to preserve their gains, and Bulgaria, a loser, was determined to recover her losses. The worst feature of this policy of "the spoils to the victor" was the incorporation of national minorities in states of other nationalities. Nearly 1.2 million Magyars and 600,000 Germans, to Yugoslavia, and about one quarter of the Bulgarians, to Greece and other states. The situation was aggravated by this fact that most of the nations did not pursue a liberal policy towards the minorities despite their promises to do so. This not only increased the discontent among the minorities, but also strengthened the determination of the various national states to redeem these minorities.

After the settlement of 1919 at Versailles, the Balkan equilibrium became more sensitive than before and border incidents increased. The governments of Yugoslavia, Romania, and Czechoslovakia formed a defensive alliance as a means of frustrating the designs of the vanquished states. This alliance, known as the *Little Entente,* was concluded by a series of treaties in 1920 and 1921. While the general purpose was the maintenance of the status quo, the more specific aim was the prevention of attempts to restore the power to the Habsburgs either at Budapest or Vienna. Such a restoration, it was feared, would lead to an attempt to regain the territories which were distributed to the victorious states after the collapse of the Habsburg empire in 1918. The Little Entente played a role in the period between the two world wars.

But, problems of territory and of national minorities were not the only ones confronting the Balkan states. In addition to the general upheaval caused by the War, the collapse of the Habsburg Empire and the creation of national states, upon its ruins brought in their train such difficulties as the transfer of land to the peasantry, the transfer of power to new classes, the creation of new bureaucracies, revision of many fundamental institutions, establishment of internal unity through the fusion of the old and the new elements in the population, and the restoration of commercial and financial stability. In most of the states, financial conditions were serious as a result of the disorder produced by four years of war and the dislocation caused by the increase in the number of tariff walls. There were also religious problems. Although most of the inhabitants of the Peninsula were as least nominal members of the Eastern Orthodox Church, the number of Roman Catholics, particularly in Yugoslavia (Croatia), was considerable. Then there were Muslims, who were convinced of their duty to go on being loyal and consistent professors of their religion, Islam. Another major problem was the conflict between radicalism and conservatism.

OTTOMAN RULE & MUSLIM QUESTION

It may be recalled that Muslims in the Balkans are far too different from those in the Arab land or in Malaysia or India. But Muslims continued to remind the Serbs and Croats of their defeat in 1389, in the battle at Kosuro when the Turks were the conquerors who ruled a good part of the area. The fall of the Ottoman Empire, which was complete by the end of World War I (1918), left some Muslims behind in the Balkans. The Ottoman Turks, (Mongols by origin), were so powerful that they conquered Egypt, Syria, Arabia, Mesopotamia, (Iraq), Tripoli and most of Hungary in the Balkans. They conquered Cyprus in 1571 and Crete in 1669. However, Christians launched a counter-offensive in 1683 and by 1699 Turks lost Hungary. There was a revolt against Muslims in Serbia in 1894 and in 1821, Greece threw off the Turkish rule. The Bulgarian rising of 1876 led to a new war between Turkey and Russia ending in the Treaty of Berlin (1878), according to which Turkey lost Bulgaria, Bosnia and Herzegovina. A militant nationalist group, *Young Turk,* secured a constitution. (The term 'Young Turk' is used in India for those who oppose the existing order). In 1912 and 1913, the Balkan States expelled Turk Muslims from Albania and Macedonia. Turkey fought World War II with Germans and as a result lost Syria, Arabia, Mesopotamia and a part of Egypt after Hitler's defeat.

KEMAL ATATURK, A REFORMER

There has been a sea-change with the coming to power of Mustafa Kemal Ataturk (1920) after which Turkey ceased to be an Islamic country. Polygamy

MUSTAFA KEMAL ATATURK
FOUNDER OF TURKEY

Mustafa Kemal Ataturk

Mustafa Kemal Ataturk (1881–1938) was a Turkish army officer, revolutionary statesman, and founder of the Republic of Turkey as well as its first President. Ataturk became known as an extremely capable military officer by being the only undefeated Ottoman commander during World War I. Following the defeat of the Ottoman Empire, he led the Turkish national movement in the Turkish War of Independence. Having established a provisional government in Ankara, he defeated the forces sent by the Allies. His successful military campaigns led to the liberation of the country and to the establishment of Turkey. During his presidency, Atatürk embarked upon a program of political, economic, and cultural reforms. An admirer of the Age of Enlightenment, he sought to transform the former Ottoman Empire into a modern, democratic, and secular nation-state. The principles of Atatürk's reforms, upon which modern Turkey was established, are referred to as Kemalism. Born as *Mustafa*, his second name *Kemal* (meaning *Perfection* or *Maturity*) was given to him by his mathematics teacher in recognition of his academic excellence. In his early years, his mother encouraged Mustafa to attend a religious school, something he did reluctantly and only briefly.

was abolished and a new legal code was introduced by Kemal's People's Party which ruled until 1950, after which there had been political uncertainties. Now, Turkey has a very small area and a few fortresses in the European part of the country. However, a large Muslim population lives in Bosnia. And, thereby hangs a tale of the Bosnian massacre. The fact is, that Europeans never accepted Muslims in the *Continent of Destiny,* largely because they were of a different cultural group although Slav Muslims have nothing in common with mainstream Muslims of the Arabian variety. The German-Turkey alliance in World War II only worsened the matter. The US gave money under the Marshall Plan to re-build Europe but not to Turkey or to the Muslim-dominated areas of the former Ottoman empire. It was only when President Milosevic started slaughtering Muslims, whose corpses were brought alive on TV screens in homes all over the world, that the US and NATO powers realised that it was yet another Holocaust, which could put the West in the dock. And, that marked a shift in Europe's (and American's) perception of the Balkans which have always been boiling over the brims.

WHERE MELTING POTS DON'T MELT

There is yet another lesson to learn from the unfinished Balkan tragedy;

that different cultural groups don't mix. (Prof. Samuel Huttington of *"Clash of Civilizations"* fame should have the last laugh). The former Soviet Union sought to put together under an empire of more than 50 racial groups divided in 15 Soviet republics and many autonomous regions to produce a multi-racial neo-communist society but failed. Marshal Tito, also tried to put the warring racial groups together but the system could not survive him. Former Czechoslovakia consisted of two racial groups, Czech and Slovak, and they separated although without conflict because they could be clinically separated which was not the case in former Yugoslavia where Muslims and Serbs were inter-mixed inextricably. And, hence, the ethnic cleansing and the continuing conflict.

The fact is, that the Balkan countries have always been fighting with others, if not among themselves. Geography and history have conspired to make this mountainous and drought-prone area the most dangerous flash-point of the world which has caused many wars, including the first global one in which about 10 million people died; the injured were never counted. Having read it through, one is left more confused than before about the Balkan tragedy. And this confusion is the source of Balkan conflicts. The fact is that ethnic fault-lines have only deepened the already divided region which witnessed the genocide, the like of which has not been seen after World War II. To be true, the Balkans have been the stomping ground of imperial powers in the past which nobody can remember without wondering how mysteriously history is made. And, how helpless are the people of the Balkans in its making.

The Turkish empire (1300-1920) reached the greatest extent to include Hungary part of South Russia and right up to north Africa. When it fell, the thud was heard all over the world.

32

Ottoman Empire: its triumph and tragedy

The Ottoman Turks, who ruled the Balkans for a long time, owed their power not entirely to bravery and strategy but by converting the Slav youths to Islam and making them slaves sworn to fight for their masters which they did until the last of the Turks was thrown out after the Balkan Wars.

In one time, the Turkish (Ottoman) empire spread almost all over the Balkans. The two Balkan Wars (1912 and 1913) finally resulted in the expulsion of Turks from the Balkans. Although the Turks left the Balkans, retaining only Thrace (modern Bulgaria) they left a large population of converted Muslims in all the countries under their control. And, the Muslims don't fit into the Orthodox Christian social structure. Hence, the continuing conflict in the Balkans.

The name "Balkan" has been in use since the early 19th century; it is a Turkish for "mountains". The Balkan peninsula is defined physiographically by the lower Danube and Sava rivers (north), the Black Sea (east), the Aegean Sea (southeast), the Mediterranean Sea (south), the Ionian Sea (southwest), and the Adriatic Sea (west). Its area within these limits is about 505,000 sq. km. Politically however, the Balkans also extend beyond these limits to include all of former Yugoslavia, Romania, Albania, Bulgaria, Greece and the European part of Turkey. The population of the peninsula so mentioned in the early 1980s was approximately 72 million and its area was about 305,000 sq.miles.

One has to hurriedly go through part of the Ottoman empire history, whose expansion during 1330-1481 was the highest, to be able to understand the problems of the Balkans, the most troubled peninsula in the world. The

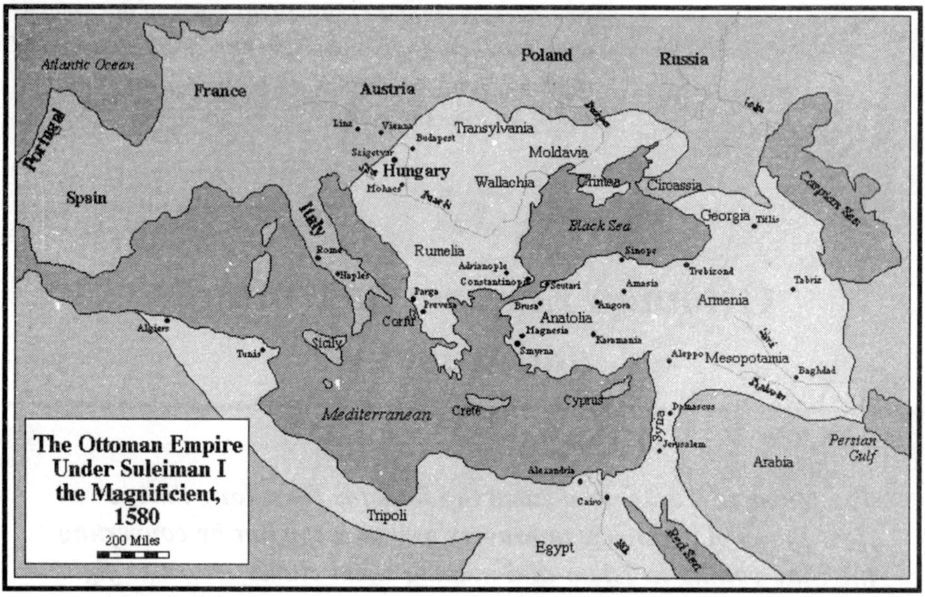

The Ottoman Empire Under Suleiman I the Magnificient, 1580

Ottomans had adopted unique military and administrative forms to win wars. The most notable included the *devsirme* system, whereby Christian youths from the Balkans were drafted and converted to Islam for a life-time of slavery. The military arm supplied by the *devsirme* system was the *Janissary* corps, an infantry group attached to the sultan. Mehmed-II developed the practice of requiring all members of the government and army, Turkish or Balkan, Muslim or non-Muslim, to accept the status of personal slave of the sultan. Thus, he hoped to ensure the indivisibility of power, with the entire ruling class sworn to absolute obedience to the ruler.

Under Selim-I (1512-20), Ottoman's victory over the Mamluks in 1516-17 doubled the size of the empire at a stroke by adding to it Syria, Palestine, Egypt, and Algeria. The reign of his son Suleyman-I (1520-66), known in Europe as "the Magnificent," was a golden age of Ottoman power and grandeur. He conquered Hungary from the Habsburgs, annexed Tripoli, extended the empire southeastward through Mesopotamia to the Persian Gulf, and made the Ottoman navy dominant in the eastern Mediterranean. After Suleyman's reign, the decline set in. Even though territorial expansion continued for a while – Murad-III (1574-95) conquered the Caucasus and seized Azerbaijan from Iran – administrative and social weaknesses became clear.

The causes of the decline of the empire after Suleyman include lack of ability of the succeeding sultans, the ever-increasing power of the *devsirme*

> **THE TURKISH EMPIRE**
>
> The Ottoman was Muslim empire of the Turks (1300-1920), the successor of the Seljuk Empire. It was founded by Osman I and reached its height with Suleiman in the 16th Century. The Capital was Istanbul (formerly Constantinople). At its greatest extent the Ottoman Empire's boundaries were Europe as far as Hungary, part of south Russia, Iran, the Palestinian coastline, Egypt and north Africa. From the 17th century it was in decline. There was an attempted revival and reform under the Young Turk Party 1908, but the regime crumbled when Turkey sided with Germany in World War I. And, lost. The sultanate was abolished by Kemal Ataturk in 1922; the last sultan was Muhammad VI.

(slave) class and the tensions it created within the ruling class, the erosion of Ottoman industry, the decline of Ottoman-controlled trade routes with the development of better navigation, and sudden leaps in population and the subsequent decline of urban centres. The powerful nation-states, arising in Europe during this period, formed alliances to drive the Ottoman out of the continent. The 18th century saw the decay of rural administration into small, feudal-like states and increased unrest in the cities, disrupting food supplies and leading to widespread famine. No innovations in technology that supported Europe's prosperity made their way into the Turkish empire.

REVOLT BY YOUNG TURKS

By the accession of Mahmud-II in 1808, the Ottoman situation appeared desperate. Local authorities openly opposed the central government, while the empire was at war with both England and Russia. In the next few decades, Mahmud-II re-established some order with military modernization and governmental reorganization, but the boundaries of the empire continued to shrink, Mahmud's sons, Abdulmecid-I and Abdulaziz, enacted a series of liberal and modernizing reforms called the *Tazimate,* which were widely viewed in the West as an effort to encourage friendly relations with European powers. Among the reforms were the first comprehensive education system and the westernization of commercial, maritime, and penal codes.

In 1876, Abdulhamid-II agreed to the first constitution in any Islamic country. Two years later, by the *Treaty of San Stefano* and negotiations at the Congress of Berlin, the empire was forced to give up Romania, Serbia, Montenegro, Bulgaria, Cyprus and other territories. Abdulhamid was able to hold the empire together for the rest of the century by telling Europeans that the Turks kept peace in Europe but the final years of reign were marked by revolts, notably by the *Young Turks,* in 1908. The Balkan wars of 1912-13 completed the empire's expulsion from Europe. After disastrous defeat in World War I and a revolution immediately after, the 36th and final Ottoman emperor, Mehmed-VI Vahideddin, was overthrown in 1922 and modern Turkey formed.

EASTERN QUESTION : It indicated diplomatic problem in the 19th and early 20th centuries posed by the disintegration of the Ottoman Empire. Any internal change in the Turkish domains caused tension among the European powers, each of whom feared that one of the others might take advantage of the political disarray to increase its own influence. This question arose periodically during the 19th century – e.g., during the Greek War of Independence in the 1820s; in the Crimean conflict (1853-56), the Balkan crisis of 1875-78, the Bosnian crisis of 1908, and the Balkan Wars of 1912-13 which marked the end of the Ottoman rule in the Balkans. The eventual distribution of the Ottoman empire after its disintegration was as follows: the Balkan provinces emerged as independent states, often under the influence of Russia or one of the other great powers; Great Britain occupied Cyprus in 1878 and Egypt in 1882 and acquired Palestine and Iraq as mandates after World War I and France took over Syria and Lebanon in 1920. Turkey, the heart of the Ottoman state, won recognition as an independent republic in 1923. This is how the great Ottoman empire finally became an ordinary state, a tiny part (Turkey) in Europe and the rest is Anatolia, mountainous, rugged and poor.

SOME IMPORTANT DATES – OTTOMAN EMPIRE

1st C BC	Asia Minor (Turkey) became part of the Roman Empire, later passing to Byzantine Empire.
6th C AD	Turkish peoples spread from Mongolia into Turkestan, where they adopted Islam.
13th C	Ottoman Turks, driven west by the Mongols, became vassals of the Seljuk Turks.
c. 1299	Osman-I founded a small Ottoman kingdom, which displaced the Seljuks to include all Asia Minor.
1354	Ottoman Turks captured Gallipoli and began their conquests in Europe.
1389	Battle of Kossovo: Turks defeated the Serbs to take control of most of the Balkan peninsula.

1453	Constantinople, capital of the Byzantine Empire, fell to the Turks; became capital of Ottoman Empire as Istanbul.
16th C	Ottoman Empire reached its zenith under Suleiman the Magnificent 1520-66; Turks conquered Egypt, Syria, Arabia, Mesopotamia, Tripoli, Cyprus and most of Hungary.
1683	Failure of the Siege of Vienna marked the start of the decline of the Ottoman Empire.
1699	Treaty of Karlowitz: Turks forced out of Hungary by Austrians.
1774	Treaty of Kuchuk Kainarji: Russia drove Turks from Crimea and won the right to intervene on behalf of Christian subjects of the sultan.
19th C	'The Eastern Question': Ottoman weakness caused intense rivalry between the great Powers to shape the future of the Near East.
1821-29	Greeks defeated the Turks with help of Russia, Britain and France.
1854-56	Crimean War: Britain and France fought to defend the Ottoman Empire from Russians.
1877-78	Russo-Turkish War ended with the Treaty of Berlin and the withdrawal of Turks from Bulgaria.
1908	Young Turk revolution forced sultan to grant a constitution; start of political modernisation.
1911-12	Italo-Turkish War: Turkey lost Tripoli (Libya).
1912-13	Balkan War: Greece, Serbia and Bulgaria expelled the Turks from Macedonia and Albania.
1914	Ottoman Empire entered World War I on German side.
1919	Following Turkish defeat, Mustapha Kemal launched nationalist revolt to resist foreign encroachments.
1920	Treaty of Sevres partitioned the Ottoman Empire, leaving no part of Turkey fully independent.
1922	Kemal, having defied the Allies, expelled Greeks, French and Italians from Asia Minor; sultanate abolished.
1923	Treaty of Lausanne recognised Turkish independence; secular republic established by Kemal, who imposed rapid Westernisation.
1935	Kemal adopted the surname Ataturk ('Father of the Turks').

1938	Death of Kemal Ataturk.
1952	Turkey became a member of NATO.
1960	Military coup led by General Cemal Gursel deposed Menderes, who was executed in 1961.
1961	Inonu returned as prime minister; politics dominated by the issue of Cyprus.
1965	Justice Party came to power under Suleyman Demirel.
1974	Turkey invaded northern Cyprus.
1984	Kurds began guerrilla war autonomy.
1989	Application to join European Community rejected.
1990-91	Turkey joined UN coalition against Iraq in Gulf War.
1997	Agreement with Greece on peaceful resolution of disputes.
1998	Islamic Welfare Party (RP) banned.
1999	Coalition government formed in January, headed by Bulent Ecevit.

PART – II

The British Empire is lost in history, but it has left lasting imprints without which globalization would not have been possible. Among British legacies are; the English language; English forms of land tenure; Scottish and English banking; the Common Law; Protestantism; team sports; the limited or 'night watchman' state; representative assemblies and the idea of liberty, says Niall Ferguson in his book, Empire.

33

British islanders, strange people and stranger legacies

This island state was the last frontier of the Roman empire and it continues to be the extremity of the European landmass, cut off by the English Channel which also marks the emotional disconnect between Great Britain and Europe. Britain is an intensely virile nation in the realm of ideas and scientific inventions which respects non-conformist views.

Wet and windy between the North Sea and the Atlantic Ocean, the British Isles are perhaps the most fateful of all the world's islands, standing in a unique relationship to the rest of Europe. Four nations occupy these relatively uninviting islands – the English, Irish, Welsh and the Scots – and they are grouped into two States: 60 million people live in the *Kingdom of Great Britain and Northern Ireland* and four and a half million live in the Republic of Ireland. The mutual attitudes of the two are notoriously equivocal. The islands have not been occupied by an outside power since 1066 AD, and for several centuries they have been governed by systems of parliamentary democracy.

Most of the land is good for farming, well-watered and easy to grow crops. But in Wales and in much of Scotland, along the Atlantic shore of Ireland, rough highlands predominate the landscape which accentuate the chief ethnic division of the population between the Anglo-Saxon, deriving from Teutonic

invaders, and the Celtic who came, from far in earlier waves of Mediterranean immigration. It was here that the Roman Empire reached its final frontier. The legions never controlled northern Scotland, and they never crossed the Irish Sea. The archipelago was an extremity of the Roman world then, and it remains an extremity of Europe still, never quite assimilated into the European consciousness.

Several of Europe's great historical trends, nevertheless, are epitomized in the British Isles. The continent's ancient dynastic fervours survive here in a rich and ostentatious monarchy. The feudalism that once dominated Europe finds its mementoes still in the class system of England and in the kilts, tartans and rituals of the Scottish clans. The religious struggles of the continent, mostly ended elsewhere, survive here in a violent, and stylized conflict between Catholics and Protestants in Northern Ireland. Europe's instinct for aggression and expansion has found some of its most vigorous exponents among these islanders – from the sixteenth century to the twentieth, the British were engaged in a career of conquest which made them once the most powerful people on earth, ruling territories in every continent and brazenly commanding all the oceans. It was here that Europe first mechanized itself when the power of steam was harnessed by British scientists and engineers at the end of the eighteenth century. The mastery of technique not only made the British wealthy, but it made them primarily an urban nation – the first in Europe. Today England, in particular, is one of the most crowded of all countries, and the vast city of London, sprawling in the southeast corner of the islands, is an example of crowded urban life.

> **CHANNEL TUNNEL**
>
> Channel tunnel, a land link, was first suggested by a Frenchman, Mathieu, to Napoleon-I in 1802. And after signature at an Anglo-French convention in 1875, excavations began in 1882, but abandoned in 1883 when a House of Commons Committee rejected the idea as a military hazard. In 1972 England and France signed an agreement for the construction of a rail tunnel but owing to economic difficulties, the project languished until a revival of interest in 1980.
>
> The tunnel is built beneath the English Channel, linking Britain with mainland Europe. It comprises twin rail tunnels, 50 km long and 7.3 metres in diameter, located 40 metre beneath the seabed. Construction began in 1987, and the French and English sections were linked in December 1990. It was officially opened on May 6, 1994. The shuttle train service, *Le Shuttle*, opened to lorries in May 1994 and to cars in December 1994. The tunnel's high-speed train service, *Eurostar,* linking London to Paris and Brussels, opened in November 1994. The estimated cost of the tunnel was continually revised upwards reaching £8 billion in 1995.

The British attitude to Europe remains ambivalent. No other European power is an island state, and none has looked so instinctively to the sea for its fortunes. For centuries, the British tried to stay clear of continental involvements, intervening only when it seemed that one European power or another was becoming dangerously dominant. Now their empire has gone, and their industrial capacity has long been overtaken, but their overseas investments are still enormous, and many older citizens still feel that they have more in common with the other English–speaking peoples, scattered across the world, than with their continental neighbours. In 1990, the British Isles were for the first time linked by a tunnel to France – opening out the possibility of their joining the pan-European system while old-school Britons, remember with nostalgia the days when Britain ruled the waves. Britain during their long rule over many parts of the world, almost as long as Romans did (350 years) has left behind many legacies in their former colonies. Some of these are:

COMMON LAW

Blame it on Henry-II, if you must. It was England's first King who prepared the ground for the Common Law system that replaced the practice of justice being dispensed on the basis of disparate customs by feudal and county courts. While his bold reforms in the 12th century led to the creation of a strong and unified legal framework under the Common Law, the people were still expected to treat judges as if they were nobility and address them with titles such as *"Milord"* and *"Your Lordship"* which implied that judges were divine and infallible. Old habits are notoriously hard to break, but it has taken India almost a millennium to dispense with the use of such forms while addressing judges. Or, not yet!!

The Common law is the typical system of British law based on precedent rather than written codes or statutes; it is the basis of the English legal system and that of most former British colonies; including the United States. In contrast, most European and Latin American countries, and some in Africa and Asia, operate under a system of *civil law,* rooted in the ancient Roman legal code, emphasizing statutory dictates over precedents set by decisions in previous cases. *Common law means the law that is common to and accepted throughout the realm.* It flows from the idea that legal principles are established on a case-by-case basis, over time (as Chief Justice Oliver Wendell Holmes observed in The Common Law 1881) not by logic but by experience. In Britain, Common Law has evolved since the 12th century and there is no written constitution, all law was *"judge-made"* – based on the interpretation of prior precedents – until the 19th century when parliamentary statutes began to supplement case law. Even today, when most law is statutory even in the common-law systems, appellate courts' review of lower-court decisions is based on precedent.

The cornerstone of Common Law is *stare decisis* (Latin, "to stand by settled decisions"), that judicial decisions must follow established precedents unless they are outmoded or unjust. This allows for flexibility and growth in the law through the setting of new precedents, and is related to equity, the equally ancient doctrine that conforms to the strict application of law to principles of *"natural justice."* In the United States, common law is influenced by the Constitution that, on the one hand, sets inviolable principles of law and, on the other, grants some legislative and judicial automony to the states which can enact different laws and interpret them in different ways, so long as they do not conflict with federal law. At first, this freedom resulted in widely diverging court decisions from state to state, but uniform procedure codes have now been accepted by most states in areas such as criminal and commercial law, and much of the Common Law has been supplanted by statute.

SOURCES OF BRITAIN'S UNWRITTEN CONSTITUTION

The constitution of a country is the document of fundamental laws, laying down the system of government, and defining the relations of the legislative, executive and judiciary to each other and to the citizens. The British Constitution is unique; in that it does not exist in the form of a single document. It consists rather of an accumulation of customs and precedents which have arisen in the course of national development together with a number of laws, defining some of its aspects. Among the most important of the latter are Magna Carta (1215) and the Habeas Corpus Act (1679), limiting the royal powers of taxation and imprisonment; the Bill of Rights (1689) and the Act of Settlement (1701), establishing parliamentary supremacy and the independence of the judiciary; and the Parliament Acts (1911 and 1949), limiting the powers of the Lords. The Triennial Act (1694), the Septennial Act (1716), and the Parliament Act (1911) limited the duration of parliament, while the Reform Acts of 1832, 1867, 1884, 1918, and 1928 extended the electorate.

Relations between the states of the Commonwealth are regulated by the Statute of Westminster (1931). By the Republic of Ireland Act (1948), South Ireland ceased to be a member of the Commonwealth, but neither the Irish Republic nor the UK regards the other as a foreign state. The adoption of republican status by India (1950) and others does not affect their membership and they accept the Queen as Head of the Commonwealth. In some countries of the 'old Commonwealth', such as Canada, the Queen, as Queen of Canada, is represented by a Governor-General, appointed on the recommendation of the country concerned. Constitutional crises in this connection are rare but one occurred in 1975 when the Australian Governor-General dismissed the Prime Minister after deadlock between the two Houses of Parliament and the Prime Minister refused to call a general election.

PARLIAMENTARY MONARCHY

The British commonwealth is that of a parliamentary monarchy, sovereignty being vested in the Queen, Lords, and Commons. The legislature consists of the House of Lords and the elected House of Commons. Considerable numbers of Life Peers, specially since 1958, have modified the hereditary basis of the Lords, but the natural bias of the House towards conservative-type legislation led to friction with the Wilson govt. in 1968 and 1975, and with that of Callaghan in 1976, when demand for its abolition was made. Nevertheless, creation of Labour peers continued. All legislation requires the royal assent of the Queen as the head of the executive, she appoints her ministers, but since the revolution of 1688 it has become customary for her to choose them from the party commanding a majority in the Commons and on the advice of the leader of the party. The judges are appointed by the Crown for life, and can be removed only on a petition from both Houses.

The Constitution of the USA, adopted in 1787, is the oldest written Constitution in existence. Subsequent modifications include the Bill of Rights in 1791 which contains 12 amendments, of which 10 were adopted, in the "5th amendment". It included the provision that none should be compelled "to be a witness against himself", abolition of slavery (1865), equal rights for white and coloured (1870), and limitation of presidential terms to two, which came into effect in 1951. This was inspired by F.D. Roosevelt's unique achievement in being elected for a 4th term. The majority of judges are elected by popular vote.

CONSERVATIVE PARTY

It is one of the two historic British parties, the name replacing *'Tory,'* in use since 1830. Traditionally, this has been the party of landed interests, opposed to the *laissez-faire* of the Liberal manufacturers who supported the struggle of the working-class against the harsh working conditions, during the Industrial Revolution. The split in 1846 over Peel's Corn Law policy led to the party remaining out of office for 20 years, until Disraeli "educated" his party into accepting parliamentary and social change, and extended the franchise to workers. The Home Rule issue of 1886 drove old-fashioned Whigs into alliance with the Conservatives and, consequently, had nearly 20 years in office. But, Joseph Chamberlain's proposals for Imperial Preference and the general fear that protection meant higher prices led to a Liberal landslide in 1906.

Margaret Thatcher

During 1915-45, (except briefly in 1924 and 1929-31), the Conservatives were in office alone, or as part of a coalition, the main reason in maintaining this ascendance being the break-up of the traditional two-party system following the rise of Labour. At the elections, following the end of the World War II, Labour came to power. After the defeat the Conservative Party formulated a new policy in their Industrial Charter of 1947, visualizing an economic and social system in which employers and employed, private enterprise and the State, work together to mutual advantage. Antagonism to workers and nationalization reduced the Labour majority in the 1950 election and in 1951 returned the Conservatives to power with a small majority. This increased slightly in the general elections of 1955 and 1959 – despite such setbacks as Suez. Narrowly defeated in 1964, the party chose in 1965 its first elected leader, Edward Heath, and was again defeated in 1966, but in 1970, achieved a small majority. However, the Conservative govt's imposition of wage controls led to confrontation with the unions and, when Heath sought a mandate in Feb. 1974, a narrow defeat repeated in a further election later in 1974. Margaret Thatcher replaced Heath, and in the general election of May 1979, the Conservative Party won a working majority of 43 over all other parties. Heath remained outside the new government.

In the 1980s, the party's economic policies increased the spending power of the majority, but also the gap between rich and poor; nationalised industries were sold off, military spending and close alliance with the USA were favoured; and the funding of the local government was overhauled with the introduction of the poll tax. The Conservative government under John Major 1990-97 repudiated some of the extreme policies of Thatcherism, notably the poll tax; it introduced the new Citizen's Charter, and promoted further privatisation of public services. In the May 1997 general election, the party suffered a landslide defeat, and its parliamentary seats were reduced to the smallest number since 1906. John Major resigned and was succeeded by William Hague as party leader. The rest is a known story.

LIBERALISM

It is a political and social theory associated with the Liberal Party in Britain, and similar parties elsewhere. Liberalism developed during the 17th-19th centuries as the distinctive theory of the industrial and commercial classes, in their struggle against the power of the monarchy, the Church, and the feudal landowners. In politics, it stood for parliamentary govt, freedom of the press, speech and worship, and the abolition of class privileges. Economically, it was associated with laissez-faire, a minimum state interference in economic life, and international free trade. In the late 19th and early 20th centuries, these ideas were modified by the acceptance of universal suffrage, hitherto opposed by most Liberals, and a certain level of state intervention to ensure a minimum standard of living and to remove extremes of poverty and wealth. The classical statement of Liberal principles is found in "On Liberty" and other works of J.S. Mill.

LIBERAL PARTY

It is the successor to the Whig Party. The term liberal was used officially from 1840 (and unofficially from 1815), marking the transfer of control from aristocrats to industrialists, backed by the Benthamites, non-conformists and the middle classes During the Liberal's first period of power (1830-41), they promoted parliamentary and municipal govt. reform and the abolition of slavery, but their utilitarian and *laissez-faire* theories led to the harsh Poor Law of 1834. Liberal's pressure forced Peel to repeal the Corn Laws in 1846, thereby splitting the Tory Party, and except for two short periods, the Liberal's were in power during 1746-66, but the only outstanding figure of the period, Palmerston, was very conservative and the only major change was the general adoption of free trade.

Gladstone

It extended franchise in 1867 and Gladstone's emergence as leader began a new phase, dominated by the *'Manchester school'* with a programme of 'peace, retrenchment, and reform'. Gladstone's 1868-74 govt. introduced many important reforms, including elementary education and vote by ballot. The party's left, mainly composed of working-class radicals led by the Bradlaugh and Chamberlain, repudiated the laissez-faire ideology and inclined towards republicanism, but the Liberals were split over Home Rule in 1886 and many joined the Conservatives. Except for 1892-5, the Liberals remained out of power until 1906, when reinforced by Labour and Irish support, they returned with a huge majority: Old-Age Pensions, National Insurance, limitation of the powers of the Lords, and the Irish Home Rule Bill followed.

From 1914, the Liberal Party declined Lloyd George's alliance with the Conservatives (1916-22), divided between himself and Asquith, and although reunited in 1923, they continued to lose votes. They briefly joined the National

Govt (1931-2), but after World War II they were reduced to a handful of MPs. A revival began under the leadership (1956-67) of Grimond, and continued under Jeremy Thorpe, who resigned after controversy within the party in 1976. After a 'caretaker' return by Grimond, David Steel became the first party leader in British politics to be elected by party members. In 1977-8, Steel entered into an agreement to support Labour in any vote of confidence in return for consultation on measures undertaken. In the 1979 general election, the Liberal Party lost some seats but retained much of the Liberal vote.

LABOUR PARTY

It is the British working-class and Socialist party. Although Keir Hardie and John Burns entered Parliament independently as Labour MPs in 1892, it was not till 1900 that a conference, representing trade unions, the independents, Labour Party and the Fabian society, founded the Labour Party. All, but a pacifist minority of the party, supported the World War I and in 1918 a Socialist programme was first adopted with local branches of the party being set up. By 1922, the Labour Party was recognized as the official Opposition and in 1924, it formed a minority govt (with Liberal support) for a few months under J.R. MacDonald. A second minority govt in 1929 followed a conservative policy, completely failing to deal with unemployment, and in 1931, MacDonald and other leaders, faced with a financial crisis, left the party to support the national government in 1932. In 1936-9, there was internal dissension on foreign policy, the leaderships' support of non-intervention in Spain being strongly criticized, and Sir Stafford Cripps, Aneurin Bevan and others being expelled for advocating an alliance of all Left-wing parties against the Chamberlain govt.

Labour P.M. Gordon Brown

The Labour Party supported Churchill's wartime coalition, but then withdrew and took office for the first time as a majority govt. under Attlee after the 1945 elections. The Welfare State was developed by nationalisation of essential services and industries, and a system of national insurance (1946) and a National Health Service (1948). Defeated in 1951, the party was split by disagreements on further nationalisation and unilateral/multilateral disarmament, but achieved unity under Gaitskell's leadership (1955-63), and under Wilson returned to power (1964-70) and, very narrowly, (1974-9). Callaghan, who had been elected by labour MPs to succeed Wilson in 1976 (the first British PM to be elected to the office) attempted to retain power by a consultative pact with the Liberals (1977-8). But, he was forced to a general election in May 1979 and lost.

In the Opposition, he confronted the pressure from the constituency organisations and the trade unions (who form a large part of the Labour Party membership and contribute largely to its funds by a political levy) for increased control. Demands included the election of future party leaders by an electoral college, instead of by MPs alone; the college (and not as previously the leader) would also prepare the party manifesto, some form of control would also be exercised over the leader's choice of his Cabinet as PM (In Opposition, there is already an annual ballot among MPs to elect members of the Parliamentary Committee or *'Shadow Cabinet',* who each take responsibility for covering one aspect of govt.); and Labour MPs themselves would have to submit themselves for re-selection at each election. Michael Foot was elected to the leadership by MPs in Nov. 1980, Denis Healey becoming his deputy. The Labour Party, the TUC and the Co-operative movement together form the National Council of Labour in order to co-ordinate political activities and take joint action on specific issues. The Fabian Society is the most important affiliated political body. The party adopted the policy of unilateral nuclear disarmament in 1986, a major factor in the 1987 general election. Under Tony Blair's leadership, Labour launched a campaign to revise the party's Constitution by scrapping clause 4, concerning the common ownership of the means of production and ending Trade Union's direct sponsorship of Members of Parliament. And, a new Labour Charter was approved in 1995. Thus, *New Labour* was born, fathered by Tony Blair (Anthony Charles Lynton) who won the election and became Prime Minister in 1997, after a landslide victory. And, also won the second term. And third term in 2005.

Britain's empire, in the sense of oversea territories under United Kingdom sovereignty, has shrunk and shrunk: it now consists of just 14 islands, rocks and barely inhabited strips of land, the biggest of them in Antarctica.

34

British ruled by parades and pageants more than by arms

Britain had never had army and navy large enough to control its widely dispersed empire by force. Hence, it tied the colonies in different relationships, some of them seemed to be independent but they were not. The British ruled these colonies more by parade, pageants, ceremonies, flags, costume and uniforms than by arms. The British imperial spectacle has been dazzling which finally created the grand delusion of invincibility and that proved the undoing of the British empire.

The varied nature of the British Empire in 1914, which the steamship and railway had brought together, was a quite unique political combination; nothing of the sort had ever existed before. First, the majority in the British Parliament, made up of the three united parliaments of England & Wales, Scotland and Ireland, decided the British domestic politics. It had the power of peace and war over the empire. Next in order of political importance were the "crowned republics" of Australia, Canada, Newfoundland (the oldest British possession of 1583), New Zealand, and South Africa which were self-governing states but subordinate to Great Britain. Next was the Indian Empire, with about 500 protected princely states, stretching from Baluchistan to Burma, including Eden which was governed from Bombay. The Indian empire was ruled by the India Office in London. Then came Egypt, still nominally part of the Turkish Empire but retaining its own monarch, the *Khedive,* but under almost despotic British rule.

EAST INDIA COMPANY

And, 100 years later in 1815 the British Empire consisted of the thinly populated coastal regions of Canada, a third of India under the rule of the East India Company, Cape of Good Hope, inhabited by blacks and rebellious Dutch settlers; a few trading posts on the coast of West Africa, the rock of Gibraltar, Malta, Jamaica, a few minor slave labour possessions in the East Indies and British Guiana in South America. On the other side of the world, the British colonies included two dumps for convicts at Botany Bay in Australia and in Tasmania, an island state of Australia, Spain retained Cuba and a few settlements in the Philippine Islands. Portugal had in Africa some vestiges of her ancient claims. Holland had many islands and possessions in the East Indies and Dutch Guiana, while Denmark had an island in the West Indies, France had two West India Islands and French Guiana. These were the colonies European powers had at that time.

However, while Europe was busy with the Napoleonic wars, the East India Company was expanding its control in India. The British Company's power spread to Assam, Sind and Oudh in India. A patchwork of native states were held together under direct British rule until 1859. After a serious mutiny of troops in India in 1857, the East India Company empire was annexed to the British Crown by an Act entitled *An Act for the Better Government of India.* The Governor-General became a Viceroy, representing the Sovereign, and the place of the Company Chairman was taken by a Secretary of State for India, responsible to the British Parliament. In 1877, Queen Victoria was proclaimed Empress of India. And, thus India and Britain were linked in an imperial bond.

Apart from India, there was no great expansion of any European empire until the railways and the steamships came in effective action. The Australian settlements developed slowly until in 1842 when the discovery of valuable coppermines, and in 1851 of gold, gave them a new importance. Improvements in transport were also making Australian wool an increasingly marketable commodity in Europe. Canada, too, was not remarkably progressive until 1849; it was troubled by dissensions between its French and British inhabitants. There were several serious revolts; but in 1867, a new constitution was made, creating a Federal Dominion of Canada which eased its internal strains. Railway enabled Canada, just as it enabled the United States, to expand westward, to market its corn and other produce in Europe. The railway, steamship, and the telegraph cable were helping empire to grow far beyond the capacity of the colonial powers to manage and control them with arms.

Before 1840, English settlements had already begun in New Zealand, and a New Zealand Land Company had been formed to exploit the possibilities of the island. In 1840 New Zealand also was added to the colonial possessions of the British Crown. Canada, as has been noted, was among the first of the British possessions to open new economic possibilities that the new methods of transport provided. Then republics of South America, and particularly Argentine, began to see in the cattle trade and coffee growing the increased nearness of the European market. Hitherto the chief commodities, that had seduced the European powers into unsettled and barbaric regions had been gold or other metals, spices, ivory, or slaves. But in the latter quarter of the nineteenth century the increase of the European populations was obliging their governments to look abroad for staple food also. The growth of scientific industrialism was also creating a demand for new raw materials like fats, cotton, greases, rubber, and other commodities. It was plain that Britain and Holland and Portugal were getting commercial advantages from their colonies in Africa. After 1871, Germany and France and later Italy, began to look for raw material areas in the poor countries. And, thus began a fresh scramble for colonies all over the world, except in the American region where the Monroe Doctrine had barred such adventures in the politically unprotected lands.

Close to Europe was the continent of Africa, full of vaguely known possibilities. In 1850, it was a continent of black mystery; only Egypt was known to the West. There were stories of the amazing explorers and adventurers who first pierced the African darkness and also the stories of the pygmies, strange beasts, fruits and flowers, insects, terrible diseases, astounding scenery of forest and mountain, enormous inland seas and gigantic rivers. Even the remains in Zimbabwe of some vanished civilization, the southward enterprise of an early people, were discovered. Into this new and void world came the Europeans, only to find the guns already there in the hands of the Arab slave-traders.

By 1900, all Africa was mapped, explored, and divided among European powers, without caring for the welfare of the natives. The Arab slaver was indeed curbed rather than expelled, but the greed for rubber, which was a wild product collected by enslaved natives in the Belgian Congo, led to horrible atrocities. No European power had perfectly clean hands in this matter. All of them sinned in Africa. Great Britain got the possession of Egypt in 1883 and remained there, as said earlier, in spite of the fact the Egypt was technically a part of the Turkish Empire, Scramble led to war between France and Great Britain in 1898, when Colonel Marchland, crossed in Central Africa from the west coast, and tried to seize the Upper Nile.

In a quarter of century, the partition of Africa was completed. There remained unannexed three small countries: Liberia, a settlement of liberated negro slaves on the west coast; Morocco, under a Muslim Sultan, and Abyssinia, a very poor country, with an ancient and peculiar form of Christianity, which had successfully maintained its independence against Italy at the Battle of Adowa in 1896. Except these, the entire Africa was subjugated and lost its freedom without much resistance. This was how the European imperialism expanded.

BRITISH PAGEANTRY

FRIGHTENED NATIVES

In the context, it may be mentioned that the British forces in India seldom exceeded 50,000 troops and they defeated large Indian armies many times its size. In the decisive battle of Plassey in 1757, the British used very primitive guns and defeated a mighty army of West Bengal governor. It is said Robert Clive had recruited gardeners from South India and trained them to fire guns. When the battle began, he went to sleep with his mistress (*a lass and a lakh a day*) and woke up only to count the dead. And, India lost its freedom for about 200 years. All for lack of technology.

The British pomp, pageantry and parades also frightened the native Indians into submission with fighting. Patrick French writes: "King George V's coronation in 1911 was a spectacular propaganda coup, with myriad Indian princes and imperial prime ministers filling Westminster Abbey for the seven hour ceremony... A giant Durbar was subsequently held in Delhi which was attended by all the Indian princes". Gita Mehta, an Indian writer has given a good description of the incredibly profligate life styles of Indian princes with a princely dog "marriage" as an example. "The marriage of the two dogs *Roshanara*, veiled and covered in gems, to *Bobby* in red silk pyjamas (to make sure he does not violate the bride before the wedding!) was conducted with all the ceremony that would have accompanied the marriage of a royal princess. A court minister solembly read out a list of the wealth *Roshanara* was bringing to the marriage, including a golden palanquin... At the end of the ceremony, the visiting rulers circled the dogs with gold coins and their aides placed gifts in a large basket. The strains of Mendelsohn's Wedding March were faintly audible... An enormous rectangular table for 200 guests dominated the banquet hall for the nuptial dinner. In the centre, dancing girls sang and danced for the dogs".

BRITISH EMPIRE NOT ALL THAT BAD, SAYS NIALL FERGUSON

The atrocities during the British Empire are many, so also plundering by the East India officials, including Lord Clive. But Niall Ferguson, in his beautifully nuanced book, *Empire,* says British legacies include, the English language, English forms of land tenure, British and Scottish banking system, the Common Law, Protestantism, idea of liberty and parliamentary system of Govt.

True the great Bengal famine of the late 18th century was a direct consequence of East India Company policies; of the 10 million Africans shipped across the Atlantic in the 18th and 19th centuries, a very large proportion were by the British. The book does not whitewash the history of the British empire. On the contrary it is a balance sheet of empire that looks both at the liabilities and the assets. What I reject is the argument that empire is all bad, that every single thing about imperialism is wicked. What did the Romans ever do for the British? Well, aqueducts. Apart from aqueducts? Well, roads. Well, apart from roads, public health. Well, apart from public health... That is exactly the sort of things we should be asking about the British Empire.

"You only have to ask yourself about the world of 1940-41. If you have no British empire in the wake of the fall of France and on the eve of Japan's expansion, it is very hard to see how the Axis power can be stopped. The only thing at that point standing between Hitler, Mussolini and Tojo and world domination happened to be Winston Churchill, the ultimate apologist for empire. If don't know what is, world renowned Scottish historian says in an interview. Would the world have been better off if the Great Rebellion in 1857 had been so successful that British rule not only collapsed in India, but the British Empire was wiped out? What would our world have been like? One thing is very clear. The great age of global economic expansion of the late 19th and early 20th century would not have happened had the British empire not created the liberal order of free trade, factual that gets rid of the British empire has an economic downside as well as a geopolitical one". Says Ferguson.

That raw, mist-bound little island has done more to spread the European civilization over the earth than all the countries of the rest of Europe together.

– Arnold Toynbee

35

The making of Great Britain (The United Kingdom of Great Britain and Northern Ireland)

Virtually a mere dab on the map, Britain had captured the world's surface, almost 135 times its size and ruled it for over 350 years, holding the peoples hostage to her glory. It was because of the enterprise of the people, their hard work, ambition or pure greed. However, after World War II ended in 1945, it has nothing to celebrate except its survival.

The name is derived from the Roman name *Britannia* which, in turn, is derived from the ancient Celtic name of the inhabitants, *Bryttas.* Although the once Great Britain is now reduced to become a small England, it continues to play an important role in European politics. British culture, habits and institutions are there to see in all its former colonies and, instead of declining, the British influence is expanding although its empire has vanished. Very rightly, the line marking the centre of the world map (zero degree longitude) has been drawn through Greenwich, a London suburb. So, let us know more about Britain, its geography, people, institutions and everything else that went into making it the largest empire in the world in the past.

Britons, more than any people in the world, are products of geography. Their coming together was also more of an accident than a conscious act. The *United Kingdom of Great Britain and Northern Ireland* is the official name of the political union of England, Scotland, Wales and Northern Ireland. This name had many *avatars*. Wales was united with England in 1301 after which it became Great Britain under a royal proclamation issued in 1604 when

James-VI of Scotland succeeded the throne of England. When Ireland joined Great Britain in 1821, the official name became the United Kingdom of Great Britain and Ireland. In 1922, as many as 26 Irish counties (all Catholic Christians), separated from the United Kingdom and Eire State, (Republic of Ireland) came into existence in 1949. Again, there was a change in the title. By a royal proclamation on May 29, 1953, Ireland became Northern Ireland. So let there be no confusion; Northern Ireland is a British unit while Eire, (Republic of Ireland or Ulster) is an independent republic of Catholic Christians who live in the 26 counties separated from the mainland in 1922.

GEOGRAPHY: Anybody would have listed Britain among the geographical areas least likely to succeed. It is the same size and is situated in the same Siberian latitude as the peninsula of Kamchatka, opposite Alaska. It is an Island nation in the Atlantic Ocean, covering an area of 244,100 sq.km. The United Kingdom, as said earlier, comprises the Island of Great Britain, consisting of England, Scotland and Wales; Northern Ireland, (also known as Ulster) and smaller Islands, including the Crown dependencies of Guernsey, Jersey and the Isle of Man. Except for coal, it had no natural riches until the North Sea Oil was found. Its soil and climate are not favourable for growing important staples that support a large population; yet this bleak outcrop from the sea sustains a population 235 times that of Wyoming which is also as much a rocky and semi arid US state. With more than 3,000 inhabitants to the arable per square mile, England is said to be the most densely populated country on the earth, relative to its cultivable land.

Community of interests, arising out of geographical proximity, and detachment from the mainland of Europe makes for its homogeneity. The inhabitants draw a sharp line between themselves and those living on the European mainland. This is one reason why Britons find Europeans uncomfortable companions while trying to work together. This dislike was the one reason which provoked Mrs. Margaret Thatcher, Prime Minister (1979-90), to call Europeans *"Ogres and conspirators"*. And, that, among other reasons, led to her fall on November 28, 1990 on the issue of joining the European Union.

A HOME-GROWN CULTURE

Being Islanders, people of Britain developed their own institutions, largely uninfluenced by the European civilization although historically, they have been in touch with the European mainland and felt the effect of all major cultural and political developments there. However, being separated by water, they have enjoyed a degree of independence because continental ideas were always late in reaching the islands. And, when they did, they were changed to suit the British needs.

Much of the Englishman's independence, his devotion to precedents, and his conservatism flow from the conviction that their culture is home-grown. The water barriers provided security from invasion and also ensured continuity in national life. In fact, there were no sharp breaks in the history of the English people, after the Norman conquest in the 11th century. It may be interesting to know that the British race is not pure. Peoples from all countries and continents came to the islands. As Danial Defoe says: *"Thus, from a mixture of all kinds began that heterogenous species called Englishman".*

The Englishman represents the fusion of innumerable invading groups which include virtually every known branch of the white race. By far the largest single body of invaders were, however, the Celtic-speaking Nordics who came from Northern Europe in the Iron Age and most Britons owe most of their physical features to the Nordics. Ethnically, the population of the British Isles is an integration of minorities. There are four chief types, English, Welsh, Scottish and Irish, representing four geographical divisions. Among the English, the Germanic element is distinctive and it provided a basis for a common language; in Wales, the Mediterranean type predominates and in the highlands of Scotland, Scandinavian invaders left their influence. However, it

THE GREAT FIRE OF LONDON (1666)

At 2 a.m. on September 2, 1666, a fire was discovered in the house of John Farynor, the king's baker in Pudding Lane, a narrow street east of London Bridge. Fanned by a strong east wind, the flames spread rapidly through the city. For four days, the fire raged. Even king, Charles-II and his brother turned out to fight it. First it reached London Bridge, which had wooden buildings upon it, and then it spread northward to Lombard Street and Cornhill. On the third day, it destroyed Cheapside and Fleet Street before continuing on to the Inner Temple and Newgate.

Over 121 hectares, containing more than 13,000 houses, were destroyed. The fire was not, however, a complete disaster; for, it destroyed many of the main areas of infection remaining from the Plague and made it possible to create a new city with wider streets and brick buildings to replace the cramped medieval streets and wooden buildings. Between 1664 and 1645, as many as 68,000 people had died in London alone because of plague which had infected the entire Europe. It was controlled by 1667.

was the coming of the Nordics in Iron Age which integrated these people to produce Englishmen.

ENGLAND: England has more than four-fifths of UK's total population that has increased, so also its wealth because of London, the national capital. London is spread over an area of 950 km in radius. It was the biggest town in the Roman Britain and has been the capital of unified England since the Norman conquest in 1066. Romans-built roads in radial pattern persist even today. The Roman rule extended to the Scottish and the Welsh borders of today. The frontiers of Roman rule in Britain was close to those of England of today. There is something like the "Englishness" of Great Britain which is not Scottish and Welsh. Shakespeare and Shaw were English and the Scots are not very enthusiastic about it. And, Sir Walter Scott, among others, was a Scottish poet and Englishmen are not very enthusiastic about it. English qualities include remarkable capacity to work hard, absorb other cultures and still stay English. England is in a temperate zone, but it has erratic weather, coldest is 4°C and warmest 17°C. It is a wet country; lowland England suffers from drought and, hence, needs irrigation water. The weather, being erratic, is the much widely discussed subject. Dr. Samuel Johnson said: "When two Englishmen meet, their first talk is about the weather."

SCOTLAND: (Capital – Edinburgh) Scotland is cool, hilly and wet. It is about one-third of Great Britain. Earlier it was a known as *Caledonia.* The name "Scotland" was given in 11th century when the name *Scotia* was given to the south western area settled by a tribe, Scots, who had migrated from Ireland. After being independent until 1707, Scotland became an integral

THE ISLE OF MAN

The *Isle of Man* is about 48 km long by 16 km wide, with a rocky coastline enclosing a central highland area at Snaefell. Low-lying land on either side produces cereals and potatoes. It was settled as early as 2000 to 1500 BC. The next wave of settlers were the Celts, and their language, Gaelic – known on the island as Manx – remained in daily use until the 19th century. In the 5th century AD, the island was settled by Irish missionaries and in the 9th century it was invaded by Vikings from Norway. It remained a Norwegian dependency until it was sold to Scotland in 1266. It came under English control in the early 15th century. It has its own two-chamber parliament, which dates from the 9th century. The legislative council, or upper house, and the elected lower house, the House of Keys, sometimes assemble as the Court of Tynwald, but they normally operate as separate bodies. The Isle's chief industry is tourism, and its Tourist Trophy (TT) motorcycle races attract many visitors.

part of the United Kingdom through something of a curiosity. It is smaller than like Jammu and Kashmir's. Scotland retains some powers, indicating its sovereignty in its own legal and educational system, a national Presbyterian church and a separate administration. Scotland's economy is integrated with that of the rest of Britain. However, it has preserved its identity in international scene. Some of its products, specially whisky (Scotch) and tweeds are internationally known and generations of Scots talked of their separate culture as stern, wild and romantic. The famous people of Scotland include Robert Bruce, Walter Scott, Robert Burns, Robert Louis Stevenson and Adam Smith. It sends 72 members to the UK Parliament. Scotland has a legal system which is different from the rest of the UK, being based on 'civil law' (not common law). The separate existence was guaranteed by the Act of Union with England in 1707.

Scotland is divided into three geographical areas; the highlands, the lowlands, and the southern uplands. The coastal plain is a flat expanse of the northern highland regions. Scotland has many lakes, the largest of which is *Loch Ness*, famous for its mythical monster. The north-western part is barren, separated by glens, (valleys) carved out of glaciers, granulated and layered rocks. Further inland areas are spectacular sandstone mountains, weathered into cliffs, rock terraces and pinnacles. In the centre are bogs, moors, bleak expanse rocks, and barren land. Agriculture is done only on the river mouths. Climate is temperate, oceanic and mild. There are considerable variations in climate.

WALES: (Capital: Cardiff). Wales is a squat peninsula with an area of just over 21,000 sq. km. jutting westward from England into the Irish Sea. It is, thus, an integral part of the British Islands. Wales is full of plateau and hills, coastal areas and valley lowlands, surrounded by seas on three sides which has given Wales an Atlantic character. It has a maritime climate dominated by Atlantic air masses. Rainfall is high, the mean temperature is 10.4°C ranging from 5°C in January to 10°C in July-August. It has vast grasslands, plantations and woodlands. It has pastoral economy and is sparsely populated. The shadows of clouds racing across the wild moorlands in the bright afternoon sun present the great beauty of Wales which is quite distinct from England and Scotland. There are large farmlands and settlement areas, also marked by dairy farming. The oil terminals at coastal areas have thriving trade. Wales has lots of minerals, including coal. Villages are as attractive as cities are glittering. Unlike Scotland, the Welsh economy is totally integrated with the larger unit. It is divided into eight regions for administrative reasons. Wales sends 38 members to the UK Parliament. In 1996, the eight counties established in 1774 were replaced by 22 unitary authorities. It is fully integrated with the British economy, unlike Scotland and Ulster.

NORTHERN IRELAND (Capital: Dublin). The geographical position of Northern Ireland accounts for much of her social, economic and political problems, a process which explains the ingrained antagonism. The country was created in 1920, as a self-governing state within the United Kingdom. Northern Ireland is also referred to as the province of Ulster because its inhabitants are Ulstermen. It contains only six of the nine counties which make for the Irish entity. The majority of the people are Catholic and this is the principle reason for the running battles between two sections, Protestants and Catholics. Its area is 14,120 sq.km., or one-sixth of the whole area of the Island and separated from Scotland by the narrow North Channel. *(See also Ireland)*

WALPOLE BECAME THE FIRST BRITISH PRIME MINISTER IN 1721

Sir Robert Walpole

When the South Sea Bubble burst in 1720 the task of sorting out the financial tangles fell to Robert Walpole (1676-1745) who was appointed First Lord of the Treasury and Chancellor of the Exchequer in 1721. Walpole held this post from April 3, 1721 to February 12, 1742 and is generally regarded as the first British prime minister although the post was not officially recognized until 1905. The office evolved as a result of George-I's unwillingness to attend cabinet meetings because of his difficulties with the English language.

Walpole had entered Parliament in 1701 and very quickly became renowned for his wizardry with figures, his accurate judgement of people, and his shrewd capability. In 1708, he became secretary of war in the Whig administration but four years later was sent to prison on a charge of corruption. He returned to office in 1714 when George-I came to the throne. Walpole's premiership, the longest in British history, lasted until he was defeated in Parliament in 1742.

Despite poor domestic resources, Britain has long kept her people the wealthiest in the world; created one of the richest cultures, built and maintained its supremacy for centuries through the world's strongest armed forces, including the British Fleet. Virtually a dab of red on the map, she ruled over the world's largest empire, 135 times its size having a quarter of the earth's total population. *(See also Rise and Fall of British Empire).*

Accident of Geography

The great British saga began by the accident of its geographic location. When the medieval powers discovered the new world, Britain, then no more important than Iceland is today, stood across the richest trade route. Being an Island and difficult to access, Britain had tough and adventurous seamen for whom the western ocean posed no problem. Several timely accidents assisted her. In the Wars of Roses, the feudal barons conveniently killed one another, without seriously harming the population. An early breach with Roman Church kept her out of the religious wars which ravaged Europe. The Hundred Years War, (a name given to the struggle between England and France, between 1337 and 1453 over the claim of Edward-III to the crown of France), also helped Britain. As a matter of fact, it was that war which destroyed the French desire for expansion and left Britain alone to conquer the world.

Quite about the time when European trade with primitive America became profitable, British farmers found that wool paid more than grain and began to convert farmland into pastures, shifting population from villages to cities. Consequently, great pressure was created on city centres and people began to migrate to America. While Germany languished in religious wars, Britain started out to create an empire for its expanding population.

Inevitably, Britain was the first to feel the pressure from increase of population. When the British scientists invented the steam locomotion, they found that they had enough coal to run it. With plenty of raw materials and virgin markets all over the world, she built an industrial economy that no one could compete with. Other nations raised tariff walls to keep Britain from flooding markets with cheap goods. But so strong was the British trading position that it was not until 1931 that her monopoly was substantially threatened by Germany which was one of the reasons for World War II.

LEISURE CLASS CREATED ARTS

The intellectual achievements are due to her wealth which created a large leisure class that pursued arts and science and a larger wealthy class which patronised them. The bastard dialect of the English language was refined into the richest language of world literature and the first language of world commerce and science. Wealth, also made for social health. When the demands of a lower class for a larger share in the national wealth became too strident,

CIVIL WAR IN BRITAIN (1642);
KING CHARLES BEHEADED

The struggle between King Charles-I and his Parliament was reaching a climax; for, he believed in the divine authority of king whilst his Parliament believed in the democratic right of Englishmen to be governed by their elected representatives. Charles's tax called Ship Money widened the gulf between king and Parliament.

Charles-I on the scaffold—a sketch

The near-penniless king was forced to call Parliament but when he tried to arrest five members, England was thrust into a Civil War that was to last from 1642 until 1649. At first, the victories were all Royalist ones, the dashing cavalry led by Charles's nephew Rupert, sweeping aside the poorly armed, mainly peasant soldiers. But his opponent, Cromwell, slowly developed a new breed of fighting men, a psalm-singing but tough and well-drilled *"New Model Army"* and with them he won a series of important victories - Marston Moor (1644), Naseby (1645), Preston and Colchester (both 1648).

Charles sought refuge in Scotland but he was handed over to England. When Charles-I was returned to London, it was decided to bring him before a Court of Commissioners. The trial opened on January 20, 1649, and the king was blamed for causing all the misfortunes that had befallen the nation since the beginning of the Civil War. For his part, the king claimed that the court was illegal, because the House of Commons was not a court of law. Charles refused to plead "not guilty" when brought before the court again on January 27 and was then declared guilty.

He was kept under close guard for three days although he was allowed to say goodbye to his children and then, on January 30, 1649, the king left St. James's Palace, walking on foot with a large escort. Taken to the Banqueting House in Whitehall, he stepped out onto a scaffold that had been erected in the street and after a brief speech he said; "I shall say very short prayers, and then thrust out my hands." The king knelt with his head on the block and soon stretched out his hands. The axe fell and a groan rose from the thousands who thronged the street. Then, with many weeping, the crowd silently dispersed.

there was always a surplus from colonies to give to them, instead of fighting over the demand as it happened in France where *Queen Marie Antoinette* refused to give bread because she had none and the French Revolution broke out in 1789. For this reason, Britain holds the world record for having undergone no violent changes for more than 300 years. Her empire, which created wealth, stood between Britain and revolution. No wonder, Britain had evolution instead of revolution. The miraculous creation of British greatness was less astonishing than her ability to maintain it. The world has been a jungle of kings and queens and the only medium of their dealing was strength. The British empire was not in one piece but loosely scattered all over the world and, therefore, vulnerable at many points. More vulnerable than any other part has been the motherland itself. With big expansions in commerce, Britain abandoned agriculture, which constituted the smallest part of the economy. In 1939, only seven per cent of people (against India's 95 per cent then) were employed in agriculture.

A NATION OF CITY DWELLERS

No wonder, Britain became a land of city-dwellers with four out of five persons living in urban areas, the highest degree of urbanisation on earth. Therefore, Britain depended on import from overseas for 60 per cent of her food, 80 per cent of raw material (1950s) which was the highest level of dependence by any country, on overseas trade. She feared that the arteries of the empire might have been pinched shut. And to ensure that it did not happen, a large fleet was raised to protect the British empire and its trade on

BETWEEN ENGLISH AND BRITISH

Two hundred years ago, the British abolished the slave trade though not slavery itself. Its celebration fits well with the notion of Britain as a successful multicultural society and marks the end to the cruel history of the African-Caribbean black population. Britishers also celebrated the anniversary of the foundation of the British State.

Scotland and England were united by the Treaty five Union in 1707. Which means that Great Britain is three hundred years old in May, 2009. Most people however, may not know the difference between the words "England" and "Britain" which so often mean the same thing. Even a perceptive writer such as George Orwell tended to think of Britain as simply a greater England. Scotland and England, however, were two separate nations with two separate monarchs (until 1603) and two separate parliaments (until 1707), and even after their political union they each maintained - and still maintain - different systems of education, law and the Christian religion. They are in an uneasy relationship even today when Scots are clamouring for more autonomy (or separation) because they feel exploited by their richer half down South.

Scotland means whisky, kilts and the poetry of Burns. But England invokes wider range of topics, anything from Dickens to the Rolling Stones, Churchill, Mountbatten, Kipling, George Harrison and the Queen. British has looser and more capacious identity, less grounded in ideas of blood and soil. This is why most of Britain's immigrants prefer British as a label to "English", including the descendants of Britain's slave traders who are being reminded in the bicentenary year of the crimes and cruelties their forefathers committed to get rich.

which depended its survival. The British fleet created its own industries, protected dominions from its local enemies and bonded them together. Churchill has described the role of the British fleet in his book *"The World Crisis"* thus: *"Let the British fleet sink beneath the surface and the whole outlook of the world would change. The British empire would dissolve like a dream... the central power of union will break."*

SOME RANDOM HIGHLIGHTS

1707	Scotland and England were joined together under the name of *Great Britain.*
1876	The Royal Titles Bill was passed by the British Parliament, entitling Queen Victoria to call herself *Empress of India.*
1963	Sir Winston Churchill announced his retirement from the House of Commons.
1997	Tony Blair's Labour Party won a landslide victory in Britain's general election. In 2005, he was re-elected for the third term.

The source of the British miracle was also their attitude of mind; as seven-day week, all-night alertness and an unremitting concentration to draw the last ounce of advantage out of every change in the world situation. Britain followed no long-term policy: it always acted on a day-to-day basis. A German statesman summed it up thus: "The English, those inscrutable politicians, know that there is no such thing as solution. They know that the best of solutions get out of date and, thus, must be continually renewed and re-adapted to new conditions. The British can never relax. Even after they have completed work, they will like to do it over again". "England", Lord Palmerston once said, "has no permanent friend. She has only permanent interests". It has been the widely known British policy to keep potential enemies small and divided. To that extent, the tiny island has done more than any other nation to carve out new frontiers in the world. In addition to conquering a fifth of the world, her command over the seas has allowed the other great overseas empires (Portuguese, Dutch and Belgians) to exist under the British protection. And as a price for this favour, these nations had to play the occasional role of British satellites in European politics.

UNITED KINGDOM, at a glance

THROUGHOUT THEIR HISTORY, the British Isles have been subject to frequent invasions. In turn, Celts, Romans, Anglo-Saxons, and Vikings invaded the islands and established their rule. In 1066, the Normans invaded and subjugated England which emerged as the strongest nation, conquering first Ireland, and then Wales, before joining with Scotland in 1603. The United Kingdom thus formed the leading industrial and colonial power in the world, maintaining a supremacy that was to last into the present century.

Ancient Britain

The earliest inhabitants of Britain were nomadic hunter-gatherers, who moved from place to place in search of food. In about 4000 BC, people began to settle in villages, farm the land, and raise animals.

Roman Britain

Julius Ceasar invaded Britain in 55 and 54 BC to stop local Celtic tribes helping the Gauls in France to undermine the Roman Empire. In AD 43, England and Wales were conquered and made part of the empire. The Romans built many towns and roads, and encouraged trade.

Anglo-Saxon Invasions

After the Romans left in 410, Germanic Anglo-Saxons from northern Europe began to invade Britain. By 613, the Anglo-Saxons had conquered all of England, dividing it into seven kingdoms.

Norman England

In 1066, William Duke of Normandy invaded England to claim the throne. Near Hastings, he defeated the English army led by King Harold, and conquered the country. The Normans built castles to enforce their rule, and provided England with strong central government.

Magna Carta

Under Norman rule, arguments frequently occurred between the king and his most powerful lords. In 1215, at Runnymede in Surrey, King John signed the Magna Carta with his royal seal. This document drawn up by senior lords, laid down the responsibilities and rights of citizens and the Church in relation to the crown. The Magna Carta is still one of the major constitutional documents of English government.

Roman Towns

The Romans built a network of towns as centers of trade and local government. Among these were Londinium (London) on the River Thames, and Aquae Sulis (Bath) in the west.

St. Augustine

Under Roman rule, most of Britain was Christian, but the Anglo-Saxons had their own gods. Christian missionary St. Augustine came to Canterbury in 597 and began to convert the area to Christianity.

William I

William I (c. 1027-87) was a descendent of Vikings who had settled in Normandy in northern Europe. As king of England, he was a strong ruler who brought stability to the country. He died after falling from his horse at Nantes, France.

Vikings and Cnut

In 787, Viking sailors made their first raid on the English coast, and soon controlled the north and east of the country. In 1013, they seized the entire kingdom; under King Cnut, England was part of a Viking empire called the Danelaw that included much of Scandinavia.

Parliament

In 1265, Henry III called representatives of the towns, lords, and clergy, to the first parliament in London to advise the government. Within a century, parliament had the right to make laws and levy taxes.

Wales

England tried to rule Wales from Saxon times, but the Welsh princes resisted. In 1282, Edward I conquered the country, and built many castles to keep the Welsh subdued. An act of Union in 1536 formally joined Wales to England. The Welsh language was suppressed for centuries afterwards.

Tudors and Stuarts

Henry VII, the first Tudor king, seized power in 1485. He curbed the power of the lords, restored royal finances, and ruled strongly. The Tudors ruled until 1603. They were followed by the Stuarts, under whom England tried to keep its leading role in Europe, in spite of a bitter civil war.

Dissolution of the Monasteries

In 1534, Henry VIII broke with the Roman Catholic Church because it refused to grant him a divorce. He created the Church of England, with him as its supreme head, dissolved the monasteries to get money for his court, and seized Church lands.

English Civil War

Conflicts between parliament and Charles I over the government of the country broke out into open war in 1642. The king was defeated and was executed in 1649. England became a republic until 1660.

Scotland

Scotland first became a kingdom in 843, and remained independent for centuries despite constant invasions by England. In 1603, the Scottish king, James VI, inherited the English throne from the Tudor queen Elizabeth I; in 1707, the two countries were formally united.

Industrial England

In the 18th century, Britain became the world's first industrialized country. Millions of people moved from the countryside to the towns to work in new factories and workshops. Canals and railways moved raw materials and finished goods around the country. By 1850, Britain was the "workshop of the world".

Victorian England

During the reign of Queen Victoria (1837-1901), Britain became the world's richest country, with an empire that covered one-quarter of the globe. Despite this wealth, living conditions were poor for many people in the cities.

Chartists

In the early 19th century, demands grew for better representation of working people in government. In the 1830s and 1840s, groups such as the Chartists campaigned for reform. They were named after the People's Charter, drafted by William Lovett in 1838. Reforms were only granted much later.

Modern Britain

During the 20th century, Britain underwent many changes. It granted much of its empire independence, lost control of most of Ireland, and struggled to cope with economic decline. In the late 20th century, Britain became a more multi-cultural society, as many immigrants arrived from the country's former colonies in Africa, Asia, and the Caribbean. In the 21st century, Britain remains almost unchanged.

Wartime Britain

In 1940, Britain stood alone in the fight against Nazi Germany. British fighter pilots fought off a planned German invasion during the Battle of Britain, but British cities were heavily bombed throughout World War II.

Welfare state

In the early 20th century, Britain introduced national pensions and insurance schemes to protest workers against poverty, ill health, and unemployment. In 1948, a national health service established free medical treatment.

Entry into Europe

After a referendum of the adult population, Britain joined the European Community (now called the European Union) in 1973. Membership brought many benefits, but the role of Britain in Europe has remained one of the most controversial issues for British political parties.

Timeline

54 BC Julius Caesar leads exploratory invasion of England.

AD 43-410 England and Wales are part of the Roman Empire.

613 Anglo-Saxons complete their invasion of England.

787 Vikings begin to raid coastline.

1016-35 Cnut rules England as part of large Scandinavian Empire.

1066 Battle of Hastings: Normans rule England under William.

1455-85 War of the Roses: the Houses of York and Lancaster, represented by a white and a red rose respectively, fight for the English throne.

1603 James I (James VI of Scotland), the first Stuart king, comes to the English throne, uniting the English and Scottish thrones.

1707 The Act of Union between England and Scotland creates the United Kingdom of Great Britain.

1800 Union between Great Britain and Ireland.

1837-1901 Reign of Queen Victoria. British Empire at its height.

1922 Most of Ireland gains its independence from Britain and is called the Irish Free State.

1973 United Kingdom joins European Community, later called the European Union.

NATIONAL INDICATORS – UNITED KINGDOM

Area 244,100 sq.km.; capital London; major towns Birmingham, Glasgow, Leeds, Sheffield, Liverpool, Manchester, Edinburgh, Bradford, Bristol, Belfast, Newcastle, Cardiff; territories Anguilla, Bermuda, British Antarctic Territory, British Indian Ocean Territory, British Virgin Island, Cayman Islands, Falkland Islands, Gibraltar, Hong Kong (until 1997), Monteserrat, Pitcairn Islands, St. Helena and Dependencies (Ascension, Tristan da Cunha), Turks and Caicos Islands. The Channel Islands and the Isle of Man are not part of the UK but are direct dependencies of the crown; head of the state Queen Elizabeth-II from 1952; head of government Gordon Brown; political system liberal democracy; administrative divisions England: 35 counties, 27 unitary authorities, 6 metropolitan counties, Scotland: 32 unitary authorities, Wales: 22 unitary authorities; Northern Ireland: 26 districts within 6 geographical counties; political parties Conservative and Unionist Party, right of centre; Labour Party, moderate left of centre; Social and Liberal Democrats, centre-left; Scottish National Party (SNP), Scottish nationalist; Plaid Cymru (Welsh Nationalist Party), Welsh nationalist; Official Ulster Unionist Party (OUP), Democratic Unionist Party (DUP), Ulster People's Unionist Party (UPUP), all Northern Ireland right of centre, in favour of remaining part of United Kingdom; Social Democratic Labour Party (SDLP), Northern Ireland, moderate left of centre; Green Party, ecological; literacy rate 99%; languages English, Welsh, Gaelic; religions Church of England (established church); other Protestant denominations, Roman Catholic, Muslim, Jewish, Hindu, Sikh; GDP (US $) 1,278.4 billion (1997); GDP per capita (PPP) (US $) 18,360 (1995); growth rate 2.4% (1994-95).

HISTORY

c. 400-200 BC	British Isles conquered by the Celts.
55-54 BC	Romans led by Julius Ceasar raided Britain.
AD 43-60	Romans conquered England and Waves, which formed the province of Britannia; Picts stopped them penetrating further north.
5th-7th Cs	After Romans withdrew, Anglo-Saxons overran most of England and formed kingdoms, including Wassex, orthumbria and Mercia; Wales was stronghold of Celts.
500	The Scots, a Gaelic-speaking tribe from Ireland, settled in the kingdom of Dalriada (Argyll).

5th-6th Cs	British Isles converted to Christianity.
829	King Egbert of Wessex overlord of all England.
c. 843	Kenneth McAlpin unified Scots and Picts to become first king of Scotland.
9th-11th Cs	Vikings raided British Isles, conquering N and E England and N Scotland.
1215	King John of England forced to sign Magna Carta, which placed limits on royal powers.
1284	Edward I of England Invaded Scotland; Scots defeated English at Battle of Stirling Bridge 1297.
1455-85	Wars of the Roses: House of York and House of Lancaster disputed the English throne.
1513	Battle of Flodden: Scots defeated by English; James IV of Scotland killed.
1529	Henry VIII founded Church of England after break with Rome; Reformation effective in England and Wales, but not in Ireland.
1603	Union of crowns: James VI of Scotland became James I of England also.
1607	First successful English colony in Virginia marked start of three centuries of overseas expansion.
1610	James I established plantation of Ulster in Northern Ireland with Protestant settlers from England and Scotland.
1642-52	English Civil War between king and Parliament, with Scottish intervention and Irish rebellion, resulted in victory for Parliament.
1649	Execution of charles I; Oliver Cromwell appointed Lord Protector 1653; monarchy restored 1660.
1689	'Glorious Revolution' confirmed power of Parliament; replacement of James II by William III resisted by Scottish Highlanders and Catholic Irish.
1707	Act of Union between England and Scotland created United Kingdom of Great Britain, governed by a single parliament.

1721-42	Cabinet government developed under Robert Walpole, in effect the first prime minister.
1745	'The Forty-five': rebellion of Scottish Highlanders in support of Jacobite pretender to throne; defeated 1746.
c. 1760-1850	Industrial Revolution: British became the first industrial nation in the world.
1775-83	American Revolution: Britain lost 13 American colonies; empire continued to expand in Canada, India and Australia.
1793-1815	Britain at war with revolutionary France except for 1802-03.
1800	Act of Union created United Kingdom of Great Britain and Ireland, governed by a single parliament effective 1801.
1832	Great Reform Act extended the franchise; further extensions 1867, 1884, 1918 and 1928.
1846	Repeal of the Corn Laws reflected shift of power from landowners to industrialists.
1870	Home Rule Party formed to campaign for restoration of a separate Irish parliament.
1880-90s	Rapid expansion of British Empire in Africa.
1906-14	Liberal governments introduced social reforms and curbed power of House of Lords.
1914-18	United Kingdom played a leading part in World War I; Empire expanded in the Middle-East.
1919-21	Anglo-Irish war ended with secession of south Ireland as Irish Free State; Ulster renamed within United Kingdom of Great Britain and Northern Ireland with some powers devolved to a northern Irish parliament.
1924	First Labour government led by Ramsay MacDonald.
1931	National Government coalition formed to face economic crisis; unemployment reached 3 million.
1939-45	United Kingdom played a leading part in World War II.
1949-71	Decolonisation and end of British Empire.
1969	Start of the Troubles in Northern Ireland; Northern Irish Parliament suspended 1972.

1973	UK joined European Economic Community. (Now EU)
1979	Referenda failed to approve devolution of power to Scottish and Welsh Assemblies.
1979-90	Conservative government of Margaret Thatcher pursued radical free-market economic policies.
1982	Falklands War.
1991	British troops took part in US-led war against Iraq under United Nations umbrella.
1993	Peace proposal for Northern Ireland, the Downing Street Declaration, issued jointly with Irish government.
1994	Irish Republican Army and Protestant paramilitary declared cease-fire in Northern Ireland.
1997	Labour Party landslide victory in general election. Tony Blair became prime minister defeating John Major (1990-97).
1998	Historic multiparty agreement (known as the Good Friday Agreement) was reached on the future of Northern Ireland. Peace plan approved by referenda in both Northern Ireland and the Irish Republic. UUP leader, David Trimble, elected first minister. 'Real IRA' exploded large bomb in Omagh, Northern Ireland. Strong anti-terrorist legislation passed. Nobel Peace Prize jointly awarded to John Hume and David Trimble.

(Source; Hutchinson Encyclopedia)

The whole world perished in one city, Rome, in 476 AD when the last Roman emperor in the West, Romulus was deposed by barbarians.

– *Gibbon*

36

When Britain was part of the Roman Empire

Britain, formerly Albion, was a Roman colony which Julius Caesar rampaged through many times over, leaving behind Roman law, Roman names, Graeco-Roman culture, and dumping them in the junkyard which later became the rich heritage of Britain.

The Island of Britain was known to Greeks and Romans as *Albion*. (Britain is derived from the Roman name *Britannia* which, in turn, is derived from the ancient Celtic name of the inhabitants of Bryttas). As stated earlier, it was once the end of the known world. Its history began about 330 B.C. when the explorer Pytheas was sent by the merchants of the Greek city of Massilia to find the unknown islands from which daring traders brought amber and tin and pearls. In those days, the coasts of the Mediterranean included the whole of the Western civilisation. Then the young Alexander marched to the conquest of Asia and Aristotle, the founder of scientific enquiry, lectured at Athens. The cities of Greece had an age of culture and refinement which surpassed, in many ways, our own age. The books by explorer Pytheas are lost, but many quotations from them are found in ancient Greek literature. And his discovery of Britain has became a fact of its known history. The little we know of Britain from Greek writers, before the Roman conquest, has been interpreted and expanded by archaeologists to put in place the history of ancient Britain. But, for the purposes of this narrative, let us begin by talking about British history, beginning from Julius Caesar.

Julius Ceasar, born in 100 BC, was a Roman citizen of ancient lineage and great wealth. He spent his youth in extravagance and luxury. At forty, he was elected Consul and used his political influence to get command of an army in the Roman province of southern Gaul (modern France and Belgium). He defeated the *Helvetii,* a wandering tribe who threatened to invade the Roman frontiers, marched north against the Celts to conquer Gaul and sailed for Britain in 55 BC. After making two raids through Kent and across the Thames, he returned to Gaul where people had again risen in rebellion behind him; he defeated them and marched south to Italy. The Roman Republic had for thirty years been harassed by wars between rival generals who, by means of their armies, had become the masters, instead of the servants of the Senate and people of Rome. Ceasar decided to plunge into these wars and crossed the *Rubicon*, the legal boundary of his authority, to advance against Pompey, the conqueror of Syria who dominated Rome. Rubicon is the ancient name of the small river flowing into Adriatic which marked the boundary between Italy and Gaul. When Caesar led his army across it in 49 BC, he declared war.

Julius Caesar was murdered by conspirators led by Brutus and Cassius. – A sketch

Pompey was defeated and killed, leaving Ceasar master of Rome. However, Caesar, had to wage wars in Spain and Egypt before becoming the master of Rome. During the last three years of his life, Ceasar was all-powerful. Though he did not put an end to the Republic, he had full control over power, liberating the whole Roman world from the corrupt officials and Senate. Caesar was murdered in the Senate House of Rome on the *"Ides of March"* 44 BC by Brutus and Cassius. Ceasar's successor, *Octavianus,* (later, he became Augustus) defeated Brutus and turned to Ceasar's friend, Antony, who was in love with Cleopatra, the Egyptian queen and wife of Caesar. He won the sea battle of Actinum 31 BC. He called himself Octavianus, and still later called *Augustus.* Historians trace the foundation of the Roman Empire, to him when the world enjoyed four centuries of law and order such as it had never known before.

KEY DATES OF ROMAN RULE OVER BRITAIN	
44 BC	Murder of Julius Caesar
31 BC	Victory of Augustus at Actium
29 AD	Probable date of the Crucifixion
43 AD	Conquest of Britain by Aulus Plautius
61 AD	Boadicea's (Queen Warrior) Revolt
78-85 AD	Final Conquest by Agricola
122 AD	Hadrian's visit to Britain
303 AD	Possible date of St. Alban's death
323 AD	Christianity established by Constantine throughout the Roman Empire
395 AD	Final division between Eastern and Western Empires Roman legions withdrawn from Britain and
410 AD	Rome was sacked by Visigoths, a Germanic tribe
476 AD	Deposition of Romulus, last Western Emperor

As soldier and statesman, Ceasar is one of the greatest of men of all time. His thin aquiline face was similar to that of his fellow-countrymen; his native tongue was the language of the Briton's Roman Catholic Church; his very name ("Kaiser," "Czar," "Kaisar-e-Hind") has become a monarch's proudest title. By his conquests, he bequeathed the extended Graeco-Roman culture to the Western World. For 1,800 years, the boundaries of the old Roman Empire contained almost all the world's civilisations. Only during the last 300 years have the European races made fresh advances in the *"regions Caesar never knew"*.

CEASAR'S VOYAGES TO BRITAIN: During Caesar's first campaigns in Gaul, (France) his enemies, the *Belgae* a tribe, depended on their relatives in Britain for supplies, and to whom they could flee for refuge. Gaining what information he could from merchants and warships that he sent to reconnoitre the British coast, Ceasar prepared his invasion plan with two legions (10,000 men). On August 26, 55 BC, his fleet crossed the straits, intending to land in Kent at a point near Dover. The cavalry, however, came late. Hence, a desperate fight took place in the surf below the white chalk cliffs of Dover. Until the Tenth Legion led the way, the Roman soldiers shrank from the waves of attacks by the Britons who fought from war chariots on the beach. At last, covered by discharges from catapults on the warships, the Roman legions landed, and fortified a camp. And, captured the enemy. After some time, they rose in revolt again. And, again, Caesar marched rapidly through Kent, crossed the Thames, stormed the camp of Cassivellaunus of the rebel leader and dissolved the league of the British tribes. The enemies surrendered to Rome. He ordered hostages to be delivered and fixed the amount to be paid to Rome by way of tribute and left Britain.

DESTRUCTION OF THE PROVINCE OF BRITAIN: During the second half of the fourth century, the barbarians overran the Roman Wall. There are signs that many fortresses were stormed and sacked in 360 AD. At Whittinghame on the border, a large treasure was found recently, apparently the spoil of a raiding tribe who buried for safety the loot of a Roman town: Saxon pirates from the East, Picts (Roman term for the people of Northern Scotland) from the North and the Scots, a tribe, invaded and gave their name to North Britain (Scotland). Meanwhile troops were recalled from the boundaries of the Empire to protect Rome from the Goths. In 406, the regular legions were withdrawn from Britain to defend Rome itself from the barbarian tribe. Deserting the frontier, they failed to save the city. The whole Western Empire fell to Lombards, Goths, Franks, Vandals and Anglo-Saxons who destroyed the organisation of the Roman Empire though they never ceased to revere the name of Rome. In 475, Odaacer, the Lombard, deposed the puppet Emperor, Romulus, and sent his crown and robes to the Eastern emperor at Constantinople. By that time Britain had ceased to be a part of the Roman world. This, in brief, is the history of Romanised Britain – a Roman colony which colonised one-fifth of the world, later, much later.

CONSTANTINE SAW THE CROSS IN HIS DREAMS AND ROMAN EMPIRE BECAME CHRISTIAN

Diocletian made the last serious attempts to suppress Christianity. During the third century many oriental religions had spread through the Empire, which were not discouraged by the authorities, since they did not forbid the worship of the *Guardian Spirit* (a god) of the Emperor that was done by all Roman citizens, whatever other gods besides. Jews and Christians alone refused to worship the Roman god and, hence, they were persecuted as traitors, though the persecuting governors, from *Pontius Pilate* onwards, could find no other fault in them. When Diocletian died, Constantius, the Caesar of the West, set himself up as *Emperor at York* and ruled the West for several years.

His son, Constantine the Great, set out from York in 313 to reunite the world. At the battle of the Milvian Bridge, near Rome, he defeated his rival who had staked his claim to the throne. It is said on the eve of the battle,

Constantine saw the Cross in his dream and won the battle to become a Christian. Since then, the Roman Empire became a Christian empire. After 323, Christianity became the official religion of the Roman Empire.

This was the golden age of the Roman empire. The power of Rome, growing for a thousand years, had given to the whole known world one church, one government, one law, one currency, one system of trade and communication. Never again has there been so great an opportunity for peace and prosperity. But, within 200 years, Rome had been twice looted by barbarians, the Church was deeply divided and the western half of the Empire had sunk back into savagery and decline.

DECLINE OF THE ROMAN EMPIRE

The greatest of all historians, *Edward Gibbon,* has written many volumes to explain why and how the power of Rome declined and fell. Some reasons are shortly indicated here.

(1) Constantine moved the capital of the Empire from Rome to Byzantium, which he called *Constantinople.* From that time on the Empire split into two halves, a Greek-speaking Byzantine empire, which survived many more years, and a Latin-speaking empire which was overthrown by the barbarians in 410. In 395, Emperor Theodosius made a final division between East and West. Under different governments, the Greek and Latin Churches gradually separated : one has become the *Eastern Orthodox Church,* the other the *Catholic Church of Rome.*

(2) The worst weakness of the Roman Empire was military mutiny. Many times, the armies on the frontiers attempted to set popular generals on the throne. Several mutinies of this kind occurred in Britain, under Carausius (287), Maximus (380) and Constantine who gained the throne and became a great emperor.

(3) In the third century, the population of Europe was much reduced by pestilence. It was perhaps at this time that malaria ravaged Levant, making a desert of what was once the centre of the world, green and prosperous. (Levant was the Mediterranean coastal region of Turkey, Syria, Lebanon and Israel).

(4) The finances of the Empire broke down for several reasons. Taxation was unjust. Farming decayed, as it always did in old and rich countries

CLEOPATRA, QUEEN OF EGYPT

CLEOPATRA-Caesar launched a thousand ships in the Mediterranean to see the Queen of Egypt.

Regarded as the most famous woman in history, Cleopatra (c. 68-30 BC) was the daughter of Ptolemy V although, like her father, she was entirely Greek, not Egyptian. In 51 BC, she became joint ruler of Egypt with her young brother but they quarrelled and she was forced to leave and go to Syria. At this time, Julius Caesar arrived in Alexandria and Cleopatra, using her charms, persuaded him to make war on her behalf. Her brother was killed and she become Queen of Egypt once more. Caesar took her to Rome with him, but following his assassination, she returned to Egypt. She then became the mistress of Marcus Antonius (Mark Antony, c. 83-30 BC) and added her fleet to his at the Battle of Actium (31 BC), where she fought against Octavian (later to become Caesar Augustus). Realising all was lost, she poisoned herself with a viper; the line of Ptolemies ended with her death and Egypt became a Roman province.

because the peasants preferred the excitement of town life to the drudgery of agriculture. What farms survived were mostly great estates owned by rich capitalists and worked by slaves. Slavery degraded the people and produced poor results and discontent.

(5) In the fourth century, tribes of barbarians were often encouraged to do service in the Roman army and settle in deserted places. Having discovered the nakedness of the land, they often looted the rich provinces. These tribes included the Franks, who settled between the Rhine and the Seine, the Goths who sacked Rome in 410 and the Vandals who marched through Spain into Africa, leaving behind their name as a byword for wanton destruction.

ROMAN LEGACIES

Britain prospered during the Roman rule. Roman roads, still the most permanent relics of Roman occupation, were built from all outlying towns to London, from where they lead on to Dover and to Rome. Ermine Street from the north, and Watling Street from the north-west, are still the mainlines of English communication largely on the modern lines of road and railway.

The main forum in Rome, originally smaller than five acres, was expanded under the dictator Sulla in 78 BC and later by Julius Caesar to include many of the empire's administrative buildings. – A sketch

London grew in size and commerce till it became one of the largest cities of the Roman Empire. Verulam (St. Albans), Lindum (Lincoln), Glevum (Glouchester), and York were self-governing municipalities. For the most part, Britain was a land of farms and market towns and country houses, but by the third century British cloth had become famous. Social life in all Roman towns centred in baths which were clubs and meeting-places as well. Amid Roman ruins exist baths. In London; just off the Strand, a small Roman bath is still in use. Gladiatorial shows were arranged in Britain as is evident from a gladiator tomb in London. There are also remains of amphitheatres at Dorchester, Silchester and Cirencester.

The Roman Empire reached its highest stage of development under Diocletian, (284-303 AD) who redistributed the provinces under the new name of dioceses, each under a vicar, thus introducing names still surviving in the Church which owed so much of its organisation to the Roman Empire. He appointed three assistants who governed a quarter of his Empire. Constantius was Caesar of Britain and Gaul. The British diocese, besides its vicar or civil governor, had three military officials, the Duke of Britain who guarded the northern frontier, the Count of Britain who commanded the legions, and the count of the Saxon shore who held the narrow seas against Saxon pirates. Britain was threatened more from the north Sea raiders than from Scotland.

The responsibility for governing India has been placed by the inscrutable decree of providence upon the shoulders of the British race. Thus, Britain has the right to rule India without law.

— Rudyard Kipling

37

The rise and fall of the British Empire

Queen Victoria's Diamond Jubilee, held in London on June 22, 1897, was one of the grandest fetes the world has ever seen: 46,000 troops and 11 colonial prime ministers arrived from the four corners of the earth to pay homage to their sovereign. The event was as much a celebration of Victoria's 60 years on the throne as it was of Britain's superpower status. In 1897, Queen Victoria ruled over a quarter of the world's population and a fifth of its territory. An 8-year-old boy, Arnold Toynbee, who became a great historian later, watched the parade while sitting on his uncle's shoulders. "I remember the atmosphere", he later wrote. "It was as if we are on the top of the world, and we have arrived at this peak to stay there forever!" But, the empire, which they took 350 years to build vanished in three years after World War II ended in 1945.

British Empire consisted of various territories conquered or colonized by Britain from about 1600, most of them are now independent or ruled by other powers. The British Empire was at its largest at the end of World War I, consisting of a quarter of the world's population and a fifth of its area. The British Empire lasted more than three and a half centuries = almost as long as the Roman Empire. By the time the British began colonizing overseas, the Portuguese and Spaniards had already divided a considerable part of the Earth's land surface between them. The Empire grew quickly with acquisitions in North America and India, as well as some small settlement in Africa in the 17th and 18th centuries.

The 19th century saw the largest expansion of the Empire as the Briish took many former French possessions in the West Indies and began to settle in large numbers in Australia in the early part of the last century and later competed fiercely with other European powers for territory in Africa. At the same time, there was serious expansion in Asia, notably after the acquisition of Singapore (1824), Hong Kong (1841), and Burma (1886), and the South Pacific, particularly the settlement of New Zealand (1840). The only serious loss of territory was the loss of the 13 American colonies after the American Revolution 1776.

The first successful British colony was Jamestown, (now Virginia), founded in 1607, although there was an earlier settlement at Newfoundland (Canada) in 1583. Settlements were made in Gambia and on the Gold Coast of Africa in 1618; Bermuda in 1609 and other islands of the West Indies; Jamaica was taken from Spain in 1655; Acadia (Nova Scotia in Canada), was secured from France by the Treaty of Utrecht in 1713, which recognised Newfoundland and Hudson Bay (as well as Gibraltar in Europe) as British possessions. New France (Quebec), Cape Breton Island, and Prince Edward Island became British as a result of the Seven Years' War (1756-63).

WEST INDIES: Following the early settlement in Virginia, British colonies spread up and down the east coast of North America and by 1664, when the British secured New Amsterdam (now New York) from the Dutch, there was a continuous fringe of colonies from the present South Carolina in the south to what is now New Hampshire. The attempt of George III and his minister Lord North to coerce the colonists into paying special taxes to Britain aroused them to resistance which resulted in the American War of Independence (1775-83) and birth of the United States of America from the 13 English colonies then lost. Constitutional development in Canada started with an act of 1791 which set up Lower Canada (Quebec), mainly French-speaking, and Upper Canada (Ontario), mainly English-speaking. In the War of 1812, the US wrongly assumed that Canada would join the union. But there was sufficient discontent there to lead to rebellion in 1837 in both Canadas. After the suppression of these risings, the two Canadas were united in 1840 and given a representative legislative council, which marked the beginning of colonial self-government. With the British North America Act in 1867, the self-governing dominion of Canada came into existence; to the original union of Ontario, Quebec, New Brunswick, and Nova Scotia were later added further territories until the federal government of Canada controlled all the northern part of the continent except Alaska.

AUSTRALIA: In Australia, colonisation began with the desire to find a place for penal settlement after the loss of the original American colonies. The first shipload of British convicts landed in Australia 1788 on the present site of city of Sydney. New South Wales was opened to free settlers in 1819, and in 1853 transportation of convicts was abolished. Before the end of the last century, five Australian colonies – New South Wales, Western Australia, South Australia, Victoria, Queensland – and the island colony of Tasmania had each achieved self-government; the federal commonwealth of Australia, an independent dominion, was created in 1901. New Zealand, annexed in 1840, was at first a dependency of New South Wales. It became a separate colony in 1853 and a dominion in 1907. It may be noted that in 1817 Governor Lachlan Macquarie formally adopted the name "Australia" for the British colony.

SOUTHERN AFRICA: the Cape of Good Hope in South Africa was occupied by two English captains in 1620, but the Dutch seized it in 1650 and it remained with them until 1795 when the British seized it again from the French. Under the Treaty of Paris in 1814, the UK bought Cape Town from the new Kingdom of the Netherlands for $6 million. British settlement began 1824 on the coast of Natal, proclaimed a British colony in 1843. The need to find new farmland and establish independence from British rule led a body of Boers (Dutch farmers) from the Cape to make the Great Trek northeast in 1836, to found Transvaal and Orange Free State. Conflict between the British government and the Boers culminated, after the discovery of gold in the Boer territories, in the South African War in 1899-1902, which brought Transvaal and Orange Free State under British sovereignty. Given self-government in 1907, they were formed, with Cape Colony (self-governing in 1872) and Natal (self-governing in 1893), into the Union of South Africa's 1910. Cecil Rhode's British South Africa Company, registered in 1889, extended British influence over Southern Rhodesia (a colony 1923) and Northern Rhodesia (a protectorate in 1924); with Nyasaland, taken under British protection in 1891, the Rhodesias were formed into a federation in 1953-63 with representative government. Uganda was made a British protectorate in 1894. Kenya, formerly a protectorate, became a colony in 1920, but certain districts on the coast forming part of the sultan of Zanzibar's dominions remained a protectorate.

WEST AFRICA: The British showed little interest in Africa outside the Cape until the scramble for territory in the 1880s, although a few forts were kept in West Africa, where gold and ivory remained important after the slave trade was ended by Britain in 1807. An early exception was the colony of

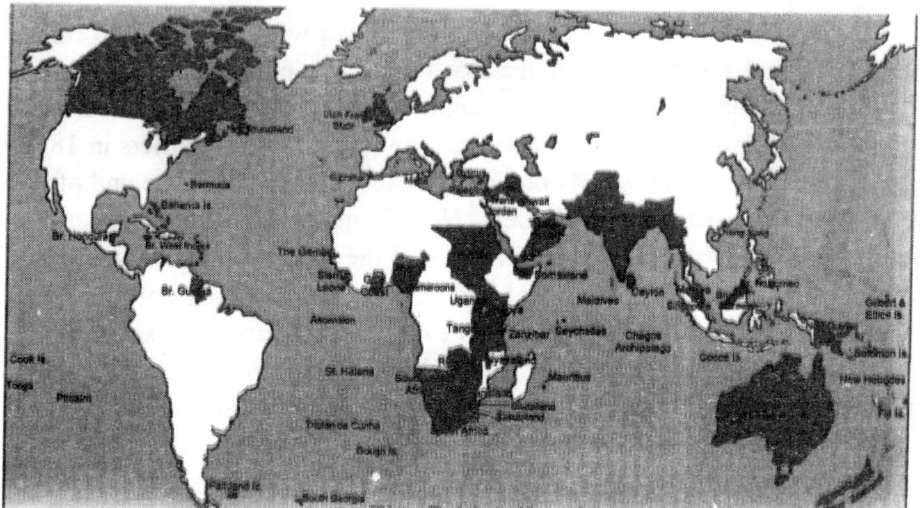

The British Empire in the 1920's

Sierra Leone founded in 1788. British influence in Nigeria began through the activities of the National Africa Company (the Royal Niger Company from 1886), which bought Lagos from an African chief 1861 and steadily extended its hold over the Niger Valley until it surrendered its charter in 1899; in 1900 the two protectorates of North and South Nigeria were proclaimed. In 1921-22, under a League of Nations mandate, Tanganyika (now Tanzania) was transferred to British administration, and south-west Africa (Namibia) to South Africa; the Cameroons and Togoland (now Togo), in West Africa, were divided between Britain and France.

EAST AFRICA: Private companies under charter from the British government established their control over Kenya in 1888 and Uganda in 1890. Northern Somalia came under direct control of the British government in 1884 and in 1890 Germany, which had already relinquished its interests in Uganda, ceded Zanzibar to Britain in exchange for Heliogoland, an island off the German coast.

DOMINION STATUS: The concept of self-government for some colonies was first formulated in the Lord Durham "Report on the Affairs of British North America" 1839 which recommended that responsible government (the acceptance of rule by governors on the advice of local ministers) should be granted to Upper Canada (Ontario) and Lower Canada (Quebec). This pattern was subsequently applied to the other Canadian provinces and to the Australian colonies by 1859, except for Western Australia (1890). New Zealand obtained responsible government in 1856 and the Cape colony in 1872, followed by Natal in 1893. A further intermediate form of government, dominion status, was devised in the late 19th and early 20th century at a series of Colonial Conferences (renamed Imperial Conferences 1907). Canada became a dominion in 1867, Australia in 1901, New Zealand in 1907, and South Africa by 1910. These four self-governing countries were known as Dominions within the British Empire. Dominion status was very inexactly defined until the Statute of Westminster 1931 established it as synonymous with complete independence.

EAST INDIA: Ceylon (now Sri Lanka) was annexed to the East India Company in 1796. When the British government took it over from the company, it also acquired the Straits Settlements and by 1914 all Malaya was under British control. Britain gained Hong Kong as a result of the Opium Wars (1839-42) and Kowloon was added to the colony after a second Opium War (1856-58).

INDIA: India was at the heart of the British Empire but it was originally controlled by the East India Company. This huge company, registered in 1600 set up a number of factories and steadily increased its possessions and the territories over which it held treaty rights until its power extended from Aden in Arabia to Penang in Malaya. The East India Company was the most powerful private company in history, controlling India, partly by direct rule and partly by a system of alliances with Indian princes and protected by the Company's powerful army. The company's political power was ended by the Indian Mutiny 1857. Although this revolt was put down, it resulted in the crown taking over the government of India in 1858; Queen Victoria was proclaimed empress of India on 1 Jan. 1877.

The East India Company received its official sanction on December 31, 1599, when Queen Elizabeth-I signed a royal charter assigning it exclusive trading rights with all countries beyond the Cape of Good Hope for an initial period of 15 years. Eight months later, a ship named, *Hector*, dropped anchor in the little port of Surat. It was August 24, 1600 when the British had arrived in India. Their initial landing was a modest one. William Hawkins, Captain of the Hector, was more of a pirate than explorer. Hawkins marched off into the interior, prepared to find rubies as big as pigeons' eggs, pepper, ginger, indigo, cinnamon, trees whose leaves were so enormous, that the shade they cast could cover an entire family, potions derived from elephants' testicles to give him eternal youth. The Captain later went to Agra where he found himself face to face with a sovereign. Reigning over 70 million subjects, Emperor Jehangir was the world's richest and most powerful monarch, the fourth and last of India's great Moghul rulers.

The first Englishman to reach his court, was greeted with a gesture which might have disconcerted the 125 worthy shareholders of the East India Company. The Moghul made him a member of the royal household and offered him, as a welcome gift, the most beautiful girl in his harem, an Armenian Christian. But, profit inspired Hawkins more than sex. Jehangir signed an imperial firman, authorizing the East India Company to open trading depots north of Bombay. Its success was rapid and impressive. Soon, two ships a month were unloading mountains of spices, gum, sugar, raw silk and muslin cotton on the docks along the Thames and sailing off with holds full of English goods. A deluge of dividends, some of them as high as 200%, came pouring down on the firm's fortunate shareholders.

PLASSEY PAVES WAY FOR EMPIRE: The British were welcomed by Indian rulers and the population. Unlike the zealous Spaniards who were conquering South America in the name of God, the British said they came to India for "trade, not territory," and the company's officers never ceased repeating this policy. However, as their trading activities grew, the company's officers became involved in local politics and were forced to intervene in the squabbles of the petty sovereigns on whose territories they operated. Thus began the irreversible process which would lead England to conquer India almost by "inadvertence." On June 23, 1757, marching through drenching rain at the head of 900 Englishmen and 3000 Indian sepoys, an audacious general, named Robert Clive routed the army of a Nawab in the rice paddies outside a Bengali village called Plassey. Clive's victory opened the gates of northern India. With it, the British conquest of India truly started.

The century that followed was one of conquest. Although they were instructed by London to avoid "schemes of conquest and territorial expansion," a succession of ambitious governor-generals relentlessly embraced the opposite policy. In less than a century, a company of traders was changed into a sovereign power, its accountants and traders became generals and governors, its race for profit turned into a struggle for imperial authority. But, the British intent had always been to relinquish the possessions she had so inadvertently acquired. As early as 1818, Hastings noted: "A time, not very remote, will arrive when England will, on sound principles of policy, relinquish the domination which she has gradually and unintentionally assumed over India." Empires, however, were more naturally acquired than disposed of and the moment foreseen by Hastings was to be considerably more remote, than he might have imagined. The British rule nonetheless brought some benefits also, like the British legal, administrative and educational systems. It gave India the gift that was to become the common bond of its diverse peoples and the conduit of their revolutionary aspirations, the English language.

OVER TO BRITISH CROWN: The first manifestation of imperial aspirations came from the savage mutiny of 1857. As stated earlier, Its most important result was an abrupt change in the manner in which Britain governed India. After years of fruitful rule, the East India Company's existence was, finally, terminated and the responsibility for the governance of 300 million (of the then) Indians was transferred to the crown by Queen Victoria. Henceforth, Britain's authority was exercised by the *crown*, represented in India by the Viceroy. With that change began the Victorian Era.

Ultimately, responsibility was exercised at any given time by about 3,000 members of the Indian Civil Service, ICS, and 10,000 British officers of the Indian Army. Their authority over 300 million people was sustained by 60,000 British soldiers and 200,000 men of the Indian Army. India for them was picturesque and romantic of Kipling's tales. Theirs was the India of gentleman officers at the head of their turbaned sepoys; of district magistrates lost in the torrid wastes of the Deccan; of sumptuous imperial balls in the Himalayan summer capital of Shimla; cricket matches on the manicured lawns of Calcutta's Bengal Club; polo games on the sun-burnt plains of Rajasthan; tiger hunts in Assam; young men sitting down to dinner in black ties in a tent in the middle of jungle, solemnly proposing their toast to the King Emperor. Those men were, generally, the products of families of impeccable breeding but of less certain wealth; the offsprings of good Anglican country churchmen; talented second sons of the landed aristocracy; sons of schoolmasters, professors of the classics and above all of the previous generation of the British in India. "India," said James S. Mill, "was a vast system of outdoor recreation for Britain's upper classes."

MONEY, ADVENTURE AND EVERYTHING ELSE: These well-bred Britons enjoyed challenge and adventure, and used India's boundless spaces as an arena in which England's young men could find fulfilment of their dreams, that the restricted shores of Britain always denied them. They arrived on the docks of Bombay (Mumbai) at nineteen or twenty years of age, barely able to raise a stubble on their chins, and went home thirty-five or forty years later with their bodies scarred by bullets, disease, a panther's claws or by a fall on the polo field; their faces ravaged by too much sun and too much whisky, but proud of having lived a romantic life.

The parties and receptions in imperial India's principal cities – Bombay, Calcutta, Lahore, Delhi, Simla – were lavish affairs. "Everyone with any standing had a ballroom and a drawing-room at least eighty feet long," wrote a British general who lived in Victorian India. In those days, there were none of those horrible buffets where people go to a table with a plate and stand around, eating with whomsoever they choose. The average private dinner was for thirty-five or forty with a servant for each guest. Shopkeepers and commercial people were never invited nor, of course, did one ever see an Indian socially accepted anywhere. The great pastime of the British in India was sport. A love of cricket, tennis, squash and hockey would be the most enduring heritage they have left behind. Golf was introduced in Calcutta in 1829, 30 years before it reached New York, and the world's highest course was laid out in the Himalayas at 11,000 feet. "No gold bag was considered more chic on those courses than one made of an elephant's penis – provided, of course, its owner had shot the beast himself."

The British played in India and died there, too, in very great numbers, often young. Every cantonment church had its adjacent graveyard to which the little community might carry its regular flow of dead, victims of India's cruel climate, her peculiar hazards, her epidemics of malaria, cholera, jungle fever. No more poignant account of the British in India was ever written than that inscribed upon the tombstones of those cemeteries. Their rule was paternalistic, that of the old public schoolmaster disciplining an unruly band of boys, forcing on them the education he was sure was good for them. With some exception, they were able and incorruptible, determined to administer India in its own best interests – but it was always they who decided what those interests were, not the Indians they governed.

DECLINE AND FALL OF BRITISH EMPIRE

FINANCIAL CRISIS: Yet another reason for the fall of the British empire was the financial crisis. Right through history, imperial powers clung to their possessions to death. Why then did Britain in 1947 give up the jewel in its crown, India? It was for many reasons. One being that the independence struggle exposed the hollowness of the white man's burden. Provincial self-rule since 1935, paved the way for full self-rule. Churchill resisted independence, but the Labour government of Attlee was anti-imperialist by ideology. And, he paved the way for independence. The Royal Indian Navy mutiny in 1946, also raised fears of a second sepoy mutiny, and convinced British waverers that it was safe to withdraw gracefully.

BRITISH LEFT INDIA ALSO BECAUSE IT WAS NOT PROFITABLE TO KEEP AFTER WAR

To be true, the basis of empire has always been money. The end of empire had much to do with the fact that British imperialism had ceased to be profitable. World War II left Britain victorious but deeply indebted, needing Marshall Aid and loans from the World Bank that constituted a strong financial case for ending the no-longer-profitable empire. Empire-building is expensive. The US spent one billion dollars a day to stay in Iraq since 2003. And, it was not imperialism. Through the centuries, empire-building had been costly, yet constantly undertaken because it promised high returns. The investment was in armies and conquest. The biggest conquerors were revered. Hence, titles like Alexander the Great, Akbar the Great, and Peter the Great. This mindset gradually changed with the rise of new ideas about equality, the ideas that culminated in the French and American revolutions. Robert Clive was impeached for making money, so was Warren Hastings. The white man's burden was sought to be made a moral rationale for conquest. It was supposedly for the good of the conquered. The empire had to yield profitable returns.

The sepoy mutiny though crushed, reminded the British that they were a tiny ethnic group, who could not rule a gigantic subcontinent without the support of important locals. Hence, after 1857, the British stopped annexing one princely state after another, and instead treated the princes as allies. Land revenue was fixed in absolute terms, partly to prevent local unrest and partly to promote the notion of the white man's burden. The empire proclaimed itself to be a protector of the Indian peasant against exploitation by Indian landlords. This was denounced by nationalists like Dadabhoy Naoroji in the 19th century, who complained that land taxes led to an enormous drain from India to Britain. Objective calculations by historians like Angus Maddison suggest a drain of perhaps 1.6 per cent of Indian GNP in the 19th century. But land revenue was more or less fixed by the Raj in absolute terms, and so its real value diminished rapidly with inflation in the 20th century. By World War II, India had ceased to be a profit centre for the British Empire. Historically, conquered nations paid taxes to finance fresh wars of the conqueror. India was asked to pay a large sum at the end of World War I to help repair Britain's finances. But, as shown by historian Indivar Kamtekar, the independence movement led by Gandhiji changed the political landscape, and made mass taxation of India increasingly difficult. By World War II, this had become politically impossible.

Far from taxing India to pay for World War II, Britain actually began paying India for its contribution in men and materials. Troops from white dominions like Australia, Canada and New Zealand were paid for entirely by those countries, but Indian costs were shared by the British government. Britain paid in the form of non-convertible sterling balances that mounted swiftly. The conqueror was paying the conquered, undercutting their profitability on which an empire is founded. But money could not be a recompense to what Indians did to the British in their hours of crisis. *Pax Britannica* – lasting from Waterloo (1815) to the shooting of Archduke Ferdinand at Sarajevo (1914) and after – would not have been possible without Royal Navy, British diplomacy and the Indian Army which was the foundation on which the British empire was built.

Even then Churchill opposed money being given and wanted to tax India rather than pay money to it. But he was overruled by Indian voices who said India would resist payment, and paralyse the war effort. Leo Amery, secretary of state for India, said that when you are driving in a taxi to the station to catch a life-or-death train, you do not loudly announce that you have doubts about whether to pay the fare. Thus, World War II converted India from a debtor to a creditor with over one billion pounds in sterling balances. Britain, meanwhile, became the biggest debtor in the world. No debtor ever ruled the people whom they owed money and Britons were no exception.

THE LAST GASP

On November 10, 1942, Sir Winston Churchill made a celebrated speech at Mansion House, London, in which he said defiantly: "I have not become the first minister of the Crown to preside over the liquidation of the British Empire". And, in fewer than six years, a quarter of the earth, inhabited by about half of the then population of the world, became free from British control. Churchill was, however, never known for his political maturity. He made more mistakes than any wartime leaders did; the one most unforgivable was his call for unconditional surrender which drove Germans to fight the battle to the last ditch. If this "*total surrender*" call had not been given by the Allied on the explicit persuasion of Churchill, there would been revolt against Hitler within Germany (which did take place) and the War would possibly have ended soon after America joined it. Beinz Guderian, a close associate of Hitler and the founder of the Panzer division, and Liddell Hart, an expert on war strategy, bear it out in ample measure in their books *"Panzer Division and the Current of War"* considered the most authentic account of the World War II.

While making the grandiose statement (liquidation of the British empire), Churchill did not remember that British strength largely flowed from its alliance with America. Tony Blair who was sworn in for third term as British Prime Minister in 2005, however, did not forget it and joined the Iraq war with the US in 2003, despite opposition at home, (and London shooting) riding piggy back to the US and staying a global power. And. American President Woodrow Wilson (1856-1924) had announced in Paris in 1919 that the right of small nations to self-determination was absolute and *"colonialism is morally wrong, unworkable and as archaic as slavery."* Churchill also forgot that America always represented the conscience of the world; it fought World War I to make *"the US an arsenal of democracy"* (Wilson); it fought World War II to *"make the democracy safe in the world"* (Roosevelt). To be true, the Anglo American alliance has always been an uncomfortable friendship until the last of the British colony was freed.

However, all Britons were not as unwise as Churchill. Many sensible Britons thought that once an underdeveloped community became educated to the ways of modern world, it would be impossible to suppress nationalism except at an exorbitant cost in money, manpower, arms and blood. Ernest Bevin (1881-1951) talked of *"give and keep"*. That is, by getting out in time, and fulfilling the nationalist aspirations of colonial peoples, early rather than late, Britain would continue to retain trade advantages with these countries. And, for that matter, some political link can also be retained. (British Commonwealth is the product of this thought) If Indian relation with Britain is good now, it is because of the doctrine of *"give and keep"*.

Let us also remember those Britons who did not figure prominently in history books, but they did a lot to free the colonies. One such man was a remarkable young Scot, Norman Macleod, who became Secretary of State for Colonies in 1959. Macleod (1913-70) was an able British subject, cheerful, bright, confident and very tough, intellectually. He came to prominence by taking on no less a person than Aneurin Bevan in a debate on health. Even though Bevan was good debator, Macleod annihilated him in the House of Commons. The stunned Bevan, looking in amazement at this young highlander, said, "It seems the younger generation of politicians are ready to take over from us. And, they show promise to do better than we did". Macleod had very impressive credentials, a brilliant chess player, voracious reader and a formidable debator, who came from a middle class family and joined the War to suffer a severe leg wound in France. He was later assigned to a staff college, rose to be a major and landed in Normandy with his regiment on D-Day. He was a combat officer on the beachhead and saw much action until the end of the War. Macleod might well have become foreign secretary in 1960 but Prime Minister Macmillan said: "He is too young (39 years) to be eligible," to which Churchill retorted: "He is too eligible to be too young". Macleod passionately pleaded that the way to save Britain was to free colonies and establish relations with them. The highlander talked a lot about British idealism and stirred the conscience of islanders.The British had the illusion that despite their vast empire, they were the most fair-minded people in the world. And for this reason, the British continued to respect and elect those who expressed non-conformist views, either in the House of Commons as Macleod did, or in the Hyde Park where Krishna Menon and other Indian leaders pleaded for India's freedom. However, to be fair to our former masters, we have to accept the fact that Britain has always been a country with conscience. And, a section of people always fought for it. No country in the world, for instance, has such a zealous pride in civil liberties and this was one reason she went to war on behalf of Belgium in 1914 and for Poland in 1939, though other motivations played a role. No doubt, Britain is a virile nation in the realm of ideas and scientific inventions which respects non-conformist views.

THE LONGEST-LIVED EMPIRES

The longest-lived empire was the Holy Roman Empire, which may be dated from 9th century until its dissolution by Napoleon in 1806. The Ming dynasty in China (1368-1644) and its immediate successor, the Manchu or Qing dynasty, which lasted together more than five hundred years, as did the Abbasid caliphate (750-1258). The Ottoman Empire (1453-1922) lasted for about five hundred years. The continental empires of the Habsburgs and the Romano's each existed for more than three centuries, expiring in rapid succession at the end of the First World War. The Mughals ruled a substantial part of India for around two hundred years. Of similar duration were the rule of the Mamluks in Egypt (1250-1517) and the Safavids in Persia (1501-1736). The Spanish, Dutch, French and British empires may be said to have lasted for three hundred years, the Portuguese empire lasted for five hundred. The empires created in the twentieth century, by contrast, were all of comparatively short duration. The Bolsheviks' Soviet Union (1922-1991) lasted less than seventy years. The German Reich founded by Bismarck (1871-1918), lasted forty-seven years. Japan's colonial empire, which can be dated from 1905, lasted just forty. Most ephemeral of all modern empires was the so-called Third Reich of Adolf Hitler which lasted just twelve years. Hittler said it would last for a thousand years. It was the dream of a dictator which died unborn.

But it should be remembered that over a great part of the globe, it was imperialism that brought the modern world, with all its mixture of blessings and curses. Even in 'independent' China and Japan, modern progress was forced down their throats. And, once the draught has been swallowed, there is no turning back. What the "victims" of imperialism wanted and still want is a mastery of technology to conquer and rule the world. But technology was with the West and, hence, their empires. Sir Henry Maine once wrote that "except the blind forces of Nature, nothing moves in the world which is not Greek in its origin". Nothing moves today, no political system, no system of technology and of law, of science that is not European or American in origin. And if these systems have been imposed on a great part of the world by force, it is too late to waste time on regretting it. After all, it was by force that the ideas and the systems of the Graeco-Roman world were spread from the Euphrates in Iraq to the Clyde in Ireland. And, even the modern world and all other changes for good were forced upon the unwilling conservative world by law or revolution. Here Newton's *First Law* – that all material bodies tend to stay in a state of rest until forced to change by external intervention – comes into force. The only difference was that Western imperialism was science and art both.

BRITISH EMPIRE

Current Name	*Colonial names and history*	*Colonised*	*Independent*
India	British East India Company	18th C-1858	1947
Pakistan	British East India Company	18th C-1858	1947
Myanmar	Burma	1866	1948
Sri Lanka	Portuguese, Dutch 1602-1796; Ceylon 1802-1972	16th C	1948
Ghana	Gold Coast; British Togoland integrated 1956	1618	1957
Nigeria		1861	1960
Cyprus	Turkish to 1878, then British rule	1878	1960
Sierra Leone	British protectorate	1788	1961
Tanzania	German E Africa to 1921; British mandate from League of Nations/UN as Tanganyika	19th C	1961
Jamaica	Spanish to 1655	16th C	1962
Trinidad & Tobago	Spanish 1532-1797; British 1797-1962	1532	1962
Uganda	British protectorate	1894	1962
Kenya	British colony from 1920	1895	1963
Malaysia	British interests from 1786; Federation of Malaya 1957-63	1874	1963
Malawi	British protectorate of Nyasaland 1907-53; Federation of Rhodesia & Nyasaland 1953-64	1891	1964
Malta	French 1798-1814	1798	1964
Zambia	N Rhodesia - British protectorate Federation of Rhodesia & Nyasaland 1953-64	1924	1964
The Gambia		1888	1965
Singapore	Federation of Malaya 1963-65	1858	1965
Guyana*	Dutch to 1796; British Guiana* 1796-1966	1620	1966
Botswana	Bechuanaland - British protectorate	1885	1966
Lesotho	Basutoland	1868	1966
Bangladesh	British East India Company 18th century-1858; British India 1858-1947; E Pakistan 1947-71	18th C	1971
Zimbabwe	S Rhodesia from 1923; UDI under Ian Smith 1965-79	1895	1980
Belize	British Honduras	17th C	1981

**Guyana is the name of the country NE coast of South America occupied by British in 1796 and established as colony of British Guiana in 1813.*

**Guiana is the name of the region in northern part of South America comprising Guyana, Suriname, French Guiana and northern Brazil'.*

Have you heard of Sinn Fein in Ireland? It is the most interesting movement and resembles very closely the so-called extremist movements in India. Their policy is not to beg for favours, but to wrest them by force.

– Jawaharlal Nehru (aged 18) to his father from London, September 12, 1907

38

Ireland
Irish Republic
(Republic of Ireland)

Since Reformation, Ireland is the only country where conflict and tension between the Catholics and Protestants still continue despite fragile peace. Which is amazing for Europe which claims to be a secular continent.

Ireland is occupying the greater part of an island west of Great Britain. The republic's only neighbour is Northern Ireland, which occupies the northeastern portion of the island. Although it has been invaded and colonized by Celts, Norsemen, Normans, English and Scots, ethnic distinctions are nonexistent. Languages: Irish and English (both official). Religions: Roman Catholicism (95%), Church of Ireland Episcopalianism, Presbyterianism, Methodism, Judaism. Ireland's topography consists largely of broad lowlands drained by river that include the Shannon; its coasts are fringed with mountains. Nearly three-fifths of the population is urban. Ireland is a republic with two legislative houses; its chief of state is the president, and the head of government is the prime minister. Ireland's independence ended in 1171 when the English King Henry-II proclaimed himself overlord of the island. Beginning in the 16th century, Irish Catholic landowners had fled religious persecution by the English and were replaced by English and Scottish Protestant migrants. The United Kingdom of Great Britain and Ireland was established in 1801.

FROM IRELAND TO EIRE

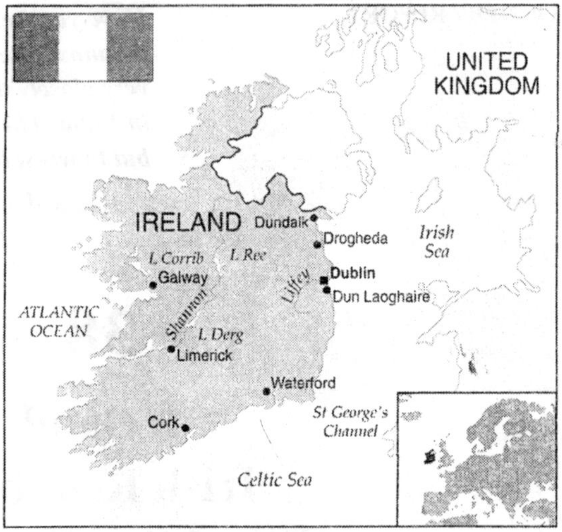

Southern Ireland was granted dominion status and became the Irish Free State in 1921, and in 1937 it adopted the name Eire and became a sovereign independent country. It remained neutral during World War II. Britain recognised the status of Ireland in 1949 but declared that cession of the northern six counties (Northern Ireland) could not occur without the consent of the Parliament of Northern Ireland. In 1973 Ireland joined the European Economic Community (later the European Community); it is now a member of the European Union. The last decades of the 20th century were dominated by sectarian hostilities between the island's Catholics and Protestants. The Irish government played a pivotal role in negotiating and winning public support for the Belfast Agreement (1998), which gave the country a consultative role in the affairs of Northern Ireland and modified Ireland's constitution to remove its claim to the territory of the entire island.

Ireland is a republic with two legislative houses; its chief of state is the president, and the head of government is the prime minister. Human settlement in Ireland began in c.6000 BC, and Celtic migration dates from c.300 BC St. Patrick is credited with Christianizing the country in the 5th century. Norse domination began in 795 and ended in 1014, when the English Henry II proclaimed himself overlord of the island. Although, Ireland has turbulent history of bloodshed, religious conflict and the fight for independence, it today is a stable democracy. The earliest known occupants of Ireland date back to about 7000 BC, and Bronze Age artifacts from Ireland were traded all over Europe. In about 300 BC, Celtic iron workers arrived from Europe and gradually became organised into five tribal groups or kingdoms. The Irish Celts were unaffected by the Roman conquest of Britain in the 1st century AD. Converted to Christianity in the 5th century, they remained a centre of faith despite the collapse of the Roman empire and several centuries of raids by

Vikings, who established a fortified base in Dublin before they were finally defeated by Brian Boru (941-1014), the first king of all Ireland, in 1014.

England's break with the Roman Catholic Church in 1533 under King Henry-VIII (1491-1547), increased the resentment of the Irish, who remained firmly Catholic. Repeated uprisings took place, often aided by Catholic Spanish or French troops. Many Irish Catholics emigrated to Europe. When the earls of Ulster in the north chose this course, James-I of England (1566-1625), encouraged Scottish Protestants to settle on the vacated lands. In 1641, an uprising among the Irish of Ulster led to the massacre of thousands of colonists. An equally savage massacre of the Irish was at the hands of Parliamentary forces fighting in Ireland under Oliver Cromwell (1599-1658). In 1690 an uprising, led by England's deposed Roman Catholic king James II (1633-1701) was defeated at the Battle of the Boyne by the Protestant forces of King William-III (1650-1702). The English government imposed civil disabilities and land confiscations (known as the penal laws) on Irish Catholics, but uprisings continued. In 1801, an Act of Union abolished Ireland's parliament, integrating it with that of Britain.

A MILLION DIED IN FAMINE; SINN FEIN BORN

Under English rule, Ireland was divided into large estates owned by absentee landlords and farmed by local Irish peasants. From 1846 to 1851, the potato crop – the Irish staple food – was destroyed by a fungal disease, leading to the Great Famine. More than a million people died; many more emigrated to the United States, halving the population in Ireland. From about 1870, the movement for Irish Home Rule gathered momentum, led in the British House of Commons by the Irish Member of Parliament Charles Stewart Parnell (1846-91). Home rule was finally granted in 1914, though violently opposed by Ulster's majority Protestant population. World War I delayed its implementation, fuelling discontent. In 1916 an armed insurrection was suppressed by the British army; 14 leaders were executed. Eamon de Valera (1882-1975), a survivor, formed the Sinn Fein party and in 1919 set up a provisional Irish government. After a bitter civil war, Britain agreed to partition the island. The six northeastern countries became Northern Ireland, a province of the United Kingdom. The self-governing Irish Free State was created in the south.

As stated earlier, in 1937, the Irish Free State renamed itself Eire and adopted a new constitution with an elected president, severing its links with the British crown. In 1949, on leaving the British Commonwealth, it declared itself an independent republic. Economic development was slcw, and large numbers continued to emigrate in search of work, particularly to Britain. In 1973 Ireland joined the European Community (EC) now the European Union (EU). The Republic has never formally renounced its claim to Northern Ireland.

Sinn Féin is a political party in Ireland. Originating in the Sinn Féin organisation founded in 1905 by Arthur Griffith, it took its current form in 1970 after a split within the party. Sinn Féin is led by Gerry Adams. It is the major party of Irish republicanism and its political ideology is left wing. The party has historically been associated with the Provisional IRA. The name is Irish for "ourselves" or "we ourselves", although it is frequently mistranslated as "ourselves alone".

Gerry Adams

Sinn Féin is currently the second-largest party in the Northern Ireland Assembly, where it has four ministerial posts (including deputy First Minister) in the power-sharing Northern Ireland Executive. It is the fifth-largest party in Dáil Éireann, the lower house of the Oireachtas, the parliament of the Republic of Ireland. In the 2009 European Parliamentary elections the party's candidate in Northern Ireland, Bairbre de Brún, topped the poll, the first time for Sinn Féin in any Northern Ireland election.

NATIONAL INDICATORS - IRELAND

Area 70,282 sq.km.; capital Dublin; physical features central plateau surrounded by hills; rivers Shannon, Liffey, Boyne; ethnic distribution, most of the population has Celtic origins; education (compulsory years) 9; literacy rate 99%; languages Irish Gaelic and English (both official); religions Roman Catholic 95%, Church of Ireland, other Protestant denominations.

HISTORY

3rd C BC — The Gaels, a Celtic people, invaded Ireland and formed about 150 small kingdoms.

C. AD 432	St. Patrick introduced Christianity.
5th-9th Cs	Irish Church remained a centre of culture and scholarship throughout the Dark Ages.
9th-11th Cs	The Vikings raided Ireland until defeated by High King Brian Boru at Clontarf 1014.
14th-15th Cs	Irish chieftains recovered their lands, restricting English rule to the Pale around Dublin.
1541	Irish Parliament recognised Henry-VIII as king of Ireland.
1610	James-I established plantation of Ulster with Protestant settlers from England and Scotland.
1641	Catholic Irish rebelled against English rule; Oliver Cromwell brutally reasserted English control 1649-50; Irish landowners evicted and replaced with English landowners.
1720	Act passed declaring British Parliament's right to legislate for Ireland.
1739-41	Famine killed one-third of population.
1798	British suppressed revolt by Society of United Irishmen led by Wolfe Tone.
1800	Act of Union abolished Irish parliament and created United Kingdom of Great Britain and Ireland, effective 1801.
1846-51	Potato famine reduced population by 20% through starvation and emigration.
1870	Land Act increased security for tenants but failed to halt agrarian disorder; Isaac Butt formed political party to campaign for Irish Home Rule (devolution).
1885	Home Rulers, led by Charles Stewart Parnell, held balance of power in parliament; first Home Rule Bill rejected 1886; second defeated 1893.
1905	Arthur Griffith founded the nationalist movement *Sinn Fein* ('Ourselves Alone').
1914	Ireland came close to civil war as Ulster prepared to resist Home Rule Act.
1916	Easter Rising: British crushed revolt, executed 15 leaders.

1919	Sinn Fein MPs formed an Irish parliament in Dublin in defiance of the British government.
1919-21	Irish Republican Army (IRA) waged guerrilla war against British forces.
1922	*Irish Free State* proclaimed; IRA split over Anglo-Irish Treaty led to civil war 1922-23.
1932	Anti-Treaty party, *Fianna Fail,* came to power under Eamonn de Valera.
1937	New constitution established Eire (Gaelic name for Ireland) as a sovereign state and refused to acknowledge partition.
1949	After remaining neutral in World War II, Eire left the Commonwealth and became the Republic of Ireland.
1990	Mary Robinson became the first woman president of Ireland.
1994	Cease-fire announced by Catholic and Protestant paramilitaries in Northern Ireland.
1995	Ulster framework peace document issued.
1997	Fianna Fall leader Bertie Ahern became prime minister; Mary MacAleese elected President.
1998	Historic, multiparty agreement (the Good Friday Agreement) was reached on the future of Northern Ireland. Referendum showed large majority in favour of dropping Ireland's claim to the North.
1999	Power was devolved to an elected assembly after peace talks between British Govt. and IRA. Sporadic strife continues till 2006 during the process of IRA disarmament.

France is led by dreams. Hence, it is a great responsibility to be French.
– Francois Rene de Chateaubriand

39

France, a twice-blessed land of distinctive people and culture

France has within its border a little of England in Brittany, a little of Germany in Alsace, a little of Italy in the Riviera and a little of Switzerland in Savoy. No wonder, easy living has made Frenchmen soft and isolationist and it lost all the wars it fought with tougher Germans, including two global wars after which the French population fell by 16 percent. And, never recovered again.

Now that a new Europe is emerging after the Maastricht Treaty was signed on November 1, 1993, France is transforming itself into a dynamic new nation. The French spirit is undying; a nation fed on grandeur of art, culture and revolutionary ideas is not going to give in before Europeans who have none of these. "It is a great responsibility to be French," said Charles de Gaulle in 1958, on his election as President. More than a century earlier, Alexis de Tocqueville had said: "The French are at once the most brilliant of all European nations and the most qualified to become an object of admiration, of hatred, of compassion or alarm – never of indifference." A nation that gave the world the slogan of *"Liberty, Equality and Fraternity"* and the *"Rights of Man"* is the legatee of all that is best and finest in European civilization. A country of about 58 million people, who dearly love their pet animal population of nearly 30 million cats and dogs, a country that has provided asylum to 1.5 million political refugees is certainly not going to accept the leadership of another nation – not in any case of Germans, against whom they had fought two global wars in the last centuries.

Nearly two centuries after Napoleon dominated the Continent, France in 1993 looked well placed to become more than the mere centre of gravity of a new Europe. Its standard of living is among the best in the world, and the quality of life, visitors will attest, remains as invigorating as it is gracious. Modern arts and science flourish in a landscape adorned with Gothic cathedrals, tree-lined avenues and grand chateaus. Philosophy is still in fashion. Together with modern farms, a medieval patchwork of agriculture still yields enough to feed a country better prepared for the new century than most others in Europe. A land criss-crossed by bullet trains, a nuclear electric power grid, Airbus jetliners and satellites borne aloft in Ariane rockets, these and more are the defining features of France. The French advantage in recent years has been stability: a sureness about the nation's place and purpose in the world as well as its material prospects. Inflation was reined in, exports rose comfortably and Presidents in the Elysee managed to guide France's fortunes at home and abroad with the confidence of de Gaulle. A people famous for crossing swords over the slightest trespass or ideological difference have finally settled into political stability. The undercurrent of the new dispensation is desire for a new national myth, a sense of grandeur and destiny. It was *Francois Rene de Chateaubriand*, the great Romantic writer, who said of his compatriots, "The French are led by dreams." De Gaulle gave them the illusion of victory after World War II and pride of place among the conquerors of Germany (by becoming a Security Council member) when France had been defeated. After founding the Fifth Republic in 1958 and establishing a presidential form of government verging on monarchy, he too set France apart from NATO, apart from "the Anglo-Saxons" and even, in important ways, apart from Europe, though ironically, France is among the founders of the European Union. Though the General often talked of a like-minded Europe "from the Atlantic to the Urals," he helped create the Common Market (now European Union) largely in order to control West Germany. From the visionary Jean Monnet's day on, the E.C.'s chief purpose was to bind French and Germans so tightly together economically that war would become unthinkable. In exchange, Paris would support West German interests in international councils where measures proposed by Bonn might not sound *"Teutonically threatening."*

THE GERMAN FEAR

Although relationship before France and Germany remains cordial but the French still fear a larger, unified Germany, raising some worst nightmares of an old nemesis reborn. During the centuries when Germany was fragmented into kingdoms, free cities, and principalities, France was safe. The two times in modern history when Germans ventured to consolidate – under Bismarck and Hitler – France was overrun. Apprehensions today do not envisage anything so dire as a panzer plunge through the Ardennes, but the French do not trust Germany with money, industry and technology. Germany under woman chancellor Angela Merkel (2006) is far too different from the blood-letting maniac like Hitler. Even the famous *"civilizing mission"* to the rest of the world has come under question. French policy toward the Arab world sank practically in the Gulf crisis and Iraq war in 2003 which Paris opposed and which the US won with the UK. An ex-ambassador with close links to the Socialists says. "For, most of our statesmen, whether they belonged to the left or the right, France was always strong, feared, respected, admired and envied – until the Iraq War taught us otherwise". A conservative commentator laments in his book *Is God Still French?* "We are no longer criticized; worse, we are ignored".

FRENCH DELUSION OF GRANDEUR

The French have had many illusions, one of them is that they are revolutionaries although no revolution has taken place since 1789 when a handful of convicts, jobless wanderers, carpenters and political novices attacked the Bastille prison, setting off the French Revolution which changed the world beyond recognition. Bastille is not a fort now; it is a metro station where the tourists are taken round a non-existent fortress by the guide who scratches the ground to show the remains of the area where once the prison stood. Stones of the demolished Bastille Fort have been used in a bridge over the Seine *Pont de la Concorde* which has become a Bastille monument. It is only a fantasy which all Frenchmen love to remember on every July 14, *Bastille Day,* an equivalent to our Independence Day.

Charles de Gaulle, (1890-1970) President of France - A dreamer

A highly mercurial people, with pride in their culture, art, literature and cheese, Frenchmen love to say that they are a people apart, the French exceptionalism. Yes, in someway they are. Their Gaullist features, highly sensitive look, humility and misty depth in their blue eyes make them different from others in Europe, of which they are part. (France has in double measure all that the rest of Europe lack. In the beginning when God was distributing the bounties, it is said, France slipped into the queue twice). It is the biggest

European nation. However, it is not too big; it possesses enough people (about 58 million) and it had the second largest empire in the world next to Britain's. France has the rare advantage of good, solid natural frontiers except in the north from where all invasions have taken place. She has inherited the tradition of two rich civilisations; when the Mediterranean was in the Centre of the world, France was a Mediterranean country and when the source of civilisations shifted to the Atlantic, she became an Atlantic power.

IS PARIS BURNING?

"Jodi," Hitler shouted, smashing his fist on the table: – "I want to know – Is Paris burning? Is Paris burning right now, Jodi?" Hitler's Reich was to have lasted a thousand years. And, Paris was to have been its showpiece. Now, in the fury and despair of retreat, Hitler was determined to destroy the city. But it was too late in the day because the Allied had landed on the Normandy beaches and much of the German troops, stationed in Paris, were moved to the battlefield. Insurrection, lack of adequate troops, and chaos in the city made it difficult for the Germans to start the destruction of Paris. Maybe, the German officer incharge of Paris destruction, was emotionally moved and became hesitant when it came to destroying this beautiful city. It was August 1940. The Vichy Government Mayor Rierre Charles Taittenger, pleading with Nazi General Dietrich van Choltitz, pointed to the grey wings of the Louvre holding its green gardens between them in their cold stone embrace; to the right, the flawless symmetry of the *place de la Concorde* said: "It is always given to a general to destroy, rarely to preserve. Imagine that one day you may stand on this balcony again as a tourist to look once more on these beautiful monuments and say, 'one day, I could have destroyed all this, but I preserved it as a gift for humanity.' All generals are not worth a conqueror's glory but you can be one." Von Choltitz was silent; then he turned to Taittinger, his voice softer now. "You are a good defender for Paris, Mr Taittinger," he said. "You have done your duty well. Now, as a German let me make a history." And, Paris was saved. (It is quoted from the book: *Is Paris Burning*?)

FRANCE, A DREAMLAND

The French are thrifty and hardworking. The country has the most perfect climate in Europe and the most fertile soil, east of the Ukraine. France produces all the food she needs and almost completely meets her industrial requirements. More than 2,000 years ago, Julius Ceasar said: "France has all the nature's gift; it is a human organism with no unnecessary flesh and limbs

– all well turned and none superfluous." Despite all these advantages, the French have always been plagued by unstable political and social conditions. The homogeneity of the social structure could not ensure political stability. Revolution is a romantic concept and the French always had great passion for it although in all its practices, social and economic, they have been very conservative. The French Revolution did bring about changes, but for the worse. If Bastille continues to haunt the Gauls, it is because Napoleon sought to conquer the entire Europe for them which was an exciting idea for the French. After a time, revolutions ceased to fire the imagination of people.

The French Revolution was an act of middle classes of towns and the peasants working in the field who carried forward and suffered most in the violence sparked off after the fall of the Bastille Fort on July 14, 1789. Later, the revolution was taken over by the elite who handed it over to Napoleon, a subaltern from Corsica. Having succeeded, the revolutionaries proceeded to establish political institutions and traditions, leaving no room for newcomers. In order to ensure that each person has a share in the making of the Government, they adopted the proportional representation system which is a source of political instability in France. Political writer Gordon Wright says that an average size of a French political party is himself and his voters. Revolution has done no good to France; beneficiaries were the world. Rather, revolution has produced a culture of street protest which was evident even today (2006) when the entire people of Paris poured into the streets to protest against Prime Minister Villepin's move to change the labour laws. Villepin's plan was dropped and the Jacque Chirac Govt. suffered humiliation.

A SERIES OF REPUBLICS

The course of political development in France has been marked by a series of changes in regimes. Between 1875 and 1890, the average life of a French Govt. was ten months. Between two world wars, it was four months; since World War II, it was three months. Although the question of national identity has never been a question of political importance, the form of the Government has always been in dispute. The Revolution of 1789 was transformed into the plebiscitary regime of Napoleon. Following the overthrow of Napoleon in 1815, the monarchy was restored, though in 1830 popular uprisings led to a transfer of the crown from the Bourbon to the Orleans branch with some limitations on the role of the monarchy. In 1848, another revolution took place; first to restore the republic, then to restore the Napoleonic dynasty under the Emperor Louis Napoleon-II. This was Second Republic *(see National Indicators)*. His reign was terminated by defeat in the Franco-Prussian war. The *Third Republic* lasted from 1871 to 1940 when the French forces surrendered to Germany and a part of France was subjected to the direct rule by German forces and a part was ruled by Vichy France, a puppet state by Marshal Petain and his head of the Government, Pierre Laval. Vichy is a health resort spa town in south central France. During the World War II, it was the headquarters of the regime set up after the German occupation of northern France to administer unoccupied France; the regime functioned as a puppet government for the Nazis.

Eiffel Tower - An icon of Paris

FIFTH REPUBLIC: After World War II, the *Fourth Republic* was established in 1946 which suffered from chronic instability with 25 governments in 12 years before the Fourth Republic ended in 1958 and Charles de Gaulle, France's war-time hero was brought from retirement to become the country's leader. He introduced a new regime, the *Fifth Republic*. His domineering style of leadership was challenged in May 1968 by street demonstrations and strikes but he survived and the Fifth Republic proved to be stable. The Fifth Republic Presidents are: Charles de Gaulle (accession date 1959); Georges Pompidou (1969); Valery Giscard d' Estang (1974); Francois Mitterrand (1981); Jacques Chirac (1995). Despite the conflict and changes in regimes, the French Govts. did not abandon the original concept of revolutionaries and they continued to have the Declaration of the Rights of Man, universal suffrage, plural political systems and referendum as the guiding principles of the French political life. In working the political system, unchanged in spirit since 1789, peasantry and middle class played a crucial role. Unlike the working class which tends to put all eggs in one basket, the French peasantry distributes its votes among many parties. No wonder, there is no party in France which can antagonise the twin support pillars – peasantry and middle class – and still stay in power. And, these two classes sponsored the Revolution. Their influence on the system has been enormous. Having defeated the "royal tax-collector" (Louis-XVI) in the Revolution, they resisted taxes during the following regimes.

DE GAULLE ABOVE LAW: The first election was held in October 1942 and the three great parties to the Resistance, the Catholics, Socialists and the Communists, won equal seats in the Constituent Assembly but the Communists were first with thin margin. According to tradition and constitutional practice, the Communists were to name the premier and had first choice of the cabinet posts. De Gaulle declined to oblige them and threatened to resign his post as provisional president. The Communists relented and said in despair that constitutional provisions applied to all except them. A draft constitution was ultimately prepared after lots of squabbling in the Assembly. It was a hodge-podge of more checks than balances which placed a premium on instability of the Govt. At the request of de Gaulle, the make-shift constitution was rejected by the people in a referendum on May 5, 1946. A new Constituent Assembly was elected on October 13, 1946 and a new constitution was formally accepted, but in fact two-thirds of the people rejected it. Under this basic law, it was said, a bastard was born of an unknown father and unwilling mother and that spelled instability in France. On November 10, 1946, France's first Parliament under the new Constitution was elected. France began moving to extremes – the Catholics (extreme conservatives) and Socialists and Communists, extreme leftists. Despite the growing division, the three parties of the Resistance continued to govern the country. Thus began the *Fifth Republic* with de Gaulle as President of France.

In sum, the French political culture is republican, affected by the ***"myth of the revolution"***. The idea is that if things go wrong, the ultimate recourse to revolution is available. It is a political culture that stresses the distinction between public and private life; many French people would be averse to discussing their political sympathies to friends, let alone to strangers. It is a political culture marked by traditional loyalties, many of which go back to the nineteenth century. This culture is marked by nationalism, radicalism and by the membership of the Resistance group, of which de Gaulle was the leader.

QUASI-POLITICAL SYSTEM

The French political system is a quasi-presidential regime; the Fifth

Republic replaced the parliamentary system (Fourth Republic) of 1946. The Fourth Republic had been losing the support of the people for many years because of the inability of the Govt. to solve problems. The Fifth Republic was based on a written constitution, part of which had been amended since 1958. On the left, the Communist Party competed for support with the Socialist Party. On the right, the Republican Party combined with smaller centrist parties to compete for power. The authorities in France depend on direction of the President who is elected directly by the people for a seven-year term, and is the effective head of the government as well as the head of the state. The President appoints the Prime Minister. A government is then chosen by the Prime Minister who takes charge of the various departments of state. Ministers may address the National Assembly and its committees, but must not be members of it.

The National Assembly is elected for a five-year term (unless dissolved earlier). It debates laws and the budget. But its powers have been restricted substantially by the constitution of the Fifth Republic so as to provide greater stability than existed prior to 1958. If the government has a majority in the National Assembly, it need not fear defeat of its policies in the legislature. France is governed through a system of regions and departments, the responsible officers of which until 1982 were the prefects, appointed by and answerable to the government in Paris. There is also a system of local government to run affairs of local importance. The civil service is headed by a number of highly-qualified administrators, and these may change with the political composition of the government. But each ministry has a small group of administrators appointed by the minister to act as his "personal office", and these do change when the minister changes. The decisions of the French authorities are communicated to the public through the broadcasting networks, and the Press. In general, political communication is more restricted and controlled than in the UK; de Gaulle, Pompidou and Giscard d'Estaing all made blatant efforts to interfere with the mass media.

A COUNTRY OF MIDDLE CLASS AND PAMPERED PEASANTRY

There is no effective law to make middle-class shopkeepers pay taxes. The peasants are taxed on the assessment of their property which was carried out by Napoleon. It was a very generous assessment. The trade war between EU and the US started when French peasants resisted withdrawal of subsidy to their oil-bearing crops as demanded by the US. Normandy, once declared as barren heath, now yields a handsome income although at the "Napoleonic rates," so also the slopes of Midi, once a rocky area and now rich vineyards. As a result of special tax relief to middle class and peasantry, the state had to depend on printing notes to meet the ever-increasing expenditure. And, higher taxes on the working class which is constantly in revolt against the Govt. The birth of the Communist Party in France (and, consequently, *Eurocommunism*) owes its origin to this skewed tax regime. The revolution makers – peasantry and petty bourgeoisie – likewise made no allowance for the industrial age; rather they have been essentially hostile to it in many ways. They have denied industries their capital. By influencing legislation to perpetuate and strengthen their own position, they deprived the industry of the labour force. To protect agriculture, they periodically passed laws, setting up tariff barriers even against their own colonial produce from across the Mediterranean. These laws made French farming community happy and stable for generations. And, their agriculture non-competitive. No wonder, one American farmer feeds more than twenty people while one French farmers feeds only five.

Due to heavy stress on agriculture, industrialisation in France could not keep pace with the rest of Europe. Germany, a traditional rival of France, always depended on trade in finished goods unlike the French emphasis on agriculture. The amount of capital invested in French industries between the two world wars was only 27 per cent of that of Great Britain which itself was inadequate compared to Germans. No wonder, Germany took less than a month to defeat France, a trauma from which it took long to recover. When a nation is prosperous and there is an increasing flow of wealth from colonies, the rigid social structure becomes more rigid. But after the colonies became free one after other, the French began to show their feet of clay. It is said that Frenchmen will die for their country but they won't pay for it.

NATURE'S BOUNTIES MADE FRANCE A SOFT NATION

The sense of complacency came to Frenchmen because of the nature's bounties. They have within their borders a little of England in Brittany; a little of Germany in Alsace; a little of Italy in the Riviera and a little of Switzerland in Savoy. Everywhere, they have the best food and the most sparkling company. It is said that walking along Champ Elysee, one can see persons worth seeing pass by – painters, poets, politicians, thinkers, novelist and maniacs. Generations of luxurious living have made this great nation soft and isolationist. No wonder, they continued to lose wars to their tougher and alert neighbour, Germany. France had been invaded and beaten five times during the past 200 years. But, due to the resilience of the people, and the richness of the land, it bounced back to its shape. After the long and exhausting Napoleonic wars and a crushing defeat, France staged a remarkable recovery. Ten years after Bismarck invaded and prostrated the country in 1870, France was richer and stronger than before.

GLOBAL WARS & LOST COLONIES ALMOST CRIPPLED FRANCE

But it happened twice too often. After World War I, France did not snap back into shape. The wars ruined French economy. It was fought over ten of her richest agricultural and industrial areas. Furthermore, France had long been pouring its investment in Russia. It was for that reason that it intervened in the October Revolution of 1917 to throw out Bolsheviks. She failed and the French economy was never the same again. In the World War I, a million and a half of her able-bodied men were killed; four million were wounded and a million of them were maimed for life. Thirty years later, French buses and trains had numbered seats set apart for those crippled in the war. The French population, consequently, dropped by 16%. When the World War II began, the French recruiting stations discovered that they had fewer able-bodied men to enlist than in 1914. World War II was a decisive blow although hostility in France was brief, consisting of one month of invasion and defeat by Germany in 1940 and two months of counter-invasion by the Allies in 1944. In a shorter period, twice as many buildings were destroyed as in the previous War. In addition, the Germans took away a good deal of best plants and during the two years of occupation, German sucked out of France more than France could receive in reparation later.

A still greater blow came from her empire. The World War II fanned nationalism in her colonies. North Africa rumbled periodically from discontent. Madagascar broke out in open revolt for independence. Syria and Lebanon did the same and won independence. Rebellion on a large scale in Indo-China, France's richest colony, almost ended the colonial status of France. At one time, France had to keep more men in armies them in domestic industries and, consequently, she had to spend more on guns than on education. And that brought about ruin to the country. After the colonies became free, the trade flow dried up. French productive machinery decayed from lack of investment in renewals and a large part of it was taken away by Germans. The War nearly destroyed her other sources of income. The rich tourist trade fell off. Her luxury industry like cosmetics, perfumes and fashions faced stiff competition.

FRENCH MORALE DESTROYED IN WAR:

2.5 MILLION TAKEN PRISONERS

Mercifully, World War II did not kill more men relatively because the French never fought it seriously. But, the morale of Frenchmen was destroyed. Two and a half million of them were taken to Germany as slave labourers. The family, basic unit of social organism, was broken up. Those who stayed home learnt the patriotic trick to deceive the Nazis; the peasants developed the skill to hold back goods from market, shopkeepers helped thrive black market. But, it was difficult to give up those tricks after the war ended. In post-War France, it was said that all gears of society moved but they didn't mesh. The Frenchmen had lost all sense of belonging to a social organism demanding a certain degree of cooperation. It was every man for himself as never before. There was little faith in Govt. and still less respect for it. In the general dispersion of interest, the two great classes of the French Revolution – peasantry and bourouisie – became an obstacle in finding a solution to French problems. Peasants, in the war-time tradition, refused to deliver goods; shopkeepers refused to distribute them at reasonable prices and together they created artificial food crises. For example, the peasants, for a long-time, preferred feeding their grains to cattle because bread prices were low while meat prices in black market was high. French farms were stocked with grain but still the country had to import food from the US. Thus, the trade position weakened.

During the first year of German occupation in 1940, France was a weak and lost country. But when the War became global, the Nazis lacked labour and they began combing France for slave labour to be taken to Germany. The youth of France began moving into mountains with no higher motive than to hide. But as the number grew and the sacrifices had to be shared, the motive changed; they became dominated by the desire to re-make France. *"Get it out of mind that we are fighting a war; we are fighting a revolution."* In the name of revolution, the bell began to ring in the French mind and the 1789 tumult came alive.

RESISTANCE GROUPS

Those who had moved into mountains to save life became heroes of the resistance groups in the name of revolution. Selfishness and indiscipline, which had marked the French character before the War, disappeared. A commander of the Resistance group has written in his memoire that when he went to inspect the resistance troops in the mountains, he found the youths with sticks in hand to salute the commander and barefoot in the snow. The commander of the mountain troops requested the Allies to send shoes, *"...hell with shoes; we want guns."* When the commander pointed out to the two boys with guns, a sergeant replied: *"Three of them were killed the other day in the streets; if they are old enough to die, they are old enough to fight as well."* This was France in 1942, a divided, vanquished and weak nation. When the war became a revolution, all Frenchmen were fighting on the same side of the barricade. The myth of the French being revolutionaries worked wonders.

Perhaps the greatest achievement of the Resistance group was sinking of political differences and the adoption of a common plan for the regeneration of their ancient glory and power. All over eastern France, the partisan groups liberated their areas much before the Allied armies came. In much of the rest of France, their assistance to Allied troops was decisive. France came out of its liberation struggle with its honour washed clean and ready to begin anew. One very clear gain was the end to old corrupt bureaucracy and the birth of a new crop of leadership which led the country back to glory.

FRANCE, at a glance

THE LARGEST COUNTRY in western Europe, France has dominated European history ever since the Franks conquered the country in the 5th century. Its vast natural wealth and large population have enabled a succession of rules, such as Charlemagne in the 9th century, Louis XIV in the 17th, and Napoleon in the 19th, to create powerful empires that spanned Europe. Despite three bitter wars with Germany between 1870 and 1945, France emerged as one of the world's superpowers. Today, France is a leading member of the European Union, and one of the wealthiest countries in the world.

Medieval France

In common with other European rulers, the power of the French kings was always limited by the strength of local nobles. Despite this weakness, France became one of the richest countries in Europe during the 11th century. Major trade fairs in the Champagne region attracted merchants from all over

Europe, and trade and commerce flourished.

Angevin Empire

As a result of marriage and war, Henry II of England (r. 1154-89) ruled much of western and northern France. His vast realm was called the Angevin Empire, after the country of Anjou. For years, it was a threat to French unification.

Bourbons

Under the Bourbon kings, France emerged as the major power in Europe during the 17th century. The Habsburg-ruled Spain and Austria – enemies of France – were defeated, and all power was centralized under the king. Industry and commerce were supported, and France established colonies in North America and India.

Palace of Versailles

In order to increase his own power, and reduce that of the nobility, Louis XIV built this vast new palace outside Paris. Some 36,000 people worked on the building, decorating it with the best examples of French art and design. At the centre was the king's bed chamber where Louis received guests.

Prehistoric France

The first inhabitants of France were prolific artists. More than 20,000 years ago, they adorned caves at Lascaux and elsewhere with lifelike pictures of animal. They also carved likenesses of animal heads from bone, antler, and rock.

Roman France

Between 58 and 51 BC, a Roman army led by Julius Caesar conquered France. The new province of Gaul was one of the richest in the Roman empire. Trade flourished, and the Romans built many roads and bridges. They also started growing grapes for wine.

Franks

In 486, the Franks from Germany routed the last Roman governor of Gaul and took control, giving France its name. At first, the Franks continued with Roman customs, but their empire broke up in civil wars. The 8th-century kings Charles Martel, *Pepin the Short*, and Charlemagne restored order.

Renaissance France

Joan of Arc, who fought the English for independence, was burnt at the stake in 1431. During the 15th century, the French kings drove out the English, and united their country. They also crushed the power of the nobles. During the next century, the ideas of the Italian Renaissance entered France. New chateaux were built, and the arts flourished.

Religious Wars

The Reformation split France, with many Catholics becoming Huguenots (Protestants). In 1562, civil war broke out between the two sides; religious tolerance was agreed by the Edict of Nantes in 1598, but tension remained high. In 1685, Louis XIV revoked the Edict, and many Huguenots fled to England and Holland.

Golden Age

The 17th and 18th centuries were a golden age of arts. Royal support led to the founding of the Goblins tapestry works in 1602 and the royal pottery at Sevres in 1756. The nobility supported artists such as Watteau and Fragonard, dramatists such as Racine, Moliere and Corneille, the writer Montaigne, creator of the essay, and the fable-writer La Fontaine.

Louis XIV

During the long reign of Louis XIV (r.1643-1715), the power of the French kings reached its height. Louis believed in the divine right of kings to rule, and governed without parliament. He reorganized the army and expanded French territory. But his lavish lifestyle left France almost bankrupt.

French Revolution

After the defeat of Napoleon in 1815, France had a series of short-lived, weak governments. The restored Bourbon monarchy was overthrown in 1830 and King Louis Philippe lost his throne in 1848. The resulting Second Republic collapsed when its president, Louis-Napoleon (r. 1852-70), became emperor. In spite of these problems, France grew prosperous.

Revolution of 1848

In February 1848, Parisians rose up against their ineffectual king, Louis Philippe. A republic was set up, with Louis-Napoleon, a nephew of Bonaparte, as president. Radical reforms were promised, but in 1852 Napoleon became emperor.

Dreyfus Case

In October 1894, French army captain Alfred Dreyfus was court-martialled for treason, for passing military secrets to Germany. But a mistake had been made, and a campaign to free Dreyfus began. He was cleared in 1906, but the case split the nation between his supporters and those who refused to change the verdict.

Vichy France

In 1940, German forces invaded France. French general and right-wing politician Marshal Petain set up a government in Vichy, central France. This government collaborated with the occupying forces; opposition was led from London by Charles de Gaulle, leader of the Free French. Vichy France was occupied by the Germans in 1942.

Franco-Prussian War

Although successful at home, Napoleon III was no match for Bismarck, chancellor of Prussia. In 1870, rivalry between France and Prussia led to war, but the French armies were unprepared and were soon defeated. France lost the provinces of Alsace and Lorraine to Germany.

Modern France

After the liberation of France from German occupation in 1944, a Fourth Republic was set up to govern the country. Like its predecessor, it was weak and was brought down by the unrest caused by the Algerian war in 1958. Charles de Gaulle then set up the Fifth Republic, aiming to restore French prestige and prosperity.

Charles de Gaulle

Charles de Gaulle (1890-1970) trained as a soldier, rising to command an armoured division. On the fall of France in 1940, he fled to Britain and called on French people to resist German occupation. As leader of the Free French, he did much to boost French morale during the war. In 1958 he became president, leading his country until he resigned in 1969.

Algerian war

In 1954, Algeria, one of several African countries colonized by France, demanded that it be granted its independence. This led to conflict with the many European settlers in the country. The French army supported the settlers in their wish to remain French and waged a vicious war against the Algerian rebels, Algeria finally won its independence in 1962.

May 1698

In May 1968, students demanding more money for education

demonstrated against high defense spending. Riots broke out in Paris and elsewhere, with fighting between police and students. A general strike ensued, and de Gaulle's government was weakened.

Timeline

58-51 BC Gaul (present-day France) becomes part of the Roman Empire.

AD 486 The Franks take control of the country.

1337-1453 France and Britain fight the Hundred Years' War.

1589 Henry IV becomes first Bourbon king.

1643-1715 France reaches height of its power under Louis XIV.

1789 Revolution breaks out in Paris.

1848 After a revolution the short-lived Second Republic is established.

1870-71 Third Republic set up.

1870s Impressionist movement founded by Claude Monet and other French painters.

1914-18 France fights Germany in World War I.

1946 Fourth Republic established after World War II.

1958 De Gaulle takes power and introduces Fifth Republic.

1950s-90s France is a leading member of European Union.

NATIONAL INDICATORS - FRANCE

Area (including Corsica) 543,965 sq.km.; capital Paris; major towns Lyon Lille, Bordeaux, Toulouse, Nantes, Strasbourg; major ports Marseille, Nice, Le Havre, physical features river Seine, Loire, Garonne, Rhone, mountain ranges Alps, Massif Central, Pyrenees, Jura, Vosges, Cevennes, Auvergne mountain region; Mont Blanc (4,810 m.); Ardennes forest; Riviera, caves of Dordogne with evidence of early humans, including paleolithic cave art at Lascaux, the island of Corsica; territories Guadeloupe, French Guiana, Martinique, Reunion, St. Piterre and Miquelon, Southern and Antarctic Territories, New Caledonia, French Polynesia, Wallis and Futuna, Mayotte; political system liberal democracy; administrative divisions 22 regions containing 96 departments, four overseas departments, two territorial collectivities, and four overseas territories; political parties Rally for the Republic (RPR), neo-Gaulist conservative; Union for French Democracy (UDF), centre-right;

Socialist Party (PS); left of centre; Left Radical Movement (MRG), centre-left; French Communist Party (PCF), Marxist-Leninist; National Front, far-right; Greens, fundamental-ecologist; Generation Ecologie, pragmatic ecologist, Movement for France, right-wing, anti-Maastricht; population 58,330,000 (1996); population growth rate 0.4% (1990-95); 0.2% (2000-05); ethnic distribution predominantly French ethnic, of Celtic and Latin descent; Basque minority in the southwest; 7% of the population are immigrants – a third of these are from Algeria and Morocco and reside mainly in the Marseilles Midi region and in northern cities, a fifth originate from Portugal and a tenth each from Italy and Spain; languages French (regional languages include Basque, Breton, Catalan and Provencal); religion Roman Catholic; also Muslim, Protestant and Jewish minorities;

HISTORY

5th C BC	Celtic people invaded the region.
58-51 BC	Romans conquered the Celts and formed province of Gaul.
5th C AD	Gaul overrun by Franks and other Germanic tribes.
481-511	Frankish chief, Clovis, accepted Christianity.
751-68	Pepin the Short usurped the Frankish throne, reunified the kingdom, and founded the Carlingian dynasty.
768-814	Charlemagne conquered much of west Europe and created the Holy Roman Empire.
843	Treaty of Verdun divided the Holy Roman Empire into three, with the western portion corresponding to modern France.
9th-10th Cs	Weak central government allowed the great nobles to become virtually independent.
1337	Start of the Hundred Years' War: Edward-III of England disputed the Valois succession and claimed the throne. English won victories at Crecy 1346 and Agincourt 1415.
1429	Joan of Arc raised the siege of Orleans; Hundred Years' War ended with Charles-VII expelling the English: 1453.
16th-17th Cs	French kings fought the Habsburgs (of Holy Roman Empire and Spain) for supremacy in west Europe.
1562-98	Civil wars between nobles were fought under religious slogans,

	Catholic versus Protestant (or Huguenot).
1589-1610	Henry IV, first king of Bourbon dynasty, established peace, religious tolerance and absolute monarchy.
1701-14	War of the Spanish Succession: England, Austria and allies checked expansionism of France under Louis XIV.
1756-63	Seven Years' War: France lost most of its colonies in India and Canada to Britain.
1789	French Revolution abolished absolute monarchy and feudalism; *First Republic* proclaimed and revolutionary wars began: 1782.
1799	Napoleon Bonaparte seized power in coup; crowned himself emperor in 1804; France conquered much of Europe.
1814	Defeat of France; restoration of Bourbon monarchy; Napoleon defeated at Waterloo in 1815.
1830	Liberal revolution deposed Charles X in favour of his cousin Louis Philippe, the 'Citizen King'.
1848	Revolution established *Second Republic,* conflict between liberals and socialists; Louis Napoleon, nephew of Napoleon-I, elected president.
1852	Louis Napoleon proclaimed Second Empire, taking title Napoleon-III.
1870-71	Franco-Prussian War: France lost Alsace-Lorraine; Second Empire abolished; Paris Commune crushed; Third Republic founded.
late 19th C	France colonised Indo-China, much of north Africa, and the south Pacific.
1914-18	France resisted German invasion in World War I; Alsace-Lorraine recovered 1919.
1939	France entered World War II.
1940	Germany invaded and occupied north France; Marshal Petain formed right-wing puppet regime at Vichy; resistance maintained by Maquis and Free French; Germans occupied all France 1942.

1944	Allies liberated France; provisional government formed by General Charles de Gaulle, leader of Free French.
1946	*Fourth Republic* proclaimed.
1949	Became a member of NATO; withdrew from military command structure 1966.
1954	French leave Indo-China after eight years of war; guerrilla war against French rule in Algeria.
1957	France was a founder member of the European Economic Community.
1958	Algerian crisis caused collapse of Fourth Republic; De Gaulle took power, became president of the *Fifth Republic* in 1959.
1962	Algeria achieved independence.
1968	'May events': revolutionary students rioted in Paris; general strike throughout France.
1981	Francois Mitterand elected Fifth Republic's first socialist president.
1995	Conservative Jacques Chirac elected president. Widespread condemnation of government's decision to resume nuclear tests in Pacific region.
1996	End to nuclear-testing in south Pacific.
1997	General election called by President Chirac. Unexpected victory for Socialists; Lionel Jospin appointed prime minister.
1998	Protests by the unemployed. Law passed to reduce working week to 35 hours, from 2000. Far-right National Front (FN) held balance of power in 19 regions after March elections, and caused divisions within 'mainstream right' on issue of whether or not to accept FN support to form administrations.
2006	Massive Protest against new labour laws, introducing flexibility in service tenure. The Govt. had to withdraw the law proposal and suffer consequent humiliation. This has left Jacques Chirac, president since 1995, a lame-duck president, also because he was voted out on the EU constitution issue in a referendum in 2005.

"Being and Nothingness" is not all about Jean-Paul Satre but about the French mystery.

-The New York Times

40

France (French Republic)

France is the largest country in the European Union and the second largest in Europe. It has been a major power for many centuries. During the 17th and 18th centuries, France colonized much of North America; during the 19th and early 20th centuries, France built the third largest empire of the time, including large portions of North, West and Central Africa, Southeast Asia, and many Pacific islands.

France has border with Belgium, Luxembourg, Germany, Switzerland, Italy, Monaco, Andorra, and Spain. France's overseas departments and collectivities also share land borders with Brazil and Suriname (bordering French Guiana), and the Netherlands Antilles (bordering Saint-Martin). France is linked to the United Kingdom by the Channel Tunnel, which passes underneath the English Channel.

France is a developed country and possesses the fifth largest economy by nominal GDP and eighth largest economy by purchasing power parity. It is the most visited country in the world, receiving 82 million foreign tourists annually. France is one of the founding members of the European Union, and has the largest land area of all members. It is also a founding member of the United Nations, and a member of the Francophonie, the G8, NATO, OECD, WTO and the Latin Union. It is one of the five permanent members of the United Nations Security Council and owns the largest number of nuclear weapons with active warheads and nuclear power plants in the European Union.

The name "France" comes from Latin *Francia*, which literally means "*land of the Franks*" or "Frankland". There are various theories as to the origin of the name of the Franks. One is that it is derived from the Proto-

Germanic word *frankon* which translates as *javelin* or *lance* as the throwing axe of the Franks was known as a francisca. Another proposed etymology is that in an ancient Germanic language, Frank means *free* as opposed to slave. This word still exists in French as *franc*, it is also used as the translation of "Frank" and to name the local money, until the use of the euro in the 2000s.

The borders of modern France are approximately the same as those of ancient Gaul, which was inhabited by Celtic *Gauls*. Gaul was conquered for Rome by Julius Caesar in the 1st century BC, and the Gauls eventually adopted Roman speech (Latin, from which the French language evolved) and Roman culture. Christianity first appeared in the 2nd and 3rd centuries AD, and became so firmly established by the fourth and fifth centuries that St. Jerome wrote that Gaul was the only region "free from heresy". In the 4th century AD, Gaul's eastern frontier along the Rhine was overrun by Germanic tribes, principally the Franks, from whom the ancient name of "Francie" was derived.

The modern name "France" derives from the name of the feudal domain of the Capetian Kings of France around Paris. The Franks were the first tribe among the Germanic conquerors of Europe after the fall of the Roman Empire to convert to Catholic Christianity rather than Arianism (their King Clovis did so in 498); thus France obtained the title "Eldest daughter of the Church" (*La fille ainée de l'Église*), and the French would adopt this as justification for calling themselves "the Most Christian Kingdom of France". Existence as a separate entity began with the Treaty of Verdun (843), with the division of Charlemagne's Carolingian Empire into East Francia, Middle Francia and Western Francia. Western Francia approximated the area occupied by modern France and was the precursor to modern France.

MONARCHY TO REPUBLIC

The monarchy ruled France until the French Revolution, in 1789. Louis XVI and his wife, Marie Antoinette, were executed (in 1793), along with thousands of other French citizens. After a series of short-lived governmental schemes, Napoleon Bonaparte seized control of the Republic in 1799, making himself First Consul, and later Emperor of what is now known as the First Empire (1804–1814). In the course of several wars, his armies conquered most of continental Europe, with members of the Bonaparte family being appointed as monarchs of newly established kingdoms.

Following Napoleon's final defeat in 1815 at the Battle of Waterloo, the French monarchy was re-established, but with new constitutional limitations.

Versaille Palace, near Paris, where peace treaty was signed, ending World War I.

In 1830, a civil uprising established the constitutional July Monarchy, which lasted until 1848. The short-lived Second Republic ended in 1852 when Louis-Napoléon Bonaparte proclaimed the Second Empire. Louis-Napoléon was unseated following defeat in the Franco-Prussian war of 1870 and his regime was replaced by the Third Republic.

FOURTH REPUBLIC

France had colonial possessions, in various forms, since the beginning of the 17th century until the 1960s. In the 19th and 20th centuries, its global overseas colonial empire was the second largest in the world behind the British Empire. At its peak, between 1919 and 1939, the second French colonial empire extended over 12,347,000 square kilometres (4,767,000 sq mi) of land. Including metropolitan France, the total area of land under French sovereignty reached 12,898,000 square kilometres (4,980,000 sq mi) in the 1920s and 1930s, which is 8.6% of the world's land area.

France was a victorious nation in World War I and World War II. The human and material losses in the first war exceeded largely those of the second, even though only a minor part of its territory was occupied during World War I. The interbellum phase was marked by a variety of social reforms introduced by the Popular Front government. Following the German *blitzkrieg* campaign in World War II metropolitan France was divided in an occupation zone in the north and Vichy France, a puppet regime loyal to Germany, in the south.

The Fourth Republic was established after World War II and, despite spectacular economic growth (*les Trente Glorieuses*), it struggled to maintain its political status as a dominant nation state. France attempted to hold on to its colonial empire, but soon ran into trouble. The half-hearted 1946 attempt at regaining control of French Indochina resulted in the First Indochina War, which ended in French defeat at the Battle of Dien Bien Phu in 1954. Only months later, France faced a new, even harsher conflict in Algeria.

The debate over whether or not to keep control of Algeria, then home to over one million European settlers, wracked the country and nearly led to civil war. In 1958, the weak and unstable Fourth Republic gave way to the Fifth Republic, which contained a strengthened Presidency. In the latter role, Charles de Gaulle managed to keep the country together while taking steps to end the war. The Algerian War and Franco-French civil war that resulted in the capital Algiers, was concluded with peace negotiations in 1962 that led to Algerian independence.

In recent decades, France's reconciliation and cooperation with Germany have proved central to the political and economic integration of the evolving European Union, including the introduction of the euro in January 1999. France has been at the forefront of the European Union member states seeking to exploit the momentum of monetary union to create a more unified and capable European Union political, defence, and security apparatus. The French electorate voted against ratification of the European Constitutional Treaty in May 2005, but the successor Treaty of Lisbon was ratified by Parliament in February 2008.

While Metropolitan France is located in Western Europe, France also has a number of territories in North America, the Caribbean, South America, the southern Indian Ocean, the Pacific Ocean, and Antarctica. These territories have varying forms of government ranging from overseas department to overseas collectivity.

The debate over whether or not to keep control of Algeria, then home to over one million European settlers, wracked the country and nearly led to civil war. In 1958, the weak and unstable Fourth Republic gave way to the Fifth Republic, which contained a strengthened Presidency. In the latter role, Charles de Gaulle managed to keep the country together while taking steps to end the war. The Algerian War and Franco-French civil war that resulted in the capital Algiers, was concluded with peace negotiations in 1962 that led to Algerian independence.

Metropolitan France covers 547,030 square kilometres (211,209 sq mi), having the largest area among European Union members and slightly larger than Spain. France possesses a wide variety of landscapes, from coastal plains in the north and west to mountain ranges of the Alps in the south-east, the Massif Central in the south-central and Pyrenees in the south-west. At 4,807 metres (15,770 ft) above sea-level, the highest point in Western Europe, Mont Blanc, is situated in the Alps on the border between France and Italy. Metropolitan France also has extensive river systems such as the Loire, the Garonne, the Seine and the Rhône, which divides the Massif Central from the Alps and flows into the Mediterranean sea at the Camargue, the lowest point in France (2 m / 6.5 ft below sea level). Corsica lies off the Mediterranean coast.

> French politics are characterised by two politically opposed groupings: one left-wing, centred around the French Socialist Party, and the other right-wing, centred previously around the Rassemblement pour la République (RPR) and now its successor the Union for a Popular Movement (UMP). The executive branch is currently composed mostly of the UMP.

France's total land area, with its overseas departments and territories (excluding Adélie Land), is 674,843 square kilometres (260,558 sq mi), 0.45% of the total land area on Earth. However, France possesses the second-largest Exclusive Economic Zone (EEZ) in the world, covering 11,035,000 square kilometres (4,260,000 sq mi), approximately 8% of the total surface of all the EEZs of the world, just behind the United States (11,351,000 km² / 4,383,000 sq mi) and ahead of Australia (8,232,000 km² / 3,178,000 sq mi).

Metropolitan France is situated between 41° and 51° North, on the western edge of Europe, and thus lies within the northern temperate zone. The north and northwest have a temperate climate, while a combination of maritime influences, latitude and altitude produce a varied climate in the rest of Metropolitan France. In the south-east a Mediterranean climate prevails. In the west, the climate is predominantly oceanic with a high level of rainfall, mild winters and cool to warm summers. Inland the climate becomes more continental with hot, stormy summers, colder winters and less rain. The climate of the Alps and other mountainous regions is mainly alpine, with the number of days with temperatures below freezing over 150 per year and snow cover lasting for up to six months.

FIFTH REPUBLIC

The French Republic is a unitary semi-presidential republic with strong democratic traditions. The constitution of the Fifth Republic was approved by referendum on 28 September 1958. It greatly strengthened the authority of the executive in relation to parliament. The executive branch itself has two leaders: the President of the Republic, currently Nicolas Sarkozy, who is head of state and is elected directly by universal adult suffrage for a 5-year term (formerly 7 years), and the Government, led by the president-appointed Prime Minister, currently François Fillon.

The French parliament is a bicameral legislature comprising a National Assembly (*Assemblée Nationale*) and a Senate. The National Assembly deputies represent local constituencies and are directly elected for 5-year terms. The Assembly has the power to dismiss the cabinet, and thus the majority in the Assembly determines the choice of government. Senators are chosen by an electoral college for 6-year terms (originally 9-year terms), and one half of the seats are submitted to election every 3 years starting in September 2008. The Senate's legislative powers are limited; in the event of disagreement between the two chambers, the National Assembly has the final say, except for constitutional laws and *lois organiques* (laws that are directly provided for by the constitution) in some cases. The government has a strong influence in shaping the agenda of Parliament.

French politics are characterised by two politically opposed groupings: one left-wing, centred around the French Socialist Party, and the other right-wing, centred previously around the Rassemblement pour la République (RPR) and now its successor the Union for a Popular Movement (UMP). The executive branch is currently composed mostly of the UMP.

CIVIL LEGAL SYSTEM

France uses a civil legal system; that is, law arises primarily from written statutes; judges are not to make law, but merely to interpret it (though the amount of judges' interpretation in certain areas makes it equivalent to case law). Basic principles of the rule of law were laid in the Napoleonic Code. In agreement with the principles of the Declaration of the Rights of Man and of the Citizen law should only prohibit actions detrimental to society. As Guy Canivet, first president of the Court of Cassation, wrote about the management of prisons:

Freedom is the rule, and its restriction is the exception; any restriction of Freedom must be provided for by Law and must follow the principles of necessity and proportionality.

That is, Law should lay out prohibitions only if they are needed, and if the inconveniences caused by this restriction do not exceed the inconveniences that the prohibition is supposed to remedy. French law is divided into two principal areas: private law and public law. Private law includes, in particular, civil law and criminal law. Public law includes, in particular, administrative law and constitutional law. However, in practical terms, French law comprises three principal areas of law: civil law, criminal law and administrative law.

France does not recognise religious law, nor does it recognise religious beliefs or morality as a motivation for the enactment of prohibitions. As a consequence, France has long had neither blasphemy laws nor sodomy laws (the latter being abolished in 1791). However "offences against public decency" (*contraires aux bonnes moeurs)* or disturbing public order (*trouble à l'ordre public*) have been used to repress public expressions of homosexuality or street prostitution.

Laws can only address the future and not the past (ex post facto laws are prohibited) ; and to be applicable, laws must be officially published in the *Journal Officiel de la République Française.*

SIXTH LARGEST ECONOMY

A member of the G8 group of leading industrialised countries, it is ranked as the sixth largest economy by nominal GDP. France joined 11 other EU members to launch the euro on 1 January 1999, with euro coins and banknotes completely replacing the French franc (£) in early 2002.

France's economy combines extensive private enterprise (nearly 2.5 million companies registered) with substantial (though declining) government intervention (see dirigisme). The government retains considerable influence over key segments of infrastructure sectors, with majority ownership of railway, electricity, aircraft, and telecommunications firms. It has been gradually relaxing its control over these sectors since the early 1990s. The government is slowly selling off holdings in France Télécom, Air France, as well as the insurance, banking, and defence industries. France has an important aerospace industry led by the European consortium Airbus, and has its own national spaceport, the *Centre Spatial Guyanais*.

According to the OECD, in 2004 France was the world's fifth-largest exporter and the fourth-largest importer of manufactured goods. In 2003, France was the 2nd-largest recipient of foreign direct investment among OECD countries at $47 billion, ranking behind Luxembourg (where foreign direct investment was essentially monetary transfers to banks located in that country) but above the United States ($39.9 billion), the United Kingdom ($14.6 billion), Germany ($12.9 billion), or Japan ($6.3 billion). In the same year, French companies invested $57.3 billion outside of France, ranking France as the second most important outward direct investor in the OECD, behind the United States ($173.8 billion), and ahead of the United Kingdom ($55.3 billion), Japan ($28.8 billion) and Germany ($2.6 billion).

France is also the most energy independent Western country due to heavy investment in nuclear power (Nuclear power in France), which also makes France the smallest producer of carbon dioxide among the seven most industrialized countries in the world. As a result of large investments in nuclear technology, most of the electricity produced in the country is generated by 59 nuclear power plants (78% in 2006, up from only 8% in 1973, 24% in 1980, and 75% in 1990). In this context, renewable energies (see the power cooperative Enercoop) are having difficulties taking off the ground.

Large tracts of fertile land, the application of modern technology, and EU subsidies have combined to make France the leading agricultural producer and exporter in Europe. Wheat, poultry, dairy, beef, and pork, as well as an internationally recognised foodstuff and wine industry are primary French agricultural exports. EU agriculture subsidies to France total almost $14 billion. Since the end of the Second World War the government made efforts to integrate more and more with Germany, both economically and politically. Today the two countries form what is often referred to as the "core" countries in favour of greater integration of the European Union.

The French GDP per capita is similar to the GDP per capita of other comparable European countries such as Germany and the United Kingdom, and is 30% below the US level. GDP per capita is determined by (i) productivity per hour worked, which in France is the highest of the G8 countries in 2005, according to the OECD, (ii) the number of hours worked, which is one the lowest of developed countries, and (iii) the employment rate. France has one of the lowest 15–64 years employment rates of the OECD countries: in 2004, only 68.8% of the French population aged 15–64 years were in employment, compared to 80.0% in Japan, 78.9% in the UK, 77.2% in the US, and 71.0% in Germany.

This gap is due to the very low employment rates at both age extremes: the employment rate of people aged 55–64 was 38,3% in 2007, compared to 46,6% in the EU15; for the 15–24 years old, the employment rate was 31,5%

in 2007, compared to 37,2% in EU25. These low employment rates are explained by the high minimum wages which prevent low productivity workers – such as young people – from easily entering the labour market, ineffective university curricula that fail to prepare students adequately for the labour market, and, concerning the older workers, restrictive legislation on work and incentives for premature retirement.

FROZEN POPULATION GROWTH

With an estimated population of 65.1 million people, France is the 19th most populous country in the world. France's largest cities are Paris, Marseille, Lyon, Lille, Toulouse, Nice, and Nantes. In 2003, France's natural population growth (excluding immigration) was responsible for almost all natural population growth in the European Union. In 2004, population growth was 0.68% and then in 2005 birth and fertility rates continued to increase. The natural increase of births over deaths rose to 299,800 in 2006. The total fertility rate rose to 2.02 in 2008, from 1.88 in 2002.

In 2004, a total of 140,033 people immigrated to France. Of them, 90,250 were from Africa and 13,710 from Europe. In 2005, immigration level fell slightly to 135,890. France is an ethnically diverse nation. According to the French National Institute for Statistics and Economic Studies, it has an estimated 4.9 million foreign-born immigrants, of which 2 million have acquired French citizenship. France is the leading asylum destination in Western Europe with an estimated 50,000 applications in 2005 (a 15% decrease from 2004). The European Union allows free movement between the member states. While Ireland did not impose restrictions, France put in place controls to curb Eastern European migration.

A perennial political issue concerns rural depopulation. Over the period 1960-1999 fifteen rural *départements* experienced a decline in population. In the most extreme case, the population of Creuse fell by 24%.

According to Article 2 of the Constitution, French is the sole official language of France since 1992. This makes France the only Western European nation (excluding microstates) to have only one officially recognised language. However, 77 regional languages are also spoken, in metropolitan France as well as in the overseas departments and territories. Until recently, the French government and state school system discouraged the use of any of these languages, but they are now taught to varying degrees at some schools. Other languages, such as Portuguese, Italian, Maghrebi Arabic and several Berber languages are spoken by immigrants.

"Bliss was it in that dawn to be alive,
But to be young was very heaven !"
– Wordsworth

41

World benefited from Revolution while France suffered it alone

The French Revolution was the first major social movement for ideas as abstract as liberty, equality and fraternity which later caught up across the world and many social movements had been launched to promote these ideals. The Revolution, however, caused huge sufferings to the French people while the world benefited from it immensely.

Between 1789 and 1799, when the Revolution lasted, France witnessed events which toppled monarchy, created a republic, ended feudalism and produced a Charter of Human Rights amid turmoil of mob rule, and the guillotine. Most institutions of freedom and human rights that we have today have their origin in the French Revolution, after which the world was never the same again.

In 1789, a political upheaval began in France that changed the face of Europe. Some contemporaries regarded it with admiration: "It was the greatest event that ever happened in the world" declared the English politician Charles James Fox. Others looked upon it with horror; for, although it swept away entrenched privileges and injustice, it ushered onto the political stage the intimidation, ideological struggles and ruthless killing. English poet William Wordsworth says it was blissful at *"that dawn to be alive."* Edmund Burke denounced the *Rights of Man* as a "monstrous doctrine" that "endangered every nation in Europe." Catherine the Great frowned: "Better the foolishness of one ruler than the madness of many." Russia, like France, much later subjected her revolution of 1917, to painful re-examination. "We are not going to hide that the Revolution denied what it approved," said Jean-Noel Jeanneney. "We shall not try to explain what went wrong. Nor are we interested in a chauvinistic celebration. We're not praising the Terror of 1793-94. We hail 1789 and its

Declaration of the Rights of Man – the year when so much good emerged for France and the world" says Jeanneney, Director Bicentennial Mission. A contemporary French writer, when asked to comment on the Revolution, said: "*We have survived.*"

The revolutionary leader Georges Danton who was fond of boasting that he had been responsible for the overthrow of the French monarchy. He was beheaded at the guillotine.

The sequence of events leading to the French Revolution began with Louis XVI's announcement that the States-General, (French Assembly), would meet on May 5, 1789, for the first time in 175 years. The king summoned the assembly because his treasury was empty and he hoped to persuade the delegates to grant him funds. The peasantry could no longer raise enough revenue to support the government, specially in the wars against England. Lafayette, a marquis from the rural Auvergne, played the key-role. He wrote to George Washington: "I persuaded Parliament to begin with a Declaration of Rights, consonant with the most perfect principles of Natural Rights" based on the doctrine set out by his American friend Thomas Jefferson in his Declaration of Independence.

On August 26, 1789, the Assembly adopted the landmark Declaration of the *Rights of Man and of the Citizen.* It proclaimed that laws were the expression of Rousseau's General Will and that all men are born equal in the eyes of the law and in opportunity and have rights to liberty, property, security, and resistance to oppression. They have also freedom of opinion, religion, speech, writing, and are taxed according to capacity to pay. And they are presumed innocent until proved guilty. This idealism, born of the Enlightenment, became a beacon that shines down the centuries.

SAYS ROUSSEAU

"Men are born free and equal in rights." Like the U.S. Declaration of Independence, this keystone of the Declaration of the Rights of Man and of the Citizen – adopted by the Assembly in August 1789 – reflects the influence of philosopher Jean-Jacques Rousseau (1712-1778).

FISHERWOMEN AND WANDERERS CAPTURED THE KING

Bastille Fort, the fall of which sparked off the French Revolution

In Paris, angered that the king brought in troops instead of food, a crowd of women – fisherwomen and stall-keepers, harlots and wanderers of Paris – streamed toward Versailles, 6,000 in number armed with pikes, cudgels, and scythes. Milling around the palace gates, demanding bread, they shouted for *"the baker"* and *"the baker's wife"* – the king and queen, who famously (as widely believed) said, "If there is no bread, ask them to eat cake." Next morning, October 6, 1789, the crowds found a side gate open and burst into the palace. Waving the heads of two guards on pikes, they captured the royal family and put them in the Tuileries Palace where they could keep an eye on them. Parisian mobs ensured that Louis XVI would never see Versailles again. The king made an attempt to escape, but the royal carriage was intercepted and the royal family was brought back in disgrace. The Assembly completed its long deliberations on a constitution. Attempts were made during 1787 to reform state finances and the tax system, but the privileged classes demanded constitutional reform against the government's attempts to break their immunity from taxation. With the calling of Assembly (States-General), these attempts were abandoned and the Swiss banker Jacques Necker, who until 1781 had handled finance by raising loans, was recalled.

FOOD RIOTS AND FALL OF BASTILLE

The turmoil was all the greater because the harvest in 1788 had been disastrous. Peasants were required to hand over money or grain to the owner of the land, to the Church and to the State, while speculators in the towns sold food at high prices. Bad harvests also provoked riots in France. Desperate people sacked food shops, assaulted grain merchants, hijacked convoys on road and river, tore down toll barriers that checked smuggling and hiked prices. Just days before the storming of the Bastille on July 14, 1789, furious mobs wrecked customs posts in the 18-mile wall surrounding Paris. Guards were called out to quell the riot. Pelted with roof tiles and stones, they opened fire, and in the fighting several hundred people were killed or wounded.

"LET THEM EAT CAKE"

All subjects of Louis XVI and Marie Antoinette were welcomed to tour Versailles if they were decently dressed and did not beg. The queen granted private audiences in her bedroom. On the morning of October 6, 1789, she escaped through a passageway to the king's apartment as a mob of women threatening to "make lace out of her entrails" burst into her quarters. Enraged by lack of bread and by rumours of the queen's indifference – the unfounded "Let them eat cake" retort – as many as 6,000 women had marched from Paris the day before. With Lafayette's National Guard desperately trying to keep order, they escorted the royal family back to Paris to live in the Tuileries Palace, next to Louvre. "We will not lack bread in the future," they told the waiting crowd. "We are bringing you the baker and the baker's wife."

Early on July 14, a swollen crowd burst into the *Invalides,* the old soldiers' home and weapons depot across the Seine, and carried away 30,000 muskets and five cannon. But they needed powder which was stored in the Bastille, where they converged. By the end of the afternoon, with 170 casualties, the old fortress was captured by crowds. They emerged with the governor of the Bastille, whose head they cut off and impaled on a pike. The prisoners they freed were four forgers, two lunatics and a debauched count imprisoned at his family's request. In the days that followed, delirious crowds would parade the streets with other heads on pikes, including those of high officials. The French Revolution was in full sway. This was all about the beginning of the revolution. Nothing was inevitable about the French Revolution. A striking feature was the unpredictable nature of events. The French are volatile, energetic, unruly people. There were lots of peasant and urban revolts under the *ancien régime.* The Revolution could have begun at any time. The date July 14, was simply incidental. (The French celebrate July 14 as national day which is like August 15 for India).

INCOMPETENT KING, EXTRAVAGANT QUEEN

Louis XVI used to be out hunting most days, when not drinking or womanising. The day the Bastille fell, he records: "You don't need a good honest man as king, you need a competent one". He was neither. The queen was frivolous, extravagant, pretty, and influenced the king to resist reforms but she was not cruel. Marie Antoinette was a spoiled child of Austria. Although well-intentioned, the king had neither the experience nor the ability to lead the State out of crisis. He had assumed that when the Assembly met, it would sit, as before, separately in three sections: clergy, nobility and *'Third Estate'* – commoners. But the Third Estate was inspired by thinkers of the Enlightenment who believed that the State should be run on modern, rational principles rather than by a privileged hereditary elite.

In the following months, the Revolution took a radical turn. Three representative leaders emerged : Danton, Marat, and Robespierre. None could inflame a throng more effectively than Danton. He was a giant of a man, robust, sensual and swaggering, outgoing and strong, *"booming, flawed, florid-faced man of the people, dressed like an unmade bed"*. No journalist called for blood more than Marat. The Swiss-born doctor, and scientist was described as a "sallow man with pock-pitted countenance, black flat hair, bloodshot eye and twitching mouth." He suffered from an incurable skin disease and could find relief only in warm medicated baths in a tub. However, no one was more effective in making himself the interpreter of "the will of the people" than Robespierre. Slight, squeaky-voiced, frugal, perfectionist, self-righteous, intolerant, sexually repressed, Robespierre dressed like a gentleman lawyer. As a boy, deprived of parental affection by death and desertion, he lavished loving care on sparrows and pigeons he raised in his native Arras.

The other development was the outbreak of war. Some politicians hoped that war would allow the revolution to go forward by spreading its principles across Europe. In August 1792, the French declared war against Austria, whose forces invaded France and threatened to destroy Paris if the royal family were harmed. The ensuing conflict, in which Britain, Holland and Spain joined Austria and Prussia in a coalition against France, threw the people behind the revolution in a struggle for national survival.

CONSTITUTION ABOLISHED; KING EXECUTED

The tempo quickened. The constitution was abolished and a new National Convention was elected. The enemy was now seen not only to be foreign powers; it was also the enemy within. Rooting out internal opponents was the job of the Terror and its weapon – the guillotine. The king was executed on January 21, 1793. The republic was proclaimed. France declared war on Britain. Spain joined France's foes. Making the war a crusade, the Committee of Public Safety, dominated by Robespierre, introduced mass conscription, economic mobilisation, ruthless centralisation, to crush evil forces, real and imagined. Meanwhile, taking his cue from Rousseau's *Social Contract* (the only true sovereign is "the will of the people"), Robespierre and his Jacobin disciples, such as the fanatical Saint-Just, attempted with increasing frenzy to create a new world in which good men, rid of the corrupting influence of aristocratic and ecclesiastic oppressors, will find happiness.

HOW THE QUEEN DIED

The Queen faces quillotine

"My father cried not out of fear of death," the 14-year-old princess wrote of their last meeting with the King. Her brother died in prison in 1795. Before going to the guillotine on October 16, 1793, the Queen cried: "My God, have pity on me! My eyes have no

REIGN OF TERROR

To the rumble and the thud of the guillotine, the *Reign of Terror* became the interpreters of "the people's will". As the condemned aristocrats, priests, young women, commoners, a general who lost a battle, women's rights activist Olympe de Gouges, Counselor Dupin, age 97, Charles Dubost, 14, the astronomer Bailly, first president of the Assembly and former mayor of Paris, the famous chemist Lavoisier, the young poet Andre Chenier, one father who had taken the place of his son to die – rode unsteadily, hands tied, in the tall red horse-drawn carts, crowds in the streets screamed insults and pelted them with rotten fruits. Some cursed back, others wept and prayed. The Duke of Orleans and the Marechale de Noailles remained impassive. The Girondist leaders sang *"La Marseillaise."* Madame du Barry, former royal mistress, pleads, "Save me, friends... I beg you!" Lucile, the 23-year-old wife of Desmoulins, pleaded with Robespierre to spare his friend from school days, a staunch Jacobin supporter. But Desmoulins had published his and Danton's view that the Terror should be moderated. Robespierre had him guillotined. Lucile soon followed. Amid the growing paranoia, the deputies who anticipated being killed, plotted to strike first. On July, 27 with cries of "down with the tyrant," they seized Robespierre, along with a hundred others. And, killed them.

Some people relished watching executions with women knitting stockings while people were being killed. In 11 months of the Terror, 300,000 were arrested, 170,000 were put to death, another 35,000 perished in prisons and in summary executions. The majority of deaths occurred in five of the nation's 86 departments (provinces). Like a genie released from the bottle, the Revolution's energies, once unleashed, were hard to control. Throughout France, the breakdown of old-regime institutions and the upsurge of radicalism created a political cauldron that gave opportunists a chance to seize power and institute reign of terror. The longest, most searing of the counter-revolutionary struggles ravaged the Vendee region of Western France. The Vendee is a county of small holdings contrasting with open wheatlands to the east.

THE BOURBON DYNASTY

The Bourbon is a royal house of Europe whose members have occupied the thrones of France, Spain, Naples and ruled several Italian duchies. The name comes from *Bourbon l'Archambault,* chief town of the feudal lordship of *Bourbonnais* in central France. Antoine de Bourbon became king of Navarre by marriage in 1554, and his son became king of France in 1589 as Henry IV. The last of the French line was Louis-Philippe, who abdicated in 1848. The present Bourbon Pretender to the French throne is Henry, Count of Paris. The Spanish Bourbons are descended from Philippe, duke of Anjou, younger son of Louis, Dauphin of France (died in 1711); he became Philip-V of Spain in 1700. The Spanish king, Alfonso-XIII, lost his throne in 1931, but the monarchy was fully restored under his grandson Juan Carlos in 1975. The Bourbons ruled France when the Revolution took place.

NEW REPUBLIC, NEW CULT AND NEW RELIGION IN OLD FRANCE

France was ruled by the Committee of Public Safety. Robespierre was the dominant figure from the spring of 1793 to the summer of 1794. A new calendar was introduced; a new religion was organised, the *Cult of the Supreme Being*. The Republic was made of the peasantry of Brittany and the Vendee because they would not accept the rule of Paris. When this conflict

was won, it was seen that the Republic was no longer in danger and the need for the Terror had passed. All men feared Robespierre, and he was himself guillotined in 1794. The killer was finally killed. The revolution began to stabilise. From 1795 to 1799, France was ruled by five directors of *the Directory* who ensured that there would not be another Robespierre, or by a two-chamber parliament based on wealth. It was a time of corruption. Royalist plots continued. French armies fought in Europe. As dissension grew, politicians turned to the army to maintain control.

COMES NAPOLEON

At the end of 1799, a coup by Napoleon Bonaparte toppled the government and established the consulate with himself as First Consul. Some scholars stop the story of the French Revolution here, considering Napoleon the consolidator of revolutionary reforms and codifier of French law. Others see him as the "Revolution betrayed" – subverting its humanitarian, egalitarian, and universal principles by bringing back the church establishment and the trappings of monarchy, and feeding his megalomania with blood drenched wars of conquest. Many consider this dictatorship, xenophobic nationalism, and imperial expansion a natural outgrowth of the Revolution. Napoleon considered himself *"a Revolution in boots."* And the upstart Corsican brought to heel most of Europe, "first in the guise of liberator, then as forger of chains."

The Revolution had its price. Economic historian Rene Sedillot added it up in his *Cost of the French Revolution.* "For two centuries, we have been living with a legend. Now historians are dealing with facts, not poetry." He details staggering loss of life (two million French slaughtered in the revolutionary, imperial, and civil wars between 1789 and 1815) and the destruction of art and architecture. In the name of liberty, liberties disappeared. In the name of equality, he says, the rich became richer, the poor poorer. This era set French industry 20 years back, shook the nation with inflation, took steps backward in women's and workers rights, suffrage, learning, the arts and sciences. Rival England pushed ahead in industry and world trade while France fought revolution.

And yet there's no going back from the Revolution: Many of its goals have been achieved through a century and more of social, economic, and political struggle, with France itself undergoing the pendulum swings of revolutions, monarchies, empires, and republics before arriving at relative stability under the constitution of its Fifth Republic later. In an era when revolution is talked about in terms of changes in science, fashion, communications, we tend to ignore the gains in political democracy, the personal rights and freedom that are our heritage from the French revolution. Replacing a hereditary divine-right monarchy with elected constitutional government that created a new society by *General Will,* an example was set for world change which became a virtue rather than a threat; the idea of progress a creed, fanning the faith that technological, economic, educational, and political innovation would bail mankind out of any dilemma, and that the good life could be legislated or decreed and drilled. Few modern regimes, no matter how dictatorial, fail to include "democratic," "republic," or "people's" in their official titles.

"The Legacy of the Revolution is still very much alive," said Jean-Noel Jeanneney, director of the Bicentennial Mission, headquartered near the Eiffel Tower. "A nation is rich in its memory. And the roots of the 20th-century France are its founding myth. I'd like all the youth of this nation to know its story – so full of passion and surprise. The French people shared the gains of the revolution with the whole world but suffered its consequences alone, says Jeanneney.

FRENCH REVOLUTION

IN 1789, REVOLUTION BROKE OUT in France when people rose up against poverty and injustice. The French Revolution swept away the power of the monarchy and ended the traditional social order. When the revolution began, poverty was widespread, the king was unpopular, and people resented the clergy and nobility. Following the formation of the National

Assembly, France was declared a republic, the king was executed, and, for a while, terror reigned. In 1799, Napoleon came to power, and the revolution ended.

National Assembly

In 1788, France ran out of money, and King Louis XVI called the Estates General, representing clergy, nobility, and middle classes. The Third Estate formed a National Assembly, seized lands, and drew up a new constitution.

Rights of Man

The National Assembly issued the *Declaration of the Rights of Man and the Citizen,* stating that "Men are born and remain equal". Women's rights were not included, but the ideals of "liberty, equality, and fraternity" inspired everyone.

groups emerged: the Girondins and the more radical Jacobins.

Guillotine

Named after a French doctor, the guillotine consisted of a wooden frame, with a sharp blade mounted on it, which sliced off the victims' heads. This killing machine was quicker than previous methods of execution and was, therefore, thought to be more humane.

Revolutionary Paris

The key events of the revolution occurred on the streets of Paris. Various political groups sprang up, such as the Jacobin Club, which relied on the Parisian *sans culottes* for support.

Storming of the Bastille

In 1789, angry demonstrators seized the Bastille, a prison that had been a symbol of oppression for many years. This act sparked a wave of rebellion. Outside Paris, peasants attacked the country houses of the nobility they hated.

Robespierre

A lawyer by profession, Maximilien Robespierre (1758-94) was one of the leaders of the revolution. He headed the Jacobin Club, and by 1793, was leader of the Committee of Public Safety that conducted the Reign of Terror. In 1794, he, too, went to the guillotine.

Marseillaise

From 1792, revolution spread outside French borders. A soldier composed the *Marseillaise* as a revolutionary marching song. Today, it is France's national anthem.

Timeline

1788 France bankrupt. Louis XVI summons Estates General.

May 1789 Third Estate forms National Assembly,

14 July, 1789 Paris mob storms the Bastille; French Revolution begins.

27 August, 1789 National Assembly issues Rights of Man.

October 1789 Women march to Versailles from Paris to demand bread.

1791 The French revolution inspires a slave rebellion in Haiti.

1792 National Assembly abolishes monarchy. France becomes a republic and goes to war with Austria and Prussia.

1793 Louis XVI executed. Counter-revolution breaks out. Revolutionary war spreads across Europe.

1793-4 Reign of Terror.

1795 The Directory, a more moderate board of governors, is formed and takes power.

1799 Napoleon overthrows Directory and takes power.

1798-99 Revolution inspires uprisings in Ireland.

FRENCH REVOLUTION 1789-99 - SOME IMPORTANT DATES

1789 May	Meeting of States General called by Louis XVI to discuss reform of state finances. Nobility opposed reforms.
June	Third (commoners) estate demanded end to system where first (noble) estate and second (church) estate could outvote them; rejected by Louis. Third estate declared themselves a national assembly and 'tennis-court oath' pledged them to draw up new constitution.
July	Rumours of royal plans to break up the assembly led to riots in Paris and the storming of the Bastille. Revolutionaries adopted the tricolour as their flag. Peasant uprisings occurred throughout the country.
1789-91	National-assembly reforms included abolition of noble privileges, dissolution of religious orders, appropriation of

	church lands, centralization of governments, and limits on the king's power.
1791 June	King Louis attempted to escape from Paris in order to unite opposition to the assembly, but was recaptured.
September	The king agreed to a new constitution.
Oct	New legislative assembly met, divided between moderate Girondists and radical Jacobins.
1792 Jan	Girondists formed a new government but their power in Paris was undermined by the Jacobins. Foreign invasion led to the breakdown of law and order. Hatred of the monarchy increased.
August	The king was suspended from office and the government dismissed.
September	National Convention elected on the basis of universal suffrage; dominated by Jacobins. A republic was proclaimed.
December	The king was tried and condemned to death.
1793 Jan	The king was guillotined.
April	The National Convention delegated power to the Committee of Public Safety, dominated by Robespierre. The Reign of Terror began.
1794 July	Robespierre became increasingly unpopular, was deposed and executed.
1795	Moderate Thermidoreans took control of the convention and created a new executive Directory of five members.
1795-99	Directory failed to solve France's internal or external problems and became increasingly unpopular.
1799	Coup d'etat overthrew the Directory and a consulate of three was established, including Napolean as First Consul with special powers.

A nation, like stardust, has survived because of the oversight of conquerors. Now, it is a heritage piece, more of a historical curiosity than a country.

42

Andorra (Principality of Andorra)

That a country with a "mohalla" population of a mere 60,000 people and without an army of its own has survived as an independent nation in a quarrelling continent is an amazing fact of European history.

Andorra is an independent principality in the southeastern Europe. Lying on the southern slopes of the Pyrenees Mountains, it consists of a cluster of mountain valleys whose streams form the Valira River. It is bounded by Spain and France. Much of the population is Spanish; a minority is Andorran. Language is Catalan and religion is Roman Catholicism. Andorra's independence is traditionally ascribed to Charlemagne, who recovered the region from the Muslim in 803 AD. It was placed under the joint rule of the French counts of Foix and the Spanish bishops of Urgel in 1278, to be subsequently governed jointly by the Spanish bishop and the French head of state.

Andorra had the feudal system of government which lasted until 1993, when a new constitution was adopted that transferred powers to the Andorran General Council, which is elected by universal suffrage. Andorra has long had a strong affinity with Catalonia (an autonomous region in northeast Spain) and its institutions are based in Catalonian law. The traditional economy is based on sheep raising, but tourism grew in importance since the 1950s to become central to Andorra's economy by the early 21st century.

During Andorra's 700 years, people lived in their six villages by raising sheep and growing tobacco. Then dirt roads were built in place of mule tracks connectiong Andorra with France and Spain. First, the people got ideas and had a "revolution" whose main consequence was the introduction of universal male suffrage to elect the country's 24-man parliament. When Hitler occupied France and moved to the Pyrenees in 1940, the revolution was promptly reversed and the vote once again was restricted to heads of families. By charging no customs, Andorrans imported goods from Spain cheap and then smuggled them across the French border at night, to be sold at a good profit.

Andorra is an isolated principality in the heart of the eastern Pyrenees around the Valira river which flows south into Spain and forms the only breach in the surrounding mountains. The landscape is rugged, with high peaks towering above deep valleys and gorges carved out by glaciers. No part of the country lies below 900 metres. The climate is alpine, but with variable rainfall. Winters are cold, with heavy snow usually blocking the only pass into France. Spring and summer are mild and sunny. Hardy trees such as pine, fir and birch have been largely cleared, giving way to extensive mountain pastures on the slopes where Spanish goat roam wild.

It has strong cultural links with the neighbouring Catalonia. Catalan is the main language, though French and Spanish are also spoken. Most of the population are Roman Catholic, and Andorra belongs to the diocese of Urgel across the border in Spain. The only large town is the capital, *Andorra la Vella.* In recent decades the population has been greatly swelled by immigrants, mostly from Catalonia, lured by the growing tourist industry and the promise of jobs. Immigrants now make up some two-thirds of the population.

NATIONAL INDICATORS - ANDORRA

Area 468 sq km; Capital Andorra la Vella (20,000); Major town Les Escaldes; Physical features mountainous, with narrow valleys; the East Pyrenees, Administrative divisions seven parishes; Ethnic distribution 25% Andorrans,

75% immigrant Spanish workers; Languages Catalan (official), Spanish, French; Religion Roman Catholic.

HISTORY

AD 803 Holy Roman Emperor Charlemagne liberated Andorra from Muslim control.

819 Louis-I, 'the pious', the son of Charlemagne, granted control over the area to the Spanish bishop of Urgel.

1278 Treaty signed making Spanish bishop and French count joint rulers of Andorra (through marriage the king of France later inherited the count's right).

1806 After temporary suspension during the French Revolution, (1789) the feudal arrangement of dual allegiance to the co-princes (French and Spanish rulers) was re-established by Napoleon.

1976 First political organisation, Democratic Party of Andorra, formed.

1977 Franchise extended to first-generation Andorrans.

1981 First prime minister appointed by General Council.

1991 Links with European Community formalized.

1993 New constitution legalized political parties, introduced first direct elections, leading to coalition government being formed under acting prime minister, Oscar Ribas Reig. Became a member of United Nations.

1994 Joined Council of Europe.

1997 Liberal Union (UL) won assembly majority in general election.

Yet another small enclave of a country with the population of a mere 30,000 people and without army which indicates how the balance of power concept worked in the stormy politics of Europe.

43

Monaco (Principality of Monaco)

This is a country which lives off stamps duty and gambling income, and also earns from "polite" smuggling of wine. The people live well and happily.

Monaco is an independent enclave on the Mediterranean Sea of the France-Italy border. The majority of Monaco's population is composed of French citizens, with a small minority of Italians. Language is French (official) and Religion is Roman Catholicism. Inhabited since prehistoric times, the area was known to the Phoenicians, Greeks, Carthaginians, and Romans. In 1191 the Genoese took possession of it; in 1297 the reign of the Grimaldi family began. The Grimaldis allied themselves with France except for the period between 1524 and 1641, when they were under the protection of Spain. France annexed Monaco in 1793, and it remained under their control until the fall of Napoleon, when the Grimaldis returned to power. In 1815 it was put under the protection of Sardinia. A treaty in 1861 called for the sale of the towns of Menton and Roquebrune to France and the establishment of Monaco's independence. Monaco, is one of Europe's most luxurious resorts, known for its Monte-Carlo gambling centre, international sports-car races, and beaches. In 1997, the 700-year rule of the Grimaldis, under Prince Rainier, was celebrated.

Monaco is in customs and monetary union with France. Until 1962, its tax-exempt status provided a haven for the world's rich to put their money, black and white, fuelling the town's prosperity. Taxes have since been introduced, though native Monegasques are exempt from income tax. Monaco is also a major international business center, drawing revenue from taxes from radio and television franchises and from state-operated businesses such as tobacco, postage stamps and the casino. And the chief industry is tourism

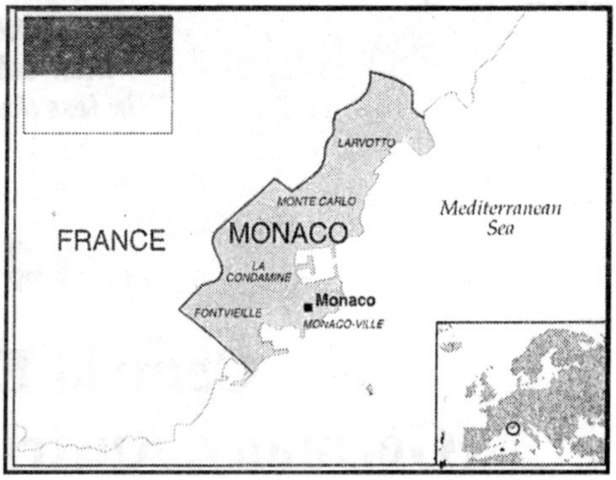

because of its location and climate. Monte Carlo contains world famous casino, a theatre that is renowned for its opera and ballet. It is also known for two international motor sports events, Monte Carlo car rally and Monte Carlo grand priz. That a country with only two km of area, smaller than a mohalla, makes world headline, speaks of ingenuity of its people. Although it has no basic attributes of an independent sovereign nation, it lives as a progressive political unit and is growing.

NATIONAL INDICATORS - MONACO

Area 1.95 sq km; Capital Monaco-Villie; Major towns/cities Monte Carlo, La Condamine; Head of State Prince Rainier-III from 1949; Political system, constitutional monarchy under French protectorate; Administrative divisions no local or regional government; Population 31,000 (1993) Ethnic distribution 58% French; 19% Monegasque (local); Literacy rate 99% (1985); Languages French (official), English, Italian; Religion Roman Catholic.

HISTORY

1191	The Genoese took control of Monaco, formerly been part of the Holy Roman Empire.
1297	Came under the rule of the Grimaldi dynasty.
1641	Came under Spanish protection.
1793	Annexed by France during the French Revolutionary Wars.
1815	Placed under the protection of Sardinia.
1865	Customs union established with France.
1918	France given a veto over succession to the throne.
1941-45	Occupied by Italians and Germans during World War II.
1949	Prince Rainier-III ascended the throne.
1956	Prince Rainier married US actress Grace Kelly.
1959	Constitution of 1911 suspended and National Council dissolved.
1982	Princess Grace died in a car accident.
1993	Joined the United Nations.

PERSPECTIVE

As many as 500 small kingdoms were forcibly integrated to make a strong Germanic nation which came close to conquering Europe twice in less than 20 years.

– Joseph S. Roucek

44

Central Europe (Germany, Austria, Switzerland and Liechtenstein)

Many kinds of terrain are found in Germany. There are Baltic ports and North Sea beaches, the Alps of Bavaria and the forests of Baden-Wurttemberg. Hamburg, in the northwest, is a famously liberal and outward-looking seaport with old British connections; Munich, in the southeast, is a model of German continentalism close to Switzerland, Austria, Italy and Czechoslovakia. The eastern provinces, so long stifled by communism, remain way behind other areas in development. In the Western provinces, the cult of materialism is at its glitziest and most successful.

In the very heart of Europe, lies a language – German – the language of Goethe, Schiller, Beethoven, Martin Luther, Einstein and Benz, and of Adolf Hitler. The energy of this powerful tongue, which inspires a particular loyalty among all who use it, has frequently governed the course of history and binds these territories together, not only linguistically but also in style and emotion. However, in one of the States of this Germanic core, Switzerland, three other national languages are officially recognised as well – French, Italian and Rominish – but then Switzerland, which is not even a member of the United Nations, stands outside every norm in its wealth, beauty and conservatism, as in its constitutional neutrality. Austria is also a state or country, being the rump of the once mighty Habsburg empire. And, Liechtenstein is a State only in name; for, its foreign affairs, defence, postal services and even its currencies are managed by the Swiss.

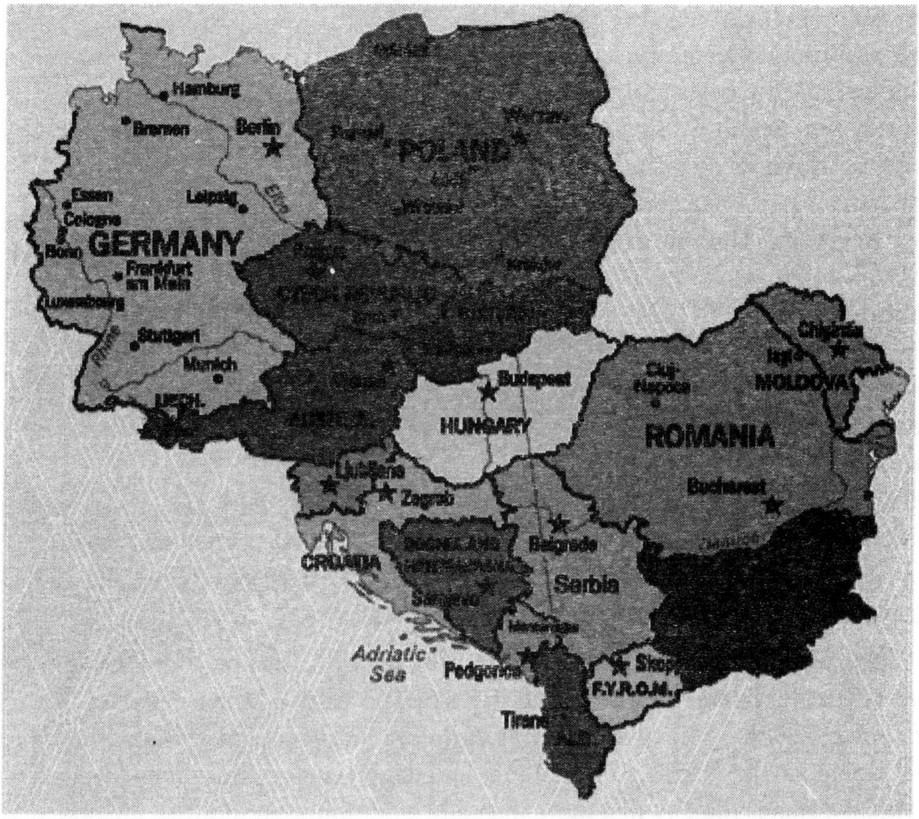

But Germany, the cradle of the language, has played a key part in the history of the last century and its status has become almost a metaphor for the destiny of Europe. In 1990, its two halves were reunited after thirty years of Cold War; this event more than any other seemed to carry the promise of a Europe reconciled; for, without a strong, stable and peaceful Germany at its centre, the idea of a united Europe loses its meaning.

Germany, however, is a newcomer among the nation-states, so also among democracies. Split for centuries into fissiparous principalities, disrupted again by the 16th-century Reformation, which later divided Europe, saddled by countless wars and dynastic settlements, Germany became a modern unified State in 1871. Even into the 20th century, Prussians, Saxons and Bavarians hardly recognized them-selves as being of the same nationality despite their common language. Hence, Germany remained a federation of disparate provinces.

Albert Einstein

Many kinds of terrain are found in Germany. There are Baltic ports and North Sea beaches, the Alps of Bavaria and the forests of Baden-Wurttemberg. Hamburg, in the northwest, is a famously liberal and outward-looking seaport with old British connections; Munich, in the southeast, is a model of German continentalism close to Switzerland, Austria, Italy and Czechoslovakia. The eastern provinces, so long stifled by communism, remain way behind other areas in development. In the Western provinces, the cult of materialism is at its glitziest and most successful.

The Germans have concerned themselves with Europe although their overseas colonialism was brief and limited. The work of their geniuses has, of course, become part of the world's cultural inheritance; Mozart and Freud are global in their appeal. But, their language remains European. And in Germany, stands the city that more than any other thing exemplifies the mixed significance of this continent. Berlin, standing at its epicentre because of Adolf Hitler, is a place of evil memory. Now, reunited, Berlin is around the Brandenburg Gate, with its tragedy, hopes and distrust. Backed by the wealth and power of Germany, Berlin, now capital of Germany, seems to be the natural capital of united Europe also. Or, so it seems.

The unification has cost Germany dear. Its growth rate has declined, so also productivity. Its strong economy was not strong enough to support the backward eastern Germany where people, during their Soviet control of 70 years, had lost the initiative to grow and heavily depended on state subsidy. That being not available easily in the united Germany, the former East Germans looked poor and deprived. Now, in the united European economy, Germany in unlikely to achieve pre-eminence that made it fight two global wars and suffer the consequences. And, its memory still hurts.

In other cases, it is the state which has the army; in case of Germany, it is the army which has a state.

– Robert Ergang

45

Germany (Federal Republic of Germany)

Conflict is built into the German history and geography. It is a borderless country with German-speaking people spreading all over in the neighbouring countries. Add to it the German philosophy, including that of Nietzsche, and it becomes easy to understand why Germans were the first to start the two global wars in the last century. And, they lost both and a generation of German youth perished in the battlefields. Some landmark events.

Geography has played a critical part in determining the course of events in Germany. The advantages of an insular position, so helpful to the British during the formative period of their national life, have never been enjoyed by the Germans. Traversed by numerous rivers and overland trade routes, Germany has always had the economic advantage of being located on the crossroads of Europe; but has often had to suffer for its central location by becoming a battleground in which non-Germans fought on soil and its own people fought one another. The development of political unity, long delayed by rivalries among the German states and by interference from the outside, thus, assumed a new and perhaps an exaggerated value in the minds of many Germans. The nationalism which the French had learned to take for granted, and the security from invasion which the people of Great Britain had always counted on, was not available to Germans. Nationalism had to be cultivated in Germany for the sake of strength and security and both nationalism and security were more talked about than achieved except by force.

NINE NEIGHBOURS AND A BRIDGE TO THE EAST

Being in the centre of Europe, no other European country has as many neighbours as Germany; the count is nine, including Denmark, to the north; the Netherlands, Belgium, Luxembourg and France to the west, Switzerland and Austria to the south and Czechoslovakia and Poland to the east. This central location also makes Germany a transit country both from Scandinavian to the Mediterranean and from western to eastern Europe. At the same time, Germany, integrated into the European Community and NATO, forms a bridge to the east European countries.

RHINE AND ELBE IN THE WEST AND EAST NEARLY MARK BORDERS

Some of the country's greatest rivers flow through the North German plain. The Rhine in the west, the Ems, the Weser and the Elbe – all flow into the North Sea. In Germany, these mountains rarely rise above 1,000 m (3,300 ft), producing slopes separated by fertile valleys. The rugged Harz Mountains, the northern uplands, straddle the east-west German border and some of the highest peaks.

Farther south, the main river valleys divide the upland belt into ranges. In the far west, the Eifel and Hunsruck mountains are separated by the deep river valley of the Moselle. The Rhine valley divides both these ranges from the Sauerland and Westerwald massifs. South of the ancient city of Koblenx, where the Moselle joins the Rhine, the spectacular scenery of the Rhine gorge separates the Hunsruck from the Taunus range. In the center of Germany are two massive volcanic plateaus – the Vogelsberg and the Rhon. Much of central-southern Germany is a low plateau divided by deep, winding river valleys. Most of the rivers, notably the Main and the Neckar, flow westward to join the Rhine which itself flows north and extends from the Swiss border to Frankfurt. In the south-west, where the Rhine forms the border with France, the rounded peaks of the Black Forest look across to their French counterparts, the Vosges. Farther east are the parallel ranges of the Bavarian Forest and the Bohemian Forest.

Germany's most dramatic scenery lies in the far south, on the border with Austria, where the Bavarian plateau rises toward the northern Alps. The area contains numerous high peaks, such as the Zugspitze, the highest of Germany's mountains at 2,963 m (9,720 ft). Lake Constance, bordered by Germany as well as Switzerland and Austria, is where the Rhine begins its long journey through Germany. The great river, Danube, (twice as long as the Rhine) rises on the east slope of the Black Forest. Germany's climate becomes continental, with colder winters and warmer summers, toward the south and east of the country. Rain falls throughout the year, and there is frequent snow in the winter; the driest areas are in the northern lowlands. The Bavarian plateau has cold winters but early springs, partly as a result of the *fohn* – a warm, dry wind that blows down from the Alps. The Rhine valley, protected by mountains, enjoys warm summers, relatively dry winters and plenty of sunshine. *(The Danube flows 2,820 km, the holy Ganga 2,506 km and the Rhine flows, 1,300 km.)*

DIVIDED IN FOUR AREAS

Germany can be divided into four areas: the North German plains; the central uplands; southern Germany; and the Bavarian plateau bordering the Alps along the Austrian border. In many places the Rhine, Elbe and smaller rivers have carved out a landscape of their own. Germany's two coasts are quite different. The Baltic coast is flat, with some low chalk cliffs and long, white, sandy beaches. The shallow North Sea coast has dikes protecting farmland reclaimed from marshes. Beyond its extensive tidal flats lie the East Frisian Islands and farther out to sea the rocky island of Helgoland. The German state of Schleswig-Holstein, at the base of the Jutland Peninsula, has coasts facing both seas, with the tidal western coast flanked by the North Frisian Islands.

The northern German plains are part of a massive lowland belt that stretches from northern France into Russia. Ice-age glaciers left ridges and depressions, notably in Mecklenburg in the northeast, which has numerous small lakes amid rolling farmland and wooded hills. Farther south there is another hilly stretch running from the sandy Luneburg Heath in central-northern

Brandenburg Gate, which once stood between east and west Berlin

Germany and continuing southeast toward the Polish border. Northwestern Germany is more level, alternating between sandy heath-land and marshy peatlands.

A region named Germania inhabited by several Germanic peoples has been known and documented before AD 100. Beginning in the 10th century, German territories formed a central part of the Holy Roman Empire that lasted until 1806. During the 16th century, northern Germany became the centre of the Protestant Reformation. As a modern nation-state, the country was first unified amidst the Franco-Prussian War in 1871. In 1949, after World War II, Germany was divided into two separate states—East Germany and West Germany—along the lines of Allied occupation. The two states were unified in 1990.

The English word "Germany" derives from Latin name Germania. The name "Germania" came into use after Julius Caesar adopted it from a Gallic term for the peoples east of the Rhine that probably meant "neighbour". The ethnogenesis of the Germanic tribes is assumed to have occurred during the Nordic Bronze Age, or at the latest, during the Pre-Roman Iron Age. From southern Scandinavia and northern Germany, the tribes began expanding south, east and west in the 1st century BC, coming into contact with the Celtic tribes of Gaul as well as Iranian, Baltic, and Slavic tribes in Eastern Europe. Little is known about early Germanic history, except through their recorded interactions with the Roman Empire, etymological research and archaeological finds.

Under Augustus, the Roman General Publius Quinctilius Varus began to invade Germania (a term used by the Romans to define a territory running roughly from the Rhine to the Ural Mountains), and it was in this period that the Germanic tribes became familiar with Roman tactics of warfare while maintaining their tribal identity. In AD 9, three Roman legions led by Varus were defeated by the Cheruscan leader Arminius in the Battle of the Teutoburg Forest. Modern Germany, as far as the Rhine and the Danube, thus remained outside the Roman Empire. By AD 100, the time of Tacitus' *Germania*, Germanic tribes settled along the Rhine and the Danube (the Limes Germanicus), occupying most of the area of modern Germany. The 3rd century saw the emergence of a number of large West Germanic tribes: Alamanni, Franks, Chatti, Saxons, Frisians, Sicambri, and Thuringii. Around 260, the Germanic peoples broke through the Limes and the Danube frontier into Roman-controlled lands

BASIC LAW

Germany is a federal, parliamentary, representative democratic republic. The German political system operates under a framework laid out in the 1949 constitutional document known as the *Grundgesetz* (Basic Law). By calling the document *Grundgesetz*, rather than *Verfassung* (constitution), the authors expressed the intention that it would be replaced by a proper constitution once Germany was reunited as one state. Amendments to the *Grundgesetz* generally require a two-thirds majority of both chambers of the parliament; the articles guaranteeing fundamental rights, the separation of powers, the federal structure, and the right to resist attempts to overthrow the constitution are valid in perpetuity and cannot be amended. Despite the initial intention, the *Grundgesetz* remained in effect after the German reunification in 1990, with only minor amendments.

The *Bundeskanzler* (Federal Chancellor)—currently Angela Merkel (2009) is the head of government and exercises executive power, similar to the role of a Prime Minister in other parliamentary democracies. Federal legislative power is vested in the parliament consisting of the *Bundestag* (Federal Diet) and *Bundesrat* (Federal Council), which together form a unique type of legislative body. The *Bundestag* is elected through direct elections, yet abiding proportional representation. The members of the *Bundesrat* represent the governments of the sixteen federal states and are members of the state cabinets. The respective state governments have the right to appoint and remove their envoys at any time.

The *Bundespräsident* (Federal President)—currently Horst Köhler (2009) is the head of state, invested primarily with representative responsibilities and powers. He is elected by the *Bundesversammlung* (federal convention), an institution consisting of the members of the *Bundestag* and an equal number of state delegates. The second highest official in the German order of precedence is the *Bundestagspräsident* (President of the *Bundestag*), who is elected by the *Bundestag* and responsible for overseeing the daily sessions of the body. The third-highest official and the head of government is the Chancellor, who is nominated by the *Bundespräsident* after being elected by the *Bundestag*. The Chancellor can be removed by a constructive motion of no confidence by the *Bundestag*, where constructive implies that the *Bundestag* simultaneously elects a successor.

Since 1949, the party system has been dominated by the Christian Democratic Union and the Social Democratic Party of Germany with all chancellors hitherto being member of either party. However, the smaller liberal Free Democratic Party (which has had members in the *Bundestag* since 1949) and the Alliance '90/The Greens (which has controlled seats in parliament since 1983) have also played important roles, as they are regularly the smaller partner of a coalition government.

MOST SKILLED TALENTED PEOPLE

Before the last War, it was not America but Germany which led the world in production of steel. Germany is, after America, also the most populated nation in the Western world. And, its people are most skilled, industrious and ingenious in Europe. Their ingenuity, combined with curious imperfections in their social development, makes them the most deadly soldiers on the earth. Twice they very nearly conquered Europe almost single-handedly. And, twice they lost in the wars only to rise again like a phoenix. Germany by virtue of its central location, economic power and the number and quality of its people, is the balancing factor which would enable any other power to dominate not only Europe but the whole of Northern Hemisphere. No wonder, the Berlin crisis of (1948-49) did more than anything else, aggravate the Cold War and start an armament race between the two superpowers.

500 KINGDOMS, MUNICIPALITIES, DUKEDOMS WERE UNITED INTO A MIGHTY NATION

For centuries, Germany was a patchwork of rival city-states, principalities and kingdoms that slowly coalesced into a loose confederation. The price of nationalism was high. At the end of World War II, Germany lay in ruins, divided between the eastern and western blocs. Between1945 and1990, the gulf between the two Germanys widened until the collapse of communism in Eastern Europe made re-unification possible. Germanic peoples living along the shores of the Baltic gradually migrated down into the lands east of the Rhine, the Carpathians and the territories north of the Black Sea. In the 4th century AD, the Germanic peoples were displaced westward by nomadic Huns invading from central Asia. In 410 AD, the Germanic Visigoths from the Black Sea region sacked Rome. The collapse of the western Roman empire had begun, and by 500 a patchwork of Germanic kingdoms stood in its place.

Most of these kingdoms were short-lived until the Frankish kingdom, comprising most of modern France and much of Germany was formed. Charlemagne (c. 742-814), the greatest Frankish ruler, built an empire that stretched from Rome to the North Sea and from the Elbe to beyond the Pyrenees. The empire survived until 888, when it was divided into the separate kingdoms of *East Francia* (modern Germany), *West Francia* (modern France), Italy, Burgundy and Provence (ancient province of France on the Mediterranean). When Charlemagne's line died out, the crown passed on, in 919, to Henry Duke of Saxony (c. 876-936) who became the first true German ruler. His son Otto I (912-973) is regarded as the founder of the *Holy Roman Empire* which united Germany, Burgundy and Italy under a single ruler, but by 1254 the empire was fragmented. In 1273, Rudolf-I (1218-91), the first of the Austrian Habsburg rulers, was elected to the imperial throne. With one exception, his descendants retained the title of Holy Roman Emperor until 1806 but the empire was never unified, under their control.

CHARLEMAGNE WAS THE GREATEST RULER

In the 16th century, Emperor Charles-V (1500-58) inherited Luxembourg, Burgundy and Spain. But the territories were scattered, disparate and often rebellious. Instability intensified as a growing movement for religious change – the Protestant Reformation – gripped Europe. An increasing sense of national awareness made Protestantism the focus of opposition both to the Roman Catholic Church and its champion Charles V. To oppose the emperor, the

Protestant princes united in 1530 to form the Schmalkaldic League under the leadership of John Frederick, Elector of Saxony (1503-54). The Peace of Augsburg in 1555 fully recognized Lutheranism in those states with a Protestant leader. Among the peasants and the urban poor, Protestantism inspired social revolutionary movements. In 1618 Emperor Ferdinand II (1578-1637) started a long campaign against the Bohemian Protestants, plunging Europe into the Thirty Year's War (1618-48). Over the next three decades, the region's population declined from 21 million to 13.5 million. The Peace of Westphalia (1648) recognized the sovereignty of some 300 German principalities and free cities, preserving the fragmented character of the empire. (see Treaty of Westphalia in earlier pages).

The weakening of the Habsburg empire allowed other leaders to increase their influence and power. The Hohenzollern rulers of Brandenburg-Prussia in the northeast made territorial gains along the Baltic coast of Poland. Under Frederick the Great (1712-86) Prussia began to accelerate its remarkable rise to military power. During his reign, Prussian territory extended from modern Lithuania to Magdeburg on the Elbe in the west. Prussia's

ALSACE AND LORRAINE

For centuries, control of the provinces of Alsace and its larger western neighbour Lorraine swung to and fro between the rulers of France and Germany. The two nations contended for the region's rich iron, coal and potash resources. Alsace and Lorraine remain industrial, but traditional heavy industries are giving way to chemicals, textiles and electronics. And the fertile land still supports the vineyards of Alsace and the orchards and grain fields of Lorraine.

Alsace and Lorraine were part of Roman Gaul and later of the medieval Holy Roman Empire. France acquired the territory during the 17th and 18th centuries. Germany annexed Alsace and part of Lorraine in 1871, after winning the Franco-Prussian War.

They were restored to France in 1919 at the end of the First World War, and a movement began for autonomy. After Germany annexed them again during the Second World War – and after 20,000 of their citizens died in the German army on the Eastern Front – the two provinces were content to become French once again.

Today, Alsace and Lorraine have become a symbol of European unity. Their turbulent history has created a region where the two languages are spoken more or less equally and whose traditions, culture, and architecture reflect both French and German influences.

As a gesture of reconciliation after the end of the Second World War, the Alsatian capital Strasbourg became the seat first of the Council of Europe and then of European Parliament.

transformation into a major European power was checked temporarily by the invasion of Napoleon's army in 1806. Austria was defeated by the French, and Francis-II of Austria (1768-1835) was forced to abandon the title of Holy Roman Emperor. In the following year, most of the minor German states became members of the French-dominated Rhine confederation.

CONGRESS OF VIENNA AND OTTO VON BISMARCK

One of the results of the Congress of Vienna (1814-15) after the defeat of Napoleon was the formation of a loose German Confederation of 39 independent states dominated by Austria. In 1834, a German "customs union" was formed, creating a unified inland market. Prussia, meanwhile, grew in strength. The Austro-Prussian War of 1866 led to Austria's expulsion from the Confederation, and the subsequent Franco-Prussian War (1870-71) finally established Prussian domination of Europe. By this time, the Prussian chancellor Otto von Bismarck (1815-98), had forged a unified Germany of about 50 nations, which began to build an overseas empire and a powerful navy to defend it.

Between 1871 and 1907 Italy and Austria-Hungary aligned against Britain, France and Russia. The assassination of the Austrian Archduke Franz Ferdinand (1863-1914) in Sarajevo by a Serbian nationalist finally pushed the two alliances into war in 1914. Germany's defeat in 1918 led to the abolition of its monarchy and the French occupation of the Rhineland, its industrial heart. In February 1919 a new constitution established the democratic Weimar republic. Its problems were considerable, compounded by massive reparations and boundary changes imposed on Germany. By November 1923, high inflation produced extremist parties. A brief economic recovery collapsed with the Depression, and in 1933 Adolf Hitler (1889-1945), leader of the National Socialist (Nazi) Party, became chancellor. Hitler's *Third Reich* soon threw Europe into the World War II. Dissidents were ruthlessly suppressed and millions of Jews and other minorities killed in extermination camps. The rest is the known history.

EAST AND WEST GERMANYS CREATED IN 1952

At the end of World War II (1939-45), Germany lost all territories east of the Oder and Neisse rivers, and was divided into zones of occupation by Britain, France, the United States and the Soviet Union. In 1949, the British, French and Americar zones were consolidated to form the Federal Republic of Germany (West Germany). The Soviet Union responded by creating the communist German Democratic Republic (East Germany). In 1952, the Soviet Union established a heavily guarded cordon of land along the whole border. West Berlin – an isolated enclave 190 km into East Germany – became the favored destination for refugees. An uprising against the communist regime in June 1953 was crushed by Soviet tanks. In 1955 the Warsaw Treaty Organization unified the military command structure of the Eastern bloc countries. West Germany achieved full sovereignty, and became a member of the North Atlantic Treaty Organization (NATO).

In order to stem the exodus of East Berliners to West Berlin, East Germany built the massive Berlin Wall in 1961. In 1968, a thaw in relations between East and West was interrupted by the Soviet invasion of Czechoslovakia, in which East German troops played a role. Cool relations lasted until 1970, when a treaty confirmed the existing German frontiers and renounced the use of force for political purposes. Two years later, a pact between East and West Germanys opened the door to cooperation. The 1980s, saw a slowly increasing wave of pressure for reform in the Soviet bloc. In 1989, a wave of demonstrations was followed by large-scale resignations in both national and local governments. In November 1989, the border with West Germany was opened, releasing a flood of emigrants. East Germany's communist government finally collapsed in the spring of 1990. On October 3, 1990, East and West Germany were formally reunited.

German Federal Republic (West Germany) was created in 1949 by the British, French and US zones of occupation after the World War II, and the Soviet dominated German Democratic Republic (East Germany) was created in eastern Germany. The federal republic became a sovereign state in 1955 when ambassadors were exchanged with world powers. As First Chancellor (1949-63), Konrad Adenauer worked to ensure the eventual reunification of Germany, and, hence, refused to recognise East Germany as an independent state. In 1961, the USSR started building the Berlin Wall to separate the East from the rest.

WILLY BRANDT PAVED THE WAY FOR REUNIFICATION

Tensions over Berlin began to ease in 1971, during the chancellorship of the Socialist Chancellor Willy Brandt with his policy of *Ostpolitik* – the opening of relations with the Eastern Bloc. This led to treaties with the Soviet Union, Poland and Czechoslovakia and one of mutual recognition and cooperation with East Germany. Economic recovery was assisted after the World War II by the Marshall Plan. Shattered cities were rebuilt, many millions of refugees from Eastern Europe were absorbed into the system of social welfare and health which provided social security. The Federal Republic joined NATO in 1955, and in 1957 it signed the *Treaty of Rome,* becoming one of the founder-members of the then *European Economic Community,* now the European Union. The pace of economic growth slackened, but the economy remained one of the strongest in the world, under a stable democratic regime. Following economic and monetary union with East Germany in June 1990, the *Treaty of Unification* was signed in August and unification took place in October 1990 under Chancellor Helmut Kohl. The first free elections were held in March and October 1990, East Germany was absorbed into the West to become a united country. A number of trials opened in 1992 involving East German politicians, including Eric Honecker, the former head of state. Extra measures were taken in 1993 to fund the restructuring of the eastern German economy, notably the imposition

THIRTY YEARS' WAR (1618-48)

The Thirty Years' War (1618-48) was a major war in central Europe. Beginning as a German conflict between Protestants and Catholics, it was gradually transformed into a struggle to determine whether the ruling Austrian Habsburg family could gain control of all Germany. Under the Peace of Westphalia the German states were granted their sovereignty and the emperor retained only nominal control.

1618-20 A Bohemian revolt against Austrian rule was defeated. Some Protestant princes continued the struggle against Austria.

1625-27 Denmark entered the war on the Protestant side.

1630 Gustavaus Adolphus of Sweden intervened on the Protestant side, overrunning N Germany.

1631 The Catholic commander Tilly stormed Magdeburg.

1632 Tilly was defeated at Breitenfeld near the river Lech, and was killed. The German general Wallenstein was defeated at the Battle of Lutzen; Gustavus Adolphus was killed.

Reich is German state; First Reich Holy Roman Empire, 962-1806; Second Reich under Hohenzollern emperors, 1871-1918, and Third Reich as a dictatorship under the Nazi regime, 1933-45.

of a 7.5 per cent *'solidarity surcharge'* on income tax and cuts in social welfare spending and unemployment benefits.

FIRST GERMAN WOMAN CHANCELLOR

Ms. Angela Merkel, a physicist, and leader of the Christian Democratic Party, was the first woman in German history to become Chancellor in November 2005. She is also the first from East Germany to replace Gerhard Schroder, the last of the post-War survivors who still breathed war rhetorics and was obsessed with German power. She is daughter of a Protestant Minister who took his family from Hamburg to East Germany when Ms. Merkel was a child. Helmut Kohl had discovered the political talent of Ms. Merkel in 1991 among those young people who came from East Germany's communist regime. He made her his Minister for the Environment and called her *Mein Madchen* (my girl): this was the greatest mistake of his life. For, it was Ms. Merkel who, almost single-handedly, removed Kohl from the leadership of his party after the election defeat of 1998, when it became known that Kohl had illegally accepted anonymous party donations.

GERMANY UNITED ON OCTOBER 3, 1990

Germany became a united country on October 3, 1990. At midnight the previous evening, the federal colours were hoisted in front of the Reichstag building to the cheers of tens of thousands of spectators. Celebra-tions were held all over the country. This was the end of German division. "Policy," the 19th-century Austrian Foreign Minister Metternich once wrote, "is like a play in many acts which unfolds inexorably once the curtain is raised. To declare that the performance will not go on and on is an absurdity. The play will be completed either by the actors or by the spectators who storm the stage." In German case, both the things happened. Germans mounted the Berlin Wall while the play of national consolidation continued to succeed.

On 27 February 1933, the Reichstag went up in flames. Afterwards an emergency decree was made and some basic democratic rights were quickly abrogated. An Enabling Act gave the Hitler-led government full legislative power. Only the Social Democratic Party of Germany voted against the measure and the Communists, who were thought to be behind the fire, were not able to present opposition due to the Reichstag Fire Decree. A centralised totalitarian state was established by a series of moves and decrees making Germany a single-party state. Industry was revitalised, with a focus on military rearmament. In 1936, Germany reacquired control of the Rhineland, the first of several expansionist moves to establish Greater Germany.

THIRD REICH (1933–1945)

GERMAN STATES		
State	**Capital**	**Area in sq. km**
Baden-Wurttemberg	Stuttgart	35,800
Bavaria	Munich	70,600
Berlin	Berlin	880
Brandenburg	Potsdam	25,900
Bremen	Bremen	400
Hamburg	Hamburg	760
Hessen	Wiesbaden	21,100
Lower Saxony	Hanover	47,400
Mecklenburg-West Pomerania	Schwerin	22,900
North Rhine-Westphalia	Dusseldorf	34,100
Rhineland-Palatinate	Mainz	19,800
Saarland	Saarbrucken	2,570
Saxony	Dresden	17,050
Saxony-Anhalt	Magdeburg	25,900
Schleswig-Holstein	Kiel	15,700
Thuringia	Erfurt	15,500

In 1939, growing tensions from nationalism, militarism, and territorial issues and a pact promising support from the Soviet Union led the Germans to launch a blitzkrieg ("lightning war") against Poland, which was followed by declarations of war from Britain and France. This marked the beginning of World War II in Europe. As the war continued, Germany and its allies quickly gained direct or indirect control of the majority of Europe.

On 22 June 1941, Hitler broke the pact with the Soviets and invaded the Soviet Union. The same year, Japan attacked the American base at Pearl Harbor, and Germany declared war on the United States. Although the German army advanced into the Soviet Union quite rapidly, the Battle of Stalingrad marked a major turning point in the war. Subsequently, the German army started to retreat on the Eastern front. D-Day marked another major turning point in the war, opening up a Western front; the Allied forces landed on the beaches of Normandy and made advances towards German territory. Germany's defeat soon followed. On 8 May 1945, the German armed forces surrendered after the Red Army occupied Berlin.

In what later became known as The Holocaust, the Third Reich regime enacted governmental policies directly subjugating many dissidents and minorities. About eleven million people were murdered during the Holocaust, including six million Jews. World War II and the German Nazi regime were responsible for about 35 million dead in Europe.

DIVISION & REUNIFICATION (1945–1990)

The war resulted in the death of nearly ten million German soldiers and civilians; large territorial losses; the expulsion of about 15 million Germans from the former eastern territories and other countries; and the destruction of multiple major cities. The remaining national territory and Berlin were partitioned by the Allies into four military occupation zones.

The western sectors, controlled by France, the United Kingdom, and the United States, were merged on 23 May 1949, to form the *Federal Republic of Germany* (*Bundesrepublik Deutschland*, or BRD); on 7 October 1949, the Soviet Zone became the *German Democratic Republic* (*Deutsche Demokratische Republik*, or DDR). They were informally known as "West Germany" and "East Germany", and the two parts of Berlin as "West Berlin" and "East Berlin". East Germany selected East Berlin as its capital, while West Germany chose Bonn. However, West Germany declared the status of its capital Bonn as provisional, in order to emphasise its stance that the two-state solution was an artificial *status quo* that was to be overcome one day.

West Germany, established as a federal parliamentary republic with a "social market economy", was allied with the United States, the UK and France. The country came to enjoy prolonged economic growth beginning in the early 1950s (*Wirtschaftswunder*). West Germany joined NATO in 1955 and was a founding member of the European Economic Community in 1958.

East Germany was an Eastern bloc state under political and military control by the USSR via the latter's occupation forces and the Warsaw Treaty. While claiming to be a democracy, political power was solely executed by leading members (*Politburo*) of the communist-controlled SED (*Socialist Unity Party of Germany*). Their power was ensured by the Stasi, a secret service of immense size, and a variety of SED suborganizations controlling every aspect of society. In return, the basic needs of the population were satisfied at low cost by the state. A Soviet-style command economy was set up; later, the GDR became a Comecon state. While East German propaganda was based on the benefits of the GDR's social programs and the alleged constant threat of a West German invasion, many of her citizens looked to the West for political freedoms and economic prosperity.The Berlin Wall, built in 1961 to stop East Germans from escaping to West Germany, became a symbol of the Cold War.

Tensions between East and West Germany were somewhat reduced in the early 1970s by Chancellor Willy Brandt's *Ostpolitik*, which included the *de facto* acceptance of Germany's territorial losses in World War II. In the summer of 1989, Hungary decided (May 2) to dismantle the Iron Curtain and open the borders (August 23), causing an exodus of thousands of East Germans (September 11) going to West Germany via Hungary. The effects of the Hungarian events had devastating effects on the GDR, with mass demonstrations. The East German authorities unexpectedly eased the border restrictions in November, allowing East German citizens to travel to the West. Originally intended as a pressure valve to retain East Germany as a state, the opening of the border actually led to an acceleration of the *Wende* reform process in East Germany, which finally concluded with the *Two Plus Four Treaty* a year later on 12 September 1990, under which the four occupying powers renounced their rights under the Instrument of Surrender, and Germany regained full sovereignty. This permitted German reunification on 3 October 1990, with the accession of the five re-established East German states (New Länder or "new federal states").

BERLIN REPUBLIC AND EU INTEGRATION (1990)

Based on the Bonn-Berlin Act, adopted by the Parliament on 10 March 1994, Berlin was chosen to be the capital of the unified state, while Bonn obtained the unique status of a *Bundesstadt* (federal city) retaining some federal ministries. The relocation of the government was completed in 1999. Since reunification, Germany has taken a more active role in the European Union and NATO. Germany sent a peacekeeping force to secure stability in the Balkans and sent a force of German troops to Afghanistan as part of a NATO effort to provide security in that country after the ousting of the Taliban. These deployments were controversial, since after the war, Germany was bound by law only to deploy troops for defence roles. Deployments to foreign territories were understood not to be covered by the defence provision; however, the parliamentary vote on the issue effectively legalised the participation in a peacekeeping context.

HISTORY MADE UNITY HAPPEN, NOT GERMANS

The Germans did not make unity happen: it happened to them. It was not the result of West German policy; rather it was the outcome of a fortuitous combination of factors: reforms in the Soviet Union, upheaval in Eastern

Europe, and, most of all, the determination of the East Germans. What started as an assertion of the democratic spirit against a dictatorial regime soon turned into a national uprising against division. "We did not goose-step in where angels feared to tread", said German politicians. In 1990, the West Germans were not embittered and embattled; they lived in peace with themselves and their neighbours. Their commitment to democracy and free enterprise, to social caring and the rule of law, were beyond doubt. And, they were not ready for fight for them because they were there. It began in 1871, thanks to Bismarck, Prussia's chancellor, and ended after World War II, a failed experiment with democracy (Weimar Republic), and the collapse of Hitler's *"thousand-year Reich"* in 1945. For centuries before Bismarck, Germany's division into small states was seen by other Europeans as a necessary ingredient in the continental balance of power. And, since 1945, the existence of two German states had been widely regarded in the same way. The western allies, America, Britain and France, had backed the cause of peaceful German reunification for decades. But their attitude, and that of Russians was ambivalent.

The year 1989 was quite about the time when Mikhail Gorbachev was shaking things up in the Communist world. And, this set off the process of unification which had been in three phases, beginning with Konrad Adenauer, a Christian Democrat, who became its first chancellor (head of government). In the first phase Adenauer took West Germany into NATO and into the then European Community (EC), arguing that only firm backing in the West would make reunification possible. But, there is no evidence to suggest that he really believed the country's unification would happen. As a Rhinelander, his instincts drew him more to the West. Hence, his special push for friendship with the old arch-enemy France than to Prussia in the east, for which he had no liking. "You can smell Prussia when you cross the Elbe," he once remarked with distaste. Adenauer's policies, especially rearmament and NATO membership, were attacked by opposition Social Democrats who thought that German integration with Western Europe would block German unity. They wanted a united, neutral, social-democratic Germany closely linked to similar states throughout Europe – east and west. Prussia, like Haryana in India, is a special cultural bloc and its people, again like Haryana, have different features, intellectually and physically very tough, aggressive and intolerant. Despite unification, Prussians united with the rest of Germans only by language. And, nothing else. They have also a different history and geography situated as it is east of the Elbe while most of Germany is west between the Elbe and the Rhine.

Adenauer was an admirer of eminent American diplomat George Kennan who says that it is a myth that religion and language are basis for unity. It was true not only of two German States, but of the entire English-speaking world which, in the past, had been at war with itself for power, money and more. India and Pakistan have common background, so also China and Taiwan, countries of Middle East, North and South Korea but they are locked in eternal conflict. This is to quote only a few cases.

GERMAN EMPIRES (REICH);

BLOOD AND IRON POLICY

However, in order to give a perspective to the story, we may go back again to know how it all began. The *First German Empire* (Reich) was the Holy Roman Empire (962-1806). The *Second German Reich* (1871-1918) was between the end of the German Confederation and the setting up of the Weimar Republic when Germany rose to become an industrial and colonial power. The *Third Reich* was the Nazi regime (1933-45). The German Confederation of 25 states was created by Chancellor Otto von Bismarck. The Prussian King became the first emperor, Kaiser Wilhelm-I.

The growth of industry between 1871 and 1910 made Germany the greatest industrial power in Europe, and the search for new markets led to tension with other powers. Bismarck won important allies in the *Triple Alliance* (Germany, Austria and Italy) and in the Three Emperors' League between Germany, Austria and Russia. After Kaiser Wilhelm-II forced Bismarck to retire in 1890, he let the alliance with Russia lapse in favour of Austria, and turned to Admiral Alfred von Tirpitz, to launch a naval arms race with Britain. He also plunged into colonial adventures which antagonised both Britain and France and led to the *Entente Cordiale* between the two countries. In 1914, Germany declared war on Russia and France in support of its Austrian ally's dispute with Russia over Serbia. By 1918, Germany had lost its overseas colonies, and the German people, long deprived of democratic reforms and starved of food during wartime shortages, rose in revolt against their leaders. Wilhelm-II went into exile, and the Weimar Republic was proclaimed by the Social Democrats.

By depriving Germany of the areas in which most of her alien population lived, the Treaty of Versailles practically solved her national minorities problems, although a considerable number of Poles and Danes were left within her borders. Dissident political groups, however, were more numerous than ever;

and the framers of the *Weimar Constitution* tried scrupulously by proportional representation to give all of them a voice in the government. It remained for the National Socialists (read Nazis) to focus attention, not for the first time in history but more sharply than before, upon what they called a "racial" minority, specially the Jews. Nazis said, they should be eliminated. All other minorities were to be "coordinated," or subordinated to the majority.

EU MEMBERS SINCE 1957

West Germany was a founding member of the European Community (EC) in 1957, which became the European Union in 1993. It is part of the Schengen zone and adopted the European currency, the euro, in 1999. Germany is a federal parliamentary republic of sixteen states (*Länder*). The capital and largest city is Berlin. Germany is a member of the United Nations, NATO, G8 and the OECD. It is a major economic power with the world's fourth largest economy by nominal GDP and the fifth largest in purchasing power parity.

It is the largest exporter and second largest importer of goods. In absolute terms, Germany allocates the second biggest annual budget of development aid in the world, while its military expenditure ranked sixth. The country has developed a high standard of living and established a comprehensive system of social security. It holds a key position in European affairs and maintains a multitude of close partnerships on a global level. Germany is recognised as a scientific and technological leader in several fields.

HOLY ROMAN EMPIRE (962–1806)

On 25 December 800, Charlemagne founded the Carolingian Empire, which was divided in 843. The medieval empire resulted from the eastern portion of this division and existed in varying forms from 962 until 1806. Its territory stretched from the Eider River in the north to the Mediterranean coast in the south. Often referred to as the Holy Roman Empire (or the Old Empire), it was officially called the *Sacrum Romanum Imperium Nationis Germanicæ* (Holy Roman Empire of the German Nation) starting in 1448, to adjust the title to its then reduced territory.*(More about it in other chapter)*

Under the reign of the Ottonian emperors (919–1024), the duchies of Lorraine, Saxony, Franconia, Swabia, Thuringia, and Bavaria were consolidated, and the German king was crowned Holy Roman Emperor of these regions in 962. Under the reign of the Salian emperors (1024–1125), the Holy Roman Empire absorbed northern Italy and Burgundy, although the emperors lost power through the Investiture Controversy. Under the Hohenstaufen emperors (1138–1254), the German princes increased their influence further south and east into territories inhabited by Slavs, preceding German settlement in these areas and further east *(Ostsiedlung)*. Northern German towns grew prosperous as members of the Hanseatic League. Starting with the Great Famine in 1315, then the Black Death of 1348-50, the population of Germany plummeted.

The edict of the Golden Bull in 1356 provided the basic constitution of the empire that lasted until its dissolution. It codified the election of the emperor by seven prince-electors who ruled some of the most powerful principalities and archbishoprics. Beginning in the 15th century, the emperors were elected nearly exclusively from the Habsburg dynasty of Austria.

The monk Martin Luther publicised his 95 Theses in 1517, challenging practices of the Roman Catholic Church, initiating the Protestant Reformation. A separate Lutheran church became the official religion in many German states after 1530. Religious conflict led to the Thirty Years' War (1618–1648), which devastated German lands. The population of the German states was reduced by about 30%. The Peace of Westphalia (1648) ended religious warfare among the German states, but the empire was *de facto* divided into numerous independent principalities. From 1740 onwards, the dualism between the Austrian Habsburg Monarchy and the Kingdom of Prussia dominated German history. In 1806, the *Imperium* was overrun and dissolved as a result of the Napoleonic Wars.

RESTORATION AND REVOLUTION (1814–1871)

Following the fall of Napoleon Bonaparte, the Congress of Vienna convened in 1814 and founded the German Confederation (Deutscher Bund), a loose league of 39 sovereign states. Disagreement with restoration politics partly led to the rise of liberal movements, demanding unity and freedom. These, however, were followed by new measures of repression on the part of the Austrian statesman Metternich. The *Zollverein*, a tariff union, profoundly furthered economic unity in the German states. During this era many Germans had been stirred by the ideals of the French Revolution, and nationalism became a more significant force, especially among young intellectuals. For the first time, the colours of black, red and gold were chosen to represent the movement, which later became the national colours.

In light of a series of revolutionary movements in Europe, which successfully established a republic in France, intellectuals and commoners started the Revolutions of 1848 in the German states. The monarchs initially yielded to the revolutionaries' liberal demands. King Frederick William IV of Prussia was offered the title of Emperor, but with a loss of power; he rejected the crown and the proposed constitution, leading to a temporary setback for the movement. Conflict between King William I of Prussia and the increasingly liberal parliament erupted over military reforms in 1862, and the king appointed Otto von Bismarck the new Prime Minister of Prussia. Bismarck successfully waged war on Denmark in 1864. Prussian victory in the Austro-Prussian War of 1866 enabled him to create the North German Federation (Norddeutscher Bund) and to exclude Austria, formerly the leading German state, from the affairs of the remaining German states.

GERMAN STATE AND EMPIRE

There was no country like Germany until the unification of German speaking areas in 1871. It was Branderburg Prussia which finally grew to become what is the United Germany today. After unification in 1871, Germany was rapidly industrialized, a process in which the iron ore of Alsace-Lorraine floated cheaply down the Rhine and was smelted with the coking-coal of the Ruhr. Railroads were built and state railway systems were coordinated to supplement the rivers and canals which had long been some of Europe's busiest inland waterways. As commerce expanded and capital accumulated, the north seaports of Bremen and Hamburg gained a position in world trade. As world trade interest in colonies and sea power grew, Kiel and Wilhelmshaven were developed as naval bases. By 1914, with Germany still growing industrially, pan-German expansionists were constantly calling attention to her alleged need of a larger *"working space"*. With territorial expansion on the continent blocked by the Franco-Russian alliance, Germany resorted to force.

The state known as *Germany* was unified as a modern nation-state in 1871, when the German Empire was forged, with the Kingdom of Prussia as its largest constituent. After the French defeat in the Franco-Prussian War, the German Empire was proclaimed in Versailles on 18 January1871. The Hohenzollern dynasty of Prussia ruled the new empire, whose capital was Berlin. The empire was a unification of all the scattered parts of Germany except Austria (*Kleindeutschland*, or "Lesser Germany"). Beginning in 1884, Germany began establishing several colonies outside of Europe.

In the *Gründerzeit* period following the unification of Germany, Emperor

William I's foreign policy secured Germany's position as a great nation by forging alliances, isolating France by diplomatic means, and avoiding war. Under William II, however, Germany, like other European powers, took an imperialistic course leading to friction with neighbouring countries. Most alliances in which Germany had been previously involved were not renewed, and new alliances excluded the country. Specifically, France established new relationships by signing the Entente Cordiale with the United Kingdom and securing ties with the Russian Empire. Aside from its contacts with Austria-Hungary, Germany became increasingly isolated. Germany's imperialism reached outside of its own country and joined many other powers in Europe in claiming their share of Africa. The Berlin Conference divided Africa between the European powers. Germany owned several pieces of land in Africa including German East Africa, South-West Africa, Togo, and Cameroon. The Scramble for Africa caused tension between the great powers that may have contributed to the conditions that led to World War I.

The assassination of Austria's crown prince on 28 June 1914 triggered World War I. Germany, as part of the unsuccessful Central Powers, suffered defeat against the Allied Powers in one of the bloodiest conflicts of all time. The German Revolution broke out in November 1918, and Emperor William II and all German ruling princes abdicated. An armistice putting an end to the war was signed on 11 November and Germany was forced to sign the Treaty of Versailles in June 1919. Its negotiation, contrary to traditional post-war diplomacy, excluded the defeated Central Powers. The treaty was perceived in Germany as a humiliating continuation of the war by other means and its harshness is often cited as having facilitated the later rise of Nazism in the country.

WEIMAR REPUBLIC (1919-1933)

At the beginning of the German Revolution, Germany was declared a republic and the monarchy collapsed. However, the struggle for power continued, with radical-left communists seizing power in Bavaria, but failing to take control of all of Germany. The revolution came to an end in August 1919, when the Weimar Republic was formally established. The Weimar (a town) Constitution came into effect with its signing by President Friedrich Ebert on 11 August 1919.

Suffering from the Great Depression, the harsh peace conditions dictated by the Treaty of Versailles, and a long succession of unstable governments, the people of Germany increasingly lacked identification with their political system and the "Establishment Parties" in their parliamentary democracy. This was exacerbated by a widespread right-wing (monarchist, *völkisch*, and Nazi) *Dolchstoßlegende*, which promoted the view that Germany had lost World War I because of the efforts and influence of those who wanted to overthrow the government. The top brass of the Weimar government was accused of betraying the German Nation by signing the Versailles Treaty, while the radical left-wing communists, such as the Spartacist League, had wanted a revolution to abolish "capitalist rule" in favour of a *Räterepublik*, and were also targeted.

Nevertheless, discontentment with the new Weimar government helped fuel the growth of the German Communist Party. Many conservatives were drawn towards the reactionary/revolutionary right, particularly the National Socialist German Workers Party—the Nazi Party. By 1932, these two parties controlled the majority of parliament (296 total parliamentary seats by July 1932). After a series of unsuccessful cabinets, President Paul von Hindenburg made a crucial decision: on 30 January 1933, seeing little alternative and pushed by right-wing advisors, von Hindenburg appointed Adolf Hitler as Chancellor of Germany, honoring Hitler's request.

LARGEST ECONOMY

Germany is the largest national economy in Europe, the fourth largest by nominal GDP in the world, and ranked fifth by GDP (PPP) in 2008. Since the age of industrialisation, the country has been a driver, innovator, and beneficiary of an ever more globalised economy. Germany is the world's top exporter with $1.133 trillion exported in 2006 (Eurozone countries are included) and generates a trade surplus of €165 billion. The service sector contributes around 70% of the total GDP, industry 29.1%, and agriculture 0.9%. Most of the country's products are in engineering, especially in automobiles, machinery, metals, and chemical goods. Germany is the leading producer of wind turbines and solar power technology in the world. The largest annual international trade fairs and congresses are held in several German cities such as Hanover, Frankfurt, and Berlin. Of the world's 500 largest stock market listed companies measured by revenue, the Fortune Global 500, 37 companies are headquartered in Germany. In 2007 the ten biggest were Daimler, Volkswagen, Allianz (the most profitable company), Siemens, Deutsche Bank (2nd most profitable company), E.ON, Deutsche Post, Deutsche Telekom, Metro, and BASF. Among the largest employers are also Deutsche Post, Robert Bosch GmbH, and Edeka. Well known global brands are Mercedes Benz, SAP, BMW, Adidas, Audi, Porsche, Volkswagen, and Nivea.

Germany is a strong advocate of closer European economic and political integration, and its commercial policies are increasingly determined by agreements among European Union (EU) members and EU single market legislation. Germany uses the common European currency, the euro, and its monetary policy is set by the European Central Bank in Frankfurt. Even after the German reunification in 1990, the standard of living and annual income remains significantly higher in the former West German states.The modernisation and integration of the eastern German economy continues to be a long-term process scheduled to last until the year 2019, with annual transfers from west to east amounting to roughly $80 billion. The overall unemployment rate has consistently fallen since 2005 and reached a 15-year low in June 2008 with 7.5%. The percentage ranges from 6.2% in former West Germany to 12.7% in former East Germany. The former government of Chancellor Gerhard Schröder launched a comprehensive set of reforms of labour market and welfare-related institutions while the current government runs a restrictive fiscal policy and has cut regular jobs in the public sector.

GERMANY, at a glance

ALTHOUGH THERE HAVE ALWAYS been German speakers living in Europe, a single German country did not exist until 1871. For much small kingdoms, duchies, and other states, kept apart by rivalries. Unification was eventually achieved under the diplomatic and military leadership of the north German state of Prussia. German industrial strength allowed the new nation to dominate Europe, but defeat in two world wars left country divided again. In 1990, Germany reunited, and once more became the major economic power of Europe.

German Renaissance

In the 15th century, the Renaissance spread to Germany. Artists such as Albrecht Durer (1471-1528) perfected the technique of the woodcut, Hand Holbein (1498-1543), working mostly in Switzerland and England, produced superb portraits, and Mathias Grunewald (1480-1528) painted religious masterpieces.

Peasants' War

In the 16th century, there was much tension between Catholics and Protestants in Germany. In 1524, peasants in southern Germany exploited the confusion to rise up and demand social reforms. The revolt was crushed in 1526.

German Tribes

In about 370, Huns from Asia swept into Germany, forcing native German tribes to pour into the neighbouring Roman Empire. Within a century, Rome had collapsed, and Germanic tribes such as the Visigoths and Franks controlled much of western Europe.

Medieval Germany

In 962, Otto I of Saxony united the German kingdoms in the Holy Roman Empire. This empire was long-lasting but weak, as local rulers fought to protect and increase their own power. Despite this disunity, the country became increasingly rich. By the late 15th century, German cities such as Augsburg controlled European banking and finance.

Hanseatic League

The cities of northern Germany worked together to support their trading interests. In 1241, Lubeck and Hamburg concluded a treaty that led to the growth of the Hanseatic League, a trading alliance that dominated commerce in northern Europe. At its height there were 160 cities in the League.

Coming of Christianity

From the 5th century onwards, individual Germans became Christian. Some churches, such as Ulm Cathedral, were founded in the early 7th century, but it was not until the mission of St Boniface in the early 8th century that most of the people converted to Christianity.

Thirty Years' War

In 1618, a revolt broke out in the Protestant province of Bohemia against the rule of the Catholic Habsburgs. War spread through Germany as Protestant princess rebelled against the Habsburgs. Other nations, notably France and Sweden, entered the war on the Protestant side to end Habsburg domination of Europe.

Rise of Prussia

Prussia was one of the few German states to emerge from the Thirty Years' War with increased power. Under successive rulers, Prussian territory expanded across most of northern Germany and, by 1795, also included western Poland.

Treaties of Westphalia

When the treaties ended the Thurty Years' War in 1648, German agriculture and commerce were in ruins, and the population had been reduced by half. The Habsburgs were seriously weakened by the years of conflict and Germany was more disunited than ever before, split into no fewer than 234 states and 51 independent cities.

Frederick the Great

Frederick, King of Prussia from 1740-86, laid the foundations of later-day Prussian greatness. An inspired military leader, his diplomacy enabled to outwit Austria and Russia. At his death, Prussia was Europe's foremost power.

German Unification

After Napoleon's defeat in 1815, many Germans wanted to unite as one nation. A confederation of states was set up, but it was too weak to last. In 1861, Wilhelm I became king of Prussia. Prussia's strength grew, and the other German states agreed to unite with Prussia. At last, in 1871, Wilhelm was made emperor of a united Germany.

Prussian Power

A strong army gave Prussia the power to defeat France in the Franco-Prussian War of 1870-71. Prussian strength also enabled the newly-united Germany to negotiate a powerful and advantageous alliance with Austria-Hungary and Russia in 1881. This gave Germany great influence throughout the Continent.

Otto von Bismarck

Otto von Bismarck (1815-98) became chief minister of Prussia in 1862. In a brilliant series of diplomatic and military campaigns, he removed all foreign influence from Germany, making Prussia the leading German state. He was chancellor of Germany for 19 years.

Imperial Germany

Under Wilhelm I and Wilhelm II, Germany became the leading power in Europe. Germany sought its "place in the sun" by acquiring colonies in Africa, China, and the Pacific, but its aggressive foreign policy led to the world war in 1914 and the collapse of its empire in 1918.

Weimar Germany

In 1918, following its defeat in World War I, Germany became a republic. A new constitution was agreed in 1919 in the town of Weimar, where the National Assembly met until it moved back to Berlin in 1920. However, Germany was badly affected by economic problems in the 1920s and by 1932 over 5 million people were unemployed.

The rise of the Nazis

The unfavourable terms of the peace settlement after World War I, together with the economic failures of the 1930s, saw Germany crippled by high unemployment and hyper-inflation, which led to a desire for change among the people. Support grew for the Nazis, an extreme nationalist party led by Adolf Hitler who took power in 1933. The Nazis promised to rebuild Germany's strength and power. It was Hitler's imperialist ambitions that were one of the causes of World War II.

Modern Germany

After World War II, the country was occupied by French, British, US, and Russian troops. In 1949, Germany was divided in two, with a communist, Russian-backed state in the east and US-backed capitalist state in the west. Living conditions in West Germany were much better than in the east.

Reunification

In the late 1980s, Russian control over East Germany weakened. The Berlin Wall, which divided the former capital, was felled in November 1989, and free access between the two countries was guaranteed for the first time. By October 1990, the two halves of Germany were politically united once more.

Timeline

962 Otto I of Saxony establishes Holy Roman Empire.

1241 Hamburg and Lubeck combine to form Hanseatic League; German trade prospers.

1517 German monk Martin Luther begins Protestant Reformation.

1618-90 Thirty Years' War devastates Germany.

1740-86 Frederick the Great rules Prussia.

1815-66 German Confederation tries to unite Germany.

1871 Wilhelm I is made German emperor.

1871-90 Bismarck governs as chancellor.

1914-18 Germany fights in World War I, is defeated, and empire collapses.

1919 Weimar Republic is established.

1931 German economy crashes; prices rise, the currency becomes worthless, and many suffer unemployment.

1939-45 Germany fights in World War II.

1949 Germany divided into East and West.

1989 The Berlin Wall fell.

1990 East and West Germany reunited as a single state.

The great questions of Europe will not be decided by resolutions and speeches but by blood and iron.

– Otto von Bismarck

46

Making of German Reichs and rise of Hitler

The Prussian question took Europe to wars many times since 1870 when Bismarck formed a federation of neighbouring political units and gave it a name, Germany. And, when the German question was finally solved after her re-unification in 1990, Europeans hurried up efforts to integrate the countries of the continent if only to ensure that it does not happen again.

It occupied them for 184 years – the *German question*. It arose on August 6, 1806 when Franz II, the last Emperor of the Holy Roman Empire, bowed down to an ultimatum from Napoleon; laid down his crown, and dissolved the "Old Empire". The German question was resolved on October 3, 1990, with the reunification. Between 1871 and 1918, the era of the German Reich, nobody would have dreamed of referring to an unresolved German question. The German question resurfaced on May 8 and 9, 1945 when the Third Reich surrendered unconditionally to the victors of the World War II. The division of Germany into two states was a preliminary answer to the German question. The final answer came in the form of the merger of the two states, together with the recognition under international law of the borders of 1945. After October 3, 1990, German borders were finally drawn. The following are landmark events of Germany.

PARLIAMENTARY MOVEMENT 1830-1848

For the Germans, there were always two sides to the German question: of territory and constitution and the question of the relationship between unity and freedom. At the heart of the territorial question was the problem of a "larger Germany" or "smaller Germany." If it were possible to replace the Holy Roman Empire with a German national state, it would have included German-speaking Austria. And, possibly World War II would have been averted. Unity and freedom first emerged as issues in the wars of liberation against Napoleon. The French Emperor was defeated but the removal of the foreign rulers neither united Germany nor created liberal conditions for a German confederation. Yet the call for unity and freedom could no longer be suppressed. In the early 1830s, it became louder after the French won struggle for a liberal constitutional monarchy after the July 1830 revolution. Inspired by events in France, there was a revolution in Germany in March 1848 too and unity and freedom once again became an issue.

To make Germany both a nation and a state was a far more ambitious goal than what the French revolutionaries had set themselves to achieve in 1789. Anyone demanding unity and freedom for the Germans had to clarify what was actually to be part of Germany. In simple words: what constituted Germany. This was never the case with France. In the first freely-elected National Assembly, it was stated that a German nation state should include the German-speaking part of the Habsburg monarchy. But, it was only in 1848 that a majority of the Deputies realised that it was not within their power to break up the multi-nation state of Austro-Hungary. (Reich is the term used to describe the German Empire. The Holy Roman Empire was the First Reich and the unified Germany after 1870 was the Second Reich. After 1933, the enlarged Hitler's Germany was the Third Reich.)

The German state according to the desire of the National Assembly in Frankfurt, was to be headed by Frederick William IV of Prussia, as a liberal constitutional state with a strong parliament which would have the government under its control. And the German Emperor, the King of Prussia of the House of the Hoenzollern, would have had to forget God and submit himself to the will of the people. On April 28, 1849, the monarch rejected this notion sealing the fate of the revolution which had, thus, brought the Germans neither unity nor freedom. What remained among the bourgeois liberals was a feeling of political failure: they had chased down countless illusions in that "mad year" and the realities of power proved them wrong.

A few years after the 1848 revolution, "*Realpolitik*" was to become a political catchword. This was first used in an article titled "*The Principles of Realpolitik as Applied to Conditions in the German States*," which the Liberal publisher Ludwig August von Rochau printed in 1853. Parliament had, in fact, already had pursued a policy of "realpolitik" when it ignored the right of self-determination of other peoples (the Poles in the Prussian Grand Duchy of Posen, the Danes in North Schleswig, and the Italians in "Welsch Tyrol") and decided to define the borders of the future German Reich in line with supposedly German national interests. As such, unity was for the first time given a higher status than freedom. The freedom of other ethnic groups was subordinated to the goal of German unity.

FOUNDING OF THE GERMAN REICH IN 1871

In the 1860s, Germany likewise took the decision to prioritize unity over freedom. This was the result of the "revolution from above," by which Otto von Bismarck, the Prussian Prime Minister, solved the *German question* in his own way. The Prussian constitutional conflict, (1862-1866), enabled Bismarck to solve the question of domestic power in favour of the Executive against Parliament and this was strengthened by foreign policy including the Prussian victory in 1866 which was considered as a war for the "smaller Germany" (the exclusion of Austria) and in the Franco-Prussian war (1870-71) against Napoleon's France, which had vetoed the creation of a united German nation-state. One goal of the 1848 Revolution, unity, was thus achieved. However, the demand for freedom, inasmuch as it denoted a government responsible to parliament, remained unmet. Even if he had wanted, Bismarck would not have been able to solve the freedom question by ceding power to Parliament because it was opposed not only by the ruling class in old Prussia, army, the landed gentry, and civil servants but also by other German states, including Bavaria, Saxony, and Württemberg. For, thus, they enjoyed a major share of the executive power in the German Reich, they were not inclined to forgo power and concede it to the Reichstag, elected on the basis of universal suffrage. This was in line with the Reich Constitution of

Otto von Bismarck

1849, which never actually gave the Germans more democratic rights than those enjoyed at the time by the citizens of liberal model monarchies such as Great Britain and Belgium.

WORLD WAR I

It was not until October 1918, when there was no longer any doubt about Germany's military defeat in the World War I, that the decisive change to the constitution took place, making the Reich Chancellor dependent on the confidence of the Reichstag. This act of making him responsible to parliament was intended to encourage the victorious Western democracies to make a lenient peace agreement and preempt a revolution from below. It failed on both counts, after which it was easy for the opponents of democracy to denounce the parliamentary system as "Western" and "un-German." The revolution from below broke out in November 1918. The army was unwilling to subordinate itself to political control of Reich leaders who were responsible to Parliament. However, the German Revolution of 1918-19, giving power to parliament, cannot be considered as one of the major or classic revolutions of world history, for, Germany was too radical to break with its political and social structure along the lines of the French Revolution of 1789 or the October Revolution of 1917 in Russia.

THE WEIMAR REPUBLIC 1919-1933

There was, in fact, a continuity between the German Reich and the Weimar Republic, which emerged following the fall of the monarchy in November 1918 and the January 1919 elections after which the German National Assembly drew up a constitution known as the Weimar Republic, named after the Weimar city in south Germany on the Rhine. To a certain extent, the institution of monarchy simply persisted in a different form. The office of Reich President, who was elected by the people, came with such huge powers that there was talk of a "substitute emperor." Nor was there any emotional break with

FALL OF BASTILLE AND BERLIN WALL

The infamous Berlin Wall fell in 1989, when the French were celebrating 200 years of the fall of Bastille in 1789. Both events are momentous. The former marked the end of Communism in Europe and the latter marked the beginning of the French Revolution. Both the events changed the world as nothing did before. The first breach in the Wall was made on November 9, 1989, and soon even East German soldiers were joining the heady race to break down the hated symbol of division.

the German Reich. Almost all Germans saw the Treaty of Versailles, which Germany was forced to sign on June 28, 1919, as a blatant injustice. This was primarily as a result of the territories the country had to cede, in particular to the newly established Poland. The hardships in the form of reparation payments, the loss of colonies, and the military restrictions – all these were justified by citing the guilt of the German Reich for the War although the war started after the assassination on June 28, 1914 in Sarajevo of the successor to the Austro Hungarian throne. The Germans, very clearly, were not the first to shoot.

SOME KEY DATES OF GERMAN UNIFICATION

Sept. 10, 1989	Hungary opens its borders to Austria, allowing thousands of east Germans to escape to the West.
Sept. 30, 1989	West German Foreign Minister Hang-Dietrich Genscher told East German refugees, holed up at the West German embassy in Prague, that they were free to go West.
Oct. 7, 1989	Soviet President Mikhail Gorbachev visits East Germany's 40th anniversary ceremonies in East Berlin. Thousands of East Germans shout *"Glasnost";* police beat and arrest demonstrators.
Oct. 18, 1989	East Germany Communist leader Erich Honecker is forced out of office after 18 years in power.
Nov. 9, 1989	East Germany's desperate Communist regime opens the Berlin Wall and border points in a bid to halt growing discontent.
Dec. 22, 1989	Berlin's Brandenburg Gate, a symbol of division, opened.
Feb. 13, 1990	The World War II Allies – France, Britain, the US and the Soviet Union – approve German unification.
March 18, 1990	A conservative coalition comes out as the strongest force in East Germany's first free elections.
April 24, 1990	Helmut Kohl and Lothar de Maiziere, the democratically elected East German Prime Minister, agree on July 1 as the date for merging the two countries' economics.
July 1, 1990	The West German mark becomes the East German currency.
Aug. 23, 1990	East German law-makers agree to Oct. 3 as the date for German unification.
Aug. 31, 1991	The two Germanys sign a state treaty on unification.
Sept. 12, 1990	The four victorious World War II Allies and the two Germanys sign a treaty restoring Germany's sovereignty.
Oct. 3, 1990	East and West unite, ending 45 years of German division.

The fact that Austria was forbidden according to the Treaty to unite with Germany was also considered to be unjust. Once the downfall of the Habsburg monarchy removed the major obstacle to a solution for a greater Germany, the revolutionary governments in Vienna and Berlin had spoken out in favour of the two German-speaking republics uniting. They could be assured of the popularity of the demand in both countries. The fact that the Treaties of Versailles had forbidden the union did not however, discourage the notion of a greater Germany which gained momentum. Germany which was attracted to the idea of German unity had been beaten and was suffering the consequences of defeat. The Holy Roman Empire in the Middle Ages had not been a nation-state but rather a supranational structure. After 1918, conservative political forces made increasing reference to their imperial past. In Europe, they suggested, Germany should establish itself as the upholder of law and order in the struggle against Western democracy and Eastern Bolshevism which, they said, was anarchy.

As a parliamentary democracy, the Weimar Republic survived mere 11 years. At the end of March 1930, the last majority government, headed by Hermann Müller, a Social Democrat, collapsed on an argument that the unemployment insurance system had to be restructured. The Grand Coalition, that had been in power until then, was replaced by a center-right minority cabinet under a politician from the Catholic Zentrum Party, Heinrich Brüning. From the summer of 1930, this government ruled with the help of emergency decrees issued by Field Marshall General Paul von Hindenburg, the aging Reich President. His age and political weakness paved the way for the rise of Hitler.

HITLER IN WAITING

At the Reichstag elections on September 14, 1930, Adolf Hitler's Nationalist Socialist Party (NSDAP) became the second largest party. The Social Democrat Party (SPD), which was still the largest party, decided to tolerate the Brüning cabinet in order to prevent further drift to the right and preserve democracy in Prussia, then the largest constituent state where the SPD ruled jointly with Brüning's Catholic Center Party, and the center-right Democrats. Following the transition to a presidential system based on the emergency decree regime, the Reichstag had less influence than it had during the constitutional monarchy of the German Reich. The reduced influence of parliament meant that the electorate no longer played any major role in the running of the country. Of these, the National Socialists (Nazis) benefited the most. And, when the Social Democrats supported Brüning, Hitler was able to present his party as the people's only alternative to Marxism. Hitler was liked by the people for their widespread resentment against parliamentary democracy which had by now failed. The idea of people's participation in the shape of universal suffrage did not attract people. Thus, Hitler became the greatest beneficiary of a dysfunctional German democracy as conceived at Weimar.

THE ERA OF NATIONAL SOCIALISM 1933-1945

Hitler did not come to power after any major election victory but he would not have become Reich Chancellor in January 1933 had he not been the leader of the strongest party. After the last Weimar Republic Reichstag (Parliament) elections on November 6, 1932 the National Socialists (Nazis) had lost in the July 31, 1932 elections, while the Communists gained 100 seats which whipped up fears of a civil war. And, this fear made Hitler the most powerful ally, particularly among the Conservative elite. It was on their recommendation to Chancellor Hindenburg that Hitler assumed power. Hence, on January 30, 1933 the Reich President appointed Hitler as Chancellor at the head of a predominantly conservative cabinet though Hitler had no majority in Parliament. Here, the story of German suffering begins.

Hitler was immediately able to beat unemployment problem through a rearmaments programme, thereby winning the support of large sections of the working classes. As a result of the ruthless exploitation of workers and natural resources in the occupied territories, he was able to spare the German masses the hardships they had to endure after the World War I, ensuring that he could count on their support even during the World War II. The major successes in foreign policy during the pre-War years, headed by the re-occupation of the de-militarized Rhineland in March 1936 and the Austrian "*Anschluss*" in March 1938 took Hitler's popularity to record levels in all classes of society. The legend of the Reich and its historic mission, which Hitler was a master in propagating, influenced educated Germans. The charismatic "Fuhrer" (leader) needed their assistance if he was to make Germany a power in the European order, and they needed him, too, because otherwise, it seemed, there was nobody in a position to make the dream of a great German Reich a reality.

Anschluss was the concept of union between Austria and Germany, expressly forbidden by the Treaty of Versailles 1919, but with some support in both countries after the collapse of the Habsburg Empire, Hitler pursued the idea once in power, and in 1938, after the resignation of Austrian Chancellor

Schuschnigg, the Germans were "invited" to occupy Austria. The union of Austria and Germany was formally proclaimed on March 13, 1938).

Even though he did not focus on it in the electoral campaigns in the early 1930s, Hitler had made no secret of his anti-Semitism. His slogans would not have won him votes of the working classes, something he was extremely keen to get. Among educated, property-owning classes, small businessmen and farmers, anti-Jewish prejudice was widespread. Since the Nuremberg Race Laws of September 1935 had deprived Jews of their civil rights, Hitler's plans against the Jews met with no major opposition. The violent disturbances on November 9, 1938 were not popular, but the "Aryanization" (takeover) of Jewish property, for distribution was widely acclaimed by the people.

In German history the downfall of Hitler's Greater German Reich in May 1945 signifies a far deeper damnation than that of the German Reich of November 1918. The Reich as such continued to exist after the World War I. Following the unconditional surrender after World War II, governmental power and the decision-making powers as to the future of Germany, were assumed by the four occupying powers, the United States, the Soviet Union, Great Britain and France. Unlike 1918, in 1945 the German political and military leaders were stripped of their powers and sent for trial at Nuremberg. The landowners east of the Elbe, who had contributed more than any other powerful elite to the destruction of the Weimar Republic and the transfer of power to Hitler, lost everything. The giving away of territories east of the Oder and Neisse Rivers to Poland and northeastern Prussian, Soviet administration, caused considerable dissatisfaction.

As opposed to the aftermath of 1918, after 1945, it was just clear that Nazi Germany had unleashed the World War II. In both the World Wars I & II, German propaganda had portrayed the democratic Western powers as imperialist plutocrats, and their own law and order as an expression of a high level of social justice. After 1945, renewed attacks on the Western democracies would have been crazy: The price paid for the contempt shown for the West's political ideas was too high for a return to the slogans of the past to promise any success.

THE TWO GERMAN STATES 1949-1990

In 1948-49, representatives of the freely elected parliaments of the federal states in the American, British and French zones of occupation met in the Parliamentary Council in Bonn and devised a constitution that drew logical conclusions from the mistakes made in preparing the Reich Constitution of 1919 and the failure of the Weimar Republic: the Basic Law of the Federal Republic of Germany. The second German democracy was to be a functioning parliamentary democracy with a strong Federal Chancellor, who could only be toppled by a "constructive vote of no confidence," i.e. by a successor being voted, and a Federal President who played a nominal role earlier. As opposed to Weimar days, parallel legislative powers for the people were not envisaged. The revised Basic Law laid very strong foundations for democracy in West Germany by making it impossible for a majority party to change the constitution as was the case in 1933.

While West Germany drew "anti-totalitarian" conclusions from the most recent German history, the East, that is the Soviet zone of occupation and later East Germany, had to put up with "anti-fascist" consequences. These served to legitimize a Marxist-Leninist-influenced party dictatorship. The break with the principles of Nazi rule was to be achieved primarily through class struggle and by dispossessing large landowners and industrialists. Former Nazi "supporters", by contrast, were allowed to prove their worth to society by helping "build socialism". Once the process of "denazification" had been completed in East Germany, former Nazi party officials managed to occupy leading positions. To be true, but for the "economic miracle" in the 1950s and 1960s, the longest boom period in the 20th century, there would not have been success story of West Germany. The booming economy gave legitimacy to the model of a social market economy as promulgated by Ludwig Erhard, the first Federal Economics Minister. It enabled the swift integration of the eight million displaced persons from the former Eastern territories of the German Reich, Sudetenland and other areas of East and Southeast Europe.

REUNIFICATION 1990

With the Wall having fallen in 1989, (see more about it in other chapters) it was to be another 11 months before Germany was reunited. Germans in both German states welcomed it. In the first (and last) free elections to East Germany's *Volkskammer* (parliament) on March 18, 1990 the East German electorate voted by an overwhelming majority for those parties that demanded swift accession to West Germany. In summer 1990 a treaty to this effect was negotiated by the two Germanys. Parallel to this in the two-plus-four-treaty, West and East Germany reached agreement with the four powers responsible for Berlin and Germany as a whole, also on the conditions with regard to foreign and security policy determining German unity.

There is no evidence to suggest that there is any advantage in belonging to a pure race. The purest races, now in existence, are the Pygmies in equatorial Africa, Hottentots in South Africa and Namibia and Australian aborigins. The Greeks, who were most civilized, were most mixed.

– Bertrand Russell

47

Adolf Hitler (1889-1945)

"A political genius formed in gutter"

A tramp, a failed painter, a street brawler and a fanatic Austrian of German origin finally became a soldier to fight in the World War I in which he was injured. One more bullet would have killed Hitler and saved the world from another world war in which millions of people died. But, that bullet never came. Of all infamous men of our time, none affected world history more violently than Adolf Hitler. Yet Hitler was born without any advantages of birth or education. He was a soldier in the World War I but never rose beyond the rank of corporal. He never studied anything for its own sake or achieved any degree of intellectual excellence. But, he learned how to gain power over people. He was a political genius formed in the gutter. Of lower middle-class origin, Adolf Hitler was born in 1889 at Braunau in Austria. He quarrelled with his father, a minor State official, because he wanted to be a painter. Having failed to get admission to an art school, he spent his early manhood in various cheap houses in Vienna living like a tramp, painting post-cards for a living. He was lazy, feckless and moody. He had no interest in women – neither smoked nor drank. His passion was talking politics and he would hang around night shelters where free soup was distributed, often getting involved in street brawls.

He left Vienna for Munich in 1913, where he lived by painting cards. This part of his life ended in August, 1914, when he wrote a petition to King Ludwig-III of Bavaria, asking permission as an Austrian to join the German Army. It was granted. And, thereby hangs a trail. For all its triviality and sordidness, the early period of Hitler's life was of fundamental importance.

Adolf Hitler - the mass killer

Here among the *lumpen proletariat,* he learnt his hatred for the Jews. After the Jews, he hated the "lower" races, such as the Poles and the Czechs. The politics he picked up were those that fortified his hates. He saw how the leader must rule the mob. His idle life gave him time to read ancient history, particularly Roman history, books on occultism, yoga and astrology. Here too, he developed ability to argue powerfully enough to attract the low mind. This environment taught him his basic philosophy which he expounded in his book, *Mein Kempf,* the basic tenet which produced this monster.

He made a good soldier, winning the Iron Cross in 1918. His fellow-soldiers found him far too keen on war and far too serious to fight it. He would harangue them occasionally, saying that the invisible foes of the German people, the Jews and Marxists, were a greater threat to victory than the enemy's guns. After the World War I, he was employed by the German Army in Munich where he founded the *National Socialist Party,* a combination of various patriotic groups of working men and ex-soldiers, all thriving in the atmosphere of revolutionary and counter-revolutionary conspiracy which characterized the early days of the German Republic.

The French occupation of the Ruhr in 1923 was an enormous fillip to the German nationalist extremists. By then Hitler, whose supporters included Rosenberg and Goering, attempted *a coup d'etat* which very nearly succeeded against the Bavarian Government. Hitler spent just over two years in prison at Landsberg. It was a comfortable prison and Hitler as the leader of a party had a room to himself. He began the composition of *Mein Kampf,* a work which is clearly that of a semi-educated man. His 35th birthday was spent in prison. From 1924 until the end of the twenties, Hitler had a hard period in rebuilding the Nazi Party, (National Socialist German Workers' Party) fighting off rivals, and getting money for his movement from industrialists and the propertied classes.

Nazis fought Socialists and Communists throughout Germany and even, on occasions, joined Communists in strikes designed to produce a breakdown of public order. President Hindenburg and his advisers tried to keep Hitler out of power. But in 1932, the Nazis won 230 seats in the Reichstag and were stronger than the Socialists and Communists combined. In January, 1933,

Entrance gate to the Auschwitz concentration camp, a sign reads, "Work Makes One Free" giving prisoners the false hope that they would be rewarded for their hard work.

Hindenburg, unwillingly, made Hitler Chancellor of the Reich. In 1934, Hindenburg died and Hitler secured his appointment not as President but as Fuhrer (leader) of the German people and Reich Chancellor for life. Hitler's success was due above all to his power to appeal to the powerful irrational feelings of the people. The technique of Nazi crowd management has never since been matched – mass bands, drum beats, huge slogans, standard bearers and the stalwart bodyguards of splendid young men, parading the strength of the German race.

NAZIS SEIZE POWER: The Nazis set fire to the Reichstag building and the Communists, accused of this crime, were deprived of their seats. In May, trade unions were abolished and on July 14, 1933, the Nazi Party was made the only legal party in the Reich. In February, 1934, Hitler made the governments of the States of Germany completely subordinate to the Reich, thus completing the work of unification and carried out a purge of the Nazi Party in which hundreds of his followers were summarily shot. This was to get rid of certain elements in the Party whom the German Army leaders disliked and to ensure Hitler's complete domination. He now had at his back the Army, the powerful Gestapo of which Himmler was, for a while, the Chief, as well as the elite force of young men recruited from the Nazi Party. They were the killers in concentration camps. Hitler re-occupied the Rhineland in

March 1936. In 1938, he took over Austria. Mussolini, the Fascist dictator of Italy, had made common cause with France and Britain in defending Austria when Germany appeared to threaten that country's independence in 1935. But Mussolini later became an ally of Hitler (read the chapter on World War II).

THIRD REICH – HITLER BECAME CHANCELLOR BY DEFAULT

The *Third Reich of Hitler* came into being on January 30, 1933. The new system was formally established by the *Enabling Law* approved by the Reichstag on March 24, 1933, for a period of four years. When Hindenburg died, no successor to the Presidency was appointed, and later, by a combination of conspiracy, fraud and murder, Hitler became head of the state, head of the government, and head of the army. *"His will is my law,"* declared Goring in 1933. "Our Constitution is the will of the Fuhrer," (leader) he added. The Reichstag survived, not as an assembly of elected people responsible to the people, but as a gathering of party nominees who ratified the Fuhrer's decisions without debate. The chief novelty in Nazi political ideology was the *"Fuhrerprinzip,"* which assumed an uninterrupted succession of supermen of which Nietsche spoke of. *Hitler was his creation.*

HITLER WAS VEGETARIAN AND A TEETOTALLER

Hitler, throughout his life, was a vegetarian, teetotaller and a non-smoker. He was inclined to hypochondria, suffered from bad stomach. The woman who most deeply affected his life was Geli Raubal, his sister's daughter who, with her mother, lived in Munich. She was twenty years his younger. He was intensely jealous of her and tried to keep her away from all male contacts; whether or not she was his mistress is uncertain. In 1931, she was found shot dead in Hitler's Munich flat and suicide was considered likely. Eva Braun was flaxen-haired woman with whom Hitler had a liaison dating some years before the War. It was a well-kept secret. Hitler made it clear that he had no intention of marrying her as it would destroy his prestige. She suffered greatly from the isolation which this liaison entailed. However, she loved Adolf Hitler and willingly agreed to die with him.

HITLER'S FINAL DAYS

As Allied troops closed in on Berlin in April 1945, Adolf Hitler sank into depression to become a shaking and weakened man, according to a nurse who worked in his bunker. "The circle (in the bunker) got increasingly small,"

Erna Flegel (92) said in an interview with *Guardian* published in the 60th year of Hitler's death on April 30, 2005. As the German army collapsed, Hitler stayed in Berlin continuously from November 1944, eventually retreating into the bunker with his entourage. In the middle of April 1945, Joseph Goebbels, the Nazi propaganda chief and a prime killer, his wife Magda and their six children moved in. Hitler "aged greatly in the last days; he now had a lot of grey hair, and gave the impression of a man at least 15 to 20 years older. He shook a good deal, walking was difficult for him, his right side was still very much weakened as a result of the attempt on his life" Flegel said. Hitler's decision to marry Braun made it "immediately clear that the end of the Third Reich had come", she said.

By April 29, 1945, the once mighty Third Reich had been reduced to an area the size of a large football field, stretching between Potsdamer Platz and Friedrichstrasse. Fighting engulfed the city center. Radio communications with the outside world ceased. At 10.30 pm that evening, Flegel was summoned with the rest of the medical team to line up and take their leave of the Führer. "He came out of the side room, shook everyone's hand, and said a few friendly words," she said. The next afternoon (April 30, 1945) Hitler shot himself. Hitler's body was taken out to the Chancellery garden and burned. The next morning, the survivors were told that they were released from their oath of loyalty and some made the ill-fated attempt to fight their way out to the West. Others shot themselves.

Nurse Flegel stayed and witnessed the deaths of the Goebbels family. Dr. Helmut Kunz, a dentist, injected the children, aged four to 12, with poison. Later the same evening, their parents killed themselves. On the morning of May 2, 1945 Russian soldiers reached the bunker and seized the half-burnt body of Hitler, the greatest killer of history. This is how the Third Reich ended in six years in ignominy and defeat – a regime which Hitler had set up to last for "a thousand years." There is no survivor in Hitler's family. Hitler's grandson William Patrick Hitler vanished into the life of anonymity in Long Island and his three sons decided not to have children so that the ignominious bloodline could end.

WAR ENDS FINALLY

On May 8, 1945, World War II officially ended. Germans surrendered in France on May 16, 1945 and on May 9, 1945 Soviet troops finally completed the conquest of eastern Germany. As many as 13.6 million Soviet troops had to die (7.7 million civilians were killed or missing. See chart) before they could capture Hitler's bunker. "If each soldier had five kg. of blood, do your maths to know how much blood had to be spilt to control the madness of one man – Adolf Hitler", says the Russian news agency, *Novosti,* on the celebrations of the 60th year of Soviet conquest of Germany in World War II.

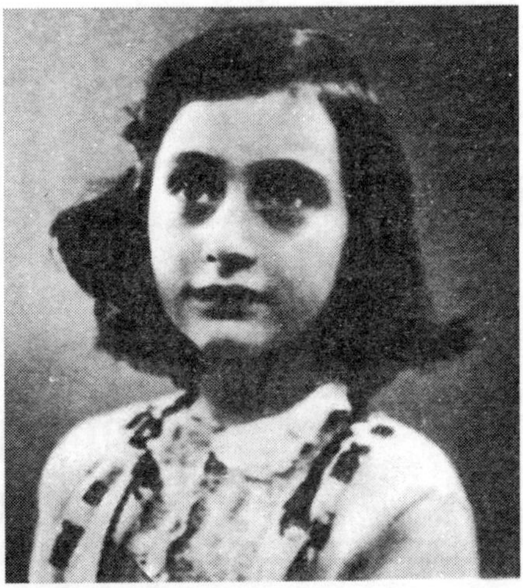

Anne Frank, who hid from the Nazis for two years in Amsterdam, finally died in the Belsen death camp. Her diary gives the daily account of sufferings. It is a historical document.

HUMAN COST OF THE WAR

During six years of fighting, some 24 million service personnel, Allied and Axis, were killed. Even more civilians – perhaps more than 40 million – died in fighting on the ground or in bombing raids, in forced-labour or extermination camps, of starvation or disease, or executed as hostages or partisans. The Eastern Front, where Russians mostly fought, saw the heaviest losses, both military and civilian. Brutal treatment of local populations – especially Jews – by their own governments swelled the numbers. Luxembourg's fighters were almost all forced to serve in the German Army – and a quarter deserted. The armed forces of Poland were at peak size before the German blitzkrieg of September 1939. A Polish army-in-exile grew first in France, then in Britain, numbering over 100 000 by 1942 and over double that by the end of the war. The French story was similar. The armed forces were at peak size before the German occupation in June 1940. By December that year, a Free French force of 35 000 had formed, which doubled by mid-1942 and swelled to well over 300 000 by the war's end.

In the Philippine, a US possession, 11 000 Philippine Scouts were part of the US Army and more than 160 000 Filipinos fought in the Philippine Army. No reliable records exist, but some claim a million Filipinos, soldiers and civilians, died at Japanese hands. The number of armed forces wounded listed in the chart gives only an indication of what the troops suffered, not an accurate count. The wounds recorded might vary from slight to permanently disabling. Some people were injured more than once, or died subsequently and were recorded among both wounded and dead.

One only thing that is stronger than all the armies in the world is an idea whose time has come.
– *Victor Hugo*

48

German political ideas that changed Europe

German thinkers and philosophers have radiated glory of humankind (Immanuel Kant) and have produced dictators (Nietzsche) who together have set trends in the history of Europe and the world.

On September 17, 1789, George Washington told the delegates from 13 American states: *"Should the States reject this excellent constitution, the next one will be drawn in blood"*. The American Constitution was, thus, made to be a model for democracies of the world. Every country has its governing principles; the US has economy, France has revolution, the UK has Common Law, Muslim countries have Islam and Germany has *obedience* which is the basis of its political thought and behaviour.

The fundamental cause of the different attitude of the average modern German to political authority must be sought in its place on the map. Geography is the mother of history. The central European plain, stretching without a break from the Bay of Biscay to the Urals, and inhabited by many different stocks, is a standing invitation to strife. Lacking well-defined frontiers of mountains and sea, Germanic tribes were continually at war with their neighbours or with one another. The *Holy Roman Empire* strove in vain to organise the territories inhabited by men of German race. The Reformation introduced a new source of discord between north and south. The devastation of the Thirty Years' War was the grim penalty of external and internal disunion, and the Austro-Prussian rivalry, dating from Frederick

MARTIN LUTHER (1483-1546), AN ICONOCLAST

Martin Luther was a German Christian church reformer and the founder of Protestantism. While he was a priest at the University fo Wittenberg, he wrote an attack on the *sale of indulgences* (remissions of punishment for sin for money). The Holy Roman empror Charles V summoned him to the Diet (meeting of dignitaries of the Holy Roman Empire) *of Worms* in Germany in 1521 where he refused to retract his objections. His protest led to schism. Luther is regarded as the instigator of the Protestant revolution, (Lutheranism) which is now the predominant religion of many north European countries, including Germany, Sweden and Denmark.

Luther was born in Eisleben as the son of a miner; he studied at the University of Erfurt, spent three years among the Augustinians, and in 1507 he was ordained as priest. Shortly after, he attracted attention as a teacher and preacher at the University of Wittenberg, and in 1517, after returning from a visit to Rome, he attained nationwide celebrity for his denunciation of the Dominican monk Johann Tetzel (1455-1519), one of those sent out by the pope to sell indulgences as a means of raising funds for the rebuilding of St. Peter's Basilica in Rome.

On October 31, 1517, Luther nailed on the church door in Wittenberg a statement of 95 theses concerning indulgences, and the following year he was summoned to Rome to defend his action. His reply was to attack the papal system even more strongly, and in 1520 he publicly burned in Wittenberg the *papal bull* (edict) that had been launched against him. On his way home from the imperial *Diet of Worms,* he was taken into 'protective custody' by the elector of Saxony in the castle of Wartburg. After the Augsburg Confession 1530, Luther gradually retired from the Protestant leadership.

the Great, postponed the creation of a nation-state to a period centuries later than in England and France, Spain and Russia.

Italy alone of the Great Powers had to wait so long to create unity behind the Alps. If Germany became a nation-state like the rest, it was only through the power of a formidable army, and a disciplined people. A country with open frontiers, surrounded by unfriendly neighbours, was always conscious of its dangers to a degree not easily envisaged by Englishmen who evolved the theory and practice of self-government in leisurely ways of islanders. National strength, not internal self-determination, was the watchword. This difference of atmosphere and historical experiences were behind the evolution of political ideas in Germany in the Age of Nationalism.

The Middle Ages knew nothing of the doctrine of absolute state. All human authority, it was believed, was limited, and all political authority was derived from the community itself. The King had two superiors – God and the law. The medieval order, symbolised by the Papacy and the Holy Roman

Empire, collapsed in the sixteenth, and the familiar world of sovereign states took its place. A new era of thought was inaugurated by Machiavelli, whose gospel of an unfettered executive has dominated the practice of large portions of the world since. The supreme achievement of the Reformation was the modern state. The community continued to be thought as an organic whole. But while medieval thinkers regarded society as a church, and a community bound together by a common faith, modern thinkers envisaged it as a secular state. The craving for prosperity and peace facilitated the transition from feudalism to nation-states.

IMPACT OF FRENCH REVOLUTION ON GERMAN THOUGHT SYSTEMS

The impact the French Revolution was greater in Germany than in any other country. It was as if a huge rock had been hurled into a stagnant pool. The opening scenes were watched with delight not only by the average citizen, but also by the rulers. *The Declaration of the Rights of Man* put into words the muffled aspirations of the masses and brought a new sense of human dignity in its train. The windows of the prison house seemed to fly open, and the common man felt that he had come of age. Poets exclaimed that the angels must be singing in the heaven, and "mankind had awakened from its long sleep." The dream, however, faded soon and people began to curse the revolution. Yet the fascination continued to work and Germany produced treatises on the nature and functions of the state in line with the French revolutionary ideas. The transition from the eighteenth century to the nineteenth, from the Age of Rationalism to the Age of Nationalism, from the old Germany to the new is reflected in the political writings of Kant, and Fichte.

FALL OF BISMARCK (1890)

After the peace of Frankfurt, Bismarck's policy, both domestic and foreign, concentrated on consolidating and securing the young German empire. His domestic policy was marked by universal suffrage, nationalization of the Prussian railways, codification of the law and many attempts to combat socialism. However, he distrusted movements with international affiliations and quarrelled bitterly with the Roman Catholics in the 1870s (Bismarck feared the political power of the Vatican) and with the Socialists in 1880s. In 1888, Kaiser Wilhelm-II (1859-1941) came to the German throne as emperor. A wilful and stubborn personality, Wilhelm dismissed Bismarch two years later. The Chancellor now found himself out of step with the younger generation in Germany and quarrelled with Whilhelm over home and foreign policy. And, he lost his job.

LUTHER WANTED TO BE GOVERNED BY LIGHT WITHIN

The claim of the *Prince* to unchallengeable power, put forward in most continental countries, was an innovation and Martin Luther was its prophet. Not that he was in a systematic political thinker: he was indeed so obsessed with problems of the religious life and papal "indulgences" that he had little time for politics except insofar as they helped the cause of the Reformation. The good, Luther believed, needed no state, no law, no punishment, since they were steered by the *light within;* his ideal was a community ruled by God and the natural law. Thus, the state was a necessary evil, approved by God to meet the needs of erring man, and, as such, its orders had to be obeyed. Resistance to the constituted authority was condemned by Scripture. State commands, contrary to divine law, could not be obeyed because the magistrate possessed no authority over the *Christian conscience, worship and belief,* even in regard to which Scripture was supreme. Resistance, however just, should be passive and unjust punishments must be patiently borne. Caring nothing for political liberty, Luther was satisfied with the rule of a virtuous prince like his patron *Frederick, the Wise,* Elector of Saxony. Never for a moment did he advocate political responsibility for the common man. Or, his Prince.

Though his ideal was the Christian Prince, Luther had no illusions about character and capacity of the ruler. Princes, for him, were far from divine; a clever prince was rare, a pious prince rarer still. "Let no one think the land and people are mine." The duty of the ruler was to protect the good and punish the wicked without respect for persons, whether popes, bishops, monks, nuns or anyone else. One law should prevail, and all must obey it. The conception of Christendom faded away and a mosaic of sovereign states took its place. Yet the state was more than a purely secular institution, for, among its tasks, as the Reformers saw it, was to protect true religion against its domestic and foreign foes.

POWER AS A TRUST & SOCIAL CONTRACT

Opinions on the nature and functions of the state have differed widely in Germany between libertarian and authoritarian apologists. The former were more numerous till the beginning of the nineteenth century, when the Napoleonic rule revived German nationalism. The concept of social contract, which played such a vital part in the controversies in the seventeenth and eighteenth centuries, rested on a legal fiction and, except in case of Hobbes, embodied the principles of agreement and limited power. The task of government is the execution of the law and the law is made by the community, hence, the supreme magistrate is bound by contract embodied in solemn oaths taken by the magistrate and the people on his accession or their election. Power is a trust, not a right. No individual is wise enough to rule without control. "What concerns all should be determined by all, because the many are wiser than the few, and it is by such a form of government that the liberty of the people is protected because they compel the officials to recognise that the people is their master." Luther approved of the definition of liberty as power divided into units. His unit of authority was not the individual but the group – the family, the city, the province, or the federal state.

HUMBOLDT: (ALEXANDER VON – 1769-1859)

MAN, NOT THE STATE, MATTERS

The true end of man, says Humboldt, is the harmonious development of his powers, and reason demands a condition in which every one enjoys abundant opportunities of self-realisation. The unceasing effort of the state to promote the welfare of its citizens is harmful; for, it creates uniformity, suppresses spontaneity, discourages energy, and thereby hinders the natural growth of the individual. What a man does under instruction or guidance fails to enter into his being and remains alien to his true nature. Legislation necessarily bears a general character and, therefore, fails to meet the need of particular cases. He says the liberty of people decline with the increase in the power of the state. "The state should not proceed a step further than is necessary for the protection of its citizens against foreign enemies." Voluntary associations are better than any arrangement that the Government can make. Civilisation has reached a point beyond which it cannot aspire to achieve still loftier heights, save through the development of individuals and, therefore, all institutions which obstruct this development must be abolished. National education turns out scholars on the same pattern. The Church, by encouraging the same opinions, discourages the people to think free and differently. National supervision of morals might produce a prosperous community, but its members would be like a flock of sheep. "The state is merely an agency for which man must never be sacrificed," says Humboldt.

KANT: (IMMANUEL 1724-1804)

CATEGORICAL IMPERATIVE

By his individualism and cosmopolitanism, Kant, no less than Humboldt, belongs to the eighteenth century, but this great philosopher, was also one of the boldest political thinkers. His interest in political affairs was aroused by the American War of Independence (1775-83) which won his whole-hearted sympathy. Though he welcomed the outbreak of the French Revolution (1789-99), when he was 70, his talk was mainly of politics. His pen was as bold as his tongue. In his *Study of Religion,* published in 1793, he counters the argument that the French are not ripe for liberty with the axiom that men become ripe for liberty when they were set free. *"We must be free in order to use our powers wisely in freedom. The first attempts will naturally be imperfect, but experience will show the way; for God has created mankind for freedom."* Kant talked of *categorical imperatives* which, he says, "*when you are in doubt, turn into your conscience and a bell will begin to ring on what is right and what is wrong: follow – that divine ring. His categorical imperative is the absolute, unconditional command of the moral law – a law binding universally on every rational will. Among his best known books are the Critique of Pure Reason, and Metaphysic of Ethics.*" In his *Philosophy of Law,* he said that liberty, equality and personal independence are the inalienable attributes of citizens. Since man is a rational and a moral being, politics should be based on reason and morality. ("Anything which is morally wrong, cannot be legally right.") Kant is the greatest philosopher of all time who gave inspiration to all philosophers and thinkers, including Karl Marx. He was a thinker of the Enlightenment who supported pure reason and not empiricism. He never travelled beyond East Prussia which became a Soviet territory after 1946, but guided the thinkers, and philosophers all over the world. He was, to begin with, a student of physics and mathematics and later switched over to philosophy which he interpreted scientifically. He said "God's existence could be proved theoretically, but here emotion and feelings work. Not knowledge." His last words were: *"It is good."* On his grave

Immanuel Kant

is inscribed *"The starry heavens above and the moral law within, fill my being."*

FICHTE: (JOHANN GUTTIEB – 1762-1814)

NAPOLEON SHOOK HIS IDEALISM

The battle of Jena, where Napoleon defeated Prussians, turned Fichte into the most eloquent champion of the national-state; and his *Address to the German Nation,* delivered in 1807-8 within earshot of the French garrison in Berlin, proclaimed the political gospel of which his countrymen were later to become devotees. He no longer painted his princes black and their subjects white. "Those who were responsible for the great collapse were slack and selfish, all must co-operate in the work of reconstruction". The nation must become self-conscious, the school system must be reformed, and the state must be strong enough to defend its citizens. It was not merely the state which he had learned to respect: he shed his cosmopolitanism like an old garment. The man, who in his youth, had desired to become a French citizen, woke up to the fact that the Germans were a great people. Germans had a peculiarly important part to play; for, they had retained their language untainted by alien influences and could, therefore, give expression to the soul of the people. It was paradoxical that although Fichte was a supporter of *"trascendental idealism"* of Kant, he supported state power because he saw at Jena, where he was a teacher, the defeat of Germany. His *"ethical idealism"* collapsed at the Jena battlefield. His writings are taken as his support for dictatorship, though he was a great admirer of Kant.

FATHER OF MODERN PRINTING

In the German city of Mainz on the west bank of the Rhine river, an obscure pensioner was found dead in February 1468. For some years this destitute, half-blind old man had received an yearly allowance of cloth, grain and wine from the local ruler who held court just across the Rhine at Weisbaden. But few people remembered who he was, or what he had achieved. His name was Johannes Gutenberg (c.1395-1468), and he was the father of modern printing.

STEIN: (KARLY FREIHERR VON 1875-1831)

CREATOR OF MUNICIPAL GOVERNMENT

He was the most imposing figure on the German political stage between Frederick the Great and Bismarck who distrusted political theories. As a student of Burke and Montesquieu, and an admirer of English institutions,

Stein dreamed of far-reaching reforms. Rejecting monarchical absolutism, feudal privileges and the sovereignty of the people, he wished the middle classes to have their chance. "If the nation is to be uplifted," he declared, "the submerged part must be given independence and property should be protected by law." His chief monument is the creation of municipal self-government and his role in the emancipation of serfs, links him with modern concept of equal rights and self-determination; yet he was rooted in the past. Stein, a civil servant who advised Tsar Alexander-I, wished to revive the Empire, and envisaged the citizen as a member of some corporate body rather than as an isolated unit. These corporations, he believed, should advise the ruler on legislation and give their consent to taxation. Even this shade of liberal conservatism was too bright for the princes and the junkers (German noblemen), who angrily denounced him as a Jacobin French radicals. (Jacobin was a democratic republican club during the French Revolution in 1789. The name "Jacobin," a Dominican friary, is used for supporters of the French Revolution.)

HEGEL (GEORG WILLHELM FRIEDRICH 1770-1831)

The German philosopher was born at Stuttgart; he lectured at Jena and Nuremberg, and was professor of philosophy at Heidelberg and Berlin. His writings include, the Phenomenology of Spirit, Encyclopaedia of the Philosophical Sciences (1817), and Philosophy of Right. His German disciples split into "Right Hegelians," who like himself championed religion, the Prussian State and the existing order, and "Left Hegelians," included Marx, who used Hegelian dialectic to show the inevitability of radical change and criticized both religion and society. Hegel conceived of consciousness and the external object as forming a unity, in which neither factor can exist independently. Mind and nature are two abstractions of one indivisible whole. Thus, the world is the expression of one all-embracing absolute idea, an organism constantly developing by its own internal necessity so as to become the gradual embodiment of reason. The laws of thinking are, in principle, the laws of reality, e.g. logic must

Hegel

reflect the contradictions within nature, whereby everything is not only something, but is striving to become something else. The whole of history is realization of the *absolute* through phases of culture, each of which is embodied in a great nation. Each system by its own development brings about its opposite (antithesis), and finally a synthesis which unifies and includes both. These are the philosophical abstractions, hypotheses and assumptions that pass over the heads of ordinary mortals.

BISMARCK (OTTO VAN 1815-98)

A "BLOOD & IRON" CHANCELLOR

In 1848, the year of revolutions, the German people were politically more advanced than their rulers. The educated bourgeoisie looked with envy on the constitutional monarchy of Victorian England. The professors, then

HOW BISMARCK WAS SAVED FROM DROWNING

He was the man who famously unified Germany and ended France's domination of Europe. But new documents found in a dusty town hall reveal that Otto von Bismarck nearly drowned while swimming at the French seaside resort of Biarritz, an event that could have profoundly changed the course of European history.

Records found in the archive of the local swimming committee, reported in August 2006, show that a quick-thinking French lifeguard, Pierre Lafleur, plucked a floundering Bismarck from the waves. Lafleur also rescued Bismarck's mistress - 21-year-old Katharina Orloff - who had also got into difficulties during the trip in August 1862.

"The weather was good and the ocean was calm. But somehow Bismarck got swept into the sea by a strong current," Monique Beaufils, archivist at Biarritz's town hall, said. "Lafleur rescued the unconscious princess first. He then went back for Bismarck who was waving his arms for help. This wasn't easy. Bismarck was a big man, 1.9 metres tall, and weighed 100 kg. By the time Lafleur got him back to the beach he had passed out. A doctor revived him a few minutes later."

The rescue of Bismarck - then Prussia's ambassador in Paris in his mid-40s - would prove costly for France. Eight years later, in 1870, he masterminded Prussia's swift, crushing defeat of France in the Franco-Prussian war, ending French primacy in Europe. The Iron Chancellor went on to unify Germany, something that had eluded its kings and rulers since Charlemagne.

The story, meanwhile, did not end happily for Lafleur, the lighthouse keeper. He also drowned in the Atlantic four weeks later and there was nobody to rescue him. Bismarck agreed to be godfather to Lafleur's baby son, while his mistress - the wife of an elderly Prussia war hero, Prince Orloff, who apparently tolerated the affair - became godmother. Bismarck later recalled his time in Biarritz, where he met the French emperor Napoleon III, as the happiest of his life.

the most influential factor in the formation of opinion, were adherents of moderate liberalism. A new era in the life of the German people and the Prussian state opened with the accession of Wilhelm I and the summoning of Bismarck to the helm in 1862. Bismarck explained his view at a budget committee meeting in a few challenging sentences which echoed through Europe like a thunderclap. "The great questions of the time will be decided not by speeches and resolutions of majorities but by *blood and iron.*" He had championed the royal prerogative in the United Diet of 1847 in a series of speeches which marked him out as the leader of the extreme Right. The surrender of Frederick William IV to the Berlin mob in the *"March days"* of 1848 filled him with contempt. *(Wilhelm is also spelt as Willian because of their English connection with Queen Victoria).*

Bismarck declares: "Absolutism will neither be desirable nor successful in Germany in the long run. Absolutism would be the ideal form of government if the King and his officials are endowed with superhuman wisdom, and justice. But, since the most experienced and well-meaning absolute rulers are subject to human imperfections, this is not possible. Monarchy and the most ideal monarch, such as the Emperor Joseph II, stand in need of criticism which sets them right when in danger of losing their way, but this function is more efficiently discharged by a wise Minister than by elected assemblies." The grant of suffrage in 1866, he explained, was merely a tactical manoeuvre against Austria and a threat to use all weapons in a struggle against possible coalitions. The principle was sound if accompanied by open voting – a condition which he had reluctantly to omit. The masses were too easily moved by greed and rhetoric. Eveıy state which lost the restraining influence of the propertied classes was bound to come to grief. Revolution would be followed by dictatorship because in the end even the masses realise from bitter experience the need of order, and cheerfully sacrifice freedom for stability.

Here then was the *Iron Chancellor's* ideal state: hereditary monarchy, an invincible army, a prudent Chancellor with security of tenure, the preponderance of property, a representative assembly to let off steam, and social legislation for the working classes. Bismarck secured Austria's support in his war of 1863-4 with Denmark, but in 1866 he went to war with Austria and her allies. Prussia's victory brought about the unification of the northern German states under Bismarck's chancellorship (1867). The proclamation of the German Empire in 1871 and the annexation of Alsace and Lorraine crowned his work. As Imperial Chancellor, he sought to secure the peace settlement by forming the Triple Alliance with Austria and Italy (1882). At home, he became involved in conflicts with the church, and with the socialist movement, in both of which he was defeated. Kaiser Wilhelm II dismissed him in 1890.

NIETZSCHE (FREIDRICH WILHELM 1844-1900)
SUPPORTER OF SUPERMAN

Nietzsche expounded the philosophy of power. Hence, he was only interested in the superman. "Creative activity, not renunciation, is our duty and our right. Doctrines that create power are good, those which discourage it are bad. Of the latter, the worst is Christianity, *a fiction for weaklings,* a conspiracy of the feeble against the strong. The religion of pity is religion of slaves. "Ignorance and fear are the basis of all religions," he says. The man of genius is the creator of all values and, therefore, he is a law unto himself. *"The many must be sacrificed for the few."* This gospel of anarchy makes Nietzsche as much of a rebel in political theory as in ethics. He despises democracy as the *cult of numbers,* socialism as the superstition of equality. He abhors standardisation and the factors that produce it – custom, religion, law, public opinion, the state – for all of them tend to fetter the superman. The bureaucratic machine encourages the citizen to crave its aid instead of elbowing its way through the throng. The schools and universities teach mere erudition, the army is a great leveller. For Nietzsche, it was the superman all the way. The state, the Fatherland and the army were too firmly entrenched in the generation of 1870, yet he exerted an indirect political influence which cannot be ignored. The concept of will to power, the emphasis on personal prowess, contempt for compromise coloured the thought and hardened the heart of Bismarckian and post-Bismarckian Germany. And, of all of the political writers and philosophers, Nietzsche did most to produce dictators in Germany, including Hitler.

Nietzsche

> ***We know no spectacle so ridiculous as the British public in one of their periodical fits of morality.***
>
> – *Thomas Macaulay (Literary Essays)*

49

Winners are not sinless either; the war-dead also "speak"

After the war ended, official historians began distorting facts to tell the world that Allied were warriors in shining armours, fighting to defend democracy and freedom. This is not true. Hitler was trying to do what imperialists did before but with greater cruelty.

After the end of World War II in 1945, the victor powers started spinning the war history to prove their innocence. In Britain and the US, less flattering memories were suppressed. Robert Lilly, a distinguished American sociologist, wrote a book in 2000 which is a study of the rapes committed by American soldiers in Europe between 1942 and 1945. He submitted his manuscript in 2001. But after November 9, 2001 (Trade Tower bombing in US), its US publishers suppressed it. It finally appeared in 2003 in a French translation.

We knew about the sexual violence unleashed by the Red Army, but not about the mass rape committed by American and British troops. Lilly suggests a minimum of 10,000 American rapes. *Time* magazine reported in September 1945: *"we too are considered an army of rapists."* Americans also committed war crimes in the 1940s. Edger Jones, an "embedded" (the reporters who travel with army, hidden in tanks etc.) Pacific war correspondent, wrote in 1946; "We shot prisoners in cold blood, destroyed hospitals, strafed lifeboats, killed enemy civilians, finished off the wounded enemy, tossed the dying into holes with the dead, and boiled the flesh of enemy skulls to make table ornaments." The United States had got killed Allende in Chile and handed the country to a commerce-friendly, torture-loving, far-right junta in Argentina in 1973. The *My Lai* horror, committed by the US army in Vietnam in 1968, is still fresh in the popular memory.

The Big Three: Churchill, Roosevelt and Stalin at Yalta

The US was a colonial power in the Philippines and other former Dutch colonies. It fought in the Korean peninsula in 1950 and left it divided along 38th Parallel. Guam, Puerto Rico, and many of the 2,360 islands, islets and Pacific atolls were acquired or purchased by the US between 1856 and 1945 under various acts of Congress, including Guano Act 1856. America has supported dictators, including Duvaliers, Pinochet, Marcos, Yahya Khan, Lon Nol, Syngman Rhee, Mobutu, Shah of Iran and Saddam Hussein who has finally been dislodged by his patron in the war that George Bush started on March 19, 2003.

However, the British and American public share a sunny view of the World War II. Movies, popular histories and political speeches framed the war as a symbol of Anglo-American courage. We were told it was, "a war for democracy." Americans believe that they fought the war to save the world from Hitler. For the apologists of the British Empire, such as Niall Ferguson, the war was "an ethical battle where the sins of centuries of the British conquest, slavery and exploitation were washed away." It had become an ethical approval for the British-US power. The supporters of *"democratic imperialism"* prefer to forget that Hitler's dream was inspired, in part, by the British Empire. In eastern Europe, the Nazis sought to make their versions of America and Australia where ethnic cleansing and slave labour could create space for new settlements. In western Europe, Hitler sought to create an India from which he could get revenues, labour and conscripted soldiers. American imperialism in Latin America set an example for Germany's and Japan's claims to supremacy in their neighbouring regions. The British and Americans were key theorists of eugenics (racial superiority) and had made racial segregation respectable. The Nazi concentration camp was a British invention, tried out in many countries, induding South Africa.

IRAQ AND AFGHANISTAN

In Iraq and Afghanistan, the British were the first to use air power to suppress partisan resistance. The American *gulag* at Guantanamo Bay (Cuba) and Abu Ghraib in Iraq are the latest proofs to American guilt. British and US leaders gave assistance to Fascists. Capital and technology flowed freely, and Fascist despots received dignified treatment in Washington and London. Henry Ford gave Hitler birthday gifts of 50,000 German marks. The US carpet-bombed the industrial German city of Dresden in February 1945 when the war was almost over. And, 135,000 industrial workers and their family members were killed. The US also dropped atomic bomb in Hiroshima and Nagasaki in August 1945, killing over a million civilians, again when the war was almost over.

After Saddam was dislodged, leading nations of the world were re-aligning their relations with the victor if only to find a common ground for working together in the post-war re-construction of Iraq which, unlike Rwanda, Cameroon, Angola and Uganda, has plenty of oil to pay for construction. The victor set the moral standards and made the rules of the game to suit their interests. To be agreeable to the US, French President Jacques Chirac (who became president in 1995) welcomed the toppling of Saddam against whom he opposed military action. Russia sent its nuclear fleet in the international

> One British historian Andrew Roberts argues in his articles that for "the vast majority of its half-millennium-long history, the British empire was an exemplary force for good. The British gave up their empire largely without bloodshed, after having tried to educate their successor governments in the ways of democracy and representative institutions". In another, he insists that "the British empire delivered astonishing growth rates, at least in those places fortunate enough to be coloured pink on the globe." (compare this to Mike Davis' central finding, that "there was no increase in India's per capita income from 1757 to 1947.")

Soviet soldiers raise their flag over the Reichstag in Berlin in 1945

waters in 2004 to demonstrate that she was not entirely a diminished force in the Central Asia where it stayed for 10 years, promoting communism in Afghanistan and opposing the Baghdad Pact. The then German Chancellor Gerhard Schroder talked of peace in Iraq which was not very convincing despite his claim to have lived down the past since Bismarck who created modern Germany (1870-71) by violence from what was then known as little Prussia, a duchy of Teutonic order.

BRITISH ATROCITIES AND RUSSIAN DECEIT

More than 35,000 Indian soldiers in British army perished in the World War II and no mention has been made in any global list of war heroes. Imperial historian Niall Ferguson also admits that over one lakh Indian soldiers went to Mesopotamia (Iraq) in 1923 to fight for the British and 40,000 of them never came back home.

Not only historian Ferguson but many others, including Indian Prime Minister Manmohan Singh mentioned in 2005 while accepting the doctorate degree at Oxford the good work that Britishers did during their rule in India, including setting up the civil service, introducing English and setting up many institutions. That is true. But not the whole truth.

In his book *Late Victorian Holocausts*, published in 2001, Mike Davis tells the story of famines that killed between 12 million and 29 million Indians. When an *El Nino* drought destituted the farmers of the Deccan plateau in 1876, there was a net surplus of rice and wheat in India. But Viceroy Lord Lytton insisted that nothing should prevent their export to England. In 1877 and 1878, at the height of the famine, grain merchants exported a record 320,000 tonnes of wheat. As the peasants began to starve, officials were ordered "to discourage relief works in every possible way." The Anti-Charitable Contributions Act of 1877 prohibited "at the pain of imprisonment private relief donations that potentially interfered with the market fixing of grain prices." The only relief permitted in most districts was hard labour. In 1877, monthly mortality in the camps equated to an annual death rate of 94 per cent.

FAMINE: MILLIONS DIED

As millions died, the imperial government launched a militarized campaign to collect the tax arrears accumulated during the drought. The money, which ruined those who might otherwise have survived, was used by Lord Lytton to fund his war in Afghanistan. Even in places that had produced a crop surplus, the government's export policies, such as Stalin's in Ukraine, manufactured hunger. In the north-western provinces, Oud, and the Punjab, which had record harvests in the preceding three year, at least 1.25 million people died, says the book.

Three recent books – *Britain's Gulag* by Caroline Elkins, *Histories of the Hanged* by David Anderson, and *Web of Deceit* by Mark Curtis show how white settlers and British troops suppressed the Mau Mau revolt in Kenya in the 1950s. Thrown off their best land and deprived of political rights, the local people started to organize against colonial rule. The British responded by driving up to 320,000 of them into concentration camps and more than a million were held in "enclosed villages."

However, one British historian Andrew Roberts argued in his articles that for "the vast majority of its half-millennium-long history, the British empire was an exemplary force for good. The British gave up their empire largely without bloodshed, after having tried to educate their successor governments in the ways of democracy and representative institutions".

COUNTRY REPORT

The legend has it that in 1307 William Tell, a warrior, was forced to shoot the apple off his son's head for his refusal to pay taxes levied on the Swiss. He later defied both the Austrian army and tax collectors. And, it was out of this struggle that Switzerland was born.

50

Switzerland (The Swiss Confederation)

A group of cantons have joined together to become a testing ground of how human differences are managed. Switzerland is a country where direct democracy is practised as Athenians did before. But, Athenians failed and the Swiss have succeeded.

Switzerland is a land in central Europe. It is divided into three regions: the meadow-covered Jura Mountains; the central Mittelland, a rich agricultural and urbanised area; and the lofty crags of the Alps. It is one of the world's major financial centres whose economy is based largely on international trade and banking. Manufactures include watches, precision instruments, machinery, and chemicals. Tourism and agriculture are also important. Despite diverse ethnic groups, religions, and languages, Switzerland has maintained the world's oldest democracy for some 700 years. It is federal state with two legislative houses; its head of state and government is the president.

Switzerland is a federal republic. National policy is decided by the Federal Assembly: the 200-member National Council is elected every four years. The Council of States has 46 members appointed by the cantons. Federal government is administered by the Federal Council, consisting of seven members, each from a different canton, whom the Federal Assembly elects for four-year terms. Each year, a member of the Council is elected federal president. Major issues, such as constitutional changes, are decided by popular referendum. Women were denied voting rights until 1971.

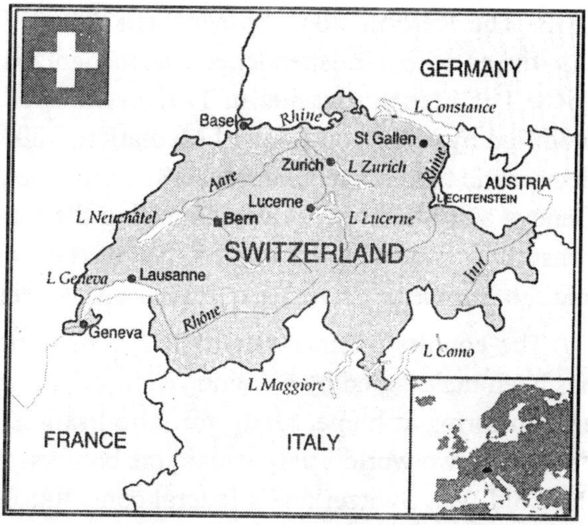

In 1798-1803, Napoleon gave the Swiss their first written constitution. The federal constitution of 1814-1815 which restored the old aristocratic and oligarchic cantonal governments fostered dissatisfaction among the people and in 1830 popular pressure resulted in the peaceful transformation of these illiberal governments into liberal democracies. Out of the brief civil war of 1847 came the democratic constitution of 1848 which, with some revisions in 1874, remains the fundamental law of the Swiss republic.

The original inhabitants were the Helvetians, who were conquered by the Romans in the Ist century BC. Germanic tribes penetrated the region from the 3rd to the 6th century AD, and Muslim and Magyar raiders ventured in during the 10th century. It came under the rule of the Franks in the 9th century and the medieval empire (later to become the Holy Roman Empire) in the 11th century. In 1291 three cantons formed an anti-Habsburg league that became the nucleus of the Swiss Confederation. It was a centre of the Reformation, which divided the confederation and led to a period of political and religious conflict. The French organised Switzerland as the Helvetic Republic in 1798. In 1815 the Congress of Vienna recognised Swiss independence and guranteed its neutrality. A new federal state was formed in 1848 with Bern as the capital. Switzerland remained neutral in both World War I and World War II and has continued to defend this neutrality. It joined the European Free Trade Association in 1960, but it has opted against joining the European Union. It joined the United Nations in 2002.

Switzerland became a political unit in 1291, when the 'forest cantons' of Schwyz, Uri, and Lower Unterwalden formed the *Everlasting League* for the defence of their liberties against their Habsburg (Austria) overlords. Practical freedom from Habsburg control was secured in 1389, (and earlier in 1307) and from the suzerainty of the emperor in 1499. The entry of new towns and districts brought the number of cantons to 8 by 1353 and to 13 by

1513. The Reformation was accepted during 1523-9 by Berne, and Basle. But, the complete independence was recognized by the Treaty of Westphalia, 1648. The French invasion in 1798 established a centralized govt; this was modified by Napoleon's Act of Mediation (1803), which made Switzerland a democratic federation. Under the 1815 peace settlement, Switzerland received Geneva and other territories, increasing the number of cantons to 22; a new constitution was adopted whereby Switzerland again became a confederation, and the European powers guaranteed Swiss neutrality.

The country's famed neutrality – proclaimed first in the 16th century – has been maintained by a countrywide militia which keep arms, ammunition and uniforms at home, ready for mobilisation. The army was strengthened during the two world wars to guard the borders, and it remained on alert during the Cold War. Switzerland's federal constitution says that "every Swiss male is liable for military service" and can be conscripted from the age of 20 to 42. Everyone must pay a military tax. Women can join army, but not for combat duties. The cantons – the constituent regions of the Swiss Confederation – provide their local soldiers with physical training under federal government supervision and the defence department then gives regular military training. All military personnel do regular target practice while off duty. They also perform civil protection duties in catastrophes or other emergencies. At the beginning of the 21st century, Switzerland was preparing to ease its policy of "security through autonomy" and replace it with "security through cooperation" – prompted partly by events in the Balkans, less than an hour's flight away. It planned to cooperate with friendly nations in military training exercises and peace-support operations to expand its participation in international security organisations. Switzerland is not a member of the European Union.

Switzerland is a small country that has been a testing ground for those profound problems in human relations which stem from differences in language and religion. The Swiss have gradually resolved these in an enlightening and pragmatic fashion. Independence and democracy, as stated earlier, began for the Swiss in 1291 when the freemen of the three forest cantons of Uri, Schwyz, and Unterwalden bound themselves into an *Everlasting League*. This was a loose confederation of practically sovereign communities. By 1513, it had thirteen members. Until the end of the eighteenth century Switzerland was a preponderately Germanic country. On the eve of the French Revolution, six of the cantons were direct democracies, four were aristocracies and three oligarchies. Switzerland's climate is temperate and continental, but the weather varies depending on terrain and altitude. Midwinter temperatures normally fall below freezing everywhere. The highest Alps lie under perpetual snow and ice. Summers in the Mittelland, however, are warm, and in the southern valleys they are often quite hot. Rain falls throughout the year. Over the centuries, grazing sheep and goats have stripped much of the country's original plant cover, although rare plants, and flowers can still be found above 2,000 m (6,500 ft.). The lower slopes support woodland; the southern valleys contain trees, such as cypresses and figs. Switzerland harbors many species familiar in other parts of Central Europe.

THE CANTONS

In the 13th, 14th and 15th centuries the Swiss cantons struggled to achieve independence. Since then, they have kept that freedom, forging disparate cultures, religions and languages into a strong national identity. In 58 BC, the Romans placed permanent garrisons in the Alpine passes of Helvetia – modern Switzerland. In 259 AD, the Alemanni were the first of several successive waves of German invaders to arrive. The area later came under Frankish rule, and by 1033 it had become a part of the Holy Roman Empire. In 1291 three cantons around Lake Lucerne – Uri, Schwyz and Nidwalden formed a confederation to break free of Habsburg rule. In 1332 Lucerne joined; Lurish joined in 1351, followed by neighbouring Glarus, Zug and Bern. By 1388 the Swiss Confederation was firmly established. During the next 150 years the Confederation grew in power and influence, while continuing to struggle for independence against the threat of warring neighbouring states.

The rise of Protestantism led to open conflict between cantons. Yet, while religious wars ravaged Europe, the Swiss remained neutral, patching up their domestic differences. The Peace of Westphalia (1648) finally acknowledged the cantons' freedom from imperial rule. Switzerland maintained its neutrality well into the 18th century. Then in 1794 revolutionary France occupied much of Switzerland, establishing the puppet Helvetic Republic four years later. In 1815 the last remaining cantons were admitted to the confederation, and Switzerland regained its neutrality.

NEUTRAL BY LAW

The Great Powers, by an Act of November 20, 1815, made the neutrality of Switzerland an essential part of the then international law of Europe. The Swiss Diet had already adhered to this principle on May 27, 1815. In May,

A lovely Swiss mountain

1848 the Swiss reaffirmed this policy. After the World War I, the National Council and the Council of States voted to join the League of Nations. The people affirmed this move on May 16, 1920. Article 435 of the Treaty of Versailles and Article 21 of the Covenant of the League emphasized the neutrality of Switzerland, which was to be exempt from participating in military sanctions. There was some inconsistency between League membership and traditional Swiss neutrality, particularly as long as the defeated powers were outside the League.

Switzerland, therefore, welcomed the entry of Austria in 1920 and Germany in 1926, and greatly deplored the subsequent withdrawals of Germany and Italy. Switzerland opposed League efforts to enforce peace through collective action. Indeed, as Professor Rappard points out, neutrality and collective security are, for Switzerland, mutually exclusive. He describes the Swiss policy vividly: "For Switzerland, neutrality is the parachute which she will not abandon until international flying becomes safer." "On May 14, 1938 the Council of the League of Nations, complying with a Swiss request, exempted Switzerland from participating in economic sanctions. Since Hitler's invasion of Poland in September, 1939 and subsequent German conquests, Switzerland has naturally felt uneasy concerning her safety. Swiss neutrality made the country a haven for many international bodies, such as the

International Red Cross and the short-lived League of Nations. The Geneva Convention of 1864 established laws for the conduct of war. Today United Nations and other international agencies have offices there. Even so, a referendum in 1986 rejected United Nations' membership as a threat to Swiss neutrality. (It joined UN in 2002).

A PROSPEROUS NATION AND CENTRE OF WORLD FINANCE

Switzerland is one of the most prosperous nations in the world. Its strategic location at the crossroads of Europe, combined with its political stability and tradition of confidentiality, has boosted its development as a centre of international finance. Switzerland's few flat areas are heavily populated, leaving little fertile land for farming. Nearly half the nation's food has to be imported. However, Swiss cheese and chocolates are exported all over the world. Mountain slopes provide pasture for beef and dairy cattle. Forests-protection against avalanches and floods covers many valley slopes, and clearance is forbidden by law. The welfare system provides child allowances and pensions; all salaried workers must take unemployment insurance. Education is free and compulsory from the age of 7 to 14, and secondary education is either academic or vocational. Higher education attracts an unusually large number of foreign students. The Swiss lead simple, democratic, creative lives in their narrow valleys. They have learned to harmonize their deep linguistic, religious, and political differences. As one authority has remarked: "The Swiss are fond of likening their country to a rambling old bungalow of twenty-two rooms, all strikingly peculiar but all under the same broad and sheltering roof." Their political experiments and cultural activities have flourished because of the enduring peace that has been preserved amidst belligerent neighbours.

In sum, Switzerland is the most democratic of all nations with its citizens showing a higher political intelligence and keener interest in public affairs than in other countries. Switzerland teaches us how traditions and institutions together can develop in the average man the qualities that make him a good citizen – shrewdness, moderation, common sense and a sense of duty to the community. It is because these have happened in Switzerland that democracy there is more democratic than in any other country of the world.

NATIONAL INDICATORS - SWITZERLAND

Area 41,300 sq.km.; capital Bern (Berne); major towns Zurich, Geneva, Lausanne; major ports river port Basel (on the Rhine); physical features most mountainous country in Europe (Alps and Jura mountains); highest peak Dufourspitze 4,634 m. in Apennines; administrative divisions 20 cantons and six demi cantons; armed forces No army: only on mobilisation; conscription 17 weeks' recruit training, followed by refresher training of varying length according to age; population growth rate 1.1% (1990-95); 0.5% (2000-05); ethnic distribution majority of Alpine descent; sizeable Nordic element; life expectancy 75 (men) 81 (women); education (compulsory years) 8-9 (depending on canton); literacy rate 99%; languages German 64%, French 19%, Italian 8%, Romansch 0.6%, (all official); religion Roman Catholic 50%, Protestant 48%

HISTORY

58 BC	Celtic Helvetii tribe submitted to Roman authority after defeat by Julius Caesar.
4th C AD	Region overrun by Germanic tribes, Burgundians, and Alemannians.
7th C	Formed part of Frankish kingdom and embraced Christianity.
9th C	Included in the Holy Roman Empire.
13th C	Habsburgs became dominant as overlords of eastern Switzerland.
1291	Cantons of Schwyz, Uri and Lower Underwalden formed Everlasting League, a loose confederation to resist Habsburg control.
1315	Battle of Morgarten: Swiss Confederation defeated Habsburgs.
14th C	Luzern, Zurich, Basel and other cantons joined Swiss Confederation, which became independent of Habsburgs.
1648	Treaty of Westphalia recognised Swiss independence from Holy Roman Empire.
1798	French invasion established Helvetic Republic, a puppet state with centralised government.
1803	Napoleon's Act of Mediation restored considerable autonomy of cantons.

1814	End of French domination; Switzerland reverted to loose confederation of sovereign cantons with a weak federal parliament.
1815	Great powers recognised 'Perpetual Neutrality' of Switzerland.
1845	Seven Catholic cantons founded Sonderbund league to resist any strengthening of central government by Liberals.
1847	Federal troops defeated Sonderbund in brief civil war.
1848	Bern chosen as capital.
1874	Powers of federal government increased; principle of referendum introduced.
late 19th C	Development of industry, railways and tourism led to growing prosperity.
1920	League of Nations selected Geneva as its headquarters.
1923	Switzerland formed customs union with Liechtenstein.
1960	Joined European Free Trade Association (EFTA).
1971	Women gained right to vote in federal elections.
1986	Referendum rejected proposal for membership of United Nations (UN).
1992	No to EC in a national referendum.
1999	Ruth Dreifuss elected as president, the first woman to hold this office.
2002	Joins the UN.

A country as small as any small Indian town (30,000 people) has stayed independent and free in the midst of rise and fall of many empires in Europe.

51

Liechtenstein
(The Principality of Liechtenstein)

It is the country of a mohalla size with very high per capita income. Its survival indicates how balance of power worked in Europe where nation-states fought over land, wealth or religion.

Liechtenstein, a principality in western Europe, is located between Switzerland and Austria. The Liechtensteiners are descended from the Alemanni tribe that came into the region after AD 500. The eastern two-third of Liechtenstein's small territory is composed of the foothills of the Rhaktikon Massif, part of the central Alps. The western section of the country is occupied by the Rhine river floodplain. It has no natural resources of commercial value, and virtually all raw materials, including wood, have to be imported. Manufacturing includes metalworking, pharmaceuticals, optical lenses, electronics and food processing.

The area was first settled by the Alemanni, a Germanic tribe, in about 500 AD, and Liechtensteiners still speak an Alemannic dialect of Germans. Under Charlemagne (742-814), it became part of the Carolingian Empire, and, for centuries, the land was divided between two independent counties based at Vaduz (present capital) and Schellenberg in the north. In 1719, these two counties were joined to form the principality of Liechtenstein, which remained a part of the Empire. In 1806 the Austrian king abondoned the title of Holy Roman Emperor, and Liechtenstein became part of the Rhine Confederation. In 1815 it joined the German Confederation, and achieved full independence in 1866 when the Confederation was dissolved.

Liechtenstein measures about 25 km from north to south, and is 6 km wide. To the north and west the land is part of a broad plain bordering the

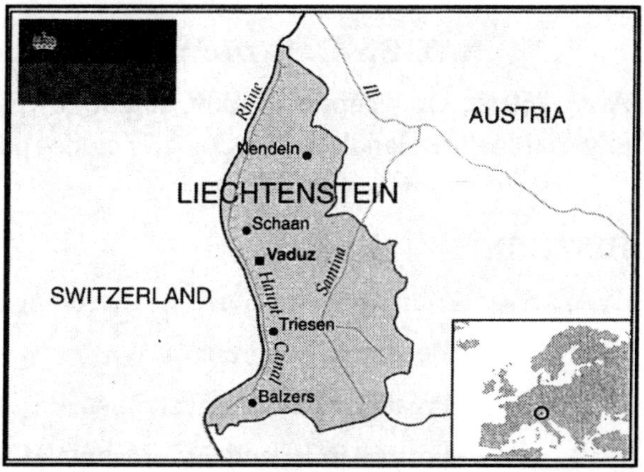

Rhine. Once marshy, it was drained in the 1930s for agricultural purposes. To the east, the foothills of the Alps rise to snow-capped peaks along the southern border. The climate is mild, and rainfall is plentiful. The valley suffers from sharp frosts, but a warm, dry wind that blows from the south brings an early spring. These conditions allow a rich variety of plant life, with Alpine plants at higher altitudes, and forests of beech, and ash on the lower slopes. The forests cover two-fifths of the land area, and are rigorously protected.

Liechtenstein is a constitutional monarchy with a single-chamber parliament, whose 25 members are elected every four years. There are 11 local authorities, each controlled by an elected mayor and council. Women may vote only in national elections. The official language is German, and most people are Roman Catholics, but fewer than two-thirds of the population are native Liechtensteiners; most of the rest are foreign industrial workers. No town in the country has more than 5,000 inhabitants.

Since 1921, Swiss currency has been used in Liechtenstein now that *euro* is the European currency, things have changed. Its advantageous tax and company legislation have made the principality an important banking center. Revenue also comes from the registration of foreign firms, and from a thriving government-sponsored tourist industry. Liechtenstein is particularly famous for its decorative postage stamps which add to the government revenue. Good roads provide excellent access from neighbouring countries, and the Paris-Vienna railroad crosses its territory. In 1930, the great majority of Liechtensteiners were farmers. Today, fewer than one in 40 of the population work on the land, and farms are being enlarged to improve efficiency, notably in stock breeding and dairy farming.

NATIONAL INDICATORS - LIECHTENSTEIN

Area 160 sq.km.; capital Vaduz; major towns Balzers, Schaan, Ruggell; physical features landlocked, Alpine; includes part of Rhine Valley in west;.

HISTORY

C. AD 500	Settled by the Germanic-speaking tribe.
1342	Became a sovereign state.
1434	Present boundaries established.
1719	Former independent lordships of Schellenberg and Vaduz were united by the Princes of Liechtenstein to form the present state.
1815-66	A member of the German Confederation.
1868	Abolished its standing armed forces.
1871	Liechtenstein was only German principality to stay outside German Empire.
1919	Switzerland replaced Austria as foreign representative of Liechtenstein.
1923	United with Switzerland in a customs and monetary union.
1938	Prince Franz Josef-II came to power.
1978	Joined the Council of Europe.
1984	Prince Franz Josef-II handed over power to Crown Prince Hans Adam. Vote extended to women in national elections.
1989	Prince Franz Josef-II died and was succeeded by Hans Adam-II.
1990	Became a member of the United Nations.
1991	Became seventh member of European Free Trade Association.
1993	Mario Frick of the VU became Europe's youngest head of government, aged 28.

As the one between two massive powers, I have always lived a life for whom neutrality could not save, nor could freedom cheer.

– C. Day Lewis, an Austrian poet

52

Austria (Republic of Austria)

Once the greatest Empire of Europe, Austria is now reduced to a rump of its former self but still radiating the light of all that is best in the European civilization-music, literature, painting and architecture. And, much else besides.

Austria is a republic with two legislative houses. Austria's chief of state is the president and its head of government is the chancellor. Its greatest cultural contribution has been in music. Major cultural figures in other fields include Oskar Kokoschka in art, Sigmund Freud in psychoanalysis, and Ludwig Wittgenstein in philosophy. Settlement in Austria goes back some 3,000 years, when Illyrians were probably the main inhabitants. The Celts invaded c. 400 BC and established the kingdom of Noricum. The Romans arrived after 200 BC and established the provinces of Raetia, Noricum, and Pannonia; prosperity followed and the population became Romanised. With the fall of Rome in the 5th century AD, many tribes invaded, including the Slavs; they were eventually subdued by Charlemagne, and the area became ethnically Germanic.

The distinct political entity that would become Austria emerged in 976 with Leopold-I of Babenberg. In 1278 Rudolf-IV of Habsburg (later Rudolf-I of the Holy Roman Empire) conquered the area; Habsburg rule lasted until 1918. While in power, the Habsburgs created kingdom centered on Austria, Bohemia, and Hungary. The Napoleonic Wars brought about the end of the Holy Roman Empire (1806) and the creation of the Austrian Empire. Count von Metternich tried to assure Austrian supremacy among Germanic states, but war with Prussia led Austria to divide the empire into the Dual Monarchy of Austria-Hungary.

Nationalist sentiment plagued the kingdom, and the assassination of Francis Ferdinand by a Servian nationalist in 1914 triggered World War I, which destroyed the Austro-Hungarian Empire. In the postwar carving up of Austria-Hungary, Austria became an independent republic. It was annexed by Nazi Germany in 1938 and joined the Axis powers in World War II. The republic was restored in 1955 after 10 years of Allied occupation. Austria became a full member of the European Union (EU) in 1995. After a half-century of military neutrality, Austria was one of the few members of the EU that was not a member of NATO at the outset of the 21st century.

ONCE WORLD'S GREATEST EMPIRE

Austria-Hungary Empire at one time included Austria and Hungary, Bohemia, Moravia, Bukovina, Transylvania, Carniola, Kustenland, Dalmatia, Croatia, Fiume and Galicia. The Dual Monarchy, formed by the compromise of 1867, created a king of Hungary in addition to the existing Austrian emperor; though these were the same person, Hungary was granted its own parliament and considerable autonomy. Francis Joseph held both titles from Austria-Hungary's inception until his death in 1916. Up to 1914, the monarchy maintained a balance among its many minorities; that year, as stated earlier, saw the balance toppled with the assassination of the Austro-Hungarian Francis Ferdinand by a Serbian nationalist that precipitated World War I. Following the defeat in the War and nationalist revolutions by the Czechs, Yugoslavs, and Hungarians, the monarchy collapsed in 1918.

HABSBURG DYNASTY

Habusburgs are European royal family to which the former imperial house of Austria-Hungary belongs. The name comes from the family castle in Switzerland. The Habsburg held the title of Holy Roman Emperor – 1273-91, 1298-1308, 1438-1740 and 1745-1806. They ruled Austria from 1278 and in 1806 adopted the title of emperor of Austria, which they held until 1918. The archduke Otto, son of the last emperor, Charles, is the present Habsburg pretender and became a Euro-M.P. in 1979.

Austria was one of the greatest empires in the history of Europe which also included the present-day Germany and most East European countries. Although its power has declined today, its geographical situation on the frontier of Western and Eastern Europe ensures its continuing influence on the continent's political and economic life. Mountainous and landlocked Austria is bordered by Switzerland and Liechtenstein to the west, Germany to the northwest, the Czech Republic and Slovakia to the north and northeast, Hungary to the east, Slovenia to the southeast, and Italy to the south. Its geographical location is also a source of its pre-eminence in European politics. Austria can be divided into three main topographical areas: the Alps; the lowlands in the east; and the hill country along the borders with the Czech Republic and Slovakia.

The Alps cover nearly two-thirds of the country, stretching from west to east in several major ranges. The central mountain chain (Tauern) includes some of the highest peaks. On either side of the Tauern, separated by deep river valleys, their streams fed by snowfields and glaciers, are two younger, more rugged limestone ranges. Some of the most majestic scenery is in the Otztaler Alps, near the borders with Switzerland and Italy. The mountains gradually fall away into the Danube valley in the north and to the Vienna basin in the east. These lowlands are Austria's main agricultural area, with vineyards on the valley slopes, the forested hills north of the Danube become more mountainous along the frontier with Slovakia, the Czech Republic and Germany. The Danube, Europe's second longest river, flows west to east across northern Austria, its tributaries draining much of the country. (Volga is the longest river 3,685 km; Danube is 2,820 km. But, in the 37 countries we discuss in this book, Danube is the longest). Most of Austria's lakes are around the Alpine ranges.

Austria is made up of nine semi-autonomous *Lander,* or provinces. The president and head of state is elected for a six-year term; he appoints the chancellor and cabinet, who must command a majority in the National Council (183 members), the more influential of the two legislative houses, elected every four years by a system of proportional representation. The Federal Council represents the Lander and its 64 members are elected by the provincial assemblies. The Lander is responsible for implementing local legislation, each has its own administration led by a governor elected by the provincial assembly which is itself elected by popular vote. The Socialist Party of Austria has for many years been the largest single party in government. The main party is

SIGMUND FREUD WHO INTREPRETED DREAMS

After escaping from the Nazis in 1938, Freud went straight back to work at his desk in Hampstead, London.

Born in Austria to Jewish parents, Sigmund Freud (1856-1939) was trained as a doctor in Vienna before specialising in the study of the brain and its disorders. Freud believed that human behaviour is rooted in sexual desire, present from infancy. He argued in *The Interpretation of Dreams* (1900) that the dream, like neurosis, was a disguised manifestation of repressed desire and provided the "hidden meaning" to behaviour. His excellence as a writer won him the *Goethe Prize* in 1930. He was an inspired phrase-maker, coining the terms *Oedipus complex*, *guilt complex*, *sublimation* and *death psychology*. He used his own patients' case histories to great effect. He shocked his readers when, in *The Future of an Illusion* (1927), he declared that religion was a *mass-delusion.*

Sigmund Freud deserves a place alongside Einstein, Newton, Darwin and Kant as the man who recognised and tried to map the way our primeval and dark impulses interact with our intellects to deliver results ranging from war to individual psychosis.

Nobody has been untouched by his findings. There would have been no sexual revolution without his insistence that the repression of our deepest primal sexual urges can be profoundly costly. Without his introducing us to the world of the subconscious and how it responds to our deep twin urges, we would have understood ourselves immeasurably less well. And although contemporary society has its psychoses, they are nothing besides the way earlier civilisations created mental demons that twisted peoples' minds and crushed their chance of happiness. Freud permitted a collective escape. We are incomparably happier and more peaceful as a result.

Yet for decades, he has been derided and scorned. He is one of the Europe's Right's deadliest iconic enemies and the more European conservatism grows in influence, the more Freud is taking cultural and intellectual hits. In its lexicon, he undermined morality and hypocrisy. He is the author of cultural relativism because his preoccupation is not with facts and reason, but the psychological drives of why anybody takes the position he does.

the centre-right Austrian People Party which has regularly featured in coalition governments with the Socialist Party. Other parties include the right-wing Freedom Party of Austria and the Green Party, which first won parliamentary representation in 1986.

Austrian garden at twilight, Vienna

Post-War Austria has become increasingly urbanized, with nearly one-fifth of the population living in the capital, Vienna. The vast majority are German-speaking Austrians, with a few minorities, mainly of neighbouring nationalities such as Hungarians, Croats and Slovenes. German is spoken in a variety of dialects; those of Tirol, Carinthia and Vorarlberg are particularly strong. Although most Austrians are Roman Catholic, the Lutheran Church has a significant membership; the 12,000 members of the Jewish community, much diminished since World War II, are concentrated in Vienna.

RICH IN MINERAL AND ENERGY RESOURCES

Austria is rich in mineral and energy resources, and both mining and energy production are nationalised industries. The country is the world's largest producer of magnesite, used in the chemical industry. Other materials mined include iron ore, lignite (brown coal), graphite, salt, quartz and clay. Austria is one of Europe's leading oil producers, although reserves of both petroleum and natural-gas are diminishing. Hydroelectric power supplies most of the country's electricity. The nationalised iron and steel industry is a model of efficiency, and nearly half of the annual production of 3.1 million tonnes of pig iron and 4.6 million tonnes of crude steel is exported. Austria also has one of the world's largest aluminium plants. There are important petroleum and chemical industries, as well as plants manufacturing plastics and electrical goods. Optical instruments for export are assembled near Salzburg. Austria, like most European countries, has extensive welfare network.

NATIONAL INDICATORS - AUSTRIA

Area 83,500 sq.km.; capital Vienna; population 8,106,000 (1996); major towns Graz, Linz, Salzburg, Innsbruck; physical features landlocked mountainous state, with Alps in west and south (Austrian Alps, including Grossglockner and Brenner and Semmerging passes, Lechtaler and Allgauer Alps north of river inn, Carnic Alps on Italian border) and low relief in east where most of the population is concentrated; river Danube; population density 94 (per sq.km.); urban population 56 % of total (1995); labour force 46% of population: 8% agriculture, 38% industry, 55% services (1990).

HISTORY

14 BC	Country south of river Danube conquered by the Romans.
5th C AD	Region occupied by Vandals, Huns, Goths, Lombards and Avars.
791	Charlemagne conquered the Avars and established the East Mark, the nucleus of the future Austrian Empire.
976	Holy Roman Emperor Otto-II granted the East Mark to the House of Babenburg, which ruled until 1246.
1282	Holy Roman Emperor Rudolf of Habsburg seized Austria and invested his son as its duke; for over 500 years most rulers of Austria were elected Holy Roman emperor.
1453	Austria became an archduchy.
1526	Bohemia came under Habsburg rule.
1529	Vienna besieged by the Ottoman Turks.
1618-48	Thirty Years' War: Habsburgs weakened by failure to secure control over Germany.
1713	By the Treaty of Utrecht, Austria obtained the Spanish Netherlands (Belgium) and political control over most of Italy.
1804	Francis-II took the title Emperor of Austria.

1806	Holy Roman Empire abolished.
1809-48	Guided by foreign minister Prince Klemenc von Metternich, Austria took a leading role in resisting liberalism and nationalism in Europe.
1815	After the Napoleonic Wars, Austria lost Netherlands but received Lombardy and Venetia.
1866	Seven Weeks' War: Prussia defeated Austria, which ceded Venetia to Italy.
1878	Treaty of Berlin: Austria-Hungary occupied Bosnia-Herzegovina; annexed 1908.
1914	Archduke Franz Ferdinand, the heir to the throne, assassinated by a Serbian nationalist; Austria-Hungary invaded Serbia, precipitating World War I.
1918	Austria-Hungary collapsed in military defeat; empire dissolved; republic proclaimed.
1919	Treaty of St. Germain reduced Austria to its present boundaries and prohibited union with Germany.
1934	Political instability culminated in brief civil war; right-wingers defeated socialists.
1938	The Anschluss: Nazi Germany incorporated Austria into the Third Reich.
1945	Following World War II, the victorious Allies divided Austria into four zones of occupation (US, British, French and Soviet); Second Republic established under Karl Renner.
1960-70s	Austria experienced rapid industrialisation and prosperity under governments dominated by moderate socialists and centrists.
1986	Election of Kurt Waldheim as president, despite allegations of war crimes during World War II, led to a measure of diplomatic isolation until Waldheim's replacement in 1992.
1995	Became a full European Union (EU) member.
1998	President Klestil re-elected.

PERSPECTIVE

The vanishing common culture of Nordic countries is becoming a midsummer night's dream. I guess this is a postmodern phenomenon.

– Walter C. Langsam

53

Five countries united in Nordic culture

It is a cultural group of people with shared history and a perception of common future, united in their social preferences and political choice, based on democracy and liberalism, the like of which is not found in other countries of Europe. The Nordic race is characterised by tall stature, long head, fair skin, hair and eyes, found chiefly in Scandinavia and the adjoining parts of Europe.

The 24 million people of the five Nordic countries – Norway, Sweden, Denmark, Finland and Iceland – are united in their cultural practices and social preferences despite enormous changes brought about by their becoming members of the European Union. The fact is that this had been a cultural group of people who had always had a shared history, too mixed to study separately. The Swedes, Danes, Norwegians, Finns and Icelanders celebrate the midnight sun when the night is longest. On this night, the Swedes dance around maypole, Danes light greatfires on beaches, Norwegians take their sailing boats to the fjords and people everywhere move to their cottages in the woods. They call it the "day of leaving cities, drinking, making love, drowning and bonfire". It is the night of exuberant pagan Nordic self-assertion.

The pan-Nordic identity is built on common culture, geography, history, ethnicity, homogeneity, love of nature and a shared Scandinavian language – except Finland. These roots go back to 1397 when they had a common union of kingdoms. Nordic people are good-looking, hard drinking, heavily taxed and prone to suicide due to depression caused by weather. Norsemen of olden time were greedy, psychopaths, fierce warriors, pillagers and traders. Vikings sacked Paris in 861, conquered much of England and northern France, settled in Iceland and Greenland, and raided Baghdad. But, there is an identity change now. Nordics are peace-lovers. During the Cold War, these five countries built a series of alliances and adopted neutrality. Denmark, Norway and Iceland joined NATO while Sweden and Finland adopted neutrality as policy. Now, EU is the catch phrase; it is commerce and security as well. But, for now Iceland and Norway remain outside EU; one doesn't know for how long. There is a Nordic model of social care. Support for high rate of trade union membership, high quality of public service and high taxes seem part of Nordic identity. The peoples in this region have free schooling, quality health care, generous unemployment and sickness benefits, state-funded maternity and paternity leave, universal pension and more. Norway, with oil, is the richest, and Sweden comes next.

PRIMACY OF THE ENGLISH LANGUAGE

Now things are changing. English is fast becoming the lingua franca of the Nordic countries. In Europe, nobody can hope to prosper without knowing good English. The immigrants are also changing the situation, specially in Sweden. A closer relationship with EU has led to the partial surrender of sovereignty and local preferences. The inroad of Americanism, IT culture, expanding pan-European concept, flight of Norwegians and Swedes to America for jobs and warmer climate are changing the complexion of Nordic countries. And, the changes may be enormous to finally destroy the common identity of Nordic Countries.

Scandinavian governments are typically European, in that they are parliamentary democracies, regardless of their monarchical or presidential form. Like the British and American governments, they are true democracies as the voice of the people, freely expressed at the polls, is the final power in the state. Like the British government, each Scandinavian government is headed by a premier and a cabinet which must command parliamentary confidence in order to continue in office. Perhaps nowhere in the world has the social role of government been so widely accepted and developed while still preserving free enterprise, including most of the forms of enlightened capitalism. Many of the parties are organised on a socio-political basis, unlike American and British political parties. The cooperative movement has been injected into practically all phases of life.

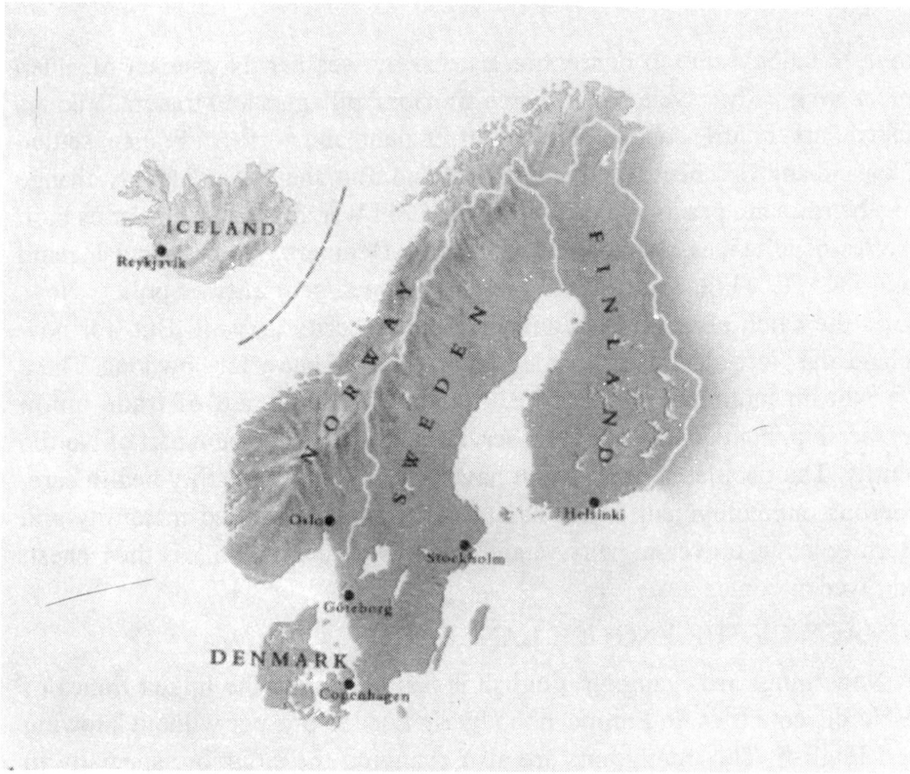

Denmark, Finland, Norway and Sweden located in northern Europe and once combined into the most powerful state on that continent, have much the same background of history and culture. Their total population is about 17,000,000 people related in race and language except for the Finns (Finno-Ugrians) and the Laplanders. The common religion is Lutheran, and education and culture are well advanced. All four countries run north and south. The terrain is varied and ranges from the flat rolling terrain of Finland or the sandy stretches of Denmark to the towering mountains of Sweden and Norway with their deep fjords and precipices. All lie around the Baltic Sea with the exception of Norway, which faces the North Sea.

From the standpoint of government they have been one of the most successful testing grounds for democratic principles. Three of the governments are constitutional monarchies and one a parliamentary democracy. The Scandinavians have a deep respect for freedom and a fine sense of social responsibility, and because of necessity they have developed cooperatives to a highly advanced stage regulated by the governments.

The Scandinavian peninsula comprises Norway and Sweden but politically and culturally, it also includes Denmark, Iceland, the Faroe Islands and Finland.

54

The Scandinavian conquests dwarf those of Caesar's

The Scandinavian people of Nordic stock had made history well before it was written with so much of drama and romance as about Columbus who could never excel what Scandinavians did before him.

Scandinavia's history is an epic of conquests that dwarf Caesar's and modern dictators. Norsemen ruled the dark, open seas when Britons timidly stayed home. They discovered America five centuries before Columbus seized most of the islands in the Atlantic and invaded and conquered Britain several times. At the other extremity of Europe, they founded the first Russian state, ruled it for four centuries and shook Constantinople at the prime of its power. In between, they terrorized the whole continent, plundering Paris no fewer than three times, and overran Italy, Sicily, Spain and North Africa. The institution of feudalism was largely a reaction to irresistible Scandinavian rapacity. The Pope called for the Crusades, which marked the end of feudalism, partly to divert the ravaging energies of the Scandinavians away from Italy.

These countries of the north are difficult terrain of mountainous, sparse and forested land. Only Denmark and southern Sweden offer rich pasture land. Scandinavians have traditionally been obliged to earn their livings as fishermen, seamen, lumbermen or graziers. Coupled with a paucity of winter sunshine, or even daylight, this has made for the characteristics of strength, taciturnity, introspection and sudden exuberance that the whole world recognizes as Nordic qualities. Nobody knows the origins of the Sami, or Lapps, who live in the extreme north of Sweden, Finland and Norway, sometimes nomadically with reindeers. The Finns evidently originated somewhere in the east. The others, however, are quintessentially Nordic. Except again for the Finns, whose language is akin to Hungarian, they all speak a variety of the same Germanic language.

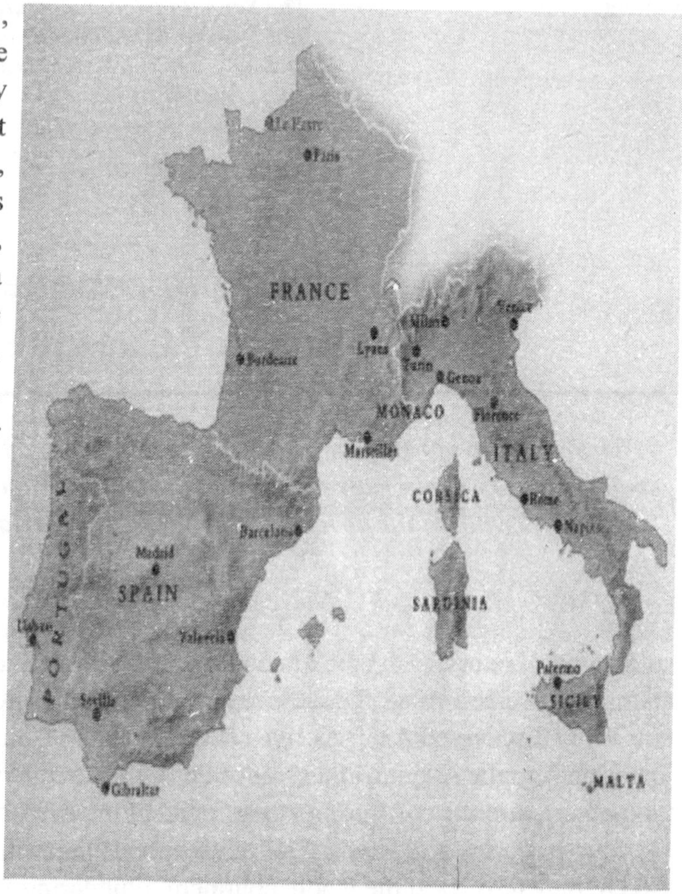

At one time or another, most of them have occupied each others' territories or have formed part of the same State – even Iceland was constitutionally subject to Denmark until 1944 – and this has given them, willy-nilly, similar styles of government. Norway, Sweden and Denmark have monarchies of the most self-effacing kind, with their kings and queens preferring populist activities to parades and pageantry. All the Nordic States are governed by democratic systems. Iceland claims to have the oldest elected assembly in the world – the Alting having been in existence for more than a thousand years.

SOCIAL JUSTICE MOST

PRACTISED IN REGION

This was the homeland of the Vikings, the bravos of medieval Europe, whose trading settlements extended as far as the eastern Mediterranean.They reconnoitred Greenland and North America, and their occupation of Normandy (Norseman's land) led to the conquest of England. The characteristics of a fighting aristocracy are found in Scandinavia, but are remembered always through the great works of medieval literature, the Icelandic Sagas, which record the high-flown pugnacity of the Norwegian kings living in Iceland, and the exploits of legendary heroes.

Today, the Scandinavian is about the most wholesome thing in Europe. It is mainly in Scandinavia that serious progress has been made in social fields. The maldistribution of wealth hardly exists. It is said that out of 13 Danish high court judges, only one can afford a car but few Danish workmen cannot afford more than a bicycle. According to a survey, the highest paid government official in England earns twenty-four times more than the lowest paid. In Sweden, the highest paid earns only six times more than the lowest, and the lowest is paid nearly twice as much as the lowest in England. Earlier, Sweden was one of the first five nations in Europe in wealth per capita. Sweden has also been more successful than any other nation in reducing disparities by means of systematic and carefully-timed launching of public works projects.

PEOPLE LIVE BY WATER

The Scandinavian's character flows from the sea. The coastline of minuscule Denmark is longer than that of England. The coast-line of Norway, with her barely five million people, is longer than that of all the United States. Nature forced the people to live by water: the glaciers scraped the Scandinavian peninsula clean of fertile top-soil, depositing it in Germany. Retreating glaciers left the Peninsula a long, nearly barren spine of rock shredded with lakes and fjords. Only 9 per cent of Sweden's area is arable, and only 3 per cent of Norway's. Denmark is wholly arable, but the soil varies from only average to below average in richness. Arid rock pressed the people into the sea and made them the world's best sailors, which they remain today. Until the outbreak of the last war, Norway had the largest merchant fleet in the world per capita of population. Her annual fishing catch was the world's biggest. The sea is responsible not only for the material, but also for the spiritual health of Scandinavians.

NORDIC TYPE

It is a racial group characterised by tall stature, long head and fair skin and eyes, found chiefly in Scandinavian and the adjoining parts of Europe. The Nordic type is present in its purest form among the Swedes and Finns, somewhat less in Norway, Denmark, and the coastal region of Germany, and among the Baltic peoples. It is well represented in Britain, specially in the north of England and the Western Isles of Scotland. The term "Nordic" is, however, no longer in current scientific use. "Nordic" is a "racial type" while Scandinavian is a political term.

SCANDINAVIANS UNITED MUCH BEFORE EUROPEANS DID

The sea has been for Scandinavia what the great western frontier was for America. It was an outlet to freedom which destroyed tyranny at source – for a tyrant must first be able to keep his people in before he can keep them down. Like the American frontier, it was also an attraction, competing with rising industry for labour power: if wages were not high and conditions of work were not good, Scandinavians had the world for a playground and ships for legs to take them there. There is indubitably a direct relation between the sea and the broad-mindedness that distinguishes Scandinavian morals and her people's breadth of international sympathies. The sea-faring Scandinavians with the world for a school learned too much from the follies and triumphs of man in his many different environments to nourish much vanity or many delusions about themselves at home. No wonder happiness and prosperity are found in the Scandinavian countries in much greater measure than anywhere else in Europe.

In modern times, these States have been among the least aggressive of all the European countries, devoting themselves chiefly to social progress and enrichment. They were relatively unharmed by the great twentieth-century wars, and they have been famous pioneers of public welfare and successful economic specialists: the Danes as agriculturists, the Norwegians as shipowners, the Swedes as manufacturers of cars, aircraft and machinery, the Finns as lumbermen and shipbuilders. And in the European context they have chiefly been successful, perhaps, in cooperating among themselves. Long before Europe began its present movement towards unity, the Scandinavian countries had established common institutions of their own and had managed to present themselves to the world as a bloc – the first to prove, despite all the historical evidence, that Europeans need not be endemically at each others' throats.

SCANDINAVIA, at a glance

DESPITE ITS SMALL population, Scandinavia has had a huge impact on European history. The Vikings of Denmark and Sweden raided most European nations in the 9th and 10th centuries, leaving their mark wherever they landed. During the 16th century, Sweden emerged as one of Europe's most powerful nations, creating an empire that lasted for200 years. In the 20th century, Scandinavian nations led the way in establishing welfare states to support their people, and Norway was the first European nation to give women the vote.

Sweden

During the 16th and 17th centuries, Sweden took over Norwegian cities such as Trondheim and rose to become one of the most powerful states in Europe. The country adopted the Lutheran faith, and championed the Protestant cause. A succession of able kings carved out a vast empire that surrounded the Baltic Sea and included Finland and parts of Russia and northern Germany.

Modern Scandinavia

Norway broke free from Swedish rule in 1905; Finland won independence from Russia in 1917. Later, the Scandinavia nations worked together, setting up the Nordic Council in 1952 to improve relations between them. Denmark, Sweden, and Finland have joined the European Union.

Scandinavia in World War II

Denmark and Norway were occupied by Germany from 1940-45; Finland was occupied by the Russians. Sweden stayed neutral. Most people defied the occupied forces- King Christian X and other Danes helped Jews to escape to Sweden but a collaborationist government was set up by fascist politician Vidkun Quisling (1887-1945) in Norway.

Empire of Canute

In 1016, the throne of England fell vacant. It was seized by Canute, brother of the Danish king. Within a few years, Canute added Denmark, Norway, and southern Sweden to his empire, ruling with great skill until his death in 1035.

Coming of Christianity

The nations of Scandinavian became Christian during the 9th and 11th centuries although remote regions kept their traditional beliefs until much later. In Norway, initially churches were built of wood.

Union of Kalmar

In 1397, in Kalmar, Sweden, Margaret of Denmark persuaded Norway and Sweden to unite. Kingship was elected in all these countries, so the union could not be maintained. It collapsed in 1523, when Gustavus I became king of Sweden.

Great Northern War

In 1700, Sweden's neighbours joined together to break its stranglehold on the Baltic and its trade. When peace finally came in 1721, Sweden lost its supremacy in the region, and Russia achieved its "window on Europe" by gaining access to the Baltic.

Welfare States

The Scandinavian states were among the first to introduce a strong welfare system. Good child care and facilities for the sick and elderly were provided and unemployment has been kept low. High taxes were needed to pay for these benefits.

Gustavus II Adolphus

Gustavus Adolphus (1594-1632) became king of Sweden in 1611. Aided by his chancellor Axel Oxenstjema, he improved the economy and extended the Swedish empire in northern Poland. In 1630, he entered the Thirty - Year War on the side of the German Protestants fighting against Catholic Habsburg domination. In a few months, he won a series of battles that changed the map of Europe.

Timeline

700s Vikings raid Europe's coast line.

1016 Canute rules Denmark, Norway and England.

1397 Kalmar Union between Denmark, Sweden and Norway.

1523 Sweden leaves union and gains independence.

1658 Swedish Empire reaches its greatest extent in Europe.

1700-21 Great Northern War: Sweden fends off an attempted takeover from neighbouring countries.

1814 Norway is transferred from Denmark to Sweden.

1905 Norway gains independence.

1917 Finland gains independence from Russia.

1940-45 Germany occupies Denmark and Norway; Russia occupies Finland.

1967 Denmark joins European Union.

1995 Sweden and Finland join European Union.

Once united by force into a single union, Norway, Sweden and Denmark are now independent countries, independently pursuing happiness in their own ways.

55

Norway (Kingdom of Norway)

Although not much different from other Nordic countries, Norway, however, has its own stories of failure and success.

Norway is in the northwestern Europe. Most people are of Germanic origin and the largest minority goup is the Sami (Lapps). Language: Norwegian. Located in the western part of the Scandinavian Peninsula, Norway is Europe's fifth largest country. It is a mountainous land with extensive plateau regions in its southwestern and central parts. Traditionally a fishing and lumbering country, it has greatly increased its mining and manufacturing activities since World War II. It has a developed economy largely based on services, petroleum and natural gas production, and light and heavy industries. Literacy is virtually 100%. Norway is a constitutional monarchy with one legislative house; its chief of state is the king, and the head of government is the prime minister. Several principalities were united into the kingdom of Norway in the 11th century. It had the same king as Denmark from 1380 to 1814, when it was ceded to Sweden. The union with Sweden was dissolved in 1905, and Norway's economy grew rapidly.

It remained neutral during World War I, although its shipping industry was destroyed by German troops. Norway maintains a comprehensive welfare system and is a member of NATO. Its citizens rejected membership in the European Union in 1994. The Norwegian sea is an Open Sea, bordered by Greenland, Iceland, Spitsbergen and Norway. A submarine ridge linking Greenland, Iceland, the Faeroe Islands, and northern Scotland separates the Norwegian Sea from the Atlantic Ocean. The sea is crossed by the Arctic

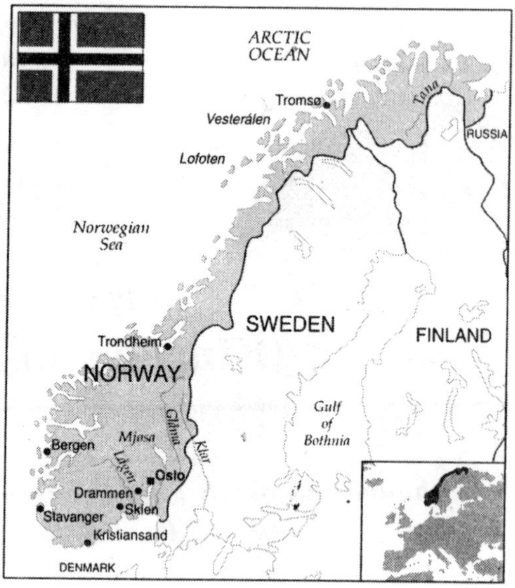

Circle, but the warm Norway Current that flows northeast off the Norway coast produces generally ice-free conditions. Colder currents mixing with this warm water create excellent fishing grounds.

Along its shores, are 150,000 islands. The climate is mild, being influenced by the Gulf Stream. Coal, gypsum, granite, iron ore and zinc are among the natural resources. For the most part, the land has a generous covering of forests. The Norwegians are of the same stock as the Swedes, blond Nordics, occasionally crossed with groups from other countries. The language bears a close resemblance to Swedish, as does the culture as a whole.

The Kingdom was consolidated from several small groups during the ninth or tenth centuries. In the fourteenth century, Sweden, Norway and Denmark were combined into a single union under Queen Margareta's centralized rule. In 1449, Sweden broke away from that union, but Norway and Denmark continued their partnership until the nineteenth century. In 1536, Denmark terminated the independent existence of Norway, but by 1660, a joint central administration for both kingdoms was established, and in the Peace of Kiel Jan. 14, 1814, Norway was ceded to Sweden, while Iceland, Greenland, and the Faeroe Islands, which had formerly belonged to Norway, were retained by Denmark. Finally, in 1905, as a result of a consolidation of the Liberal party with other political groups Norway broke away from Sweden and set herself up as an independent state.

Norway lies along the Western coast of the Scandinavian peninsula. Its spectacular rugged land supports a small population. Long and thin – only 450 km across at its widest point – Norway narrows in places to 80 km. Norway's ancient granite bedrock was eroded by Ice Age glaciers and shaped into high mountains and deep valleys. There are more than 160,000 lakes; the largest is lake Mjosa in the southeast. Fjords (highwalled sea lakes in glacial valleys) turn the coastline into a maze flanked by some 50,000 islands.

Oslo, the capital, is in the lowlands. Important lowland farming is in central Norway, and near Stavanger in the southwest. Glacial erosion has flattened some mountains, creating large plateaus such as the Hardangervidda in southern central Norway. Farther north lies the Jotunheimen mountain range. Towards the coast is the Jostedalsbreen icefield with its flowing glaciers. Northern Norway, lying mostly above the Arctic Circle, ends in the Finnmark Plateau. Norway also includes the bleak Arctic islands of Svalbard and Jan Mayen.

Below the Arctic Circle, the North Atlantic Drift gives western Norway a relatively temperate climate. Eastern Norway has colder winters, warmer summers and lower rainfall. About one-quarter of the country is forested. The richly varied vegetation includes blueberries, cranberries and cloudberries – the fruits of Scandinavian delicacies. Recently, large areas have been damaged by acid rain from industrial air pollution originating in neighbouring countries. Large predatory animals such as wolves, bears and lynx have been hunted almost to extinction in the southern forests.

THE VIKINGS

Norway's immense mountains and deep fjords have always made land travel and communications extremely difficult, so it is not surprising that the country has a long maritime and seafaring history. Norway's earliest settlers, Central European hunter-gatherers, gradually moved north as the last Ice Age ended. By the 9th century AD, people settled on farms. As the population expanded, settlers began trading and raiding Scotland, Ireland, northern England and parts of northern France (Normandy). They also settled in Iceland and Greenland, and crossed the Atlantic to North America.

NORWAY'S ISLAND POSSESSIONS

A group of Arctic islands north of mainland Norway was recognised as a Norwegian possession by international treaty in 1920, and contains the Spitsbergen group of islands as well as White Island, King Charles island and the southerly Bear Island. Well known to the Vikings, the islands were only rediscovered in 1596. At first, they were centres for whaling, and later for hunting and trapping. Since 1773, they have been used as a base for explorations to the North Pole. But it was the discovery of coal in the early 20th century that brought the islands to international prominence. The extreme winter weather conditions mean that the population is entirely seasonal; few, if any, would wish to stay permanently. In the brief summer months, however, the North Atlantic Drift can raise the temperature to 15°C.

The Norwegian Fjord is the beauty unmatched by any in the world

The name Viking comes from Skagerrak, the strait between Norway and Denmark, then called the Vik.

The decline of the Viking era strengthened the monarchy, but the country was devastated by the bubonic plague which reached Norway in 1350. The Kalmar Union of 1397 combined the royal lines of Norway, Sweden and Denmark. In 1814, Norway was forced into a union with Sweden but did gain limited internal self-government. After a series of popular protests, Sweden recognised Norway's independence in 1905. Norway, which sought to remain neutral in World War II, was occupied by the German army from 1940 to 1945. After the War, Norway joined the North Atlantic Treaty Organisation (NATO) and the European Free Trade Association (EFTA).

Norway had adopted in 1814 the constitutional monarchy which remains today. The parliament, (or Storting), is elected by universal adult suffrage for a 4-year term and, in turn, selects a prime minister and cabinet. The king acts as head of state but his functions are mainly ceremonial. Most Norwegians share common ethic and linguistic origins with their Scandinavian neighbours. Most Norwegians belong to the national Lutheran Church. Some 20,000 Sami (Lapps) and 10,000 Finns make up the main ethnic minorities with their own languages. They live mainly in traditional homelands in the far north. Some 2,000 Sami on the Finnmark Plateau are semi-nomadic herders of reindeer.

Only 5 per cent of the land area is farmed. The rest is forest. Norway's economy is chiefly industrial. Nearly half of the small southern coastal agricultural area provides pasture; the rest is used to grow cereals, potatoes and animal fodder. Most holdings are small. Metallic ores are the only substantial mineral resources on the mainland. Iron and steel production, once the most important industries, have been replaced by aluminium production from imported bauxite. Norway is still a leading exporter of nickel, copper and zinc. During the 1970s, deposits of natural gas and oil were found in the Norwegian North Sea sector. Norway became a significant exporter of oil and gas, while other industries suffered from lack of investment. The oil-dependent economy was hit very hard by falling oil prices in the late 1970s. Today much of the country's energy is produced by hydroelectric plants on the many fast-flowing rivers.

Norway's large merchant fleet, though declining in size, still makes a large contribution to the balance of payments. Trade has been affected by Norway's decision in 1994 not to join the European Union, but free-trade agreements have been concluded. The magnificent scenery and outdoor sports facilities draw tourists year-round. It is a welfare state. There is compulsory insurance, education and highly subsidized higher education.

NATIONAL INDICATORS - NORWAY

Area 3,87,000 sq.km.; capital Oslo; major towns Begen, Trondheim, Stavanger; physical features mountainous with fertile valleys and deeply indented coast; forest cover 25%, extends north of Arctic Circle; territories dependencies in the Arctic (Svalbard and Jan Mayen) and in Antarctica (Bouvet and Peter I Island, and Queen Maud Land); political system constitutional monarchy; administrative divisions 19 countries; population 4,337,000 (1995); ethnic distribution majority of Nordic descent; Lapp minority in the far north; urban population (% of total) 73 (1995); education (compulsory years 9), literacy rate 99%; languages Norwegian (official).

HISTORY

5th C First small kingdom established by the Goths

8th-11th Cs Vikings from Norway raided and settled in many parts of Europe.

1217-63 Haakon-VI established royal authority over nobles and church and made the monarchy hereditary.

15th C Norway was increasingly treated as an appendage of Denmark.

1661	Denmark restored formal equality of status to Norway as a twin kingdom.
1814	Treaty of Kiel: Denmark ceded Norway (minus iceland) to Sweden.
1905	Union with Sweden dissolved.
1935	First Labour government took office.
1940-45	German occupation.
1949	Became a founding member of the NATO.
1952	Joined Nordic Council.
1960	Joined European Free Trade Association (EFTA).
1972	National referendum rejected membership of European Economic Community (EEC).
1975	Export of North Sea oil began.
1981	Gro Harlem Brundtland (Labour) became Norway's woman prime minister.
1991	Olaf-V succeeded by his son Harald-V.
1994	National referendum rejected membership of European Union (formerly EC).
1996	Brundtland resigned; succeeded by Thorbjoern Jagland.
1997	Jagland failed to win decisive majority in general election. Khell Magne Bondevik became prime minister.

A land of lakes, rivers and high mountains, Sweden remains a torch-bearer in Europe in respect of social justice and economic security to become a model for the world in these troubled times.

56

Sweden
(Kingdom of Sweden)

Sweden is a constitutional monarchy with a parliamentary system of government and a highly developed economy. It ranks first in the world in The Economist's Democracy Index and 7th in the United Nation's Human Development Index. "Work and safety, for all" is Social Democratic slogan from the election, 1936 and the basic message is still the same.

Sweden is located on the Scandinavian Peninsula in the northern Europe. The population is largely homogenous, although there are Finnish and Sami minorities and about 10% of the inhabitants are immigrants or their descendants. Language: Swedish (official). Religions: Church of Sweden (Lutheran), Islam, Roman Catholicism, Pentacostalism. Sweden has three traditional regions. Mountainous Norrland covers about three-fifths of the country and has vast forests and large ore deposits. Svealand has undulating glacial ridges and contains most of the country's 90,000 lakes. Gotaland comprises the stony Smaland highlands and the rich Skane plains. About 15% of Sweden lies north of Arctic Circle. The economy is largely based on services, heavy industries and international trade. Sweden has large deposits of iron ore; industries include mining, lumbering, steel manufacturing, and tourism. Important agricultural products include grains, sugar beets, potatoes, and livestock.

Sweden is a Nordic country and has land borders with Norway, to the west, and Finland, to the northeast. It is connected to Denmark by the Öresund Bridge in the south. At 450,000 km, Sweden is the third largest country in the

European Union in terms of area, and it has a total population of over 9.2 million. Sweden has a low population density of 20 people per km, but with a considerably higher density in the southern half of the country. About 85% of the population live in urban areas, Sweden's capital is Stockholm, which is also the largest city in the country (population of 1.3 million in the urban area and with 2 million in the metropolitan area). The second and third largest cities are Gothenburg and Malmo. Sweden has been a member of the European Union since 1 January 1995 and is a member of the OECD.

CONSTITUTIONAL MONARCHY

Sweden is a constitutional monarchy with one legislative house; its chief of state is the king, and the head of government is the prime minister. The first inhabitants were apparently hunters who crossed a land bridge from Europe c. 12,000 BC. During the Viking era (9th-10th centuries AD), the Swedes controlled river trade in eastern Europe between the Baltic Sea and the Black Sea; they also raided western European lands. Sweden was united and christianised in the 11th-12th centuries. It conquered the Finns in the 12th century, and in the 14th century it united with Norway and Denmark under a single monarchy. Sweden broke away in 1523 under Gustav-I Vasa. In the 17th century it emerged as a great European power in the Baltic region, but its dominance declined after its defeat in the Second Northern War (1700-21). It became a constitutional monarchy in 1809 and united with Norway in 1815; it acknowledged Norwegian independence in 1905. Sweden maintained its neutrality during both World Wars. It was a charter member of the UN but abstained from membership in NATO and the European Union until the 1990. A new constitution drafted in 1975 reduced the monarch's powers to those of a ceremonial head of state. In 1997 Sweden began the controversial shutdown of its nuclear power industry. By the early 21st century it had emerged as a European centre of telecommunications and information technology.

Sweden emerged as an independent and unified country during the Middle Ages. In the 17th century the country expanded its territories to form the Swedish empire. Most of the conquered territories outside the Scandinavian Peninsula were lost during the 18th and 19th centuries. The eastern half of Sweden, present-day Finland, was lost to Russia in 1809. The last war in which Sweden was directly involved was in 1814, when Sweden by military means forced Norway into a personal union with Sweden, a union which lasted until 1905. Since then, Sweden has been at peace, adopting a non-aligned foreign policy in peacetime and neutrality in wartime.

ONCE EUROPE'S GREAT POWER

During the 17th century Sweden emerged as a European Great Power. Before the emergence of the Swedish Empire, Sweden was a very poor, scarcely populated, barely known of country in northern Europe with no significant power or reputation. Sweden rose to European power during the tenure of king Gustavus Adolphus, thanks to territories seized from Russia and Poland-Lithuania and the Thirty Years' War. These military, victories made Sweden the continental leader of Protestantism until the Empire's collapse in 1721.

Gustav Adolphus' war against the Holy Roman Empire had a high cost; during the Thirty Years' War, a third of the population of the Holy Roman Empire died, and the Holy Roman Empire lost its position as the mightiest country in Europe. Sweden managed to conquer approximately 50 percent of the Holy Roman states. Gustav Adolphus planned to become the new Holy Roman Emperor over a united Scandinavia and the Holy Roman states; however, after his death in 1632 at the Battle of Lützen, this plan was scrapped. After the Battle of Nördlingen, Sweden's only military disaster, the pro-Sweden feeling among the German states was severely injured. These German provinces excluded themselves from Swedish power one by one, leaving Sweden with only a couple of northern German provinces: Swedish Pomerania, Bremen-Verden and Wismar.

In the middle of the 17th century Sweden was the third largest country in Europe by land area, only superseded by Russia and Spain. Sweden reached its largest territorial extent under the rule of Charles X (1622–1660) after the treaty of Roskilde in 1658. The foundation of Sweden's success during this period is credited to Gustav I's major changes on the Swedish economy in the mid-1500s, and his introduction of Protestantism.[15] The 17th century saw Sweden engaged in many wars, for example with the Polish-Lithuanian Commonwealth with both sides competing for territories of today's Baltic states, with the disastrous Battle of Kircholm being one of the highlights.

Strong grassroots movements sprung up in Sweden during the latter half of the nineteenth century (trade unions, temperance groups, and independent religious groups), creating a strong foundation of democratic principles. In 1889 The Swedish Social Democratic Party was founded. These movements precipitated Sweden's migration into a modern parliamentary democracy, achieved by the time of World War I. As the Industrial Revolution progressed during the twentieth century, people gradually began moving into cities to work in factories, and became involved in socialist unions. A socialist revolution was avoided in 1917, following the re-introduction of parliamentarism, and the country was democratized.

NEUTRAL IN WAR

Sweden remained officially neutral during World War I and World War II, although its neutrality during World War II has been debated. Sweden was under German influence for much of the war, as ties to the rest of the world were cut off through blockades. The Swedish government felt that it was in no position to openly contest Germany, and therefore made some concessions. Sweden also supplied steel and machine parts to Germany throughout the war. However, Sweden supported Norwegian resistance, and in 1943 helped rescue Danish Jews from deportation to concentration camps. Toward the end of the war, Sweden began to play a role in humanitarian efforts and many refugees, among them many Jews from Nazi-occupied Europe, were saved partly because of the Swedish involvement in rescue missions at the internment camps and partly because Sweden served as a haven for refugees, primarily from the Nordic countries and the Baltic states. Nevertheless, internal and external critics have argued that Sweden could have done more to resist the Nazi war effort, even if risking occupation.

A WELFARE GOVT

Since World War II, Sweden's predominately socialist governments have provided ample welfare provisions for its citizens. The early history of Sweden apart from legends and mythology, is not well documented, but even before the Viking age (9th to 11th centuries) Swedish chieftains had exerted overlordship around the Baltic and beyond. Their Viking descendants opened up trade routes along rivers across Europe to Byzantium (modern Istanbul) and Baghdad, and established new centres of power in Russia. Christianity fared badly in this strongly pagan society, and the church was not established until King Olof Skotkonung (d. 1022) was baptized in the 11th century. A period of instability and civil war came to an end in the mid-13th century, but the struggle for power between Sweden's nobles and kings continued into the 14th century. In 1397, Erik of Pomerania (c.1381-1459) was crowned king of Norway, Denmark and Sweden at Kalmar, in southwestern Sweden. The Kalmar Unison sought to counter the might of the Hanseatic League, a confederation of north German towns and merchants.

In the long term this was an expensive triumph, demanding a continuous Swedish presence in Germany and the Baltic. In 1700 Charles XII (1682-1718) gained a string of initial victories against the united armies of Denmark, Poland and Russia in the Great Northern War. However, after 1709 the fortunes of war went against Sweden and the country continuously lost territorial possessions. Charles was killed at the siege of Frederiksten, three years later in 1721 Sweden ceded its Baltic provinces, part of Karelia and the city of Vyborg (near St. Petersburg) to Tsar Peter the Great (1672-1725) of Russia. Parliamentary power became stronger after Charles's death, but a second war with Russia (1741-43) left Finland, then a duchy of Sweden, occupied by Russian troops, while war with Prussia (1757-62), the rising power in northern Germany, put a heavy strain on the country's finances. Gustav-III (1746-92) restored absolute rule and attempted major social reforms. His efforts to regain the Finnish provinces were foiled by treason in 1788, and four years later he was assassinated.

During the Napoleonic wars at the beginning of the 19th century, Sweden aligned itself with Britain, but its ally could offer little support against the combined forces of France, Russia and Denmark. In 1809 Finland and the Aland Islands at the southern end of the Gulf of Bothnia were ceded to Russia, and in 1810 one of the emperor Napoleon's marshals, Jean-Baptiste Bernadotte (1763-1844), was chosen as crown prince, taking the name of Charles John. He failed to negotiate a return of the ceded territories, but in 1813 took a combined Prussian, Russian and Swedish army into Denmark, forcing its king, Frederik-VI (1768-1839), to surrender Norway under the *Treaty of Kiel* in

1814. Shortly afterward, following a brief rebellion, Norway was forced into political union with Sweden. Liberal reforms in the 19th century included free trade (1846) and a two-chamber parliament (1865-66). In 1905 Oscar-II (1829-1907) dissolved the union of the Swedish and Norwegian crowns. Sweden remained neutral throughout both world wars. It later joined the United Nations (UN), but stayed outside the North Atlantic Treaty Organisation (NATO). From 1946 onward the Social Democratic Party developed a comprehensive welfare system. The murder of prime minister Olof Palme (1927-86) deprived the Social Democrats of their most charismatic leader.

A bursting real estate bubble caused by inadequate controls on lending combined with an international recession and a policy switch from anti-unemployment policies to anti-inflationary policies resulted in a fiscal crisis in the early 1990s. Sweden's GDP declined by around 5%. In 1992, there was a run on the currency, the central bank briefly jacking up interest to 500% in an unsuccessful effort to defend the currency's fixed exchange rate. Total employment fell by almost 10% during the crisis. The response of the government was to cut spending and institute a multitude of reforms to improve Sweden's competitiveness, among them reducing the welfare state and privatizing public services and goods. Much of the political establishment promoted EU membership, and the Swedish referendum passed with 52% in favour of joining the EU on 13 November 1994. Sweden joined the European Union on 1 January 1995.

COLD AND VERY COLD

Forestry resources are vast and regulated by excellent legislation as well as being cared for by the most advanced forest management and forestry methods. Agriculture is varied, producing grain, peas, beans, potatoes, sugar beets, fodder, fruits, limestock and dairy products. Industry too is excellent, including activities in the fields of mining, machines, electrotechnical work, timber, foodstuffs, textiles, tailoring, leather, rubber, chemicals and minerals. Foreign trade is extensive and has been on the increase for years. About 45 per cent of Sweden's shipping is devoted to the service of other countries. Exports include matches, copper, ball-bearings, telephone equipment, illuminating gas equipment and electrical equipment. Sweden is the fourth largest country in Europe. Its people enjoy a very high standard of living, a highly developed welfare system and one of the highest average incomes in the world.

Almost 15 percent of Sweden's land area lies within the Arctic Circle, while its southern tip is on the same latitude as Copenhagen in Denmark. This long north-south extent gives the country a varied climate. Southwestern Sweden benefits from the warm winds associated with the North Atlantic Drift. These bring mild, wet winters and cool summers. The north and east areas, affected by cold air masses from Siberia, are significantly cooler than the south. The northern Baltic is usually icebound throughout the winter.

NATIONAL INDICATORS - SWEDEN

Area 4,50,00 sq.km.; capital and port Stockholm; major towns Uppsala, Norrkoping, Vasteraos, Linkoping, Orebro; major ports Helsingborg, Malmo Goteborg; physical features mountains in west; plains in south; thickly forested; more than 20,000 islands off the Stockholm coast, lakes including Vanern, Vattern, Malaren and Hjalmaren; Political system constitutional monarchy; Administrative divisions 24 counties; Population 8,780,000 (1995); Ethnic distribution predominantly of Teutonic descent, with small minorities of Saami (Lapps), Finns, and Germans; education (compulsory years) 9; literacy rate 99%; languages Swedish; there are Finnish-and Saami-speaking minorities; religion Evangelical Lutheran (established national church).

HISTORY

9th-11th Cs	Swedish Vikings raided and settled along the rivers.
c. 1000	Olaf Skotkonung, king of the Svear, adopted Christianity and united much of Sweden (except the south and west coasts, which remained Danish until the 17th century).
11th-13th	Cs Sweden existed as an isolated kingdom under the Stenkil, Sverker, and Folkung dynasties; a series of crusades incorporated Finland.
1523	Gustavus Vasa, leader of insurgents, became king of fully independent Sweden.
1527	Swedish Reformation: Gustavus confiscated church property and encouraged Lutherans.
1544	Swedish crown became hereditary in House of Vasa.
1709	Battle of Poltava: Russians inflicted major defeat on Swedes under Charles-XII.

1720	Limited monarchy established; political power passed to Riksdag (parliament) dominated by nobles.
1721	Great Northern War ended with Sweden losing nearly all its conquests of the previous century.
1741-43	Sweden defeated in disastrous war with Russia.
1771-92	Gustavus-III increased royal power and introduced wide-ranging reforms; assassinated at a masked ball.
1809	Russian invaders annexed Finland: Swedish nobles staged coup and restored powers of Riksdag.
1810	Napoleonic marshal, Jean-Baptiste Bernadotte, elected crown prince of Sweden, as Charles-XIII had no heir.
1812	Bernadotte allied Sweden with Russia against France.
1814	Treaty of Kiel: Sweden obtained Norway from Denmark.
1818-44	Bernadotte reigned in Sweden as Charles-XIV John.
1905	Union with Norway dissolved.
1907	Adoption of proportional representation and universal suffrage.
1920s	Economic boom transformed Sweden from an agricultural to an industrial economy.
1940-43	Under duress, neutral Sweden permitted limited transit of German forces through its territory.
1946-69	Social Democrat government of Tage Erlander developed comprehensive welfare state.
1959	Sweden joined the European Free Trade Association.
1969-76	Olof Palme, head of Social Democratic Party, prime minister.
1975	Remaining constitutional powers of monarch removed.
1982	Palme regained premiership.
1986	Prime Minister Olof Palme assassinated.
1995	Sweden became a member of the European Union.

COUNTRY REPORT

A land of lakes, forests, rivers and swamps, Finland has been fighting with winter and unfriendly neighbours and has finally survived to be a growing and prosperous nation of Europe.

57

Finland (Republic of Finland)

Once part of Sweden, a kingdom, and then a duchy of Russia, Finland has always been in the eye of storm with European powers which have been rampaging through its natural wealth.

Finland is situated in northern Europe. The majority of the people are Finns; there is a small Sami (Lapp) population in Lapland. Languages: Finnish, Swedish (both official); the Sami speak a Finno-Ugric language. Religions: Lutheranism, Finnish (Greek) Orthodoxy. Finland is about 1,165 km long and a maximum of 550 km. wide; one-third of the country is north of Arctic Circle.

Heavily forested, Finland contains thousands of lakes, numerous rivers, and extensive areas of marshland. Except for a small highland region in the extreme northwest, most of the country lies less than 600 ft. above the sea level. The south has relatively mild weather; the north has severe and prolonged winters and short summers. Finland has a developed free-market economy combined with state ownership of a few key industries. Among the wealthiest countries in Europe, Finland is a republic with one legislative house; its chief of state is the president, and the head of government is the prime minister. Archaeological discoveries suggest that human habitation in Finland dates back at least 100,000 years. Ancestors of the Sami apparently were present in Finland by about 7000 BC. The ancestors of the present-day Finns came from the southern shore of the Gulf of Finland in the 1st millennium BC. The people were gradually Christianised from the 11th century AD. From the 12th century, Sweden and Russia contested for supremacy in Finland until in 1323 Sweden ruled most of the country.

Sweden had a series of wars which made Finland a part of the Kingdom of Sweden but Finland enjoyed a substantial degree of independence under this arrangement, and it was in the latter part of the sixteenth century, that she was closely integrated into the Swedish kingdom. There she remained until the Napoleonic wars and in 1809 she was transferred to Russia. Czar Alexander gave her autonomy, made her a grand duchy, and permitted her to retain her own constitution.

BETWEEN WAR AND PEACE

Although Finland has been made independent only in the early 20th century, its people retain a proud and enduring sense of national identity. Finland was first inhabited by Neolithic nomadic hunter-gatherers, probably ancestors of the present-day Sami. Later, settlers came from around the Baltic area, speaking a Finno-Ugaric language that is closely related to Estonian but is unrelated to the Scandinavian languages, which are Indo-European in origin. Finland remained outside the cultural orbit of Europe until the 12th century when the Swedish kings launched a crusade to subdue and convert its "pagan" inhabitants. The Swedes' English-born bishop, Henry, murdered by a Finnish peasant, later became Finland's patron-saint between the 13th and 19th centuries.

Russia, however, continually eroded parts of Finnish territory, and in 1809, when Sweden failed to defend Finland, the Finns accepted an offer by Tsar Alexander-I (1777-1825) to make the country an autonomous grand duchy. Finland enjoyed considerable political freedom, and prospered under the favourable rule of Alexander-II (1818-81). He encouraged wider use of Finnish, which had survived only as the language of the working people; this was partly to weaken links with Sweden, and partly to foster a sense of nationalism and new belief in a Finnish cultural identity. Harsh moves by his successor, Nicholas-II (1868-1918), to Russify the country only encouraged a growing nationalist movement that united all sections of society.

At the outbreak of the Russian revolution (1917), Finland seized the opportunity to declare its independence; a communist coup was defeated and a republic established in 1919. The people of *Aland Island* (land of waters) in 1917 sought to become part of Sweden, with which they had economic and cultural links dating back to the 12th century. Finland granted them autonomy in 1920, but refused to allow them to secede; today they remain an autonomous part of the state of Finland. In 1939 the Soviet Union took advantage of its pact with Nazi Germany to seize much of the eastern Finland. With the Allies unable to help, Finland had to turn to Germany, for which the Soviet Union imposed heavy post-War reparations. During Cold War, Finland managed to steer a delicate course, maintaining its democratic tradition and mixed economy without offending the Soviet Union. The term "Finalization" came to describe the situation of a small, neutral country co-existing beside a communist power.

CULTURE AND LIFESTYLE

Finland's culture and language are quite distinct from those of the other Nordic countries. For long periods of its history it was ruled by Sweden and Russia, but neither was able to subdue the Finnish spirit. Finland is the sixth largest country in Europe. One-third of the country's area lies within the Arctic Circle. Finland is landlocked to the north and east; to the south lies the Gulf of Finland and to the west the Gulf of Bothnia. The Aland Islands, lying at the entrance to the Gulf a few miles off the southwestern coast of Finland, are an extension of the coastal lowland. Some 80 of the 3,000 islands in the archipelago are inhabited. Apart from a small hilly area in the northwest, Finland is lowlying, its ancient granite rocks ground down by the glacial icesheets.

Separated from the Atlantic by the Scandinavian Peninsula, Finland's climate is influenced by the continental weather system. Above the Arctic Circle, the weather is extreme; very cold winters are matched by short summers in which temperatures often soar during the long days. Farther south, the climate is moderated by the proximity of the sea. The mild summers allow Finland's agricultural area to extend farther north than in the other Nordic countries. However, from mid-November until April the whole country is snow-covered and the sea is frozen.

The country is heavily forested, chiefly with pine, spruce and other conifers. Hardy broadleaf trees grow in the south. In the extreme north the forests give way to swampy tundra, a landscape of few trees but rich in lichens and berry producing plants, especially cloudberries. The woodlands are home to many animal species, including bears, wolves and lynx; elk and reindeer are common. The rivers are rich in salmon and trout, and they also support ducks and other waterfowl. Forests, lakes and rivers show signs of environmental damage from acid rain, caused by windblown air pollution originating outside the region. In addition, radiation from the Chernobyl nuclear disaster in the Ukraine in 1986 still affects Sami (Lapp) reindeer herds.

The country has extensive road network. The state-owned rail network is extensively developed in the southwest, and is undergoing modernization and electrification elsewhere. The inland waterway network of lakes and rivers is an important transportation route for the timber industry, and its scenic beauty also attracts tourists. Finland's state welfare system offers a wide range of benefits. Elderly people enjoy good pensions and generous care provisions. The nine-year comprehensive free and compulsory education system has made the country fully literate, enterprising and competitive in Europe. The novelist Emile Sillaupaa (1888-1964) was awarded Nobel Prize.

NATIONAL INDICATORS - FINLAND

Area 338,145 sq.km.; capital Helsinki; major towns Tampere, Espoo, Vantaa; major ports Turku, Oulu; physical features, most of the country is forest, with low hills and about 60,000 lakes; one third is within the Arctic Circle; archipelago in South includes Aland islands; Helsinki is the most northerly national capital on the European continent – at the 70th parallel there is constant daylight for 73 days in summer and 51 days of uninterrupted night in winter; administrative divisions 12 provinces; population 5,126,000 (1996); ethnic distribution majority descended from Finno-Ugric inhabitants; arable land 9% (1993); agricultural products oats, sugar, beet, potatoes, barley, hay, forestry and animal husbandry.

HISTORY

1st C	Occupied by Finnic nomads from Asia who drove out native Sami (Lapps).
12th-13th Cs	Series of Swedish crusades conquered Finns and converted them to Christianity.
16th-17th Cs	Finland was a semi-autonomous Swedish duchy with Swedish landowners ruling Finnish peasants; Finland allowed relative autonomy, becoming a grand duchy 1581.

1700-21	Great Northern War between Sweden and Russia; half of Finnish population died in famine and epidemics.
1788-90	Further Russo-Swedish wars; much of the fighting took place in Finland.
1808	Russia invaded Sweden (with support of Napoleon).
1812	Helsinki became capital of grand duchy.
1904-05	Policies promoting Russification of Finland provoked national uprising; Russians imposed military rule.
1917	Finland declared independence.
1918	Bitter civil war between Reds (supported by Russian Bolsheviks) and Whites (supported by Germany); Baron Carl Gustaf Mannerheim led Whites to victory.
1919	Republican constitution adopted.
1927	Land reform broke up big estates.
1939-40	Winter War: USSR invaded Finland.
1940	Treaty of Moscow: Finland ceded territory to USSR.
1941	Finland joined German attack on USSR, in hope of regaining lost lands.
1944	Finland agreed separate armistice with USSR; German troops withdrawn.
1947	Finno-Soviet peace treaty: Finland forced to cede 12% of its total area to pay $ 300 million in reparations.
1948	Finno-Soviet Pact of Friendship, Cooperation, and Mutual Assistance (YYA treaty): Finland pledged to repel any attack on USSR through its territories.
1955	Finland joined United Nations (UN) and Nordic Council.
1973	Trade agreements signed with European Economic Community (EEC) and Comecon.
1991	Big swing to Centre Party in general election.
1994	Martti Ahtisaari (SSDP) elected president.
1995	Finland joined European Union (EU).

Denmark has adopted all that is best in the socialist system without becoming one. Most schools are free, so also vocational training with extensive social entitlements network. No wonder, there is full literacy and a stable social order – a model state in Europe, for that matter.

58

Denmark (Kingdom of Denmark)

The smallest Scandinavian country, Denmark has the highest standard of living in Europe and an extensive network of welfare programmes, making people happy and secure.

The Kingdom of Denmark is a constitutional monarchy in north-central Europe. Its territory includes Greenland and the Faeroe Islands, which are self-governing dependencies. The majority of the population is Nordic; language is Danish (official); religion evangelical Lutheranism. Lying between the North and Baltic seas, it occupies the Jutland peninsula and an archipelago to its east. The two largest islands, Zealand (Sjaelland) and Funen (Fyn), together make up more than one-fourth of the country's total land area. With a 7,300 km coastline, it has a generally temperate and often wet climate. Mainland Denmark, the Jutland Peninsula, extends 300 km north from the border with Germany. Dunes, lagoons and sandbars shelter the west coast from North Sea storms; the eastern plains face the Baltic sea and an archipelago of 483 islands, of which 97 are inhabited. Denmark is only about 100 ft above sea level. Its landscapes are the product of Ice Age glaciation; glacial debris divides eastern and western Jutland. Denmark's largest lagoon, *Lim Fjord,* cuts north across the country.

Denmark has a mixed economy based on services and manufacturing. It has one of the world's oldest and largest social welfare systems, and its standard of living is among the highest in the world. Most schools are free; private schools receive state support. Youth schools offer both vocational and other trainings. The traditional folk high schools, provide a broad-based curriculum of adult education. There are five universities and a number of

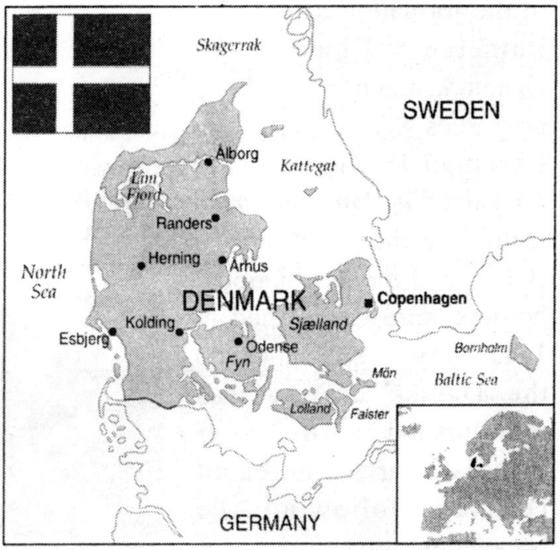

professional institutions, commercial and technical colleges. And, about 100% literacy which provides a strong foundation for democracy. Its chief of state is the Danish Monarch, while the head of government is the prime minister. Inhabited from 1,00,000 BC, it was settled by Danes, a Scandinavian branch of the Teutons, c.6th century AD. During the Viking period, the Danes expanded their territory, and the 11th century United Danish kingdom included parts of what are now Germany, Sweden, England and Norway.

Scandinavia was united under Danish rule from 1397 to 1523, when Sweden became independent and a series of wars with Sweden in the 17th century resulted in the Treaty of Copenhagen (1660), which established the modern Scandinavian frontiers. Denmark gained and lost many territories, including Norway, in the 19th and 20th centuries. It went through three constitutions between 1849 and 1915 and was occupied by Nazi Germany in 1940-45. A founding member of NATO (1949), Denmark adopted its current constitution in 1953 to became a member of the European Union in 1973 and modified its membership during the 1990s. The island of Zealand, on which Copenhagen stands, was connected to the central island of Funen by a rail tunnel and bridge in 1997. This ended more than 100 years of ferry service and cut the crossing time to less than 10 minutes. Progressive, but deeply interested in their past, the Danes have achieved a healthy and equitable society. Reliable historical accounts began in the 9th century when the Danes resisted the northward expansion of the Frank King, Harald Bluetooth of Jutland, (c.910-985) who sought to impose Christianity on his people. His son Sweyn Forkbeard (d.1014) conquered England, creating an empire that lasted for two generations. Norway and Sweden were united under the crown of Denmark by the Kalmar Union (1396-1523), which tried to counter the commercial power of the German-based Hanseatic League. Civil War in 1534-36 resulted

COPENHAGEN. At the entrance to the harbour stands Edvard Eriksen's famous statue of Hans Christian Andersen's "Little Mermaid."

in the formation of the new Lutheran Church of Denmark, and many Catholic properties were seized. King Christian IV (1577-1648) tried and failed to re-establish Danish authority over the Baltic, and modern national borders were established in 1645. Norway, still subject to the Danish crown, was relinquished in 1813 after Swedish forces defeated Denmark following the Napoleonic wars.

In 1864, war broke out with Prussia and Austria over long-disputed Schleswig and Holstein at the southern tip of Jutland. Denmark lost, but in 1920 a plebiscite returned Schleswig to Danish rule. Although neutral in World War II, Denmark was occupied by German troops in 1940 and had an active resistance movement. As a member of the North Atlantic Treaty Organisation (NATO) from 1949, Denmark refused to allow United States' air bases on Danish soil. In 1973, Denmark joined the European Community (EC) and was one of the 15 member countries of the European Union (EU) in 1995.

A NORDIC NATION

As stated earlier, the Danes are a Nordic nation, numbering about 5 million. Once a formidable power on the continent of Europe, they are now one of the smaller groups. In the tenth century the Danes occupied substantial part of Europe and England, and in the twelfth century, under the leadership of King Valdemar, they challenged the might of the Teutonic Knights and took most of Estonia from them. Then they were at the peak of their strength. At the end of the fourteenth century, the three Scandinavian countries, Denmark, Norway and Sweden (of which Finland was a part) were joined in the Kalmar Union. When Sweden broke away, Norway remained attached to Denmark until 1814. Denmark meanwhile gradually lost power, and in the middle of the nineteenth century she lost both Schleswig and Holstein to Prussia. Part of

Schleswig was regained from Germany after World War I. In 1940 Denmark was occupied by German forces. Iceland, which had been under Danish rule since 1264, was recognised as an independent state under the Danish king in 1918 and declared its complete independence from Denmark on June 17, 1944. Allied forces had occupied Iceland after the German invasion of Denmark.

Copenhagen, the capital city, is on its eastern coast. Suburbs now cover most of the coast from Copenhagen to Helsingor (Elsinore). Far out in the Baltic lies the granite island of Bornholm. Denmark's cool and temperate climate is warmed by the North Atlantic Drill. Summers are warm, with high rainfall. Conifer plantations have replaced the natural deciduous woods, and trees have been planted as windbreaks on the North Sea coast. Few large mammals have survived in the wild. Pollution has affected marine and freshwater animal life.

THE FAEROES – ISLANDS OF SHEEP

The Faeroes are a group of 22 islands lying in the Atlantic between Scotland and Iceland, formed by the basaltic lavas similar to those found in Iceland. Some 18 of the islands are inhabited. The characteristic landscape is harsh and rugged with high coastal cliffs and treacherous straits between islands.

The climate, with mild winters and cool summers, benefits from the warm North Atlantic Drift. Fog and rain are frequent. Native wildlife consists mainly of seals and a rich variety of seabirds, including puffins and eider, valued for their feathers. There are no native land mammals: rats and mice were introduced by early settlers, and Viking colonizers in the 9th century brought sheep to the islands. An old proverb says that *"sheep's wool is Faeroe gold"*, and the islands' name even means "sheep islands".

In about 100 AD the Faeroese were converted to Christianity. The islands came under Norwegian rule in 1035, and passed to Denmark in 1380. From 1709 to 1856 a Danish royal trade monopoly held back economic development and impoverished the population. In the 19th century a growing nationalist movement led to the creation of the written Faeroese language, based on Old Norse. Demand for home rule strengthened, and in 1948 the Faeroes became a self-governing dependency of Denmark. Today the Faeroes have their own 32-member parliament, the Lagting, which elects the Landsstyri, an administrative committee.

CONSTITUTIONAL MONARCHY; AN INDUSTRIAL SOCIETY

Denmark has been a constitutional monarchy since 1849. The monarch appoints the prime minister and the cabinet, who are accountable to the 179-member single-chamber parliament or Folketing. Legislation passed by the

Folketing must be signed by the monarch before it becomes law. Parliamentary elections based on proportional representation are held every four years. All citizens aged 18 and over may vote. Greenland and the Faeroes each have two representatives in the Folketing but follow Danish foreign affairs, defence, financial and legal policies. Denmark's non-nuclear policy has led to debates over the presence of nuclear weapons on visiting warships. The Danes are closely related to the other Scandinavian peoples, and there is a significant German minority. Both German and English are taught in Danish schools. More than 90 percent of Danes belong to the national Lutheran church. The country has produced internationally renowned writers including philosopher Soren Kierkegaard (1815-55) and Hans Christian Andersen (1805-75). The Royal Danish Ballet preserves 19th century choreographic tradition. Denmark is an industrial society, but agriculture still plays a vital role.

The country's mineral resources include granite, boulder clay, white chalk and kaolin. North Sea gas and oil supply about half of Denmark's energy. Surplus energy is sold to Germany and Sweden. Wind turbines are increasingly common in flat, windy Jutland, and new houses have solar heating. Industrial products include cement, crude steel, machinery and transportation equipment, processed foods, chemicals, paper and furniture. Shipping and tourism are also important.

LAND OF BICYCLES

Denmark trades almost entirely within the European Union, particularly with Germany, Britain and Sweden. High consumer spending in the 1980s caused a severe balance-of-payments problem. The government responded with tax cuts and reductions in welfare expenditure. The sea has always been central to Denmark's mainlines of communication. In addition to sea routes, there are about 420 km of inland waterways. Two bridges connect Jutland with Fyn, and

Cycling in way of life in Denmark

in 1989 a massive project was launched to make a permanent link between Fyn and Sjaelland, formerly accessible only by ferry. Road and railroad networks are extensive and well maintained. There are approximately twice as many bicycles as automobiles. Denmark has 13 airports. Kastrup, near Copenhagen, serves Jutland and Bornholm as well as international traffic, and is a major base for the co-owned SAS (Scandinavian Airlines System). Until the 1980s, Danish broadcasting was controlled by Danmarks Radio, an independent public body funded by license fees. A second television channel with commercial advertising was launched in 1988, and Danes can receive broadcasts from Sweden, Norway and Germany. There are about 60 newspapers.

DENMARK, at a glance

THE SMALLEST, flattest, and most southerly country in Scandinavia, Denmark occupies the Jylland peninsula, the islands of Sjaelland, Lolland, Falster, and Fyn, and more than 500 smaller islands. The Faeroe Islands and Greenland in the North Atlantic are self-governing Danish territories. A prosperous, environmentally conscious, and liberal nation, Denmark offers its people a high standard of living and was one of the first countries to set up a welfare system in the 1930s.

Copenhagen

Denmark's capital is also its most important port and Scandinavia's largest city. Criss-crossed with a network of canals, quaint alleys, and cycle path, Copenhagen has many historic buildings and churches. It also boasts the Tivoli Gardens, an amusement park that attracts millions every year.

Physical Features

Denmark's flat landscape is broken by low, rolling hills and gentle valleys with shady beech forests. There are also extensive areas of heathlands, a beautiful lake district, and a coastline of cliffs, dunes, and broad sandy beaches.

Jylland (Jutland)

The Jylland peninsula makes up about 70 per cent of Denmark's land. Its west coast is edged with beaches and the southwest has a sandy plain. Strong winds sweeping across the land drive windmills for generating electricity.

Baltic Islands

The steep, chalk cliffs on the Baltic island of Mon contrast with the gentle dunes on other islands. The Danish take great care of their environment and beaches.

Climate

Denmark's usually mild and damp climate is dominated by stiff westerly winds. In many coastal areas, to prevent sand from the dunes from blowing over the land, the Danes have planted conifers as windbreaks.

Land use

Over four-fifths of Denmark is farmland, including lush pasture for grazing cattle and for raising pigs. Denmark's land yields few natural resources, although high winds are harnessed to produce power.

People

Only four per cent of the population is foreign mainly Europeans. The only minority groups are Turks and Inuit from Greenland. The Danish have liberal policies on homosexuality and marriage, with a high divorce rate. Today, 47 per cent of all children are raised by unmarried couples or single parents. Three- quarters of all women work, and Denmark has the best child- support system in the world.

Farming and Industry

Danish farming is efficient and often run by co-operatives. Only about four per cent of the work –force is employed in farming, mainly of dairy cattle and pigs, yet agriculture accounts for much of the country's export income. Denmark also has successful fishing, manufacturing, and food industries for processing bacon and dairy products. Service industries employ 79 per cent of workers.

NATIONAL INDICATORS - DENMARK

Area 43,075 sq.km.; capital Copenhagen; major ports Aarhus, Odense, Aalborg, Esbjerg; physical features comprise the Jutland peninsula and about 500 islands (100 inhabited) including Bornholm in the Baltic Sea; the land is flat and cultivated; sand dunes and lagoons on the West coast and long inlets (fjords) on the East; the main island is Sja(lig)lland (Zealand), where most of Copenhagen is located and the rest is on the island of Amager; territories the dependencies of Faeroe islands and Greenland; head of state Queen Margrethe-II from 1972; political system liberal democracy; administrative divisions 14 countries, one city and one borough; population 5,215,718 (1995); life expectancy 73 (men), 79 (women); education (compulsory years) 9; literacy rate 99%; languages Danish (official); there is a German-speaking minority; religion Lutheran 97%; resources crude petroleum, natural gas, salt, limestone; industries mining, food precessing, machinery, textiles, furniture, electronic goods and transport equipment, chemicals and pharmaceuticals, printing and publishing;.

HISTORY

5th-6th Cs	Danes migrated from Sweden.
8th-10th Cs	Viking raids throughout Europe.
c. 940-85	Harald Bluetooth unified Kingdom of Denmark and established Christianity.
1014-35	King Canute-I created empire, collapsed after his death.
12th C	Denmark re-emerged as dominant Baltic power.
1397	Union of Kalmar: Denmark, Sweden and Norway (with Iceland) united under a single monarch.
1449	Sweden broke away from union.
1523	Denmark recognised Sweden's independence.
1536	Lutheranism established as official religion of Denmark.
1563-70	Unsuccessful war to recover Sweden.
1625-29	Denmark sided with Protestants in Thirty Years War.
1643-45	Second attempt to reclaim Sweden ended in failure.
1729	Greenland became Danish province.
1780-81	Denmark, Russia and Sweden formed 'Armed Neutrality' coalition to protect neutral shipping during War of American Independence.
1788	Serfdom abolished.
1800	France persuaded Denmark to revive Armed Neutrality against British blockade.
1801	First Battle of Copenhagen: much of Danish fleet destroyed by British navy.
1807	Second Battle of Copenhagen: British seized rebuilt fleet to pre-empt Danish entry into Napoleonic War on French side.

1814	Treaty of Kiel: Denmark ceded Norway to Sweden as penalty for supporting French in Napoleonic War; Denmark retained Iceland.
1914-19	Denmark neutral during World War I.
1918	Iceland achieved full self-government.
1919	Denmark recovered northern Schleswig under peace settlement after World War I.
1929-40	Welfare state established under left-wing coalition government dominated by Social Democrat Party.
1940-45	German occupation.
1944	Iceland declared independence.
1949	Denmark became a founding member of North Atlantic Treaty Organisation (NATO).
1960	Denmark joined European Free Trade Association (EFTA).
1973	Withdrew from EFTA and joined European Economic Community (EEC).
1981	Greenland achieved full self-government.
1992	Referendum rejected Maastricht Treaty on European union.
1993	Second referendum approved Maastricht Treaty after government negotiated a series of 'opt-out' clauses.

With "shaking" land and hot water springs, the Icelanders' lifestyle has not changed much despite growth and modernisation.

59

Iceland
(Republic of Iceland)

A land of ice, cold winds and snow, Iceland has been on the invasion route of Vikings who had rampaged Europe and beyond. But, ironically, the world's first Parliament (Althing) was set up in Reykjavik, first to settle local disputes and, later, to govern the country with a population of less than three lakh hardy people who live in volcanically active conditions. There are no railroads on the island, nor any complaint about it.

The Republic of Iceland is situated in the northern Atlantic Ocean between Norway and Greenland. The people are overwhelmingly Nordic. One of the most active volcanic regions in the world, Iceland contains about 200 volcanoes and accounts for one-third of the earth's total lava flow. One-tenth of its area is covered by cooled lava beds and glaciers. Its rugged coastline is 6,000 km. long. The economy is based heavily on fishing and fish products but also includes hydropower production, livestock and aluminium processing.

Iceland is a republic with one legislative house; its chief of state is the president, and the head of government is the prime minister. Iceland was settled by Norwegian seafarers in the 9th century and was Christianised by 1000. Its legislature, the Althing, was founded in 930, making it one of the oldest legislative assemblies in the world. Iceland united with Norway in 1262 and with Denmark in 1380. It became an independent state of Denmark in 1918, but it severed those ties to become an independent republic in 1944. Vigdis Finnobogadotir became the world's first female elected president in 1980.

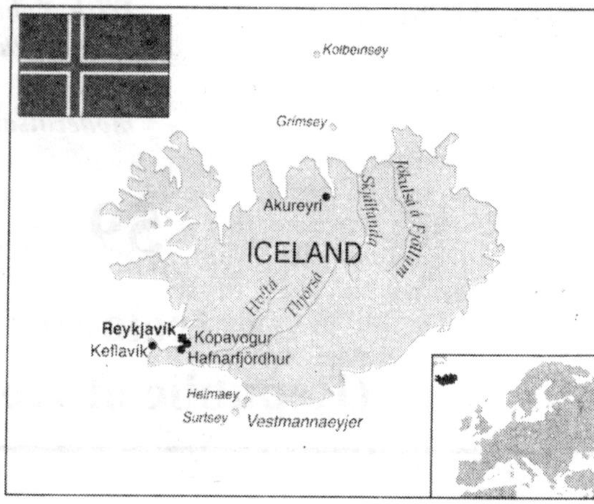

Geologically Iceland is very young. It has been built up by a series of volcanic eruptions from the mid-Atlantic ridge – the boundary of two of the Earth's tectonic plates. Earth tremors are frequent, and hot springs are common in volcanic areas, most notably at Geysir in the southwest. Similar springs gave the capital its name – Reykjavik, or "Smoky Bay" – and today they provide most of the country's hot water and heating. The island is a high plateau partly covered by a glacier and surrounded by mountains. Glaciers account for over one-tenth of Iceland's total land area. The largest is Vatnajokull in the southeast. Most of the population live on the narrow Reykjavik in the southwest. In the north steep valleys penetrate deep into the interior. The northwest of the island tends to be cooler than the southeast, and snowfall frequent. Only one percent of the country is forested. The vegetation is mosses and lichens with a few shrubs. Sparse grassland is limited to valleys and the coastal plain. Foxes are Iceland's only native mammal.

The first settlers in Iceland were Irish monks. They were followed in about 870 AD by Vikings from Norway, Ireland and Scotland. The chieftains in each district set up a local assembly to settle quarrels and feuds common among landholders, and about 930, a national assembly, the *Althing,* was established – the basis of Europe's oldest parliament. It was through a decision reached in the Althing that the population accepted Christianity in 999-1000. During the 13th century, Iceland's Chieftains accepted Norwegian rule in order to preserve domestic peace, but in 1380, Norway itself fell under Danish sovereignty, and Iceland entered a long period of decline, exacerbated by the Danish crown's commercial monopoly, which crippled trade.

INDEPENDENT SINCE 1940

During World War II, British and American forced invasion of Denmark in 1940 had covered communications with the island, and in 1944 the *Althing* cut the last ties with Denmark by declaring Iceland an independent republic. Since 1951 there has been an American military base at Keflavik; this, and

Golden Falls, Iceland

Iceland's membership of the North Atlantic Treaty Organisation (NATO), have been hotly debated political issues. Fishery protection is another major concern. In 1975, the government declared a 370-km fishing limit – a decision that led to one of several "cold wars" with the United Kingdom. However, in 1976 the British government recognised the new international limit.

Icelanders are proud of their Viking roots and many can trace their ancestry back to the earliest settlers, whose names are recorded in the *Landnama Bok,* or Book of Settlement. The modern Icelandic language is directly descended from Old Norse, the language of the Vikings. The medieval sagas, which mingle imagination and folklore with historical facts of the early settlers, can be easily read by modern Icelanders. Most of the islanders belong to the Lutheran Church. Fishing is the cornerstone of Iceland's economy, accounting for three-quarters of its exports. There are no railroads on the island and in many places Icelandic ponies still provide an important means of local transportation. Icelanders operate domestic and international flights. Icelanders are among the healthiest people in the world. Compulsory health insurance allows many medical services to be offered at minimal cost, and hospital care is free. Education is also free, and compulsory. There is a university at Reykjavik. Traditionally, other nations including Britain, used to fish Iceland's rich water and the extension of Iceland's fishing limit led to 'cod war' dispute with Britain in 1952-56, 1871-73 and 1975-76.

NATIONAL INDICATORS - ICELAND

Area 103,000 sq.km.; capital Reykjavik; major towns Akureyri, Akranes, physical features warmed by the Gulf stream, glaciers and lava fields cover 75% of the country; active volcanoes, geysers, hot springs, and new islands created offshore (Surtsey in 1963); sub-terranean hot water heats 85% of Iceland's homes; political system democratic republic; administrative divisions 23 counties; US forces under NATO are stationed there: 2,500 military personnel and a 130-strong coastguard (1995); death penalty abolished 1928; population 269,000 (1995); age distribution (% of total population) <15 24.5%, 15-65 64.3%, >65 11.2% (1995); ethnic distribution most of the population is descended from Norwegians and Celts.

HISTORY

7th C	Iceland discovered by Irish seafarers.
874	First Norse settler, Ingolfr Arnarson, founded a small colony at Rekyavik.
c. 900	Norse settlers came in larger numbers, mainly from Norway.
930	Settlers established an annual parliament, the *Althing,* to make laws and resolve disputes.
1000	Icelanders adopted Christianity.
1397	Norway and Iceland united with Denmark and Sweden under a single monarch.
15th C	Norway and Iceland were increasingly treated as appendages of Denmark, especially after Sweden seceded in 1449.
1814	Norway passed to the Swedish crown; Iceland remained under Danish rule.
1918	Iceland was granted full self-government under the Danish crown.
1940	British forces occupied Iceland after Germany invaded Denmark; US troops took over 1941.
1944	Iceland became an independent republic.
1949	Became a member of NATO.
1958	Introduction of exclusive 19 km fishing limit led to first 'Cod War'.
1980	Vigdis Finnogadottir became the first woman president of Iceland.
1985	Iceland declared itself a nuclear-free zone.
1992	Iceland defied world ban to resume whaling.

These are the countries scooped out of the sea with spades and pumps. They are called low countries because they are below the sea level.

60

About low countries
(The Netherlands, Belgium, Luxembourg)

Once a united kingdom, the three low-land countries are now independent nations. The Netherlands (Holland) had the colonies all over the world, from South Africa to Latin America, where they planted their culture, customs and language (Afrikaans). Belgium had been the battlefield of Europe where Waterloo, Ypres and Ardennes tell their own stories. And, Luxembourg is a Grand Duchy now: it was grander before.

The Low Countries – also called the *Benelux* countries from the initial letters of their names Belgium, the Netherlands, and Luxembourg – are situated in central Europe. Enjoying a favoured position on the North Sea coast, the Low Countries have long been economically important. The addition of a network of the canals and other artificial waterways and the establishment of a system of dikes and pumps to hold back the seas and reclaim the land have provided an impressive history of human control over nature.

On the map, the Low Countries look as though they are a single State. And once they were. They are the flatlands that surround the North Sea estuaries of three rivers, the Rhine, the Meuse and the Scheldt. At the end of the nineteenth-century Napoleonic wars, after a complex history of dynastic exchange and rivalry, they were briefly united as the *Kingdom of the Low Countries;* but in the old ways of Europe, the federation did not last, and they are now divided into the kingdoms of Belgium and the Netherlands, and the Grand Duchy of Luxembourg.

They have, however, much in common. They are all small countries – Luxembourg, with an area less than 1,000 square miles (about 2600 square kilometres, half of Delhi's area) – is the smallest and independent, sovereign State in Europe. Their histories have often coincided. Their countrysides are mostly uniformly flat. Their peoples are Germanic in origin, and, long before the European Common Market (now, European Union) came into being, they had established their own customs union.

Pre-eminent among the three is the Netherlands, more accurately but less officially known as Holland, which has a population of less than 16 million (about Delhi's population), but has been one of Europe's power-houses. Great sailors, merchants, engineers, patrons and practitioners of art, the Dutch literally created their own country because a quarter of it has been reclaimed from the sea. It is the most densely populated state in Europe. From this precarious seashore base, the Dutch sailed out to seize for themselves one of the largest overseas Empires. The language of the South Africa's Afrikaners is a kind of Dutch (It is called Afrikans). With the spoils of the colonies, they made themselves rich, and they have remained rich by clever trading, innovative industry, and by exploiting the geographical advantage of their position at the mouth of the Rhine. Huge industries have grown up around the port of Rotterdam, chief outlet to the sea for Germany, and one of the world's busiest seaports, and some of the great Dutch companies are worldwide in their presence.

BENELUX CUSTOMS UNION

Benelux is the abbreviated word for Belgium, the Netherlands, the Luxembourg customs union. This term was adopted by the exiled governments of these countries in 1944, and ratified by them after the World War II, hoping that they will join together to become a customs union. But because of post-War economic difficulties, it did not happen. However, the abbreviation stays, instead.

A PLACE OF MANY BATTLES

No such case with Belgium which is not an assertive country, and no place in Europe had been more cruelly ravaged by the comings and goings of foreign armies. Waterloo is in Belgium, and so is Ypres, and here are the forests of the Ardennes where Hitler's armies made their last counter attack in the West. Belgium is Europe's cockpit. A nation–state since 1831, when it was separated from the Netherlands, Belgium is inhabited partly by the Flemings of Latin origin who speak Dutch and partly by the Walloons of Celtic origin who speak French. Thickly populated, heavily industrialized, producing few things that most

Wellington at Waterloo, Belgium - a low country

of us know about, boasting few heroes that we have heard of, Belgium came out of obscurity when its capital, Brussels, became the administrative headquarters of the European Union.

And, what about Luxembourg? Oddly enough, for many decades it was a prime symbol of Europeanism. The Grand Duchy was once very much grander than Belgium, and it has remained a formidable little state. Its steel production is said to be the highest per capita in the world; it is a busy centre of international finance and the legal capital of the European Union. However, what made it seem long ago a supra-European State was the presence there of an international commercial broadcasting industry, transmitting news in many languages. In the days when a united Europe seemed no more than a pipedream, the familiar name of Radio Luxembourg carried to listeners far away the first faint inkling of Europeans coming together.

In 1944, during World War II, the governments of Belgium in-exile, the Netherlands, and Luxembourg signed an agreement to establish a post-War customs union, which became operative in 1948. The progressive end of economic barriers led to the signing in 1958 of the comprehensive Treaty of the Benelux Economic Union, which took effect on November 1, 1960. So, in fact, Benelux's problem is simply that of amalgamating two economic units: Belgium-Luxembourg with the Netherlands. There is nothing dramatic in the first serious effort to demolish a difficult economic frontier by mutual consent. The decision to do so was not the result of sudden and spectacular calamity. Belgians and Dutchmen remained unified as one country for 15 years after the Napoleonic wars, after which the Belgians broke away. For the past hundred-years or so, they have been talking about getting back together again. Once, when the talk seemed likely to succeed, Germany stopped it. Between the two world wars, when the two nations began lowering their customs barriers, America and Britain protested and said that this amounted to discrimination and they put a stop to it again.

During World War II the two governments, exiled in London, decided to take the step. Their main assumption was that Germany would be defeated and both would lose a valuable market. By unification they might, however, turn the loss into gain and capture many German markets. Together they would constitute a unit of 20 million people to be the third largest trading nation on earth. Their traditions were fairly uniform. More than half the population of Belgium is Flemish, more closely related in language and race to the Dutch than to their own Belgian compatriots. Their politics was nearly identical, both countries leaning to the conservative side and both are governed by a coalition of Catholics and Socialists. Their economic conceptions provided no obstacle; both are doggedly faithful to the principles of free enterprise. Fifty years ago, their economies were complementary, Holland being agrarian and Belgium being industrial. That has changed, but still there are no grave conflicts.

Belgium had an empire 25 times its size, including Belgian Congo (Congo Free State), now Zaire. But when the empire was lost, the country did not falter, thanks to the ingenuity and hard work of the people of Belgium.

61

Belgium a survivor of many crises

The European Union is largely about six countries – Britain, Germany, France, Poland, Italy and Spain – which account for 74% of its population. But, the other countries also have useful roles to play. Among them is Belgium.

Belgium, like most other small countries of Europe, was a battlefield for its larger neighbours. Czechoslovakia was dismembered after a shabby deal between the big European countries in 1938; the Baltic States simply disappeared into the Soviet Union after Hitler-Stalin Pact in 1939. After the European Union came into being, things improved. Europe's small countries see the EU as a guarantee that the continent will be run by law rather than force. The six bigs, Britain, Germany, France, Poland, Italy and Spain account for 74% of the population, with others making up the rest of it. The small countries of the Continent had been struggling for retaining their existence. Belgium had been the one. After the last War, it was proposed to form an economic union of Belgium, the Netherlands and Luxembourg. Their plan for union – called Benelux – was made independent of the Marshall Plan.

Belgium provides the most flattering example of human ingenuity in the contemporary world. With over 700 people to a square mile, it claims to be the most densely populated country on earth in relation to absolute area – sixteen times as densely populated as the USA. Belgium was for years the world's biggest exporter of steel. In Antwerp, it had the busiest port in the world. In Flanders, near the coast, it has the most intensively cultivated patch of soil on earth with the world's highest output of garden produce per acre. Her businesslike monarch, Leopold-I, developed an early interest in Africa. He summoned a journalist, Henry Stanley, fresh from a visit to the dark continent, to the Belgian court and asked his advice on carving out of the Congo an empire 25 times bigger than Belgium. In twenty years, Belgium grew into a rich modern nation on par with Britain in industrialization.

Belgium's was the only national economy that emerged from the last War in a healthy condition and ready to expand. This was partly due to the skill of the Belgians, but in greater part due to a set of fortunate circumstances. Firstly, her colony in Africa was most backward and unaffected by the post-War wave of nationalism that swept Asia and deprived other European empires of much of their colonial flow of wealth. Throughout the War, the Belgian Congo (Congo Free State) now Zaire, produced raw materials that brought in foreign currency for reconstruction of Belgium. Its chief products were copper and the new fissile element, uranium, which America bought in large quantities at good prices. Congo became poorer and Belgium became richer.

COLONY-BASED ECONOMY;
POST-WAR BONANZA

Belgium had also the advantage of being liberated almost literally between sunrise and sunset. Having been beaten as far as the Franco-Belgian frontier, the Germans abandoned the hopeless job of trying to defend flat Flanders and fled back to the security of the German Siegfried Line, leaving Belgium almost unharmed. Belgium had enjoyed an uncommon war-time advantage, shared only by Denmark among the occupied countries. The Nazis did not remove or convert to war purposes the Belgian industry. They allowed Belgian factories to produce for the German home market. When the War was over, the Belgian productive apparatus was all in place and there was no great problem in starting production again.

Finally, the structure of Belgian industry was favourable for a post-War period. While many other European countries get their foreign currency by selling foodstuffs and luxuries abroad, Belgium's main export was steel. While other steel-making nations required most of their steel for domestic rebuilding, Belgium needed only 20 per cent of her steel at home and, thus, could export the rest to earn foreign exchange. When Britain collapsed in the winter crisis, she cut off her imports of Dutch cheeses and radios; but she actually increased purchases of Belgian steel. In normal times, the top-heaviness of Belgian industry is a disadvantage, for no phase of production is so sensitive to the trade cycle as steel. But in the abnormal post-War period, it gave Belgium a spurt, which no other European country enjoyed.

LOW COUNTRIES, GIVEN AWAY IN DOWRY

Following the death of the last Burgundian duke, Charles the Rash (1433-77), in the battle at Nancy, the Low Countries passed to the Habsburg line through the marriage of Charles' daughter, Mary (1457-82) to Maximilian of Austria (1459-1519), the heir to the Holy Roman Empire. Under Habsburg Empress Maria Theresa (1717-80), the modernization of agriculture brought prosperity and stimulated new industries in the region. Roads and waterways were built during the period. But in 1792, war broke out between revolutionary France and Austria. The French defeated the Austrians in June 1794, a prelude to the French annexation of Belgium. After Napoleon's defeat in 1814, the Congress of Vienna united Belgium with the Netherlands. However, the two regions had conflicting interests and religions. Belgium proclaimed national independence in 1831, when Prince Leopold of Saxe-Coburg (1790-1865), was chosen as the first ruler of the new kingdom. In 1885, in a bid to make Belgium a colonial power, King Leopold II (1835-1909) acquired the vast territory of the Congo in Central Africa; this became the Belgian Congo in 1908. The Congo brought Leopold great wealth from rubber production, but the African labourers suffered atrocities against them by overseers, causing an international scandal.

QUICK RECOVERY AFTER WAR

In Belgium, the quick return of free enterprise resulted in maldistribution of income in favour of those who already had money and were able to make profitable use of the new freedom. The middle-class became poorer. Worker wages never rose. Consequently, there were continuous strikes for higher pay in the post-War years and unemployment grew. In the German invasion of 1940, King Leopold had surrendered to the Germans without awaiting the consent of his British and French allies, or that of the Belgian cabinet. The Belgian cabinet in Limoges, where it had fled, voted to condemn his action. Animosity mounted when Leopold rejected an opportunity to leave the country as most other monarchs of occupied countries did. He chose to remain in Belgium. The King of Denmark, too, remained in his country and continued to be popular. This act of bravery added to the powers of the King. Belgium, no wonder, is among the most porsperous countries of Europe.

Once a marshy land, Belgium now boasts of beautiful places in Europe. The country is named after a tribe, "Belgae". Caesar had destroyed them, but their name endures.

62

Belgium
(Kingdom of Belgium)

Belgium is a founding member of the European Union and hosts its headquarters, as well as those of other major international organizations, including NATO. Belgium covers an area of 30,528 square kilometers (11,787 sq mi) and has a population of about 10.7 million. It is monarchy; the current King is Albert II.

Belgium is situated in the northwestern Europe. The population consists mostly of Flemings and Walloons. The Flemings, more than half of the population, speak Flemish (Dutch) and live in the northern half of the country; the Walloons, about one-third of the population, speak French and inhabit the southern half. Language: Dutch, French, German (all official). Religions: Roman Catholicism (90%), Islam, Protestantism.

Belgium can be divided into several geographic regions. The southeast consists of the forested Ardennes highland, which extends south of the Meuse River valley and includes Belgium's highest Mount Botrange (2,277 ft). Middle Belgium is a fertile region crossed by tributaries of the Schelde River. Lower Belgium comprises the flat plains of Flanders in the northwest with their many canals. Maritime Flanders borders the North Sea and is agriculturally prosperous; the chief North Sea port is Oostende but Antwerp, near the mouth of the Schelde, has much greater grade. Belgium has minimal natural resources, so the manufacture of goods from imported raw materials plays a major role in the economy, and the country is highly industrialised.

The country derives its name from the Latin name of Gaul, *Gallia Belgica*, named after a group of Celtic tribes, *Belgae*. Historically, Belgium has been

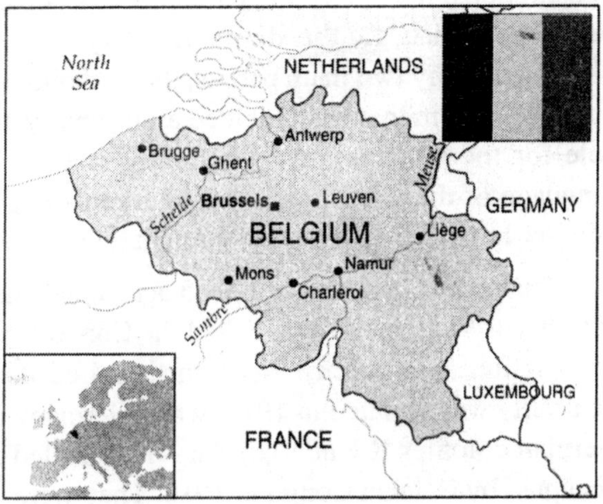

a part of the Low Countries, which also include the Netherlands and Luxembourg. From the end of the Middle Ages until the seventeenth century, it was a prosperous centre of commerce and culture. From the sixteenth century until the Belgian revolution in 1830, (the area then called the Southern Netherlands), was the site of many battles between the European powers, and has been dubbed "the battlefield of Europe" or "the cockpit of Europe".

Overrun by the Germans in World Wars-I and II, it was the scene of the Battle of the Bulge (1944-45), the most fiercely fought battle between the Allied and Axis powers. Internal discord led to legislation in the 1970s and 1980s that created three nearly autonomous regions in accordance with language distribution; Flemish Flanders, French Wallonia, and bilingual Brussels. In 1993, Belgium became a federation comprising the three regions, which gained greater autonomy at the outset of the 21st century. Belgium is a founding member of the European Union.

The history of Belgium can be distinguished from that of the Low Countries from the 16th century. The Eighty Years' War (1568–1648), divided the Seventeen Provinces into the United Provinces, in the north, and the Southern Netherlands, in the south. The southern provinces were ruled by the Spanish and the Austrian Habsburgs. Until independence, the Southern Netherlands was sought after by numerous French conquerors and was the theatre of most Franco-Spanish and Franco-Austrian wars during the 17th and 18th centuries. During the 1794 French Revolutionary Wars, the Low Countries were overrun by France, ending Spanish-Austrian rule in the region. The reunification of the Low Countries as the United Kingdom of the Netherlands occurred at the end of the Napoleon's Empire in 1815.

The 1830 Belgian Revolution also led to the establishment of an independent Catholic and neutral Belgium under a provisional government. Since the installation of Leopold I as king in 1831, Belgium has been a constitutional monarchy and parliamentary democracy. Between independence and World War II, the democratic system evolved from an oligarchy, characterised by two main parties, the Catholics and the Liberals, to a universal suffrage system that has included a third party, the Labour Party, and a strong role for the trade unions. Originally, the French, which was the adopted language of the nobility and the bourgeoisie, was the official language. The country has since developed a bilingual Dutch-French system.

The Berlin Conference of 1885 agreed to hand over Congo to King Leopold II as his private possession, called the Congo Free State. In 1908, it was ceded to Belgium as a colony, henceforth called the Belgian Congo. Belgium's neutrality was violated in 1914, when Germany invaded Belgium. The former German colonies Ruanda-Urundi – now called Rwanda and Burundi – were occupied by Belgian Congo in 1916. They were mandated in 1924 to Belgium by the League of Nations. Belgium was again invaded by Germany in 1940. The country was occupied until the winter of 1944-45 when it was liberated by Allied troops. Belgian Congo gained its independence in 1960 and Ruanda-Urundi became independent in 1962.

After World War II, Belgium joined NATO and, together with the Netherlands and Luxembourg, it formed the Benelux group of nations. Belgium is also one of the six founding members of the 1951 established European Coal and Steel Community, and of the 1957 established European Economic Community and European Atomic Energy Community. Belgium hosts the headquarters of NATO and many European Union's institutions and offices, including the European Commission, the Council of the European Union and the extraordinary and committee sessions of the European Parliament, as well as parts of its administration.

BORN BY ACCIDENT:

Belgium was born by accident, different peoples cobbled together speaking different languages and with different cultures. Belgians have nothing in common except "the king, the football team, some beers". No wonder Belgium is facing the problem of separation of Dutch-speaking Flanders from French-speaking people Wallonia. The latest crisis was born out of the June 10, 2007 legislative polls which resulted in the victory of Yves Leterme, leader of the Flemish Christian Democratic Party, which wants more autonomy for the wealthy Flemish in northern region. The Walloon Christian Democrats are deeply suspicious of Mr. Leterme.

Separation and conflict have been a constant factor in Belgium's 170-year-old history. The north and the south have been divided along social, philosophical, linguistic and political lines. And the Flemings even today continue to decry the "arrogance" of the Franco phones while calling for greater autonomy, if not outright separation.

The origin of this opposition goes back to 1815, some 15 years before the formal creation of Belgium when the victor nations, which defeated Napoleon Bonaparte, decided to re-fashion Europe in order to create a buffer zone between France and its enemy in further north. They put together the principality of Liege, the United Provinces of the Netherlands and the Austrian Low Countries to create the United Kingdom of Netherlands. Largely French speaking people in South rebelled against the union with The Netherlands and declared Belgian independence.

Former Belgian Prime Minister Herman Van Rompuy is currently serving as the President of the European Council. (January 1, 2010)

The new kingdom was placed under the reign of William I of Orange. William I turned out to be a short-sighted leader, imposing on the French-speaking Catholic south Dutch language by making it the official language. This deepened the divide. But it was not until 1939 under the *Treaty of London* signed by the major European powers (including The Netherlands), that Belgium was recognized as an independent and neutral country,. The new nation comprised the provinces of East and West Flanders, Brabant, Antwerp, Hainaut, Liege, Namur as well as that of Luxemburg and Limburg.

To be true Belgium was "established as an independent state after a historic accident that came to be known as the Belgian Revolution." The new state was unwanted by both the Dutch-speaking majority and the French speaking minority. The latter, in fact, wanted to join France. But it was forced into a compromise by the Great Powers who tuned Belgium into a neutral independent kingdom with a non-indigenous prince, the German Leopold of Saxe-Coburg, who became the first King of the Belgians. And because of the artificial nature of Belgium, its King has more power than any other constitutional monarch. Power is vested not in the country's Constitution but in the monarchy. The King is neither Fleming nor Walloon but German, hence,

European Union office in Brussels

is the only true Belgian institution in the land. Because of the fragile nature of the state, Belgian Kings over the past century-and-a-half have used various methods to impart a sense of "nationhood" to this totally artificial creation.

Leopold I tried to bind the people together through religion. His son, Leopold II, used outside conquest especially the colonies in Africa as a means to fan nationalist feelings. Albert I, who reigned from 1909 to 1934 tried to unify his people by creating entrenched vested interests through a system of division of the spoils. In fact, he laid the foundations of a welfare state. Over the years, the French-speaking regions (which once boasted heavy industries such as steel and coal) have lost out economically and it is now the Flemings who call the Wallons as "lazy socialists."

Belgium has an extremely complicated system of governance called "double federalism". Each of the three regions (Flanders, Wallonia and Brussels) has a "government" while there are three language "communities" (Dutch, French and German)along with a federal government which represents the nation as a whole on the world stage but which is often at loggerheads with this or that regional or communal government. Flanders-wealthy, right wing enterprising and business-headed-have nothing in common with Wallonia which is left-leaning, slow to modernize and whose politics is dominated by the Socialist party. The federative model was once a seductive solution but it appears less efficient and rational today in the face of growing conflict.

The First World War was fought to preserve Belgium's neutrality and independence. A break-up now for purely petty nationalistic and economic reasons would be a betrayal of all those who fought and died in the killing fields of Flanders. If split takes place, an independent Flanders will become "a small insignificant state" whereas a "little Belgium will continue with Wallonia, Brussels and its periphery." Never has mutual suspicion appeared so strong. The Walloons suspect that the Flemings have made up their mind to break apart and await their next moves with trepidation. The Flemings are convinced that the Walloons are cynically hoping to take advantage of Flemish wealth and industry for as long as possible. And, thus, the future of Belgium hangs in balance.

If we compare the Belgium crisis with India's diversities, we begin to discover how pluralism has best served us. India has 12 major languages and over two thousand dialects and here all the major religions of the world are practiced with tolerance and respect; people of one part, say south India, have nothing in common with those, say, in north-east and mind-boggling varieties of cultural practices, cuisines, festivals, faiths and follies are being practiced by over a billion people. India is tapestries where individual identities are not lost while woven together. If you compare these with those in Belgium, a country of only 10 million, you will begin to wonder how magic works!!

NATIONAL INDICATORS - BELGIUM

Area 30,510 sq.km.; capital Brussels; major towns Ghent, Liege, Charleroi, Bruges, Mons, Namur, Leuven; major ports Antwerp, Ostend, Zeebruge; physical features fertile coastal plain in northwest, central rolling hills rise eastwards, hills and forest in southeast, Ardennes Forest, river Scheldt and Meuse; head of state King Albert from 1993; political system federal constitutional monarchy; administrative divisions ten provinces within three regions; population 10,113,000 (1995); education (compulsory years) 12; literacy rate 99%.

HISTORY

57 BC Romans conquered the Belgae (the indigenous Celtic people), and formed province of Belgica.

3rd-4th Cs AD	Region overrun by Franks and Saxons.
8th-9th Cs	Part of Frankish Empire; peace and order fostered growth of Ghent, Bruges and Brussels.
843	Division of Holy Roman Empire; became part of Lotharingia, but frequent repartitioning followed.
10th-11th Cs	Seven feudal states emerged: Flanders, Hainaut, Namur, Brabant, Limburg and Luxembourg, all nominally subject to French king or Holy Roman emperor, but in practice independent.
12th C	Economy began to flourish; textles in Bruges, Ghent, and Ypres; copper and tin in Dinant and Liege.
15th C	One by one, states came under rule of dukes of Burgundy.
1477	Passed into Habsburg dominions through marriage of Mary of Burgundy to Maximilian, archduke of Austria.
1555	Division of Habsburg dominions; Low Countries allotted to Spain.
1648	Independence of Dutch Republic recognised; South retained by Spain.
1713	Treaty of Utrecht transferred Spanish Netherlands to Austrian rule.
1792-97	Austrian Netherlands invaded by revolutionary France and finally annexed.
1815	Congress of Vienna reunited north and south Netherlands as one kingdom under House of Orange.
1830	Largely French speaking people in south rebelled against union with Holland and declared Belgian independence.
1831	Leopold of Saxe-Coburg-Gotha became first king of Belgium.
1839	Treaty of London recognised independence of Belgium and guaranteed its neutrality.
1847-70	Government dominated by Liberals; growth of heavy industry.
1870-1914	Catholic Party predominant.
1914-18	Invaded and occupied by Germany. Belgian forces under King Albert-I fought in conjunction with Allies.
1919	Acquired Eupen-Malmedy region from Germany.

1940	Second invasion by Germany; King Leopold-III ordered Belgian army to capitulate.
1944-45	Belgium liberated.
1948	Belgium formed Benelux customs union with Luxembourg and the Netherlands.
1949	Belgium was a founding member of North Atlantic Treaty Organisation (NATO).
1951	Leopold-III abdicated in favour of his son Baudouin.
1958	Belgium was a founding member of European Economic Community (EEC) which made Brussels its headquarters.
1967	NATO made Brussels its headquarters.
1971	Constitution amended to safeguard cultural rights of the Flemish (in Flanders in the north) and French speaking communities (Walloons in the southeast) in an effort to ease the linguistic dispute.
1974	Separate regional councils and ministerial committees established for Flemings and Walloons.
1980	Open violence over language divisions; regional assemblies for Flanders and Wallonia and a three-member executive for Brussels created.
1993	Federal system adopted, based on Flanders, Wallonia and Brussels. King Baudouin died, succeeded by his brother, Albert.
1995	Dehaene-led coalition re-elected.

Once a great colonial power, having an empire 60 times its size, the Netherlands has survived the loss of its empire and is growing faster than most countries of the Continent. The monarchy is leading the country in most enlightened ways.

63

The Netherlands (Holland)

The Dutch created the richest part of their country by recovering it from the sea with spades and pumps. All the country's chief cities stand, and three-quarters of the population live, behind dykes below sea level. Though only 30 per cent of Holland's sandy surface is arable, it yields some of the biggest grain crop per acre in the world. Her tulip and dairy farms are among her largest industries of Europe.

Unlike Belgium, Holland has seldom been passive in history. She was a great commercial sea power before Britain became one. Her sons, who settled in the US, pulled the wildest real estate deal on record, by buying a wild island called Manhattan, from the Indians for about 25 dollars worth of trinkets. Today all of Holland cannot buy it back. Holland had an empire sixty times her own size, scattered over three continents. Lacking a basis for heavy industry, Holland lived by selling colonial raw materials and domestic foodstuffs to the rest of the world.

Holland came out of the war in a very different condition from Belgium. The Nazis in their retreat from France stopped in Holland and built their defence lines along the broad river mouths of the southern part of the country. For nine terrible months, the Germans looted and destroyed her and Allied bombers pounded her. Maastricht was headquarters of the American Ninth Army. Even in that privileged town, people lived on less than 900 calories a day (standard: 2,600). In German occupied Holland, people starved. By the time the Germans were thrown out, 30 per cent of its domestic national wealth was destroyed.

INDONESIA WAS THE CHIEF COLONY

As an overpopulated and essentially agrarian economy, Holland before the War leaned on urban markets for sales and foreign exchange. The most important nearby market was the Ruhr. The second most important was Britain. Holland also lived by her ports, Rotterdam and Amsterdam. The worst blow was the rise of nationalism after the last War in her rich colony of Indonesia. A total of one sixth of her wealth was invested in Indonesia and from it she derived annually 15 per cent of her national income. The loss of Indonesia had reduced the Dutch domestic standard of living 30 per cent below pre-War level. Indonesia – formerly a rich source of dollar-earning rubber – has become a net loss to Holland.

During the war the population of Belgium increased by 100,000 people while that of Holland went up to 600,000. The state of Holland illustrated the extent to which morality had become a luxury in international affairs. There were no more moral people in Europe than the Dutch. Yet their attitude towards the Indonesians and their defiance of the UN in putting down the Indonesian republicans has been flagrant. Their aim was simply to exploit a colonial people and derive benefit of their own wealth for a change. But direst domestic necessity dictated Dutch behaviour, and even induced Dutchmen to think that their cause was just.

ONCE THIRD LARGEST COLONIAL POWER IN THE WORLD

Before World War II, the republic formed the Netherlands Indies, which was occupied in 1942-5, by the Japanese and they promoted the movement for independence from the Dutch. At the end of the fighting, Indonesia included all the Netherlands Indies except western New Guinea, which was recognized by the Dutch in 1949 and a union set up between the two countries at the same time was abrogated by Indonesia in 1956. Under the leadership of President Sukarno, the republic laid claim to Netherlands' New Guinea which in 1962 was ceded, to the UN and in 1963 to Indonesia, but the confrontation of Malaysia over Sabah and Sarawak 1963-6 ended in a truce. This was a consequence of a revision of policy by Gen. Suharto who took power 1966 and banned the Communist Party. He became president in 1968 (re-elected for a third term in 1978), and encouraged investment and commerce. Indonesia, formerly called *Dutch East-Indies*, was the third largest colonial power in the world.

As a part of the Kingdom of the Netherlands, the *Netherlands Indies,* inhabited predominantly by Muslims of Malay stock, was subject to the legislation of the home government. The Crown appointed a Governor-General to rule the area. An advisory council and a council of the heads of the government departments assisted him. There was also a consultative body called the *Volksraad* (People's Council) which was partly appointed and partly elected by local councils. The less developed, or so-called "outposts," like Borneo and the Celebes, had been generally ruled by natives, supervised by governors under treaties or contracts. The mother country would never have attained its pre-eminent position without the colonies. They did not have dominion status, but the Dutch had not attempted to monopolize their trade or forced it to give special favours to the mother country. Since the debacle of May 10, 1940 the Indies had pursued a course quite independent of the mother country, and acquired a dominion status.

CHALLENGES OF THE 21ST CENTURY

A flat Netherlands, inhabited by well-off people, has been a peaceful, prosperous place and a bastion of liberalism, social tolerance, softdrugs and ethnic minorities. But, the assassinations of Pim Fortuyn, (2002)

THE DUTCH EAST INDIA COMPANY

Spice trade led to empire

By the end of the 15th century, Dutch commercial explorers were keen to challenge Portugal for a share of the spice trade. To divide the risks – as well as the profits – involved in trading with the East Indies, rich Amsterdam merchants invested in a joint-stock company called the Dutch East India Company. The government granted the company a trading monopoly between the Cape of Good Hope and the Straits of Magellan, with the right to make treaties with neighbouring provinces, maintain armed forces and appoint officials in new territories.

In 1603, the Dutch seized the island of Amboina from the Portuguese. Malacca fell to the Dutch in 1644, and control of Ceylon, with its precious stones, pearls and cinnamon trees, was finally wrested from the Portuguese in 1656. By 1755, most of the island of Java was in Dutch hands.

In the 18th century, the company began purchasing local produce which went to Europe, and the profits remained in Dutch hands. But, these measures could not halt the company's slow decline. Its monopoly was broken, first by smuggling, and then, after the Treaty of Paris in 1784, by its old rivals, Britain, who were granted the right to trade in the East Indies.

In 1799, while the Netherlands lay under the dominion of the French Napoleonic Empire, the company was finally wound up by the Dutch goverment which acquired all its debts and possessions.

an anti-immigrant populist, and Theovan Gogh, (2004) an anti-Muslim leader, has set the anti-immigration pot boiling in the country. The conundrum facing the Netherlands and also the other countries of Europe, is how to manage a growing minority that is itself becoming intolerant. Ever since van Gogh's murder, Dutch society has been in a funk and the specture of Islamist terrorism only has made it worse. Attempts to coerce Muslims into adopting Western values seems to be failing. Europe needs to come to terms with Islam as a European religion. It is amazing that the most radical Muslims are not immigrants but the second generation – those who grow up in Europe, disaffected, rootless and often jobless. These are the people who must be persuaded that they have a stake in a modern, liberal democracy. For the Netherlands, as for all of Europe, that requires better education, better housing, lower crime and more job opportunities.

These questions are relevant because the Dutch economic miracle of the 1990s is over, although the country is still richer than its German and French neighbours. Its unemployment, poverty and need for generous welfare state are most needed by immigrants. Economic reform and faster growth may be the best way to combat radical Islam, but it is not clear now the Dutch government will be able to deliver them because of a slowdown in its economy and its unwillingness to accept Islam as a European religion. Growing influence of radical Islam is the biggest challenge of the Netherlands, so also of the entire Europe.

COUNTRY REPORT

Once part of the Roman Empire, the Netherlands has a long history of fighting against many rulers and conquerors to finally emerge as a beautiful and prosperous country.

64

The Netherlands (Kingdom of the Netherlands)

A country of dikes, drains and windmills, a quarter of Holland lies below sea level, making people fight to stay safe on the land. It also faces the threat from climate change when warm surging water may threaten its existence. However, the ingenious and hardworking people are far ahead of nature's fury to stay prosperous and happy.

The Netherlands is situated in northwestern Europe; its southern and eastern region consists mostly of plains and a few high ridges; its western and northern region is lower and includes polders on the site of the Zuiderzee and the common delta of the Rhine, Meuse, and Schelde rivers. Building dike was first conceived as early as 1891, to reclaim land from what was then the Zuider Zee, and to link the province of North Holland with the northwestern province of Friesland. While the dike was under construction the shallow Wieringermeer, to the southwest, was drained. This became the first of four large polders (low lying areas) to be reclaimed, and today they cover an area of more than 2,000 sq km. The western provinces of North and South Holland are reclaimed lands. About 27% of its area and 60% of its population is located below sea level.

The rivers Rhine, Schelde and Meuse flow out into the North Sea by way of a delta made up of estuaries and islands. After disastrous flooding in 1953, most of the estuaries and sea-arms were sealed off by 32 km of new dikes, and a tidal barrage. The New Waterway, linking Rotterdam with the sea, and

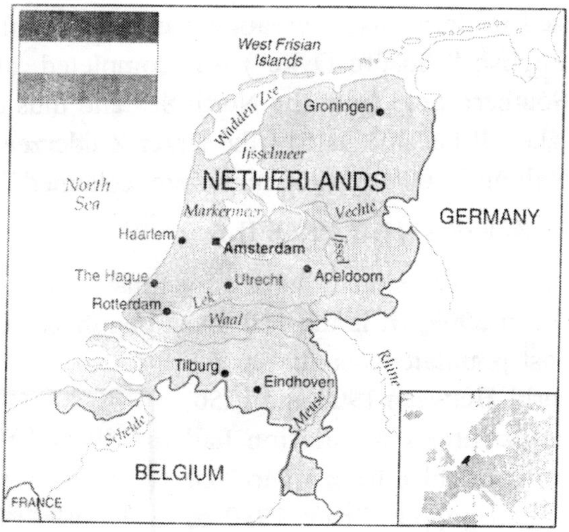

the Western Schelde, give access to the Belgian port of Antwerp. In early 1995, the government declared a state of emergency during severe flooding. Coastal areas are almost completely below sea level and are protected by dunes and artificial dikes.

In years past, the Dutch coastline has changed considerably as a result of human intervention and natural disasters. Most notable in terms of land loss is the 1134 storm, which created the archipelago of Zeeland in the south west. The St. Elizabeth flood of 1421 and the mismanagement in its aftermath destroyed a newly reclaimed polder, replacing it with the 72 square kilometres (28 sq mi) *Biesbosch* tidal floodplains in the south-centre. Most recently parts of Zeeland were flooded during the North Sea Flood of 1953 when 1,836 people were killed, after which the *Delta Plan* was executed.

The disasters were partially increased in severity through human influence. People had drained relatively high lying swampland to use it as farmland. This drainage caused the fertile peat to compress and the ground level to drop, locking the land users in a vicious circle whereby they would lower the water level to compensate for the drop in ground level, causing the underlying peat to compress even more. The problem remains unsolvable to this day. Also, up until the 19th century peat was mined, dried, and used for fuel, further adding to the problem.

To guard against floods, a series of defences against the water were contrived. In the first millennium AD, villages and farmhouses were built on man-made hills called *terps*. Later, these terps were connected by dikes. In the 12th century, local government agencies called *"waterschappen"* (English "water bodies") or *"hoogheemraadschappen"* ("high home councils") started to appear, whose job it was to maintain the water level and to protect a region from floods. (These agencies exist to this day, performing the same function.) As the ground level dropped, the dykes by necessity grew and merged into an integrated system. By the 13th century, windmills had come into use in order to pump water out of areas below sea level. The windmills were later used to drain lakes, creating the famous polders. In 1932, the *Afsluitdijk* (English "Closure Dyke") was completed, blocking the former *Zuiderzee* (Southern Sea) from the North Sea and thus creating the IJsselmeer (IJssel Lake). It became part of the larger Zuiderzee Works in which four polders totalling 2,500 km^2 (965 mi^2) were reclaimed from the sea.

DEMOGRAPHIC PROFILE

The Netherlands have an estimated population of 16,491,852 (as of 8 March 2009). It is the 11th most populated country in Europe and the 61st most populated country in the world. Between 1900 and 1950, the country's population had almost doubled from 5.1 to 10.0 million people. From 1950 to 2000, the population further increased from 10.0 to 15.9 million people, but the population growth decreased compared to the previous fifty years. The estimated growth rate is currently 0.436% (as of 2008). The fertility rate in the Netherlands is 1.66 children per woman (as of 2008), which is high compared to many other European countries, but well below the 2.1-rate required for natural population replacement. Life expectancy is high in the Netherlands: 82 years for newborn girls and 77 for boys (2007). The country has a migration rate of 2.55 migrants per 1,000 inhabitants.

> **HOLLAND OR THE NETHERLANDS?**
>
> Holland, North and South, are two provinces of the Netherlands, which occupy the Peninsula jutting northwards between the North Sea and the Ijsselmeer. Most of it is below the sea-level, protected from water by a series of sand dunes and artificial dykes. South Holland is also low-lying. The Hague is its capital. Because the provinces of North and South Holland have always been the wealthiest part of the Netherlands, the name Holland is frequently used for the whole country – even by Dutchmen. The people of Holland are called Dutchmen or Dutchwomen. The term "Dutch" is used as an adjective like the Dutch Government, or the Dutch trade.

The majority of the population of the Netherlands are ethnically Dutch. A 2005 estimate counted: 80.9% Dutch, 2.4% Indonesian (Indo-Dutch, South Moluccan), 2.4% German, 2.2% Turkish, 2.0% Surinamese, 1.9% Moroccan, 0.8% Antillean and Aruban, and 6.0% others. The Dutch people are among the tallest in the world, with an average height of about 1.85 m (6 ft 1 in) for adult males and 1.68 m (5 ft 6 in) for adult females. People in the south are on average about 2 cm shorter than those in the north.

The Netherlands is the 25th most densely populated country in the world, with 395 inhabitants per square kilometre or 484 people per square kilometre if only the land area is counted. It is the most densely populated country in Europe with a population over 1 million. The Randstad is the country's largest conurbation located in the west of the country and contains the four largest cities: Amsterdam in the province North Holland, Rotterdam and The Hague in the province South Holland, and Utrecht in the province Utrecht. The Randstad alone has a population of 7 million inhabitants and is the 6th largest metropolitan area in Europe.

The Netherlands is known for its traditional windmills, tulips, cheese, *clogs* (wooden shoes), delftware and gouda pottery, for its bicycles, and in addition, traditional values and civil virtues such as its social tolerance. The country has more recently become known for its liberal policies. It also has one of the most free market capitalist economies in the world, ranking 12th of 157 countries in one index.

The Netherlands has a long tradition of social tolerance. In the 18th century, while the Dutch Reformed Church was the state religion, Catholicism and Judaism were tolerated. In the late 19th century this Dutch tradition of religious tolerance transformed into a system of pillarisation, in which religious groups coexisted separately and only interacted at the level of government. This tradition of tolerance is linked to the Dutch policies on recreational drugs, prostitution, LGBT rights, euthanasia, and abortion which are among the most liberal in the world.

CONSTITUTIONAL MONARCHY

The Netherlands has been a constitutional monarchy since 1815 and a parliamentary democracy since 1848; before that it had been a republic from 1581 to 1806, a kingdom between 1806 and 1810, and a part of France between 1810 and 1813. The Netherlands is described as a consociational state. Dutch politics and governance are characterised by an effort to achieve broad consensus on important issues, within both the political community and society as a whole. In 2008, The Economist ranked The Netherlands as the fourth most democratic country in the world.

The monarch is the head of state, at present Queen Beatrix. Constitutionally, the position is equipped with considerable powers, but in practice it has become a ceremonial function. The monarch can exert most influence during the formation of a new cabinet, where they serve as neutral arbiter between the political parties.

In practice, the executive power is formed by the ministerraad, the deliberative council of the Dutch cabinet. The cabinet consists usually of thirteen to sixteen ministers and a varying number of state secretaries. One to three ministers are ministers without portfolio. The head of government is the Prime Minister of the Netherlands, who often is the leader of the largest party of the coalition. In fact, this has been continuously the case since 1973. The Prime Minister is a *primus inter pares*, meaning he has no explicit powers beyond those of the other ministers.

The cabinet is responsible to the bicameral parliament, the States-General which also has legislative powers. The 150 members of the House of Representatives, the Lower House, are elected in direct elections, which are held every four years or after the fall of the cabinet (by example: when one of the chambers carries a motion of no-confidence, the cabinet offers her resignation to the monarch). The States-Provincial are directly elected every four years as well. The members of the provincial assemblies elect the 75 members of the Senate, the upper house, which has less legislative powers, as it can merely reject laws, not propose or amend them.

While historically the Dutch foreign policy was characterised by neutrality, since the Second World War the Netherlands became a member of a large number of international organisations, most prominently the UN, NATO and the EU. The Dutch economy is very open and relies on international trade.

A CHEQUERED HISTORY

Under Charles V, Holy Roman Emperor, and king of Spain, the region was part of the Seventeen Provinces of the Netherlands, which also included most of present-day Belgium, Luxembourg, and some land of France and Germany. The Eighty Years' War between the provinces and Spain began in 1568. In 1579, the northern half of the Seventeen Provinces formed the Union of Utrecht, a treaty in which they promised to support each other in their defense against the Spanish army. The Union of Utrecht is seen as the foundation of the modern Netherlands. In 1581 the northern provinces adopted the Act of Abjuration, the declaration of independence in which the provinces officially deposed Philip II. Philip II the son of Charles V, was not prepared to let them go easily and war continued until 1648 when Spain under King Philip IV finally recognised the independence of the seven northwestern provinces in the Treaty of Münster. Parts of the southern provinces became de facto colonies of the new republican-mercantile empire.

DUTCH GOLDEN AGE

Since their independence from Phillip II in 1581 seven provinces formed the Republic of the Seven United Netherlands. The republic was a confederation of the provinces Holland, Zeeland, Groningen, Friesland, Utrecht, Overijssel and Gelre. All these provinces were autonomous and had their own government, the "States of the Province". The States-General, the confederal government, were seated in The Hague and consisted of representatives from each of the seven provinces. The Dutch grew to become one of the major seafaring and economic powers of the 17th century during the period of the Republic of the Seven United Netherlands. In the so-called Dutch Golden Age, colonies and trading posts were established all over the globe (see Dutch colonial empire). During the 17th century, the Dutch population increased from an estimated 1.5 million to almost 2 million.

The Netherlands is regarded as the first thoroughly capitalist country in the world. In early modern Europe it featured the wealthiest trading city (Amsterdam) and the first full-time stock exchange. The inventiveness of the traders led to insurance and retirement funds as well as such less benign phenomena as the boom-bust cycle, the world's first asset-inflation bubble, the tulip mania of 1636–1637, and according to Murray Sayle, the world's first bear raider - Isaac le Maire, who forced prices down by dumping stock and then buying it back at a discount. The republic went into a state of general decline in the later 18th century, with economic competition from England and long standing rivalries between the two main factions in Dutch society, Republicans and the Royalists or Orangists as main factors.

A UNITARY STATE

On 19 January 1795, one day after William V of Orange fled to England, the Batavian Republic was proclaimed, rendering the Netherlands a unitary state. From 1795 to 1806, the Batavian Republic designated the Netherlands as a republic modelled after the French Republic. From 1806 to 1810, the Kingdom of Holland was set up by Napoleon Bonaparte as a puppet kingdom governed by his third brother, Louis Napoleon Bonaparte, in order to control the Netherlands more effectively. The name of the leading province, Holland, was now taken for the whole country. The Kingdom of Holland covered the area of the present day Netherlands, with the exception of Limburg, and parts of Zeeland, which were French territory. In 1807, Prussian East Frisia and

Jever were added to the kingdom. In 1809 however, after an English invasion, Holland had to give over all territories south of the river Rhine to France. King Louis Napoleon did not meet Napoleon's expectations—he tried to serve Dutch interests instead of his brother's—and the King had to abdicate on 1 July 1810. He was succeeded by his five year old son Napoleon Louis Bonaparte. Napoleon Louis reigned as Louis II for just ten days as Emperor Napoleon Bonaparte ignored his young nephew's accession to the throne. The Emperor sent in an army to invade the country and dissolved the Kingdom of Holland. The Netherlands then became part of the French Empire. From 1810 to 1813, when Napoleon Bonaparte was defeated in the battle of Leipzig, the Netherlands were part of the French Empire.

In 1795 William V of Orange fled to England. His son returned to the Netherlands in 1813 to become William I of the Netherlands, Sovereign Prince of the Netherlands. On 16 March 1815, the Sovereign Prince became King of the Netherlands. In 1815, the Congress of Vienna formed the United Kingdom of the Netherlands, by expanding the Netherlands with Belgium in order to create a strong country on the northern border of France. In addition, William became hereditary Grand Duke of Luxembourg. The Congress of Vienna gave Luxembourg to William as personal property in exchange for his German possessions, Nassau-Dillenburg, Siegen, Hadamar and Diez. Belgium rebelled and gained independence in 1830, while the personal union between Luxembourg and the Netherlands was severed in 1890, when King William III of the Netherlands died with no surviving male heirs. Ascendancy laws prevented his daughter Queen Wilhelmina from becoming the next Grand Duchess. Therefore the throne of Luxembourg passed over from the House of Orange-Nassau to the House of Nassau-Weilburg, another branch of the House of Nassau.

THE KINGDOM AND ITS COLONIES

The largest Dutch settlement abroad was the Cape Colony. It was established by Jan van Riebeeck on behalf of the Dutch East India Company at Cape Town in 1652. The Prince of Orange acquiesced to British occupation and control of the Cape Colony in 1788. The Netherlands also possessed several other colonies, but Dutch settlement in these lands was limited. Most notable were the vast Dutch East Indies (now Indonesia) and Suriname (Suriname was traded with the British for New Amsterdam, now known as New York City). These 'colonies' were first managed by the Dutch East India Company and the Dutch West India Company, both collective private enterprises. Three centuries later these companies got into financial trouble and the territories in which they operated were taken over by the Dutch government (in 1815 and 1791 respectively). Only then did they become official colonies.

The Netherlands remained neutral in World War I and intended to do so in World War II. There were, however, contingency plans involving the armies of Belgium, France and Great Britain. Regardless, Nazi Germany invaded the Netherlands in 1940 in the Western European campaign of the Second World War. French forces in the south and British ships in the west came to help, but turned around quickly, evacuating many civilians and several thousand German prisoners of war from their elite airborne divisions. In spite of fierce fighting and victory in several local battles the country was overrun in five days, far longer than the German High Command and Hitler had planned for. Only after, but not because of, the bombing of Rotterdam, the army's main force surrendered on 14 May, although a Dutch/French allied force held the western part of Zeeland for some time after the surrender. The German Luftwaffe and Airborne regiments suffered very heavy losses. The Kingdom as such continued the war from the colonial empire; the government in exile resided in London.

During the occupation, over 100,000 Dutch Jews were rounded up to be transported to Nazi concentration camps in Germany, Poland and Czechoslovakia. By the time these camps were liberated, only 876 Dutch Jews survived. Dutch workers were conscripted for forced labour in German factories, civilians were killed in reprisal for attacks on German soldiers, and the countryside was plundered for food for German soldiers in the Netherlands and for shipment to Germany. Although there were many Dutch who risked their lives by hiding Jews from the Germans, as in the diary of Anne Frank, there were also Dutch who collaborated with the occupying force in hunting down hiding Jews. Local fascists and anti-Bolsheviks joined the Waffen-SS in the 4th SS Volunteer Panzergrenadier Brigade Netherlands, fighting on the Eastern Front as well as other units.

The government-in-exile lost control of its major colonial stronghold, the Netherlands East Indies (Indonesia), to Japanese forces in March 1942. "American-British-Dutch-Australian" (ABDA) forces fought hard in some instances, but were overwhelmed. During the occupation, the Japanese interned Dutch civilians and used Dutch and Indos alike as forced labour, both in the Netherlands East Indies and in neighbouring countries. This included forcing women to work as "comfort women" (sex slaves) for Japanese personnel.

Some military personnel escaped to Australia and other Allied countries from where they carried on the fight against Japan. The Japanese furthered the cause of independence for the colony, so that after VE day many young Dutchmen found themselves fighting a colonial war against the new republic of Indonesia.

PROSPEROUS PEOPLE, GROWING ECONOMY

The Netherlands has a prosperous and open economy in which the government has reduced its role since the 1980s. Industrial activity is predominantly in food-processing (for example Unilever and Heineken International), chemicals (for example DSM), petroleum refining (for example Royal Dutch Shell), and electrical machinery (for example Philips). The Netherlands has the 16th largest economy in the world, and ranks 10th in GDP (nominal) per capita. Between 1998 and 2000 annual economic growth (GDP) averaged nearly 4%, well above the European average. Growth slowed considerably in 2001-05 due to the global economic slowdown, but accelerated to 4.1% in the third quarter of 2007. Inflation is 1.3% and is expected to stay low at around 1.5% in the coming years Unemployment is at 4.0% of the labour force. By Eurostat standards however, unemployment in the Netherlands is at only 2.9% - the lowest rate of all European Union member states. The Netherlands also has a relatively low GINI coefficient of 0.326. Despite ranking only 10th in GDP per capita, UNICEF ranked the Netherlands 1st in child well-being. On the Index of Economic Freedom Netherlands is the 13th most free market capitalist economy out of 157 surveyed countries.

After the war, the Dutch economy prospered by leaving behind an era of neutrality and gaining closer ties with neighbouring states. The Netherlands was one of the founding members of the Benelux (Belgium, the Netherlands and Luxembourg) grouping, was among the twelve founding members of the North Atlantic Treaty Organisation (NATO), and was among the six founding members of the European Coal and Steel Community, which would later evolve, via the EEC (Common Market), into the European Union.

The last major flood in the Netherlands took place in early February 1953, when a huge storm caused the collapse of several dikes in the southwest of the Netherlands. More than 1,800 people drowned in the ensuing inundations. The Dutch government subsequently decided on a large-scale program of public works (the "Delta Works") to protect the country against future flooding. The project took more than thirty years to complete. According to Dutch government engineers, the odds of a major inundation anywhere in the Netherlands are now 1 in 10,000 per year. Following the disaster with hurricane Katrina in 2005, an American congressional delegation visited the Netherlands to inspect the Delta Works and Dutch government engineers were invited to a hearing of the United States Congress to explain the Netherlands' efforts to protect low-lying areas.

The 60s and 70s were a time of great social and cultural change, such as rapid *ontzuiling* (literally: depillarisation), a term that describes the decay of the old divisions along class and religious lines. Youths, and students in particular, rejected traditional mores, and pushed for change in matters like women's rights, sexuality, disarmament and environmental issues. Today, the Netherlands is regarded as a liberal country, considering its drugs policy and its legalisation of euthanasia. Same-sex marriage has been permitted since 1 April 2001.

The House of Orange

Profile of H.R.H. Prince Willem-Alexander

The House of Orange is the princely dynasty which derives its name from the medieval principality of Orange. In the 16th century, through a marital alliance with the German House of Nassau, the House of Orange became involved in the history of the Netherlands. In 1544 a Count of Nassau who became Prince of Orange as Willem I led the Netherlands revolt against Spain (1568 to 1584) and held the office of stadholder (Dutch viceroy or provincial governor) in four of the rebelling provinces. This was the start of a tradition in the Dutch Republic whereby the stadholderships were for long periods held by the princes of Orange and counts of Nassau. As heir to the Dutch throne, Prince Willem-Alexander's official title is His Royal Highness the Prince of Orange, which was automatically conferred to him when his mother became Queen of the Netherlands on 30th April 1980. It has been borne by the sovereign's oldest son ever since the Netherlands became a monarchy in 1815. The male line ended in 1890 when Wilhemina became queen. In 1908 Queen Wilhemina decreed that her descendants should be called princes or princesses of Orange-Nassau.

Prince Willem-Alexander, as the eldest child of Queen Beatrix, is first in line of succession to the throne. Since his mother's investiture on 30 April 1980, he has borne the title Prince of Orange, which has been held by the heir to the throne since 1815. The Prince is married to Princess Maxima. They have three daughters, Princess Catharina-Amalia, Princess Alexia and Princess Ariane. Willem-Alexander Claus George Ferdinand, Prince of the Netherlands, Prince of Orange-Nassau and Jonkheer van Amsberg, was born in the University Hospital, Utrecht, on 27 April 1967, the first child of Princess Beatrix and Prince Claus. He spent his early childhood at Drakensteyn Castle in Lage Vuursche. Prince Willem-Alexander has two brothers: Prince Friso (born in 1968) and Prince Constantijn (born in 1969). In 1981, the royal family moved from Drakensteyn Castle to Huis ten Bosch Palace in The Hague.

Prince Willem-Alexander received his primary education at the Nieuwe Baarnse School in Baarn and completed secondary education at Atlantic College in Llantwit Major, Wales, where he gained an International Baccalaureate in 1985. The Prince concluded his studies with a dissertation on the Dutch response to France's decision under President de Gaulle to leave NATO's integrated command structure. He was awarded a degree in history in 1993. The Prince has been active in this field, in the Netherlands and elsewhere, since 1998. At present, the prince is Chair of the UN Secretary-General's Advisory Board on Water and Sanitation. (Sources: Encyclopedia Britannica & www.koninklijkhuis.nl).

NETHERLANDS, at a glance

THROUGHOUT THEIR HISTORY, the Dutch have been influenced by the sea. At first, they had to reclaim their low-lying land from beneath the North Sea and protect it from flooding. Then they used their maritime skills to create a rich, worldwide trading empire. In the 16th and 17th centuries, cities such as Amsterdam and Rotterdam prospered on the spice trade with the East, and merchants patronized the arts and science. Despite a decline during the 18th century, the Netherlands has kept its close relationship with the sea to this day.

William the Silent

Prince William (1533-84) came from Orange in southern France, but was a major landowner in the Netherlands and resented Spanish rule. In 1576, he became leader of the Dutch United Provinces and proved to be a superb general. He was assassinated before the Dutch won their independence.

Golden Age

Freed from Spanish rule, the Dutch state became wealthy. Merchants grew rich on overseas trade, while skilled Jewish and Protestant refugees flooded in, fleeing persecution in Catholic Europe. The openness of Dutch society encouraged a free exchange of ideas. Science flourished and painters such as Vermeer and Rembrandt produced masterpieces for the rich middle classes.

Dutch Wars

As the leading maritime trading nation in Europe, the Dutch had to fight to protect their wealth. Commercial rivalry, first with England and then France in the late 17th century, led to wars, that weakened Dutch power.

Dutch Water Engineering

During the 13th century, the Dutch began to reclaim land from the North Sea by building a series of dykes and drainage canals. Dutch engineers became so good at designing drainage schemes that their skills were in demand throughout Europe.

Revolt Against Spain

In 1556, the Netherlands became part of the Spanish branch of the Habsburg Empire. The Protestant Dutch resented being ruled by Catholic Spain. A revolt broke out and in 1581 the seven northern provinces declared independence from Spain. After a long and bloody war, a truce was announced in 1609. Independence from Spain was finally agreed in 1648.

Dutch Empire

In the late 1500s, Dutch merchants sailed into the Indian Ocean in search of spices from Asia. In 1602, the Dutch East India Company was set for trade. Trading posts were set up in India, China, Japan, and what is now Indonesia. By 1650, the Dutch ruled a vast empire in eastern Asia.

Spice Trade

Spices such as pepper, cloves, and nutmeg fetched huge prices in the 16th and 17th centuries. The Dutch defeated the Portuguese and the British to control the spice trade with Europe. They set up an empire in southeast

Asia where they also grew crops such as coffee.

Wealth of Empire

The Dutch merchants grew rich on the trade in the East. Although some were based in the capital of the Dutch eastern empire, Batavia (now Jakarta, Indonesia), most built large houses for themselves in Amsterdam. These houses had to be lightweight in construction, because they were sited on unstable, reclaimed land next to the city's canals. They were, therefore, built of light materials with large windows.

20th Century

The Netherlands was neutral in World War I but was invaded and occupied by Germany from 1940-45. Since World War II, the Dutch have created one of the most successful economies in Europe. During the government of the Social Democratic Party, a welfare state was introduced. The Netherlands is a keen supporter of closer integration within the European Union.

Timeline

1300-1400s Netherlands is part of Burgundy.

1477 Netherlands becomes part of the Habsburg empire.

1555 In the partition of the empire, Netherlands is ruled by Spain.

1568 Revolt against Spanish rule begins.

1579 Seven northern provinces unite in the Union of Utrecht.

1581 The United Provinces declare their independence from their Spanish rulers.

1648 The Treaty of Westphalia recognizes Dutch independence from Spain.

1830 Belgium, its Catholic citizens resenting Protestant rule, at last gains its independence from the northern Netherlands.

NATIONAL INDICATORS - THE NETHERLANDS

Area 41,863 sq.km.; capital Amsterdam; major towns The Hague (seat of government), Utrecht, Eindhoven, Maastricht; major ports Rotterdam; physical features flat coastal lowland; river Rhine, Scheldt, Maas; Frisian Islands; territories Aruba, Netherlands Antilles (Caribbean); head of state Queen Beatrix Wilhelmina Armgard from 1980; head of government Wim Kok from 1994; political system constitutional monarchy; administrative divisions 12 provinces; life expectancy 74 (men), 81 (women); education (compulsory years) 11; literacy rate 99%; language Dutch; religions Roman Catholic, Dutch Reformed Church.

HISTORY

55 BC	Julius Caesar brought lands of Rhine under Roman rule.
4th C AD	Region overrun by Franks and Saxons.
843-12th	Cs Division of Holy Roman Empire; the Netherlands repeatedly partitioned, not falling clearly into either French or German kingdoms.
15th C	Low Countries (Holland, Belgium and Flanders) came under rule of dukes of Burgundy.
1477	Low Countries passed by marriage to Habsburgs.
1555	The Netherlands passed to Spain upon division of Habsburg domains.
1579	Union of Utrecht: seven northern rebel provinces formed United Provinces.
1648	Treaty of Westphalia: United Provinces finally recognised as independent Dutch Republic.
1652-54	Commercial and colonial rivalries led to naval war with England.
1665-67	Second Anglo-Dutch war.
1672-74	Third Anglo-Dutch war.
1672	William of Orange became stadholder (ruling as chief magistrate) of the Dutch Republic, an office which became hereditary in the Orange family.
1672-78	The Netherlands fought to prevent domination by King Louis XIV of France.

1688-97 & 1701-13	War with France resumed.
1795	Revolutionary France conquered the Netherlands and established the Batavian Republic.
1806	Napoleon made his brother Louis king of Holland.
1810	France annexed the Netherlands.
1848	Liberal constitution adopted.
1894-96	Dutch suppressed colonial revolt in Java.
1914-18	Netherlands neutral during World War I.
1940-45	Occupied by Germany during World War II.
1948	The Netherlands formed Benelux customs union with Belgium and Luxembourg; Queen Wilhelmina abdicated in favour of her daughter Juliana.
1949	Became a founding member of North Atlantic Treaty Organisation (NATO); most of Dutch East Indies became independent as Indonesia.
1953	Dykes breached by storm; nearly two thousand people and tens of thousands of cattle died in flood.
1958	The Netherlands became a founding member of European Economic Community (EEC).
1963	Dutch colony of Western New Guinea ceded to Indonesia.
1975	Dutch Guiana became independent as Surinam.
1980	Queen Juliana abdicated in favour of her daughter Beatrix.
1994	Following inclusive general election, three-party coalition formed under PvdA leader Wim Kok.
1998	Gains for Labour in May general election.

Luxembourg was a fortress where Roman troops stayed and later it became a country.

65

Luxembourg (Grand Duchy of Luxembourg)

A duchy of about five lakh people and the size of a small Indian town, Luxembourg has survived as a separate political unit more by accident than by choice. Which also indicates how power balance has worked in Europe which has always been at war against itself.

Luxembourg is situated in Western Europe. Most of the population is ethnically French or German. It is 82 km long and 56 km wide and is divided into two regions: the Oesling, an extension of the Ardennes Mountains in the northern part of the country consisting of a high plateau dissected by river valleys; and the Bon Pays, or Gutland, a rolling plateau that occupies the rest of the country. Luxembourg's economy is largely based on heavy industry and international trade and banking, and its per capita income is among the highest in the world.

After AD 400, Germanic tribes invaded the region. It later came under Charlemagne's empire. Made a duchy in 1354, it was ceded to the house of Burgundy in 1441 and to the Habsburgs in 1477. In the mid-16 century it became part of the Spanish Netherlands. The Congress of Vienna in 1815 made it a grand duchy and gave it to The Netherlands. After an uprising in 1830, its western portion became part of Belgium, while the remainder was held by The Netherlands. In 1867 the European powers guaranteed the neutrality and independence of Luxembourg. In the late 19th century it built a great steel industry by exploiting its extensive iron ore deposits. It was invaded and occupied by Germany in both world wars. Following World War II, it abandoned its neutrality by joining NATO in 1949. It joined the Benelux

Economic Union in 1944 and the European Coal and Steel Community, a forerunner of the European Union, in 1952. Luxembourg ratified the Maastricht Treaty on European Union in 1992 and adopted the euro as its official monetary unit in 1999.

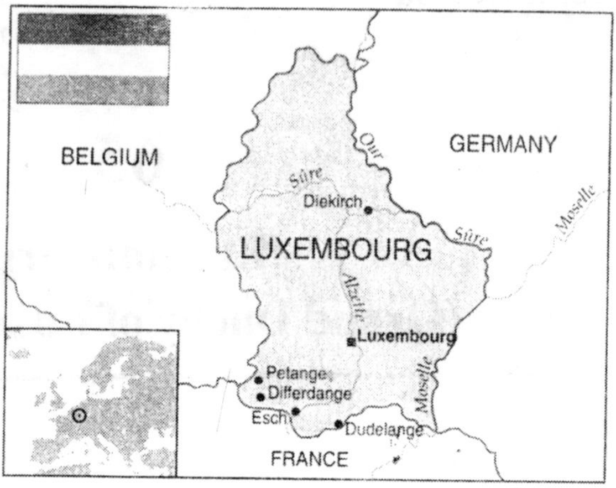

Luxembourg City (pop.76,833), capital of Luxembourg was the site of a Roman fortress and later of a Frankish castle, around which the medieval town developed. Siegfried, count of Ardennes, purchased this castle and made the duchy of Luxembourg independent in 963. The stronger in Europe after Gibraltar, the castle was garrisoned by the Prussians as a bulwark of the German confederation (1815-66); it was dismantled by treaty in 1867. For long an important road and railway focus, the city is also an important industrial and financial centre. It is the seat of the European Court of Justice and several administrative offices of the European Union.

Luxembourg is one of Europe's smallest states, landlocked between France, Germany and Belgium. Luxembourg means *Little Castle or Fortress.* It is in an impregnable defensive position where natural barriers between France and Germany end. They fought over it so often that eventually the powers decided to make it independent of either, as a duchy. Luxembourg has made its marks on history. When in 1346, the Count of Luxembourg died fighting in the Battle of Crecy, the Prince of Wales in admiration, plucked three feathers from the Count's helmet and used them as the Count's motto, *'Ich Dien'*, on the Welsh coat of arms. During World War II, Luxembourg was the first occupied country to organize a general strike against the Nazis and to print its own underground newspaper. In 1922, Luxembourg entered into a customs union with Belgium to which she remains virtually an economic appendage.

HISTORY AND PEOPLE

Luxembourg, whose history is closely intertwined with those of its more powerful neighbours – France, Belgium and Germany – retains a keen sense of its cultural identity and independence. When the Romans colonized the region in about 50 BC, Celtic peoples inhabitated it. Some 450 years later, the region became part of the Frankish kingdom of Australasia. Originally called Lucilinburhuc, or *"Little Fortress"* Luxembourg became a county within the Holy Roman Empire in 963. In the 14th century Henry IV, Count of Luxembourg (1269-1313) became Holy Roman Emperor as Henry VII. His descendant, Emperor Charles-IV (1316-78) made Luxembourg an independent duchy in 1354. Subsequently it became a political pawn in the power struggle between Europe's ruling houses.

In the 16th century Luxembourg passed from the Austrian Habsburgs to the rulers of Spain, before being returned, together with Belgium, to the Austrian Habsburgs in 1713. Luxembourg was later under the rule of revolutionary France, but with the fall of Napoleon in 1814, it came under the control of the Dutch king William-I (1772-1843). After a revolt in 1830, Luxembourg was split into the French-speaking Belgian province of Luxembourg and the smaller Grand Duchy, centring on the capital. In 1867, the Grand Duchy was given to the House of Nassau. Despite its neutrality, Luxembourg was occupied by Germany in both world wars. In 1949 Luxembourg abandoned its neutral status to become a founder member of the North Atlantic Treaty Organization (NATO) and, later, of the European Union (EU). The Grand Duchy is the seat of the European Court of Justice created in 1958.

Luxembourg is a constitutional monarchy with a democratically elected Government headed by the Grand Duke. His power is exercised through ministers, council headed by a Prime Minister. These, in turn, are responsible to 60-member Chamber of Deputies, who are directly elected, under a system of proportional representation for a five year term. In Luxembourg, voting is compulsory. People speak their native language and also French and German; minorities speak the other two official languages, Italian and Portuguese. Most people are Roman Catholic. Luxembourg enjoys close ties with European countries. The multi-lingual Radio Luxembourg has become an institution throughout Europe. Luxembourg has no university, but the arts, culture and sciences are promoted by the *Institute Grand-Ducal*, the state library and museums.

INDUSTRY-BASED ECONOMY

Although Luxembourg is still strongly agricultural, its prosperity depends almost entirely on heavy industry and international finance. (Arcelor is Europe's biggest steel industry which India's Mittal Steel took ever). Farm output meets domestic needs. The Gutland provides the richest pasture for both beef and dairy cattle, and the best land for grains and fodder crops. Fruit is grown here, too, especially grapes for the wine industry. Luxembourg's main mineral resource is iron ore from deposits in the southwest, but most of these have been depleted. For energy, the country depends heavily on imported fuels and hydroelectricity. Luxembourg's road and rail networks provide major links with neighbouring countries. Barge traffic on the river Moselle carries import and export freight. The national airline, Luxair, operates from Findel airport near the capital. Health and social security schemes, which were first introduced after World War I, are comparable with others in Western Europe. Education is compulsory.

NATIONAL INDICATORS - LUXEMBOURG

HISTORY

963	Luxembourg became autonomous within the Holy Roman Empire under Siegfried, Count of Ardennes.
1060	Conrad, descendent of Siegfried, took the title Count of Luxembourg.
1354	Emperor Charles IV promoted Luxembourg to status of duchy.
1441	Luxembourg ceded to duke of Burgundy.
1482	Luxembourg came under Habsburg control.
1555	Luxembourg became part of Spanish Netherlands on division of Habsburg domains.
1684-97	Much of Luxembourg occupied by France.
1713	Treaty of Utrecht transferred Spanish Netherlands to Austria.
1797	Conquered by revolutionary France.
1815	Congress of Vienna made Luxembourg a grand duchy, under King William of the Netherlands.
1830	Most of Luxembourg supported Belgian revolt against the Netherlands.
1839	Western part of Luxembourg assigned to Belgium.
1867	Treaty of London confirmed independence and neutrality of

	Luxembourg to allay French fears about possible inclusion in a unified Germany.
1914-18	Occupied by Germany.
1919	Plebiscite overwhelmingly favoured continued independence; Marie-Adelaide abdicated after allegations of collaboration with Germany; succeeded by Grand Duchess Charlotte.
1921	Entered into close economic links with Belgium.
1940	Invaded by Germany.
1942-44	Annexed by Germany.
1948	Luxembourg formed Benelux customs union with Belgium and the Netherlands.
1949	Luxembourg became a founding member of North Atlantic Treaty Organisation (NATO).
1958	Luxembourg became a founding member of European Economic Community (EEC).
1964	Grand Duchess Charlotte abdicated in favour of her son Jean.
1974-79	Christian Social Party outside governing coalition for first time since 1919.
1994	Former premier Jacques Santer became president of European Commission (EC).
1995	Jean-Claude Juncker became prime minister.
2006	Luxembourg's largest steel industry, Arcelor, was taken over by India's Mittal Steel.

PERSPECTIVE

The Mediterranean Sea is an inland water area, separating Europe from north Africa with Asia to the east. It is linked to the Atlantic Ocean (at the strait of Gibraltar), Red Sea and the Indian Ocean (by the Suez Canal), and the Black Sea at the Dardanelles and Sea of Marmara. It is a tideless sea. Great civilizations, including Greek, prospered on the Mediterrean shore which shaped Europe.

66

Mediterranean was incubator of Western civilisation

This is almost a landlocked water area in the midst of landmass of Europe and Africa where glorious and great things happened, many of which shaped the human civilization since ancient time.

The Mediterranean Sea is the great expanse of waters that stretches from the Atlantic Ocean, on the west, to Asia, on the east, separating Europe from Africa. It has been called the incubator of Western civilisation. This ancient "*sea between the lands*" occupies a deep, elongated, and almost landlocked irregular depression lying between 30° and 46° N and between 5°50¢ W and 36° E. Its east-west extent, from the Strait of Gibraltar to the shores of the Gulf of Iskenderum, is 2,500 miles, while its average north-south extent, between the shores of Yugoslavia and Libya, is about 500 miles. The Mediterranean Sea is an area of 1,145,000 square miles.

The western extremity of the Mediterranean connects with the Atlantic Ocean through the narrow and shallow channel of the Strait of Gibraltar, which is only eight miles wide at its narrowest point, and the depth of the sill, or submarine ridge separating the basins, is 320 metres. To the northeast, the Mediterranean Sea is connected with the Black Sea through the Dardanelle's (with a sill depth of 230 feet), the Sea of Marmara, and the strait of Bosporus. To the southeast, it is connected with the Red Sea by the Suez Canal.

The coasts of the western Mediterranean, just as those of the eastern basin, have been subjected to the uneven action of deposition and erosion. This action, together with the movements of the sea and the emergence and submergence of the land, resulted in a rich variety of coasts. The Italian Peninsula underwent considerable uplift in the post-Pliocene times (2,500,000 years), as a result of which a strip of Late Tertiary rocks has been exposed on the Adriatic flank of the Apennies. Examples of coasts, the outline of which is due to submergence, are the granite coast where the eroded land surface has been sunk, producing elongated islands parallel to the coast. The deltas of the Rhone, Po, Ebro, and Nile rivers are examples of coasts resulting from silt deposit.

THE EASTERN MEDITERRANEAN

The Sicilian straits scarcely exceed 1,500 feet in depth; hence, there is essentially a shelf from Tunisia to Sicily separating the Mediterranean into two parts. South of the straits, the shelf widens to 170 miles off the Gulf of Gabes on the eastern coast of Tunisia. The first mud appears on the approach in the Nile delta, and the shelf widens again to 70 miles, off Port Said, at the entrance to the Suez Canal. The shelves continue to be narrow along most of the northern shore of the Mediterranean. An exception is the broad shelf extending for 300 miles along the inner portion of the Adriatic Sea. Relatively deep water is found along much of the coast of former Yugoslavia and along the Italian coast. The northern shores of the eastern Mediterranean have multi-fold mountains that offered favourable sites for the development of the Mediterranean civilisations.

The north coast of Africa, bordering the eastern Mediterranean, is low-lying and of monotonous uniformity except for the Barqah highlands in Libya, which lie to the east of the Gulf of Sidra. The largest islands of the eastern Mediterranean are Crete and Cyprus, both of which are mountainous. The 2,000 mile access that the Mediterranean offers in the temperate zone to rain-bearing westerly winds; the ease of communications across its western, central, and eastern straits; and its prevailing freedom from storms in the summer months-all these have made it the *"inland sea"* of early civilisations. The revolutionary development of a higher civilisation based on agriculture originated in the lands beyond the eastern Mediterranean.

The western Mediterranean lands followed the eastern into the full light of history in the 1st millennium BC with the expansion of Semitic Carthage in North Africa and into Spain and the establishment of Greek colonies as far

west as the Gulf of Lions. By 300 BC, the eastern Mediterranean basin belonged to the Greek kingdoms of Alexander, and his successors. In the following two centuries, the expanding Roman Republic annexed the Carthaginian Empire and began the absorption of the Greek world. When the Christian era opened, the entire Mediterranean basin as far south as the Sahara was, for the first time, politically and economically unified under the Roman Empire, a circumstance that greatly facilitated the expansion of Christianity.

By AD 400, however, the Germanic migration that pushed forward from central Asia was breaking down the northern defences of the Roman Empire. While its western half collapsed, the Byzantine (Eastern Roman) Empire survived; but Levantine separatists found expression in the schism of the eastern churches and welcomed the 7th-century Muslim Arabs as liberators. The Arab rapidly advanced through North Africa, conquered Spain and Sicily, and harassed Italy. Although the Mediterranean basin was, thus, partitioned between a Christian north and a Muslim south, common economic interests reasserted themselves, notably through Jewish intermediaries. By the 11th century, the Arab empire was lapsing into disorder, and the Christian conquest of Spain and Sicily began.

The Crusades were designed to win safe access to the Christian holy places and also offered land to landless and commerce to the Mediterranean trading cities, notably Venice, Genoa, and Barcelona. The Crusades failed militarily after two centuries of struggle, completed the schism between Latin and Greek Christendom, marked the doom of the Byzantine Empire, and heightened the enmity between Christendom and Islam. Meanwhile, western Christendom emerged from adolescence into maturity, and the widening of its cultural horizons heralded both the humanist Renaissance and the religious.

Until the 15th century, Constantinople, Barcelona, and the Italian commercial states assumed the role of intermediaries between the Orient and northwestern Europe. In the 15th century, however, the rise of the Ottoman Turks brought a second period of eclipse in the Mediterranean as well as an era of severe rivalries. Turkish conquest of the Levant, the Balkans, and North Africa was through the hazardous sea. The discovery of the route to Asia around the Cape of Good Hope at the end of the 15th century created a safer and easier sea route connecting northwestern Europe directly with the East. Mediterranean lands lost their commercial function as intermediaries between Europe and Asia, and for more than two and a half centuries, the Mediterranean Sea remained a backwater of world ocean trade and traffic.

The opening of the Suez Canal in 1869, together with the advent of the steamship, promoted industrialization in northwestern and central Europe. In 1857, it came under British control and its nationalisation by Egypt in 1956 created Suez crisis. The French colonization in North Africa made the Mediterranean again one of the busiest sea-lanes of the world. Much of the traffic, however, passed through the sea between Asia and northwestern Europe. Countries in the Mediterranean basin had not been able to industrialise and, consequently, had retained their agricultural and artisan economies, which limited their purchasing power and reduced their ability to trade. Nevertheless, a fierce competition ensued among ports in northwestern Europe and Mediterranean Europe for the capture of transit trade to and from the industrialized areas of western and central Europe, a rivalry that has continued to this day.

BRITISH DOMINATION IN 19TH AND 20TH CENTURIES

From the 18th century until World War II, the Mediterranean was dominated by Great Britain which had gradually acquired control over several strategic points along the sea route so vital to its empire trade; among them was Gibraltar (1704), Malta (1800), Aden (1839), Cyprus (1878), and finally Egypt (1882). Egypt, of course, first became a kingdom (1922), and then a republic (1953). After World War II Cyprus and Malta gained independence, Aden became the People's Democratic Republic of Yemen, and the status of

Gibraltar was challenged seriously by Spain. The Suez Canal was closed to all traffic from 1967 to 1975, as a result of the continuing conflict between Israel and its Arab neighbours.

Britain lost its supremacy in the Mediterranean, and a new era began with U.S. entry into North Africa in 1942. After the last War, it became clear that only the United States was strong enough to oppose the Soviet Union, which made repeated attempts to expand into the Mediterranean sphere economically and politically. Thus, with the view to keeping the Mediterranean under non-Communist control and to protect Western interests in the Middle East and its oilfields, the United States took a leading role in the security of the Mediterranean and its borderlands by launching the Marshall Plan and the Truman Doctrine, Harry Truman, 33rd US President, said the US would support free people against tyranny by participation in the North Atlantic Treaty Organization and by the enactment of the Eisenhower Doctrine (Dwight David Eisenhower, 34th US President, who said the US would protect Middle East against Communists for the Middle East). The sharpening of the Arab-Israeli conflict and the persistence of inter-Arab rivalries, most notably in the ravages of Lebanon, threatened to make the Mediterranean a backwater for World Ocean shipping once again and to bring chaos and destruction to its eastern shores. Now, the Mediterranean is more of a historical interest than a major trade channel, thanks to the development of communication technologies and science of aviation.

EUROPEAN ROOTS LIE IN THE MEDITERRANEAN

Between the Adriatic Sea and the Atlantic Ocean, lived the people commonly called the Latins, stereotyped often as hot-blooded, romantic and artistic. In fact, they are related more by the common Latin of their languages than by anything else, and the five countries they inhabit are as ethnically complex. Greeks, Phoenicians, Celts, Arabs have all settled in these parts at one time or another, adding their own elements to the common stock.

Geographically, too, the region is many–faced. Its southern shores are pure Mediterranean. These are the lands of oranges, perfumed shrubs and scraggy goats, tinged by memories of classical Greece. The sea is not always as clear as it used to be, the beaches are often hideously developed, but still over much of these coasts, there hangs a myth. Corsica, the largest island of the region, is clad with the aromatic *maquis*, the tangle of thyme, oleander, lavender, mint and myrtle that gave its name to the French resistance movement of the World

War–II. It was here, that Christianity, the chief coalescing force of Europe, developed its power and its aesthetic. From the village churches of Malta to the immense and marvellous cathedrals of Spain and France, from lonely mountain shrines to the Vatican itself at the centre of it all, the old consequence of this faith proclaims itself here as nowhere else. Here, too exploded the Renaissance, that surge of all the arts and sciences which was at once to challenge and glorify the Christian creed, and which now makes all Europe a treasure house of its artefacts. Much of the artistic genius of Europe has come from this corner of the world. The navigators of Portugal and Spain opened the rest of the world to European exploration, creating the first of the great maritime empires of history; later the French flag too would fly over colonies across the world; and almost until the last gasp of the imperial age, Italy was still conquering territories overseas.

LATIN LANGUAGE: Latin was spoken by the Romans, and it is the parent of the Romance languages, e.g. Italian, French, Spanish, and Portuguese. As Latin literature had influence on all subsequent European civilizations Latin remained for long as the vehicle for learned works. The striking merits of Latin. are its clarity and conciseness. Like Greek, it is a highly inflected language, i.e. the grammatical functions of nouns, verbs, pronouns, and adjectives in a sentence is indicated by terminations which vary according to the meaning. Latin, however, was not native to Italy. It was brought there about 1000 BC by wandering tribes from the North who settled in Latium near the mouth cf the Tiber in Rome. With the growing power of Rome, it spread throughout Italy, and other competing languages gradually disappeared. The conquest of Spain and Gaul by Romans exended the use and influence of Latin outside Italy, but the Roman hold on Britain (AD 43 - AD 410) was not firm enough to submerge completely the Celtic speech of the islanders.

Italy had 34 prime ministers between 1946 and 2000, most of them lasted only months.

67

Italy-a country always at war against itself

Italy has inadequate resources; add to it the unstable politics and growing population and the story of Italy will be complete but only by half. The other half remains to be told by Italians themselves.

Italy is a country different from other countries of Europe. The World War II splintered Italy into some 300 parts. Italy is only half the size of her neighbour, France, but she has to feed some six million more mouths than France. More than half the gaunt Peninsula is rock. It is lush and verdant with grain fields, olive groves and vineyards. But the feast is for the eye, not for the stomach. The grain is of low quality and the wheat for the Italian staple, pasta, must be imported. Italy's per capita farm yield is lower than that of the backward Balkan neighbour, former Yugoslavia. It is but one-third that of her advanced neighbour, France.

Industry is unable to absorb growing population. Italy has meagre raw materials and no mineral fuel. There is a macabre saying that Italy is self-sufficient only in hemp, a fibre used in making rope to hang men with, and marble to make their tombstones. Considering the paucity of resources, the country has done very well in the building industry. She has a well-developed hydro electric industry, has domesticated the silkworm as a means of getting raw material for a very fine textile industry, and has good chemical and automobile factories. With little productive employment available, men learn to live by their wits. The most obvious way is by becoming middle men, inserting themselves into the distributive process and taking a toll on national wealth, some do this on a big scale buying up automobiles, and withholding them from the market to create a scarcity and then letting the prices go up.

It had also been the practice in India until privatisation was launched in 1991. However, it was done on a small scale.

The social consequences of the struggle for survival inside Italy are obvious. It induces the privileged to hold on blindly to every advantage they possess in the struggle; to the point, if necessary, of supporting right-wing dictatorship to guard it for them. In desperation, it drives the poor to the other extreme – towards Communism and confiscation. The room necessary for social compromise, which is the first requisite for democracy, does not exist. No wonder the Italians are caught in an impossible situation. We know of no people in Europe who so painfully want to be democratic. They have had their dictatorship, and the people are sick of it. Unlike the French, the Italian people are not demoralized; the speed with which they rebuilt their damaged country after the War, largely with their bare hands, is adequate evidence of their faith in their future.

ITALY-NORTH AND SOUTH;
AMERIGO VESPUCCI AND COLUMBUS

There are two Italys – north Italy and south Italy. There is a tendency to overlook how little north Italy belongs to the Mediterranean and how completely it is a part of the heart of Europe with France and Germany. The city of Florence, with half the Peninsula below and half above it, is on a latitude with Marseilles. Italy's northern-most towns are more northerly than Geneva. Her great northern cities, Milan, Turin and Venice are on a level with Bordeaux. North Italy is a European nation. The Renaissance which marked the beginning of European civilization, began in the city-states of north Italy. The revival of commerce which laid the basis for the beginning of European civilization began in the North and spread from there over the continent. It was north Italy that gave birth to the dominant European civilization of today. While all this was in progress, south Italy languished with the rest of Mediterranean civilizations from the end of the Roman Empire onwards. It was ruled until the last century by dictators. From northern Italy, America got its name – from the Florentine explorer, *Amerigo Vespucci* – and its discovery by the Genoese sailor, *Columbus*. Northern Italy creates wealth; southern Italy consumes it. Northern Italy is a land of efficient industry. Its farms are modern and very productive. Southern Italy is a land of inefficient feudal plantations, dominated by landlords whose tenures date from the Middle Ages, and peopled by peasantry. The difference in outlook between the two Italys was never so clearly attested as in the referendum of June 1946, on whether or not to keep the monarchy,

The Trevi Fountain in Rome

which had licked Mussolini's boots for twenty-five years. South Italy favoured keeping the discredited institution. North Italy wanted to abolish it.

OVERPOPULATION

Italy's problem is overpopulation. The average size of a family in Italy is four persons. But south of Rome, among the oppressed peasantry of the South, the average size of the family is seven. Italy's problem is the South; the remedy is to turn the South into a modern country. The magnates of the South are the most blindly resistant elements in Italy to the changes and reforms that this policy would require. And due to an unfortunate circumstance, it is they who dominate the government structure of Italy. The circumstance is inherent in the nature of the two Italys; when the son of a Northern merchant comes of age, he seeks to do business. When the son of a Southern landowner comes of age, he reaches for the gun because farming is already overcrowded. So he goes to Rome and pulls strings to get into government service. The Italian civil service is run by the southerners, who carry their feudal resistance to change their executive functions. Therefore, it is difficult to get a progressive government elected in the first place. North Italy has its normal quota of conservatives. The South has an abnormal quota of them with a powerful popular support among easily intimidated peasantry. Together, the rightists outweigh the progressives who are confined largely to north Italy. This is also a source of political instability.

ITALIANS EXHAUSTED IN AFTER MANY WARS

After the Allied captured Italy, the Germans invaded and *occupied* it. They rescued Mussolini from his mountain prison and set-him up as a figure-head of an *'Italian Social Republic'* in the North. But Nazis and Mussolini together could get no support from the North Italian people. So they resorted to recruiting desperadoes from prisons to constitute neo-Fascist police and army. Almost the entire population of North Italy went into service as resistance-bankers, workers, priests and peasants, in the most unanimous effort Italians have ever made. In Switzerland, Italians created the best and bravest partisan movement against Mussolini and Hitler. The *Economist* commented on the activity of the North Italian Resistance, *"It was one of the greatest feats ever achieved by a people in arms."*

The partisans put themselves in position to paralyse the Germans at almost any time they chose. When the allies began their northwards offensive against the German *'Gothic Line'*, the partisans started shooting. On 25 April 1945, they seized Milan, the biggest Northern city, from the Germans, and proceeded to wrest other cities without outside aid. It was solely due to their action that most industries were captured and held intact during the last destructive phase of the Italian war. Italy was close to exhaustion when Mussolini carried her into Hitler's war in 1940. The conquest of Ethiopia had been a heavy drain on her resources and morale. The Spanish Civil War, having dragged on far longer than Mussolini had anticipated, added its strain on the nation. The bloated artificial economy, too long on a war footing, and a series of wars in which the people felt no real interest, had left them weary and spiritless. The Italian army won no battles, not even small ones, to stir its spirit. Greece, a third of Italy's size and wealth, not only contained Mussolini's attack on her, but also threw the Italians back into Albania by the time Germany intervened to save the Italian Army. There was no incentive for Italians. There was nothing like fight for democracy.

CRISIS AFTER WAR WHEN BREAD WAS SOLD BY SLICE

When the Allies arrived, a new Italy awaited them. Local committees of liberation, representing the six democratic parties, had constituted local governments. They had already purged some 30 per cent of the managerial staff of industry. The factories were operating to the limit of their resources under the management of workers' committees. The economic situation, however, deteriorated rapidly. With no more German coal coming in, and the Allies able to deliver only 50,000 tons a month instead of the 1,000,000 tons necessary for Italian industry, factories barely ran. Food was short everywhere and for some time bread was sold by the slice. The inept bureaucracy was unable to enforce rationing and controls, and shops blossomed with luxuries for those who could pay for them. Returning prisoners of war became disillusioned at the injustice and withdrew to the mountains to form robber gangs. As late as the summer of 1947, allied troops were required to carry arms while travelling in certain parts of Italy and were ordered not to travel at night.

On this poor foundation, the new Italy followed the pattern of France in its political development. The first elections, on June 2, 1946, brought to power the Catholic Christian Democrats, the Socialists and the Communists. As in France, the three formed a coalition. The discontent among the masses was far more intense in Italy than in France and, thus, there was a far more fertile field open to the Italian Communists than to the French. The Italian offensive had great success. It was one of the few countries in the Marshall Plan that had not been able to reach pre-war levels of production. This failure had been due partly to Communist-supported strikes. Partly, it was due to the refusal of investors to lend their funds to industry. Investment had reached only 70 per cent of pre-war level; people preferred to put their money where it would do them more private good; for example, in Switzerland. After the war Italy continued to be an object of pity for many years.

The foundation of the western civilisation was laid on the Italian Renaissance in art, science and literature. But, Italians benefited the least from these developments.

68

Italy (Italian Republic)

As the power base of Europe, the birthplace of Roman Catholic Church and Renaissance, Italy has always played a key role in the making of the European history until the World War II which has reduced it to become a poor cousin in Europe with zero growth in 2006.

Italy, situated in southern Europe, comprises the boot-shaped peninsula extending into the Mediterranean as well as Sicily, Sardinia and a number of smaller islands. More than three-fourths of Italy is mountainous. The Alps stretch from east to west along Italy's northern boundary. Most of the country's lowlands lie in the valley of river Po. Three tectonic plates converge in southern Italy and Sicily, creating intense geologic pressure. Italy's four active volcanoes include Mount Vesuvius and Mount Etna.

The peoples, living in Tuscany, Latins and Sabines in middle Italy, Greek colonies in Sicily, and Gauls in the north, were united under the Roman rule during the 4th-3rd century BC. With the decline of the Roman Empire, and its final extinction in AD 476, Italy became exposed to the attacks of the barbarians, and passed, in turn, under the rule of the Ostrogoths and the Lombards. The 8th century witnessed the rise of the papacy as a territorial power, the annexation of the Lombard kingdom (central Italy) by Charlemagne, and his coronation as emperor of the west in 800.

Until 1250, Italian history turned on the relations, at first friendly and later hostile, between the papacy and the Holy Roman Empire. During this struggle,

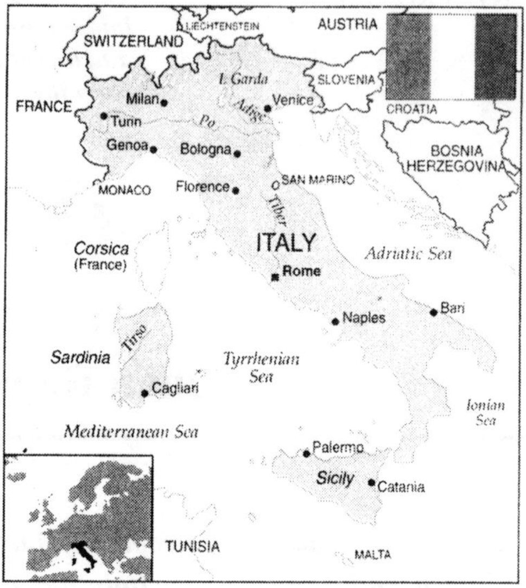

the Italian cities seized the opportunity to convert themselves into self-governing republics *(city republics)*. By 1300, five major powers existed in Italy: the city republics of Milan, Florence and Venice; the papal state; and the kingdom of Naples. Their mutual rivalries and wars laid Italy open during 1494-1559 to invasions from France and Spain. As a result Naples and Milan passed under Spanish rule. After 1700 Austria secured Milan and replaced Spain as the dominating power, while Naples passed to a Spanish Bourbon dynasty, and Sardinia to the dukes of Savoy.

GARIBALDI UNIFIED ITALY

The period of French rule (1796-1814) temporarily unified Italy, and introduced the principles of the French Revolution but after Napoleon's fall Italy was again divided between Austria, the Pope, the kingdoms of Sardinia and Naples, and 4 smaller duchies. Nationalist and democratic ideas nevertheless remained alive, and inspired attempts at revolutions in 1820, 1831 and 1848-9. After this last failure, the Sardinian monarchy assumed the leadership of the national movement. With the help of Napoleon-III, the Austrians were expelled from Lombardy (inhabited by Germanic tribes) in 1859; the duchies joined the Italian kingdom. Garibaldi overthrew the monarchy and Victor Emmanuel-II of Sardinia was proclaimed king of Italy at Turin in 1861. Venice and part of Venetia was secured by another war with Austria in 1866; in 1870 Italian forces occupied Rome, thus completing the unification of Italy, and the Pope ceased to be a temporal ruler until 1929. In 1878, Victor Emmanuel-II died, and was succeeded by Humbert (Umberto), his son, who was assassinated in 1900.

Meanwhile, the formation of a colonial empire had begun in 1869 with the purchase of land on the Bay of Assab, on the Red Sea, from the local sultan. In the next 20 years, the Italians occupied Eritrea which was made an Italian colony in 1889. An attempt to seize Ethiopia was decisively defeated

GARIBALDI WHO UNITED ITALY

Italian hero

Giuseppe Garibaldi (1807-82) was an Italian patriot. Born in Nice, he became a sailor, and in 1834 joined Mazzini's Young Italy society. Condemned to death for treason, he escaped to South America where he lived the life of a soldier of fortune. He returned to Italy during the 1848 revolution, served with the Sardinian army against the Austrians, and commanded the army of the Roman republic in its defence of the city against the French. He subsequently lived in exile until 1854, when he settled on Caprera.

He again fought against the Austrians in the war of 1859; and in 1860, at the head of his 1,000 Redshirts, conquered Sicily and Naples for the new kingdom of Italy. He led two unsuccessful expeditions to liberate Rome from papal rule in 1862 and 1867. His enthusiastic leadership and colourful exploits fired the imagination of Italians. He never wavered from his single purpose, the unification of Italy under Italian rule, and he did more than any other person to bring it about.

Garibaldi's most spectacular achievement was in 1860, when he unified small states of northern Italy. Leading red-shirted volunteers known as the thousand heroes, Garibaldi, aided by Count Cavour (1820-78), set out to capture the south which was held by the King of Naples. Within three months he had conquered Sicily; he soon entered Naples in Triumph, and Victor Emmanuel was proclaimed King of Italy.

Twice in later years Garibaldi tried to take the city of Rome from the Pope, believing that only then would Italy be truly independent and united. Both attempts failed and Garibaldi devoted his last years to writing on oppressed nations.

at Adowa in 1896. War with Turkey in 1911-12 gave Tripoli and Cyrenaica. Italy's intervention in the World War I on the Allied side secured her Trieste, the Trentino and South Tirol, (a part of Austria).

MUSSOLINI'S DICTATORSHIP

The post-war period was marked by intense political and industrial unrest, culminating in 1922 in Mussolini's Fascist dictatorship. The regime embraced a policy of aggression with the conquest of Ethiopia in 1935-6 and of Albania in 1939, and Italy entered the World War II in 1940 as the ally of Germany. Defeat in Africa 1941-3 and the Allied conquest of Sicily in 1943 resulted in Mussolini's downfall; the new govt. declared war on Germany, and until 1945 Italy was a battlefield between German occupying forces and the advancing Allies. In 1946 Victor Emmanuel-III, who had been king since 1900, abdicated in favour of his son Humbert (Umberto)-II, who abdicated later in 1960 when a referendum rejected the monarchy. A peace treaty between Italy and the Allies was signed and ratified in 1947. It deprived Italy of its colonial empire and transferred to Yugoslavia Zara (Zadar) and part of Venezia Guilia; to France 4 small areas in the Alpes Maritimes; and to Greece the Dodecanese. Trieste, which the Allies proposed to make a free territory, was in 1954 returned to Italy.

ITALIAN COMMUNIST PARTY

Italy had the largest Communist party in Europe led by Enrico Berlinguer. There was a 'historic compromise between Communists and Christian Democrats (1973-9), which resulted in a fall of the Communist support from the high reached in the elections of 1976. In 1979, the Communists withdrew from the official parliamentary majority. By 1980 the Socialists had associated themselves with the Christian Democrats govt., but the situation remained unstable and when Arnaldo Forlani became PM later in the year; he was the fortieth premier to

BENITO MUSSOLINI (1883-1945)

Mussolini postures in 1938 as the Fascists prepared for the war.

Benito Mussolini was born on July 29, 1883 at Predappio, Italy, and publically executed in Milan on April 28, 1945. An unruly but intelligent youth, he became an ardent socialist and served as editor of the party newspaper, *Avanti* (1912-14). When he reversed his opposition to World War I, he was ousted by the party. He founded the pro-war-Il *Popolo d'Italia*, served with the Italian Army (1915-17), then returned to his editorship. Advocating government by dictatorship, he formed a political group in 1919 that marked the beginning of Fascism. A captivating orator at rallies, he organised the *March on Rome* (1922) to prevent a socialist-led general strike. After the government fell, he was appointed prime minister, the youngest in Italian history. He obtained a law to establish the fascist as the majority party and became known as *Duce* ("The Leader").

His dreams of empire led to the invasion of Abyssinia (later Ethiopia) in 1935. Supported by Adolf Hitler, Mussolini agreed to the Rome-Berlin Axis and declared war on the Allies in 1940. Italian defeats in Greece and North Africa led to growing disillusionment with Mussolini. After the Allied invasion of Sicily (1943), the Fascist Grand Council dismissed him from office. He was arrested and imprisoned but rescued by German commandos. As German defenses in Italy collapsed in 1945, Mussolini tried to escape to Austria but was captured and executed.

hold office since the end of the dictatorship.

NORTH AND SOUTH DIVIDE

Centuries of foreign domination have left a distinctive mark on the Italian people and their dialects. In the south and in Sicily, Greek and Arab influences are strong, while in the north people tend to be taller and fair-skinned. In the post-War period, these distinctions became blurred as many people from the rural areas of the south migrated to the industrialized cities of the north, such as Milan and Turin. In the Valle d'Aosta and Trentino-Alto Adige (South Tyrol) regions – isolated enclaves in the high Alps on the northern borders – there are long-established French and German-speaking communities. The Alto Adige only became part of Italy after World War I, as a reward for victory over Austria, and many of its inhabitants resented the transfer of authority. There are also significant ethnic minorities from neighbouring states such as Albania and

FLORENCE; A CITY OF DANTE, MEDICI, MICHELANGELO AND DA VINCI

During the Middle Ages, Florence, a town on the river Arno at the foot of the Apennines, emerged as one of the most powerful city states in Italy. Its wealth was based on woollen cloth and international banking. Its merchant aristocracy supported social improvements, ranging from street paving to schools, hospitals and one of Europe's foremost universities. These turbulent and exciting times produced many talents, notably the painter and architect Giotto (1266-1337) and two of the world's greatest writers, *Dante* Aleghieri (1265-1321) and Giovanni Boccaccio (1313-75). The city entered a period of financial eclipse in the mid-4th century, but recovered under the powerful merchant princes of the Medici family.

The *Medicis* were the patrons of artists, writers and thinkers who symbolised "Renaissance men" – widely talented creators who were deeply interested in all aspects of humanity and human knowledge. *Leonardo* da Vinci (1452-1519) – artist, inventor, writer – exemplified the Renaissance man, as did Lorenzo de' Medici himself, a notable poet and naturalist. Other Renaissance artists included the architect Filippo Brunelleschi (1377-1446) and innumerable painters, among them the Della Robbia family; Tommaso Masaccio (1402-28); Sandro Botticelli (1445-1510); Raffaello Sanzio, known as *Raphael* (1483-1520); and *Michelangelo* Buonarroti (1475-1564).

Later, Florentine art declined, and by the 17th century it had stagnated altogether. Its influence, however, had spread far beyond Italy, and stagnation preserved many Renaissance treasures intact, to the benefit of the thriving tourist trade which began in the 18th century. Modern Florence still owes its rich character and its distinctive skyline to the Renaissance churches, palaces and public buildings that are its living inheritance from the Medici.

Slovenia.

Each of the former independent city states boasts a distinctive character and dialect, but the Tuscan form of the Italian language, which was used by the 14th century poet Dante in his masterpiece, *Divine Comedy*, has become the literary standard.

The Roman Catholic Church has played a major part in the shaping of the country. Until 1870, part of the country was under direct papal rule. More than 90 percent of Italians are Catholic, though in the post-War period, the authority of the church has declined, particularly over controversial moral issues such as divorce, contraception and abortion. Religious respect for the sanctity of family life is still important, specially in rural communities.

RENAISSANCE

The Italian Renaissance of the 14th to 16th centuries created an astonishing wealth of paintings and sculpture, as well as a school of music that dominated Europe throughout. The artists of Florence, in particular, turned to the art of classical Greece and Rome for inspiration. It was also a period that saw the growth of skepticism and free-thinking, belief in the individual and new discoveries in science and mathematics. Opera is an Italian invention. It is still a national passion today and, like the rest of the country's magnificent heritage, is a tourist attraction.

20 AUTONOMOUS REGIONS

The present structure of the Italian government was adopted in the

GALILEO GALILEI

Galileo Galilei

Galileo Galilei (1564-1642), Italian scientist. Born at Pisa, he studied at the university there to become professor of mathematics. A demonstration by dropping two stones of unequal weight from the top of the *Leaning Tower*, confirmed his view that all falling bodies, great or small, descend with equal velocity, making him unpopular with the orthodox scientists, and he resigned his chair in 1591. From 1592 to 1610, he was professor of mathematics at Padua. He improved the recently invented telescope, and, with it, he became the first man to see Jupiter. His astronomical observations led him to accept the Copernican system, which he advocated in his *Dialogues* on the two chief systems of the universe, published in 1632. The book was banned, and Galileo was summoned to Rome by the Inquisition, and eventually made to recant his views while Bruno, his follower, later refused to recant and was burnt alive at the stake in 1593.

Republican constitution of 1947. The country is divided into 20 autonomous regions (or States), each with its own legislature and executive council, headed by a regional president. The national parliament consists of a lower chamber of deputies with 630 members elected for a five-year term, and an upper house of 315 senators elected for five-year term. There are also 11 life senators appointed by the president, who is elected by both chambers for a seven-year term.

The two largest parties are the conservative Christian Democrats and the Communists, renamed the Socialist Unity Party in 1990. Election by proportional representation, together with fierce regional self-interest and tension between religious and socialist ideals, has denied either party an absolute majority. Between 1945 and 1993, Italy had 52 governments, mostly coalitions which has also hampered attempts to address national problems. These include poverty in the south, the infiltration of the mafia – a secret criminal organization – into both business and government, and political corruption at all levels. In 1993, the government was rocked by many allegations of corruption. In the same year, a referendum was held in which there was a substantial majority in favour of changing the system of election from proportional representation to first-past-the-post. Under these reforms (first election 1994), 75 percent of members of both houses are elected by first-past-the-post, the rest by proportional representation. Yet, another confusion.

Since 1980, Italians have enjoyed a comprehensive national health service that provides free medical care for all citizens. Welfare includes unemployment and disability benefits, as well as retirement pensions and family allowances, and there is a scheme for industrial injuries. Education is compulsory between the ages of 6 and 14. Private schools, often run by the church, flourish alongside the public schools. In the bitterly fought general election in April, 2006, Silvio Berlusconi, a flamboyant tycoon, was defeated by Left leaning Romano Prodi.

NATIONAL INDICATORS - ITALY

Land area 301,277 sq km.; capital Rome; Physical features highest point: Monte Rosa 4,634 metres; longest rivers: Po 620 km.; largest lake : Lake Garda 370 sq km; Population 58,138,394; Form of government multiparty republic with two legislative houses; Large cities Rome, Milan, Naples, Turin, Palermo, Genoa; Bologna, Florence; Official language Italian; Ethnic composition Italian 94.1%; Sardinian 2.7%; Rhaetian 1.3%, others 1.9%;

Religious affiliations Roman Catholic 83.2%, non-religious 16.2%, others 0.6%.

HISTORY

C.1000	City states rise to power.
16th-18thC	Most Italian states under Spanish and then Austrian control.
1796-1815	Most of Italy ruled by France.
1848	Revolutions in major Italian cities.
1861	Most of Italy united as kingdom.
1866	Acquires Mantua and Venetia after Austro-Prussian War.
1870	Rome is made the capital city.
1915-18	Joins with Allies in First World War.
1922	Fascist Mussolini named prime minister.
1925	Mussolini becomes dictator.
1929	Independence for Vatican City.
1936	Invades Albania.
1940-3	Joins with Axis in Second World War.
1945	Mussolini executed.
1946	Republic declared
1957	Becomes a founder-member of European Economic Community. (Now EU)
1997	Leads peace keeping in Albania
2006	Romino Prodi became Prime Minister, defeating Silvio Berlusconi.—now P.M. (2010).

Christianity is not our work; it is a revelation, a message that has been received by us. Hence, we have no right to reconstruct it as we choose.
– Pope Benedict XVI

69

Vatican City (State of the Vatican City)

The Vatican has always stood for Roman Catholic traditionalism, opposing change and liberalising forces, including science, women's equality and birth control in the name of God. "A woman has a role inscribed in her own biology," says Pope Benedict XVI who was elected as the 265th Pope in May 2005, suceeding Pope John Paul II.

The Vatican City is the smallest sovereignty in Europe with an area of only 16 square miles, and little over, 1,000 inhabitants. The city is dominated by St. Peter's, the biggest Christian Church in the world. It has its own laws and administration. It has diplomatic relations with thirty-five nations, most of which maintain ambassadors to the Holy See (the headquarters of the Pope, ("see" as a noun means a district or diocese). The Pope office was also the centre of the Sacred Congregation for the Doctrine of the Faith, it was also called the Inquisition which condemned many dissidents, including Copernicus and Bruno who was burnt alive. Copernicus was saved because he recanted.

Within its walls is a miniature nation, with its own diplomatic missions, newspaper, post office, radio station, banking system, an army of more than 100 Swiss Guards, and a publishing house. There is no income tax. The Pope has absolute executive, legislative and judicial powers within the city. He appoints the members of the Vatican's government organs, which are separate from those of the Holy See. The many imposing buildings include St. Peter's Basilica, the Vatican Palace, and the Vatican Museums. Frescoes by

A view of Vatican City

Michelangelo in the Sistine Chapel, by Pinturicchio in the Borgia Apartment, and by Raphel in the Stanze are also there. The Vatican Library contains a priceless collection of manuscripts from the pre-Christian and Christian eras. The pope and other representatives of the papal state travel widely to maintain international relations.

First enclosed in 850, the irregularly walled compound contains gardens, courtyards, living quarters, galleries and other facilities. The residence, with more than 1,400 rooms, was built in the 13th century by Pope Nicholas-III. Giovanni dei Dolci built the Sistine Chapel, noted for its spectacular interior artwork including Michelangelo's ceiling; Donato Bramante completed the palace's northern facade and planned the immense Belvedere court; and Raphael painted his masterpieces in the palace. Antonio da Sangallo the Younger, designed the Sala Regia (Royal Hall) and Pauline Chapel, decorated by Michelangelo.

The Vatican State commands the religious allegiance of 320 million Roman Catholics, the largest number of followers of any religion of which records are kept (there are 220 million Muslims, 137 million Protestants in the world). It is a salient fact that its greatest accretion of converts in recent history has come from the United States. There were, at the beginning of the 1800s, only 40,000 Catholics in America. Their numbers have since increased out of proportion to the rise in total population, now being around twenty-six millions and constituting a strong balancing force in American politics. Lately, in America the Church has received converts at the rate of 85,000 a year.

POPE ALSO DOES BUSINESS

For its size, the Vatican is also among the richest states. By the Lateran treaty of 1929, which established the independence of the Holy See from Italy, Mussolini agreed to pay it a lumpsum of 750 million pre-war lire plus 1,000 million lire in Italian State. In addition, it owns the controlling interest in thirty-one Italian industries with a capital of over 300 million pre-War lire, and minority holdings in Italian banks, shipping companies, insurance firms, mines, and chemical, textile and hydro-electric industries.

In France, it owns the Franco-Italian bank and the *Semaine Sociale,* a publishing house which brings out periodicals. With 70 per cent control of the great *Societe Textiles du Nord* its total invested capital in France is around 200 million pre-War francs. It has also holdings in Belgium and Holland. In the United States, it is said to have investments totalling around 700 million pre-War lire. Its investments over the whole world are estimated at 3,000 million pre-War lire or roughly around 240 million dollars. (The figures refer only to Vatican City holdings; those of individual churches are not included.) In addition to its investment income, the Holy See receives an annual contribution of "*Peter's pence*" from every nation where there are Catholics, the largest contributions coming from America. For that matter, the Pope is a businessman also.

CHURCH BLESSED DICTATORS

Between the wars, Mussolini's legions that conquered Ethiopia were blessed by the Catholic bishops, as were the legionaries of General Franco in the Spanish Civil War. In Austria, the Catholic bishops exhorted the people to support Hitler in the plebiscite which the German Fuhrer held after his invasion of Austria. The Church later opposed Hitler, but only after the Fuhrer had opened his assault on the Church, confiscating its properties. It is

TINY CENTRE OF THE CATHOLIC WORLD

Vatican City *(Stato della Citta del Vaticano)* is the world's smallest nation. The city-state is about the size of the President estate in New Delhi. Vatican City is the surviving remnant of the Papal States that once dominated much of central Italy; in 1859, just before Italian unification, papal territory covered about 44,000 km. The Papal States were abolished in 1870, but the Vatican's Independence was guaranteed by the Italian dictator Benito Mussolini in 1929. Located in the heart of Rome, on Vatican Hill near the bank of the Tiber, the state now covers only 109 acres.

only fair to add that during the late war, parish priests widely supported the underground partisans in both France and Italy, sometimes at the cost of their lives.

DON'T STUDY BIG BANG, POPE JOHN PAUL II HAD TOLD STEPHEN HAWKING

Famous astrophysicist Stephen Hawking said (June, 2006) the late Pope John Paul-II once told scientists they should not study the beginning of the universe because it was the work of God. The British author – who wrote the best-seller, *A Brief History of Time* – said that the Pope made the comments at a cosmology conference at the Vatican, who didn't say when the meeting was held, quoted the Pope as saying, "It's OK to study the universe and where it began. But we should not enquire into the beginning itself because that was the moment of creation and the work of God.' The scientist then joked during a lecture in Hong Kong, "I was glad he didn't realise I had presented a paper at the conference suggesting how the universe began and was not created by God".

The entrance of the Church into active European politics after the War was virtually forced on it. While the two Marxist parties, Communists and Socialists, advanced in almost every country in Europe, the war very nearly left a vacuum in the centre and to the right of European politics. The old centre parties had been discredited by collaboration with the Nazis. No "bourgeois" political force remained to confront the rising tide of the left, so anti-Communists of the most diverse brands created political organizations around the remaining strong spiritual force against Marxism – the Catholic Church. The Catholic parties, many of them unheard of before the war, rose to astonishing strength: at one point shortly after the War no fewer than nine of sixteen West European countries were run by Catholic governments. The Catholic tide surged over the Iron Curtain and predominantly Catholic parties swept the elections in both Hungary and Slovakia. Poland has traditionally been a Catholic country.

The Catholic vote was enlarged by special circum-stances. First, women were allowed to vote for the first time in half a dozen European countries, and women are much more easily influenced by the Church than men. Second, the threat of Communism to private ownership of property inevitably made church a bastion of free enterprise. The present Pope Benedict XVI (a Bavarian German) has opposed Turkey joining the European Union on the ground that 68 million Turkish Muslims will dilute the Western Europe's Christian heritage. In addition to intervention in domestic politics, the Vatican mended its international fences. The administration of the Catholic Church has nearly always been Italian. Since the time of Adrian of Utrecht, who died in 1523, all popes and most cardinals have been Italians except now, when the Pope is German and Pope John Paul-II, his predecessor, was a Pole.

NATIONAL INDICATORS - VATICAN CITY

National name Stato della Citta del Vaticano; Area 0.4 sq.km.; physical features forms an enclave in the heart of Rome, Italy; Head of State John Paul-II from 1978; Political system absolute catholicism; population 1,000 (1994); languages Latin (official), Italian; religion Roman Catholic.

HISTORY

AD 64	Death of St. Peter, a Christian martyr who, by legend, was killed in Rome regarded as the first bishop of Rome. The Pope, as head of the Roman Catholic Church, is viewed as the spiritual descendent of St. Peter.
756	The Pope became temporal ruler of the Papal States, which stretched across central Italy, centred around Rome.
11th-13th Cs	Under Gregory-VII and Innocent-III in the papacy enjoyed its greatest temporal power.
1377	After seven decades in which the papacy was based in Avignon (France), Rome once again became the headquarters for the Pope, with the Vatican Palace becoming the official residence.
1860	Umbria, Marche, and much of the Emilia Romagna which, along with Lazio formed the Papal States, were annexed by the new unified Italian state.
1870	First Vatican Council defined as a matter of faith the absolute primacy of the Pope and the infallibility of his pronouncements on 'matters of faith and morals'.
1870-71	French forces, which had been protecting the Pope, were withdrawn, allowing Italian nationalist forces to capture Rome, which became the capital of Italy; Pope Pius-IX retreated into the Vatican Palace, from which no Pope was to emerge until 1929.
1929	Lateran Agreement, signed by the Italian fascist leader Benito Mussolini and Pope Pius XI, restored full sovereign jurisdiction over the Vatican City State to the bishopric of Rome (Holy See) and declared the new state to be a neutral and inviolable

	territory.
1947	New Italian constitution confirmed the sovereignty of the Vatican City State.
1962	Second Vatican Council called by Pope John XXIII.
1978	John Paul II became the first non-Italian pope for more than 400 years.
1985	New concordat signed under which Roman Catholicism ceased to be Italy's state religion.
1992	Relations with East European states restored.
2005	Pope Benedict XVI elected pope in May 2005. His earlier name was Joseph Cardinal Ratzinger of Germany.

CHRISTIAN MISSIONARIES – PROFILES

ST PAUL (died C.67): Paul, a Roman citizen, travelled widely, taking the message of Christianity to the Aegean islands, Asia Minor, Greece, Italy and Spain.

ST COLUMBA (C.521-97): Columba, an abbot of Iona, became the centre of Celtic Christianity.

ST COLUMBAN (C. 540-615): The Irish missionary monk Columban took Christianity to the pagan Franks and established monastic centres in France and northern Italy.

ST AUGUSTINE OF CANTERBURY (died 605): Augustine was sent by Pope Gregory-I to re-evangelise Britain in 597. He became the first archbishop of Canterbury.

ST BONIFACE (675-754): The English-born monk was called the 'Apostle of Germany'. Appointed as archbishop of Mainz in 751, he was killed preaching in Friesland.

CISTERCIANS: Founded in 1098 by Robert of Molesme at Citeaux, France, the Cistercian order was based on a strict interpretation of St Benedict's Rule. It was a prosperous order with large agricultural estates.

FRANCISCANS: The Franciscans (Friars Minor) were the first order of friars (mendicant or begging monks), founded in 1209 by St Francis of Assisi (1182-1226).

DOMINICANS: The Dominican order (Friars Preachers), founded in 1215 by St Dominic (1170-1221), emphasised public preaching.

AUGUSTINIANS: Augustinian canons flourished from around 1100. Their rules were based on that of St. Augustine of Hippo.

THE EASTERN ORTHODOX CHURCH: The Orthodox tradition encompasses a group of churches centred on the Patriarch of Constantinople and rejecting the supremacy of the pope. Early self-governing subdivisions include the Russian Orthodox Church founded in 998.

THE NESTORIAN CHURCH: The Nestorian church was created by the followers of Nestorius (d. 451), bishop of Constantinople. Its basic belief was that Jesus combined distinct human and divine natures. The Nestorians were expelled by the Orthodox Church in 489, and resettled in Persia; their missionaries spread to India, Sri Lanka and China.

THE COPTIC CHURCH: Traditionally founded by St Mark, the Evangelist, the Coptic Church developed in Egypt (particularly Alexandria) after the 2nd century. It split from the rest of the Church over the definition of Christ's nature, and was associated with early Christian monasticism. The Church still exists in Egypt, and is strong in Ethiopia.

THE EAST-WEST SCHISM: Bitter disputes over doctrine and papal authority began to divide the Western and Eastern Churches from the 9th century. Mutual excommunications were pronounced by Rome and Constantinople in 1054 (lifted only in 1965). This marked the first great formal split of the Christian Church into Roman Catholic, in the West, and orthodox, in the East.

St. Marino was a stone-cutter who settled in the Apennine ranges and set up a village which has now become a republic, San Marino.

70

San Marino (Republic of San Marino)

San Marino is the second smallest country in the world – rather an enclave that passes for a country. Weighed down under the load of history, the country is, however, growing along with rest of European countries. Education is free, so also many other social facilities for those who need them.

San Marino is a central Italian peninsula in southern Europe, located near the Adriatic Sea and surrounded by Italy. Capital: San Marino. Most of the people are Italian. Language: Italian (official). Religion: Roman Catholicism. The territory has an irregular rectangular form with a maximum length of 13 km. It is crossed by streams that flow into the Adriatic Sea. It is dominated by Mount Titano, 2,424 ft (739 metre) high, on which the capital, the town of San Marino, is located, surrounded by triple walls. The economy is based on private enterprise and includes tourism, commerce, agriculture, crafts, and fine printing, particularly of postage stamps. San Marino is a republic with one legislative house; its heads of state and government are two captains-regent. By the 12th century it had developed into a commune and remained independent despite challenges from neighbouring rulers. San Marino survived as a relic of the self-governing Italian City-State and remained an independent republic after the unification of Italy in 1861-70. It is one of the smallest republics in the world and may be the oldest one in Europe. Its citizens enjoy a high standard of living.

San Marino is second smallest country in the world, only an enclave in the Apennine mountains of northern Italy. The towers and battlements of the

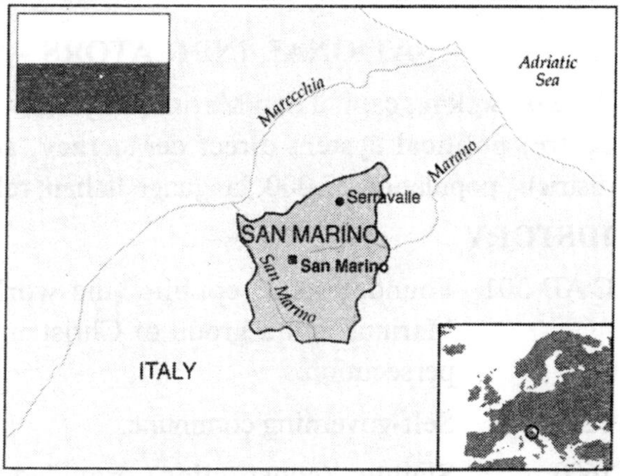

Rocca Fortress in San Marino, the capital, are perched on the rugged western slope of Mount Titano, while woods and pastureland small cover the foothills. This ancient state largely owes its survival to its rugged and isolated terrain, which helped preserve it from predatory neighbours throughout the turbulent Renaissance period and after.

Legends trace San Marino's origins to the 4th century AD, when St. Marinus, a Dalmatian (Croatia) stone-cutter, settled there with his Christian followers. It first appeared in the 12th century as a self-governing commune. In 1600, a constitution was adopted that remains broadly in force today. The Congress of Vienna (1815), which met to decide the future shape of Europe after the Napoleonic wars, agreed to preserve San Marino's independence. In the mid-19th century, the leaders of the Italian unification movement, including Garibaldi took refuge in San Marino, and this helped it to conclude favourable treaties with Italy after unification in 1861. Although many of its people have emigrated, chiefly to Italy and the United States, a large number of Italians have also moved to San Marino and settled there. Italian is the official language, though a much older dialect is also spoken.

The mountainous landscape, ancient fortification and unspoilt countryside attract increasing numbers of tourists, which enables the republic to survive as an independent state. Until this century agriculture, well suited to the mild Mediterranean climate, was the main occupation. Cattle are reared on mountain pastures and the lower slopes are planted with vines and cereals. Until the 1940s, there was no industry except stone quarries (now exhausted) on Mount Titano. Since World War II various light manufacturing industries have been introduced, though tourism is quickly overtaking them as a source of revenue. San Marino is now investing in its own resort hotel facilities. An extensive welfare system is provided; many San Marino citizens are employed in state concerns, and assisted with home ownership. Free education is provided to the age of 14, and there are grants for further study outside the republic.

NATIONAL INDICATORS - SAN MARINO

Area 61 sq.km.; capital San Marino; major towns/cities Serravalle (industrial centre) political system direct democracy; administrative divisions; nine districts; population 27,000; language Italian; religion Roman Catholic 95%.

HISTORY

C AD 301	Founded as a republic (the world's oldest surviving) by St. Marinus and a group of Christians who settled there to escape persecution.
12th C	Self-governing commune.
1600	Statutes (constitution) provided for a parliamentary form of government, based around the Great and General Council.
1815	Independent status of the republic recognised by the Congress of Vienna.
1862	Treaty with Italy signed; independence recognised under Italy's protection.
1945-57	Communist-Socialist administration in power, eventually ousted in a bloodless 'revolution'.
1971	Treaty with Italy renewed.
1986	Formation of Communist and centre-right Christian Democrat (PDCS) 'grand coalition'.
1992	Joined the United Nations. PDCS withdrew from 'grand coalition' to form alliance with Socialist Party.

Malta is a strange place – a dry, bathbrick island that glares and sets your teeth on edge; it is so dry that one expects oneself to begin to crackle.

– D.H. Lawrence in a 1920 letter to Catherine Carswell

71

Malta
(Republic of Malta)

Although a small island, but kings and conquerors have fought over it because Malta provided them with a staging post to control eastern Mediterranean. And, the countries in the region.

Malta is in the Mediterranean Sea, south of Sicily. It consists of three inhabited islands, Malta (the largest), Gozo, and Comino, and two uninhabited islets, Comminotto and Filfla. Although two-fifths of its total land area is arable, Malta imports most of its food; tourism is its major industry. It is republic with one legislative house. Inhabited as early as 3800 BC, it was ruled by the Carthaginians in 8th-7th century BC. It came under Roman control in 218 BC. In AD 60 the Apostle Paul was shipwrecked on the island and converted the inhabitants to Christianity. It was under the Byzantine rule until the Arabs seized control in 870. In 1091, the Normans defeated the Arabs, and it was ruled by a succession of feudal lords until the early 16th century. In 1530, it came under the Knights of Malta; Napolean seized control in 1978, and the British took it in 1800.

The 1802 Treaty of Amiens returned the islands to the Knights. The Maltese acknowledged the British as sovereign; this arrangement was ratified in the 1814 Treaty of Paris. It became self-governing in 1921 but reverted to a colonial regime in 1936. Malta was severely bombed by Germany and Italy during World War II. In 1964 Malta gained independece within the Commonwealth, and it became a republic in 1974. When its alliance with Britain ended in 1979, Malta proclaimed its neutral status. In 2002 it was

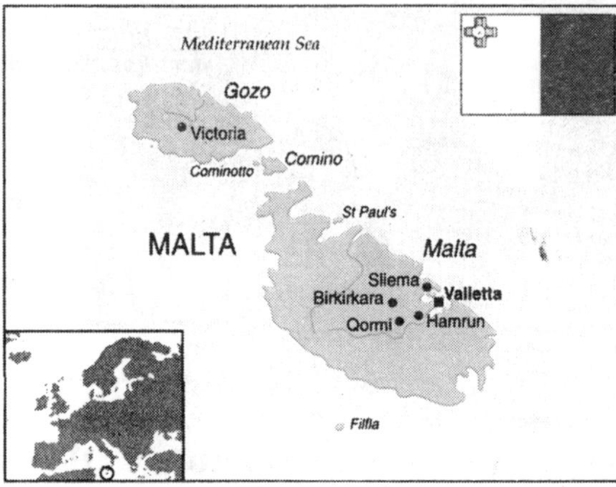

invited to join the European Union, and voters endorsed membership the following year.

Being a staging post in the Mediterranean, Malta has seen the rise and fall of many empires. Her wounds show it. The commanding position of the islands in the relatively narrow straits between Sicily and Tunisia makes them strategically important. The islands are the peaks of a massive limestone outcrop stretching south from Sicily, dissected by deep bays and valleys. With no fresh water apart from low rainfall, de-salinization plants are necessary for a potable water supply. The natural vegetation is sparse due to centuries of overgrazing and erosion. Malta, possibly a former colony of Carthage in north Africa, was part of first Roman and then Byzantine empires. Seized by the Arabs in 870, it was reconquered and ruled by Christian feudal lords until 1530, when it was ceded to the Knights of St. John, a religious and military order. Malta was seized by Napoleon in 1802. However, after a rebellion, the islands became a British colony in 1814. It became an important staging post on the sea route to India via the new Suez Canal (1869) and developed a dockyard industry. In World War II, Malta withstood repeated attacks by Germany and its allies, earning the entire population the British George Cross for bravery. Agriculture is restricted to terraced hill-sides and irrigated lowlands. Vegetables, cereals and citrus fruit are the chief crops; cattle and goats are the main livestock. Intense cultivation has brought near self-sufficiency, but agriculture accounts for only 4 percent of gross national product. Fishing is local and small-scale.

NATIONAL INDICATORS - MALTA

Area 320 sq.km.; capital and port Valletta; major towns/cities Rabat; physical features, includes islands of Gozo 67 sq.km and Comino 3 sq.km; political system liberal democracy; administrative divisions none administered from the capital; moderate, left of centre; Nationalist Party (PN), Christian, centrist, Pro-European; population 370,402 (1995).

HISTORY

7th C BC	Invaded and subjugated by the Carthaginians from North Africa.
218 BC	Came under Roman control.
AD 60	Converted to Christianity.
395	On the division of the Roman Empire, became part of the Eastern (Byzantine portion), dominated by Constantinople.
870	Came under Arab rule.
1091	Arabs defeated by the Norman count Roger-I of Sicily, and the Roman Catholic Church was re-established.
1798-1802	Briefly occupied by the French.
1814	Annexed to Britain by the Treaty of Paris on condition that the Roman Catholic Church was maintained and the Maltese Declaration of Rights honoured.
1942	Awarded the George Cross for its valour in World War II.
1947	Achieved self-government.
1955	Dom Mintoff of the left-of-centre Malta Labour Party (MLP) became prime minister.
1964	Independence achieved from Britain, within the Commonwealth.
1971	Mintoff adopted policy of non-alignment and declared 1964 treaty invalid.
1972	Seven-year NATO agreement signed.
1974	Became a republic.
1979	British military base closed; closer links established with communist and Arab states, including Libya.
1984	Mintoff was replaced by Karmenu Mifsud Bonnici as prime minister and MLP leader.
1987	Edward Fenech Adami (PN) elected prime minister and adopted a more pro-European and pro-American policy stance than the preceding administration.
1990	Formal application made for European Community membership.
2002	It was invited to join the EU. The move was endorsed in a referendum.

After being a colony almost always in its long history, when independence came in 1960 the Greeks and Turks became uncomfortable. And, the country split.

72

Cyprus
(Republic of Cyprus)

Cyprus, the outer boundary of Europe and the third largest island in the Mediterranean, is divided by the long-running conflict between the majority Greeks and minority Turkish population. And, the talks to unify the county never succeeded, indicating the fraying of Europe's eastern fringes.

Cyprus is an island country in the northeastern Mediterranean. Capital: Nicosia. Cyprus is currently divided into two de facto states. The Republic of Cyprus, the internationally recognised government, occupies the southern two-thirds of the island. its population 6,92,000 (2002) is predominantly Greek. Language: Greek (official). Religion: Eastern Orthodoxy. Currency: Cyprus pound. The Turkish Republic of Northern Cyprus occupies the northern third of the country. its population 2,15,000 (2002) is overwhelmingly Turkish. Languages: Turkish (official), English. Religion: Islam. Currency: Turkish lira.

The third largest island in the Mediterranean, Cyprus lies about 65 km. off the southern coast of Turkey. It is largely mountainous, with a fertile heartland and coastal plains. Mount Olympus is its highest peak, 6,401 ft. above sea level. The climate is Mediterranean. Cyprus is a free-enterprise economy based mainly on trade and manufacturing, and it ranks high in the world in merchant shipping. The internationally recognised government is a multiparty republic with a unicameral legislature; its head of state and government is the president.

Cyprus was inhabited by the early Neolithic period; by the late Bronze Age it had been settled by Mycenaeans and Achaeans, who introduced Greek culture and language, and it became a trading centre. By 800 BC Phoenicians had begun to settle there. Ruled over the centuries by the Assyrian, Persian and Ptolemaic empires, it was annexed by the Roman Republic and Empire in 58 BC. It was part of the Byzantine Empire in the 4th-11th centuries AD.

A CROWN COLONY

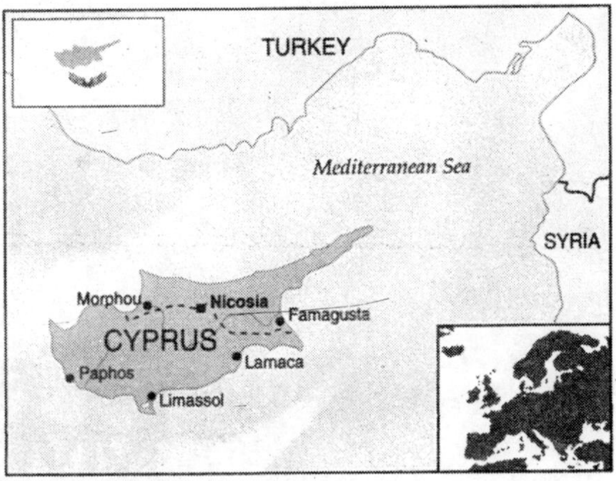

It was conquered by the English king Richard-I (the Lionheart) in 1191. A part of the Venetian trading empire from 1489, it was taken by Ottoman Empire in 1573. In 1878, the British assumed control, and Cyprus became a British crown colony in 1924. It gained independence in 1960. Conflict between Greek and Turkish Cypriots led to the establishment of a United Nations (UN) peacekeeping mission in 1964. In 1974, fearing a movement to unite Cyprus with Greece, the Republic of Turkey sent troops to occupy the northern third of the country. Turkish Cypriots established a functioning government, which obtained recognition only from Turkey. Conflict has continued, and the UN peacekeeping mission has remained in place. Negotiations to reunify the island under a single government have been inconclusive.

Cyprus is the third largest island in the Mediterranean. In the north coasts are the Kyrenia mountains; in the south, the Troodos, from which the Pedias and Kariyoti rivers flow towards the bays of Famagusta and Morphow. Four-fifths of Cypriots are of Greek descent. The Turkish-speaking minority arrived in 1573. Since 1974, many Cypriots from both communities have left to work in Britain and the Middle East. Almost all Greek Cypriots belong to the Greek (Eastern) Orthodox Church while the Turkish Cypriot community is mostly Sunni Muslim. English is the island's common language. The Republic of Cyprus still claims legitimacy under the constitution of 1960. Many constitutional provisions for Turkish Cypriot representation have been suspended, including the vice-presidency and seats in the House of Representatives. The breakaway Turkish state introduced a new constitution in 1985 and now elects its own government.

A tourist spot in Cyprus

Cyprus has history of 4,000 years. Its rulers include Greeks, Ptolemies, Persians, Romans, Byzantines, Arabs, Franks, Venetians, Turks and British. Cyprus officially became a British colony on May 1, 1925. It had been leased to Britain by Turkey in 1878 and was annexed to the British Empire in 1914. Greek Cypriots' demand for union with Greece (*enosis*) led to guerrilla warfare under Grivas and Makarios and a 4-year state of emergency (1955-9). Cyprus got independence in 1960, with Britain retaining sovereignty over bases at Akrotiri and Dhekelia. Greek-Turkish fighting continued throughout 1960s, and UN peacekeeping force was sent in 1964 but terrorists campaign continued in 1971. Turkish invasion in 1974 led to occupation of over a third of the island, resulting in displacement of over 160,000 Greek Cypriots. Island was divided into two parts by the *Attila Line*, from north-west coast above Pomos to Famagusta in the east, cutting through Nicosia (where it is called the *Green Line*). It is governed by a president elected for a 5-year term by the Greek community, and a House of Representatives of 80 elected members. Turkish members ceased to attend it in 1983, when they set up the "Turkish Republic of Northern Cyprus", recognised only by Turkey.

UNIFICATION PLAN: Greek Cypriots, on April 25, 2004, rejected a plan to reunite the island. But, the Turkish Cypriots approved it. The east-west line that divides the entire island, slashing through Nicosia, will now become an external border of Europe. EU immigration and trade controls will have to be enforced along that Green Line. The peace move was initiated by UN-Secretary-General, Kofi Annan, and its failure caused disappointment. The hope for a united Cyprus is thus lost. At least, for now.

NATIONAL INDICATORS - CYPRUS

Area 9,251 sq.km.; capital Nicosia (divided between Greek and Turkish Cypriots); major towns Morphou; major ports Limassol, Larnaca and Paphos (Greek); Kyrenia and Famagusta (Turkish); physical features central plain between two east west mountain ranges; population 756,800 (1996); literacy rate 94%; languages Greek and Turkish (official), English; religions Greek Orthodox, Sunni Muslim.

HISTORY

14th-11th Cs BC Colonized by Myceneans and Achaeans from Greece.

9th C BC Phoenicans settled in Cyprus.

7th C BC Several Cypriot kingdoms flourished under Assyrian influence.

58 BC Cyprus was annexed by the Roman Empire.

AD 45 Christianity introduced.

AD 395 When the Roman Empire divided, Cyprus was allotted to the Byzantine Empire.

7th-10th Cs Byzantines and Muslim Arabs fought for control of Cyprus.

1191 Richard-I of England, 'the Lionheart', conquered Cyprus as a base for Crusades; he later sold it to a French noble, Guy de Lusignan, who established a feudal monarchy which ruled for three centuries.

1498 Venetian Republic took control of Cyprus.

1571 Conquered by Ottoman Turks.

1914 Formally annexed by Britain after Turkey entered World War I as a Central Power.

1915 Greece rejected an offer of Cyprus in return for entry into World War I on Allied side.

1925 Cyprus became a crown colony.

1948 Greek Cypriots rejected new constitution because it did not offer links with Greece.

1951	Britain rejected Greek proposals for enosis.
1955	National organisation of Cypriot Fighters (EOKA), led by George Grivas, began terrorist campaign for enosis.
1959	Britain, Greece and Turkey agreed to Cypriot independence and partition.
1960	Cyprus became an independent republic with Archbishop Makarios as president.
1964	United Nations (UN) peacekeeping force installed.
1974	Coup by Greek officers in Cypriot National Guard installed Nikos Sampson as president; Turkey, fearing enosis, invaded northern Cyprus, military regime collapsed; President Makarios restored.
1975	Northern Cyprus declared itself the Turkish Federated State of Cyprus.
1977	Makarios died; succeeded by Spyros Kyprianou.
1983	Denktas proclaimed independent Turkish Republic of Cyprus; recognised only by Turkey.
1994	European Court of Justice declared trade with northern Cyprus illegal.
1996	Further peace talks jeopardized by boundary killing of Turkish Cypriot soldier; mounting tension between north and south.
1998	President Clerides re-elected. Denktas refused to meet British envoy. US mediation failed. The country stays divided.

Greeks were overthrown not by their enemies, but by themselves and their own internal dissension.

– Thucydides

73

The Greek tragedy

The rise and fall of ancient Greece is as legendary as its blazing comeback to the postmodern Europe is extraordinary, competing for eminence which has always been Greece's.

Greece is the mother of western civilization. Its achievements are remarkable, so also its legacy in arts, sciences, politics and everything else. Europe owes almost everything to Greeks and Romans who together laid the foundation of modern Europe. Greece's beginning, however, was inauspicious. Habitation is evident from Paleolithic times, but the Bronze Age history (3000-1000 BC) of Greece is trivial compared with the great empires of the east and Egypt. Around 2000 BC, an Aegean civilization, known as Minoan, developed on the island of Crete. The Minoans were literate, urban, and involved in maritime trade. Natural calamities and conquest brought an end to Minoan civilization after 1400 BC.

Indo-European peoples began entering Greece in about 2000 BC. The resulting Mycenaean civilization, beginning from 1600 BC, was influenced by Crete. Around 1200 BC, the Dorians, another Indo-European people, invaded Greece, and a dark age followed, known through the Homeric epics. At the end of this time, classical Greece began to emerge (750 BC) as a loose confederation of city-states with a heavy involvement in maritime trade and love for art, literature, politics, and philosophy.

This remarkable civilization reached its zenith after repelling the invasions of the Persians (5th century) but began to decline after the civil strife following the Peloponnesian War (431-404 BC). In 338 BC, the Greek city-states were taken over by Philip-II of Macedon. Though no longer an independent entity,

Greece enjoyed a measure of immortality as its culture was spread by Philip's son Alexander throughout his vast empire. The Romans, themselves heavily influenced by the Greek culture, conquered the Greek states during 205-146 BC.

The barbarian invasions of the Roman Empire found Greece reduced to a shadow of its former glory, but Greek culture, particularly the Greek language, survived in the eastern half of the Roman Empire, the Byzantine Empire. Largely through the efforts of the Byzantine Church, the peoples who invaded Greece between the 5th and the 7th century AD were converted to Greek Christianity. Thus, Greece remained an integral part of the Byzantine Empire until the attempts of the Crusaders to establish states in Greece and the Middle East from the late 11th to the 15th century. Byzantium (an ancient Greek City founded in the 7th century BC at the end of the Bosporus, it was re-named as Constantinople, now Istanbul) recaptured most of these states, but by 1460 virtually all of Greece had become part of the expanding Ottoman Empire. The Ottoman rule was harsh, but the Orthodox Church was left intact. As a result, the church came to represent Greek nationalism.

SOME KEY DATES

5thC BC	"Golden Age" of ancient Greece.
146 BC	Roman rule begins.
1453	Conquest by Ottoman empire.
1829	Independence.
1912-13	Balkan Wars, victory over Turkey and Bulgaria.
1924	Becomes a republic
1941-4	Occupied by Germany
1946-9	Civil war: rebel communists defeated.
1949	Monarchy returns.
1967	Military coup; martial law imposed.
1973	Republic declared.
1974	Martial law ends: civilian government and free elections.
1981	Joins European Community.
1995	Normal relations with Macedonia.

Revolution against the Ottomans (Turkish) came in 1821, largely as the result of Greek social developments and European interference. The struggle was long and hampered by internal dissensions, but Greek independence was recognized in 1830, and the Bavarian Otto-I was placed on the throne in 1833. Otto was deposed in 1862 and replaced by the George-I, a Dane. Greek borders expanded during his reign. But an attempt to annex Anatolia (mostly rural Turkey in the western peninsula of Asia) after World War I was unsuccessful. Instability has characterized the 20th-century Greek government. A republic was proclaimed in 1924, but the monarchy was restored in 1935. Civil unrest followed World War II and lasted until 1949, when Communist forces were defeated. There was a military coup in 1967. The military rulers abolished the monarchy and proclaimed a republic in 1973, but the military government was itself overthrown at the end of the same year; since then, democratically elected civilian *governments have succeeded one another.*

Since the entire Mediterranean basin, once the centre of civilization, is now in decline, it is difficult to say which Mediterranean country suffers most. There is, however, no doubt that Greece is in a mess. Greece has too many friends but none of them honest. For almost a decade now, the little land has been incessantly raked by indecisive warfare between friends "saving" her from a corrupt dictatorship. The British landed to save her from the Italians; the Germans re-assert their friendship and respect for the victim. Since the War, this little country has received more dollars worth of foreign aid per head than any other country in the area. But, with every friendly dollar, her misery has deepened. Greece has only one claim to attention: the accident of her geographic location. She is the stopper in the downturned bottle of the Balkans by which the West prevented Communism from flooding into the Eastern area of the Mediterranean and so damaging the West's strategic bases and rich investments in the near-east.

Eighty percent of Greece is barren rock. Only 15 per cent of her tiny surface is arable to support ten million Greeks (1996). About four million Greeks are directly engaged in agriculture – far too large a farming population for so small an area. The farmland per head of farmer population is less than one and one-half acre. The pressure on agriculture is greater than in Italy, and the resources of the country provide a still thinner basis for creating an industry to attract labour away from the overcrowded soil. While Italy has at least a good hydroelectric industry, Greece has none. Here rains come all at once in one great gush in the winter and flood the valleys for a few weeks and for the rest of the year the stream beds are bone-dry.

Greece has had the longest and most painful transition to democracy. While Spain and Portugal languished under authoritarian control, they at least, were spared the ravages of World War–II and its aftermath. Greece was not so fortunate. In 1940, Mussolini's troops invaded Greece, and though they were thrown back by a spirited Greek counterattack, the Duce's humiliation triggered

A temple to Apollo

Germany's invasion in April 1941, with far greater ruthlessness. King George-II, escaped to Crete and then to Cairo, and a collaborationist government under Gen. Georgios Tsolakoglou came to power. The country was then occupied by German, Italian, and Bulgarian forces and partitioned, with the Germans taking Athens and its hinterland. The Italians were granted control of much of the country, including the long Adriatic and Aegean coastline.

WAR DAMAGED ECONOMY

The war was a devastating experience for Greece. The Germans plundered the country, disrupted transportation and farming, and terrorized the people. The fragile Greek economy collapsed and Athens found itself in the grip of famine. Perhaps as many as 250,000 people starved to death in Greece in 1941-42 before the Red Cross was allowed to ship wheat into the country. In the face of such a ghastly occupation, many Greeks joined the resistance. In September 1941, the communists established the National Liberation Front (EAM), with a military branch, the National People's Liberation Army (ELAS). Other, non-Communist resistance organisations also sprang up, and for the next three years they fought tenaciously against the Germans, despite appalling reprisals carried out by the Germans against the civilian population. They were

> **LEGEND OF 300 SPARTANS**
>
> Some 25 centuries ago, in the narrow pass on Greece's northern coast called *Thermopylae-* the name means "the hot gates" a great event happened which has become a legend now. In August of 480 B.C., a force of about 7,000 Greek soldiers assembled there, including 300 Spartans, under the leadership of their king, Leonidas. The Spartans were great fighters, brutally trained from childhood to become the ancient equivalent of special forces. They were there to meet an army of more than 250,000 Persians under the command of Kind Xerxes. The odds were ludicrously bad, the outcome a forgone conclusion. Most of the Greeks retreated, but the 300 Spartans, the hard-core of the Greek army, chose to fight on, using the natural strategic advantage of the pass. They lasted for three days – beyond all hope, beyond what should have been militarily possible – and then they all died fighting. Their refusal to surrender their freedom to the Persians inspired the Greeks, who again rose as a nation and beat back the invaders. And, Greece became free again.

supported to some degree by Britain, but Winston Churchill remained anxious about the Communist sympathies of many resistance leaders.

The British-supported government held elections in March 1946, which the Communists boycotted. Predictably, the rightist parties won and claimed legitimacy and a popular mandate to restore order. In September, the government held a plebiscite on the monarchy, and 68 percent of the voting public favoured the return of the king. Yet the communists were still a major military force and controlled large swaths of the country. The Greek army was weak, its morale low, and its supplies poor. The guerrillas had considerable success against it, and in 1947 the Communists declared a provisional democratic government. By now, however, the Greek civil war had become tangled up in the emerging US-Soviet conflict in Europe. In 1947, the British government informed the United States that it could no longer bear the financial burden of maintaining an army in Greece. The United States, anxious about reports that the guerrillas were being supplied by the Communist governments in Yugoslavia and Bulgaria, immediately seized on the Greek case as an example of Soviet-sponsored subversion of democratic governments in Europe. Having already been put on high alert by Soviet shenanigans in Turkey and Iran, the United States announced a new policy in March 1947 – the *Truman Doctrine* – to provide military and economic aid to any government faced with internal or external threats to its liberty. Within a year, the United States had elbowed Britain aside as the chief benefactor of the Greek government.

For the United States, the stakes were high. Bordered, in the north, by Communist Albania, Yugoslavia, and Bulgaria, Greece was a western toehold on the Balkan Peninsula. The National Security Council agreed: "The defeat of Soviet efforts to destroy the political independence and territorial integrity of Greece is necessary in order to preserve the security of the whole eastern Mediterranean and Middle East, which is vital to the security of the United States." With such alarmist counsel in mind, President Truman authorized economic and military aid to Greece, which by 1953, totalled over $2 billion. The communists could not compete against such a largesse, and their fortunes worsened in mid–1948, when Tito, having been excommunicated by Stalin, closed Yugoslavia's border with Greece and cut off aid to the rebels. By 1949, the government declared victory over the insurgency.

DEATH AND DESTRUCTION

This left Greece in a shambles. During the German occupation, half a million people died; the civil war took another 160,000 lives and created 700,000 refugees. A quarter of the country's homes had been destroyed. The country was yearning for peace and stability, and with the end of the civil war, a right-wing government provided it, under the leadership of a former general, Alexandors Papagos. He promulgated a new constitution, re-established basic democratic procedures and brought Greece into NATO. Upon the death of Papagos in 1955, Konstantinos Karamanlis became premier and continued his predecessor's policies. Strongly anti-Communist, the government used forceful measures to deal with dissent and gave the police significant powers to monitor the Left. Greece began to put its house in order and during the 1950s enjoyed its first period of sustained growth in decades, led mostly by a boom in construction to replace the housing stock lost in the war.

Next to the restoration of democracy, the principal aim of the Karamanlis government was to secure entry into the European Community. In 1961, before the dictatorship, Karamanlis had successfully negotiated an association with the European Economic Community – the first country after the original six members to do so. Karamanlis hoped to gain access to Europe's markets for Greek agricultural exports, as well as secure Greek membership in "the West". The coup of 1967 put the Greek bid for full membership on hold, as the Europeans froze discussions with the military junta.

Back in power in 1974, Karamanlis believed more than ever in the imperative of EC membership. It would secure Greece's role in Europe, dampen down neutralist sentiment, counterbalance the strong anti-American sentiment that had developed as a result of Washington's support for the junta, and legitimize Greece as a member of the democratic club. It might also serve to accentuate the differences between European Greece and Muslim Turkey. Thrilled at the return of democratic rule to Greece, the EC immediately began negotiations over Greek entry to the EC, and in 1979 signed an accession agreement. Greece became a full member of the European Community on 1 January, 1981.

However, there has always been a tendency among the rich countries of Northern and Western Europe to look down at the newly democratic southern European states. Poorer, less developed, and less important in the corridors of power, Greece, Portugal, and Spain often get grouped together as Europe's laggards although these three countries have achieved more than any other European country in so short a time. Since the 1930s these three countries experienced civil war, foreign occupation, authoritarian rule, colonial war, weak economic growth, and significant political turmoil. In a mere twenty-five years, these three countries, with almost no previous experience of democracy or market capitalism, have emerged as stable democracies as any other normal European countries. In the mid-1970s, when the rest of Europe was in the doldrums, Southern Europe had set sail for freedom.

The developments were in this order. In 1973, Greece was proclaimed as a republic with Papadopoulos as President. In 1974, Constantine Karamanlis returned from exile to form the Government of National Salvation and restore democracy. In 1981, Andreas Papandreou was elected Greece's first Socialist Prime Minister and Greece entered the then European Community. In 1996, Costas Simitis succeeded Papandreau as Prime Minister. In 1997, direct talk with Turkey resulted in an agreement to settle all disputes peacefully. (See also national indicators in the next chapter).

What was discarded in the Greek backyard has become the rich heritage of Europe, in the making of which Arab scholars provided a link between Platonic philosophy and Thomas Aquinas Roman Catholic theology, thus laying the foundation of the Western civilization.

– Edward Gibbon

74

Greece (Hellenic Republic of Greece)

It is like re-living the past on the land where the Acropolis stands; where the cave of Socrates exists; where democracy and modern political thought and science originated. A land that has the legacies of Socrates, Plato, Aristotle, Aristophanes and Xenophon. A place where Homer created the Iliad and Odyssey, depicting the Battle of Troy. The expereince is intimidating.

Greece is a country in the Balkan Peninsula in the southern Europe. The people are mainly ethnic Greek. The land is closely linked with the sea; less than one-fourth of this mountainous country consists of lowland, much of which is the coastal plain along the Aegean or mountain valleys and small plains near river mouths. The country's interior is dominated by the Pindus Mountains which extend from Albania, on Greece's northwestern border, into the Peloponnese. Mount Olympus is the country's highest peak. Among its islands are the Aegean and Ionian groups and Crete. In the far north, Greek Macedonia and Thrace (an ancient country now divided between Turkey, Bulgaria and Greece) are bounded by the Rhodope Mountains, on the Bulgarian border, and the Maritsa River, on the Turkish border. East of the Pindus, the lowland plain of Thessaly, (North-east Greece) is bounded on the north by mountains.

Four fifths of Greece consist of mountains or hills, making the country one of the most mountainous in Europe. Mount Olympus, a focal point of Greek culture throughout history culminates at Mytikas peak 2,917 m (9,570 ft), the highest in the country. Once considered the throne of the gods, it is today extremely popular among hikers and climbers. Western Greece contains a number of lakes and wetlands and is dominated by the Pindus mountain range. The Pindus reaches a maximum elevation of 2,637 m (8,652 ft) at Mt. Smolikas and is essentially a prolongation of the Dinaric Alps. The Vikos-Aoos Gorge is yet another spectacular formation and a popular hotspot for those fond of extreme sports.

The range continues through the central Peloponnese, crosses the islands of Kythera and Antikythera and finds its way into southwestern Aegean, in the island of Crete where it eventually ends. The islands of the Aegean are peaks of underwater mountains that once constituted an extension of the mainland. Pindus is characterized by its high, steep peaks, often dissected by numerous canyons and a variety of other karstic landscapes. Most notably, the impressive Meteora formation consisting of high, steep boulders provides a breathtaking experience for the hundreds of thousands of tourists who visit the area each year.

Northeastern Greece features another high-altitude mountain range, the Rhodope range, spreading across the periphery of East Macedonia and Thrace; this area is covered with vast, thick, ancient forests. The famous Dadia forest is in the prefecture of Evros, in the far northeast of the country.

Expansive plains are primarily located in the prefectures of Thessaly, Central Macedonia and Thrace. They constitute key economic regions as they are among the few arable places in the country. Rare marine species such as the Pinniped Seals and the Loggerhead Sea Turtle live in the seas surrounding mainland Greece, while its dense forests are home to the endangered brown bear, the lynx, the Roe Deer and the Wild Goat.

More than 2,000 islands (only 200 of which are inhabited) account for one-fifth of the total land area. Crete, in the southern Aegean, is the largest. The lonian islands, west of the mainland, include Corfu, Levkas, Cephalonia and Zante. The two largest clusters are the Cyclades in the south Aegean and, to their east, the 12 Dodecanese. The Mediterranean climate has marked regional variations. In the northeast, cold winter is drawn in from the eastern Balkans. The icy wind, brings snow to the highest mountains. In the south, warm winds make mild winters. Rainfall is most frequent during winter, and heaviest on the western coastal ranges.

SOCRATES

Socrates (c.469-399 BC) was an Athenian philosopher who wrote nothing but was immortalized in the dialogues, of his pupil, Plato. Socrates' views are recorded in Plato's *The Republic*, in which Socrates describes the ideal state as the one where the cultivation of truth, beauty, and goodness achieves perfection. In his desire to combat the scepticism of the sophists, Socrates saw the possibility of genuine knowledge. He said that the good person never knowingly does wrong. True knowledge emerges through dialogue and systematic questioning and an abandoning of uncritical claims to knowledge. The effect of Socrates teaching was disruptive since he opposed tyranny. Accused in 399 BC on charges of impiety and corruption of youth, he was condemned by the Athenian authorities to die by drinking hemlock. And, thus, ended the life of the wisest man of the world.

"No evil can befall a good man, either in life or death."
– Socrates

The Greek are predominantly Macedonian, Turkish and Albanian. Almost all Greeks are active members of the Greek Orthodox Church. Although Greece is rapidly becoming an urban society, most Greeks feel a strong attachment to their rural roots. Strict marriage and divorce laws are enforced and the position of women has been improved by recent legislation. Greece is governed by a single-chamber parliament of about 300 members. The leader of the majority party becomes prime minister and head of government. The president is elected by parliament for a five-year term and is the supreme commander of the armed forces. Governments are elected for a four-year term, by all Greeks over 18 years. Greece is a member of the North Atlantic Treaty Organization (NATO) and also a member of the European Union (EU).

Greece's continuing involvement in Cyprus continues to cause difficult relations with neighbouring Turkey.

After the 4th century AD, Greece was part of the eastern Byzantine empire ruled from Constantinople. From the 11th century, the Byzantine emperors were unable to retain control of the Peloponnese where Norman and French adventurers established kingdoms. Venice controlled many Ionian and Aegean islands. By 1460, following the fall of Constantinople, the Ottoman empire absorbed nearly all of Greece. The Ionian islands remained in Venetian hands until 1797. During the 18th and 19th centuries, the Orthodox Church became a focus for growing nationalism. In 1830, after a bitter struggle, an independent Greek state was established in the Peloponnese, Central Greece and the Aegean. Added to these were the Ionian islands in 1863, Thessaly in 1881, Epirus and Macedonia in 1913, and Thrace in 1918. After the unsuccessful attempt to annex Anatolia from Turkey after World War I, the Greek community in Turkey was expelled.

GREECE IS CRADLE OF WESTERN CIVILIZATION

Modern Greece traces its roots to the civilization of ancient Greece, cradle of Western civilization. As such, it is the birthplace of democracy, Western philosophy, the Olympic Games, Western literature and historiography, political science, major scientific and mathematical principles, and Western drama, including both tragedy and comedy. Greece was the first in Europe where advanced early civilizations emerged, beginning with the Minoan civilization in Crete and then the Mycenean civilization on the mainland. Later, city-states emerged across the Greek peninsula and spread to the shores of Black Sea, South Italy and Asia Minor reaching great levels of prosperity that resulted in an unprecedented cultural boom, expressed in architecture, drama, science and philosophy, and nurtured in Athens under a democratic environment. Athens and Sparta led the way in repelling the Persian Empire in a series of battles. Both were later overshadowed by Thebes and eventually Macedon, with the latter under the guidance of Alexander the Great uniting and leading the Greek world to victory over the Persians, to presage the Hellenistic era, itself brought only partially to a close two centuries later with the establishment of Roman rule over Greek lands in 146 BC.

The subsequent mixture of Roman and Hellenic cultures took form in the establishment of the Byzantine Empire in 330 AD around Constantinople, which remained a major cultural and military power for the next 1,123 years, until

PLATO

Our object in the establishment of the state is the greatest happiness of the whole, and not that of any one class.

– Plato

Plato c.427-347 BC was the pupil of Socrates, teacher of Aristotle and founder of a new school of philosophy. He was the author of philosophical dialogues on such topics as metaphysics, ethics, and politics. Central to his teachings is the notion of Forms, which are located outside the everyday world - timeless, motionless, and absolutely real. Plato's philosophy has influenced Christianity and European culture, directly and through Augustine, the Florentine Platonists during the Renaissance, and countless others.

Of his work, some 30 dialogues survive. The principal figure in these ethical and philosophical debates is Socrates and the early ones employ the Socratic method, in which he asks questions and traps the students into contradicting themselves. Other dialogues include the Symposium, on love, Phaedo, on immortality, and Apology and Crito, on Socrates' trial and death. It is impossible to say whether Plato's Socrates is a faithful representative of the real man or an articulation of Plato's own thought.

Plato's philosophy rejects scientific rationalism (establishing facts through experiment) in favour of arguments, because mind, not matter, is fundamental, and material objects are merely imperfect copies of abstract and eternal "ideas." His political philosophy is expounded in two treatises, *The Republic* and *The Laws,* both of which describe ideal states. Platonic love is inspired by a person's best qualities and seeks their development.

its fall at the hands of Ottomans in 1453. On the eve of the Ottoman era the Greek intelligentsia migrated to Western Europe, playing a significant role in the Western European Renaissance through the transferring of works of Ancient Greeks to Western Europe. Nevertheless, the Ottoman millet system contributed to the cohesion of the Orthodox Greeks by segregating the various peoples within the Ottoman Empire based on religion, as the latter played an integral role in the formation of modern Greek identity.

A DEVELOPED COUNTRY

Greece is a developed country, a member of the European Union since 1981, a member of the Economic and Monetary Union of the European Union since 2001, NATO since 1952, the OECD since 1961, the WEU since 1995, a founding member of the Black Sea Economic Cooperation and a member of ESA since 2005. Athens is the capital; Thessaloniki, Patras, Heraklion, Larissa, Volos, Ioannina, Kavala, Rhodes and Serres are some of the country's other major cities. After the Greek War of Independence, successfully fought against the Ottoman Empire from 1821 to 1829, the nascent Greek state was finally recognized under the London Protocol. In 1827, Ioannis Kapodistrias, a noble Greek from the Ionian Islands, was chosen as the first governor of the new Republic. However, following his assassination, the Great Powers soon installed a monarchy under Otto, of the Bavarian House of Wittelsbach. In 1843, an uprising forced the King to grant a constitution and a representative assembly. Due to his unimpaired authoritarian rule, he was eventually dethroned in 1863 and replaced by Prince Vilhelm (William) of Denmark, who took the name George I and brought with him the Ionian Islands as a coronation gift from Britain. In 1877, Charilaos Trikoupis, a dominant figure of the Greek political scene who is attributed with the significant improvement of the country's infrastructure, curbed the power of the monarchy to interfere in the assembly by issuing the rule of vote of confidence to any potential prime minister.

BALKAN WARS AND AFTER

As a result of the Balkan Wars, Greece successfully increased the extent of her territory and population, a challenging context both socially and economically. In the following years, the struggle between King Constantine I and charismatic prime minister Eleftherios Venizelos over the country's foreign policy on the eve of World War I dominated the country's political scene, and divided the country into two opposed groups. In the aftermath of World War I, Greece fought against Turkish nationalists, led by Mustafa Kemal, a war which resulted in a massive population exchange between the two countries under the Treaty of Lausanne. Instability and successive coups d'etat marked the following era, which was overshadowed by the massive task of incorporating 1.5 million Greek refugees from Asia Minor into Greek society. On 28 October 1940 Fascist Italy demanded the surrender of Greece, but Greek dictator Ioannis Metaxas refused and in the following Greco-Italian War, Greece repelled Italian forces into Albania, giving the Allies their first victory over Axis forces on land. The country would eventually fall to urgently dispatched German forces during the Battle of Greece. The German occupiers nevertheless met serious challenges from the Greek Resistance.

After liberation, Greece experienced a bitter civil war between Royalist and Communist forces, which led to economic devastation and severe social tensions between its Rightists and largely Communist Leftists for the next 30 years. The next 20 years were characterized by marginalisation of the left in

ARISTOTLE

"Man is, by nature, a political animal."
Aristotle

Aristotle (384 BC- 322 BC) was born in 384 BC at Stagira, a Greek colony. His father, Nichomachus, was court physician to King of Macedonia. He studied under Plato. His first wife was Pythias, and second wife was Herpyllis, who bore him a son, Nichomachus. He taught Alexander the Great and died in 322 BC at Chalcis in Euboea.

Aristotle's work has been extremely relevant to the development of western thinking and beliefs. He started a school (Lyceum) where he used to walk around while giving lectures. Later, his followers came to be known as peripatetics – "*to walk about*."

Aristotle saw ultimate reality in physical objects. Objects, including organisms, were composed of potential (their matter), and of a reality (their form). In Organon, he developed a complete system of logic and reasoning to address reality. Aristotle believed that in living creatures, the form was the soul. Plants had the lowest kinds of souls, animals had higher souls which could feel, and humans alone had rational, reasoning souls.

His work in zoology was considered the last word on the subject for centuries after his death. His books on animals are the first ever recorded histories of the animal kingdom. Aristotle's thoughts on earth sciences can be found in *Meteorology* where he discusses the nature of the earth and the oceans. He worked out the hydrologic cycle, winds, earthquakes, thunder, lightning, rainbows, meteors, comets, and the Milky Way. In *Physics*, Aristotle talks about cause and effect. In *Metaphysics* (which got its name not from Aristotle, but from a librarian who needed a title for it and, because it was shelved following Physics, got the name *after-physics* or *beyond physics),* Aristotle discusses various states of being and existence. Aristotle believed that ethics were not definitive but relative. So to be good, one can't just study virtue, one has to do good deeds. But what is good? According to Aristotle, everything that is done with a good intention in mind is good.

He was the first person to define the source of true happiness – to do that what makes us human and to do it well. What is it that makes us human? Our power to reason. Aristotle said that a person who could rationalise an idea to its fullest was ultimately the happiest of them all.

the political and social spheres but also by a significant economic growth, propelled in part by the Marshall Plan. In 1965, a period of political turbulence led to a coup d'etat on 21 April 1967 by the US-backed Regime of the Colonels. On November 1973 the Athens Polytechnic Uprising sent shock waves across the regime, and a counter-coup established Brigadier Dimitrios Ioannides as dictator. On 20 July 1974, as Turkey invaded the island of Cyprus, the regime collapsed.

PARLIAMENTARY REPUBLIC

Greece is a parliamentary republic. The head of state is the President of the Republic, who is elected by the Parliament for a five-year term. The current Constitution was drawn up and adopted by the Fifth Revisionary Parliament of the Hellenes and entered into force in 1975 after the fall of the military junta of 1967–1974. It has been revised twice since, in 1986 and in 2001. The Constitution, which consists of 120 articles, provides for a separation of powers into executive, legislative, and judicial branches, and grants extensive specific guarantees (further reinforced in 2001) of civil liberties and social rights.

According to the Constitution, executive power is exercised by the President of the Republic and the Government. From the Constitutional amendment of 1986 the President's duties were curtailed to a significant extent, and they are now largely ceremonial; most political power thus lies in the hands of the Prime Minister. The position of Prime Minister, Greece's head of government, belongs to the current leader of the political party that can obtain a vote of confidence by the Parliament. The President of the Republic formally appoints the Prime Minister and, on his recommendation, appoints and dismisses the other members of the Cabinet.

Legislative power is exercised by a 300-member elective unicameral Parliament. Statutes passed by the Parliament are promulgated by the President of the Republic. Parliamentary elections are held every four years, but the President of the Republic is obliged to dissolve the Parliament earlier on the proposal of the Cabinet, in view of dealing with a national issue of exceptional importance. The President is also obliged to dissolve the Parliament earlier, if the opposition manages to pass a motion of no confidence. Women's suffrage was guaranteed with a 1952 Constitutional amendment. The Judiciary is independent of the executive and the legislature and comprises three Supreme Courts: the Court of Cassation (¢ñåéïò ÐÜãïò), the Council of State (Óõìâïýëéï ôçò Åðéêñáôåßáò) and the Court of Auditors (Åëåãêôéêü ÓõíÝäñéï). The Judiciary system is also composed of civil courts, which judge civil and penal cases and administrative courts, which judge disputes between the citizens and the Greek administrative authorities.

THE DEATH OF SOCRATES

"What!" said Socrates, "would you have me die guilty?"

On the return of the ship from Delos he was told to prepare himself for death. He invited his [193] friends to come and be with him at the end. He took with them his last meal and was as cheerful during it as if it had been a feast. One of his friends asked where he would like them to "bury him." "Bury *me?*" he said. "You cannot bury Socrates. You can bury my body; you cannot put *me* into a grave."

"No man ever behaved more grandly when unjustly condemned to die than did Socrates". - Plato

He spoke about death and the future life and said that death was only the end of sorrow and the beginning of a nobler life. When the jailer came with the cup of poison Socrates drank it as cheerfully as if it had been a glass of wine. He walked about the cell as he was bidden and then, beginning to feel sleepy, lay down. Soon after this he ceased to breathe. Plato, who was one of his pupils, says, "Thus died the man who was in death the noblest we have ever known—in life, the wisest and the best."

Before he left the court he said, "My judges, you go now to your homes—I to prison and to death. But which of the two is the better lot God only knows. It is very likely that death is our greatest blessing." Generally a person condemned to death had to drink the poison the very next day after his trial. But a sacred ship had just sailed from Athens to Delos. This ship carried every year the offerings of the Athenians to Apollo, the chief god of the island, and it was a law in Athens that no person condemned to die should be put to death while she was on her voyage to and fro. So for thirty days Socrates was kept in prison. During that time his friends were allowed to go to see him. In the prison he talked to them just as he had done in the market-place or on the streets. Some of his friends told him how sorry they were that he should die innocent.

MEDITERRANEAN CLIMATE

The climate of Greece can be categorised into three types (the Mediterranean, the Alpine and the Temperate) that influence well-defined regions of its territory. The Pindus mountain range strongly affects the climate of the country by making the western side of it (areas prone to the south-westerlies) wetter on average than the areas lying to the east of it (lee side of the mountains). The Mediterranean type of climate features mild, wet winters and hot, dry summers. The Cyclades, the Dodecanese, Crete, Eastern Peloponessus and parts of the Sterea Ellada region are mostly affected by this particular type of climate. Temperatures rarely reach extreme values along the coasts, although, with Greece being a highly mountainous country, snowfalls occur frequently in winter. It sometimes snows even in the Cyclades or the Dodecanese.

The Alpine type is dominant mainly in the mountainous areas of Northwestern Greece (Epirus, Central Greece, Thessaly, Western Macedonia) as well as in the central parts of Peloponnese, including the prefectures of Achaia, Arcadia and parts of Laconia, where extensions of the Pindus mountain range pass by. Finally, the Temperate type affects Central Macedonia and East Macedonia and Thrace; it features cold, damp winters and hot, dry summers. Athens is located in a transitional area featuring both the Mediterranean and the Temperate types. The city's northern suburbs are dominated by the temperate type while the downtown area and the southern suburbs enjoy a typical Mediterranean type.

LITERATURE AND FOLKLORE

The earliest works belonged to the oral tradition, The *Iliad* and *Odyssey* of Homer come down from 1000 BC. Lyric poetry was written from the 6th BC and reached perfection with Pindar. The great moment of Greek drama came in the 5th BC, with tragedies of Aeschylus, Sophocles, and Euripides, and the comedies of Aristophanes. Most of these plays are now lost. Simultaneous with these were the historical writings of Herodotus, to be followed within half a century by those of Xenophon; and then came the flowering of Greek philosophy with the teachings of Socrates, and the comprehensive works of Plato and Aristotle. During the Hellenistic period (327-37 BC), prose writing continued to flourish, comedy persisted with Menanden, while Theocritus introduced pastoral poetry, and revived epic verse. Greek literature survived the Roman dominance into the 2nd century AD with writers, including Plutarch, Longinus, and Aeschylus, Aristophanes and Euripides, setting trends for all time to come.

With contemporary Greeks, the problem lies in the legend of Zeus, the god of gods. As the folklore goes, Zeus, in his passion to seduce a Phoenician woman of high lineage called *Europa*, altered himself into a tame white bull and joined the herd which she maintained. Europa climbed atop the white bull one day when Zeus carried her on his back to the island of Crete and made Europa his wife. Thus was born Europe, the continent of destiny.

Ruins of ancient Greece - this is where it all began !!

ARCHITECTURE

Architecture of ancient Greece is the base for virtually all architectural developments in Europe. The Greeks invented the entablature, which allowed roofs to be hipped (inverted V-shape), and perfected the design of arcades with support columns. There were three styles, or orders, of columns; Doric (with no base), Ionic and Corinthian (with acanthus-leafed capitals). Of the Greek orders, the Doric is the oldest; it is said to have evolved from a former timber prototype. The finest example of a Doric temple is the Parthenon in Athens (447-438 BC). The origin of the Ionic is uncertain. The earliest building in which the Ionic capital appears is the temple of Artemis (Diana) at Ephesus (530 BC). The gateway to the Acropolis in Athens (known as the Propylaea) has internal columns of the Ionic order. The most perfect example is the Erechtheum (421-406 BC) in Athens.

The Corinthian order belongs to a later period of Greek art. A leading example is the temple of Zeus (Jupiter) Olympius in Athens (174 BC), completed under Roman influence AD 129. The monumental and sumptuously ornamental Mausoleum in Halicarnasus (353 BC) was one of the Seven Wonders of the world. Between 2000 and 1500 BC, Crete was the centre of the Minoan civilization, usually considered Europe's earliest. By the 16th century BC, its influence passed to Mycenae in the Peloponnese which, in turn, was overrun about 1200 BC, by Dorian warriors from the north, who had developed the use of iron weapons. The Greek city-states may have originated at this time as villages joined for self-defense within the walls of a citadel *(acropolis).*

Greece became the tenth member of the European Union on 1 January 1981, and ever since the nation has experienced a remarkable and sustained economic growth. Widespread investments in industrial enterprises and heavy infrastructure, as well as funds from the European Union and growing revenues from tourism, shipping and a fast growing service sector have raised the country's standard of living to unprecedented levels. The country adopted the Euro in 2001 and successfully organised the 2004 Olympic Games in Athens.

After World War II, Greece experienced the "Greek economic miracle"; GDP growth averaged 7% between 1950 and 1973. Since then Greece has implemented number of structural and fiscal reforms while receiving considerable European Union funding. In 2001, Greece joined the Economic and Monetary Union. Annual growth of Greek GDP has surpassed the respective levels of most of its EU partners. Today, the service industry makes up the largest, most vital and fastest-growing sector of the Greek economy, followed by industry and agriculture. The tourism industry is a major source of foreign exchange earnings and revenue accounting for 15% of Greece's total GDP and employing ,directly or indirectly, 16.5% of the total workforce.

Greece is a leading investor in all of her Balkan neighbors with the National Bank of Greece in 2006 acquiring the 46% of Turkish Finansbank and 99.44% of Serbia's Vojvođanska Bank.The manufacturing sector accounts for about 13% of GDP with the food industry leading in growth, profit and export potential. The public sector accounts for about 40% of GDP, with the government however taking measures to decrease it further. High-technology equipment production, especially for telecommunications, is also a fast-growing sector. Other important areas include textiles, building materials, machinery, transport equipment, and electrical appliances. At 10% of GDP, construction is one of the main pillars of the economy, with the sector experiencing a boom due to the Athens Olympics of 2004. Agriculture, at 7%, is the final important sector of Greek economic activity.

Greece's purchasing power-adjusted GDP per capita is the world's 28th highest. According to the International Monetary Fund it has an estimated average per capita income of $30,661 for the year 2008, comparable to that of Germany, France or Italy and approximately equal to the EU average. Greece ranks 18th in the 2006 HDI, 22nd on The Economist's 2005 world-wide quality-of-life index. According to a survey by the Economist, the cost of living in Athens is close to 90% of the costs in New York; in rural regions it is lower.

NATIONAL INDICATORS - GREECE

Area 131,957 sq.km.; capital Athens; major ports Piraeus, Thessaloniki, Patras, Iraklion; physical features mountainous (Mount Olympus); a large number of islands, notably Crete, Corfu and Rhodes and Cyclades and Ionian Islands; political system democratic republic; arable land 18.3%; agricultural products fruits and vegetables, cereals, sugar beet, tobacco, olives, livestock and dairy products.

HISTORY

c. 2000-1200 BC	Mycenaean civilisation flourished.
c. 1000-500 BC	Rise of the Greek city states; Greek colonies established around the Mediterranean.
c. 490-404	BC Ançient Greek culture reached its zenith in the democratic city state of Athens.
357-338 BC	Philip-II of Macedon won supremacy over Greece.
146 BC	Roman empire defeated Macedon and annexed Greece.
476 AD	Western Roman Empire ended; Eastern Empire continued as Byzantine Empire, based at Constantinople, with essentially Greek culture.
late 14th C-1461	Ottoman Turks conquered mainland Greece and captured Constantinople 1453.
1829	Treaty of Adrianople: Turkey recognised as Greek state.
1862	Mutiny and rebellion led King Otto to abdicate.
1863	George of Denmark became king of the Hellenes.
1864	Britain transferred Ionian islands to Greece.
1881	Following Treaty of Berlin (1878), Greece was allowed to annex Thessaly and part of Epirus.

1897	Greco-Turkish War ended in Greek defeat.
1912-13	Balkan Wars: Greece annexed a large area of Epirus and Macedonia.
1916	'National Schism': Venizelos formed rebel pro-Allied government.
1917-18	Greek forces fought on Allied side in World War I.
1919-22	Greek invasion of Asia Minor; after Turkish victory, a million refugees came to Greece.
1924	Republic declared amid great political instability.
1935	Greek monarchy restored.
1940	Greece successfully repelled Italian invasion.
1941-44	German occupation of Greece.
1946-49	Civil war: communists defeated by monarchists with military aid from Britain and USA.
1952	Became a member of NATO.
1967	'Greek Colonels' seized power, King Constantine-II exiled.
1973	Republic proclaimed with Papadopoulos as president.
1974	Cyprus crisis caused downfall of military regime; Constantine Karamanlis returned from exile to form Government of National Salvation and restore democracy.
1981	*Andreas Papandreou* elected Greece's first socialist prime minister; Greece joins EU.
1989-93	Election defeat of Panhellenic Socialist Movement (PASOK).
1993	PASOK returned to power.
1996	Costas Simitis succeeded Papandreou as prime minister.
1997	Direct talks with Turkey resulted in agreement to settle all future disputes peacefully.

Index

F

L

Y

Z

NORWEGIAN SEA
ICELAND
FAROE
ISLANDS
ATLANTIC OCEAN
NORWAY
SWE
NORTH
SEA
DENMARK
IRELAND
UNITED
KINGDOM
LONDON
THE
NETHER-
LANDS
GERMANY
BELGIUM
BERLIN
ENGLISH CHANNEL
LUXEMBOURG
ATLANTIC
OCEAN
PARIS
FRANCE
SWITZERLAND
BAY OF
BISCAY
ITALY
ANDORRA
MONACO
CORSICA
PORTUGAL
LISBON
SPAIN
VATICAN CITY
ROME
MADRID
SARDINIA
GIBRALTAR
MEDITERRANEAN SEA